Context–Aware Mobile and Ubiquitous Computing for Enhanced Usability:
Adaptive Technologies and Applications

Dragan Stojanovic
University of Nis, Serbia

INFORMATION SCIENCE REFERENCE

Hershey · New York

Director of Editorial Content: Kristin Klinger
Senior Managing Editor: Jamie Snavely
Assistant Managing Editor: Carole Coulson
Managing Editor: Jamie Snavely
Typesetter: Lindsay Bergman
Cover Design: Lisa Tosheff
Printed at: Yurchak Printing Inc.

Published in the United States of America by
        Information Science Reference (an imprint of IGI Global)
        701 E. Chocolate Avenue, Suite 200
        Hershey PA 17033
        Tel: 717-533-8845
        Fax: 717-533-8661
        E-mail: cust@igi-global.com
        Web site: http://www.igi-global.com

and in the United Kingdom by
        Information Science Reference (an imprint of IGI Global)
        3 Henrietta Street
        Covent Garden
        London WC2E 8LU
        Tel: 44 20 7240 0856
        Fax: 44 20 7379 0609
        Web site: http://www.eurospanbookstore.com

Library of Congress Cataloging-in-Publication Data

Context-aware mobile and ubiquitous computing for enhanced usability : adaptive technologies and applications / Dragan Stojanovic, editor.
      p. cm.
   Includes bibliographical references and index.
   Summary: "This book covers advanced aspects of context-awareness and up-to-date topics in context management, development and adaptation of context-aware applications and service, context-aware security and access control, incorporating context-awareness in service-oriented architectures"--Provided by publisher.
   ISBN 978-1-60566-290-9 (hardcover) -- ISBN 978-1-60566-291-6 (ebook)
   1. Context-aware computing. 2. Mobile computing. 3. Mobile communication systems. I. Stojanovic, Dragan, 1969-
   QA76.5915.C65 2009
   004.6'5--dc22
                        2008041548

British Cataloguing in Publication Data
A Cataloguing in Publication record for this book is available from the British Library.

All work contributed to this book set is original material. The views expressed in this book are those of the authors, but not necessarily of the publisher.

Editorial Advisory Board

Table of Contents

Section I
Adaptation in Context-Aware Applications

Chaper I
Davy Preuveneers, Katholieke Universiteit Leuven, Belgium
Koen Victor, Katholieke Universiteit Leuven, Belgium
Yves Vanrompay, Katholieke Universiteit Leuven, Belgium
Peter Rigole, Katholieke Universiteit Leuven, Belgium
Manuele Kirsch Pinheiro, Katholieke Universiteit Leuven, Belgium
Yolande Berbers, Katholieke Universiteit Leuven, Belgium

Chapter II
Tarak Chaari, LAAS-CNRS, France
Mohamed Zouari, IRISA-INRIA, France
Frédérique Laforest, LIRIS-CNRS, France

Chapter III
Florian Daniel, University of Trento, Italy

Section II
Advanced Context Management

Section III
Context-Aware Mobile Services and Service-Oriented Architectures

Section IV
Context-Aware Communication, Security and Privacy

Section V
Context-Awareness for Enhanced Usability and Personalization

Detailed Table of Contents

Section I
Adaptation in Context-Aware Applications

Chaper I

Davy Preuveneers, Katholieke Universiteit Leuven, Belgium
Koen Victor, Katholieke Universiteit Leuven, Belgium
Yves Vanrompay, Katholieke Universiteit Leuven, Belgium
Peter Rigole, Katholieke Universiteit Leuven, Belgium
Manuele Kirsch Pinheiro, Katholieke Universiteit Leuven, Belgium
Yolande Berbers, Katholieke Universiteit Leuven, Belgium

In recent years, many researchers have studied context-awareness to support non-intrusive adaptability of context-aware applications. Context-aware applications benefit from emerging technology that connects everyday objects and provides opportunities to collect and use context information from various sources. Context-awareness helps to adapt continuously to new situations and to turn a static computing environment into a dynamic ecology of smart and proactive applications. In this chapter, The authors present their framework that manages and uses context information to adapt applications and the content the applications provide. They show how application adaptation can be handled at the composition level, by reconfiguring, redeploying and rewiring components, e.g. to fall back into reduced functionality mode when redeploying an application on a handheld. The key features of their context-aware adaptation framework not only include local adaptations of context-aware applications and content, but also the addressing of context in large scale networks and the context-aware redeployment of running applications in a distributed setting. The authors discuss how adaptation is handled along various levels of abstraction (user, content, application, middleware, network) and illustrate the flexibility of context-aware content and application adaptation by means of a realistic use case scenario.

Tarak Chaari, LAAS-CNRS, France
Mohamed Zouari, IRISA, France, France
Frédérique Laforest, LIRIS-CNRS, France

Pervasive information systems aim to make information available anywhere and at anytime. These systems should be used in different contexts depending on the environment of the user, her/his profile and her/his device. Consequently, one of the main problems of such information systems is the adaptation to context. In this chapter, the authors propose a comprehensive and open strategy that guarantees the adaptation of applications to context on three facets: (i) the services offered to the user, (ii) the multimedia contents returned by these services and (iii) their presentation to the user. Service adaptation consists of modules that intercept the application's service calls and modify their behavior using a list of functional adaptation operators. Data adaptation consists in transforming or replacing the non-usable multimedia service outputs in the considered context situation. Presentation adaptation consists in automatically generating the complete code of the user interface that guarantees the interaction with the adapted data and services. Their adaptation strategy has achieved two goals: (i) incrementally integrate context awareness in the application and (ii) guarantee the adaptation starting from a simple description of the services offered to the user. The authors have validated this strategy by developing a platform that guarantees applications adaptation to context. They used Java, OSGi and Web service technologies to implement this platform. They have also successfully tested our adaptation approach on a home health care application concerning dialyzed persons.

Florian Daniel, University of Trento, Italy

Adaptivity (the runtime adaptation to user profile data) and context-awareness (the runtime adaptation to generic context data) have been gaining momentum in the field of Web engineering over the last years, especially in response to the ever growing demand for highly personalized services and applications coming from end users. Developing context-aware and adaptive Web applications requires addressing a few design concerns that are proper of such kind of applications and independent of the chosen modeling paradigm or programming language. In this chapter the authors characterize the design of context-aware Web applications, they describe a conceptual, model-driven development approach, and we show how the peculiarities of context-awareness require augmenting the expressive power of conceptual models in order to be able to express adaptive application behaviors.

Section II
Advanced Context Management

Chapter IV

I. Roussaki, National Technical University of Athens, Greece
M. Strimpakou, National Technical University of Athens, Greece
C. Pils, Waterford Institute of Technology, Ireland
N. Kalatzis, National Technical University of Athens, Greece
N. Liampotis, National Technical University of Athens, Greece

In ubiquitous computing environments, context management systems are expected to administrate large volumes of spatial and non-spatial information in geographical disperse domains. In particular, when these systems cover wide areas such as cities, countries or even the entire planet, the design of scalable storage, retrieval and propagation mechanisms is paramount. This Chapter elaborates on mechanisms that address advanced requirements including support for distributed context databases management; efficient query handling; innovative management of mobile physical objects and optimisation strategies for distributed context data dissemination. These mechanisms establish a robust spatially-enhanced distributed context management framework that has thoroughly been designed, carefully implemented and extensively evaluated via numerous experiments.

Chapter V

Jared Zebedee, Queen's University, Canada
Patrick Martin, Queen's University, Canada
Kirk Wilson, CA Inc, USA
Wendy Powley, Queen's University, Canada

Pervasive computing presents an exciting realm where intelligent devices interact within the background of our environments to create a more intuitive experience for their human users. Context-awareness is a key requirement in a pervasive environment because it enables an application to adapt to the current situation. Context-awareness is best facilitated by a context management system that supports the automatic discovery, retrieval and exchange of context information by devices. Such a system must perform its functions in a pervasive computing environment that involves heterogeneous mobile devices which may experience intermittent connectivity and resource and power constraints.

The objective of the chapter is to describe a robust and adaptable context management system. The authors achieve an adaptable context management system by adopting the autonomic computing paradigm, which supports systems that are aware of their surroundings and that can automatically react to changes in them. A robust context management system is achieved with an implementation based on widely accepted standards, specifically Web services and the Web Services Distributed Management (WSDM) standard.

Yuanping Li, Tsinghua University, China.
Ling Feng, Tsinghua University, China.
Lizhu Zhou, Tsinghua University, China.

Context is an essential element in mobile and ubiquitous computing. Users' information needs can be better understood and supplied by means of context-awareness. Context data may be sensed, inferred, or directly input by users, etc., which calls for specific query mechanisms to acquire context information. On the other hand, traditional non-context-aware database querying techniques need to be re-examined, taking query context into account. In order to design effective context-aware database query processing mechanism, the authors survey the latest developed context-aware querying techniques in the data management field. They outline six ways to query context directly, and provide a categorization about how to use context in querying traditional databases. The approaches of handling imperfect context in context-aware database querying are also described. They discuss some potential research issues to be addressed at the end of the chapter.

Section III
Context-Aware Mobile Services and Service-Oriented Architectures

Carsten Jacob, Fraunhofer Institute for Open Communication Systems (FOKUS), Germany
Heiko Pfeffer, Fraunhofer Institute for Open Communication Systems (FOKUS), Germany
Stephan Steglich, Technische Universität Berlin, Germany

The idea of context-aware services has been around for a long time. The rise of user mobility enabled by well-equipped mobile devices, increasing interconnectedness and available service platforms such as the mobile web offers new possibilities for context-aware computing, but, at the same time, produces a number of novel challenges. In this chapter, the authors observe current approaches in this active research area, and identify the respective challenges, achievements, and trends. They also extend the notion of context-aware services by considering service composition approaches, and present a middleware aiming at the autonomic and context-aware provision of services in mobile peer-to-peer networks. In this regard special attention is paid to a semantic blackboard concept to cache and disseminate context data and a context-aware service composition approach in terms of the identified trends and challenges.

The authors present a holistic approach for the efficient design, implementation, and validation of context-aware mobile services. The according concepts have been developed within the PLASTIC project which devises a methodology based on model-to-model transformations to be applied at different stages of the service lifecycle. Starting from a conceptual model, these models reflect characteristic properties of the mobile service under development such as context information. For the implementation of the service, a middleware suite then is used which comprises a set of constituents which significantly simplify and shorten the mobile services development cycle. They focus on demonstrating the concepts in terms of mobile business-to-business field services as opposed to business-to-consumer services. Here through the methodology and tools the dynamicity can be significantly enhanced. By using the contained adaptation mechanism, service specifications (static by nature) can be qualified to deal with additional information (e.g., context) needed for achieving a better quality of service and usability.

Chapter IX

Context-awareness is highly desired, particularly in highly dynamic mobile environments. Semantic Web Services (SWS) address context-adaptation by enabling the automatic discovery of distributed Web services based on comprehensive semantic capability descriptions. Even though the appropriateness of resources in mobile settings is strongly dependent on the current situation, SWS technology does not explicitly encourage the representation of situational contexts. Therefore, whereas SWS technology supports the allocation of resources, it does not entail the discovery of appropriate SWS representations for a given situational context. Moreover, describing the complex notion of a specific situation by utilizing symbolic SWS representation facilities is costly, prone to ambiguity issues and may never reach semantic completeness. In fact, since not any real-world situation completely equals another, a potentially infinite set of situation parameters has to be matched to a finite set of semantically defined SWS resource descriptions to enable context-adaptability. To overcome these issues, the authors propose Mobile Situation Spaces (MSS) which enable the description of situation characteristics as members in geometrical vector spaces following the idea of Conceptual Spaces (CS). Semantic similarity between situational contexts is calculated in terms of their Euclidean distance within a MSS. Extending merely symbolic SWS descriptions with context information on a conceptual level through MSS enables similarity-based matchmaking between real-world situation characteristics and predefined resource representations as part of SWS descriptions. To prove the feasibility, they provide a proof-of-concept prototype which applies MSS to support context-adaptation across distinct mobile situations.

Chapter X

Due to its nature, a mobile-enabled environment is very dynamic: reachable resources and services change very often. Users hardly know which resources they can exploit and which services they may require. In such a context, a technical support which identifies the available resources and services and indicates which resource is the best one to execute a service would be very helpful. This chapter proposes an adaptive solution to achieve these issues. Adaptivity is related to the fact that besides searching for the reachable resources or services, this approach proposes the most appropriate one for the current request by exploiting additional information about users, resources and services. Moreover, it ensures that services are delivered with the qualities requested and expected by the users. In the scientific literature adaptivity is exploited for functionality reasons (i.e., a system is not able to do what it was supposed to do) or for performance reasons (i.e., a system is not able to ensure the qualities of the services expected by the users or there is a better configuration for a given task). A challenging issue of adaptivity is the identification and design of the knowledge useful for the adaptation process and how this knowledge is exploited at run-time especially in a highly dynamic environment. This chapter proposes an approach which models the adaptation knowledge through reflective entities, qualities and properties, the management of the adaptation knowledge through views, the decision support through strategies, and the management of the functional and non-functional elements through managers.

Section IV
Context-Aware Communication, Security and Privacy

Mobile context-aware applications have specific needs regarding data communications and position sensing, that current standard hardware is still not able to fulfill. Current mechanisms are inadequate for applications that need constant communications because of their high power needs and low precision when used to measure the physical indoor position of a mobile device. For this reason the authors have created a new, flexible and inexpensive technology that aims to solve both the needs of communication and position estimation on mobile platforms. This new network type uses recently developed technology to minimize power consumption, leading to a longer battery life and maximizing the precision of the position sensing of the device. Finally, on top of their hardware platform they have devised a software layer, named Kindergarten, which allows high-level languages to interact with the underlying hardware.

Chapter XII

Laurent Gomez, SAP Research, France
Annett Laube, SAP Research, France
Alessandro Sorniotti, SAP Research, France

Access control is the process of granting permissions in accordance to an authorization policy. Mobile and ubiquitous environments challenge classical access control solutions like Role-Based Access Control. The use of context-information during policy definition and access control enforcement offers more adaptability and flexibility needed for these environments. When it comes to low-power devices, such as wireless sensor networks, access control enforcement is normally too heavy for such resource-constrained devices. Lightweight cryptography allows encrypting the data right from its production and the access is therefore intrinsically restricted. In addition, all access control mechanisms require an authenticated user. Traditionally, user authentication is performed by means of a combination of authentication factors, statically specified in the access control policy of the authorization service. Within ubiquitous and mobile environment, there is a clear need for a flexible user authentication using the available authentication factors. In this chapter, different new techniques to ensure access control are discussed and compared to the state-of-the-art.

Chapter XIII

Amr Ali Eldin, Accenture, The Netherlands
Semir Daskapan, Delft University of Technology, The Netherlands
Jan Van den Berg, Delft University of Technology, The Netherlands

With the growing interest in context-aware services, attention has been given to privacy and trust issues. Context-aware privacy architectures are usually proposed and developed without taking into account the trustworthiness of a service provider. Therefore, this chapter deals with two challenges in context-aware services. The first one is to improve privacy architectures with a trust functionality and the second one is to integrate this refined privacy architecture in larger service- oriented architectures (SOAs).

Section V
Context-Awareness for Enhanced Usability and Personalization

Chapter XIV

Adrien Joly, Alcatel-Lucent Bell Labs, France; Université de Lyon, LIRIS / INSA, France
Pierre Maret, Université de Lyon, France; Université de Saint Etienne, France
Fabien Bataille, Alcatel-Lucent Bell Labs, France

These times, when the amount of information exponentially grows on the Internet, when most people can be connected at all times with powerful personal devices, we need to enhance, adapt and simplify access to information and communication with other people. The vision of ambient intelligence which is a relevant response to this need, brings many challenges in different areas such as context-awareness, adaptive human-system interaction, privacy enforcement and social communications. The authors believe that ontologies and other semantic technologies can help meeting most of these challenges in a unified manner, as they are a bridge between meaningful (but fuzzy by nature) human knowledge and digital information systems. In this chapter, they will depict their vision of "Social Ambient Intelligence" based on the review of several uses of semantic technologies for context management, adaptive human-system interaction, privacy enforcement and social communications. Based on identified benefits and lacks, and on their experience, they will propose several research leads towards the realization of this vision.

Chapter XV

The delivery of real-time, context-aware and personalized information to end users for mobility support is a high-priority objective in improving mobility services efficiency and effectiveness. This chapter aims at providing an analysis of existing studies in the field of context awareness research targeted to the infomobility application domain. It proposes an evaluation framework for infomobility services based on the elicitation of context information items and high-level requirements. The framework is applied to some relevant state-of-the art research works among personal navigation systems, infomobility service integration frameworks and context-aware location-based communication platforms. Evaluation results are discussed in order to highlight open research challenges in the infomobility application domain.

The notion of context in context-aware applications is not merely an issue of external situational circumstances or device/channel properties, but it could also refer to a wide array of user characteristics that have an effect throughout users' interactions with a system. Human factors such as cognitive traits and current state, from a psychological point of view, are undoubtedly significant in the shaping of the perceived and objective quality of interactions with a system, and by defining context in that sense, personalization may as well become an essential function of context aware applications. The research that is presented in this chapter focuses on identifying human factors that relate to users' performance in Web applications that involve information processing, and a framework of personalization rules that are expected to increase users' performance is depicted. The environments that empirical results were derived from were both learning and commercial; in the case of e-learning personalization was beneficial, while the interaction with a commercial site needs to be further investigated due to the implicit character of information processing in the Web.

Foreword

Research on context-awareness gained a huge momentum in the early years of the new millennium. A whole community identified in context-awareness very promising approaches to solve open issues in several domains. For instance, while mobile phones started to evolve into powerful computing platforms, context-awareness delivered a tool to compensate restrictions which came along with these resource limited devices and their weak connectivity.

With devices scaling further down into smart dust, being interconnected and interwoven into the fabrics of our daily life and growing exponentially in numbers at the same time, context-awareness still offers several opportunities for original research in ubiquitous computing. Very active areas of research include, for instance, new context sensing technologies, inferring context such as human activities from low level sensor data, privacy and sharing of context information, or system design aspects.

This book, *Context-Aware Mobile and Ubiquitous Computing for Enhanced Usability: Adaptive Technologies and Applications,* draws a bow from very specific, technology-oriented aspects of recent findings in research on context-awareness to broad, application and usability-oriented aspects including also human factors. It elaborates whether ontologies and other modeling approaches can support context-based adaptation, compares different context management approaches for medium and large scale ubiquitous systems, and illustrates the applicability of context-awareness for service oriented architectures in general and specifically mobile service platforms. A large fraction of the book is dedicated to security as well as in particular typical privacy concerns and show approaches how to solve the issues. The editors awarded the importance of the interaction between the human users and any context-aware system with an interesting section on usability aspects.

Altogether, this book gives an interesting overview of recent findings in many relevant areas of research on context-awareness. Moreover, it can inspire the community to come up with entirely new ideas in this fascinating research area.

Prof. Dr. Thomas Strang
September 2008

Thomas Strang *studied computer science at the University of Technology (RWTH) in Aachen and received his Diploma degree (Dipl.-Inform.) in 1998. At this time his special interests focused on communications and distributed systems, including high speed networks and telecommunications, local area networks, multimedia communications, computer graphics and security. His diploma thesis was about a video gateway to support video streaming to mobile clients. Parallel to university he worked in industry from 1988 to 2000, where he gained experiences in design, development and management of several projects in the area of large scale security systems. Since July 2000 he has been working as a researcher in the Institute of Communications and Navigation at the German Aerospace Center (DLR) in Oberpfaffenhofen, Germany. Here his research focus has been on ubiquitous and pervasive computing, location- and context-awareness, service discovery and execution frameworks, Semantic Web and smart mobile devices. Since 2004 he has been responsible for the Institute's programme in transportation research, which includes new services for intelligent transportation systems and ad-hoc, robust and reliable vehicle-to-vehicle communications. In 2003 he was awarded a Doctor's degree in natural sciences (Dr. rer. nat.) at the University of Munich, Germany, with a dissertation on service interoperability in ubiquitous computing environments. In October 2004 he additionally accepted an appointment for a professorship in computer science at the University of Innsbruck, Austria. Since 2005, he has been an Executive Director as well as acting Head of Institute at the Digital Enterprise Research Institute (DERI) in Innsbruck, Austria, where he also leads a research group on ubiquitous services and has also given lectures at the University of Munich.*

Foreword

This book helps us understand adaptive technologies and methods at the forefront of research in context-aware mobile and ubiquitous computing. These technologies and methods can help us build adaptive systems for dynamic environments found in a wide-range of scenarios outlined in various chapters. The content of this book is thus both practical and theoretical in nature. The book thus provides solid ground both as an introduction to context-aware systems as a text-book for under-graduate education as well as an excellent reference for the professional working in the field.

In 1988, Mark Weiser coined the term "ubiquitous computing" envisioning that one day computers would become invisible and embedded in everyday objects. Ubiquitous Computing would help us focus on what is really important. This vision was published in 1991 in "Scientific American" magazine in the seminal article, *The Computer of the 21st Century*.

Weiser's vision inspired many researchers since it overall objective is clear. The research community has found that this seemingly simple vision involves many challenges. Research in the 1990's attempted to understand what kinds of services and user interaction "ubiquitous computing" would enable. It did so by including sensors in various devices and including sensor information in computing and communication. Thus spatial aspects of users, physical objects or places were linked with actions in digital services. It is clear today that the research question of the scope of services and user interaction is open-ended. This is simply due to the continuing arrival of new device and communication technologies. More importantly, we also learned that knowledge about the user's situation or context is a prerequisite to systems that support novel services and user interaction. Thus, the term context-awareness came into use.

Initially, context-awareness was used to express the ability of systems and components to respond to the situation of the user that interacted with this system. Research in context-aware computing has made numerous attempts to model not only human attributes and behavior but also how we relate to our environment. This has led to success in unexpected ways. So-called recommender engines provide those who visit digital stores or search engines with useful information, based on what the system knows about the visitor's situation. Cultural attractions such as museums often offer an interactive guide that tells the visitor something about objects close by. Thus, we see early successes in well-controlled environments with less complex relations and interactions. RFID tags and Near-Field Communication in mobile phones are transforming the way we do shopping in a very intuitive way.

Meanwhile, we recognize that our need for adaptive systems in more complex environments such as public spaces, in a home, or in an office which are very dynamic environments, with visitors, and many devices with a wide range of capabilities.

The initial three chapters in this book are dedicated to aspects of building adaptive systems in more complex environments. These aspects range from a model for orchestrating services and devices in an ecology of applications, models for adaptive presentation and interaction means with digital content, to a model-driven development of context-aware applications for the world-wide Web. This also raises questions about how to manage such information related to users, objects, and context-aware properties of system components.

Chapters IV-VI address this area with novel approaches for physically and logically distributed management and storage of context models.

Chapters VII-X provide an overview of how we may apply so-called Service Oriented Architectures for context-aware service composition in mobile services.

In the past few years even system components have been regarded as first-class objects to context-aware systems and components similar to users. This has mandated research in adding context-aware capabilities to systems and components, as well as study how system components such as mobile communication should support context-aware applications. Chapter XI provides insights by rethinking the communication mechanisms in context-aware applications. Likewise, Chapters XII and XIII provide novel approaches for privacy & access control for context information.

Final Chapters XIV-XVI present several interesting approaches to enhancing usability and personalization through applying context-awareness. In particular, Chapter XIV proposes the use of Semantics to bridge social on-line communities in order to bring about social ambient intelligence.

Considering the range and depth of the articles, written by experts yet highly readable to non-experts, this book is an important and much needed contribution for a wider audience ranging from researchers and undergraduate education. The book is also highly recommended reading for the professional who needs to understand how to build adaptive services and applications that exhibit greater utility to users and enables people to focus on what is important.

Theo Kanter,
November 2008

Theo Kanter received his MSc in electrical engineering, cum laude, from the University of Advanced Technology, the Netherlands in 1976. He completed studies in computer science and artificial intelligence at the University of Technology in Linköping in Sweden (1986, 1987), before pursuing a technical doctorate in computer communications, which he earned from the Royal Institute of Technology in Stockholm, Sweden in 2001. During his career, Kanter has held a number of leading positions in telecommunications research, earlier at Ellemtel AB, Sweden (1996-1999), where he led research in agent-based service architectures for context-aware voice service on the Internet and holds a number of patents in this area. Between 1999 and 2007, he was a senior scientist at Ericsson Research in the area of Service Layer Technologies focusing on Adaptive Mobile Services and Mobile Presence, contributing to standardization in the Open Mobile Alliance (OMA) and Third Generation Partnership Project (3GPP). From September 2007, Theo holds the position of full Professor of Computer Science –Distributed Systems within the Department of Information Technology and Media at the Mid-Sweden University. Kanter is also affiliated as guest researcher with the Wireless Center at the Royal Institute of Technology (KTH) in Stockholm, where he leads research in adaptive & context-aware mobile multimedia communication, -service architectures, & -self-organizing application infrastructures, and lectures on Mobile Presence. Kanter is an associate editor of IEEE Computer Communications magazine, and technical committee member / (co-)organizer of several well-known international conferences on wireless & mobile computing and applications, such as: IEEE Conference on Mobile and Wireless Communications Networks (MWCN), International Symposium on Wearable Computers (ISWC), IEEE Workshop on Local and Metropolitan Area Networks (LANMAN), and IEEE Vehicular Technology Conference (VTC). Kanter's current research interest involve methods for acquiring context from accumulated sensor data and utilizing context in heterogeneous wireless and mobile networks in order to enable adaptive & context-aware mobile services. Such methods are believed to enable novel distributed service delivery patterns as well as novel ways for user to interact with services.

Preface

CONTEXT IN MOBILE AND UBIQUITOUS COMPUTING

Advances in mobile and ubiquitous computing, wireless communications, mobile positioning and sensor technologies, have given a rise to a new class of mobile and ubiquitous applications and services that are aware of the context of application usage and adapt their behaviors according to that context with minimal distraction of the user.

Context-aware computing is a mobile and ubiquitous computing paradigm in which applications can discover and take advantage of contextual information (such as user location, time of day, computing and communication characteristics, nearby people, objects and devices, user activities and goals, etc.). Such applications are able to adapt their behavior, that is their functionality, content and interface according to the user's current situation with minimal intrusion. Context-aware computing is a new and rapidly evolving field and currently the focus of many recent research and development efforts. Pioneering work in context-aware computing was performed in the 1992 at Xerox PARC Laboratory and Olivetti Research, Ltd. (now part of AT&T Laboratories Cambridge), resulting in one of the first context-aware applications, *Active Badge Location System* (Want et al., 1992). Marc Weiser in his paper "The Computers of the 21st Century" (Weiser, 1991), predicted that the future computing would consist of small, interconnected computers, some integrated seamlessly in our surroundings (often invisible), and some worn by as, aiming to provide useful and effective services to the users according to their information needs and current situation. This started the vision of ubiquitous computing (also called pervasive computing) as the third wave in computing. Since then, many other researchers have studied topics surrounding context-aware mobile and ubiquitous computing and contributed to this field.

As human beings, we are aware of context, implicitly understand its importance and use it in our daily activities. We routinely use contextual information, such as, who is in our vicinity, where we are, or what is the time of the day, to modulate and adjust our interactions with other people or objects. In the same way that our gesture, activity or a word has different meanings depending on the situation and the context in which they are expressed, the user interaction with any IT application and service is influenced and determined by the situation/context in which such interaction occurs.

What is the context from the mobile and ubiquitous computing point of view? The definition given by Dey and Abowd (2000a) is the most cited one and refer to context as:

"any information that can be used to characterize the situation of an entity. An entity is a person, place, or object that is considered relevant to the interaction between a user and an application, including the user and applications themselves."

Chen and Kotz (2000) define following categories of context:

- Computing context includes network connectivity, communication bandwidth, and local computing resources such as printers, displays, memory capacity, processor speed, and so forth.
- User context includes user profile, location, preferences and people in the vicinity of the user, even the social situation.
- Physical context includes lighting and noise levels, traffic conditions, and temperature.
- Temporal context includes time of day, week, month, and season of the year.
- Context history is the recording of computing, user and physical context across a time span.

Some authors (Hofer et al., 2002; Prekop and Burnett, 2003) classify context in two dimensions: physical (external) and logical (internal). The physical (external) dimension refers to context that can be measured by hardware sensors, that is, location, light, sound, movement, touch, temperature or air pressure, whereas the logical (internal) dimension is mostly specified by the user or captured by monitoring user interactions, that is, the user's goals, tasks, work context, business processes, the user's emotional state, and so forth. However the context is defined and classified the main challenge in mobile and ubiquitous computing is how to provide intelligent context-aware applications and services, anytime, anyplace on any device, that takes into account the users' context and their current situation, increasing usability and effectiveness and minimizing distraction and needed attention.

CONTEXT-AWARE APPLICATIONS AND SERVICES

Many researchers and developers have explored context-aware computing and developed a number of context-aware applications and services to demonstrate and validate the enhanced usability, the flexibility, and adaptation of applications and services enriched with context-aware behavior. According to definition of Dey and Abowd (2000a) "a system is context-aware if it uses context to provide relevant information and/or services to the user, where relevancy depends on the user's task".

Most of the mobile and ubiquitous systems now utilize some kind of context to perform their tasks; what makes context-awareness an essential requirement of these systems. Some of them are made capable of dealing with special types of context and are well-suited for specific conditions and requirements, for example, in navigation scenario. These systems handle context in an ad hoc way and are optimized for the situations they are used in without care about extensibility and flexibility. Although there have been many context-aware systems and applications tested over the last decade, most of them are still prototypes only available in research labs and in academia. One of the main drawbacks lies in the complexity of capturing, representing, and processing the contextual data, as well as adaptation of functionality, content, and interface of applications and services to defined context. These implementations have also lacked generality and flexibility in the sense that only a predefined set of context information has been utilized, with no allowance for customization or augmenting the scope of the information as the need arises. Yet the range of potentially useful context information and the ways of adaptation of mobile and ubiquitous applications to this information is limitless and unforeseeable.

To achieve flexible, scaleable, and effective development of context-aware applications and services a more generic framework is needed. Such a generic framework should include and provide advanced methods, tools and techniques for:

- Context sensing and acquisition,
- Context modeling, representation and storing,
- Processing, aggregation and reasoning of contextual data,

- Context-aware application adaptation,
- Integration of context-awareness into service-oriented architectures
- Security and privacy of context data,
- Knowledge discovery and mining of historical context data, and
- Design and development of context-aware applications and services.

The method of context data sensing, capture and acquisition is very important when designing context-aware systems because it defines the architectural style of the system and also the capabilities of context-aware services offered. Depending of context data types defined within the particular context-aware application domain, the set of contextual data must be acquired through various sensors, either physical, logical, or virtual and represented and stored in an appropriate data store (Baldauf et al., 2007).

To efficiently manage context data and integrate it in context-aware systems the appropriate context model must be developed. The context model is needed to represent, store, and exchange contextual information in the most convenient form. To develop flexible and useable context modeling constructs that cover the wide range of possible contexts is a challenging task. Strang and Linnhoff-Popien (2004) summarized the most relevant context modeling approaches, which are based on the data structures used for representing and exchanging contextual information in the context-aware systems. The main approaches include key-value pairs, XML-based models, graphical models, object-oriented models, logic based models and ontology based models which variously fulfill requirements of the context-aware systems, such as simplicity, flexibility, extensibility and expressiveness.

To provide high-level context information from raw sensor data, such data must be appropriately processed. The data processing is responsible for transformation, reasoning and interpreting contextual information and representing it at a higher abstraction level more useful for particular context-aware system or service. Context-reasoning represents the process of deducing new and relevant information to the use of application(s) and user(s) from the various sources of context-data. For example, the exact GPS position of a person might not be of value for an application but the name and type of the room the person is in, brings greater meaning to the system. Also, if context-aware systems depend on several different context data sources, to provide useful and high-level contextual information to the other systems' components the raw context data must be aggregated and composed to generate information that is more important and advantageous to the application.

The main challenge in design and development of mobile and ubiquitous applications is the adaptation to context and context changes (Adelstain et al., 2005). Adaptation to context and its changes might happen in middleware (system), in the application level, or both. The adaptation of context-aware applications can be performed on three aspects: a) the functionality of various components (services) in the mobile application, b) the data (content) that are delivered to the application can be adapted, and c) the user interface and the ways of user interaction with the application. There is a need for concepts, methods, and tools to achieve effective and seamless integration of adaptation in design and development of context-aware applications.

Service-oriented architecture represents advanced and popular approach for the building and the rapid prototyping of context-aware mobile applications and services (Baldauf et al., 2007). Different functionalities of context-aware systems are encapsulated as low coupled services with context acquisition, context management and context adaptation roles. Usually the central services gain context data through distributed context provider services, process and aggregates it and offers it in high-abstraction and usable form to the application services. Such context-aware mobile services are located on top of the architecture, and retrieve and use contextual information to adapt their behavior according to the current and/or past context. As sensors in a distributed sensor network may fail or new ones may be added, a discovery mechanism to search for and find appropriate sensors for sensing context at runtime is important. The context-aware system must provide mechanisms and capabilities to enable discovering of new context information services using different forms of querying and lookup mechanism. Such dynamic mechanisms are important, especially in mobile and ubiquitous environments, where available sensors, the context sources, as well as their capabilities and structure, change rapidly. Also, context information obtained from context provider service in such an architecture can affect the various stages of the service provision process for example to enhance service discovery or service composition. The main challenge here is how to achieve autonomous orchestration of atomic or composite context-aware services of a service-oriented architecture into higher level services based on context information and available QoS parameters to offer adapted and more usable services.

The important aspects of context-aware mobile systems and services are security and privacy. As context may include sensitive information on people, for example, their location, their activity, the history of their context information in the form of their profile, and so forth; it is necessary to have the opportunity to protect privacy. Therefore, concepts and mechanisms are needed to express policies, to define ownership of context information and access rights for different users.

Context-aware mobile applications and services must also provide access to historical context data. The context-aware systems must provide capabilities for storing and maintenance of a context history and the facilities to query historical context data. The context histories may be used to establish trends and patterns in context changes and predict future context values by using knowledge discovery and data mining techniques. Managing and mining historical context data provides the ability to implement intelligent and highly adaptable context-aware systems and services. Furthermore, based on data mining algorithms, contextual information can be predicted to proactively provide a certain set of context-aware services to the user without his/her explicit intervention or request.

All these interesting challenges in the context-aware mobile and ubiquitous computing field have inspired the research and development community to develop many important solutions and achievements, and to report and present them in the scientific and professional publications, at workshops and conferences. Several context-aware frameworks and systems are designed and developed with some or all these functionalities in mind to enable simple and efficient development of context-aware applications. The prominent examples reported in the literature are (the list is not exhaustive):

- *Context Managing Framework* presented by Korpipää et al. (2003)
- Service-Oriented Context-Aware Middleware (*SOCAM*) project introduced by Gu et al. (2004)
- Context-Awareness Sub-Structure (*CASS*) presented in Fahy and Clarke (2004).
- Context Broker Architecture (*CoBrA*) (Chen et al., 2003)
- *Context Toolkit* (Dey and Abowd, 2000b)
- *Hydrogen* project (Hofer et al., 2002).
- *CORTEX* system based on the *Sentient Object Model* (Biegel and Cahill, 2004)
- *Gaia* Project (Roman et al., 2002)

But many open, research and development issues are still remaining. Context-aware computing is a research area that is still growing and evolving and every related study and research work contributes to richness of this field. The objective of this book is to provide throughout insight in advanced concepts of context-awareness, such as context-aware application adaptation, context management, context privacy and protection, context-awareness in service-oriented architectures, and the application of context-awareness for enhanced usability in specific application domains. The understanding of these concepts ultimately leads to more effective design and implementation of mobile and ubiquitous applications and services that can access accurate, high quality context information on the fly in highly dynamic environments and adapt their functionality, content and user interface/interaction accordingly.

BOOK OBJECTIVE AND AUDIENCE

The book relies upon a huge research in context-awareness domain during past decade which establish fundamental context-related definitions and principles, methods for context sensing and acquisition, context modeling and storage, as well as development of context-aware applications based on context frameworks. This book follows this line of research and development by presenting and describing up-to-date research and development issues in the context-aware computing community.

As such, the book covers advanced aspects of context-awareness and up-to-date topics in context management, development and adaptation of context-aware applications and service, context-aware security and access control, incorporating context-awareness in service-oriented architectures and describes how to achieve enhanced usability and personalization of context-aware applications in some actual domains such as ambient intelligence, E-Learning, infomobility, Semantic Web, and so forth.

By presenting timely and relevant information to the context-aware mobile and ubiquitous computing field, the book is expected to argue the readers that being aware of context is a key factor for enhancing usability and adaptation of contemporary mobile and ubiquitous applications and services.

The book appeals to a broad computer science and computer engineering audience. It is considerably valuable to researchers and developers in mobile and ubiquitous computing, by covering advanced aspects of context-awareness and concepts in design and development of context-aware applications and services. The reader will be able to get in touch with new and comprehensive research issues the context-aware research community is dealing with today. The book is expected to serve as guidance for researchers, software developers and practitioners in this reach and fruitful research and application field, toward making context-aware computing a full reality.

BOOK ORGANIZATION

The book consists of 16 chapters, organized into five sections. A brief description of the chapters follows.

The first section of the book presents concepts, principles and strategies for development of context-aware applications adaptation.

Preuveneers et al. (Chapter I) present the fundamental concepts of their component-based methodology and complementary context-aware adaptation framework, and discuss how the framework handles the various kinds of adaptation along multiple levels of abstraction (*content, application, framework,* and *network*). After having discussed the basic concepts of our adaptation framework, they evaluate some of the benefits of their integrated adaptation approach based on a set of QoS requirements.

Chaari et al. (Chapter II) propose a comprehensive and open strategy that guarantees the adaptation of applications to context on three facets: (i) the services offered to the user, (ii) the multimedia contents returned by these services, and (iii) their presentation to the user. They have validated this strategy by developing a platform that guarantees applications adaptation to context by using Java, OSGi and Web service technologies to implement this platform. They present a successful test of their adaptation approach on a home healthcare application concerning dialyzed persons.

Daniel (Chapter III) characterizes the design of context-aware Web applications, describes a conceptual, model-driven development approach, and shows how the peculiarities of context-awareness require augmenting the expressive power of conceptual models in order to be able to express adaptive application behaviors.

The second section of the book deals with different aspects of advanced context management, regarding the adaptive framework, distributed context and context-aware database querying methods and techniques.

Roussaki et al. (Chapter IV) elaborates on mechanisms that address advanced requirements including support for distributed context databases management; efficient query handling; innovative management of mobile physical objects and optimization strategies for distributed context data dissemination. These mechanisms establish a robust spatially-enhanced distributed context management framework that has thoroughly been designed, carefully implemented and extensively evaluated via numerous experiments.

Zebedee et al. (Chapter V) describe a robust and adaptable context management system achieved by adopting the autonomic computing paradigm, which supports systems that are aware of their surroundings and that can automatically react to changes in them. They present an implementation based on widely accepted standards, specifically Web services and the Web Services Distributed Management (WSDM) standard.

Li et al. (Chapter VI) present the latest context-aware querying techniques developed in the data management field in order to enable effective design of context-aware database query processing mechanism. They outline six ways to query context directly, and provide a categorization about how to use context in querying traditional databases. The approaches of handling imperfect context in context-aware database querying are also described.

The third section of the book is concerned with service-oriented computing in the mobile and ubiquitous settings and how to develop and seamlessly integrate context-aware mobile services in service-oriented architectures.

Jacob et al (Chapter VII) extend the notion of context-aware services by considering service composition approaches, and present a middleware aiming at the autonomic and context-aware provision of services in mobile peer-to-peer networks. In this regard special attention is paid to a semantic blackboard concept to cache and disseminate context data and a context-aware service composition approach in terms of the identified trends and challenges.

Eikerling and Mazzoleni (Chapter VIII) present a methodology based on model-to-model transformations to be applied at different stages of the service lifecycle. Starting from a conceptual model, these models reflect characteristic properties of the mobile service under development such as context information. For the implementation, a middleware suite then is used which comprises a set of constituents which significantly simplify and shorten the mobile services development cycle. They demonstrate the concepts in terms of mobile business-to-business field services in which through the methodology and tools the dynamicity can be enhanced.

Dietze et al. (Chapter IX) propose Mobile Situation Spaces (MSS) which enable the description of situation characteristics as members in geometrical vector spaces following the idea of Conceptual Spaces (CS). Semantic similarity between situational contexts is calculated in terms of their Euclidean distance within a MSS. Extending merely symbolic SWS descriptions with context information on a conceptual level through MSS enables similarity-based matchmaking between real-world situation characteristics and predefined resource representations as part of SWS descriptions. To prove the feasibility, they provide a proof-of-concept prototype which applies MSS to support context-adaptation across distinct mobile situations.

Raibulet (Chapter X) proposes an adaptive solution to enable identification of the available resources and services and indicates which resource is the best one to execute a service. She proposes an approach which models the adaptation knowledge through reflective entities, qualities and properties, the management of the adaptation knowledge through views, the decision support through strategies, and the management of the functional and non-functional elements through managers.

The fourth section of the book deals with important topics of context-aware communication, security and privacy in mobile systems and applications, which are essential prerequisites for wide use of context-aware services across the wireless Web.

Lofeudo et al. (Chapter XI) present their own hardware and software platform built to communicate and position mobile devices in an efficient way. They describe the design and implementation of their software/hardware combination, which is designed to provide a balance between network bandwidth, power consumption and roaming capabilities. They also present an example showing how the hardware is combined with their sensing layer to develop context-aware applications.

Gomez et al. (Chapter XII) present the use of context information for authentication and access control in ubiquitous and mobile environments as a way to reach a higher level of flexibility and adaptability of the systems' security. The authors propose and describe different new techniques to ensure access control, and compare them to the state-of-the-art.

Ali-Eldin et al. (Chapter XIII) deal with two challenges in incorporating privacy in context-aware services. The first one is to improve privacy architectures with a trust functionality and the second one is to integrate this refined privacy architecture in larger service- oriented architectures (SOAs).

The fifth section of the book presents application of context-awareness for enhanced usability and personalization of mobile and ubiquitous applications in specific application domains.

Joly et al. (Chapter XIV) depict their vision of "Social Ambient Intelligence" based on the review of several uses of semantic technologies for context management, adaptive human-system interaction, privacy enforcement and social communications. Based on identified benefits and lacks, and on their experience, the authors propose several research leads towards the realization of this vision.

Paganelli and Giuli (Chapter XV) provide an analysis of existing studies in the field of context awareness research targeted to the infomobility application domain. The authors propose an evaluation framework for infomobility services based on the elicitation of context information items and high-level requirements. The framework is applied to some relevant state-of-the art research works among personal navigation systems, infomobility service integration frameworks and context-aware location-based communication platforms. Evaluation results are discussed in order to highlight open research challenges in the infomobility application domain.

Tsianos et al. (Chapter XVI) put focus on identifying human factors that relate to users' performance in Web applications that involve information processing, and a framework of personalization rules that are expected to increase users' performance is depicted. The environments that empirical results were derived from were both learning and commercial; in the case of E-Learning personalization was beneficial, while the interaction with a commercial site needs to be further investigated due to the implicit character of information processing in the Web.

Dragan Stojanovic
University of Nis, Serbia

REFERENCES

Adelstain, F., Gupta, S. K. S, Richard, G. G., & Schwiebert, L. (2005). *Fundamentals of Mobile and Pervasive Computing*. New York, USA: McGraw-Hill Professional Engineering.

Baldauf, M., Dustdar, S., & Rosenberg, F. (2007). A survey on context-aware systems. *International Journal of Ad Hoc and Ubiquitous Computing, 2*(4), 263-277.

Chen, H., Finin, T., & Joshi, A. (2004). An ontology for context-aware pervasive computing environments. Special Issue on Ontologies for Distributed Systems. *Knowledge Engineering Review, 18*(3), 197–207.

Chen, G., & Kotz, D. (2000). *A Survey of Context-aware Mobile Computing Research*. Technical Report TR2000-381, Department of Computer Science, Dartmouth College, USA.

Dey, A. K., & Abowd, G. D. (2000a). Towards a better understanding of context and context-awareness. *Workshop on the What, Who, Where, When and How of Context-Awareness, as part of the 2000 Conference on Human Factors in Computing Systems (CHI 2000)*, ACM Press, New York, (pp. 304-307).

Dey, A. K., & Abowd, G. D. (2000b). The context toolkit: aiding the development of context-aware applications. *Workshop on Software Engineering for Wearable and Pervasive Computing*, Limerick, Ireland, (pp. 434-441).

Fahy, P., & Clarke, S. (2004). CASS – a middleware for mobile context-aware applications. *Workshop on Context Awareness*, MobiSys.

Gu, T., Pung, H. K., & Zhang, D. Q. (2004a). A middleware for building context-aware mobile services. *IEEE Vehicular Technology Conference (VTC)*, Milan, Italy.

Hofer, T., Schwinger, W., Pichler, M., Leonhartsberger, G., & Altmann, J. (2002). Context-awareness on mobile devices – the hydrogen approach. *36th Annual Hawaii International Conference on System Sciences*, (pp. 292–302).

Korpipää, P., Mantyjarvi, J., Kela, J., Keranen, H., & Malm, E-J. (2003). Managing context information in mobile devices. *IEEE Pervasive Computing, 2*(3), 42–51.

Prekop, P., & Burnett, M. (2003). Activities, context and ubiquitous computing. *Special Issue on Ubiquitous Computing Computer Communications, 26*(11), 1168–1176.

Roman, M., Hess, C., Cerqueira, R., Ranganathan, A., Campbell, R. H., & Nahrstedt, K. (2002). A middleware infrastructure for active spaces. *IEEE Pervasive Computing, 1*(4), 74–83.

Strang, T., & Linnhoff-Popien, C. (2004). A Context Modeling Survey. *First International Workshop on Advanced Context Modelling, Reasoning and Management, UbiComp 2004 - The Sixth International Conference on Ubiquitous Computing*, Nottingham/England.

Want, R., Hopper, A., Falcão, V., & Gibbons, J. (1992). The Active Badge location system. *ACM Transactions on Information Systems, 10(*1), 91-102.

Weiser, M. (1991). *The computer for the 21st Century*. Scientific American.

Acknowledgment

I would like to acknowledge the help of all involved in the collection and review process of the book without whose support the project could not have been satisfactorily completed. Obviously, in any project of this size, it is impossible to remember, let alone mention, everyone who had a hand in this work becoming what it is today.

First, I want to thank all of the authors. They deserve the greatest credit because their contributions ere essential, giving us great material with which to work. It was a wonderful experience to work with them, to read their contributions, and to discuss the book's overall objectives and particular ideas. Most of the authors of chapters included in this book also served as referees for articles written by other authors. Thanks go to all those who assisted us in the reviewing process by providing constructive and comprehensive reviews.

Staff members of Computer Graphics and GIS Lab at the Faculty of Electronic Engineering at University of Nis were critical in creating this final product. Their support was vital in achieving what we hope is a well-edited publication.

A special note of thanks goes to all the staff at IGI Global, whose contributions throughout the whole process, from inception of the initial idea to final publication, have been invaluable. In particular, I thank Rebecca Beistline who continuously prodded via e-mail to keep the project on schedule and promptly answers on all questions and doubts.

Finally, I wish to express great gratitude to my wife Natalija and daughter Mina for their unfailing patience, support and love.

Dragan Stojanovic
Nis, Serbia

Section I
Adaptation in Context–Aware Applications

Chapter I
Context–Aware Adaptation in an Ecology of Applications

Davy Preuveneers
Katholieke Universiteit Leuven, Belgium

Koen Victor
Katholieke Universiteit Leuven, Belgium

Yves Vanrompay
Katholieke Universiteit Leuven, Belgium

Peter Rigole
Katholieke Universiteit Leuven, Belgium

Manuele Kirsch Pinheiro
Katholieke Universiteit Leuven, Belgium

Yolande Berbers
Katholieke Universiteit Leuven, Belgium

ABSTRACT

In recent years, many researchers have studied context-awareness to support non-intrusive adaptability of context-aware applications. Context-aware applications benefit from emerging technology that connects everyday objects and provides opportunities to collect and use context information from various sources. Context-awareness helps to adapt continuously to new situations and to turn a static computing environment into a dynamic ecology of smart and proactive applications. In this chapter, we present our framework that manages and uses context information to adapt applications and the content they provide. We show how application adaptation can be handled at the composition level, by reconfiguring, redeploying and rewiring components, e.g. to fall back into reduced functionality mode when redeploying an application on a handheld. The key features of our context-aware adaptation framework not only include local adaptations of context-aware applications and content, but also the addressing of context in large scale networks and the context-aware redeployment of running applications in a distributed setting. We discuss how adaptation is handled along various levels of abstraction (user, content, application, middleware, network) and illustrate the flexibility of context-aware content and application adaptation by means of a realistic use case scenario.

INTRODUCTION

We witness nowadays a trend towards ubiquitous information and pervasive communication networks. Technology is emerging that connects everyday mobile objects and embeds intelligence in our environment. The ability to collect and combine data from various sources and adapt to changes in our surroundings is crucial to turn static environments into smart and proactive ones. In such environments, as envisioned by Weiser (1991), computing is pushed away from the traditional desktop to small embedded and networked computing devices around us. In recent years, the use of context-awareness to support non-intrusive adaptability of content and applications has received a lot of attention (Moran & Dourish, 2001; Islam & Fayad, 2003; Gheis et al. 2006; Chaari et al., 2006; Yang & Shao, 2007).

It goes without saying that context-awareness plays a key role in such systems in order (1) to meet changing user expectations, (2) to satisfy changing device and application resource constraints and (3) to optimize the quality of service.

As Chaari et al. (2006) explain, context-awareness is the capability of perceiving the user situation in all its forms, and of adapting in consequence the system behavior, i.e., the services and content supplied to the users. Or as Charles Darwin stated earlier: *"It is not the most intelligent of the species that survive the longest, it is the most adaptable."* In order to be successful,

applications need to adapt continuously to their environment and therefore require information from this environment for the adaptation to be effective.

Developing mobile and pervasive applications with support for context-driven adaptation is a daunting task. The problem is threefold. First of all, to carry out application adaptation at runtime, we require a proper application design methodology that facilitates customizing the functionality during the deployment and runtime life cycle of the application. Secondly, the design methodology needs to be complemented with runtime support that enables applications to dynamically adapt their behavior and the content they offer to the user whenever the applications' context changes. And thirdly, applications must take into account the characteristics of the systems on which they are deployed, the environment in which they are embedded, and the user expectations regarding the application in order to exhibit optimal behavior. Hence, context-awareness is a key concern that needs to be supported within the adaptation framework from the ground up. To address these challenges, we present in this chapter an integrated approach to context-aware adaptation of applications and the content they supply. The focus of our contribution is (1) a design methodology in which applications are composed out of loosely coupled distributed components, enhanced with (2) an adaptation framework that provides solutions to facilitate context-aware adaptation of applications and the content supplied by those applications. Context-aware adaptation in our framework consists of application adaptation and content adaptation and is handled at different levels.

Context-aware applications have a component-based design with basic constructs such as components, component ports, connectors, contracts and context interfaces. Components provide the functionality of the application and communicate with other components through connectors attached to their component ports.

Contracts and context interfaces ensure a specific behavior in a particular situation. These concepts are further explained in section 4. Application adaptation is handled at the architectural level by reconfiguring and redeploying components, while content adaptation is addressed internally by the components, for example, through content filtering (e.g. selecting content related to a given location, or selecting a content format that fits the capabilities of the client device) and/or content transformation (e.g. transforming content to a data format supported by the user's device).

Figure 1 shows a component-based conferencing client that is composed of 3 components: *Multimedia Player*, *Jabber Protocol* and *User Interface*. The replacement of the *Jabber Protocol* component with another instant messaging protocol component is an example of structural application adaptation, while changing the volume of the *Multimedia Player* component is an example of behavioral adaptation. Content adaptation can be achieved within the *User Interface* component by filtering or rescaling content that does not fit the size of the display.

For both application and content adaptation, the adaptation processes build upon the component philosophy and the proper runtime support within the framework to carry out the adaptation. Relevant context information is required for the adaptation to be effective. Given that this context information may not be available locally, the adaptation framework relies on mechanisms for context information collection and distribution. We will elaborate in more detail on each of these aspects in the following sections and will validate our adaptation framework with a scenario where resource conservative behavior is the requested QoS.

In the following section, we present a motivating scenario on context-aware adaptation. This scenario will be used later on to illustrate the strengths and flexibility of our integrated approach to context-aware adaptation. From this scenario we distill the fundamental requirements of the design methodology for pervasive and mobile applications and the supporting adaptation framework. Afterwards, we present the fundamental concepts of our component-based methodology

Figure 1. Adaptation with component-based applications

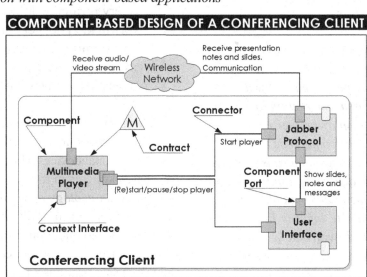

and complementary context-aware adaptation framework, and discuss how the framework handles the various kinds of adaptation along multiple levels of abstraction (*content*, *application*, *framework*, and *network*). The component-based design methodology and the corresponding basic building blocks of the framework that support context-aware adaptation are explained bottom-up. We illustrate how context information that is gathered from the environment drives the adaptation process to adapt applications to accommodate new requirements, and how context is used to optimize application deployment in a distributed setting. Context will also be a key enabler to the content adaptation process within an application to offer the most appropriate content in the most suitable format to the user. After having discussed the basic concepts of our adaptation framework, we will evaluate some of the benefits of our integrated adaptation approach based on a set of QoS requirements and end with some conclusions and future work.

MOTIVATING SCENARIO

The necessity of dealing with context-aware adaptation of applications and content supplied by those applications on different levels is illustrated in the following scenario:

Company Rising Sun organizes a large meeting for all its sales representatives where the results of a recent survey are presented and where the participants are discussing marketing strategies. All attendants use a display to interact with the shared whiteboard in the conference room. One of the sales representatives, Jim, has to leave early for an urgent dentist appointment, but he will remain in touch with his colleagues to discuss the proposals. He informs by message those managers he deals with that he is leaving. The conferencing client moves from his display in the conference room to his personal wire-less handheld device. As the capabilities of a handheld are limited, the application runs with reduced functionality. While in the dentist's seat, Jim does not want to be disturbed and will only receive the notes and a summary of the minutes on his handheld. Whenever devices with a larger display or more processing power show up in his vicinity for which he has permission to use, the application is again adapted and relocated to provide a better user experience.

In this small scenario, we observe that multiple actors on different levels of the adaptation framework can initiate the adaptation process:

- **User:** Jim is moving away, the framework should ensure that the application follows along.
- **Content:** The video stream cannot be shown on the small screen of the handheld. Unsupported content is filtered or transformed to a different format.
- **Application:** The application moves to the handheld device. Unused application components are disabled or removed from the application.
- **Middleware:** The middleware that hosts the applications monitors shared resources and notifies the applications when e.g. the battery is running low.
- **Network:** The network provides new context information about resources in the environment and triggers a relocation of the application to a new host.

This scenario illustrates how different kinds of applications may surround the user. Some run on personal devices while others are offered on shared systems in the vicinity. Together they constitute *an ecology of applications* on which a user can rely for his daily activities. Nonetheless, in order to maintain an acceptable level of user experience in pervasive computing environments, the applications and the information they provide should adapt to the current context at hand, which includes not only information about available resources, but also about the user and his preferences. The following paragraphs give an overview of the requirements that our application design methodology has to meet in order to support an ecology of context-aware adaptable applications.

REQUIREMENTS

In this section we review several non-functional concerns of context-aware adaptable applications in a mobile and pervasive computing setting. These concerns have an impact on the design and the deployment of applications and define deployment constraints in terms of the capabilities of a device as well as user preferences with respect to the application. We consider these requirements as non-functional since they are outside the application logic domain.

Context and User Personalization

A user may have requirements or preferences for the applications he is using and they should be taken into account as good as possible to help meet user expectations. For example, Jim may wish to preserve the battery power of his handheld device, which means that the highly power-consuming wireless communication should be disabled. These requirements and preferences will result in context constraints that will determine which applications are selected, how they are adapted and composed and how they behave at runtime.

Resource- and Context-Aware Deployment

While on the move Jim will mainly interact with mobile and embedded systems. This means that the applications on these devices are subject to tight resource constraints, including limited memory, processing power, network bandwidth and, last but not least, battery life time. Moreover, these devices will have to share resources when serving many applications concurrently. Hence, resource and other contextual constraints will determine whether a particular application can execute properly on a given device after deployment or if further adaptations are needed.

User Mobility and Application Relocation

The motivating scenario is an illustration of how user mobility will become an essential cornerstone to future computing. As a consequence, the amount of environmental resources the mobile device can address to extend its capabilities may fluctuate accordingly. For example, once having an application remotely deployed, a decreasing network bandwidth or network disruptions may reduce the quality of service (QoS) to an unacceptable level. Therefore, when on the move Jim may choose to run an application locally, but when stationary Jim may free up some local system resources by relocating and running one or more applications remotely on a more powerful device in the neighborhood.

Application and Content Adaptation

As the sales representative is cruising through highly dynamic pervasive computing environments, his applications will need to adapt to changing working conditions. In order to offer personalized applications and run them on devices with versatile resource characteristics, the application must be adapted to the capabilities of the device. Therefore, applications should not be monolithically designed, but rather have a modular structure that makes it possible to replace parts of the application without changing the overall intended functionality requested by the user. Moreover, the dynamism of pervasive environments, as well as the mobility of the users in such environments directly impacts the user's interests and, by consequence, the relevance of the content he expects from the applications. Thus, the way content is selected and presented to the user must also adapt whenever the context changes.

Overview of the Requirements

The previous requirements affect the whole life-cycle of an application. First of all, context information about the device, the applications, the content and the user is needed to take well-informed decisions during the adaptation process. This information is used to decide where applications are deployed. After the deployment, a changing context may affect the active applications in different ways: it may be moved to a different location or adapted to the current situation. The basic requirements for our application design methodology and complementary context-aware adaptation framework can be summarized as follows:

1. A modular application design methodology that supports runtime adaptation
2. Context management in a distributed setting
3. Context-driven content and application selection, deployment, adaptation and relocation

In the following sections we will argue how our design methodology and context-aware adaptation framework complies with these requirements.

CONTEXT-AWARE ADAPTATION IN AN ECOLOGY OF APPLICATIONS

In this section we discuss our component-based design methodology for pervasive and mobile applications and the basic building blocks within the complementary framework that support context-aware adaptation. We outline how context information is collected from the system, the user and the environment. We describe how context drives the adaptation process to structurally change applications to accommodate new requirements, optimize their deployment in a distributed setting, and personalize the content offered by the applications to the user.

A Component-Based Design for Context-Aware Adaptable Applications

In the following paragraphs we present a component-based design with support for application adaptation, interaction and composition within a mobile and pervasive context. The application design incorporates components and connectors as functional building blocks, and contracts and context interfaces as non-functional building blocks. The basic principles of the component-based design methodology are illustrated in Figure 1. It shows how the conferencing client consists of a multimedia component and an instant messaging component both wired to a user interface component. Some of these components can be disabled or replaced with compatible ones depending on the actual deployment requirements.

The following entities together form the business logic of an application and define its functional and non-functional aspects:

- **Components:** Applications are created through the assembling of components. As applications need to be deployed on devices with varying characteristics, the use of components makes it possible to dynamically adapt services either by relocating components or by replacing them with others in order to optimize deployment on a specific device.
- **Connectors:** Connectors, which are linked to the component ports of a component, provide communication channels between components within a service. They are used

to deliver asynchronous messages from one component port to another. Asynchronous messaging allows connecting to remote components and prevents the blocking of one component for another.

- **Contracts**: Contracts impose non-functional constraints on a component or a group of interacting components. Contracts can be used, for example, to guarantee memory availability or bandwidth constraints within an application internally. Contracts can be used to specify user requirements and to ensure optimal deployment on embedded devices.
- **Context Interface:** The Context Interface is a dedicated component port responsible for the sending and receiving static and dynamic context information. Among other things, it allows the application to be notified of new resources, and to inform other applications or devices about resources currently in use by this application.

This component-based design methodology for pervasive and mobile applications addresses the requirement (1) outlined in the previous section. It not only helps to compose applications using loosely coupled components, but also enables runtime adaptation by replacing components with compatible interfaces. The loose coupling and the asynchronous communication facilitates connecting to remote components in order to optimize the usage of system resources. As such, the component-based design methodology is a key enabler for requirements (2) and (3) as well.

Context Management

Context involves relevant information on real world entities that needs to be described in a structured model to facilitate the sharing of collected information. It is therefore impossible to limit context information to a fixed set of attributes or properties that would be continuously monitored for change. Several context modeling approaches have been proposed in the past: from simple key-value pairs (Schilit & Theimer, 1994) to ontologies (Preuveneers et al., 2004). They all model context in a different way, but the information that is modeled typically includes:

- **Identity:** The user himself, a person he is dealing with, user profiles and preferences
- **Activity:** Appointments, scheduled tasks in agenda, shopping, leisure pastime
- **Spatial information:** Location, direction, speed, presence, nearby items
- **Temporal information:** Date, time of the day
- **Environmental information:** Temperature, light, noise, weather
- **Social situation:** People that are nearby or with whom the user is interacting
- **Resources and services:** Devices, resources, services and applications on the network

Context management from an application perspective involves the following functional building blocks (see Figure 2), no matter whether the context information is used locally or has to be sent out to a remote entity somewhere on the network.

- **Context Retrieval:** This component gathers information from sensors, user profiles or other information providers on the system itself or in the neighborhood. In general, it monitors information, such as changes in the current network bandwidth, and receives all data that has been pushed to the system by third parties. It sends this context through a filter to make sure that only the most up-to-date and accurate information is selected when multiple external sources provide similar information in response to a particular context information request.

• **Context Storage:** A context repository ensures persistence of context information. It only saves up-to-date and relevant information in a way that queries and information updates can be handled efficiently. Therefore, context representation involves two aspects: the information itself, for example the attribute '*Age=43*', and how it relates to other concepts such as a category '*Person*', for example, the sales representative. Our context management stores context as an expandable knowledge base of ontologies for semantic modeling of concepts and as a fact container with time stamped instantiations of these concepts to exploit historic values.

• **Context Manipulation:** This component transforms and reasons on context information. Context transformation changes the way certain information is represented. For example, a temperature expressed in Celsius can be transformed into Fahrenheit using simple mathematical transformation rules. Classification is another kind of transformation, where accuracy of information is given up for the sake of more meaningful information. For example, the longitude and latitude coordinates of the dentist practice

can be replaced by the street name and city. Context reasoning derives new information based on existing facts and derivation rules. Whereas context transformation changes the way a concept is expressed, context reasoning combines derivation rules and facts into other facts which were only available implicitly.

Each of the above context managing building blocks is implemented as a composition of subcomponents that can be activated whenever an application requires them and unloaded when they are no longer needed. This way, unnecessary context managing components do not waste any resources if their function is not required by any of the context-aware applications. The component-based design is discussed in more detail in (Preuveneers & Berbers, 2005) and fulfills the requirement (2) on context management in a distributed setting. Finding context in an ad hoc network and the distribution aspect is discussed in more detail in the following paragraphs.

Context Addressing and Distribution

Context-aware applications are most useful in mobile ad hoc networks. In these networks, ap-

Figure 2. Basic composite components for context management

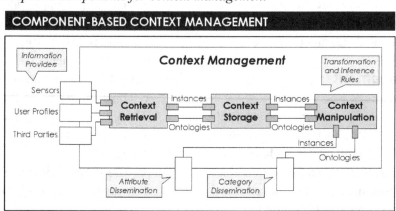

plications that respond to context changes in the network may provide functional benefits because they recognize new possibilities as opposed to applications that do not take their dynamic environment into account. A drawback of these types of networks is the difficulty of addressing relevant nodes in the network on a conceptual level and efficiently transmitting context information requests and responses to relevant nodes.

Most context-aware applications have functionality that requires information that is not available locally or that needs to be combined with other information from different sources in the network. As a result, context information may need to be combined, modified and redistributed to other actors in the network before it can be put to good use. However, querying context information is not a trivial task for context-aware applications, because the execution of the application is context data oriented, and querying context is only successful when addressed to relevant persons, objects, or other information. For example, querying for *'all managers that have to leave this room during this or the following presentation'* requires the ability to specify a query that can meaningfully express and connect *'this room'*, *'this or the following presentation'*, and *'leave'*. Each of these context constraints narrow down the possible solutions to the query for *'all managers'*.

Also the distribution of information is influenced by context-aware applications. The location of information may change depending on the location of persons, objects or other information. Also, if applications and nodes in the network nodes move, then the relevancy, accuracy and validity of context information can change.

Context addressing is not a new topic, but has been investigated before by Loke et al. (2003) and Devlic & Klintskog (2007). These schemes allow specifying the context of an object or person in a declarative way, together with a context description. For example, before leaving the meeting room Jim the sales representative sends a message to a group of people by specifying the

recipients as follows: *'All managers I work for in this meeting room'*. All objects that match this context address will receive the message. Several notations for context addressing have been studied to declaratively describe the context of an object. Below is an example of this context address in first order logic:

{ **Person** p | (p.jobtitle = 'Manager') **and** (p **in** jim.clients) **and** (p.location = jim.location) }

Considering the features of context-aware applications and the target network, a context addressing scheme should offer the following features: (1) description of the data that is sent or requested, and context data constraints, (2) specification of the environment in which the context data is relevant, (3) additional meta information about the context data or environment which may guide distribution of the query: mobility, QoS requirements such as latency, availability and accuracy. Because of the nature of context data, the context addressing should not make assumptions about the physical network (IP-addressing) or refer to services on the network. A context address can be adapted while routing the context request or the context information in the network, because nodes in the network may have more specialized information about how to interpret the address and how to adapt it to allow more efficient routing to the final destinations.

Context addresses can be combined using concept constructors, for example: *address3 = UnionOf(address1, address2)* addresses the objects in the union of the objects addressed by address1 and address2. Most context addressing schemes rely on a type system, that is shared by every node on the network. The type system may be hierarchic, and form a semantic tree. This allows semantic reasoning on the data types in the addresses and facilitates optimization of network traffic if required. For example, a search for *'Sales Manager'* and *'Sales Representatives'* may be compressed to *'Sales Staff'* (see Figure 3).

Figure 3. A hierarchic context addressing type system

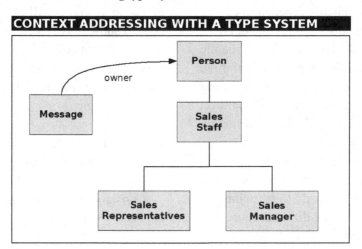

A basic building block of our addressing scheme is context grouping. Groups are formed among nodes that share a common observable context. While addressing groups, the scope of the dissemination on an abstract level is limited to well-known borders, and the underlying routing mechanism takes this into account to guide the context distribution process. Using grouping, nodes are 'joined' according to different semantic values, e.g. *'All nodes in the same room' or 'all nodes that are interested in persons leaving or entering the room'*. To define these groups, we use context operators. Context operators determine what context information needs to be retrieved from the network. They take this information as input and produce new context information as result of their operation. Context operators can be domain independent (such as Boolean operators and arithmetic operators) or domain dependent (operator *'FindClosest'* can have many implementations, depending on the context of use).

As an example, we explain the context operator that can be used to disseminate information to all nodes that are at most 20 meters away from Jim and are interested in messages from sales men:

InRange(jim, 20), (**Message** m | m.<u>owner</u>.type. <u>name</u> == "Sales Manager").

Context addresses based on context groups provide a clean way to address a number of related objects or persons, using a declarative description. As mentioned above, our context addressing scheme contains a description about the environment where the information may be found, as first described in Victor et al. (2007). This field is used by the routing algorithm to decide what search algorithm is used to execute the request, or limit the search space of the search algorithm. For example: the address

InRange(jim, 20), (**Message** m | m.<u>owner</u>.type. <u>name</u> == "Sales Manager"),
History(jim), **InRange**(**ThisTown**(), 0)

targets all nodes interested in the data type description *'Messages from sales managers'* within 20 meters of Jim, where the data is relevant for the personal log of Jim's actions, and the search space is limited to the town of the sender of the request.

In order to specify the relationships between operators and the inputs and outputs of an operator, we use an ontology based on the original proposal of Devlic & Klintskog (2007). This allows differentiating between operators on the basis of the input and output type. For example, consider the following queries: *'Find all presentation screens within a range of 5m from myself'* (e.g. to select the biggest one) and *'Find all dentists within a range of 20km'*. The inputs and outputs fed to the operator are of different types, and the reasoning process will find the appropriate operator that satisfies input and output requirements set in the query.

The context addressing scheme we present here is based on these concepts of operators and semantic type hierarchies, but we take the reasoning process one step further by not only letting the in- and outputs types select the operators, but also the semantic meaning of them. We compare the semantic meaning with the situation of the sender of the request to configure a regular operator. This allows to introduce meta-operators such as *CloseTo(), FarFrom(), InNeighbourhoodOf()*, etc. In our example, the query expressed as *'Find all dentists close to me'* can be translated to *'Find all dentists within a range of 500m from myself'* in case that I am on foot, and to *'Find all dentists within a range 20km from myself'* when by car. This may be extended by taking my situation into account, instead of the situation of the sender of the request. Using operators and meta-operators, one can specify queries that align with human questions asked in real world.

The combination of a flexible component-based context managing system and the powerful context addressing scheme to collect relevant context information in the network enable context-aware applications to adapt their behavior to changing circumstances, and both fulfill requirement (2) on distributed context management. In the following paragraphs we address various aspects that help to fulfill requirement (3) on content and application adaptation.

Deployment and Application Adaptation

One of the primary goals of context-aware adaptation is to define and to safeguard the application's quality attributes, which makes adaptation at the level of the architecture an interesting adaptation approach. Such adaptations can be performed in many of the views on the software architecture. We believe that the deployment view is one of the most appealing architectural dimensions for adapting an application because of the close relation between quality of service and resource availability. An application that provides a certain level of quality of service typically needs sufficient system resources to perform accordingly. Since resources are spread across the many nodes that comprise a pervasive environment, they create a challenge for optimizing application deployment scenario's that still meet the quality of service requirements. Such a resource-driven adaptation approach represents the first deployment adaptation track we elaborate on in this section.

The second deployment adaptation track we consider is orthogonal to the first. Where the first track considers 'where' to deploy components, the second track investigates 'when' to deploy components. A thoughtful component life-cycle manager can optimize resource allocation simply by deallocating those components that are not needed now or in the near future. By allocating components only shortly before they are expected to support the user of the system, resources are freed-up for components that are needed more urgently at the time. In order to implement a smart life-cycle manager that can do this, information is needed that expresses which functionality is required for the user's current activity. This activity-driven adaptation approach represents the second deployment adaptation track we elaborate on in this section.

Resource-Driven Adaptation

Applications that run on mobile embedded devices are often limited in the functionality they can offer because of resource constraints that characterize such devices. Component approaches separate an application's functionality into independently deployable building blocks. The ability for easy remote deployment of the functionality confined within components can greatly enhance the application's computing capabilities. This provides the application with an expanded virtual computing space. In general, we believe that good mechanisms for deploying an application in a pervasive computing environment need to be able to:

1. Optimize the deployment configuration to a stable state,
2. Exhibit self-organizing deployment behavior to perform redeployment, and
3. Deal with disconnected operation.

(1) Optimal deployment involves the deployment of the optimal amount of functionality whenever possible on the host that matches the deployment's resources needs best. It is especially important at the initial deployment to find hosts that are suited to manage the application components. A stable deployment state is a desirable condition that represents a deployment of functionality in a way that redeployment operations are unlikely to occur very often. (2) Redeployment implies the ability to change the existing deployment when the configuration of the computing environment changes with respect to resource availability so that it threatens the correct functionality of application components. Self-organizing deployment behavior stresses the fact that user distraction should be avoided in the deployment process. Cooperating middleware systems need to be able to agree upon distributed application deployment. (3) Disconnected operation enables the applications to partially or totally continue to support user tasks in the event of disconnections in the network that bears the communication load in the computing space.

In order to realize pervasive computing space that exploits remote resources, a distributed deployment mechanism is needed that is aware of the resource requirements of the application components on the one hand, and that is aware of the resources that are available in the distributed environment on the other hand. Software profiling tools can be used by designers to analyze the resource footprint of components. The resulting assessment of such analysis can then be wrapped into a component's resource contract, which is a model of the component's runtime behavior with respect to resource requirements. These resource contracts can be expressed by modeling languages such as the MARTE UML profile. This UML profile is designed to express quality attributes such as schedulability, performance, timing, memory and bandwidth for real-time embedded systems.

In Mikic-Rakic & Medvidovic (2002), the author presents a deployment solution for a distributed application that optimizes the availability of the application. The mechanism of Mikic-Rakic also deals with disconnected operations, so the solution presented is in line with our distributed deployment requirements (1) and (3). Unfortunately, their solution takes a centralized deployment approach that calculates the exact optimal deployment scenario using a constraint solver. In reality, however, we cannot assume that there exists a single coordinating entity in a distributed environment that coordinates the distributed deployment on all nodes. Firstly, this would create a single point of failure and second, a single entity will never achieve a complete view on the environment. This is why we believe that single nodes have to coordinate their deployment activities with their direct neighbors only, which calls for self-organizing deployment behavior. In Rigole & Berbers (2006), a decentralized component choreography mechanism is presented that

Figure 4. Component relocation steps with state transfer.

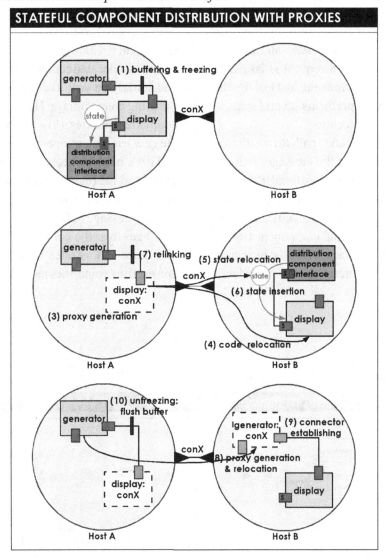

only uses local information to optimize global distributed deployment configuration. By means of a collaborative reinforcement learning mechanism, the deployment capabilities in the pervasive network are spread so that only communication with neighboring nodes suffices to optimize deployment scenarios. Although the presented solution may result in sub-optimal deployment configurations, the results are found quickly and

changes in the environment may lead to small redeployment steps that cause little overhead. This solution thus also meets the distributed deployment requirement (2).

The component model and framework presented in this chapter support component distribution with full runtime state transfer. Communication with remote components is done through proxy components to guarantee full transparency towards the underlying component framework. Figure 4 illustrates how state transfer is realized by our component framework. Initially, there are two components called *generator* and *display* located on Host A. After a request is issued to relocate the *display* component to Host B, the component framework performs several steps to realize the requested relocation.

(1) First, all communication paths to the *display* component are frozen and the messages that are still being sent over them are buffered. (2) In the second step, the component framework retrieves the component's state through a dedicated state port that is connected to the component framework's distribution interface. (3) In the next step, a proxy component is generated whose interfaces

duplicate the display component's interfaces. (4) After the proxy is available in the system, the code of the original component is relocated to Host B, (5) together with the state of the component. (6) Then, the relocated component code is instantiated and initialized with the relocated state. (7) The dangling connectors on Host A are relinked to the component proxies, (8) a proxy corresponding to the *generator* component is generated on Host B, and (9) a new connector is created between this proxy and the relocated *display* component. (10) Finally, the frozen connector on Host A is unfrozen and the message buffer is flushed by releasing the messages over the connector.

Figure 5 illustrates how component proxies are used to route messages over several hosts.

Figure 5. Component distribution with proxy components for full transparency

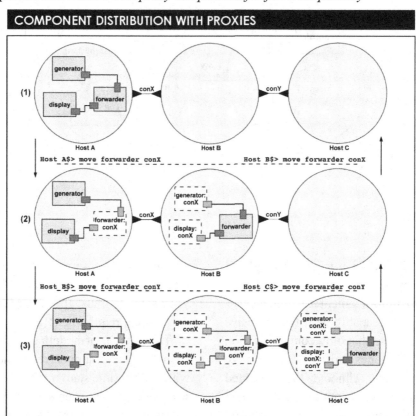

Distribution is initiated by the component framework and occurs without the relocated component being aware of it. Proxies are generated on the fly and are responsible for handling the messages to and from the real component. In the example, the messages from the generator component are forwarded over host B to the forwarder component on host C and back. The flexibility provided by this approach enables us to perform any spontaneous redistribution of components without endangering the quality attributes of the application.

Activity-Driven Adaptation

The adaptation mechanism we present here is a component life cycle managing technique that loads and unloads components based on the activities these components are needed for. Components can often be discarded when an activity finishes and new components often need to be deployed when a new activity begins. This life cycle management technique bases its deployment decisions on information deduced from an activity model that represents the activities supported by an application. The life cycle manager presented in this section is a single entity of coordination, hence the use of the term component *orchestration*.

Activity-driven software adaptation relies on the input from an activity model representing the user's activities and the relations between those. This input consists of the current activity, the software functionality needed for each activity in the activity model and the anticipated activities that may follow after the current activity. The required software functionality for each activity is expressed by a composition model that composes the expected functionality. The composition model for each activity in an activity model is typically a selective subset of the composition model for the whole application.

In the approach we present here, an activity model is transformed into a State Transition Network (STN). Each state in the STN is a collection of parallel activities that need to be available simultaneously in order for the software to support the user. Depending on the activity model used, the transformation into an STN may be more or less complex. For some activity models, there may be a simple one-to-one mapping. An example is given in Rigole et al. (2007), where we illustrate how a composition model is being mapped onto a task tree at design time, followed by a transformation into a runtime state transition network. At runtime, an instance of the STN feeds deployment

Figure 6. Activity-driven adaptation

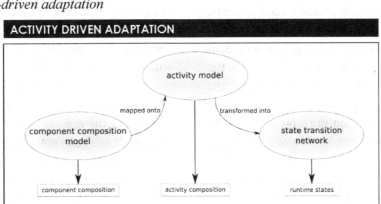

information to a life-cycle manager that executes deployment decisions. The general steps presented here are summarized in Figure 6.

The state transition network precisely knows which components need to be available to support the user's ongoing activities. In addition, it is also aware of the states, and thus the activities, that may follow from the current state. This knowledge gives room for improvement. Knowing future deployment scenarios implies that components can be instantiated even before they are needed, which may improve the availability of the application. Instantiating components only just in time may introduce latencies that bother the user. Allocating spare resources for realizing smooth transitions in the computing support for the user's activities proves to be a good deployment strategy. In Rigole et al. (2007), the next states that follow the application's current state are prioritized based on transition probabilities. Once the process has been used several times by a specific user, transition probabilities are calculated based on history information. The result is a Markov model for the state transition network that indicates the most probable next states for a given user. This way, component deployment scenarios are anticipated on a most likely basis, optimizing availability as an architectural quality attributes.

Content Adaptation

Context-aware adaptation concerns an application as a whole: its functionalities and its components, as well as the content it supplies to its users. Similarly to the application components, the content supplied by the application should also match the user's current context in order to guarantee the appropriate user experience.

Content adaptation, aiming at providing to the user a customized content, is not a new topic (see, for instance, Colajanni & Lancellotti, 2004; Villanova et al., 2003; Ardon et al., 2003). It usually involves the transformation of an original content into another version according the user's context

and preferences, or the selection of the most appropriate versions of a content item (Schilit et al., 2002; Lemlouma & Layaïda, 2004; Yang & Shao, 2007). In many cases, research on content adaptation proposes adaptation mechanisms considering the client device capabilities, involving, for instance, the selection of a given version of an object content according to the device capabilities (e.g. to choose a BMP version of an image instead of a JPEG version), or the transformation of content from an unsupported format (dimension or resolution, etc.) to a supported one.

Besides the capabilities of the client device, other elements of the user's context can also be considered for adaptation purposes. For instance, Yang & Shao (2007) adopt a broader vision of what is context, enlarging this notion with concepts such as network bandwidth, user accessibility (e.g., if the user is blind) and situation (if the user is driving, or in his office, or in a meeting, etc.). Yang & Shao (2007) propose a rule-based content adaptation mechanism in which content presentation is adapted based on a dynamically selected set of rules. Each adaptation rule is associated to a context feature and stipulates an action (for example, mute the audio or select a low quality version of a video). The adaptation strategy, which guides the adaptation process, is then dynamically defined according to the suitable adaptation rules. A planner selects the rules whose context features match the current context, and generates a proper strategy, which is a composition of these selected rules.

Works such as Lemlouma & Layaïda (2004) and Yang & Shao (2007) are mainly concerned with adapting content presentation according to the user's current context. However, the context in which the users interact with the application may affect the relevance of a given content. A content that is relevant in a particular situation can be completely irrelevant (even useless) in another situation. For example, considering the sales representative scenario presented previously, the slides from the marketing strategy meeting becomes irrelevant when Jim is in the dentist's seat. However, in other situations (for example, once he leaves the dentist), the same content becomes relevant and should be supplied to Jim.

Therefore, Kirsch-Pinheiro et al. (2006) proposes a content adaptation mechanism which filters the available content based on its supposed relevance. This relevance is determined by the user's current context and his preferences for this context. Indeed, the proposed mechanism combines traditional filtering approaches based on the user's preferences (such as in Villanova et al., 2003) with a context-aware approach, in which delivered content is adapted to the user's current context. The result is a twofold filtering mechanism in which content is filtered based on user's preferences and context.

The user's preferences are represented through a set of pre-defined profiles. User's profiles are often proposed in the literature (Daoud et al., 2007) (Kassad & Lamirel 2006) as a way to represent user's characteristics (age, spoken languages, etc.) and preferences about the supplied content. In our framework, by using a user's profile, we intend to allow users, system designers or administrators determine what information a user considers as relevant and in which circumstances. We consider a profile as the description of a potential context that might characterize a user's real situation and expresses content filtering rules that should apply when this situation happens (i.e. when the user's context matches this potential context). The filtering rules reflect the user's preferences considering the context associated with the profile. In our case, these rules indicate which content type (content classes, for instance video or text about a given topic) the user prefers to be informed of. The filtering consists in selecting relevant content instances (belonging to these classes) among the available content. We call *application context* the description of a potential context using a given context model such as the one proposed in Kirsch-Pinheiro et al. (2004). For instance, a system administrator may create a profile whose application context describes the use of a given device and whose filtering rules transform content according to the capabilities of this device.

In order to allow an improved personalization of the supplied content, we associate profiles to a progressive access model that is able to organize this content. The central idea is to progressively deliver a personalized content to the users: first, information that is essential for the users is provided, and then, some complementary information, if needed, is made available. We use a generic model, the Progressive Access Model (PAM), that is described in UML. PAM allows the organization of a data model in multiple levels of details according to the user's interests (see details in Villanova et al., 2003). Each defined organization of the data model is called stratification, which can be defined as an ordered sequence of content subsets. Each profile is then composed of a set of filtering rules, which filter the available content, and the corresponding stratifications that organize the selected content in multiple levels. As an illustration, let us consider the sales representative scenario in which Jim may define a profile for when he is out of the office. In such situations, Jim may prefer to receive first only meeting summary, leaving slides in a second level (which he may consult if necessary), and completely ignoring video related to the meetings. Thus, we assume that a profile P is defined as:

$P = \{\, o,\, C_p,\, F,\, S \,\}$, where:

- o refers to the profile owner (the user Jim);
- C_p refers to the application context in which profile can be used (user's context corresponding to out of the office context);
- F is the set of filtering rules expressing the user's preferences about available content (Jim is interested on meeting summary and slides);
- S represents a stratification of the content indicated by F, ordering this content in multiple levels (in the first level, Jim prefers

to receive first summary, then slides in a second level).

The adaptation approach we propose is based on a filtering process in two steps. The first step selects the profiles that should be applied in order to filter the available content, according the user's current context. The second step consists in applying the filtering rules defined by the selected profiles. We assume that for each user a set of pre-defined profiles is available (profiles associated to the most common situations encountered by the user).

The first step of the proposed filtering process consists in selecting the profiles which match the user's current context. This selection is performed by comparing the application context related to each available profile with the user's context. Once the profiles have been selected, the second step of the filtering process applies the filtering rules defined in the selected profiles. These rules indicate the content types considered as relevant by the profile owner. Applying these rules means selecting the content instances whose type matches those indicated in the profile rules. Once the rules are applied, the second step of the filtering process organizes the selected content

objects according to the stratifications defined in each profile. Figure 7 summarizes the algorithms for both steps of the filtering process.

At the end of the proposed filtering process, an organized (in levels of details) set of content objects is available for delivering to the mobile user, which will be able to navigate this set using the operations defined by the progressive access model (see Kirsch-Pinheiro et al., 2006 for details). Figure 8 shows a component implementing this filtering process. It also illustrates how context-aware adaptation can be addressed internally by components which handle personalized content supplied to the users.

An Integrated Approach to Context-Aware Adaptation

The whole adaptation process is entirely based on the processing of context information. The adaptation algorithm consists of the following high-level consecutive steps:

1. **Hardware:** Process the hardware of the device to discover processing power, network capabilities, and other input providers, such as a GPS module.

Figure 7. Algorithms summarizing the two steps of the proposed filtering process

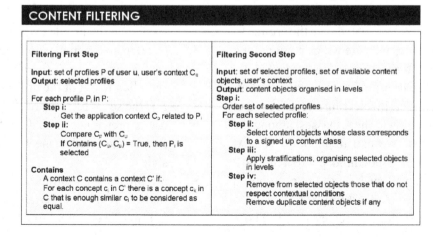

Figure 8. Internal view of a component implementing content filtering adaptation

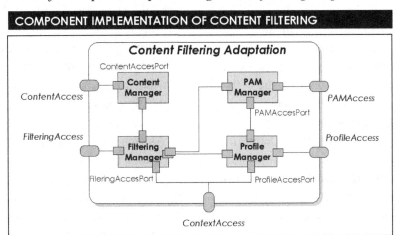

Figure 9. An integrated approach to context-aware adaptation

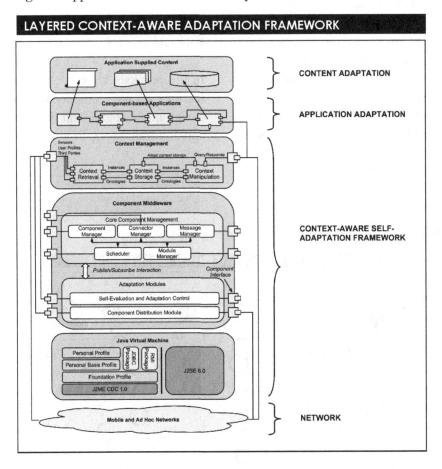

2. **Resource-awareness:** Request the current available resources on the device. This includes the CPU load, the memory and bandwidth usage, and the battery status.

3. **Context dependencies:** Check which context information is required by the active applications for personalized content and optimal component behavior.

4. **Context component selection:** Determine for each context concept the minimum resource requirements, and select the most appropriate component.

5. **Resource sharing:** Delegate context information and application components to another device in the vicinity with similar mobility patterns using location-aware resource discovery to further extend the autonomy of the device.

The context-aware adaptation framework, as illustrated in Figure 9, has a layered structure, each dealing with a particular management aspect of the adaptation process. The basic deployment constraint is that each device on the mobile ad hoc network has a Java virtual machine capable of

running our component middleware, which means it should be equipped with a J2ME CDC 1.0 virtual machine or higher. On top of the component middleware run two sets of components, one set explicitly dealing with context management and distribution, and another set of domain specific application components. The latter also take care of presenting relevant content to the user.

As such, the key features of our context-aware adaptation framework not only include local context-aware application and content adaptation, but also context management in a networked environment. These features help to optimize the user experience by automatically selecting appropriate content as well as adapting and redeploying running components to better suited hosts to further optimize their behavior.

EVALUATION

In the previous sections we discussed the key features of our component-based application design methodology and the context-aware adaptation framework. Providing a detailed and in

Figure 10. Mobility patterns for stationary and moving objects

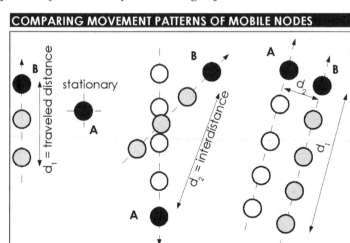

depth evaluation of these key features is beyond the scope of this chapter, but more detailed information can be found in Preuveneers et al. (2004), Kirsch-Pinheiro, Gensel & Martin (2004), Preuveneers & Berbers (2005), Rigole & Berbers (2006), Kirsch-Pinheiro, Villanova-Oliver, Gensel & Martin (2006), Victor et al. (2007), Preuveneers & Berbers (2007), and Rigole, Clerckx, Berbers & Coninx (2007). Instead, we chose to evaluate context-aware adaptation in terms of a user preferred QoS where applications are adapted on the PDA for energy and resource conservative behaviour. With these concrete goals as a given we illustrate the feasibility of our approach. We implemented the scenario presented in the second section and investigated context- and resource aware adaptation of the conferencing client in a distributed and mobile environment while trying to preserve the battery life on the PDA. Mobility patterns, as shown in Figure 10, were used to detect opportunities for collaboration.

The mobility pattern of each device is used to calculate the direction and the traveled distance of the either stationary or mobile device. For location-awareness purposes several different kinds of context components were used: WLAN, GPS and a Personal Information Manager (PIM) with locations of appointments. As the resource consumption of these three techniques differs significantly, we let the framework adapt and choose the most appropriate component in terms

of resource consumption and accuracy for location-awareness.

In our experiments the WLAN component used the most energy, not only for the wireless communication but also to compute the location through triangulation of locations and signal strengths for known access points. The PIM component was the most energy conservative. Some of the characteristics of location-awareness components are shown in Table 1.

With this context information and depending on the current conferencing client component deployment, the most optimal context component was chosen. For example, if wireless communication between a local and a remote application component is required anyway, the overhead to also use WLAN for positioning is minimal. Each request for collaboration includes the following information:

- An identifying attribute of the device (e.g. a MAC address)
- The required resources for the active application components
- The battery status and mobility pattern
- Other context data being used by the applications

Candidate remote nodes with a similar mobility pattern reply if their battery status is higher and if they can host the client's data and components. In

Table 1. Characteristics of the location-awareness components

Locating Technique	Type	Reference	Sensing Accuracy	Limitation	Sensing Frequency	Battery Usage	CPU Load
Bluetooth GPS	physical	absolute	5-10 m	outdoors	1 sec	30% / h	12 %
WLAN RSSI	physical	relative	< 10 m	indoors, ≥ 3 AP	1 sec	41% / h	17 %
WLAN MAC	physical	relative	< 100 m	≥ 1 AP	30 sec	38% / h	13 %
IP Address	symbolic	absolute	country/city	network access	4 min	34% / h	5 %
PIM	symbolic	absolute	user		4 min	12% / h	2 %

the experiment, a test person carried around two identical PDAs (a Qtek 9090) during a whole day, going from home to the office and back.

Each PDA was executing the same tasks (local weather report, restaurant finder, agenda, music player, browsing internet), but one of the PDAs was continuously using the WiFi triangulation and GPS methods for indoors and outdoors location-awareness, whereas the second PDA used the adaptive context-driven resource-aware approach and collaborated with other devices to offload context data and components in order to reduce its own energy consumption. The latter made use of notebooks in the local network at home and at the office, which had our context infrastructure deployed. Neither of both PDAs was turned off or suspended during the experiment.

The results of the performance evaluation are shown in Figure 11. The CPU load shown here is averaged over small time intervals (therefore no high peaks of short duration are shown) and includes the load of all components, including those for context management. The results in the first figure on the left show that this PDA did not make it through the day, whereas the second PDA had plenty of time left to recharge at the end of the day.

One of the coordination mechanisms for component distribution on remote nodes we have worked out consists of a distributed learning approach in which each node has a single coordinating entity that collaborates with its neighboring nodes. We used Collaborative Reinforcement Learning (CRL) in order to achieve a adaptive relocation behavior that adjusts itself to an environment in which the neighboring nodes may come and go, see Rigole et al. (2006). We compared this approach with a centralized mechanism worked out in Mikic-Rakic et al. (2002), in which the optimal solution for the deployment problem is calculated. In our comparison, we concluded that our approach finds good deployment solutions about nine times faster on average than the centralized approach. Although we often find a suboptimal solution instead of the best possible solution, our approach has the advantage that it works incremental. This means that only incremental changes are applied to existing deployment scenarios when the environment changes, which is a major advantage because component relocations imply an overhead for the availability of the application.

When reflecting back on the requirements set out in a previous section, we may conclude that our component-based design methodology and context-aware adaptation framework has proven successful for this scenario. The lightweightness of the framework made it possible to deploy it

Figure 11. Experimental evaluation of context-aware adaptation with the conferencing client.

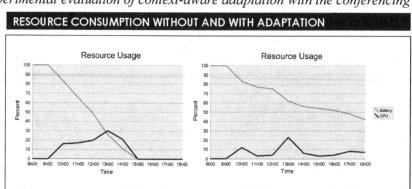

on a PDA and keep the overhead of the runtime adaptation to an acceptable level. Of course, achieving effective context-aware adaptation would not have been possible without the proper support for flexible context management in a distributed setting.

CONCLUSION AND FUTURE TRENDS

We presented a modular application design methodology supporting discovery, adaptation, relocation, composition and deployment on resource limited devices from the bottom up. This methodology is an ideal candidate for developing applications and services within ubiquitous and pervasive computing environments. The necessary flexibility for deployment on such devices is achieved through adaptation in each of the layers of the adaptation framework. Runtime adaptation ensures a resource efficient and context-aware deployment of components. Experiments have shown that our adaptation framework can more than double the autonomy of a mobile handheld device by intelligently adapting the approach for location-awareness depending on the resolution required by the applications. The result is an increased autonomy of the handheld device and a better resource usage trade-off between the component middleware, the context managing components, and the context-aware applications.

Variations on the user and the execution context not only affect the application performance (demanding deployment and application adaptation), but they also affect the relevance of the content delivered by the application to the user. This content should match the resource constraints (like available screen resolution and supported formats), as well as the user's preferences. In this chapter, we have presented a context-based filtering process that presented a way to adapt the content delivered to mobile user by filtering it according to the current user's context and pref-

erences for this context. By using context-aware profiles, this filtering process addresses the fact that the user's preferences and needs may vary according to the context during his interaction with an application. Besides, this approach illustrates how content, in the same way as the application deployment and composition, can be adapted to the user's and execution context. It also points out how content adaptation can be addressed by cooperating components in a pervasive environment. However, content adaptation itself cannot be thoroughly evaluated without involving the user himself to see if he is pleased with the end result after content adaptation. We plan to carry out an extensive user study that can provide some statistically relevant information to see whether the way content adaptation has been implemented is acceptable for the user.

The research in the area of component-based software engineering has matured over the past decade. Nowadays components are well-accepted in diverse applications domains, with wide-spread adoption established in various areas: from embedded systems to distributed enterprise application servers. Nonetheless, many challenging aspects under the hood, such as the theoretical foundations on component models, composition and verification, present further research opportunities in newly emerging software engineering developments, such as service oriented architecture and model-driven engineering. The cross-fertilization between the software and the knowledge engineering research fields may present solutions to help with formal methods of specification, ambiguity in software development, context representations, knowledge-based software systems and new methods and processes for automated software adaptation and evolution. Specifically in the area of context-aware computing, new technologies and devices for pervasive computing will continue to create innovative modes of interaction between people, mobile devices, applications and environments. It is clear that from a technological perspective the sky is the limit, but one must never underestimate the most challenging factor of all, the user.

REFERENCES

Ardon, S.,Gunningberg, P., Landfeldt, B., Ismailov, Y., Portmann, M. & Seneviratne, A. (2003). MARCH: A distributed content adaptation architecture. *International Journal of Communication Systems, 16* (1), 97-115.

Chaari, T., Dejene, E., Laforest, F. & Scuturici, V.-M. (2006). Modeling and Using Context in Adapting Applications to Pervasive Environments. In *ICPS'06 : IEEE International Conference on Pervasive Services 2006.*

Colajanni, M. & Lancellotti, R. (2004). System Architectures for Web Content Adaptation Services. *IEEE Distributed Systems On-Line*, Invited paper on Web Systems. Retrieved Mars 12 2008 from http://dsonline.computer.org/portal/pages/dsonline/topics/was/adaptation.xml.

Daoud, M., Tamine, L., Boughanem, M., & Chabaro, B. (2007). Learning Implicit User Interests Using Ontology and Search History for Personalization. In Mathias Weske, Mohand-Said Hacid, Claude Godart (Eds.): *Personalized Access to Web Information (PAWI 2007), Workshop of the 8th International Web Information Systems Engineering (WISE 2007), Lecture Notes In Computer Science, Vol. 4832* (pp. 325-336). Springer-Verlag.

Devlic, A. & Klintskog, E. (2007). Context retrieval and distribution in a mobile distributed environment, In *Third Workshop on Context Awareness for Proactive Systems (CAPS 2007).*

Dey, A. (2001). Understanding and using context. *Personal and Ubiquitous Computing, 5 (1),* 4-7.

Geihs, K., Khan, M.U., Reichle, R., Solberg, A. & Hallsteinsen, S. (2006). Modeling of component-based self-adapting context-aware applications for mobile devices. *IFIP International Federation for Information Processing - Software Engineering Techniques: Design for Quality*, Vol. 227 (pp. 85-96). Springer.

Islam, N. & Fayad, M. (2003). Toward ubiquitous acceptance of ubiquitous computing. *Communication of ACM, 46* (2), 89-92.

Kassab, R. & Lamirel, J.C. (2006) An innovative approach to intelligent information filtering. In Haddad, H (ed.), *ACM Symposium on Applied Computing 2006 (SAC 2006)* (pp. 1089-1093). ACM Press.

Kirsch-Pinheiro, M., Gensel, J. & Martin, H. (2004). Awareness on Mobile Groupware Systems. In: Karmouch, A., Korba, L. & Madeira, E.R.M. (Eds.), *1st International Workshop on Mobility Aware Technologies and Applications (MATA 2004), Lecture Notes in Computer Science,* Vol. 3284 (pp. 78-87). Springer.

Kirsch-Pinheiro, M., Villanova-Oliver, M.; Gensel, J. & Martin, H. (2006). A Personalized and Context-Aware Adaptation Process for Web-Based Groupware Systems. *4th Int. Workshop on Ubiquitous Mobile Information and Collaboration Systems (UMICS'06), CAiSE'06 Workshop* (pp. 884-898).

Lemlouma, T. & Layaïda, N. (2004). Context-Aware Adaptation for Mobile Devices. *IEEE International Conference on Mobile Data Management* (pp.106-111). IEEE Computer Society.

Loke, S. W., Padovitz, A. & Zaslavsky, A. (2003). Context-based addressing: The concept and an implementation for large-scale mobile agent systems using publish-subscribe event notification. In Stefani, J.-B., Demeure, I. & Hagimont, D. (eds.), *4th IFIP WG 6.1 International Conference on Distributed Applications and Interoperable Systems (DAIS 2003), Lecture Notes in Computer Science,* Vol. 2893 (pp. 274-284). Springer.

Mikic-Rakic, M. & Medvidovic, N. (2002). Architecture-Level Support for Software Component

Deployment in Resource Constrained Environments. In *Proceedings of the First International IFIP/ACM Working Conference on Component Deployment (CD'02)*.

Moran, T. & Dourish, P. (2001). Introduction to this special issue on context-aware computing. *Human-Computer Interaction, 16* (2-3).

Preuveneers, D. & Berbers, Y. Adaptive context management using a component-based approach. In Kutvonen, L. & Alonistioti, N. (ed.), *5th IFIP WG 6.1 International Conference Distributed Applications and Interoperable Systems (DAIS2005), Lecture Notes in Computer Science*, Vol. 3543 (pp. 14-26). Springer.

Preuveneers, D., den Bergh, J. V., Wagelaar, D., Georges, A., Rigole, P., Clerckx, T., Berbers, Y., Coninx, K., Jonckers, V. & Bosschere, K. D. (2004). Towards an Extensible Context Ontology for Ambient Intelligence. In Markopoulos, P., Eggen, B., Aarts, E. & Crowley, J. (ed.), *Second European Symposium on Ambient Intelligence (EUSAI 2004), Lecture Notes in Computer Science*, Vol. 3295 (pp. 148-159). Springer.

Preuveneers, D. & Berbers, Y. (2007). Towards Context-Aware and Resource-Driven Self-Adaptation for Mobile Handheld Applications. In *Proceedings of the 2007 ACM Symposium on Applied Computing* (pp. 1165-1170). ACM Press.

Rigole, P. & Berbers, Y. (2006). Resource-driven collaborative component deployment in mobile environments, In *Proceedings of the International Conference on Autonomic and Autonomous Systems* (pp. 1-5).

Rigole, P., Clerckx, T., Berbers, Y. & Coninx, K. (2007). Task-driven automated component deployment for ambient intelligence environments. In *Pervasive and Mobile Computing, 3* (3), 276-299. Elsevier Science Publishers B.V.

Schilit, B., Trevor, J., Hilbert, D. & Koh, T. (2002). Web interaction using very small Internet devices. *Computer, 35* (10), 37-45. IEEE Computer Society.

Schilit, B.N. & Theimer, M.M. (1994). Disseminating active map information to mobile hosts. *IEEE Network, 8* (5), 22-32.

Weiser, M. (1991). The Computer for the Twenty-First Century. Scientific American, September 1991, 99-104.

Victor, K., Pauty, J. & Berbers, Y. (2007). Context distribution using context aware flooding. In: Braun, T., Mascolo, S., Konstantas, D. & Wulff, M. (eds.), *First ERCIM Workshop on Emobility,* Vol. 1 (pp. 95-106).

Villanova, M., Gensel, J. & Martin, H. (2003). A progressive access approach for web based information systems. *Journal of Web Engineering, 2* (1&2), 27-57.

Yang, S. & Shao, N. (2007). Enhancing pervasive Web accessibility with rule-based adaptation strategy. *Expert Systems with Applications, 32* (4), 1154-1167.

Chapter II
Ontology Based Context–Aware Adaptation Approach

Tarak Chaari[1]
LAAS-CNRS, France

Mohamed Zouari[2]
IRISA-INRIA, France

Frédérique Laforest
LIRIS-CNRS, France

ABSTRACT

Pervasive information systems aim to make information available anywhere and at anytime. These systems should be used in different contexts depending on the environment of the user, her/his profile and her/his device. Consequently, one of the main problems of such information systems is the adaptation to context. In this chapter, the authors propose a comprehensive and open strategy that guarantees the adaptation of applications to context on three facets: (i) the services offered to the user, (ii) the multimedia contents returned by these services, and (iii) their presentation to the user. Service adaptation consists of modules that intercept the application's service calls and modify their behavior using a list of functional adaptation operators. Data adaptation consists in transforming or replacing the non-usable multimedia service outputs in the considered context situation. Presentation adaptation consists in automatically generating the complete code of the user interface that guarantees the interaction with the adapted data and services. The authors' adaptation strategy has achieved two goals: (i) incrementally integrate context awareness in the application and (ii) guarantee the adaptation starting from a simple description of the services offered to the user. They have validated this strategy by developing a platform that guarantees applications adaptation to context. They used Java, OSGi and Web service technologies to implement this platform. They have also successfully tested our adaptation approach on a home healthcare application concerning dialyzed persons.

INTRODUCTION

Pervasive information systems aim to providing information to users anywhere and at anytime taking account of her/his environment. Accessing web-based applications on a mobile terminal from anywhere (list of fuel stations around), using a collaborative system based on a highly dynamic peer to peer MANET architecture (collaborative writing of a tourism guide on site) or using the legacy information system in new user environments (home patients directly connected to the hospital information system) are examples of these systems. One common difficulty for establishing such systems is their context-awareness, i.e. they must have the ability to manage their utilization contexts and to adapt their behavior to their changes.

Despite a rich landscape in adaptation related contributions, a complete and generic context-aware adaptation approach is still missing (Kjaer, K. E. 2007). The existing solutions are generally proposed to incrementally create adaptive resources. They are not suitable for adapting existing systems to new utilization contexts. Moreover, the existing contributions remain very specific to proprietary models and to ad hoc needs. Like in (Rosa, L., Lopes, A. & Rodrigues, L. 2008), we target the establishment of adaptive systems where "adaptation logic can be separated from the application core. When an application needs to adapt, it is usually not because its core domain has changed but rather a non-functional requirement or behavior of some services within the application, such as the network communication protocol, needs to change."

In our opinion, to establish a generic context-aware adaptation approach, we need:

- Models and tools to describe the adaptation source (i.e. context)
- Models and tools to describe the adaptation target (applications, architectures, services, etc)

- Adaptation means and tools to modify the adaptation target when context changes
- Adaptation policies putting all the previous models and tools together

In this chapter, we present a generic and automatic ontology-based adaptation approach of existing applications to new utilization contexts. We apply our adaptation approach after the development of the applications by dynamically and automatically instantiating a software layer upon them. Our adaptation strategy is based on three main stages: service adaptation, content adaptation and user interface adaptation. Service adaptation consists in changing the behavior of the offered services to end users in order to be compatible with the utilization context of the application. Content adaptation is based on a set of transformations on the type, format and the properties of multimedia content returned by the services. Finally, user interface adaptation is the automatic generation of functional and correct user interfaces in their operating context. Our adaptation strategy is based on two ontologies describing the application architecture and its utilization context. To validate this strategy, we developed a prototype implementing its main stages to apply them on an existing medical application in order to adapt it to mobile phone utilizations.

This chapter is organized as follows: State of the art presents some interesting works related to context-awareness and adaptation. The following section entitled "Overview of our adaptation approach" gives a general overview of our context-aware adaptation approach. In section "Context Modeling", we propose an ontology based model of the utilization context. In section "Application Modeling", we present another ontology based model describing a user's view of an application. In section "Our adaptation approach", we detail how we use these models to establish a complete and a generic adaptation approach of services, multimedia content and user interfaces in context-aware applications. Finally, before concluding, we present our prototype implementing our adaptation principles and give a concrete case study to validate our context-aware adaptation approach.

STATE OF THE ART

Context is a fuzzy term that captured the attention of several software researchers. We can find many proposed definitions for this term. Most of these definitions are abstract or specific to a particular domain making context formalization and modeling very difficult. The most adopted and referenced definition in context-awareness domain is: "Context is any information that can be used to characterize the situation of an entity. An entity is a person, place, or object that is considered relevant to the interaction with an application, including the user and applications themselves" (Dey, A.K., Salber, D. & Abowd, G.D. 2001).

In literature, many platforms were proposed to facilitate creating context-aware applications. Among these platforms, we can cite: Context Toolkit (Dey, A.K., Salber, D. & Abowd, G.D. 2001), CoBrA (Chen, H. 2004), CMF (Korpipaa, P., Mantyjarvi, J., Kela, J. et al. 2004) and SOCAM (Gu, T., Pung, H.K., and Zhang, D.Q. 2005). They are based on layered architectures

where layer names and levels differ from one platform to another. However, we noticed that all these approaches are based on five principal layers (Baldauf, M., Dustdar, M.S. & Rosenberg, F. 2007): context capture (Indulska, J., Robinson, R., Rakotonirainy, A. & Henricksen, K. 2003), context interpretation/aggregation (Dey, A. K., Abowd, G. D. & Wood, A. 1998) (Kiciman, E. & Fox, A 2000), context storage (Strang, T. & Linnhoff-Popien, C. 2004), context dissemination (Bauer M., Heiber, T., Kortuem G. & Segall Z. 1998) and the application layer (Chen, H., Finin, T. & Joshi, A. 2003). Figure 1 illustrates these five layers.

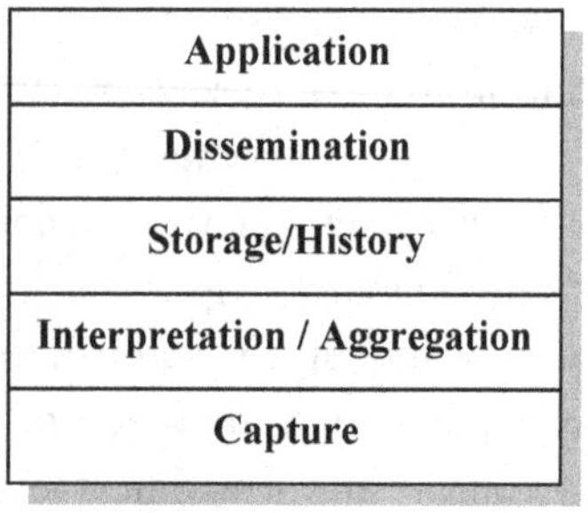

At the bottom layer of this architecture, there is a common agreement on the separation of context acquisition from its use. Indeed, it is very useful to encapsulate context acquisition mechanisms in components offering standard communication interfaces. Currently, there is not a common standard model for context acquisition and aggregation from several different sources. Each platform proposes its own model for context capturing and aggregation.

Many other researches focused on the importance of context modeling to make real advances in context-aware systems. The first attempts to model context propose simplistic models using *attribute/value* couples. Such representations can lead to complex interpretation conflicts. Consequently, even the fact that they are easy to implement, they provide an inadequate support for context interpretation and aggregation. Other approaches propose more structured models using XML-based representations. Among these models, we can cite the CC/PP profile (Composite Capabilities / Preference Profile) (W3C 2004b) and the UAProf profile (User Agent Profile) (Open Mobile Alliance 2007). These models are better than *attribute/value* representations but they don't reach the richness and the semantic expressivity of ontologies. In fact, ontologies offer a strong source for semantic reasoning and conflict resolving in context interpretations (Belhanafi Behlouli, N.,

Figure 1. General architecture of a context-aware system

Application
Dissemination
Storage/History
Interpretation / Aggregation
Capture

Taconet, C. & Bernard, G. 2006), (Baumgartner, N., Retschitzegger, W. & Schwinger, W. 2008).

Research on context modeling has been dedicated to the selection of the best model to describe context information specific to particular domains (Kirsch-Pinheiro, M., Villanova-Oliver, M., Gensel, J. & Martin, H. 2006), (Robinson, R., Henricksen, K. & Indulska, J. 2007), (Coutaz, J., Crowley, J.L., Dobson, S. & Garlan, D. 2005). This is also the first approach that we have followed and described in (Chaari, T., Laforest, F. & Celentano, A. 2007). Recently, the trend has turned to the definition of generic context models that can be the base for the construction of any applied context model (Vieira, V., Tedesco, P., Salgado, A.C. & Brézillon, P. 2007), (Hinz, M., Pietschmann, S., Fiala, Z.A 2007), (Ejigu, D., Scuturici, M. & Brunie, L. 2007), (De Virgilio, R. and Torlone R. 2006). The work we have published in (Chaari, T., Ejigu, D., Laforest, F. & Scuturici V.M. 2007) also proposes the use of ontologies to describe the application context. In this chapter, we go further by also using ontologies to describe the application and the adaptation policy too. Using an ontology allows capturing the available knowledge on the applications to adapt and integrating different information levels to adapt open applications and even legacy ones when we have too few information on their architecture and development.

The increasing need of context-awareness in the modern information systems encouraged the researchers to focus on designing architectures supporting context capture, interpretation, storage and dissemination. Many existing context-aware systems support the acquisition and the interpretation of context but the adaptation logic is still often mixed within the application code (Le Mouël, F., André, F. & Segarra, M.T. 2002), (Hinz, M., Pietschmann, S., Umbach, M. & Meißner, K. 2007), (Geihs, K., Ullah Khan, M., Reichle, R., Solberg, A., Hallsteinsen, S.O. & Merral, S. 2006), (Cheung-Foo-Wo, D., Tigli, J.Y., Lavirotte S. & Riveill, M. 2007), (Ceri, S., Daniel, F., Matera, M. & Facca, F.M. 2007). In such systems,

modifying the adaptation logic implies modifying the entire application. Moreover, they mainly propose solutions for the incremental creation and rapid prototyping of context-aware systems (Henricksen, K. & Indulska, J. 2006) (Mrissa, M., Ghedira, C., Benslimane, D., Maamar, Z., Rosenberg, F. & Dustdar S. 2007). This limits the capacity of these solutions to handle new utilization contexts that were not predicted when these applications have been developed. Consequently, we notice the absence of a complete and generic methodology to adapt applications to the context. Indeed, the majority of the existing contributions in this field are limited to composing or configuring pre-developed components depending on context. In our point of view, software components assembly is one operator among several possible adaptation actions on an application to react to context changes.

The literature shows a large scope of work on adaptation. Significant adaptation contributions can be found for the adaptive composition of services like (Benatallah, B., Casati, F., Grigori, D., Nezhad, H.R. & Toumani, F 2005), (Papazoglou, M. P. and Heuvel, W. 2007), (Cheung-Foo-Wo, D., Tigli, J.Y., Lavirotte S. & Riveill, M. 2007) and (Boussard, M. et al. 2008). We can also find other works on adapting component oriented architectures like (Aksit, M., & Choukair, Z. 2003), (Ketfi, A., Belkhatir, N. & Cunin, P. Y. 2002), (Dowling, J. & Cahill, V. 2001) and (Chefrour, D. & André F. 2002) using reflexivity (Cazzola, W., Savigni, A., Sosio, A. & Tisato F. 1999) (Maes, P. 1987), contracts (Andrade, L-F., & Fiadeiro, J.L. 2003) (Keeney, J. & Cahill, V. 2003) and aspect oriented programming (Kickzales, G., Lamping, J., Mendhekar, A. et al. 1997), (Pawlak, R., Seinturier, L., Duchien, L. et al. 2001), (Baresi, L., Guinea, S., & Tamburrelli, G. 2008). Other researches focused on content adaptation to context. Commercial products, like IBM Transcoding (IBM research 2000), Web Clipping (Hillerson, G. 2001) and WebSphere (Rodriguez, J., Dakar, B., Marras, F.L. et al. 2001) and prototypes resulting from research works, like TranSend (Fox, A., Goldberg, I., Gribble, S. et al. 1998), Odyssey (Noble, B. 2000) and Conductor (Yarvis M. 2001), were developed to provide techniques for multimedia content adaptation in heterogeneous environments. New contributions for the pervasive information systems are also proposed to adapt web documents to several types of devices and to user preferences. For example, we can cite the LiquidUI tool from Harmonia Company (Harmonia Inc. 2008). This tool is based on an XML language to produce other tagged user interfaces scripts like HTML and WAP.

The MADAM project (Hallsteinsen, S., Floch, J. & Stav, E. 2004) and its successor MUSIC (Paspallis, N., Eliassen, F., Hallsteinsen, S. & Papadopoulos G.A. 2008) are one of the very few contributions that give importance to the adaptation phase in context management. They present a framework providing the building blocks for adaptive context-aware systems. They consider the adaptation as the choice of the best version of applications according to the context. They also suppose that the applications are already configurable to handle context changes. Their approach is limited in its possible adaptation actions and it is not applicable to existing applications that were not developed to be context-aware at their first versions.

Despite all this interest in context related research, almost all the proposed solutions are still instantiated in an ad hoc manner for each application. In our opinion, the reason is: the existing works in context-awareness suppose that application adaptation to context must be ensured in a specific way by the application itself. They consider that the modification of the application's behavior according to the captured context remains a specific task to the application developer and she/he has to take it into account from the beginning of the application's life cycle (Reichle, R., Wagner, M., Ullah Khan M., Geihs, K., Lorenzo, J., Valla, M., Fra, Paspallis, N. & Papadopoulos, G.A. 2008). A question arises then:

what to do if the application has already been developed to support a particular context and we want to adapt it to new utilization contexts? We think that the existing solutions have only one answer: reconsider all the application life cycle and develop a new version. A generic solution is needed to avoid some of the tedious work that designers and developers would normally have to do. To solve this problem, we believe that adaptation and adaptability techniques have to be more studied and more integrated in context-awareness research.

OVERVIEW OF OUR ADAPTATION APPROACH

Our approach adapts the described applications on three axes: (i) their offered services to the user, (ii) the data exchanged with these services and (iii) the necessary user interfaces to interact with them. At a first step, our approach ensures the adaptation of the application's services behavior. For example, let's consider a doctor connecting to a medical application with a mobile phone having limited hardware and software capabilities. This doctor wants to invoke a service returning the list of all the patients that he supervised the last month. The considered service can return a huge amount of data that cannot be handled by the used device. In our adaptation strategy we automatically and dynamically substitute this service by another one returning the same result divided on small chunks that can be directly used on the target device. We call this first step "functional adaptation". At a second stage, our approach adapts the content exchanged with the adapted services. For example, the previous service can return the identity photograph of each patient record. The format of these photographs must be adapted to the image formats supported by the used device. We call this second step "content adaptation". The third stage consists in the automatic generation of an adequate user

Figure 2. Application adaptation process to context

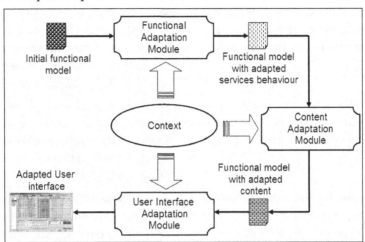

interface to the application's context in order to interact with the adapted services and data. We call this last step "presentation adaptation". Figure 2 presents our application adaptation process to context. This process requires at least a minimum functional description of the application. We call this description *functional model*. We do not make any assumption on the application architecture which can be centralized or distributed. We provide details on the functional model in the section "Application Modeling" of this chapter.

Our adaptation process does not make strong assumptions on the context acquisition and storage too. We have made choices for our prototype implementation (presented in section "SECAS platform development"), but they have no incidence on the core of our study. Our work mainly focuses on how to adapt applications to context more than context capture and management. We used a broker-oriented architecture to dissociate the context management and the context adaptation layers. A broker provides access to context information using mainly a *push* mode: adaptation modules subscribe to the broker and receive events when the context changes. In some situations,

additional context information may be required when some changes are detected. In this case, our context broker can provide this information using the *pull* mode: the adaptation modules ask for context values when required. Using this broker-oriented architecture, our adaptation approach remains open to easily integrate existing context management techniques initiated by Anind K. Dey (Dey, A.K., Salber, D. & Abowd, G.D. 2001) or others.

Before detailing each step of our adaptation process, we first present our two main models: the context model and the application model.

CONTEXT MODELING

The source and the motivation of our adaptation approach in context-aware systems are context changes during the system's runtime. To establish this approach, we need to define and model context to track these changes. The major drawback of the most adopted context definition (proposed by Dey) is the mixture between application data and context information. In our opinion, the application core should be designed in a context-independent way. This allows dissociating context management from the application logic and consequently, adding context-awareness to existing legacy applications.

We define context as the set of the external parameters that can influence the behavior of the application by defining new views on its data and its available services.

We have defined the *ContextOnto* ontology (Figure 3) to model the context structure. We have chosen ontology based models because they constitute a standard representation, reasoning and inferring scheme of knowledge. They facilitate knowledge sharing and reuse through formal and real-world semantics.

ContextOnto= ($C_{Context}$, $R_{Context}$)

$C_{Context}$ is the set of the ontology concepts and $R_{Context}$ is the set of relations between them.

This ontology is divided into a *generic ontology* (the generic level context model) and *domain specific ontologies* (the specific context model) as proposed in (Gu, T., Pung, H.K., and Zhang, D.Q.

2005). The generic ontology defines the common context concepts necessary to make an application context-aware. The specific concepts inherit from the generic ones adding properties dedicated to the considered application domain. Existing ontologies may be extended and refined to answer the needs of almost every domain. Such ontologies can be imported in our environment using the OWL-DL language (Bechhofer, S., Van Harmelen, F., Hendler, J., Horrocks, I., McGuinness, D.L., Patel-Schneider, P.F. & Stein L.A. 2004).

In the generic ontology, each concept represents a context entity. The six principal concepts of the generic ontology are: *User, Location, Device, Activity, Network* and *Physical Environment.*

The end-user is described by the concept *User* that specifies her/his basic profile (name, login, etc) and her/his preferences (language, favourite data formats, etc). The concept *Location* describes the physical space and spatial relations of involved devices and users in the system. Locations can be specified by physical representations (GPS coordinates) and symbolic representations (places identified by their names). The concept *Device* describes the hardware (like memory and CPU) and the software (like the operating system and the installed applications) capabilities of the user device. The concept *Activity* specifies some properties of the user's activity in progress as well as its starting and ending dates. The concept *Network* describes the characteristics of the network like the transport protocol, the connectivity and the QoS of the available connections. Finally, the concept *PhysicalEnvironnement* provides physical properties of the user space (like the ambient temperature) and her/his relation with her/his external environment.

Let us quote the example of a telemedicine system where a patient (*User*) is doing a dialysis (*Activity*) in his room (*Location*). This user has a PDA (*Device*) which is connected to a wireless network (*Network*). His device can receive messages that may be adapted to a rich text or a voice spelling according to her/his activity. In

Figure 3. The context ontology structure: ContextOnto

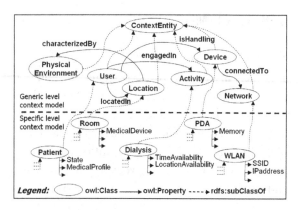

this case, the first concept *Patient* specifies the medical profile of the user. The concept *Dialysis* describes the activity steps, states as well as when and where they were scheduled. The concept *Room* gives information about the user location like specifying that he/ she is at home or in a hospital room. The last concept *Network* presents specific information of the used network like its SSID and its IP address.

After defining the terms and the structure of our adaptation source (i.e. context), we define the model of the adaptation target (i.e. applications) in the next section.

APPLICATION MODELING

To adapt a system, we must have access to some knowledge on its architecture and its structure. The granularity and the information amount representing the system may vary according to the available knowledge that we can have on its development and its lifecycle. It can be a description of the external software modules for

Figure 4. The application ontology structure ApplicationOnto

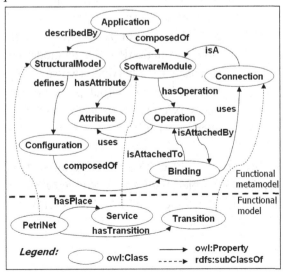

legacy applications or a detailed description of its internal classes, objects and code for open source software. We have chosen ontologies to model and to structure all the amount of information that we can have about the application's architecture. We call this application ontology *ApplicationOnto*:

$$\text{ApplicationOnto} = (C_{Application}, R_{Application})$$
$C_{Application}$ is the set of the ontology concepts and $R_{Application}$ is the set of relations between them.

We have defined two abstraction levels in *ApplicationOnto*: generic ontology (functional metamodel in Figure 3) and domain specific ontologies (functional model in Figure 3). In the generic level, we have defined the necessary classes to describe software architectures. In this level, an application is described by *software modules* that include Web services, software components, java objects, etc. The concept *SoftwareModule* represents a software module offering a set of functionalities that can be directly offered to the user or to other modules. Every module is described by a set of properties (name, type, description…) and defines one or several operations. An operation represents the interaction point of the module with its environment (other modules or end-user). The concept *Operation* represents a software entity that ensures a predefined functionality. A description of its behavior is defined by a set of input parameters *Input*, output parameters *Output* and preconditions *PreCondition* necessary to its execution.

For example, the web service *MedicalImageViewer* is a software module. This service provides a set of operations for viewing and extracting medical images and their corresponding reports and analysis. For example, the operation *getRecordImages* returns a vector of image records corresponding to a patient identified by her/his social security number. Each record contains the name, the description and the binary file of each image. A software module has a set of internal attributes represented by the concept *Attribute*.

These attributes are used in the operations code for configuration issues. For instance, the web service *MedicalImageViewer* has *ImageHostingServer* as a configuration attribute. This attribute defines where the image files are stored.

The communication mode and the interaction between modules are encapsulated by *connections* including method calls, service wrappers, connectors of components, proxies, etc. Connections guarantee content information exchange or synchronisation/control messages transmission. They are characterized by a set of properties like name (connection's name), type (method invocation, event notification…) and role (producer, consumer, transmission channel, etc). A *configuration* represents several links (*Bindings*) between the operation modules. A link is characterized by a set of properties: a *name*, a source (*FromEntity*) and a destination (*ToEntity*). A configuration is described by a structural model (graph, Petri nets, state charts…) that specifies the structure of the application. This model is detailed in the domain specific level of *ApplicationOnto*.

Our adaptation approach depends strongly on the application's functional model. In fact, it defines rules that modify and transform the different elements defined in this model. To better understand and detail our adaptation approach, we use a Petri net functional model for service oriented applications in the remaining part of this section. This choice does not affect the genericity of our adaptation approach which remains applicable if we use other architecture description models. We define an application functional model by a Petri net describing its offered services to the user and all the existing dependences between them. The places of this Petri net correspond to the application services and the transitions represent the dependencies between them. In this functional model, we consider that a service has exactly one operation. This choice remains compatible with the other existing service models: a service offering many operations can be decomposed into many mono-operation services.

We model a service by a function f. It takes a vector $INPUT=(x_1, x_2, ... x_m)$ in input and returns an output vector $OUTPUT=(c_1, c_2, ... c_n)$.

An output component c_i can be accessed using the *[]* operator ($c_i = OUTPUT[i]$). Each component c_i is associated to a vector $r_i = (r_{ia}, r_{ib}...)$ where $r_{ia}, r_{ib}...$ are the values returned by the service f and associated with the output component c_i. r_i represents the returned instances of c_i. This generic definition establishes a common exchange structure between services and facilitates their composition and adaptation.

Formally, an application functional model is a tuple $FM=(f_0, F, T)$ meeting the following recommendations:

1. F is a finite set of services $f_1, f_2, ..., f_n$
2. f_0 is the root place of the Petri net. It represents the initial service of the application.
3. T is a finite set of transitions $t_1, t_2, ..., t_m$
4. Each transition t_i is a triplet *(d, gc, A)* where:
   a. *d* is the maximum delay for passing the transition
   b. *gc* is a general condition for passing the transition
   c. *A* is a finite set of associations $a_1, a_2, ..., a_l$ between services.
   d. a_i is a finite set of pairs (inputExpression, destinationParameter) modeling an association between two services. It combines an output parameter of one service to an input parameter of another service.

In the case study section of this chapter (section "the SICOM Project Use Case"), we give a detailed description of a functional model representing a medical application.

OUR ADAPTATION APPROACH

In this section, we detail our adaptation approach based on the functional description of the application services offered to the user and the execution dependencies between them. This description (that we called functional model) is extracted from *ApplicationOnto*. Our approach adapts the described application according to three main steps: (i) its offered services to the user, (ii) the data exchanged with these services and (iii) the necessary user interface to interact with them. We detail each step in the remaining parts of this section.

Functional Adaptation

We define the functional adaptation of an application as the necessary modifications on its services behavior so that they can be used in a correct way in new operating contexts.

A functional adaptation manager applies these transformations according to an adaptation policy defined by the application administrator. This policy is based on a finite set of adaptation rules to be applied on the described entities in the functional model. An adaptation rule has the following general syntax:

On event **if** condition **do** action

In the next subsection, we detail how to model and express the three components of the functional adaptation rules: events, conditions and actions. Then, we present how to use these rules in our adaptation policy.

Context–Aware Adaptation Rules

An adaptation rule consists in performing an action when an event occurs and when a condition is satisfied. Thereafter, we present these three components of our adaptation rules (i.e. events, conditions and actions).

Event

An event signals the occurrence of a fact like a change in the context (e.g. change of the user localization). A significant event starts the activation of one or more rules. The activation of a rule can take place at anytime because events are random like the loss of connection in a wireless network for example. An event can be simple or composite, modelled using a similar algebra to SNOOP (Hanson, N.E., and Widom, J. 1992). A simple event is a symbol of a primitive event e_p or a term of the form e_p (p_1, p_2, ... p_n), where e_p is a symbol of a primitive event with N arguments $p_{i,1 \le i \le n}$ and each p_i is a constant or a variable. We distinguish between three main types of primitive events:

- Context events corresponding to value changes of context parameters.
- Application events representing changes in the state of application components like adding or retrieving a software module.
- System events happening by our adaptation approach. They usually signal errors like invocation failure of a distant service due to network problems.

A composite event is a logical combination of events (that can be simple or composite) and negation of events. This combination is ensured by using the classic disjunction (OR), conjunction (AND) and negation (NOT) Boolean operators.

Condition

A condition describes a contextual situation. It corresponds to a logical expression on the specified elements in *ContextOnto* and *ApplicationOnto*. According to the given terms and values in the condition, an adaptation rule can be generic or specific. The generic rules are applicable on several applications and several services. In this case, the condition part relates to generic properties of the application elements (like services returning image outputs for example). The specific rules relate to particular services aiming to apply an action to specific instances of *ApplicationOnto* concepts and relationships. In this case, the condition indicates the selected instances. A condition is a composition of atomic logical formulas. An atomic formula is modeled by the triplet (term, operator, term). A term can be a variable or a constant. The terms relate to the two concepts $C_{Context}$ and $C_{Application}$ and their instances. A condition operator can be (i) a relationship between instances of these concepts or (ii) a comparison operator like "greater than" (>) for example. Existential ($\exists$) or universal ($\forall$) expressions can be also used to define conditions. For example, the expression seen in Box 1 defines a generic condition concerning all the application services that provide more than one output parameter.

Action

An action specifies a list of adaptation operators calls to be applied on the functional model elements. The administrator or the developer of the adaptation rules has to specify the necessary configuration parameters for these adaptation operators to select what has to be modified in the application. These parameters depend on the variables defined in the condition (like the variable S of the given example in the "*conditions*" section). For example, lockService(S) is a simple action that blocks the access to the service S and all the services that depend on it.

An action is a conjunction of adaptation operators with a specific execution order. We defined three possible orders: sequential, concurrent and random. The sequential order executes the operators sequentially in the specified order in the rule. The concurrent order allows running the operators in different parallel threads whereas the random is used when the execution order is not important.

We model an adaptation operator by a function *operator* taking a vector of parameters in input (*input*) and producing another vector as output (*result*). The input parameters and the result of service adaptation operators are elements of the application's functional model (i.e. instances from *ApplicationOnto*) or typed variables (like Boolean, String and integer variables).

For example, the operator *lockService* takes an instance of a service from the application's functional model and blocks the access to this service. It produces a new functional model without the blocked services.

- Behavioral adaptation operators apply local transformations on a specific element of the application's functional model. These

Box 1.

$$\forall \text{ Service:S} \mid (\text{S hasOuput:O}) \text{ AND } (\text{O hasParameter:P}) \text{ AND } (\text{count(P)} > 1)$$

Box 2.

$$\text{result = operator(input) } \textbf{with}$$

$$\text{input} = \{in_i\} 1 \leq i \leq n \textbf{ and } \text{result} = \{res_j\} 1 \leq j \leq m$$

$$\textbf{where } in_i \textbf{ and } res_j \textbf{ are elements of the application's functional model}$$

transformations do not affect the generic structure of the application. In this case, the dependencies of the adapted element with the other elements of the application are not modified. The execution of these operators is ensured by an adaptation entity associated to specific elements of the application's functional model (mainly software modules). We call these adaptation entities *local adapters*. They play the role of proxies between the application's *software modules* and end users. The adaptation rules configure the local adapters to apply a list of behavioral adaptation operators on the associated application element.

• Structural adaptation operators apply transformations on the architectural model of the application. These operators take the functional model as input and produce a new modified functional model according to the operator type and its parameters. This type of operators is applied by a *global adapter*.

The application administrator defines these rules using the SWRL syntax (W3C 2004a). The header part (swrl:head) of these rules references adaptation operators. The body part (swrl:body) references the ContextOnto and ApplicationOnto elements. When events are triggered (context changes), these rules are interpreted by the integrated OWL reasoning module to make the necessary transformations on the application's functional model and to transpose them on the corresponding concrete elements.

The adaptation operators specified in these rules are defined in an extensible library containing the name, the implementing class, the input and the output parameters of each operator. The next section presents how these rules are managed in our context-aware adaptation policy.

Ontology Based Context-aware Policy

We have created the ontology PolicyOnto (Figure 5) to define the necessary terms implicated in our adaptation policy. This adaptation policy ontology includes all the rule structure that we have presented in the previous section. It also specifies how to manage and execute these rules. The ontological representation of these rules defines a semantic framework allowing the correct definition of these rules and their comprehension by human actors and by software algorithms. This ontology is divided into a common level for the general specification of the necessary terms defining the adaptation rules and a specific level implementing these terms according to the application domain. This ontology imports ContextOnto and ApplicationOnto (using the owl:import mechanisms integrated in the OWL language) to define correct rules referring the concrete concepts and relationships implementing these two ontologies. Our adaptation policy does not allow defining elements that do not exist in ContextOnto and ApplicationOnto. The adaptation rules instantiate the various concepts and relations of PolicyOnto. The specific level of this ontology must be populated by domain specific ontologies that describe the supported events, the concerned entities in the conditions and the adaptation operators that will be used (Figure 5). We give a concrete example of policyOnto in the case study section of this chapter.

Without *PolicyOnto*, the adaptation environment must be configured with specific file formats and with ad hoc parameters included in the adaptation code. Ontologies can replace these mechanisms with a formal and standardized language. In addition, they allow specifying correct adaptation rules and actions. They are also used as a reference framework to check the rules syntax and make inferences to produce new knowledge. Moreover, ontologies can ensure a separation between the definition, the implementation and the execution of the adaptation rules. Last but not least, the ap-

Figure 5. The adaptation policy ontology PolicyOnto

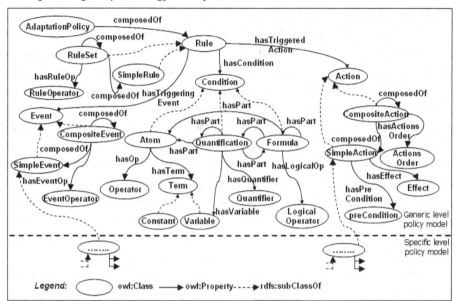

plication of reasoning techniques on *PolicyOnto* can improve the performance and the impact of the adaptation process on applications.

In *PolicyOnto*, rules are organized in sets and can be enabled or disabled. We have also defined rule operators to help administrators in managing the rule sets. For example, in certain cases, the administrator can require the execution of all the rules defined in the set. If the execution of one of these rules fails, the entire rule set is cancelled. We called this rule operator "AllOrNothing". We have also defined several other rule management operators like "All", "ExactlyOne" and "OneOr-More". This last operator is used when we should apply all the rules defined in the same set even if the execution of some of them fails. These operators can also help the administrators in writing complex rules by decomposing them into rule sets. However, guaranteeing the consistency of the adaptation results by the administrator within an increasing number of rules can be a very difficult task. Indeed, seen the dynamicity of the

adaptation process and its unpredictable results in some cases, complex adaptation actions can make the application unusable.

To address this problem, we define a *precondition* and an *effect* for each adaptation operator. Pre-conditions specify constraints on a partial state of the system before the operator execution whereas the effects describe other constraints on the system state after a successful operator execution. Pre-conditions are logical predicates that have to be valid to ensure the correct execution of the adaptation operators. They define constraints on the input parameters of these operators. Effects are conditions to be verified in order to accept the application of the operator. For example, we can have an adaptation operator (op_i) that can be applied only if all the software modules of the application are connected (i.e. there is no isolated software module). This constitutes a precondition (pre_i) for this operator. In the same rule, this operator can be preceded by another one (op_{i-1}). op_{i-1} has to provide a connected architectural model to apply the next operator (op_i). This condition constitutes the effect (eff_{i-1}) of op_{i-1}. op_{i-1} will be rolled back and the concerned rule is cancelled if it does not satisfy eff_{i-1}. Our adaptation approach refuses rules that do not satisfy the correlation (Cuppens F. and Miege A. 2002), between all the effects of their adaptation operators and the preconditions of the immediate next operators.

We used this correlation concept to automatically recognize logical dependences between the adaptation rules by analyzing the operator's preconditions and effects. In fact, in our adaptation approach, we can detect potential errors in the given set of rules by analyzing the effects and the preconditions of their adaptation operators before executing them. We also use conflict resolving strategies to enable the correct rules and to disable the other rules that caused the inconsistency. For instance, these strategies depend on the rule operators defined in the rule sets and on their execution priorities. If strategies were not specified for rule management, a choice screen is prompted to the user when the platform detects a conflict that may cause an inconsistency in the adaptation system or in the application structure. This prompt can be displayed to the administrator while deploying new adaptation rules by checking their syntax and their structure. It can also be displayed at runtime when conflicting effects and preconditions values are detected. Then, the system waits for manual user action by choosing the rules that may not be executed to resolve conflict or inconsistency problems.

After defining the guidelines of service adaptation in our approach, we give an overview on adapting their delivered content to end users in the following section.

Content Adaptation

The application services deliver a set of multimedia data (images, videos, sound, text...) to the user. These data cannot be exploitable in a particular context. For example, if the device of the end user is supporting only the PNG image format but the service delivers a different format, a transformation is necessary on this service output. Image format transcoding is not the only required adaptation operator. Indeed, several other content adaptations can be necessary to deliver directly exploitable data to the end user.

We define the application content adaptation by the necessary operations to guarantee a direct and optimal use of the delivered data to the user in a certain context.

Content Adaptation Principles

The content adaptation goal is to provide the best possible data to the end user of an application in a given context. The success and the efficiency of the content adaptation process strongly depend on the quality of transformations and the quantity of knowledge collected on: (i) the application runtime context, (ii) the available tools for adapting data and (iii) the content to adapt.

We define the content metadata as the different properties describing the exchanged data with the application's services. These properties can be: the format, the size, the dimensions, etc of a media object.

We chose the MPEG-7 format to describe these metadata. Currently, MPEG-7 is a mature standard which provides the richest and the most flexible set of descriptions of multimedia properties. It is considered as the most used and the most interoperable standard in industrial environments. We use MPEG-7 descriptors in *ContextOnto* to specify the accepted data formats by the used devices. We also use MPEG-7 to describe the input and the output parameters of the application services in the functional model.

We use web services for the implementation of the necessary transformations to adapt multimedia content. We call these services content adaptation operators (like image compression, voice synthesis, text translation, etc). Each operator takes in input the media object that will be adapted and its MPEG-7 description. The operator returns the adapted data with its new MPEG-7 description.

We designed and developed a content adaptation module based on the Distributed Content Adaptation Framework (DCAF) of (Berhe, G., Brunie, L. & Pierson J.M. 2005). This framework ensures the selection and the orchestration of content adaptation operators in order to provide adapted data to the application's context. As in the functional adaptation, we dedicate an adaptation entity for each service to adapt all the delivered contents by the considered service. We call this entity *content adapter.*

Our Content Adaptation Approach

As soon as the functional adaptation finishes, our adaptation approach solicits the content adaptation module to prepare the adaptation of each unusable output parameter in each service.

In a first step, our content adaptation module instantiates a content adapter for each specified service in the application's functional model (Figure 6).

In a second step, adapters communicate with the content adaptation framework of (Berhe, G., Brunie, L. & Pierson J.M. 2005) to adapt all the output parameters of the associated services (Figure 7).

We have configured this framework to look for the user and device profiles in the instances of the *ContextOnto's* specific level. Berhe's framework contains a content adaptation planning component to identify the sequence of the necessary content

Figure 6. General algorithm of the content adaptation preparation

```
prepareContentAdaptation(FunctionalModel FM=(f0, F, T))
{
        For each (fi ∈ F)
            {
                    ContentAdapter ca := instanciateContentAdapter(fi)
                    adaptedFunctionalModel := updateAdapter(adaptedFunctionalModel, fi, ca)
            }
        return adaptedFunctionalModel
}
```

Figure 7. General algorithm for the instantiation of content adapters

```
instanciateContentAdapter(ServiceDescription f)
{
        ContentAdapter  ca := new ContentAdapter(f)
        For each(ci ∈ f.Output)
        {
                    adaptationPlan := ContentAdaptationFramework.calculateAdaptation(ci)
                    ca.updateDescription(adaptationPlan, ci)
        }
        return ca
}
```

Figure 8. General algorithm for the calculation of a content adaptation plan

```
calculateAdaptation(MediaObjectDescriptor c)
{
      adaptationPlan :=ContentAdaptationPlanificationComponent.calculateAdaptation(c)
      intializeCache(adaptationPlan)
      return adaptationPlan
}
```

adaptation operators for each non-adapted output parameter (Figure 8). We call this sequence *content adaptation plan*. It consists of operators identified and selected from DCAF's adaptation service registry.

The adaptation plan is a point to point path in a graph representing all the possible compositions of adaptation operators providing adapted content. This graph is computed by the Multimedia Adaptation Graph Generator (MAGG) of DCAF. An adaptation plan is the optimal path to reach an adapted version for the considered media. DCAF uses a QoS model involving adaptation operator costs, response time and history to compute this optimal path. Content adapters execute their adaptation plans when en users invoke the services for the first time. After that, our content adaptation module stores the computed results in a local cache to improve response times when they will be used in the same context.

User Interface Adaptation

User interfaces ensure information exchange between the end user and the different services of the application. These interfaces must remain correctly functional when context changes. The good execution of these interfaces is conditioned by their capacity to adapt to the used device and the user preferences.

We define the presentation adaptation of an application by the necessary operations to au- *tomatically generate a functional user interface ensuring the interaction with the adapted services and content offered to the user.*

The presentation adaptation depends on the characteristics of the used device ("device" concept in *ContextOnto*) and the user preferences ("user" concept in *ContextOnto*). It also depends on the description of the adapted data produced by the content adaptation phase.

In our approach, the presentation adaptation process consists in automatically generating the complete code of the necessary user interfaces to guarantee the interaction with the application's services and content. The presentation adaptation phase is triggered just after the identification of the necessary content adaptation plans. In fact, the last content adaptation operators in these plans give MPEG-7 descriptions of the content that will be delivered to the user. Consequently, we prepare the necessary user interface components that manage the interaction between this content and end users. To generate these components, we use an abstract interaction API[1] defined in a previous work in the scope of the SEFAGI project (Chaari, T. & Laforest, F. 2005). We have specified this abstract API to overcome the heterogeneity problem of the programming APIs implemented on the available devices in the market. This API presents a generic object-oriented modeling of the different necessary entities to ensure the interaction with the adapted services and data in the functional and content adaptation steps. We detail this generic API in the following section.

User Interface Modeling in our Adaptation Approach

Our generic interaction API contains the necessary elements to guarantee the interaction between the adapted services and content. This abstract model is attached to the device concept in *ContextOnto*. It is reified for each device type to reference the concrete objects that correspond to the abstract elements of our model. For each service in the application, we associate a window that guarantees the invocation of the service and the display of its results to the user. A window is composed of two panels: an input panel and an output panel. A panel contains a set of elementary components that encapsulate the input or output parameters of the associated service. To offer navigation facilities between services, we define reactive interaction components that we called commands. In general, these components are menus or buttons. Figure 9 shows the relationships between the main elements of our abstract API.

Automatic User Interface Generation

In our adaptation approach, the automatic generation of the user interface code is based on (i) the implementation of the abstract interaction API and (ii) the functional model of the application (*ApplicationOnto* instance). For each service of

the functional model, the presentation adaptation module generates a concrete window that ensures the invocation and the display of its results (Figure 10). We use the notation L for the target library implementing the several elements of our abstract interaction API.

To organize the windows code, we use the MVC model (Krasner, G. & Pope, S. 1981). This model facilitates the code generation by separating the display, the data and service invocation. According to the MVC model, a window's code W is composed of a view V (graphical display), a model M (service invocation and data handling) and a controller C (event manager).

$$W = \{M, V, C\}$$

The controller ensures the connection between the model and the view when an event is triggered after a user action on the view (service invocation for example).

The window's view is composed of two panels: an input panel Pi and an output panel Po.

$$V = (Pi, Po)$$

The input panel Pi is composed of a display Ai and two interaction commands *InputBack* and

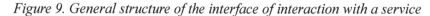

Figure 9. General structure of the interface of interaction with a service

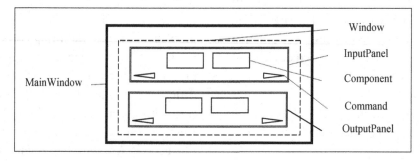

Figure 10. General algorithm for the automatic generation of user interfaces

```
generateUI(FunctionalModel FM=(f0, F, T), RunTimeEnvironmentLibrary L)
{
        For each (fi ∈ F)
        {
                        W :=generateWindow(fi, L)
                        storeInCache(W) ;
        }
}
```

Figure 11. Algorithm for the generation of window code

```
generateWindow(ServiceDescription f, RunTimeEnvironmentLibrary L)
{
        M:= generateModel(f, L)
        V:= generateView(f, L)
        C := generateController(f, L)
        W:= {M, V, C}
        return W
}
```

Figure 12. Algorithm for the window's view generation

```
generateVue(ServiceDescription f, RunTimeEnvironmentLibrary L)
{
        Pi:= generateInputPanel(f.INPUT, L)
        Po:= generateOutputPanel(f.OUTPUT, L)
        V:= {Pi, Po}
        return V
}
```

InputNext. The display *Ai* is a vector of interaction components. Each component encapsulates an input parameter of the considered service.

The InputBack command allows displaying a navigation window that lists the application's available services. The *InputNext* command triggers the service invocation with the given values in the input panel. After this invocation, the view instantiates the output panel *Po* to display its result.

The output panel *Po* is composed of a display *Ao* and two interaction commands: *OutputBack* and *OutputNext*. The display *Ao* is a vector of interac-

tion components. Each component encapsulates an output parameter of the considered service.

OutputBack is the command that allows returning to the window's input panel in order to provide new input values for another service invocation. The *OutputNext* command instantiates a navigation window that displays the list of the available services after the invocation of the current one.

The model *M* ensures the execution of the associated service to the current window. We use a single class *ServiceInvoker* to invoke all the services of the functional model. This invoker takes the description of the service and its input parameters, calls the service and returns its output values. For each target platform, the library L contains the implementation of *ServiceInvoker*. Figure 13 gives the algorithm for the automatic generation of the window's model associated with a service *f*.

In order to ensure navigation between the different application services, the presentation adaptation module offers two generic services *getPreviousServices* and *getNextServices*. These two services are respectively associated to the *InputBack* and *OutputNext* commands.

The controller C of the window contains all the necessary actions when the end user triggers a command on the window's view. Thus, the controller contains the event managers associated with the four commands of our abstract interaction API: *InputBack*, *InputNext*, *OutputBack* and

OutputNext. Figure 14 illustrates the algorithm for the generation of the window's controller.

C= {InputBackAction, InputNextAction, OutputBackAction, OutputNextAction}

After the generation of the model, the view and the controller of each window, the application is ready to be used by the target device. After a context change involving the modification in the application user interface, the presentation adaptation module notifies the end user to update her/his interface on his device.

In section "Our Adaptation Approach" of this chapter, we presented our application adaptation strategy to new contextual situations. This strategy is based on an architectural description of the offered functions to the user (*Functional Model*).

Figure 13. Algorithm for the generation of a window's model

```
generateModel(ServiceDescriptor f, RunTimeEnvironmentLibrary L)
{
M       :=generateServiceInvocation(f, L.ServiceInvoker)
/       * The generateServiceInvocation function generate the necessary code to invoke the service f using the service
        invoker of the target platform L */
r       eturn M
}
```

Figure 14. Algorithm for the generation of the window's controller

```
generateController(ServiceDescriptor f, RunTimeEnvironmentLibrary L)
{
        InputBackAction:= generateInputBackAction(f, L)
/* InputBackAction instantiates the navigation window displaying the available services before the invocation of the service f
        using the getPreviousServices(f) operation */
        InputNextAction:= generateInputNextAction(f, L)
/* InputNextAction invokes the service f and instantiates the output panel Po with the output values of the service f */
        OutputBackAction:= generateOutputBackAction(f, L)
/* OutputBackAction instantiates the input panel in order to re-invoke the service f */
        OutputNextAction:= generateOutputNextAction(f, L)
/* OutputNextAction instantiates the navigation window that displays the output services of the service f using the
        getNextServices(f) operation */
        C= {InputBackAction, InputNextAction, OutputBackAction, OutputNextAction}
        return C
}
```

Our adaptation approach comprises three main phases. First, we adapt the functional behavior of the application to the new context. Second, we adapt the delivered data to the user. Finally, we automatically generate an adapted user interface to interact with the adapted version of the application. Each phase takes the functional model of the application, applies the necessary transformations on it and passes a new version of this model to the next phase. When context changes, the functional adaptation manager re-evaluates the defined rules in phase 1. If these rules modify the functional model of the application, the content and presentation adaptation phases are re-applied.

To validate our approach, we have developed a prototype implementing our adaptation strategy to deploy applications and to adapt them to context. In the following section, we detail a complete case study presenting how we adapted an existing medical application to a new utilization context using our prototype.

IMPLEMENTING OUR ADAPTATION APPROACH

To validate our models and our approach, we developed a context-aware platform to adapt applications to new utilization contexts. We called this platform SECAS (Simple Environment for Context-Aware Systems). SECAS comprises three layers: context management layer, adaptation layer and application deployment layer. In our prototype, we focused on the adaptation and deployment layers. We guarantee the connection with context management layer using a context broker and generic publish/subscribe mechanisms. Actually, our broker is performing simple querying actions, using the Protégé OWL API (Protégé Community 2005) to get information directly from an OWL file implementing *ContextOnto*. Using SECAS, we integrated a medical application (SICOM) offering healthcare services for dialyzed persons in order to adapt it to new utilization contexts. It consists

Figure 15. Technical architecture of the SECAS adaptation layer

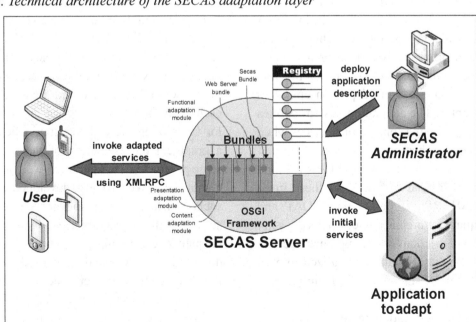

in using a dedicated application to standard PCs on mobile devices (PDAs and SmartPhones). In this section, we present how we have integrated this application in our adaptation platform.

SECAS Platform Development

We chose the Web service technology to implement the SECAS platform. This technology offers easy integration means for distributed application development (Austin, D., Barbir, A., Ferris, C. & Garg. S. 2002). Thanks to their functional description using the WSDL language, Web services are an adequate implementation for: (i) the functional services, (ii) service adapters, (iii) contents adapters and (iv) content adaptation operators. Our *SECAS* platform is deployed in an Oscar OSGI container (OSGi Alliance 2003). OSGI offers modular and dynamic facilities to application development. In our prototype, OSGI was especially very useful for the dynamic deployment of adapters.

When an administrator deploys an application's functional model, the SECAS adaptation layer instantiates a service adapter for each referenced service. These adapters are deployed into the SECAS web server hosted in the OSGI container (Figure 15). When the administrator deploys the adaptation rules or when context changes, our implemented functional adaptation module configures the service adapters and builds appropriate lists of adaptation operators in each adapter. The adaptation system applies these operators on the application services when end-users invoke them.

We have chosen the XML-RPC as a transport protocol instead of SOAP for these invocations. XML-RPC is lighter than SOAP and more adequate for mobile devices. This does not constitute a restriction for our approach because every SOAP message can be serialized into an XML-RPC format (Laurent, S.S., Dumbill, E.& Johnston, J. 2001).

Our content adaptation module guarantees the instantiation of a content adapter for each service and delegates the adaptation of its input and output data to the DCAF prototype (Berhe, G., Brunie, L. & Pierson J.M. 2005). In a last step, our presentation adaptation module generates an interaction window for each service. Currently, our prototype supports the automatic generation of java user interfaces for standard PCs compatible with J2SE (Sun Developer Network 2007), pocket PCs compatible with the CDC/PERSONNEL JAVA profile (Sun Microsystems, Inc. 2000) and mobile phones compatible with the CLDC/MIDP profile (Java Community Process 2007).

The components of our adaptation process may be centralized or distributed. For example, in our current prototype the content adaptation module is distributed; the presentation adaptation module is centralized, the functional adaptation module is on a single server.

The SICOM Project Use Case

In the scope of the SICOM project of the Rhône-Alpes region in France, we have analyzed the software needs for home healthcare of dialyzed patients. In this project, we have collaborated with the Edouard Herriot hospital, Baxter France Enterprise and the France Telecom R&D group. The developed software in this project offers a set of helpful services to the healthcare practitioners: for example, a dialysis record including the prescribed treatment and the description of each dialysis action, a list of medical images for visualizing the catheter state when needed, a graphical representation of the evolution of some parameters (temperature, weight, filtration volume, etc). We have also developed services to social assistants, nurses, and other participants for accessing the prescribed treatments, managing the medecines supplies, etc. These services were designed and developed to be used on standard PC. The healthcare practitioners expressed new needs to use these same services on PDAs and mobile phones. We validated our adaptation approach and our prototype on these services by performing these tests:

- SICOM deployment in SECAS
- Complete adaptation (services, data and presentation) of SICOM to the new context
- Test of the adapted services invocation from standard PCs and a mobile phone.

We used a PC equipped with a Pentium 4, 2.4 GHz processor and a 1 GB memory to deploy the SECAS platform and a GPRS enabled Nokia 6230 mobile phone to test the adapted application.

Used Ontologies for SICOM Adaptation

SICOM application consists of a set of Web services corresponding to software modules in *ApplicationOnto*. In the specific level of this ontology, we define all the functional model structure. Figure 4 shows the main elements of this structure. For SICOM, we have created these elements according to the available services in SICOM and the existing execution dependencies between them.

To specify the utilization context for the SICOM application, we defined these simple instances: "Doctor", "Seated", "Desk", "Desktop_PC" and "Wired_LAN". They respectively implement the User, Activity, Location, Device and Network concepts in the generic level of ContextOnto. These instances define a contextual situation where a doctor is using a desktop PC connected to the wired network of the hospital while he is seated in front of his desk. To model the context change, we have added the "GPRS_Network", "mobilePhone" and "Tramway" instances in ContextOnto. They define the new contextual situation where the same doctor is using the same SICOM application through his mobile phone while he is seated in a tramway in the direction of a patient's domicile (Figure 16).

Adaptation rules instantiate the different concepts and relations of the PolicyOnto ontology. In the specific level of this ontology, we have defined the supported events and adaptation actions that can be used in these rules. In PolicyOnto, we have instantiated the SimpleEvent concept in three types: system events, context events and application events. "User Session Start", "Device Change" and "Service added" are sample instances of these events (Figure 17).

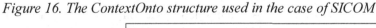

Figure 16. The ContextOnto structure used in the case of SICOM

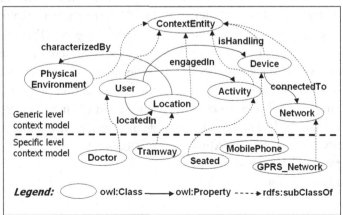

Figure 17. The PolicyOnto structure used to adapt SICOM to new contexts

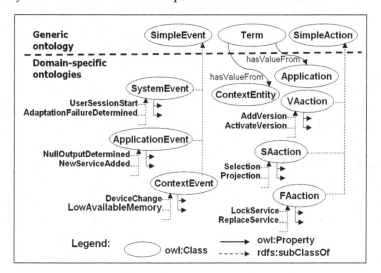

Adaptation rules instantiate the different concepts and relations of the *PolicyOnto* ontology. In the specific level of this ontology, we have defined the supported events and adaptation actions that can be used in these rules. In *PolicyOnto*, we have instantiated the SimpleEvent concept in three types: system events, context events and application events. "User Session Start", "Device Change" and "Service added" are sample instances of these events (Figure 17).

Moreover, we have developed different adaptation actions classified in three types: "FAaction", "SAaction" or "VAaction". The first type integrates the different architectural adaptation operators on the application's functional model. The second concerns the operators that can be applied locally on each service. The last type manages different possible versions and instances of a same service. For example, we can activate a specific version (using the *activateVersion* operator) for a given context (Figure 17). The association between the supported events, the contextual situations and adaptation actions are specified in the given rules to adapt the application. The

concrete rules to adapt the SICOM application are detailed in the next subsection.

SICOM Adaptation to New Utilization Contexts

We developed a deployment tool that guarantees integrating and adapting applications in our SE-CAS platform. To deploy a new application like SICOM, a SECAS administrator deploys the application description, i.e. *Functional Model,* and the necessary adaptation rules using the administration interface presented in Figure 18.

As mentioned in section "Ontologies used in SICOM Adaptation", the first context describes a doctor using SICOM from his desktop PC and the second presents the same doctor using the same application from his mobile phone. The following section presents how this application behaves in the first context and the next section details how it was automatically adapted to the new context.

Figure 18. Administration interface of the SECAS Platform

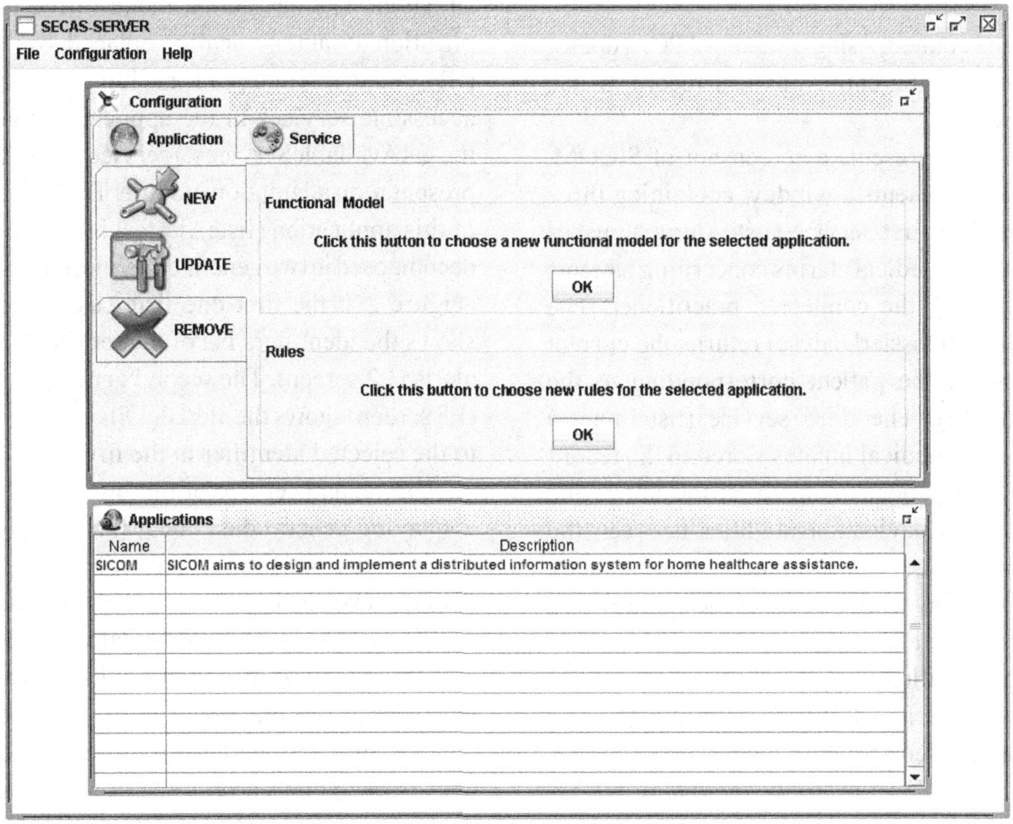

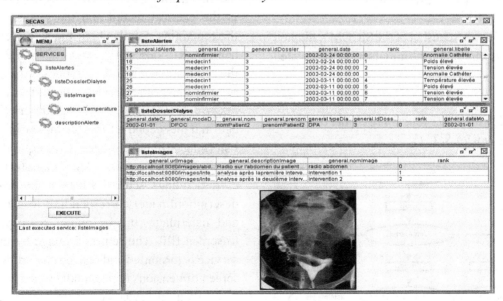

Figure 19. SICOM: visualization of a peritoneal dialysis record on a standard PC

SICOM on Standard PCs

In the first context, using a standard PC, a doctor can visualize the entire medical record in one window.

Figure 19 presents a screenshot of SICOM. This figure presents a window containing three services. The first service (listeAlertes) pushes the list of the medical alarms concerning patients supervised by the connected practitioner. The second (listeDossierDialyse) returns the current treatment of the patient corresponding to the selected alert. The third service (listeImages) presents the medical images stored in the record of the same patient. A menu (at the left of the figure) offers navigation facilities between the different services of the application. This menu presents the invocation order of the application's initial functional model.

Figure 20 illustrates the functional model of SICOM before its adaptation with SECAS. The different elements of this model are instances of the generic level in *ApplicationOnto*. We established this model after having identified the offered services of SICOM to end users.

SICOM on Mobile Phones

Figure 25 is a screenshot of the SICOM's adapted version. In this figure, the initial services presented

Figure 20. SICOM's functional model before its adaptation with SECAS

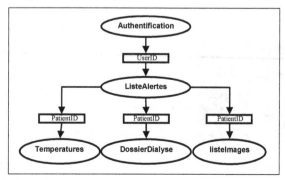

in Figure 19 are adapted to the new contextual situation. The navigation menu of the first application is automatically replaced by screens (E1), (E4), (E6) and (E7) providing the list of the accessible services in the application thanks to the getAvailableServices() service offered by the presentation adaptation module. The first service of this application (listeAlertes) is automatically decomposed in two generated services using Rule1 (Figure 21): the first one listeAlertes(idAlerte) shows the identifiers list of the returned medical alerts (E2 screen). The second generated service (E3 screen) shows the alert details corresponding to the selected identifier in the first screen.

The second service of the initial application displaying general data about the dialysis treatment corresponds to the screen E5. The data is displayed vertically whereas on the standard devices they are presented horizontally (presentation adaptation). The same initial service is used in the new context (no functional adaptation).

The third service returning the medical images is decomposed on three services after the application of Rule1 (Figure 21) followed by Rule2 (Figure 22). Indeed, the first rule decomposes the service listeImages() in two services: the first listeImages(nomImage) returns the image names in the medical record and the second returns the remaining details about the selected image name: URL, description and binary file. Then, the application of Rule2 decomposes this second service in two other services: the first returns non image data listeImages(urlImage:descriptionImage) and the second returns the binary image file listeImages(binaireImage). Consequently, we obtain the three services: listeImages(urlImage) corresponding to screen E8, listeImages(urlImage: descriptionImage) corresponding to screen E9 and listeImages(binaireImage) corresponding to screen E10. The returned image by this last service is formatted and resized according to the screen dimensions (content adaptation).

If the used device does not support displaying images, the access to the generated service

Figure 21. First adaptation rule of SICOM application

{(context.device.hardwarePlatform.memory < 1024) ∧ (∀ f∈F | f.OUTPUT.length > 1) →
firstValues=projection(f, f.OUTPUT[1]) ∧ replaceService(f, firstValues)
∧ selectedInstance=selection(f, f.OUTPUT[1] = selected(firstValues))
∧ insertServiceAfter(firstValues, selectedInstance)}

Figure 22. Second adaptation rule of SICOM application

{(context.device.softwarePlatform.acceptedDataTypes.acceptImages) ∧
(context.device.type="cldc") ∧ (∀ f∈F | f.OUTPUT.length > 1) ∧ (∃ i∈[0, f.OUTPUT.length] |
f.OUTPUT[i].type="mpeg7:binaryImage") →
(displayNonImage = projection(f, ¬(f.OUTPUT[i]))
∧ (displayImage = projection(f, f.OUTPUT[i]))
∧ replaceService(f,displayNonImage) ∧ insertAlternativeService(displayNonImage, displayImage) }

Figure 23. Third adaptation rule of SICOM application

{ (¬context.device.acceptedDataTypes.acceptImages) ∧ (∀ f∈F | ∃ i∈[0, f.OUTPUT.length] |
f.OUTPUT[i].type="mpeg7:binaryImage") → lockService(f) }

Figure 24. Adapted functional model of the SICOM application

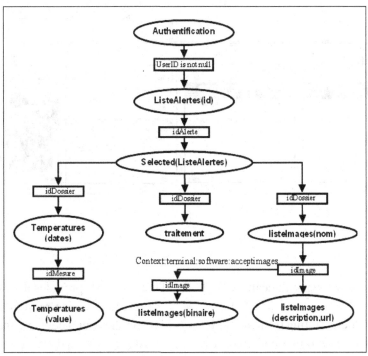

Figure 25. Visualization of the same medical record in Figure 19 on a mobile device

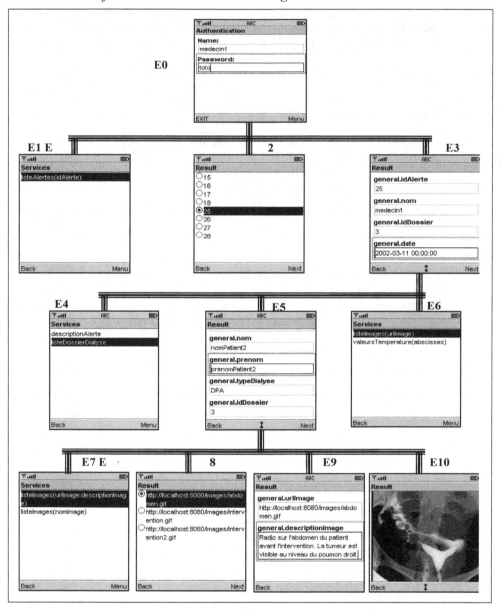

listeImages(binaireImage) is automatically locked by using *Rule3*.

The functional model resulting from the application of these three rules is illustrated in Figure 24. SECAS platform uses this functional model to adapt the data returned by its specified services.

Thus, SECAS provides a new functional model where each service returns directly exploitable data on the user's device. Finally, this new functional model is used to automatically generate the user interface that guarantees the interaction with the adapted services and data of this application (Figure 25).

To adapt this application to mobile environments, we defined generic rules (Rule1, Rule2 and Rule3) that can be used for other applications in order to adapt them for similar mobile phones. The adaptation rule base of any application can be enriched by explicit specific rules or by implicit inferred rules. In fact, the adaptation system automatically transforms these rules in SWRL syntax to look for values in ContextOnto and ApplicationOnto and to infer adaptation decisions on the given application.

CONCLUSION

In this chapter, we presented an ontology-based approach guaranteeing the adaptation of applications to context on three axes: the functional behavior of the services that applications offer to end users, the returned multimedia content by these services and the user interface that ensures the interaction with them. Unlike the major part of the existing works in context-awareness focusing on capturing, interpreting and modeling context, we propose an open platform, called SECAS, ensuring easy integration and adaptation of applications to several new operating contexts. This platform provides the necessary means and tools to adapting applications to new utilization contexts. It is based on three main layers: (i) a deployment layer to integrate new applications in the platform, (ii) an adaptation layer to dynamically adapt the integrated applications to new environments and needs and (iii) a context management layer to capture and disseminate context information to the adaptation layer. Our adaptation approach is based on simple functional application descriptions. Consequently, we gain a considerable re-engineering time to adapt the behavior of existing applications to new utilization contexts. Our platform is open and can easily evolve by integrating new adaptation actions without recompiling its code.

In order to validate our context-aware contributions, we have implemented a prototype for our SECAS platform guaranteeing application adaptation to different contexts. We used Java, OSGi and Web service technologies to implement this prototype. We have successfully applied several experiments on a home health care application demonstrating the feasibility of our approach and validating its main principles.

Actually, we are working on applying our adaptation approach in machine-to-machine environments where end users are less implicated and systems are more autonomous. We are also working on more sophisticated adaptation rule correlations to improve our adaptation process and to better control adaptation actions on the application's components. Finally, we are thinking about tools to help administrators generating the functional models of applications using reverse engineering techniques and HTTP message monitoring.

REFERENCES

Aksit, M., & Choukair, Z. (2003). Dynamic Adaptive and Reconfigurable Systems. In Overview and Prospective Vision. In *Proceedings of the International Conference on Distributed Computing Systems Workshops 03*, (pp. 84-92) IEEE Computer Society Press.

Andrade, L-F., & Fiadeiro, J. L. (2003). Architecture Based Evolution of Software Systems. In M. Bernardo & P. Inverardi (Eds.), *Formal Methods for Software Architectures: Third International School on Formal Methods for the Design of Computer, Communication and Software Systems: Software Architectures, SFM 2003, Bertinoro, Italy, September 22-27, 2003*, (pp 148-181). Advanced Lectures Series: Lecture Notes in Computer Science 2804. Springer Verlag

Austin, D., Barbir, A., Ferris, C., & Garg, S. (2002). *Web Services Architecture Requirements*. W3C

Working Draft, retrieved July 2, 2007 from http://www.w3.org/TR/2002/WD-wsa-regs20020819

Baldauf, M., Dustdar, M. S., & Rosenberg, F. (2007). A survey on context-aware systems. *International Journal of Ad Hoc and Ubiquitous Computing, 2*(4), 263-277. Inderscience

Baresi, L., Guinea, S., & Tamburrelli, G. (2008). Towards decentralized self-adaptive component-based systems. In *Proceedings of the 2008 international Workshop on Software Engineering For Adaptive and Self-Managing Systems.* (pp 57-64) ACM Press

Bauer, M., Heiber, T., Kortuem G., & Segall, Z. (1998). A collaborative wearable system with remote sensing. In *Second International Symposium on Wearable Computers (*ISWC 1998), 19-20 October 1998, Pittsburgh, Pennsylvania, USA (pp. 10-17) IEEE Computer Society Press

Baumgartner, N., Retschitzegger, W., & Schwinger, W. (2008). A software architecture for ontology-driven situation awareness. In *Proceedings of the 2008 ACM Symposium on Applied Computing* (pp 2326-2330) ACM Press

Bechhofer, S., Van Harmelen, F., Hendler, J., Horrocks, I., McGuinness, D. L., Patel-Schneider, P. F. & Stein, L. A. (2004). *OWL Web Ontology Language Reference* 10 february 2004 edition, retrieved june 17, 2008 from http://www.w3.org/TR/owl-ref/

Belhanafi Behlouli, N., Taconet, C., & Bernard, G. (2006). An Architecture for supporting Development and Execution of Context-Aware Component applications. In *International Conference on Pervasive Services*, (pp. 57-66). IEEE Computer Society Press.

Benatallah, B., Casati, F., Grigori, D., Nezhad, H. R., & Toumani, F. (2005). Developing adapters for Web services integration. In *CAiSE Conference,* (pp. 415–429) Lecture Notes in Computer Science 3520. Springer Verlag

Berhe, G., Brunie, L., & Pierson, J. M. (2005). Distributed Content Adaptation for Pervasive Systems. *International Conference on Information Technology* ITCC 2005 (pp. 234-241). IEEE Computer Society Press

Boussard, M. et al. (2008). *Service Adaptation over Heterogeneous Infrastructures*. Plastic IST project white paper. retrieved June 16, 2008 from ftp://ftp.cordis.europa.eu/pub/ist/docs/ct/whitepaper3-service-adaptation-e2r-final_en.pdf

Cazzola, W., Savigni, A., Sosio, A., & Tisato, F. (1999). *Architectural Reflection: Concepts, Design, and Evaluation*. Technical Report RI-DSI 234-99. DSI. University degli Studi di Milano

Ceri, S., Daniel, F., Matera, M., & Facca, F. M. (2007). Model-driven development of context-aware Web applications. *ACM Transactions on Internet Technologies, 7*(1).

Chaari, T., & Laforest, F. (2005). SEFAGI: Simple Environment for Adaptable Graphical Interfaces - Generating User Interfaces for Different Kinds of Terminals. In *7th International Conference on Entreprise Information Systems* (pp. 232-237).

Chaari, T., Ejigu, D., Laforest, F., & Scuturici, V. M. (2007). A Comprehensive Approach to Model and Use Context for Adapting Applications in Pervasive Environments. *Int. Journal of Systems and software 80*(12), 1973-1992. Elsevier.

Chaari, T., Laforest, F., & Celentano, A. (2007) Adaptation in Context-Aware Pervasive Information Systems: The SECAS Project. *Int. Journal on Pervasive Computing and Communications, 3*(4), 400-425. Emerald Group Publishing Limited.

Chefrour, D., & André, F. (2002). ACEEL: modèle de composants auto-adaptatifs. Application aux environnements mobiles. In *Colloque Systèmes à composants adaptables et extensibles*. October 2002, Grenoble, France.

Chen, H., Finin, T., & Joshi, A. (2003). An Ontology for Context-Aware Pervasive Computing Environments. In *Workshop on Ontologies and Distributed Systems, International Joint Conference on Artificial Intelligence*, Mexico.

Chen, H. (2004). *An Intelligent Broker Architecture for Pervasive Context-Aware Systems*. Unpublished doctoral dissertation, Baltimore County: Department of CSEE, University of Maryland.

Cheung-Foo-Wo, D., Tigli, J. Y., Lavirotte S., & Riveill, M. (2007). Self-adaptation of event-driven component-oriented Middleware using Aspects of Assembly. In *5th International Workshop on Middleware for Pervasive and Ad-Hoc Computing*, California, USA.

Coutaz, J., Crowley, J. L., Dobson, S., & Garlan, D. (2005). Context is key. *Communications of the ACM, 48*(3), 49-53

Cuppens, F., & Miege, A. (2002). Alert correlation in a cooperative intrusion detection framework. *IEEE Symposium on Security and Privacy,* (pp. 202-215).

De Virgilio, R., & Torlone, R. (2006). Modeling heterogeneous context information in adaptive web based applications. In *6th international Conference on Web Engineering, 263*, 56-63. ACM Press

Dey, A. K., Salber, D., & Abowd, G. D. (2001). A conceptual framework and a toolkit for supporting the rapid prototyping of context-aware applications. *Special issue on context-aware computing Human Computer Interaction Journal, 16*(2-4), 97–116.

Dey, A. K., Abowd, G. D., & Wood, A. (1998). CyberDesk: A framework for providing self–integrating context–aware services. *Knowledge Based Systems, 11*(1), 3-13.

Dowling, J., & Cahill, V. (2001). The K-Component Architecture Meta-Model for Self-Adaptive

Software. In *Third International Conference on Metalevel Architectures and Separation of Crosscutting Concerns*, Reflection 2001, Kyoto, Japan (pp. 81-88).

Ejigu, D., Scuturici, M., & Brunie, L. (2007). An Ontology-Based Approach to Context Modeling and Reasoning in Pervasive Computing. In *Proceedings of the Fifth IEEE international Conference on Pervasive Computing and Communications Workshops* (pp. 14-19). IEEE Computer Society Press.

Fox, A., Goldberg, I., Gribble, S. et al. (1998). Experience with TopGun Wingman: A Proxy-Based Web Browser for the 3Com PalmPilot. In *Proceedings of the IFIP International Conference on Distributed Systems Platforms and Open Distributed Processing - Middleware 98* (pp. 407-426) Lake District, England.

Geihs, K., Ullah Khan, M., Reichle, R., Solberg, A., Hallsteinsen, S. O., & Merral, S. (2006). Modeling of component-based adaptive distributed applications. In *SAC 2006:* (pp. 718-722), ACM Press.

Gu, T., Pung, H. K., & Zhang, D. Q. (2005). A service-oriented middleware for building context-aware services. *Journal of Network Computer Applications, 28*(1) 1-18. Elsevier.

Hallsteinsen, S., Floch, J., & Stav, E. (2004). A Middleware Centric Approach to Building Self-Adapting Systems. In Software Engineering. and Middleware, Lecture Notes in Computer Science 3437 (pp. 107-122) Springer Verlag

Harmonia Inc. (2008). LiquidUI. Retrieved march 19, 2008 from http://www.harmonia.com/products/index.php

Hanson, N. E., & Widom, J. (1992). *An Overview of Production Rules in Database Systems*. Technical report, University of Florida (CIS)

Henricksen, K., & Indulska, J. (2006). Developing context-aware pervasive computing applications:

Models and approach. *Journal of Pervasive and Mobile Computing, 2*(1), 37-64. Elsevier

Hillerson, G. (2001). *Web Clipping Developer's Guide.* Santa Clara, California: Palm Inc.

Hinz, M., Pietschmann, S., Umbach, M., & Meißner, K. (2007). Adaptation and Distribution of Pipeline-Based Context-Aware Web Architectures. In *Sixth Working IEEE/IFIP Conference on Software Architecture* (p. 15). IEEE Computer Society Press

Hinz, M., Pietschmann, S., Fiala, Z.A (2007). Framework for Context Modeling in Adaptive Web Applications. *IADIS International Journal of WWW/Internet, 5*(1)

IBM research (2000). LiquidUI. Retrieved June 1, 2007 from http://www.research.ibm.com/networked_data_systems/transcoding/index.html

Indulska, J., Robinson, R., Rakotonirainy, A., & Henricksen, K. (2003). Experiences in Using CC/PP in Context-Aware Systems. In *4th international Conference on Mobile Data Management*, January 21 - 24, 2003, Melbourne, Australia. (pp.247-261) Lecture Notes In Computer Science 2574, Springer Verlag

Java Community Process (2007). Mobile Information Device Profile (JSR 37) Java 2 Platform Micro Edition, Sun Microsystems. retrieved june 1, 2007 from http://java.sun.com/products/midp/

Keeney, J., & Cahill, V. (2003). Chisel: A Policy-Driven, Context-Aware, Dynamic Adaptation Framework. In *Fourth IEEE International Workshop on Policies for Distributed Systems and Networks POLICY 2003*, Italy. IEEE Computer Society Press

Ketfi, A., Belkhatir, N., & Cunin, P. Y. (2002). Adaptation Dynamique, concepts et expérimentations. In *15th International Conference on Software & Systems Engineering and their Applications ICSSEA02,* Paris, France

Kiciman, E., & Fox, A (2000). Using dynamic mediation to integrate COTS entities in a ubiquitous computing environment. In *2nd International Symposium on Handheld and Ubiquitious Computing (HUC2K).* Heidelberg, Germany : Springer London

Kickzales, G., Lamping, J., Mendhekar, A. et al. (1997). Aspect-Oriented Programming. In *ECOOP'97,* (pp. 220-242) Lecture Notes in Computer Science 1241, Springer Verlag

Kirsch-Pinheiro, M., Villanova-Oliver, M., Gensel, J., & Martin, H. (2006). A Personalized and Context-Aware Adaptation Process for Web-Based Groupware Systems. In *CAiSE'06 Workshop Ubiquitous Mobile Information and Collaboration Systems*

Kjaer, K. E. (2007). A survey of context-aware middleware. In W. Hasselbring (Ed.) 25th Conference on IASTED international Multi-Conference: Software Engineering (pp. 148-155). ACTA Press

Korpipaa, P., Mantyjarvi, J., Kela, J. et al. (2004). Managing context information in mobile devices. *IEEE Pervasive Computing,* 19(6), 21-29

Krasner, G. & Pope, S. (1981). A cookbook for using the model-view controller user interface paradigm in Smalltalk-80, *Journal of Object-Oriented Programming* (3), 26-49.

Laurent, S.S., Dumbill, E.& Johnston, J. (2001). *Programming Web Services with XML-RPC.* O'Reilly & Associates, Inc.

Le Mouël, F., André, F. & Segarra, M.T. (2002). AeDEn: An Adaptive Framework for Dynamic Distribution over Mobile Environments. *Annals of Telecommunications,* 57(11-12), 1124-1148

Maes, P. (1987). Concepts and experiments in computational reflection. In N. Meyrowitz, (Ed.) *Conference on Object-Oriented Programming Systems, Languages and Applications* OOPSLA '87 (pp 147-155). ACM Press

Mrissa, M., Ghedira, C., Benslimane, D., Maamar, Z., Rosenberg, F. & Dustdar S. (2007). A Context-based Mediation Approach to Compose Semantic Web Services. *ACM Transactions on Internet Technology* 8(1), ACM Association for Computing Machinery.

Noble, B. (2000). System Support for Mobile, Adaptive Applications. *IEEE Personal Communications*, 7(1), 44-49

Open Mobile Alliance (2007). WAP Forum. Retrieved june 1, 2007 from http://www.wapforum.org

OSGi Alliance (2003). *OSGi Service Platform*, Release 3. Amsterdam : IOS Press

Papazoglou, M. P. and Heuvel, W. (2007). Service oriented architectures: approaches, technologies and research issues. *The VLDB Journal* 16(3), 389-415

Paspallis, N., Eliassen, F., Hallsteinsen, S. & Papadopoulos G.A. (2008). Developing self-adaptive mobile applications and services with Separation-of-Concerns In: Di Nitto, R., Traverso, P., Sassen, A.M., Zwegers, A., Mylopoulos, J. & Papazoglou, M. (Eds) *At your service: Service Engineering in the Information Society Technologies Program*,. MIT Press

Pawlak, R., Seinturier, L., Duchien, L. et al. (2001). JAC: A Flexible Solution for Aspect-Oriented Programming in Java. (pp 1-24) Lecture Notes in Computer Science 2192. Springer Verlag

Protégé Community (2005). The Protégé Ontology Editor and Knowledge Acquisition System. retrieved June 16, 2005 from http://protege.stanford.edu/

Reichle, R., Wagner, M., Ullah Khan M., Geihs, K., Lorenzo, J., Valla, M., Fra, Paspallis, N. & Papadopoulos, G.A. (2008). A Comprehensive Context Modeling Framework for Pervasive Computing Systems. In *8th IFIP International Conference on Distributed Applications and Interoperable Systems* (pp. 281-295)

Robinson, R., Henricksen, K. & Indulska, J. (2007). XCML: A runtime representation for the Context Modeling Language. In *4th International Workshop on Context Modeling and Reasoning (CoMoRea), PerCom'07 Workshop Proceedings*, (pp 20-26). IEEE Computer Society Press

Rodriguez, J., Dakar, B., Marras, F.L. et al. (2001). Transcoding in WebSphere. In: *New Capabilities in IBM WebSphere Transcoding Publisher Version 3.5 Extending Web Applications to the Pervasive World. Everyplace Suite. Chapter 11.* New York: IBM Redbooks, 446 p.

Rosa, L., Lopes, A. & Rodrigues, L. (2008). Modeling adaptive services for distributed systems. In *Proceedings of the 2008 ACM Symposium on Applied Computing* (pp 2174-2180). ACM Press

Strang, T. & Linnhoff-Popien, C. (2004). A context modeling survey. In UbiComp 1st International Workshop on Advanced Context Modeling, Reasoning and Management (pp. 34-41)

Sun Microsystems, Inc. (2000). *Personal Java Application Environment Specification, Version 1.2a* (Final) retrieved from http://java.sun.com/products/personaljava/

Sun Developer Network (2007). Java 2 Platform, Standard Edition (J2SE). retrieved june 1, 2007 from http: //java.sun.com/j2se

Vieira, V., Tedesco, P., Salgado, A.C. & Brézillon, P. (2007). Investigating the Specifics of Contextual Elements Management: The CEManTIKA Approach. In Kokinov, B.; Richardson, D.C.; Roth-Berghofer, Th.R.; Vieu, L. (Eds.) *Modeling and Using Context 6th International and Interdisciplinary Conference, CONTEXT 2007* (pp. 493-506) Lecture Notes in Artificial Intelligence, Springer Verlag

W3C (2004a). SWRL: A Semantic Web Rule Language Combining OWL and RuleML, retrieved may 21, 2004 from http://www.w3.org/Submission/2004/SUBM-SWRL

W3C (2004b). Composite Capability/Preference Profiles (CC/PP): Structure and Vocabularies 1.0, retrieved june 1, 2007 from http://www.w3.org/TR/2004/REC-CCPP-struct-vocab-20040115

Yarvis M. (2001). *Conductor: Distributed Adaptation for Heterogeneous Networks*. Unpublished doctoral dissertation, Los Angeles University, UCLA Department of Computer Science.

ENDNOTES

[1] Work initiated while Tarak Chaari was in a PhD Thesis at the LIRIS lab (INSA Lyon).

[2] Work partially done when Mohamed Zouari was in a master thesis at the LIRIS lab (INSA Lyon).

Chapter III
Context–Aware Applications for the Web:
A Model–Driven Development Approach

Florian Daniel
University of Trento, Italy

ABSTRACT

Adaptivity (the runtime adaptation to user profile data) and context-awareness (the runtime adaptation to generic context data) have been gaining momentum in the field of Web engineering over the last years, especially in response to the ever growing demand for highly personalized services and applications coming from end users. Developing context-aware and adaptive Web applications requires addressing a few design concerns that are proper of such kind of applications and independent of the chosen modeling paradigm or programming language. In this chapter we characterize the design of context-aware Web applications, the authors describe a conceptual, model-driven development approach, and they show how the peculiarities of context-awareness require augmenting the expressive power of conceptual models in order to be able to express adaptive application behaviors.

INTRODUCTION

The evolution of the Information Technology in the last years has seen the World Wide Web transforming from a read-only hypertext media into a full-fledged, multi-channel and multi-service application delivery platform. Current advances in communication and network technologies are changing the way people interact with Web applications. They provide users with different types of mobile devices for accessing – at any time, from anywhere, and with any media – services and contents customized to the users' preferences and usage environments. More and more users themselves ask for services and applications highly tailored to their individual requirements and, especially due to the increasing affordability of new and powerful mobile communication devices, they also begin to appreciate the availability of ubiquitous access. In order to cope with the growing demand for novel, user-centric application features, such as adaptivity and context-awareness, appropriate development methods for Web applications are required.

Adaptivity is increasingly gaining momentum in the context of modern software systems. Runtime adaptivity provides highly flexible and responsive means for the customization of contents and services with respect to the user's identity. Varying device characteristics in mobile and multi-channel computing environments can be adequately taken into account and leveraged by means of adaptive software designs, whose development is facilitated by the availability of standardized communication protocols (e.g. HTTP) and markup languages (e.g. HTML or WML), supported by most of today's mobile devices. Multi-channel deployment does no longer require completely different, parallel design approaches and rather represents a presentation issue on top of unified engineering solutions.

But adaptivity may also enable an application to take into account a wider range of properties describing the interaction between the user and the application, thus paving the way for context-awareness. *Context-awareness* (Dey & Abowd, 2000; Schilit & Theimer, 1994) is often seen as recently emerged research field in information technology and in particular in the domain of the Web. From the perspective of application front-end development it can however be interpreted as natural evolution of personalization and adaptivity, addressing not only the user's identity and preferences, but also his/her usage environment. Personalization has already demonstrated its benefits for both users and content providers and has been commonly recognized as fundamental factor for augmenting the efficacy of the overall communication of contents. Context-awareness goes one step further in the same direction, aiming at enhancing the application's usefulness

and efficacy by combining personalization and adaptivity based on an application-specific set of properties (the context) that may affect the execution of the application.

In this chapter, we focus on the development of context-aware applications for the Web and, in particular, we describe a *model-driven* development method that allows developers to approach the problem at a level of abstraction that enables him/her to focus on the real design challenges of such class of applications, leaving low-level implementation concerns to supporting CASE (Computer-Aided Software Engineering) tools. Considering that software systems are continuously getting more complex and difficult to maintain – partly due to the previously described requirements –, we believe that efficient abstraction mechanisms and design processes, such as those provided by visual, model-driven design methods, are becoming crucial. The focus on essential design issues and the ease of reuse in model-driven design methods may significantly accelerate the overall design process. As we will show in this chapter, starting from application models, code generation techniques may then provide for the automatic generation of application code or templates, thus assuring the fast production of consistent and high quality implementations.

MOTIVATING EXAMPLES

Active application features, such as context-aware or adaptive behaviors, may augment the effectiveness of interactions and the efficiency of resource consumption in all those situations where services and contents offered by an application strongly depend on environmental situations, users' abilities or disabilities, or the state or health of a software system. For example, typical applications demanding for active features and adaptivity are:

- *Adaptive personalization.* User profile attributes for personalization purposes may present different levels of variability in time. Profile properties may be static in nature (e.g. the name of a user), slowly changing (e.g. profile data derived from a user's browsing behavior) or even fast changing (e.g. the pulse frequency of a patient). Adaptive personalization mechanisms that take into account such profile peculiarities could allow systems to go beyond the common and static tailoring or services and contents.

- *Interaction-enabling functionalities.* Context could as well consider handicaps or physical disabilities of users, such as vision problems, blindness or paralysis, to adapt the application accordingly and to provide alternative and better suited interaction mechanisms and modalities. Adaptivity could thus provide functionalities enabling handicapped users to properly interact with applications, thus fostering the accessibility of applications.

- *Effective content delivery.* In general, whatever context data may be leveraged to provide appropriate contents and program features at the right time, priority, and emphasis. For example, specifically targeted special offers could be advertised and directed more effectively, presentation properties could be adapted to varying luminosity conditions for better readability, etc. Adaptive or context-aware extensions could thus enhance the overall effectiveness of applications by adapting individual application elements to varying users or usages of the application.

- *Delivery of context as content.* Applications may depend intrinsically and in a structural manner from context data. Location-aware applications, such as city map services or navigation systems, treat position data as core contents of the application and adapt to them, supported by proper localization mechanisms. To such kind of applications,

the use of context data represents a functional requirement, rather than an optional feature.

- *Exception handling.* Critical events during the execution of a software system may raise exceptions and require prompt reactions being performed. Process-based or workflow-driven applications, for example, represent a typical class of applications that constantly have to cope with exceptional situations in order to guarantee the consistent termination of a running process. Here, adaptive or context-aware mechanisms could be leveraged to capture respective application events and to enact the pieces of application logic that are necessary to handle the exceptional situation.

- *Production and control systems.* Critical production or control systems may require, for example, highly specific sensing and alerting mechanisms to prevent production losses or product quality degradations. Context-awareness could facilitate the timeliness of reactions and the efficient handling of dangerous situations, but also proactive maintenance approaches, such as those adopted in a steadily growing number of hardware/software systems, may be achieved.

- *Self-healing software systems.* Autonomic or self-healing software systems elevate the idea of proactive maintenance from hardware to software systems and aim at the creation of computing systems that are able to configure, tune, and even repair themselves. Proactive and adaptive capabilities in this context are an essential feature.

REFERENCE SCENARIO

To exemplify the concepts introduced in this chapter and to better convey the underlying ideas, step by step we will show how we developed one of our demonstration prototypes, the PoliTour application. The application runs on a PDA with wireless Internet access and enables visitors to Politecnico di Milano, Italy, to obtain location-aware campus details (i.e. information about roads and buildings) while walking through the campus. If a user is about to leave the WiFi-covered area of the campus, an alert message is shown.

CONTEXT-AWARENESS AND WEB APPLICATIONS

Due to a lack of appropriate technologies and concepts, for a long time context-awareness has not been considered suited to the domain of the Web. Web technologies (both hardware and software) are however continuously evolving and the attitude toward reactive and context-aware behaviors in Web applications is changing. As a matter of fact, support for a multitude of non-functional requirements, whose inadequate coverage prevented the adoption of Web technologies for the implementation of reactive applications, has now been developed. Just to mention a few:

- The *reliability* of data communications has been considerably enhanced along both the software and the hardware dimension. The introduction of reliable messaging techniques (e.g. digital certificates or the WS-Reliability specification) provides for trustworthy communications on top of standard Web protocols, such as HTTP or SOAP. The success of fiber optics – as an example of hardware evolution – has allowed the Ethernet protocol (typically used in the Web) even to enter industrial production environments, where the high electromagnetic interferences that exist in the presence of high-voltage machineries practically prohibited the use of conventional, unreliable network technologies.

- The *pervasiveness* and *availability* of Web applications is continuously growing due to the introduction of novel networking technologies, such as ADSL (Asynchronous Digital Subscriber Line) or fiber optics for home and office users and WiFi and 3rd generation mobile telephony technologies (e.g. UMTS, GPRS, EDGE) for mobile users.

- Web applications have proved a high *scalability* (it suffices to think about certain portal applications that serve millions of users every day), facilitated *maintainability* and high *cost efficiency.*

Provided that technological advances enable and facilitate the development of adaptive Web applications, it is important to recognize that context-awareness, rather than being a mere technological concern, represents a true *design* issue. In the following, we will thus focus on the typical design concerns in the development of context-aware Web applications.

Enabling Context-Awareness in the Web

Developing context-aware applications for the Web demands some characteristic architectural components, in order to support adaptations to context. Figure 1 proposes a possible functional architecture that extends the traditional architecture of Web applications with components aimed at supporting the acquisition, storage, and use of context data.

The typical context-aware application's data source includes both the application data (i.e. the business objects that characterize the application domain and the user) and the context model, which offers at any moment an up-to-date representation of the context state. The context model captures all the context-characterizing properties and enables the system to adapt to

Figure 1. Context data in context-aware Web applications. Gray shaded boxes correspond to conventional, non-adaptive parts, white boxes correspond to extensions required to support context-awareness.

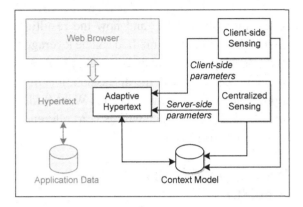

changes thereof, assuming that such changes may demand for proper reactions by the application. An application typically consists of adaptive (i.e. context-aware) and non-adaptive parts; we call the former adaptive hypertext. The pages of the adaptive hypertext present some form of adaptive behavior, i.e. they are able to react to changes in the context, while pages of the non-adaptive hypertext do not present any adaptive behavior. To decide which adaptation is required – if any –, the adaptive hypertext makes use of context data during the rendering of hypertext pages. Context data needs to be sensed (e.g. by means of suitable instruments, such as GPS positioning systems, thermometers, or similar) and communicated to the Web server that hosts the application, in order to be processed.

The above architecture allows for three main communication mechanisms to pass context data from the sensing devices to the application: (i) as parameters sensed at the *client side* and sent to the application (e.g. GPS position data); (ii) as *server-side* parameters (i.e. HTTP session variables)

provided by a centralized sensing infrastructure (e.g. system usage data); and (iii) by means of direct updates of the *context model*. Typically, client-side parameters are generated by client-side sensing solutions, server-side parameters are filled by centralized sensing solutions, and database updates may be performed by both.

Context-awareness in Web applications therefore requires addressing the following issues:

- *Context data modeling.* Context properties that are relevant for the provisioning of the context-aware behaviors of the application must be identified and represented in an application-accessible format. The result of this task is the context model that can be queried for adaptation purposes.
- *Modeling of adaptive application behaviors.* Starting from the context model, adaptation operations need to be defined in order to react to situations demanding for adaptation. That is, detected changes to the context data are translated into visible effects or operations that aim at augmenting the effectiveness and usability of the application.
- *Context model management.* The context model only captures the static aspect of context data, i.e. their structure; in order to also capture the dynamics of context data, and hence to be able to trigger adaptive behaviors, we also need to:
  - *Acquire context data* by means of measures of real-world, physical properties, corresponding to the properties of the context model. The so acquired data are then fed into the context model, so as to keep the context model up to date.
  - *Monitor context data* to detect those variations in context data that trigger adaptivity. Relevant variations are used to enact the adaptation operations in the adaptive hypertext, thus causing an automatic, adaptive behavior of the Web application.

While the definition of the context model and the monitoring of context data can easily be assisted by proper context modeling methods and a proper runtime framework providing basic monitoring functions, it is not as easy to assist designers in the development of suitable context acquisition (i.e. sensing) infrastructures. In fact, the former two activities can be generalized beyond the needs of individual applications, while the design of sensing infrastructures remains tightly coupled with individual application requirements and technological choices. The exact development of sensing infrastructures is thus out of the scope of this chapter.

Context-Aware Behaviors in Web Applications

But what exactly does it mean to adapt a Web application or to react to context? Starting from the work by Brusilovsky (1996) on adaptive hypermedia systems, in context-aware Web applications, adaptive behaviors may affect:

- *Contents and services* delivered by the accessed pages: the application may autonomously chose contents or services based on changing context data.
- The *navigation:* the application may perform automatic navigation actions on behalf of the user toward pages that better suit the current context conditions.
- The whole *hypertext structure:* the application may choose to apply coarse-grained adaptations (e.g. to the layout of the application), for example to react to changes of the user's device, role, or activity within a multi-channel, mobile environment.
- *Presentation properties*: the application may apply more fine-grained adjustments to the application's appearance (e.g. to style properties or fonts in use).
- *Generic operations*: the application may decide to enact generic operations in the

background, e.g. to log specific application events or to interact with external applications.

In this chapter, we will describe how these behaviors have been realized in the model-driven design method WebML and how the resulting extended version of the method can be leveraged for the development of context-aware applications. Before proceeding with the discussion, it is thus appropriate to shortly introduce the WebML development method, which will serve as reference throughout this chapter.

The Web Modeling Language (WebML)

WebML is a visual language for specifying the content structure of Web applications and the organization and presentation of contents into one or more hypertexts (Ceri et al., 2002).

WebML application design starts with the specification of a *data schema*, expressing the organization of the application contents by means of well established data models, such as the Entity-Relationship model or the UML class diagram. On top of such data schema, WebML design then proceeds with the specification of a so-called *hypertext model*, which describes how contents, previously specified in the data schema, are published into the application hypertext. The overall structure of the hypertext is defined in terms of *site views*, *areas*, *pages,* and *content units*. A *site view* is a hypertext, designed to address a specific set of requirements. Several site views can be defined on top of the same data schema, for serving the needs of different user communities, or for arranging the composition of pages to meet the requirements of different access devices like PDAs, smart phones, and similar appliances. A site view is composed of *areas*, which are the main sections of the hypertext, and comprise recursively other sub-areas or pages. *Pages* are the actual containers of information delivered to the user; they are made of *content units*, which are the elementary pieces of information extracted from the data sources by means of queries, and published within pages. In particular, content units denote alternative ways for displaying one or more entity instances. Unit specification requires the definition of a *source* and a *selector*: the source is the name of the entity from which the unit's content is extracted; the selector is a condition, used for retrieving the actual objects of the source entity that contribute to the unit's content. Content units and pages are interconnected by *links* to constitute site views. Besides representing user navigation, links between units also specify the transportation of parameters that can be used by the destination unit in its selector condition. Some WebML units also support the specification of content management operations. Standard operations are creating, deleting or modifying an instance of an entity or adding or dropping a relationship between two instances; custom units may be defined. Finally, WebML also allows the management of *session parameters*; parameters can be set and consumed through proper units.

In addition to the visual representation, WebML also comes with an XML-based, textual representation, which allows one to specify additional detailed properties, not conveniently expressible in the graphic notation. The availability of the XML specification enables the automatic generation of the application code (Web Models, 2008), comprising rendering formats like HTML (which is the standard choice for deployment) or WML. For a detailed description of WebML, the interested reader is referred to (Ceri et al., 2002).

MODELING DATA FOR CONTEXT-AWARE WEB APPLICATIONS

Context data can derive from several sources integrating sensed, user-supplied, and derived information (Henricksen, 2004; Henricksen,

2002). While user-supplied data are generally reliable and tend to be static, sensed data are typically highly dynamic and can be unreliable due to noise or sensor errors. The problem of unreliability has been addressed in literature for example by associating context information with quality data (Lei, 2002). Although we recognize the importance of reliable context data, in this work we rather concentrate on the exploitation of context in the design of Web applications. For simplicity, throughout this chapter we thus consider sensed data as trustworthy.

Characterizing Context Data

The main goal of context modeling is the formalization and abstraction of the context properties that affect the application. In this regard, a first characteristic distinguishing context properties is the distinction between physical and logical context. We call *physical* context those properties that are immediate representations of sensed, physical quantities (e.g. the values of an analog/digital converter), and *logical* context those properties that enrich physical context with semantics and additional abstractions of the raw sensed data (e.g. the city corresponding to physical longitude and latitude values).

A second characteristic affecting the structure of the context model is the *persistence* of context properties in the system, i.e. the property that expresses whether individual context properties represent persistent data or volatile data. *Persistent* data need to be stored in the application's data source and therefore require proper data entities being modeled as part of the context model, while *volatile* data do not need any storage and can thus be omitted from the context model. The context model therefore only captures persistent context data (indeed, in WebML the context-model is part of the database underlying the application).

Starting from these two characteristics and from the reference architecture introduced in Figure 1, Figure 2 summarizes the resulting characterization of context data:

Figure 2. Persistence of physical and logical context data

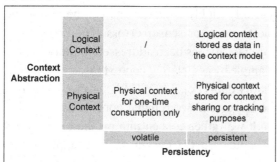

Volatile physical context. Context data communicated via client-side parameters or via server-side session parameters represent volatile data. They are immediately available during the execution of the application, independently of the underlying context model. Volatile context data are not enclosed in the context model; they might however be used during page computation to adapt the application.

- *Persistent physical context.* Context data sharing (e.g. between members of a same group) or tracking (e.g. to derive differential context properties or to keep a context history) typically require the persistent storage of data. Persistent physical context data are thus included in the context model and updated according to their dynamics.

- *Persistent logical context.* Logical context data is stored as data in the context model, so as to enable the data-driven transformation of physical context into logical context. Logical context data are typically static, as they provide abstractions of physical context; dynamic updates and/or extensions can, however, be supported as well.

Physical and logical context data therefore coexist in the application's data source. This co-

existence typically requires a transformation or mapping between raw data and information that can directly be used when specifying hypertext schemas. Consistently with the data-driven approach that characterizes WebML, we propose a formalization of such transformation at the data level by means of suitable associations between data entities representing physical and logical context data, respectively. Although technically legal, we do not expect the use of *volatile logical context*, as volatile context data typically represents sensed raw context data.

It is worth noting that even though there are several properties commonly regarded as *context attributes* (e.g. position, time, or device characteristics), there exists no universal context model that applies to all kinds of applications. For this reason, also in this chapter we do not prescribe any precise, rigid context model for WebML applications; we rather introduce some WebML-specific modeling guidelines that enable the designer to provide context-aware applications with suitable context meta-data.

Example Data Schema for Adaptation in WebML

Let's consider the PoliTour application shortly discussed in the introduction. Figure 3 illustrates a possible Entity-Relationship diagram with basic user profile data and context data, grouped in the figure into so-called sub-schemas:

- *User profile sub-schema.* Users, groups, and site views are represented as "first-class citizens" in the application data source, as required by the WebML design process. The entity User provides a basic profile of the application's users, the entity Group associates access rights to users (i.e. a role), and the entity Site View contains the site views that may be accessed by the members of a group. The relationship Membership expresses that

Figure 3. Adaptation-triggering data in WebML applications, partitioned into basic user sub-schema, personalization sub-schema and context sub-schema

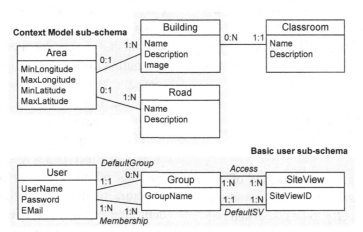

users may belong to multiple groups, which in turn cluster multiple users. The relationship DefaultGroup connects a user to his/her default role and, when logging into the application, the relationship DefaultSV allows the application to forward the user to his/her default group's default site view. The relationship Access expresses which site views a specific group is allowed to access; this relationship is required as varying context conditions may require different interaction and navigation structures for a same group. In this way, depending on the context state, the application is able to determine the most appropriate site view and to forward the user accordingly.

- *Context model sub-schema.* The context model of the application is represented by the entities Area, Building, and Road, which all provide logical context data. The actual GPS position data used for delivering the location-aware guide through the Politecnico campus (i.e. longitude and latitude) and the signal strength of the WiFi connection are not part of the context model in the application's data source; in developing the PoliTour ap-

plication, we will handle such as volatile context data. Starting from the physically sensed data, the entity Area allows the application to identify a geographical area inside the campus; an area is then associated either with a Building or a Road, meaning that starting from the user's position we can identify whether he/she is located close to a building or rather walking through one of the roads in the campus.

- *Application data.* The remaining entity Classroom represents application data that are not part of the context model. This means that from a building it is possible to access the list of classrooms of the building, but there are no adaptive behaviors associated with the entity Classroom.

MODELING CONTEXT-AWARE HYPERTEXTS

While the first step of the WebML design method, i.e. data modeling, does not require any extension of the modeling primitives for capturing context data (the standard Entity-Relationship primitives suffice), WebML hypertext modeling does require a few model extensions to express adaptivity concerns. Next we therefore introduce the new concepts and primitives that have been developed to express adaptive behaviors, and we clarify how different adaptivity policies can be used to enact adaptations.

Context-Aware Pages and Containers

Our basic assumption in the modeling of context-aware hypertexts is that context-awareness or adaptivity is a property to be associated only to some *pages* of an application (the *adaptive hypertext*), not necessarily to the application as a whole. Location-aware applications, for example, adapt core contents to the position of a user, and so-called "access pages" (e.g. containing categories or lists) typically are not affected by the context of use.

As can be seen in Figure 4, we tag context-aware pages with a C-label (standing for *context-*

aware) to distinguish them from conventional pages. The label indicates that an adaptivity rule (stylized as a cloud) is associated with the page and that during the execution of the application this logic must be taken into account when computing the page. Specifically, Figure 4 states that pages Buildings and Roads are context-aware, while the page Classrooms does not present any adaptive behavior.

There might also be the need for adaptivity rules with effects that spread over multiple pages. For this purpose, we exploit the hierarchical structure of hypertexts; that is, we allow the definition of context-aware *containers* (i.e. *site views* and *areas*, in terms of WebML). This allows the designer to insulate and to specify only once adaptivity rules that are common to multiple C-pages inside a container and thus to reduce the redundancy of the schema. Adaptivity rules associated to containers and pages are evaluated recursively, starting from the outermost container and ending with the actual pages. The site view PoliTour in Figure 4 is context-aware; we will see later on why.

Figure 4. WebML hypertext schema with one context-aware site view and two context-aware pages. The parameter P exemplifies the propagation of reusable context data by hierarchically passing context parameters from an outer area to an inner page.

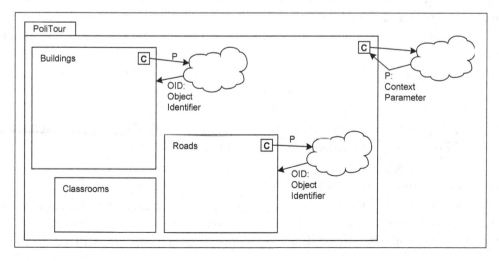

Localized and Sparse Adaptivity Rules

The adaptivity rules attached to the context-aware pages and containers in Figure 4 represent the actual adaptivity logic (i.e. the set of adaptivity actions to be performed). The adaptivity logic is external to the page or container, and the chain of adaptivity actions it clusters is kept separate from the page or container specification. The aim is to highlight the two different logics deriving from the role played by pages/containers and adaptivity operations: while the former act as *providers* of contents and services, the latter act as *modifiers* of such contents and services.

Adaptivity actions attached to a C-page typically present effects that are visible in the page they are attached to. The notion of context-aware page and adaptation logic therefore defines what we call a *localized adaptivity rule*: the scope of a localized adaptivity rule is strictly coupled with a fixed set of hypertext pages, where "scope" refers to those (adaptive) pages to which the page's adaptivity actions are associated.

The notion of context-aware container allows us to define *sparse adaptivity rules*: we talk about *sparse* adaptivity rules in those cases, where adaptivity actions are associated to containers that contain multiple pages; the scope of such actions spans a set of pages, more precisely, all context-aware pages in the container. Coming back to the PoliTour application sketched in Figure 4, we can thus associate the logic to interpret the signal strength of the WiFi connection to the pages Buildings and Roads by applying the logic to the site view as a whole.

Parameter Passing

Adaptivity logic is associated to a page by means of a directed arrow, i.e. a link exiting the C-label. This link ensures the communication between the page logic and the adaptivity logic: it may transport parameters deriving from page contents, which may be used to compute the specified actions; in turn, a link from the adaptivity logic to the page may transport context parameters or generic values that might be required to perform the final adaptation during page computation.

But Figure 4 also illustrates the possibility of *hierarchically* passing parameters from an outer container to an inner one. More precisely, if the evaluation of outer adaptivity logic produces results to be reused at an inner level, as it might happen in the case of context parameters, it passes such values back to the C-label that activated the computation of the logic. Subsequently, such parameters can then be "consumed" by adaptivity logics of the inner levels. As for context-aware pages, parameter passing from a container to its adaptivity logic occurs through the logic-activating link. Links exiting the last evaluated logic, i.e. at the end of the last adaptivity action, might carry parameter values for the computation of units inside a page.

Typical actions to be specified at the container level are the acquisition of fresh context data and the updating of the context model, e.g. if the data are to be shared among multiple users or if a history of context data is to be tracked. Hence, especially if persistent context data are adopted, we propose two levels for adaptivity actions:

- *Actions for context model management*, addressing operations for context data acquisition and context model updating, should be associated with outer containers (site views or areas) and are inherited by inner containers (areas or pages). These adaptivity actions need to be executed prior to the execution of any other action possibly specified in an inner context cloud, as such "internal" actions could depend on context data acquired and stored in the context model through "external" actions.

- *Actions for hypertext adaptivity*, defining the rules for page and navigation adaptation (and possibly depending on persistent context data), should be associated with C-pages.

Specifying Adaptivity Logics

The main novelties for modeling context-aware pages reside in the specification of adaptivity rules by means of WebML constructs. In the following, we introduce the new WebML modeling concepts that ensure full coverage for the specification of context model management and hypertext adaptation logics. The new primitives allow designers to visually specify actions for acquiring and updating context data and to define adaptivity actions.

Managing Context Data

In order to support adaptivity with respect context, the application must be able to acquire and manage context data according to the mechanisms

illustrated in Figure 1. For this purpose, some new WebML operations have been defined, which, together with the already available operations, provide the necessary primitives for:

- *Specifying the acquisition of fresh context data through client-side parameters.* A new Get ClientParameter unit (see Figure 5) has been defined to support the retrieval of parameters generated at the client side and communicated back to the application via client-side parameters (e.g. parameter-value pairs attached to the page request query string).
- *Specifying the acquisition of fresh context data through server-side parameters.* Context data directly made available as HTTP session parameters can be accessed by means

Figure 5. WebML units that have been defined for the specification of adaptivity actions

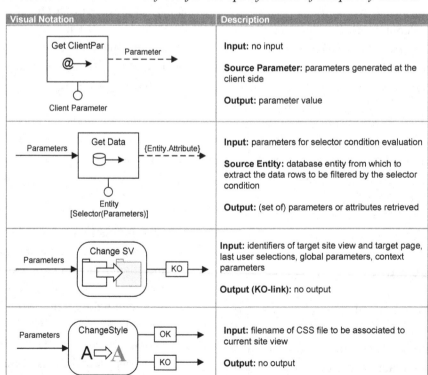

of conventional WebML Get units (Ceri et al., 2002).

- *Specifying the acquisition of context data from the context model.* The execution of adaptivity actions may require the retrieval and evaluation of context meta-data, for example, in situations where certain data are just needed to evaluate condition expressions. For this purpose, a so-called Get Data unit (see Figure 5) has been introduced, enabling the retrieval of values (both scalars and sets) from the data source according to a selector condition. The semantics of the Get Data unit is similar to the one of content publishing units (Ceri et al., 2002), with the only difference that data retrieved from the data source are not published in hypertexts, but just used as input for units or operations.

- *Updating the context model.* Once fresh context parameters have been retrieved, they can be used to update the context model at data level. This action consists in modifying values previously stored in the data source. In WebML, this is already facilitated by operation units (Ceri et al., 2002) providing support for the most common database management operations (e.g., modify, insert, delete).

Evaluating Conditions

The execution of adaptivity actions may be subject to the evaluation of some *conditions*, refining the triggering logic for context clouds. The most recurrent pattern consists in evaluating whether context changes demand for adaptation. The evaluation of conditions is specified by means of two control structures, represented by the If and Switch operation units, which have been introduced for workflow modeling in WebML (Brambilla et al., 2003).

Executing Adaptivity Actions

Once the current context state has been determined, and possible conditions have been evaluated, adaptivity actions can be performed to adapt the page contents, the navigation, the current site view structure, and/or presentation style properties. These actions are specified as follows:

- *Adapting Page Contents.* Page contents are adapted by means of proper data selectors, whose definition is based on context parameters retrieved from the context model or newly computed within the page's context logic. The use of parameterized selectors allows for both *filtering* data items with respect to the current context state and conditionally *including/excluding* (i.e. showing/hiding) individual content units.

- *Adapting Navigation.* In some cases, the effect of condition evaluation within the context cloud can be an automatic, i.e. context-triggered, navigation action, causing the redirection of the user to a different page. The specification of context-triggered navigations just requires connecting one of the links exiting the adaptivity logic of the page to an arbitrary destination page of the hypertext. Therefore, links exiting the context cloud and directed to other pages than the adaptivity logic's source page represent automatic navigation actions.

- *Adapting the Site View.* In some cases, a context-triggered switch toward a different site view may be required. Changes in the interaction context may in fact ask for a coarse-grained restructuring of the whole hypertext, for example because the user device has changed, or because the user shifted to a different activity. To switch between different site views, we have introduced a Change Site View unit (see Figure 5), which takes in input the identifiers of the target site view and the target page, to be visualized in case a switch toward the specified site view is required. In order to support "contextual" switching, the input link also transports parameters characterizing the current state of interaction, i.e.:

1. The input parameters of the source page, which represent the last selections operated by the user;
2. Global parameters, representing session data (e.g. user identifier and group identifier), as well as past user selections that have been used for the computation of the current page;
3. Client-side and server-side context parameters retrieved during the latest performed data acquisition cycle and characterizing the current context state.

- *Adapting Presentation Style.* Sometimes context changes may require only fine-grained adaptations of presentation properties (e.g. due to varying luminosity conditions), not a complete restructuring of the overall hypertext. We have defined a Change Style unit for dynamically assigning presentation style properties (see Figure 5). Style properties are collected in proper .css (Cascaded Style Sheet) files, and the unit enables the application to change its associated style sheet at runtime.
- *Enacting generic operations.* The context-triggered invocation of generic operations or, for instance, external Web services can easily be specified by placing the respective WebML operation unit into the page's adaptivity logic and by providing the unit with the necessary input parameters.

Triggering Adaptivity Rules

But *when* do we enact an adaptivity rule? In this regard, it is possible to define two different *adap-*

tivity policies for context-aware pages, assigning different priorities to users and context:

- *Deferred Adaptivity*: the *user* is granted the highest priority. Therefore, after the user has entered the page and the page has been rendered according to the user's selections, the page's adaptivity logic is evaluated at periodic time intervals, enabling the application to possibly adapt the already rendered page. Periodically evaluating the adaptivity logic means periodically refreshing the page visualized in the browser.
- *Immediate Adaptivity*: *context* is granted the highest priority. The page's adaptivity logic is evaluated each time the page is accessed, being the access due to the user or to the periodic refresh of the page. This means that the page is subject to adaptation each time it is rendered, even at the first time the page is accessed by the user.

Consider for example our PoliTour guide that shows contents about the buildings and roads in the Politecnico campus. At a given point, the user might want to get information about a specific building located in a road that is not related to his/her current position; such a preference is typically expressed by selecting a link to that building from a list. With a deferred policy, the requested page shows the building information as requested by the user, without taking into account the user's current location. Only after expiration of the refresh interval, the page becomes subject to adaptivity and the contents are adapted to the user's location. With an immediate policy, context is granted higher priority with respect to the user and, thus, the user's request for the building would be overwritten by the context and the application would show the building or road associated to the user's current location, discarding the user's selection.

Note that in addition to these adaptivity policies, we recognize that there may be situations that demand for an explicit control of the adaptation dynamics through the user. Therefore, should for example a user temporarily not be interested in having the contents adapted to his/her location, he/she can simply disable/enable adaptivity at will. In WebML, the adaptivity policy for context-aware pages and containers is declared by means of the Adaptivity_Policy property of context-aware pages and containers.

Adaptivity policies can also be associated to context-aware containers. When a C-page is requested, also the possible context clouds of its containers are evaluated recursively (from the outermost one to the innermost one), according to the adaptivity policy associated to each container. In general, a container's adaptivity policy is independent of the policy of inner containers and pages (if not, this must be taken into account by designers when associating policies to containers and pages). Therefore, it may happen that the actions in a container's context cloud are evaluated immediately, even if the actions associated to inner containers or pages adopt a deferred evaluation, or vice-versa. If, for example, the adaptivity actions associated to the container serve for tracking a context history, they could require an immediate policy, while inner adaptivity actions keep their deferred policy for front-end adaptations. The hierarchical definition of context clouds may therefore also be considered a facility to achieve different "layers" of adaptivity actions.

In our approach, we assume *deferred* adaptivity as default policy. This choice aims at minimizing application behaviors that might be perceived as invasive or annoying by users and has been experienced as the most natural for modeling adaptation. However, the *immediate* policy could be needed for handling exceptional situations, as in such cases the timely reaction to context changes could be more important than following the user's indications. We therefore, in general, recommend the selection of the adaptivity policy that is appropriate to the application requirements and that is able to minimize the application behaviors that

could be perceived as invasive or annoying by the users. In order to choose the right adaptivity policy for an adaptive page, a developer therefore needs to predict what kind of adaptive behavior a user will expect when accessing that page.

Example Hypertext Model

Figure 6 shows the adaptive WebML hypertext model of the PoliTour application. The figure provides a refinement of the coarse hypertext model introduced in Figure 4 and details the internals of pages and adaptivity logics.

The pages Buildings and Roads share the same adaptivity logic providing location-awareness to the displayed contents. The logic starts with two Get ClientParameter units accessing the user's longitude and latitude, which are then used by the Get Area unit to associate a logical area to the user's position. A further Get Data unit (the Get Building unit) then tries to retrieve a building for the identified area. If a building could be retrieved, the If unit sends the user to the Buildings page, providing updated page parameters. If instead no building could be retrieved (e.g. because the user is located in the center of a road or not close enough to a building), the If unit forwards the Area identifier to the Get Road unit, which retrieves the road associated to the current position.

Therefore, if the user views the page Buildings while walking around the campus, the application automatically updates the contents published each time a new building can be found. If only the road can be identified, the application performs an automatic navigation action toward the Roads page, where the described adaptive behavior starts again, possibly causing the adaptation of contents or automatic navigation actions. Only if the user navigates to page Classroom, no adaptations are performed, as this page is not tagged as context-aware.

The adaptivity actions associated to the surrounding site view specify how to alert users who are about to leave the WiFi-covered area.

Figure 6. Hypertext model of the PoliTour application leveraging volatile context data

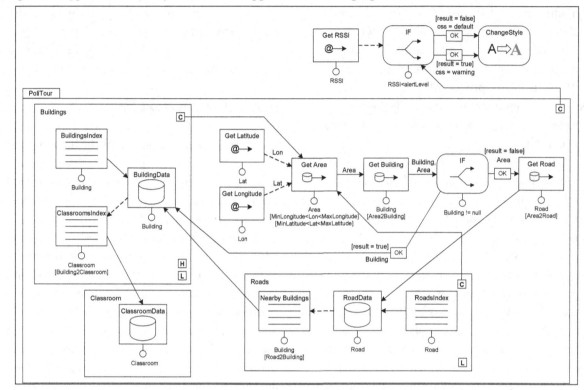

The Get RSSI unit accesses the volatile RSSI parameter sensed at the client side, and the If unit compares the retrieved value with a predefined level (alertLevel), below of which the connectivity is considered low. In case of low connectivity, the style sheet warning is adopted; otherwise, the default style sheet is adopted. We therefore model the alert of low connectivity conditions by means of a Change Style unit: under low connectivity conditions the application is rendered with a red background, under normal conditions the application is rendered with a gray background.

We recall that actions associated to containers are evaluated before any action at the page level is started. Hence, in Figure 6 the actions associated to the site view are executed before the actions associated to the pages Buildings and Roads.

RUNTIME CONTEXT MODEL MANAGEMENT

In order to manifest context-aware behaviors, the application must be equipped with the capability to monitor the context state and to trigger adaptivity actions, if required. The standard HTTP protocol underlying most of today's Web applications implements a strict *pull* paradigm, in which computations can only occur in response to client-side generated page requests. Therefore, in the classical Web architecture, lacking proper push mechanisms, context monitoring can occur only when a page is computed, i.e. when a respective page request reaches the Web server. Three main solutions can be adopted to trigger the evaluation of adaptivity rules: (i) context evaluation on user-generated page requests, (ii) periodical, automatic refreshes of viewed pages to enable context evaluation, and (iii) active context evaluation to trigger adaptivity in real time. The first solution is not able to cope with the dynamic nature of context. The periodic refresh of context-aware pages provides a way to ensure the update of the page even in absence of explicit user actions enabling the re-computation of the page. In the following, we will show an active mechanism for triggering adaptivity, which operates independently of the user in the background and comes close to the real-time triggering solution.

In absence of dedicated server-side *push* mechanisms for delivering updated pages, the HTML http-equiv META-option or JavaScript, JavaApplets, and Flash scripts, provide valuable client-side mechanisms to approximate the required active behavior. The approximation is based on periodic HTTP requests toward the application server, which are operated in the background and may serve a twofold purpose:

- On the one hand, they provide the necessary polling mechanism to query the context model and trigger the adaptivity rule attached to the page.
- On the other hand, generating page requests allows the client to transmit client-side sensed data, thus enabling the communication of context data to the application server.

Context-aware pages are therefore also characterized by an individual *refresh interval*, which can be specified as property (Refresh_Interval) of the page in the XML representation of the WebML model. Differently from C-pages, a container does not require the specification of any polling interval, which is instead derived from the interval associated to the currently viewed C-page of the container.

Context Monitoring

Context monitoring in the background (i.e. without the user observing any unwanted rendering activity) enables the application to limit the use of the refresh to those situations that really ask for adaptation and to perform context monitoring without any visual effect for users.

Figure 7 shows a functional architecture for adaptive Web applications that extends the described architecture of WebML applications (see Figure 1) with a new client-server module, called *Context Monitor* (CM), providing the necessary context monitoring logic. As further depicted by the figure, in case of client-side context sensing, the CM module also enables the communication of client-side sensed context parameters, which could be required at the server side to evaluate context changes and/or conditions over context parameters.

The CM consists of two separate modules, one on the client side and one on the server side. The CM Client module is a piece of business logic embedded into the page's HTML code and executed at the client side (e.g. a JavaScript function, a Java applet, or a Flash object), while the CM Server module works in parallel to the Web application on the same Web server. The CM Client is in charge of periodically monitoring the context state and deciding whether possibly occurring context variations demand for the adaptation of the currently viewed page.

In order to be able to take a decision about whether adaptivity actions are to be triggered or not, the CM Client is assisted by the CM Server, which has full access to the context model of the application maintained at the server side. In response to the polling executed by the CM Client, the CM Server queries the context model and provides the CM Client with an updated picture of the effective context state. By comparing the state of the (server-side) context model acquired by the current polling with the one acquired by the last polling (or the state at page computation

Figure 7. Functional architecture for background context monitoring

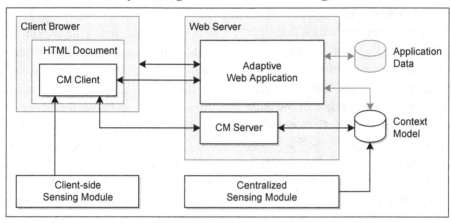

time), the CM Client knows whether the state has changed. If the state has changed, the CM Client asks the Web application for a refresh of the currently viewed page, i.e. the adaptation; if the state has not changed the CM Client proceeds with the monitoring of the context state.

Page Context

In general, the *state* of the context is expressed by the values of all the persistent parameters stored in the context model and of the volatile parameters sensed at the client or server side. However, an individual page's adaptive behavior is typically influenced by only a subset of the overall context data or, more specifically, by a function expressed over context data. The subset of context data corresponds to a page-specific view over the application's context data, narrowing the focus of the context monitoring activity. This observation leads to the definition of a new concept, i.e. page context, which can be leveraged to enhance the efficiency of the context monitoring activity: the *page context* of a page corresponds to a page-specific view over the application's context data, capturing all (and only) those context characteristics that effectively determine the adaptive behavior of the page.

Instead of monitoring the whole state of the application's context data, the definition of a page context for each adaptive page enables the context monitoring activity to focus its observation of the context state to the only page context. This implies, that during hypertext specification each adaptivity rule can be related to a subset of context parameters to be controlled, so that rule conditions do not need to check the state of the whole context model.

Page Context Parameters

In line with the idea of page context, the CM focuses its attention only to the subset of context data in the context model that really determines the adaptive behavior of the viewed page. This implies explicit knowledge of the pages' page context, which can be achieved by defining proper page context parameters for each context-aware page: p*age context parameters* define the view over the context model that captures all the static and dynamic properties of a page's page context by means of suitable queries over the context model.

This definition implies that each change to a page context parameter effectively corresponds to a need to adapt the page. The granularity of the *values* of page context parameters must thus be chosen in a way that each change of a parameter value translates into the triggering of the page's adaptivity rule. Each C-labeled page in the adaptive hypertext model is thus associated with an individual page context by means of proper page context parameters stored in the textual representation of the WebML schema, as they are not conveniently expressible in a visual manner. Page context parameters are expressed by means of parametric queries over the context data, where the parameters correspond to client- or server-side context parameters.

Context Digest

In order for the CM to be able to decide whether adaptivity is required, changes to the page context (i.e. the page context parameters) must be communicated from the CM Server to the CM Client. In order to enhance the efficiency of the overall context monitoring activity, the state of the page context is not communicated from the CM Server to the CM Client in form of the set of page context parameters, but instead it suffices to transmit and compare a numeric digest computed over the respective page context parameters, as each change to the values of the page context parameters also results in a change of the numeric digest. We call such a numeric digest context digest: the *context digest* corresponding to the page context of a page is the numeric checksum computed over the ordered list of page context parameters.

The context digest is the basis for the decisions to be taken by the CM Client: its values identify variations in the page context, which correspond to the need to adapt the page. The decision is based on the comparison of the current context digest with the last context digest; the first context digest, i.e. when the user accesses the page, is initialized with the context digest valid during page computation.

Figure 8 details the resulting flow of activities enabling the active behavior of the application and shows how the single modules cooperate in order to determine whether adaptivity is required or not. The diagram has one start node (Generate user request), which corresponds to the user's navigation to a C-page, and no end node, since the cycle in the lower part of the diagram is only interrupted by an explicit user navigation leading the user to another C-page (which corresponds to starting again from the start node of the diagram and monitoring the Page context of the new page) or to a conventional page (which does not cause any context monitoring activity).

Note that the described mechanism assumes that connectivity is available during the viewing of a C-page in order for the CM client to be able to communicate with the CM server. In case of intermittent connectivity, which is a very frequent situation in mobile environments, the CM client keeps working by periodically polling the CM Server, despite the absence of connectivity. The CM Client is however programmed to manage possible lacks of connectivity and therefore does not generate errors, with the only side effect that adaptivity is suspended until the connectivity is restored.

APPLICATION IMPLEMENTATION

The extensions that have been introduced into the WebML development method to cope with the new requirements posed by context-awareness and adaptivity in Web applications have been implemented as prototype extension of the WebRatio CASE tool, the official WebML modeling tool, equipped with a powerful automatic code generator. Due to implementation restrictions imposed by the modeling tool, the implementation of the adaptivity logic slightly differs from the models described in this paper (e.g. it was not possible to implement context-aware containers or to place all the adaptivity operations outside

Figure 8. Background context monitoring for active context-awareness (with client-side context sensing): communicating context data and triggering adaptivity

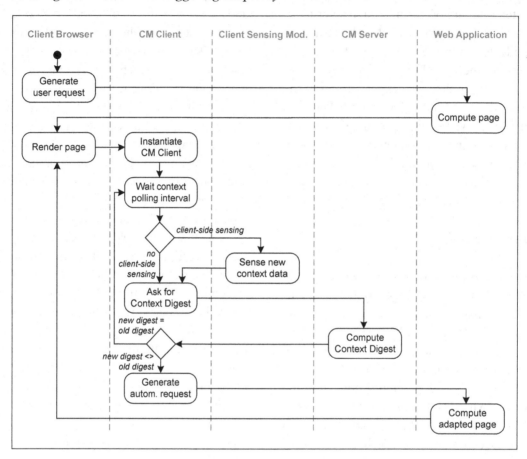

pages). Nevertheless, the described expressive power for the specification of adaptivity rules could be preserved.

Figure 9 shows a screenshot of the WebRatio tool at work. The figure shows the WebML hypertext model of the Buildings page of the PoliTour application, along with its adaptivity logic: two Get ClientParameter units access the GPS coordinates and pass them to the C-label, which forwards them to the outer adaptivity logic (cf. Figure 6). Starting from the shown hypertext model, the PoliTour application has been automatically generated on top of a J2EE platform. The configuration of the Context Monitor has been performed manually.

To access GPS position data, we leverage a client-side Bluetooth GPS device, interfaced via the Chaeron GPS Library (http://www.chaeron. com/gps.html) and wrapped by means of Flash (to exchange position data between the CM Client and the GPS library). The WiFi RSSI indicator is acquired in the PDA using Place Lab (http://www. placelab.org).

RELATED WORKS

Several other well-established, conceptual design methods have been so far extended to deal with

Web application adaptations. Frasincar & Houben (2002), for example, extend the Hera methodology with two kinds of adaptation: adaptability with respect to the user device and adaptivity based on user profile data. Adaptation rules (and the Hera schemas) are expressed in RDF(S) (Resource Description Framework/RDF Schema), attached to slices and executed by the AHA engine (De Bra et al., 2003). The UWA Consortium proposes WUML (Kappel et al., 2001) for conceptual hypertext design. Adaptation requirements are expressed by means of OCL-based customization rules, referring to UML class or package elements. Casteleyn et al. (2003) present an extension of WSDM (De Troyer & Leune, 1998) to cover the specification of adaptive behaviors. In particular, an event-based Adaptive Specification Language (ASL) is defined, which allows designers to express adaptations on the structure and the navigation of the Web site. Such adaptations consist in trans-

formations of the navigation model that can be applied to nodes (deleting/adding nodes), information chunks (connecting/disconnecting chunks to/from a node), and links (adding/deleting links). Baumeister et al. (2005) explore Aspect-Oriented Programming techniques to model adaptivity in the context of the UML-based Web engineering method UWE. Recently, WebML (Ceri et al., 2002) has been extended to cover adaptivity and context-awareness (Ceri et al., 2007). New visual primitives cover the specification of adaptivity rules to evaluate conditions and to trigger some actions for adapting page contents, navigation, hypertext structure, and presentation. Also, the data model has been enriched to represent meta-data supporting adaptivity.

Recently, active rules, based on the ECA (Event-Condition-Action) paradigm, have been proposed as a way to solve the previous problem. Initially exploited especially in fields such

Figure 9. The WebRatio CASE tool showing the hypertext model of the buildings page with respective adaptivity actions and the generated PoliTour application running on a PDA

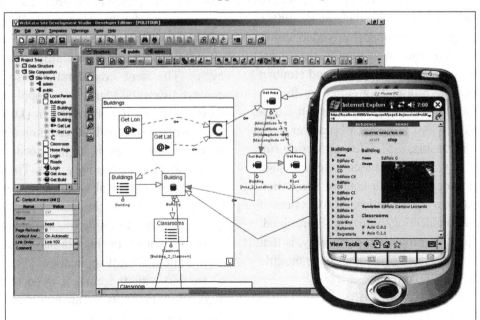

as content evolution and reactive Web (Alferes et al., 2005; Bailey et al., 2002; Bonifati et al., 2002), ECA rules have been adopted to support adaptivity in Web applications. In particular, the specification of decoupled adaptivity rules provides a way to design adaptive behaviors along an orthogonal dimension. Among the most recent and notable proposals, the work described in (Garrigos et al., 2005a) enriches the OO-H model with personalization rules for profile groups: rules are defined in PRML (Personalization Rule Modeling Language) and are attached to links in the OO-H Navigation Access Diagram. The use of a PRML rule engine is envisioned in (Garrigos et al., 2005b), but its real potential for adaptivity management also at runtime remains unexplored.

The previous works benefit from the adoption of conceptual models, which provide designers with powerful means to reason at a high-level of abstraction, independently of implementation details. There are however also co-called transcoding solutions, which adopt active rules for adapting Web pages. Most of them focus on the presentation layer and provide mechanisms to transform HTML pages according to (possibly limited) device capabilities (Hori et al., 2000) or users' visual disabilities (Yesilada et al., 2004). Moreover, they typically support only adaptability and modify Web pages in relation to a static set of user or device parameters. Fiala and Houben (2005) adopt the transcoding paradigm for the development of the Generic Adaptation Component (GAC). GAC provides a broad range of adaptation behaviors, especially supporting run time adaptivity. An RDF-based rule language is used for specifying both content adaptation and context data update rules. A collection of operations implementing these rules is provided. A notable feature, promoting portability, is that GAC can be integrated as a stand-alone module into any Web site architecture.

CONCLUSION AND FUTURE TRENDS

In this chapter, we have proposed a model-driven approach to the development of context-aware Web applications, an increasingly relevant kind of applications on the Web. We have shown that context-awareness is a first-class design concern that can considerably be aided by model-driven development techniques. But we have also shown that properly dealing with context-awareness and adaptivity at the conceptual level requires extending the expressive power of the adopted conceptual application model, so as to provide developers with suitable modeling constructs and implementation abstractions, proper of such new class of application features. In this chapter, such extensions have been introduced into the already well-established WebML modeling language, but in a similar way we could have also opted for another modeling language, as the ideas and concepts introduced in this chapter are general enough in nature to be applied to other conceptual models as well.

For the future, we believe that a *decoupled runtime management* of adaptivity features will represent a next step in the area of adaptive Web applications. The development of Web applications is more and more based on fast and incremental deployments with multiple development cycles. The same consideration also holds for context-aware and adaptive Web applications and their adaptivity requirements. In (Daniel et al., 2008) we describe our first results obtained with a decoupled environment for the execution and the administration of adaptivity rules. The described approach allows us to abstract adaptive behaviors, to extract them from the main application logic, and to provide a decoupled management support, finally enhancing the maintainability and evolvability of the overall application.

In line with the current hype of so-called Web 2.0 applications, we are also working on the *mash-up* of context-aware Web applications, in the context of our component-based development method for Web applications called Mixup (Yu et al., 2007). The final goal of the work is to enable even end users to mash up their own context-aware applications, starting from a set of so-called context components and other components equipped with own user interface (which is used to build up the user interface of the mash-up application). Mash-up development is assisted by an easy-to-use and intuitive graphical development environment that supports a drag-and-drop development and by a light-weight runtime environment that is able to interpret and run the mashup, both fully running in the client browser and based on AJAX technology.

REFERENCES

Alferes, J. J., Amador, R., & May, W. (2005). A General Language for Evolution and Reactivity in the Semantic Web. In *PPSWR'05* (pp. 101–115). Dagstuhl, Germany: Springer.

Bailey, J., Poulovassilis, A., & Wood, P. T. (2002). An Event-condition-action Language for XML. In *WWW'02* (pp. 486–495). Honolulu, Hawaii: ACM.

Baumeister, H., Knapp, A., Koch, N., & Zhang, G. (2005). Modelling Adaptivity with Aspects. In *ICWE'05* (pp. 406-416). Sydney, Australia: Springer.

Bonifati, A., Braga, D., Campi, A., & Ceri, S. (2002). Active XQuery. In *ICDE'02* (pp. 403-412). San Jose, California: IEEE.

Brambilla, M., Ceri, S., Comai, S., Fraternali, P., & Manolescu, I. (2003). Specification and Design of Workflow-Driven Hypertexts. *Journal of Web Engineering, 1*(2), 163-182.

Brusilovsky, P. (1996). Methods and Techniques of Adaptive Hypermedia. *User Modeling and User-Adapted Interaction, 6*(2-3), 87-129.

Casteleyn, S., De Troyer, O., & Brockmans, S. (2003). Design Time Support for Adaptive Behavior in Web Sites. In *SAC'03* (pp. 1222-1228). Melbourne, Florida: ACM.

Ceri, S., Fraternali, P., Bongio, A., Brambilla, M., Comai, S., & Matera, M. (2002). *Designing Data-Intensive Web Applications*. San Francisco, CA: Morgan Kauffmann.

Ceri. S., Daniel, F., Matera, M., & Facca, F. M. (2007). Model-driven Development of Context-aware Web Applications. *ACM Transactions on Internet Technologies, 7*(1), article no. 2.

Daniel, F., Matera, M., & Pozzi, G. (2008). Managing Runtime Adaptivity through Active Rules: the Bellerofonte Framework. *Journal of Web Engineering, 7*(3), 179-199.

De Bra, P., Aerts, A. T. M., Berden, B., de Lange, B., Rousseau, B., Santic, T., Smits, D., & Stash, N. (2003). AHA! The Adaptive Hypermedia Architecture. In *Hypertext'03* (pp 81-84). Nottingham, UK: ACM.

De Troyer, O., & Leune, C. J. (1998). WSDM: A User Centered Design Method for Web Sites. *Computer Networks, 30*(1-7), 85-94.

Dey, A. K., & Abowd, G.D. (2000). Towards a Better Understanding of Context and Context-Awareness. In *CHI'00 Workshop Proceedings*, The Hague, The Netherlands.

Fiala, Z., & Houben, G.-J. (2005). A generic transcoding tool for making web applications adaptive. In *CAiSE'05 Short Paper Proceedings*, volume 161 of CEUR Workshop Proceedings. CEUR-WS.org.

Frasincar, F., & Houben, G.-J. (2002). Hypermedia Presentation Adaptation on the Semantic Web. In *AH'02* (pp. 133-142). Málaga, Spain: Springer.

Garrigós, I., Casteleyn, S., & Gómez, J. (2005a). A Structured Approach to Personalize Websites Using the OO-H Personalization Framework.

In *APWeb'05* (pp. 695-706). Shanghai, China: Springer.

Garrigós, I., Gómez, J., Barna, P., & Houben, G.-J. (2005b). A Reusable Personalization Model in Web Application Design. In WISM'05 (pp. 40-49). Sydney, Australia.

Henricksen, K., & Indulska, J. (2004). Modelling and Using Imperfect Context Information. In *PERCOMW'04* (pp. 33-37). Washington, United States: IEEE.

Henricksen, K., Indulska, J., & Rakotonirainy, A. (2002). Modeling Context Information in Pervasive Computing Systems. In *Pervasive'02* (pp. 167-180). London, UK: Springer.

Hori, M., Kondoh, G., Ono, K., Hirose, S., & Singhal, S. K. (2000). Annotation based Web Content Transcoding. *Computer Networks, 33*(1-6), 197-211.

Kappel, G., Pröll, B., Retschitzegger, W., & Schwinger, W. (2001). Modelling Ubiquitous Web Applications - TheWUML Approach. In *ER'01 Workshops* (pp. 183-197). Yokohama, Japan: Springer.

Lei, H., Sow, D. M., Davis, J. S. II, Banavar, G., & Ebling, M. R. (2002). The design and applications of a context service. *SIGMOBILE Mobile Computing and Communications Review*, 6(4), 45-55.

Schilit, B.N., & Theimer, M.M. (1994). Disseminating Active Map Information to Mobile Hosts. *IEEE Network*, 8(5), 22-32.

Web Models s.r.l. (2008). WebRatio Site Development Studio. Retrieved January, 2008, from http://www.webratio.com.

Yesilada, Y., Harper, S., Goble. C. A., & Stevens, R. (2004). Screen readers cannot see: Ontology based semantic annotation for visually impaired web travellers. In ICWE'04 (pp. 445-458). Munich, Germany: Springer.

Yu, J., Benatallah, B., Saint-Paul, R., Casati, F., Daniel, F., & Matera, M. (2007). A Framework for Rapid Integration of Presentation Components. In *WWW'07* (pp. 923-932). Banff, Canada: ACM.

Section II
Advanced Context Management

Chapter IV
Distributed Context Management in Support of Multiple Remote Users

I. Roussaki
National Technical University of Athens, Greece

M. Strimpakou
National Technical University of Athens, Greece

C. Pils
Waterford Institute of Technology, Ireland

N. Kalatzis
National Technical University of Athens, Greece

N. Liampotis
National Technical University of Athens, Greece

ABSTRACT

In ubiquitous computing environments, context management systems are expected to administrate large volumes of spatial and non-spatial information in geographical disperse domains. In particular, when these systems cover wide areas such as cities, countries or even the entire planet, the design of scalable storage, retrieval and propagation mechanisms is paramount. This chapter elaborates on mechanisms that address advanced requirements including support for distributed context databases management; efficient query handling; innovative management of mobile physical objects and optimization strategies for distributed context data dissemination. These mechanisms establish a robust spatially-enhanced distributed context management framework that has thoroughly been designed, carefully implemented and extensively evaluated via numerous experiments.

INTRODUCTION

In the emerging and challenging ubiquitous computing environment mobile users will experience the successive enlargement and refinement of their computing and communication potential beyond their vision of the future world. They will wear smart clothes that will monitor their bio signals and act accordingly. They will carry personal communicators able to support highly complex task processing. They will hold advanced cards that will automatically handle their transactions. More sophisticated navigation and control systems will be embedded into the vehicles they drive. Invisible microcomputers and other artefacts will exist everywhere in their smart homes and offices to assist them in their every day lives. The collection all these heterogeneous computing devices will interact with intelligent sensors embedded in the surrounding environment in order to form an ambient-aware pervasive environment, which supports everyday activities related to business, education, leisure, healthcare, etc. In this respect, customers will be able to enjoy new experiences in a non-obtrusive way, as the existing infrastructure will become minimally intrusive and will exhibit inherent proactiveness and dynamic adaptability to current conditions, user preferences and environment. Eventually, as traditional systems evolve into pervasive, an important aspect that needs to be pursued is context-awareness (Xynogalas et al., 2004).

According to one of the most popular context definitions, *context is basically all information that is relevant to a human-computer interaction* (Dey, 2000). Theoretically, any information can become relevant for a certain task and thus, one can hardly derive context management requirements from this definition. In any case, the detection of the most important context information for characterizing the situation of a particular entity, irrespectively of the application domain, is best achieved by considering the following criterion: Human experience is strongly interrelated with location. We work when we are in our offices, we eat in a restaurant, we sleep at home, and we dance in a bar. This common understanding also influences the manner people interact with the various computing and communications systems and therefore, the way they perceive context-awareness. A system is context-aware if it uses context to provide relevant information and/or services to the user, where relevancy depends on the user's task, and therefore, implicitly, but no exclusively, on his location. In this respect, users are more interested in context information related to their current position. Until now, the design principles in context-aware systems are mainly limited in addressing special requirements and conditions of isolated areas (e.g. smart homes, offices, artifacts, etc.) in an ad-hoc manner (Strimpakou et al., 2006). Even though the progress on this field is quite impressive, few research initiatives have attempted to design and implement a general-purpose context management system, adequate for pervasive environments. Furthermore, there are very limited or even none research efforts that have dealt with minimizing the various costs introduced during the propagation of context information to multiple remote nodes maintaining replicas of master context instances, when a multitude of different context consumers residing on these remote nodes often requests for the respective replicated context information. The research presented in this chapter focuses on developing and validating the *Context Distributed Database Management System* (CDDBMS), an efficient distributed heterogeneous spatial database management system that adopts a location-centric context view, integrates sophisticated selective context replica update policies for cost minimisation and is adequate for addressing the high and continuously expanding context consumer demands anytime, anyplace in future pervasive environments.

The rest of this Chapter is structured as follows. The second section elaborates on the motivation for the presented research work, while the third section briefly describes the overall CDDBMS architecture and context query handling approach. The fourth section outlines the basic CDDBMS approach for managing mobile physical objects. The context data dissemination problem is described in the fifth section, a heuristic solution of which is provided in the sixth section. The seventh section analyses the conducted experiments and presents the obtained evaluation results. Finally, in the eighth section, a comparison of the proposed approach with the relevant state of the art work is provided, while in the ninth section, conclusions are drawn and future plans are exposed.

MOTIVATION

In order to achieve provision of context-aware services, information originating from multiple context providers is usually required. These context providers do not necessarily belong to the same legal entity or administrative domain. In simple context federation scenarios, a user has subscribed to Operator A for mobile network services. Operator A therefore stores in its database this user's profile and also maintains a sensor infrastructure for Area A for collecting and storing physical context information. Likewise, Operator B maintains a database for storing users' profile information, as well as another database for the physical context of Area B. As long as the user is located within Area A, the scenario is quite simple as all relevant information is maintained and handled by Operator A. However, when the user moves to Area B, information of two administrative domains becomes relevant. The physical context of the user is stored in the context database of Operator B, while his/her profile information is still maintained by Operator A. In case operators A and B are competitors they probably do not wish to exchange information and the user would have to subscribe with both operators to receive both areas' physical context information. In such a federated context management environment, stakeholders will hardly agree on a single

Database Management System (DBMS). This is, however, not a strong constraint. On the one hand, most DBMS are relational databases implementing the SQL standard. On the other hand, a standardisation of the basic database structure is inevitable for an efficient information exchange. Thus, a Context Distributed Database Management System (CDDBMS) should be established that would be responsible for processing context information as if this is maintained by a single database, while in fact the context information is stored and controlled by multiple administrative domains. The CDDBMS, briefly introduced in the subsequent sections, should provide the same functionality as a centralised database management system.

Furthermore, it is a fact that information that cannot be found or is not delivered in time is of low or even no value. Approaches for the distributed storage, retrieval and timely delivery of data are therefore essential for the success of context aware computing systems. In a pervasive world with millions of moving users and billions of interacting devices, an immense amount of heterogeneous context data is likely to be requested for delivery to remote nodes every second. In particular, when context aware systems are not confined to a single building, but to cities, countries or the entire planet, scalable and efficient context distribution mechanisms are paramount to ensure instant access to any context information necessary, anytime, anywhere. Thus, devices must cope with highly dynamic environments, where both context data and source availability vary over location and time, while the required information may originate from multiple context providers that do not necessarily belong to the same legal entity or administrative domain. In such an environment, apart from a quite small part of context data that will be strictly available to its owners (private), most context information will be a commodity to be traded among either a restricted consumers' group (semi-private) or frequently, among a large consumers' group (public). Even a well designed, distributed and scalable context management infrastructure would eventually fail in answering such continuously expanding demands for context information across remote context nodes. Especially, in cases where the requested context information constitutes a frequently updated piece of context data (e.g. room temperature) that should be conveyed to the client each time a new context value is available, the context management system, as well as the underlying network will be eventually flooded with the continuous context data updates to remote consumers. Each context consumer will have different requirements with regards to the context updates he/she is willing to receive, e.g. he/she might desire to be informed once every day for the room temperature and not every second, thus making things even more complicated. Obviously, it is insufficient or even impossible to address each user's needs in full, anytime and anywhere. But if a group of users is interested in the same dynamic context information, sophisticated context dissemination mechanisms should be employed that will aim to simultaneously satisfy the entire group, although taking into consideration the individual characteristics and requirements of each user. The design and evaluation of such advanced context dissemination mechanisms is the main focus of this chapter.

CONTEXT DISTRIBUTED DATABASE MANAGEMENT SYSTEM: ARCHITECTURE AND QUERY HANDLING

The designed Context Distributed Database Management System (CDDBMS) is a peer-to-peer database comprising node servers, each of which stores information about at least one predefined information domain. Such domains include for instance: user profiles, accounting information of a telecommunication operator, service advertisements or information related to a specific geographical area. Context producers store their data with respect to domains and consumers query information accordingly. Two domains are distinguished: Logical Domains (Logic-D) and Geographic Domains (Geo-D). Logic-Ds contain non-spatial information such as user profiles and are rather independent from other domains. Geo-Ds, however, carry strong spatial inclusion relationships. For example, the suburb is geographic specialization of the city domain and thus, there is an inclusion relation between the City-Node and the Suburb-Node. Inclusion relations span a directed tree on the Geo-D space, where each CDDBMS is a node and each inclusion relation is a vertex. This graph structure perfectly matches an R-Tree (Lu & Ooi, 1993), an indexing structure of spatial databases. As a result, the geographic inclusion dependencies imply a structure which perfectly caters for spatial queries (Yeung & Hall, 2007). Different database management systems, which store context information, are deployed. Though, most databases implement the SQL standard, they provide different extensions or do not fully comply with it. Moreover, these systems do not offer federation facilities and the lack of a standardized database schema makes it almost impossible to discover the entries queried. To solve this problem, the CDDBMS nodes implement both a standardized database schema and a standardized query interface.

Figure 1 illustrates the CDDBMS architecture. It comprises multiple independent CDDBMS nodes that communicate via the internet to exchange query statements and result sets. Each CDDBMS node comprises a Node-Manager and an off-the-shelf database management system (DBMS). The Node-Manager implements the management logic and the interfaces required for exchanging information with other nodes. Synchronous and asynchronous communication of context data is supported by the Query and the Event interfaces. When a CDDBMS node receives a request for manipulating information referring to data items stored in the local repository the procedure is straightforward. When a data item is not stored in the local DBMS it has to be retrieved from a remote node. An efficient look-up mechanism for finding the item is essential for the scalability of the CDDBMS. To this end, the DBMS implements a simple look-up mechanism: each data item is associated with a Home Node that acts a master repository of the item. The Home Node actually guarantees that it stores the item and that client Nodes can retrieve the item from it. The (communication) address of the Home Node is encapsulated in the identifier of the data item. This distribution concept is inspired by the Home Location Register (HLR) and Visitor Location Register (VLR) approach of the GSM user profile database (Mehrotra, 1997). Likewise, the Home Node is also used for consistent data updates. All updates must be processed by the Home Node. As long as a data item is not updated at the Home Node, the update is not valid.

The DBMS is the actual repository of the node's context data. Basically any of-the-shelf relational database engine meets the requirements of the CDDBMS. However, as spatial queries are a major feature of the CDDBMS, all CDDBMS nodes that cover a Geo-D must implement the Simple Feature Standard SQL (SFS) of the Open Geospatial Consortium (OGC, 2005). This standard specifies SQL-like spatial query statements and 3-dimensional shapes that are used to describe

geographic areas. All major database management systems, such as Oracle (www.oracle.com), DB2 (www-306.ibm.com/software/data/db2), PostGis extension of PostgreSQL (www.postgresql.org or MySQL (www.mysql.com), are shipped with an SFS extension. The introduced context database design schema perfectly caters for two major query use cases that are subsequently presented.

Navigational queries: Starting from a known context data item, applications (or context consumers in general) can follow Associations to discover new information, i.e. Entities and Attributes. Figure 2 illustrates a use case of retrieving an entity from a remote node when the entity identifier is known. The local CDDBMS extracts the URL of the Home CDDBMS from the identifier and contacts the latter. For more details on the manner navigational queries are handled by the CDDBMS you may refer to (Pils, Roussaki & Strimpakou, 2007).

Spatial queries: As spatial inclusion relations can be directly mapped to Associations, navigational queries can also be used to look-up spatial data. However, the burden of evaluating spatial information is put on the query client. A query client must just provide a spatial description. The databases analyses this description and returns the data accordingly. To this end, the distributed spatial query processing algorithm utilizes inclusion relations. Geographic retrieval searches entities based on coordinates and geographic shapes.

Figure 1. CDDBMS high-level deployment and architecture

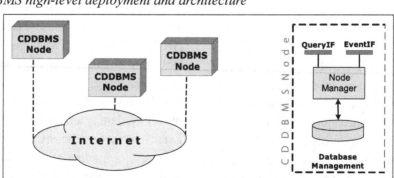

Figure 2. CDDBMS support for navigational queries

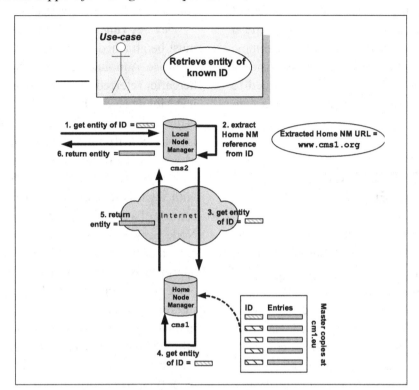

Figure 3. CDDBMS geographic DB and support for spatial queries

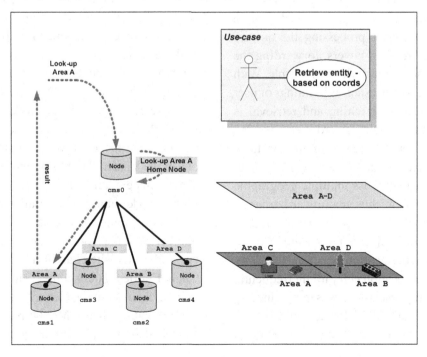

Figure 3 shows an example of the geographic database. When the user requests the content of Area A (described by a shape) from the Node at cms0.eu the latter looks-up its internal Geographic Database to find the Node that covers this area (i.e. Home Node). The request is forwarded to cms1.eu which returns the content of Area A to the requestor.

MANAGEMENT OF MOBILE PHYSICAL OBJECTS

As already stated, scalability of the distributed CDDBMS spatial database is ensured by clustering the world in geographic domains (i.e., geographic areas such as a city, a university campus or a county). Each Geo-D is associated with a CDDBMS node. Each node contains a domain data object that describes its geographical coverage, as well as the context information of all the entities (physical or not) located in its administrative domain. Leaf servers are responsible for each of these domains, node servers' group leaf servers or other node servers, thus establishing a hierarchy of spatial databases. In this perspective, each domain node is responsible for processing the queries relevant to the Geo-D it covers, forwarding the non-relevant ones to the nodes responsible. With regards to static objects, such as buildings or user preferences, context searching and retrieval is rather simple and straightforward. Yet, handling mobile physical entities (e.g. humans, portable devices, cars etc.) is quite more complicated, as these entities may cross multiple geographic domains quite often, thus making it harder to follow and locate them. This is due to the fact that every physical object is represented by two database objects: the location object and the entity object. While the location entry might frequently migrate, the entity object's entry is maintained by the same node (namely the Home Node) as it is used as a point of reference. Both location object

entries and entity object entries are interlinked and have to be synchronised.

Devices run a CDDBMS Node Server that must be attached to the hierarchy of the spatial database. A mobile device's Node Server will be hereafter referred to as a Mobile Node Server or just Mobile Node. The Geo-D of a Mobile Node is the mobile device itself. For small devices this is just a logical domain, but for large devices such as cars, aircrafts or even ships, Geo-Ds cover geographic areas, which are however mobile with regards to the outside world. The current context of a mobile device is stored in its Mobile Node Server. Thus, finding a mobile device is equivalent to finding its Mobile Node Server. The approach is depicted in Figure 4. Each Mobile Node is represented by an Entity (Visited Entity in Figure 4). The Home Node is a Node Server in the fixed network; thus the route to this server never changes. When a Mobile Node moves into a different Geo-D, the CDDBMS of the Visited Node (that is responsible for managing the visited Geo-D) inter-links the Mobile Node and the Home Node. Processing of non-spatial statements is thus similar to mobile IP (Mondal, 2003). The Home Node re-directs query statement to the CDDBMS of the visited Geo-D, which finally dispatches it to the Mobile Node.

As the Home Node stores the Master Copy of the Entity that models the Mobile Node, all statements related to the Mobile Node are send to the Home Node first. The latter looks-up the Entity and extracts the URL of the Visited Parent or one of the Visited Parent's parent Nodes (pointer chain). Since statements are directed to the actual Mobile Node, data synchronisation with the Home Node is no longer necessary. To minimize the number of Home Node updates even further, Parent Nodes of Visited Parents might carry Pointer Chain Entities. These context entities establish a pointer chain from the Home Node to the Visited Parent. Thus, when a Mobile Node changes its Visited Parent only the joint Parent of the new

Figure 4. Chain of pointers for mobile physical object handling

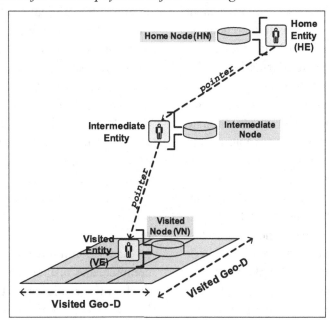

and the old Parent must be updated (rather than the Home Node). The pointer chain is sound and the Home Node still maintains a valid (indirect) pointer to the actual Mobile Node.

THE CONTEXT DATA DISSEMINATION PROBLEM

Undoubtedly, location-awareness at anytime and anyplace is a fundamental requirement in a pervasive computing environment. At the same time however, location-awareness imposes an additional degree of complexity, as it is the most dynamic context information usually involved and requires special handling to overcome the inevitable scalability problems. The CDDBMS alleviates such restrictions establishing the mobile object management mechanism described in the previous section. This approach deals with the location-awareness problem, while the invocation of multiple updates in the home node each time a mobile user changed his/her location is

reduced to minimal. However, the effectiveness of this mechanism is questionable for other types of context information, as it is not always to the interest of the consumer to communicate remotely in order to acquire context data from a different node; or for an application to be obliged to submit even the simplest context queries through a maze of pointers from the home node to the visited node of the mobile user. Furthermore, it is anticipated that in most situations many consumers will be interested in the same context information. Additionally, several such context consumers may be residing at the same node (e.g. different applications used by the same user on the same device or multiple users utilizing terminals of the same public server). In this perspective, it is much more efficient to establish context data replicas on selected context nodes that will receive updates from the home node depending on how often the original data changes and how popular it is for the various interested consumers residing at the specific node. With regards to situations involving mobile users, additional restrictions may arise (e.g.

concerning limited connectivity and bandwidth, unknown network conditions, security, agreement between administrators, etc.), thus rendering imperative the need to establish mechanisms in support of optimised context information replica dissemination and selective updates.

This section elaborates on an efficient approach for the dissemination and selective update of context objects and handles them considering their popularity and the explicit precision requirements of consumers. The proposed mechanism, which is implemented by the CDDBMS, does not encompass methods for the selection of the optimal placement of replicas on selected network nodes. On the contrary, it assumes that each consumer or group of consumers is capable of explicitly declaring its wish for the establishment of a replica on a specific context node. If this is not possible, in case a visited node faces increased demand for a specific context object, it requires the maintenance of its replica. In a nutshell, the designed and implemented framework aims at optimizing and controlling the amount of exchanged context data so that: (i) the context sources are relieved from the burden of disseminating frequent updates to the home node, while (ii) the context consumers are not overloaded with context information that does not interest them for the time being.

Problem Framework

As already presented, the home node is the main coordinator for handling any changes concerning the entities that fall in the node's administrative domain. Therefore, it is the only node responsible for securely disseminating the context updates to the respective context replicas. The home node role is twofold: (i) to instruct the relevant remote context sources about the forwarding intervals/ thresholds of the local context updates by evaluating the real update patterns in conjunction with the consumers' access patterns and requirements and (ii) to decide when to update the replicas of the context entities of its administrative domain

that reside on remote nodes. The basic motivation for this study originates from the observation that there is a fundamental trade-off between the communication cost introduced by the maintenance of fully synchronised context replicas and the degree of synchronisation that is eventually necessary. This has a strong impact on the context precision provided to the consumers and the system performance achieved. For example, when the value of a context object changes rather fast, optimal performance can only be achieved by sacrificing the precision of the copy and on the contrary, the requirement on high precision tends to degrade the performance.

As the communication resources are limited, complete and instant synchronisation of distributed context replicas with the master copy cannot be achieved when the volume of data or the rate of change is high. In the studied framework, the context information consumers play a decisive role in the selective context replica update process, as well as the update rate of the respective raw context data. In this framework, the interested consumers issue requests for the establishment of context replicas and also specify precision constraints regarding the desirable context value difference threshold above which they need to be aware about the updated context information value. Each visited context node, which hosts a context information replica can function as context source and/or context consumer and is responsible for monitoring this particular context data and record statistics with regards to the frequency of reading or writing requests, respectively. These parameters are periodically transmitted to the home node, which processes them along with the various consumers' precision constraints and determines the context update policy.

In general, requirements for strict consistency maintenance between the distributed context copies and the master copy would impose that whenever one node received an update request, initially it would be handled locally, while consequently, the new context value would be propagated to the home node. The latter would afterwards selectively inform the context replicas residing at remote context nodes about the updated context value. The introduced mechanism for selective context data dissemination supports the decision making process of the various context sources on whether/when to send the updated context values depending on the precision requirements and access behaviour of all consumers of this context data item, irrespective of the node they reside at. Furthermore, exactly the same mechanism is exploited by the home node to support its decision concerning whether/when to send the updated context values it received from the context sources to the various replicas distributed over the network. Thus, in case multiple replicas of the same context data item are established over several remote context nodes, i.e. $r = 1,2,...,R$, while numerous context sources, i.e. $s = 1,2,...,S$ are responsible for updating the respective piece of context information, the proposed optimisation algorithm should be executed one time whenever a context update request is received at any of these S context sources, and another R times whenever any of the context sources decides to update the value of the respective context information at the home node. Thus, the proposed approach is suitable for determining the overall selective context update policy both from the context sources to the home node, as well as from the home node to the nodes holding context replicas.

Formal Problem Statement

Consider a single home CM node that holds the master copy of a context data item x. Replicas of x are distributed across numerous visited CM nodes. Let V represent the current value of object x in the home CM node that undergoes updates over time, while Vn represents the value of object x residing at n node. Additionally, each context consumer request is accompanied with a precision constraint specifying the maximum acceptable divergence of the x replica's value with regards to the actual current value of x. At this point, it is assumed that all nodes are always connected to the network and that the infrastructure is robust, i.e. there is enough bandwidth available, node failures are infrequent, etc. To evaluate the proposed context replica update strategy a stochastic study is provided that considers two discrete random variables: A that represents the number of outdated retrievals of x and B that represents the number of redundant updates of the context replicas of x. The proposed strategy aims to minimise that values of both these variables. In this framework, three probabilities have been measured over various experiment settings: $P(A)$ and $P(B)$, as well as the cumulative probability $P(A + B)$. In the subsequent paragraphs, the scope of the three measured probabilities and the purpose they serve are thoroughly explained.

$P(A)$ is the probability that a consumer retrieves outdated context data. In essence, it quantifies the degree of consistency between a context master copy and its remote replica. The home CM node server propagates a selected subset of context updates to a specific replica of context data item x. Thus, only the context updates that introduce divergence between the replica's value and the current context value, which is above a predefined threshold, are propagated to the CM node of the replica. Hereafter, we will refer to the case where the context value the consumer retrieves from the visited CM node differs from the context value at the home CM node, more than the precision constraint specified by the consumer, as *outdated context retrieval*. Using the notation defined above, a context access request submitted at time t_A by consumer C with precision constraint $prec^C$, results in outdated context retrieval if $\left\| V(t_U) - V^C(t_A) \right\| > prec^C$, where $V^C(t_A)$ is the context value retrieved from the consumer C at time t_A, and $V(t_U)$ is the context value updated in the context server at the time t_U, which indicates the last context update at the server before time t_A.

$P(B)$ is the probability of redundant replica updates (i.e. propagated replica updates the values of which are never retrieved by context consumers). It indicates how sparingly communication resources are used and is a measure of the communication cost. Once a context value divergence threshold is applied, the context server disseminates updated context values that result in exceeding the predefined threshold. From these context replicas updates, users benefit only from those that modify the required context value outside the bounds of their precision constraint. Therefore, for a consumer C with precision constraint $prec^C$, the *replica update* that occurs at time t_R is *redundant* when: (i) either $t_R < t_{R'}$ and no access requests occur between replica update times t_R and $t_{R'}$, or (ii) $\left\| V^C\left(t_{A_{i-1}}\right) - V_{t_R}^C\left(t_{A_i}\right) \right\| \le prec^C$, where $t_{A_{i-1}}$ is the time of the previous access request of C, t_A is the time of the last access request of C, t_R is a replica update time that occurs between the last two access request of C (i.e. it stands that $t_{A_{i-1}} < t_R < t_{A_i}$), $V^C\left(t_{A_{i-1}}\right)$ is the context value retrieved by C at $t_{A_{i-1}}$, and $V_{t_R}^C\left(t_{A_i}\right)$ is the context value retrieved by C at t_A in case a replica update has occurred at time t_R.

When context data changes rapidly, optimised network resources utilisation can be achieved by sacrificing context replicas consistency. On the other hand, achieving high probability of consistency tends to degrade performance. Based on the aforementioned definitions of the two adopted probability metrics, we should expect $P(A)$ to continuously increase as the applied value threshold increases, while the exact opposite should take place with regards to $P(B)$. The rationale behind this assumption is straightforward: As the upper bound of the threshold increases, it is likely that more context outdated retrievals will occur and fewer replica redundant updates. In an effort to substantiate this claim, we performed some initial simulations. If the replica's context current value and the updated context value at the home CM node differ by more than ΔV, then and only then the updated value is propagated to the CM node of the replica. We define $\Delta V *$ as the

value of quantity ΔV that minimises probability $P(A + B)$. Subsequently, estimation process for the value of $\Delta V *$ is thoroughly described.

As one may easily conclude, the probability $P(A)$ for a consumer to receive outdated information increases as ΔV increases. However, as ΔV increases, the context server reduces the number of context replica updates and therefore, the probability $P(B)$ of redundant updates decreases. Obviously, these two introduced probabilities represent opposing interests. Indeed, $\overline{P(A)}$ expresses the context consumer's interest, while $P(B)$ reflects the proper utilization of the system's resources. In the established context management domain, we are interesting in satisfying both criteria simultaneously, while trying to address the context consumers' bounded precision requirements. This approach allows us to balance the benefits of both parties in order to maximize the user benefit, while avoiding redundant utilisation of the system's resources. In this respect, we conducted series of experiments to measure cumulative probability $P(A + B)$. The objective of these experiments is to observe and record the context value difference threshold that minimizes the probability $P(A + B)$. Since the two probabilities $P(A)$ and $P(B)$ have been carefully calculated taking into consideration the precision requirements of the consumers, the point where $P(A + B)$ is minimum represents the situation where the following two requirements are addressed in the best possible manner: (i) reduced communication cost that corresponds to minimum redundant replica updates and (ii) consumers' precision constraints satisfaction that results from minimizing the possibility of outdated context data access. Therefore, the ΔV value for which $P(A + B)$ curve exhibits its minimum, corresponds to the optimal threshold $\Delta V *$ above which the home CM node should propagate the context updates to the respective replicas. This selected $\Delta V *$ value will be used to establish the most efficient context consistency control policy for the specified access/update rates, and precision constraints.

HEURISTICS FOR PROBLEM SOLUTION

In order to study the problem of selective context replica update, several parameters need to be introduced. Let u represent the update rate based on which the context data item x is updated at the home CM. Hereafter, the problem of optimal update value threshold will be studied for an arbitrary CM node R that hosts a replica of context data item x. Let C_i, $i = 1, 2, ..., N$ be a consumer of context data item x residing at node R. Let a_i be the access rate based on which the consumer C_i attempts to access the value of context data item x, and p_i be the precision requirement of this consumer. This means that if x_R is the value of the replicated data item x at node R when C_i accesses x, and x_H is the value of the master data item x at the home CM node at that time then: C_i is satisfied with the retrieved value x_R, if and only if $x_R \in [x_H - p_i, x_H + p_i]$.

The selective context replica update problem that is studied hereafter, concerns the determination of the optimal context value difference $\Delta V *$ above which the server (home CM node) will propagate the updated values to the remote context replica residing at the arbitrary CM node R, given the context update rate u, the access frequency a_i for all consumers $C_i, i = 1, 2, ..., N$ and the consumers' precision constraints p_i. As already stated, $\Delta V *$ is such that the cumulative probability $P(A + B)$ is minimised. To solve the problem, four cases have been distinguished based on the ratio of the access rates a_i to the context update rate. Case 1, concerns the situation where all consumers are considerably slower with regards to the context update rate, i.e. their access rates are lower than

$$\frac{u}{2}$$

In Case 2, the access rates of all context consumers are comparable to the context update rate, thus lying in the interval:

$$\left[\frac{u}{2}, 2u \right)$$

In Case 3, all consumers are significantly faster than the context sources, i.e. their access rates are higher than $2u$. Finally, all other possible situations are classified in Case 4. These four Cases have been distinguished due to the fact that the experiments conducted indicated that quantity $\Delta V *$ varies in a similar fashion within each Case, over the access and update rates, as well as the number of context consumers and their precision constraints. In the following subsections, heuristic algorithms that solve the studied problem are provided for each of the above Cases. These heuristics have resulted from the extended experimentation conducted. This experiment framework has been built as follows: the context server update arrivals and access request arrivals have been modelled as Poisson processes, the initial values for the context information are randomly selected in the range [0,10000] and the maximum context value difference between two consecutive server updates is uniformly distributed in the interval [-0.1, 0.1], the sample values for the precision constraint for each consumer are 0:0.1:1, the sample values for threshold ΔV are 0:0.1:1, and the simulation time for each experiment has been set equal to 1 second.

Case 1: All Access Rates Lower Than Update Rate

As already stated, in *Case 1* it stands that

$$a_i < \frac{u}{2}, \forall i = 1, ..., N$$

Herewith, two sub-cases are distinguished:

Case 1.1

If $\frac{1}{N} \cdot \sum_{i=1}^{N} p_i \equiv \overline{p_i} \leq 0.23$,

Box 1. Case 1.1

$$\Delta V^* = \min\left\{\max\{p_i\},\ \max\left\{\overline{p_i},\ \left(0.006176\cdot\frac{u}{a_i}-0.0932\right)\cdot N + 0.01642\cdot\frac{u}{a_i}+0.3408\right\}\right\}$$

Box 2. Case 2

$$\Delta V^* = \min\left\{\max\{p_i\},\max\left\{\min\{p_i\},0.3201\cdot\left[\frac{\sum_{i=1}^{N}\{p_i\cdot a_i\}}{\sum_{i=1}^{N}a_i}\right]^2+0.7221\cdot\frac{\sum_{i=1}^{N}\{p_i\cdot a_i\}}{\sum_{i=1}^{N}a_i}-0.03294\right\}\right\}$$

then the selected context value update threshold is provided by the expression in Box 1.

This formula reflects the experimental observation obtained that slow consumers having very strict precision constraints result in ΔV^* that decreases as the number of the consumers increase in an almost linear fashion. The instances of the experiments conducted to support the design of this ΔV^* expression are approximately 120000.

Case 1.2

If $\overline{p_i} > 0.23$, then the following steps need to take place in order to calculate ΔV^*.

- Sort the consumers C_i, $i=1,2,...,N$, by descending order of their precision constraint p_i. Thus, the sorted list of consumers $C_{i'}$, $i'=1,2,...,N$, is such that $p_{i'} \ge p_{i'+l}$, $\forall i'=1,2,...,N$ and $\forall l=1,2,...,N-i'$.
- Select parameter k as follows: .
- Then, the selected context value update threshold is provided by the following expression:

$$k = \min\left\{ k' \Big/ \sum_{i'=1}^{k'} p_{i'} \ge 0.75\cdot\sum_{i'=1}^{N} p_{i'} \right\}$$

This formula represents the fact that when there are only slow consumers in a context node requesting the same piece of context data, then the consumers of looser precision constraints prevail in the determination of ΔV^*. This is due to the fact that the server context values change much faster than how fast they are being accessed. Thus, if the strictest precision constraints formulated quantity ΔV^*, then the cost introduced by the redundant replica updates would be overwhelming. The instances of the experiments conducted to support the design of this ΔV^* expression are approximately 170000.

Case 2: All Access Rates Comparable to Update Rate

As aforementioned, in *Case 2* it stands that

$$\frac{u}{2}\le a_i < 2u,\ \forall i=1,...,N.$$

For this case, the selected context value update threshold is provided by the expression in Box 2.

This formula reflects the experimental observation obtained that when consumers attempt to access context data almost as often as these are updated, the resulting ΔV^* increases as the access rates and the precision constraints increase. Specifically when all consumers have the same access rates, ΔV^* depends on the average consumer precision constraints based on a quadratic form. The instances of the experiments conducted to support the design of this ΔV^* expression are approximately 280000.

Case 3: All Access Rates Higher Than Update Rate

As already stated, in *Case 3* it stands that $a_i \geq 2u, \forall i = 1,...,N$. Then, the following steps need to take place in order to calculate ΔV^*:

- Select all the consumers that have access rates

$$a_i \geq \overline{a_i} \equiv \frac{1}{N} \cdot \sum_{i=1}^{N} a_i$$

Let these consumers be represented by C_j, $j = 1,2,...,M$, while the rest of the consumers are represented by $C_{j'}$, $j' = 1,2,...,N-M$.

- Sort the consumers C_j, $j = 1,2,...,M$, by descending order of quantity $a_j \cdot (1-p_j)$.

Thus, the sorted list of consumers $C_{j'}$, $j' = 1,2,...,N-M$, is such that $a_{i'} \cdot (1-p_{i'}) \geq a_{i'+l} \cdot (1-p_{i'+l}), \forall i' = 1,2,...,M$ and $\forall l = 1,2,...,M-i'$.

- Select parameter k as follows:

$$k = \min\left\{ \frac{k'}{k' \geq \frac{M}{5}} \right\}$$

- Let $a_{\max}$ be the maximum access rate for the first k consumers in the sorted list, i.e. $a_{\max} \equiv \max_{i'=1,..,k}\{a_{i'}\}$.
- Then, the selected context value update threshold is provided by the expression in Box 3.

This formula represents the fact that the faster consumers that also have the strictest precision constraints are dominant in the determination of ΔV^*. Twenty percent of these consumers are sufficient to decide on the value of ΔV^*. The instances of the experiments conducted to support the design of this ΔV^* expression are approximately 360000.

Box 3. Case 3

$$\Delta V^* = \begin{cases} \dfrac{\sum_{i'=1}^{k}\left\{ p_{i'} \cdot \dfrac{a_{i'}}{a_{\max}} \right\}}{k}, & \text{if } p_1 \cdot \dfrac{a_1}{a_{\max}} < 0.5 \text{ and } 1\sum_{i'=1}^{k}\left\{ p_{i'} \cdot \dfrac{a_{i'}}{a_{\max}} \right\} \leq \\[3ex] 0.4 \cdot \sum_{i'=1}^{k}\left\{ p_{i'} \cdot \dfrac{a_{i'}}{a_{\max}} \right\}, & \text{if } p_1 \cdot \dfrac{a_1}{a_{\max}} < 0.25 \text{ and } 1\sum_{i'=1}^{k}\left\{ p_{i'} \cdot \dfrac{a_{i'}}{a_{\max}} \right\} > \\[3ex] 1.4 \cdot p_1 \cdot \dfrac{a_1}{a_{\max}}, & \text{if } 0.25 \leq p_1 \cdot \dfrac{a_1}{a_{\max}} < 0.5 \text{ and } 1\sum_{i'=1}^{k}\left\{ p_{i'} \cdot \dfrac{a_{i'}}{a_{\max}} \right\} > \\[3ex] p_1 \cdot \dfrac{a_1}{a_{\max}}, & \text{if } p_1 \cdot \dfrac{a_1}{a_{\max}} \geq 0.5 \end{cases}$$

Case 4: Highly Diverging Access Rates

As aforementioned, *Case 4* addresses all situations that cannot be classified under *Case 1*, *Case 2* or *Case 3*. To study this case, the set of the context consumers need to be clustered. These clusters are defined as follows:

Cluster I

$$C_i \in Cluster_I \Leftrightarrow a_i < \frac{u}{2}, \ Cluster_I = \left\{ C_j^I \right\},$$

$$j = 1, 2, ..., N_I, \ \frac{1}{N_I} \cdot \sum_{j=1}^{N_I} p_j^I \equiv \overline{p_j^I}, \ \frac{1}{N_I} \cdot \sum_{j=1}^{N_I} a_j^I \equiv \overline{a_j^I}.$$

Cluster II

$$C_i \in Cluster_{II} \Leftrightarrow \frac{u}{2} \le a_i \le 2u, \ Cluster_{II} = \left\{ C_k^{II} \right\},$$

$$k = 1, 2, ..., N_{II}, \ \frac{1}{N_{II}} \cdot \sum_{k=1}^{N_{II}} p_k^{II} \equiv \overline{p_k^{II}},$$

$$\frac{1}{N_{II}} \cdot \sum_{k=1}^{N_{II}} a_k^{II} \equiv \overline{a_k^{II}}.$$

Cluster III

$$C_i \in Cluster_{III} \Leftrightarrow a_i > 2u, \ Cluster_{III} = \left\{ C_l^{III} \right\},$$

$$l = 1, 2, ..., N_{III}, \ \frac{1}{N_{III}} \cdot \sum_{l=1}^{N_{III}} p_l^{III} \equiv \overline{p_l^{III}},$$

$$\frac{1}{N_{III}} \cdot \sum_{l=1}^{N_{III}} a_l^{III} \equiv \overline{a_l^{III}}.$$

Herewith, four sub-cases are distinguished:

Case 4.1

If (i) $\overline{p_l^{III}} \le \overline{p_k^{II}}$ and $\overline{p_l^{III}} \le \overline{p_j^I}$ or (ii) and $\overline{a_l^{III}} \cdot N_{III} \ge 10 \cdot \overline{a_k^{II}} \cdot N_{II}$, then the problem is reduced

to Case 3 where only the customers in Cluster III participate, such as: $\Delta V^* = \Delta V^*_{Case3}\big|_{\left\{ C_l^{III} \right\}} \equiv \Delta V_3$.

Case 4.2

Else, if (i) $2.5 \cdot \overline{a_k^{II}} \cdot N_{II} \ge \overline{a_l^{III}} \cdot N_{III}$, $\overline{p_k^{II}} < \overline{p_l^{III}}$, and (ii) $\overline{p_k^{II}} \le \overline{p_j^I}$ or $\overline{a_k^{II}} \cdot N_{II} > 10 \cdot \overline{a_j^I} \cdot N_I$, then the problem is reduced to Case 2 where only the customers in Cluster II participate, such as: $\Delta V^* = \Delta V^*_{Case2}\big|_{\left\{ C_k^{II} \right\}} \equiv \Delta V_2$.

Case 4.3

Else, if $2.5 \cdot \overline{a_j^I} \cdot N_I \ge \overline{a_k^{II}} \cdot N_{II}$, $\overline{p_j^I} < \overline{p_k^{II}}$, $10 \cdot \overline{a_j^I} \cdot N_I \ge \overline{a_l^{III}} \cdot N_{III}$, and $\overline{p_j^I} < \overline{p_l^{III}}$, then the problem is reduced to Case 1 where only the customers in Cluster I participate, i.e.: $\Delta V^* = \Delta V^*_{Case1}\big|_{\left\{ C_j^I \right\}} \equiv \Delta V_1$.

Case 4.4

Otherwise:

$$\Delta V^* = \frac{\sum_{j=1}^{N_I} \left\{ a_j^I \cdot \left(1 - p_j^I \right) \right\} \Delta V_1 + \sum_{k=1}^{N_{II}} \left\{ a_k^{II} \cdot \left(1 - p_k^{II} \right) \right\} \Delta V_2 + \sum_{l=1}^{N_{III}} \left\{ a_l^{III} \cdot \left(1 - p_l^{III} \right) \right\} \Delta V_3}{\sum_{j=1}^{N_I} \left\{ a_j^I \cdot \left(1 - p_j^I \right) \right\} + \sum_{k=1}^{N_{II}} \left\{ a_k^{II} \cdot \left(1 - p_k^{II} \right) \right\} + \sum_{l=1}^{N_{III}} \left\{ a_l^{III} \cdot \left(1 - p_l^{III} \right) \right\}}$$

In order to determine the value of ΔV^* in *Case IV*, an attempt has been initially made to reduce it to one of the previous cases. If the cluster with the fastest consumers is either more numerous or is characterized by the lowest average precision, then the problem is reduced to Case III. Similar reductions can be made to the other two cases. However, when no cluster prevails over the other two, ΔV^* is expressed by a linear combination of the three thresholds resulting when the three consumer clusters are treated independently as instances of *Cases I, II* and *III*. In this function, the weights of the three components are formulated based on the access rates and precision constraints of the respective consumer clusters. The instances of the experiments conducted to support the design of this ΔV^* expression are approximately 320000.

EXPERIMENTAL EVALUATION

The results presented in this section attempt to evaluate the introduced formulas with regards to real data produced from a series of experiments. Our first objective is to empirically calculate parameter ΔV^* for various values of the input variables and then, study how this actual optimal threshold fluctuates with regards to the estimated ΔV^* value, as this is provided by the heuristic formulas presented in the former section. In the experiments conducted the situation studied is as follows: there is a single home CM node, which serves a multitude of context consumers that query for the same piece of replicated context information from a visited CM node. Both context server update arrivals and access request arrivals have been modelled as Poisson processes. The initial values for the context information are randomly selected in the range [0,100000] and the maximum context value difference between two consecutive server updates is uniformly distributed in the interval [-1, 1]. The sample values for the precision constraint for each consumer are 0:0.05:1, while for threshold ΔV the sample values are 0:0.01:1. The optimal context value difference threshold ΔV^* is of course the one that minimises probability $P(A + B)$ (for details you may refer to the second

subsection of third section). For all experiment families, the simulation time for each experiment has been set equal to 10 seconds.

The second objective of the experiments conducted is to calculate the resulting probabilities $P(A)$, $P(B)$ and $P(A + B)$, and compare them to the respective probabilities resulting from four alternative dissemination policies. These policies are: (i) the *fully synchronised* policy (where all context updates are disseminated irrespective of the context value difference), (ii) the *strict* policy (where the context update is disseminated if and only if the resulting context value difference is higher than or equal to the lower precision requirement $\min\{p_i\}$), (iii) the *relaxed* policy (where the context update is disseminated if and only if the resulting context value difference is higher than or equal to the higher precision requirement $\max\{p_i\}$), and (iv) the *average* policy (where the context update is disseminated if and only if the resulting context value difference is higher than or equal to the average of the precision requirements $\bar{p}_i$). It should be mentioned that the proposed solution has been implemented by the context management architecture previously presented. However, this solution approach can surely be integrated to any context management architecture that caters for distributed context handling, remote context propagation and mobile object management in order to increase its scalability and performance regarding the query handling process.

Case 1: All Access Rates Lower Than Update Rate

Aiming to evaluate the heuristics designed for Case 1, the estimated ΔV^* value, as well as the actual ΔV^* value are calculated for two families of experiments, each corresponding to one of the sub-cases distinguished in Case 1. The series of the experiments conducted for the specific case concern up to 20 consumers that all demonstrate access rates equal to 10 requests/sec (i.e. $a = 10$).

Figure 5. Mean values for ΔV^*_{actual} and $\Delta V^*_{estimated}$ depicted for various update rates over the number of consumers for Case 1.1.

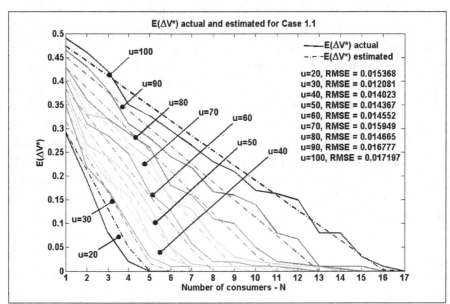

For the experiments aiming to evaluate the heuristics of sub-case 1.1, the precision constraints of the consumers have been selected so that

$$\frac{1}{N} \cdot \sum_{i=1}^{N} p_i \equiv \overline{p_i} \leq 0.23,$$

while each precision constraint lies in the interval [0,1]. To generate the specific precision constraints, a normal distribution has been used having mean value below or equal to 0.23 and standard deviation between 0.01 and 0.2. Thus, approximately 13000 combinations of up to 20 precision constraints have been produced to test sub-case 1.1. The context server update arrival has been selected as follows: $u = 20:10:100$, thus rising the overall number of the conducted experiments to 120000. For the aforementioned experiment settings, the actual ΔV^* value has been calculated, while subsequently, the estimated ΔV^* values have been produced according to the heuristic formula of sub-case 1.1 presented in the

first subsection of sixth section. In Figure 5, the mean values for quantities ΔV^*_{actual} and $\Delta V^*_{estimated}$ are depicted for the various update rates, over the number of consumers. These values have been used to calculate the root mean square error (RMSE), which is also depicted in Figure 5. As one may easily observe, the RMSEs never exceed value 0.02, which is considerably low, thus indicating the high effectiveness and suitability of the respective heuristic formula.

In conclusion, the heuristic approach designed can be safely exploited in the context management infrastructure for selectively disseminating context information in remote context nodes, when the various consumers' context access rates are significantly lower than the update rate, while their precision constraints are considerably low.

For the experiments aiming to evaluate the heuristics of sub-case 1.2, the precision constraints of the consumers have been selected so that

$$???\frac{1}{N} \cdot \sum_{i=1}^{N} p_i \equiv \overline{p_i} > 0.23,$$

while each precision constraint lies in the interval [0,1]. To generate the specific precision constraints, a normal distribution has been used of mean value lying in the interval [0.25,1] and standard deviation between 0.01 and 0.2. Thus, approximately 19000 combinations of up to 20 precision constraints have been produced to test sub-case 1.1. The context server update arrival has been selected as follows: $u = 20:10:100$, thus rising the overall number of the conducted experiments to 170000. For the aforementioned experiment settings, the actual ΔV^* value has been calculated, while subsequently, the estimated ΔV^* values have been produced according to the heuristic formula of sub-case 1.2 presented in the first subsection of sixth section. In Figure 6, the mean values for quantities ΔV^*_{actual} and $\Delta V^*_{estimated}$ are depicted over the mean value of the precision constraints of all consumers. As one may easily observe, the two curves are quite close, thus indicating the suitability of the respective heuristic formula.

The RMSE calculated is equal to 0.0258, which is rather low, thus verifying the effectiveness of the respective heuristic formula. Therefore, it can be safely stated that the heuristic approach designed can be efficiently exploited in the dissemination policies of the context management system, when the various consumers' context access rates are significantly lower than the update rate, while their precision constraints are not low.

In Figure 7, the probabilities $P(A)$, $P(B)$ and $P(A + B)$ resulting from the designed policy are depicted for Case 1 (both sub-cases), along with the respective probabilities of the four alternative dissemination policies aforementioned. As one may easily observe, the worst performance is demonstrated by the fully synchronised policy that results in $P(A + B) = 77.2\%$. On the other hand, the proposed policy outperforms all other policies, resulting in $P(A + B) = 18.1\%$.

Case 2: All Access Rates Comparable to Update Rate

A similar approach has been adopted to evaluate the heuristics designed for Case 2. Thus, the estimated and the actual ΔV^* values have been calculated for a wide family of experiments. All experiments conducted for the specific case concern

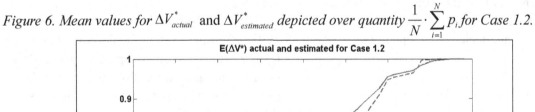

Figure 6. Mean values for ΔV^*_{actual} and $\Delta V^*_{estimated}$ depicted over quantity $\frac{1}{N} \cdot \sum_{i=1}^{N} p_i$ for Case 1.2.

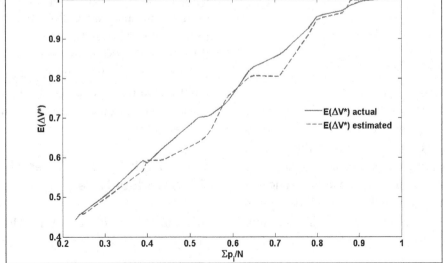

Figure 7. Probabilities P(A), P(B) and P(A + B) resulting from the designed policy, the fully syncronised, the strict, the relaxed and the average dissemination policies for Case 1.

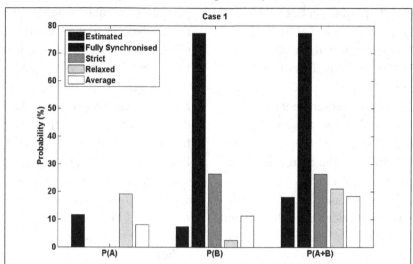

up to 50 consumers that all demonstrate access rates that lie in the interval [50,150]. The precision constraints of the consumers have been selected as follows: $p_i = 0:0.01:1$, while the context server update arrival is equal to 100 updates/sec (i.e. $u = 100$). Thus, approximately 280000 experiments with different settings have been conducted to verify the heuristic formula designed for Case 2. In Figure 8, the mean values for quantities ΔV_{actual}^* and $\Delta V_{estimated}^*$ are depicted over quantity

$$\frac{\sum_{i=1}^{N}(p_i \cdot a_i)}{\sum_{i=1}^{N} a_i},$$

along with an indication of the minimum and maximum ΔV_{actual}^* values demonstrated. As it can easily be observed, the two curves almost overlap, thus indicating that the respective heuristic formula (presented in the second subsection of sixth section) approximates very efficiently the actually observed optimal value for the minimum context value difference threshold. The RMSE

calculated is equal to 0.0169, which is significantly low, thus confirming the suitability and validity of the designed heuristic formula. Therefore, it is proved that the heuristic approach significantly optimises the context management facilities, when the various consumers' context access rates are comparable with the context update rate at the home node.

The probabilities $P(A)$, $P(B)$ and $P(A + B)$ resulting from the designed policy for Case 2, along with the respective probabilities of the four alternative dissemination policies aforementioned are illustrated in Figure 9. In this case, the worst performance is demonstrated by the relaxed policy that results in $P(A + B)$ =34.9%. On the other hand, the proposed policy outperforms all other policies, resulting in $P(A + B)$ =13.4%.

Case 3: All Access Rates Higher Than Update Rate

The heuristics designed for Case 3 have been empirically evaluated following a similar approach to

Figure 8. Mean values for ΔV_{actual}^{*} and $\Delta V_{estimated}^{*}$ depicted over quantity $\dfrac{\sum\limits_{i=1}^{N}(p_i \cdot a_i)}{\sum\limits_{i=1}^{N} a_i}$ for Case 2.

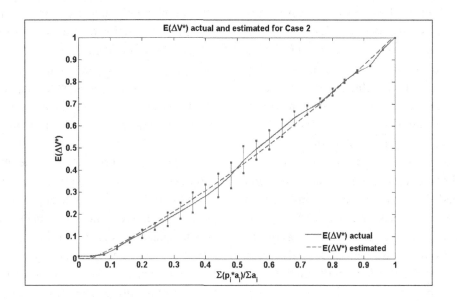

Figure 9. Probabilities P(A), P(B) and P(A + B) resulting from the designed policy, the fully syncronised, the strict, the relaxed and the average dissemination policies for Case 2.

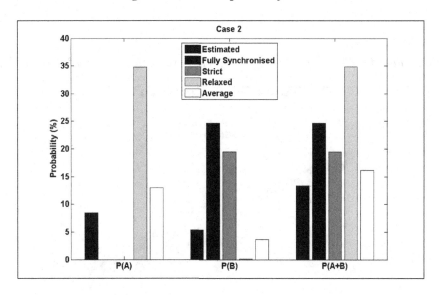

Cases 1 and 2. Thus, the estimated and the actual ΔV^* values have been calculated via a wide range of experiments involving up to 30 consumers that all demonstrate access rates that lie in the interval [200,1000]. The precision constraints of the consumers have been selected as follows: $p_i = 0:0.01:1$, while the context server update arrival is equal to 100 updates/sec (i.e. $u = 100$). Thus, approximately 360000 experiments with different settings have been conducted to verify the heuristic formula designed for Case 3.

However, as the range of both the access rates and the precision constraints is very wide, the optimal context value difference thresholds greatly varied. Thus, putting down a diagram illustrating the mean values for quantities ΔV^*_{actual} and $\Delta V^*_{estimated}$ over some function $f(p_i, a_i)$ was rather misleading, as there have been several different inputs for p_1 and a_i that result in different ΔV^*_{actual} and $\Delta V^*_{estimated}$, but the same value of $f(p_i, a_i)$. Therefore, it has been decided to depict only a narrow set of experiments in Figure 10, which presents the mean values for quantities ΔV^*_{actual} and $\Delta V^*_{estimated}$ for 10 consumers with access rates

within the interval [200,1000]. These quantities are illustrated over the two minimum precision constraints p_1 and p_2. As it can easily be observed, the two surfaces are quite close, thus indicating that the respective heuristic formula (presented in the third subsection of sixth section) is quite suitable to approximate the actually observed optimal value for the minimum context value difference threshold for this specific set of experiments. The RMSE calculated is equal to 0.0142, which is even lower that the one observed in Case 2, thus indicating that the designed heuristic formula is very efficient in approximating the actual optimal context value difference threshold. Therefore, it is proved that the heuristic approach designed is highly effective, when the various consumers' context access rates are significantly higher than the context update rate at the home node.

In Figure 11, probabilities $P(A)$, $P(B)$ and $P(A + B)$ resulting from the designed policy for Case 2 are illustrated, along with the respective probabilities of the four alternative dissemination policies aforementioned. As in Case 1, the worst performance is demonstrated by the fully

Figure 10. Mean values for ΔV^*_{actual} and $\Delta V^*_{estimated}$ depicted over precisions p_1 and p_2 for Case 3.

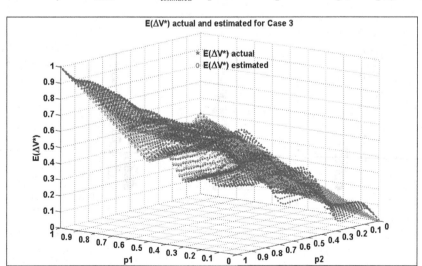

synchronised policy that results in $P(A + B) = 35.1\%$, while the proposed policy outperforms all other policies, resulting in $P(A + B) = 3.7\%$.

Case 4: Highly Diverging Access Rates

In order to evaluate the performance of the heuristics designed for Case 4, the estimated ΔV^* value, as well as the actual ΔV^* value are calculated for four families of experiments, each corresponding to one of the clusters distinguished in Case 4. The series of the experiments conducted for the specific case concern up to 50 consumers with varying access rates within the interval [50,1000]. The precision constraints for each consumer lies in the interval [0,1], while the mean context server update arrival has been selected equal to 100 updates/sec (i.e. $\bar{u} = 100$). For the four experiment families, approximately 320000 experiments have been performed to calculate the actual ΔV^* value for various combinations of precision constraints and access rates. Subsequently, the estimated ΔV^* values have been produced according to the heuristic

formulas that have been presented in the fourth subsection of fourth section. The resulting ΔV_{actual} and $\Delta V_{estimated}$ are used for calculating the RMSE for each sub-case, which is depicted in Figure 12. The RMSE values illustrated in Figure 12 clearly indicate that the introduced formulas reproduce quite successfully the actual ΔV^* value, as the RMSE does not exceed the threshold of 0.025 in any of the four clusters. Therefore, the designed heuristic approach significantly enhances the context dissemination processes, when the various consumers' context access rates vary significantly and thus, can not be treated uniformly.

The probabilities $P(A)$, $P(B)$ and $P(A + B)$ resulting from the designed policy for Case 4 (all sub-cases), along with the respective probabilities of the four alternative dissemination policies aforementioned are illustrated in Figure 13. As in Cases 1 and 3, the worst performance is demonstrated by the fully synchronised policy that results in $P(A + B) = 56.8\%$, while the Strict policy is almost just as bad. As in all Cases, the proposed policy outperforms all other policies, resulting in $P(A + B) = 6.6\%$ for Case 4.

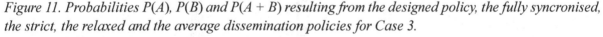

Figure 11. Probabilities $P(A)$, $P(B)$ and $P(A + B)$ resulting from the designed policy, the fully syncronised, the strict, the relaxed and the average dissemination policies for Case 3.

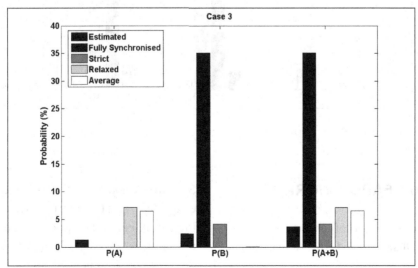

Figure 12. Root Mean Square Errors of quantity $\Delta V_{actual} - \Delta V_{estimated}$ depicted for each sub-case in Case 4.

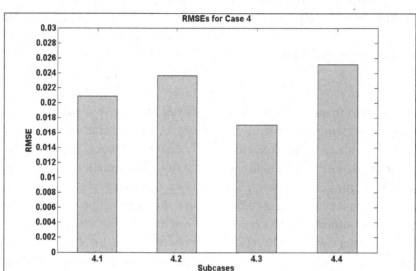

Figure 13. Probabilities P(A), P(B) and P(A + B) resulting from the designed policy, the fully syncronised, the strict, the relaxed and the average dissemination policies for Case 4.

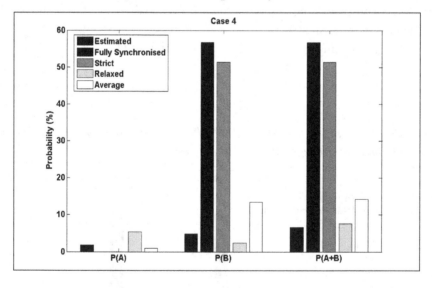

RELATED RESEARCH WORK

The research track in the field of context-awareness goes back in the '90s and includes the Active Badge System developed at Olivetti Research Lab (Want et al., 1992) and the ParcTab system developed at the Xerox Palo Alto Research Center (Schilit et al., 1994).A few years later, Cyberdesk (Dey et al., 1998) built an generic architecture to handle limited types of context. At the same time, the Cyberguide application (Abowd et al., 1997) enhanced a guidebook by adding location awareness and a simple form of orientation information. The Ektara architecture (DeVaul et al., 2000) reviewed a wide range of context-aware computing systems, identified their critical features and proposed a functional architecture for the development of real-world applications. Later on, Mediacup (Beigl et al., 2001) and TEA (http://www.teco.edu/tea/) projects tried to explore the possibility of hiding context sensors in everyday objects.

A quite promising approach was introduced by the Context Toolkit (Dey, 2000), the first one that isolated the application from context sensing. Later on, a research team in the Georgia Institute of Technology built the Context Fabric (Hong et. al., 2001) aiming in enhancing the functionality of Context Toolkit. The Aura Project (Garlan et al., 2002) at Carnegie Mellon University investigated how applications could proactively adapt to the surrounding environment. While the Context Toolkit focused on developing an object oriented framework and allowed use of multiple wire protocols, Aura focused on developing a standard interface for accessing services and forced all services and clients to use the same wire protocol. This sacrificed flexibility, but increased interoperability.

HotTown (Kanter et al., 2003) project developed an open context service architecture. All entities were represented by mobile agents. In HotTown, entities could exchange, merge and interpret context knowledge in the end devices. The Cooltown project by HP labs introduced a uniform Web presence model for people, places and things (Kindberg et al., 2002). Rather than focusing on creating the best solution for a particular application, Cooltown built a general-purpose mechanisms for providing Web presence for people, places and things, but its use was limited to tourist guide applications.

Other interesting research activities include the CoBrA, SOCAM, CASS and CORTEX projects.

CoBrA (Context Broker Architecture) (Chen et al., 2004) is an agent based architecture, which has adopted an OWL-based ontology approach and offers a context inference engine. The Co-BrA architecture lacks the necessary structure for establishing a large-scale system extending beyond a single place. Subsequently, the SOCAM (Service-oriented Context-Aware Middleware) project (Gu et al., 2005) is based on a central server that retrieves context data from distributed context providers. SOCAM also uses ontologies to model context and implements a context reasoning engine. The major disadvantage of SOCAM architecture is its centralised implementation. Another server-based middleware for context-aware mobile applications on hand-held and small mobile computers is designed within the CASS (Context-awareness sub-structure) project (Fahy & Clarke, 2004). CASS opens the way for context-aware applications configurable by users, but its use is limited to small mobile terminals. The CORTEX project is based on the Sentient Object Model (Biegel & Cahill, 2004) and is applied in ad-hoc mobile environments.

The Context Management Framework (CMF) (Korpipaa et al., 2003), designed from the VTT Technical Research Centre of Finland, presents a uniform mobile terminal software framework for acquiring and processing context information and uses ontologies to model context. The proposed approach falls short in its applicability since it concerns collection of information related to mobile terminals. The use of agents and ontologies for collecting context information is also proposed in the Agent-based Context-Aware Infrastructure (ACAI) project (Khedr et al., 2005) from the University of Ottawa. However, the approach is described quite generally without presenting implementation details and mainly without justifying the use of many agents. The project Nexus (Grossmann et al., 2005) from the University of Stuttgart, focuses on the data management aspect of large-scale pervasive computing systems using different server implementations tailored to specific classes of data. Their work is quite interesting, although their distribution concept does not ensure system scalability. Finally, the Pervasive Autonomic Context-aware Environments (Pace) project (Henricksen & Indulska, 2006) from the University of Queensland, developed a complicated layered architecture in support of a proposed graphical context model and preferences' model. The established infrastructure permits the user to control his context but does not address efficiently various critical management issues, e.g. distribution.

In an open context marketplace, where a wide variety of information types is traded, timely delivery of context information is crucial. To the best of the authors' knowledge, no prior work has been conducted to empirically measure and evaluate various selective context replica update policies over time. Thus, the short summary of related work provided subsequently, originates in traditional computing areas, such as distributed systems and the World Wide Web (WWW).

The need for performing asynchronous propagation of updates in a non-transactional fashion in WWW environments is obvious, as the minimisation of the response time and the maximisation of service availability are mandatory. This situation is further strengthened by the fact that exact consistency is virtually impossible in the presence of the high degree of autonomy, the vast data volume and the data astronomical change rates (Olston & Widom, 2005). On the Web, two forms of approximate replication are currently in heavy use: Web caching (Meneses & Torres, 2005) (Yin et al., 2002) and Web crawling (Cho & Garcia, 2003A) (Wolf et al. 2002) (Edwards et al., 2001). In general, the research work in the web domain mainly focuses on maintaining a local copy as up to date as possible. A common limitation in all these approaches is that the refreshing policies are built based solely on predictions concerning which source data objects have changed and how much (Cho & Garcia, 2003B). The goal of our research is different: we aim to maximize the freshness

of the various distributed context replicas, so as the context consumers' precision constraints are addressed, while considering the context update rate and the consumers' access patterns.

Replication is also a key enabling technology in distributed data sharing systems for improving both availability and performance. In such environments, the authors in (Olston & Widom, 2005) study adaptive refresh policies on replicated data in order to gain fine-grained control over the trade-off between precision and performance. His approach guarantees a "divergence bound" on the difference between the values of the replicated data and the source data through the cooperation of sources. The definition of "divergence" or "change" in this work is quite generic and can be also applied to our framework in case of non-numerical data. In general, the approach proposed in this paper is partially inspired by the work presented in (Olston & Widom, 2005), but the special requirements of a context management infrastructure radically differentiate the designed solution. Firstly, in our system the replica nodes are not allowed to control the update procedure as in (Olston & Widom, 2005). Instead, the client nodes are responsible only for informing the adequate context server about possible context updates, the access frequency rates, as well as the level of precision the various consumers require. Secondly, we are using different metrics for quantifying the trade-off between precision and performance. Finally, a major differentiating factor is that while we aim to address the precision requirements of various context consumers simultaneously, the research in (Olston & Widom, 2005) focuses on serving the precision requirements of a single consumer with multiple queries.

CONCLUSION AND FUTURE WORK

The essence of context-awareness is to enable applications and users to take full advantage of the context information provision and support seamless pervasive service provision users' or devices' location. The requirement for universal context access imposes a multitude of enhanced functionalities that a context-aware system should offer in order for mobile users to seamlessly experience the true benefits of a ubiquitous computing world that fades into the background and silently unfolds its potentials. The existing CA architectures and services are either not satisfactory or suitable for pervasive infrastructures viable in world scaling beyond a strictly constrained laboratory environment (Strimpakou et al., 2006). In order to address these new challenges, it is essential to establish innovative data storage and dissemination mechanisms that are applicable to any distributed context environment. The architecture of the Context Distributed DataBase Management System (CDDBMS) presented in this Chapter can be applied to a wide variety of devices ranging from resource-limited PDAs to central context servers. Moreover, the CDDBMS hides the increasing complexity of context management from external actors and incorporates advanced mechanisms for the support of mobile users, so that the various applications can operate smoothly independent of the degree of the users' mobility. In this framework, a location-based view in context data management has been adopted and therefore, the classification and storage of the context information is performed in collaborating and distributed databases, the hierarchy of which reflects the geographical structure of the physical world. A focal point in the introduced CDDBMS is that for each piece of context information monitored a master copy is maintained residing at a central point of access, the home node, while replicas of the specific data can roam and operate in a remote geographic region. The implemented mobile object handling mechanism is based on a chain of pointers from the home node to the remote mobile node and succeeds in minimising the location updates that reach the core network infrastructure.

The proposed CDDBMS does not only provide the functionality presented in this Chapter, but also implements more advanced features, such as context inference (Kalatzis et al., 2008), query extension mechanisms and free-text based query handling (Pils, Roussaki, & Strimpakou, 2006). These features are available in case the advanced Context Management layer (Pils, Roussaki & Strimpakou, 2007) is running on top of the CDDBMS and are necessary to enable applications and application developers to discover the context information they need irrespective of the data location, to prevent them from drowning in the information glut produced by large context source infrastructures and to obtain optimal context value estimations even if the necessary context sources are not available. Further research plans involve the extension of the context query processing described to incorporate facilities for identifying the result set demonstrating the highest possible Quality of Context (Zimmer, 2006). Additionally, in order to further increase the retrieval performance of the CDDBMS, the Node-Manager is being extended with OWL-based semantic matching facilities. Finally, aiming to establish a global privacy protection scheme, the establishment of an infrastructure is being studied that exploits recommender systems (Adomavicius & Tuzhilin, 2005) for controlled sharing of information concerning the trustworthiness of the various stakeholders in the context marketplace and for evaluating the potential privacy threats that may be introduced by specific parties. A prototype implementation of the presented CDDBMS has already been evaluated. This prototype has been developed based on a MySQL DBMS system that implements the Simple Feature SQL standard of the Open Geospatial Consortium (OGC, 2005). The CDDBMS prototype is built on an OSGi Service Platform (http://www.osgi.org/), using SOAP (http://www.w3.org/TR/SOAP) for remote communication, and SLP (Guttman, 1999) for the discovery of services and components.

The distributed context management systems are expected to collect, store and process context information originating from raw data generated at geographically disperse areas. Ideally, the various context objects replicas in remote databases are completely synchronised with the master copy residing at the home node. Nevertheless, the distribution of all context updates to the master copy and subsequently, to the rest of the distributed replicas is usually not practical or prohibitively expensive. In this perspective, the problem of optimally using the underlying communication resources in pervasive environments exploiting selective context update dissemination strategies is being studied in this Chapter and heuristics solutions are provided and evaluated. The designed formulas suggest a context value difference threshold over which the context update should be propagated to the remote nodes. The proposed context update policies aim to address multiple consumers' precision requirements and relieve all parties involved (i.e. context sources, consumers and home nodes) from the burden of continuously propagating remote context updates or requests. The proposed approach has been evaluated via extensive experiments conducted under 1.25 millions of different settings. The results obtained concerning the performance evaluation of this approach indicate that the designed policies approximate very accurately the optimal value difference threshold, demonstrating root mean square error lower than 0.03 in all circumstances. Furthermore, the redundant context updates are suppressed in 82.6% of the cases, while the outdated context retrievals are reduced by 91.7%. Therefore, the proposed scheme is considered of strategic importance for the viability of the context marketplace in a world-wide scale, since it successfully addresses the critical issue of efficient context data dissemination in distributed network nodes.

The authors are currently working on extending the existing approach addressing further requirements on the behalf of the consumers (e.g. response times, priority constraints), while network resources vary unexpectedly and dynamically (e.g. network failures occur) and there are limitations on the amount of overhead introduced due to replica maintenance, as well as on the number of replicas required to support the existing consumers' population. Priority constraints will be incorporated in the presented mechanism as an additional metric of the consumer's needs/desires (e.g. medical emergency) to acquire updates of a specific context data at any cost, irrespectively of the surrounding conditions. Further research plans include the extension of the introduced context dissemination strategy to integrate methods of evaluating Quality of Context parameters and study how such metrics can influence the decision about a context update policy, minimising the effect of less reliable updates and strengthening the impact of trustworthy context sources. Finally, it lies among our imminent plans to build support for automated decision making processes concerning the selection of the most appropriate network nodes to host context replicas.

REFERENCES

Abowd, G. D., Atkeson, C. G., Hong, J., Long, S., Kooper, R., & Pinkerton, M. (1997). Cyberguide: A mobile context-aware tour guide. *ACM Wireless Networks, 3*(5), 421-433.

Adomavicius, G., & Tuzhilin, A. (2005). Toward the Next Generation of Recommender Systems: A Survey of the State-of-the-Art and Possible Extensions. *IEEE Transactions on Knowledge and Data Engineering, 17*(6), 734-749.

Beigl, M., Gellersen, H. W., & Schmidt, A. (2001). Mediacups: Experience with design and use of computer-augmented everyday objects. *Computer Networks, 35*(4), 401-409.

Biegel, G., & Cahill, V. (2004)/ A Framework for Developing Mobile, Context-aware Applications. *2nd IEEE Conference on Pervasive Computing and Communications*, Orlando, FL, USA.

Buchholz, T., Küpper, A., & Schiffers, M. (2003). Quality of Context: What it is and why we need it. *Workshop of the HP OpenView University Association 2003*, Geneva, Switzerland.

Chen, H., Finin, T., & Joshi, A. (2004). An ontology for context-aware pervasive computing environments. *Special Issue on Ontologies for Distributed Systems, Knowledge Engineering Review, 18*(3), 197-207.

Cho, J., & Garcia-Molina, H. (2003A). Effective page refresh policies for web crawlers. *ACM Transactions on Database Systems, 28*, 390-426.

Cho, J., & Garcia-Molina, H. (2003B). Estimating frequency of change. *ACM Transactions on Internet Technology, 3*, 256-290.

DeVaul, R., & Pentland, A. (2000). The Ektara Architecture: The Right Framework for Context-Aware Wearable and Ubiquitous Computing Applications. *The Media Laboratory*, MIT.

Dey, A. (2000). *Providing Architectural Support for Building Context-Aware Applications*. PhD Thesis, College of Computing, GA Institute of Technology, Georgia, USA.

Dey, A., Abowd, G., & Wood, A. (1998). CyberDesk: A Framework for Providing Self–Integrating Context–Aware Services. *Knowledge Based Systems, 11*(1), 3-13.

Edwards, J., McCurley, K., & Tomlin, J. (2001). An Adaptive Model for Optimizing Performance of an Incremental Web Crawler. *WWW Conference 2001*, Hong Kong, China.

Fahy, P., & Clarke, S. (2004). CASS: Middleware for Mobile Context-Aware Applications. *ACM MobiSys Workshop on Context Awareness*, Boston, USA.

Garlan, D., Siewiorek, D., Smailagic, A., & Steenkiste, P., (2002). Project Aura: Towards Distraction-Free Pervasive Computing. *IEEE Pervasive Computing, 1*(2), 22-31.

Grossmann, M., Bauer, M., Hönle, N, Käppeler, U.P., Nicklas, D., & Schwarz, T. (2005). Efficiently Managing Context Information for Large-scale Scenarios., *3rd IEEE Conference on Pervasive Computing and Communications*, Kauai, Hawaii, USA.

Gu, T., Pung, H. K., & Zhang, D. Q. (2005). A Service-Oriented Middleware for Building Context-Aware Services. *Journal of Network and Computer Applications, 28*(1), 1-18.

Guttman, E. (1999). Service Location Protocol: Automatic Discovery of IP Network Services. *IEEE Internet Computing, 3*(4), 71-80.

Henricksen, K. & Indulska, J. (2006). Developing Context-Aware Pervasive Computing Applications: Models and Approach. *Journal of Pervasive and Mobile Computing, 2*(1), 37-64.

Henricksen, K., & Indulska, J. (2006). Developing context-aware pervasive computing applications: Models and approach. *Journal of Pervasive and Mobile Computing, 2*(1), 37-64.

Hong, J., & Landay, J. (2001). An Infrastructure Approach to Context-Aware Computing. *Human Computer Interaction Journal, 16*(2), 287-303.

Kalatzis, N., Roussaki, I., Liampotis, N., Strimpakou, M., Pils, C., & Anagnostou, M. (2008). Exploiting History of Context Data for Lightweight Inference of User Status. *ICT Mobile Summit 2008*, Stockholm, Sweden.

Kanter, T. (2003). Attaching Context-Aware Services to Moving Locations. *IEEE Internet Computing, 7*(2), 43-51.

Khedr, M., & Karmouch, A. (2005). ACAI: Agent-Based Context-aware Infrastructure for Spontaneous Applications. *Journal of Network and Computer Applications, 28*(1), 19-44.

Kindberg, T, Barton, J., Morgan, J., Becker, G., Caswell, D., Debaty, P., Gopal, G., Frid, M., Krishnan, V., Morris, H., Schettino, J., Serra, & Spasojevic, M.(2002). People, Places, Things: Web Presence for the Real World. *ACM Mobile Networks & Applications Journal (MONET)*, *7*(5), 365-376.

Korpipaa, P., Mantyjarvi, J., Kela, J., Keranen, H., & Malm, E.J. (2003). Managing Context Information in Mobile Devices, *IEEE Pervasive Computing*, *2*(3), 42-51.

Lu, H., & Ooi, B.C. (1993). Spatial Indexing: Past and Future. *IEEE Data Engineering Bulletin*, *16*(3), 16-21.

Mehrotra, A. (1997). *GSM System Engineering.* Mobile Communications Series, Artech House Publishers.

Meneses, E., & Torres-Rojas, F. J. (2005). Time and Order Considerations in Consistency Models for Web Caching. *PDPTA Conference 2005*, Las Vegas, Nevada, USA.

Mondal, A.S. (2003). *Mobile IP: Present State and Future.* Series in Computer Science, Springer Publisher.

Olston, C., & Widom, J. (2005). Efficient Monitoring and Querying of Distributed, Dynamic Data via Approximate Replication. *IEEE Data Engineering Bulletin*, *28*, 11-18.

Open Geospatial Consortium Inc. (2005). *Simple Feature access-Part 2: SQL Option.* v.1.1.0.

Pils, C., Roussaki, I., & Strimpakou, M. (2006). Location-Based Context Retrieval and Filtering. *Lecture Notes in Computer Science*, *3987*, 256-273.

Pils, C., Roussaki, I., & Strimpakou, M. (2007). Distributed Spatial Database Management for Context Aware Computing Systems. *16ᵗʰ IST*

Mobile and Wireless Communications Summit, Budapest, Hungary.

Roussaki, I., Strimpakou, M., & Anagnostou, M. (2007). Designing next generation middleware for context-aware ubiquitous and pervasive computing. *International Journal of Ad Hoc and Ubiquitous Computing*, *2*(3), 197-206.

Roussaki, I., Strimpakou, M., Pils, C., Kalatzis, N., & Anagnostou, M. (2006). Hybrid context modeling: A location-based scheme using ontologies. *3ʳᵈ Workshop on Context Modeling and Reasoning*, Pisa, Italy.

Schilit, B., Adams, N., & Want, R. (1994). Context-Aware Computing Applications. *IEEE Workshop on Mobile Computing Systems and Applications*, Santa Cruz, USA.

Strimpakou, M., Roussaki, I., Pils, C., & Anagnostou, M. (2006). COMPACT: Middleware for context representation and management in pervasive computing environments. *International Journal of Pervasive Computing and Communications*, *2*(3), 229-246.

Want, R., Hopper, A., Falcao, V., & Gibbons, J. (1992). The active badge location system. *ACM Transactions on Information Systems*, *10*(2), 91-102.

Wolf, J.L., Squillante, M.S., Yu, P.S., Sethuraman, J., & Ozsen, L. (2002). Optimal crawling strategies for web search engines. *WWW Conference 2002*, New York, USA.

Xynogalas, S., Chantzara, M., Sygkouna, I., Vrontis, S., Roussaki, I., & Anagnostou, M. (2004). Context Management for the Provision of Adaptive Services to Roaming Users. *IEEE Wireless Communications*, *11*(2), 40-47.

Yeung, A. K. W., & Hall, G. B. (2007). *Spatial Database Systems: Design, Implementation and Project Management.* Springer Series: GeoJournal Library, *87*.

Yin, J., Alvisik, L., Dahlin, M., & Iyengar, A. (2002). Engineering Web Cache Consistency. *ACM Transactions on Internet Technology, 2*, 224-259.

Zimmer, T. (2006). QoC: Quality of Context – Improving the Performance of Context-Aware Applications, *Pervasive 2006 Conference*, Dublin, Ireland.

Chapter V
An Adaptable Context Management Framework for Pervasive Computing

Jared Zebedee
Queen's University, Canada

Patrick Martin
Queen's University, Canada

Kirk Wilson
CA Inc, USA

Wendy Powley
Queen's University, Canada

ABSTRACT

Pervasive computing presents an exciting realm where intelligent devices interact within the background of our environments to create a more intuitive experience for their human users. Context-awareness is a key requirement in a pervasive environment because it enables an application to adapt to the current situation. Context-awareness is best facilitated by a context management system that supports the automatic discovery, retrieval and exchange of context information by devices. Such a system must perform its functions in a pervasive computing environment that involves heterogeneous mobile devices which may experience intermittent connectivity and resource and power constraints. The objective of the chapter is to describe a robust and adaptable context management system. We achieve an adaptable context management system by adopting the autonomic computing paradigm, which supports systems that are aware of their surroundings and that can automatically react to changes in them. A robust context management system is achieved with an implementation based on widely accepted standards, specifically Web services and the Web Services Distributed Management (WSDM) standard.

INTRODUCTION

Pervasive computing describes a state in which devices are so pervasive and critical to our activities that they are taken for granted and effectively disappear into the background (Weiser, 1991). Recent technological advances have produced devices small and sophisticated enough to provide the necessary hardware infrastructure for creating pervasive environments.

As our attention turns to the software needed to support this paradigm, we see that a key property that differentiates pervasive computing applications from traditional applications is that a pervasive application has the ability to process and share information about itself and its surrounding environment, that is, to be *context-aware*. This context-awareness acts as a cushion between the technology and the user. It allows users to interact with applications in a more intuitive way and so improves their usability.

Context has a variety of definitions in the pervasive computing literature (Chen & Kotz, 2000, Strang & Linnhoff-Popien, 2004, daCosta, Yamin & Geyer, 2008). Dey (2001) describes context as information that can be used to characterize the situation of an entity, where an entity can be a person, location or object relevant to the interaction between a user and an application. Following from this definition, we can say that a system or application is context-aware if it uses context to provide information or services relevant to the user's task (Dey, 2001). For instance, a smart thermostat's context information includes details about its location, functionality, and information on how to access its temperature controls. Upon entering the vicinity of a smart thermostat, a context-aware PDA would be able to detect its presence, determine that it is a smart thermostat, and obtain information on how to access and manipulate the current room temperature.

In this chapter we argue that context-awareness should be supported by a context management system that allows the automatic discovery, retrieval and exchange of context information by devices. Such a system must perform its functions in a pervasive computing environment that involves heterogeneous mobile devices which may experience intermittent connectivity and resource and power constraints. An effective context management system for a pervasive environment must therefore have two key properties, namely robustness and adaptability.

A robust context management system is achieved with an implementation based on widely accepted standards. While various context management solutions, such as CoBrA (Chen, Finin & Joshi, 2004) and PersonisAD (Assad, Carmichael, Kay and Kummerfeld, 2007), are available, a standardized solution has not, to the best of our knowledge, been proposed. We describe an implementation of our context management framework that integrates several existing technologies and standards and so can be used across disparate devices, software platforms and physical environments.

An adaptable context management system is able to automatically adjust to changes in its environment, for instance users disconnecting and reconnecting to the pervasive environment or a user moving around within the environment. An adaptable context management system supports context-awareness through the automatic discovery of changes in the environment and enhances usability by insulating users from the changes by automatically adjusting to them.

The objective of the chapter is to describe a robust and adaptable context management system. We first propose our Adaptable Context Management Framework (ACMF). It defines a context model and a set of context exchange protocols. ACMF views each device in terms of the *roles* it plays with respect to context management. The possible roles include client, server and proxy. A device acts as a *client* when it searches for, and retrieves, context information about devices within the local domain. A device acts as a *server* when it responds to requests about its context. A device acts as a *context proxy* when it stores and manages the context information for other devices within the domain.

The ACMF context model is used to define the various devices' contexts. Each device has a *context profile* that consists of a device schema and a context that follows the schema. Each context profile is derived from a *domain ontology*. The ontology also facilitates the exchange and understanding of context information.

The prototype implementation of the framework is based on Web services and specifically the Web Services Distributed Management (WSDM) standard (Bullard & Vambenepe, 2006). The prototype runs in a simulated pervasive environment that incorporates a device discovery and communication mechanism typical of ad-hoc networks (Frodigh, Johansson & Larsson, 2000).

The remainder of the chapter is organized as follows. The next section presents background information for context management systems in pervasive environments. The chapter then discusses our context management framework. It explains the components of our framework and describes a proof-of-concept implementation. The last section of the chapter discusses future trends in context management and summarizes the discussion.

BACKGROUND

The notion of *pervasive*, or *ubiquitous*, computing goes back to the seminal writings of Weiser (1991). He defines it to be a state where computing devices are so pervasive and critical to our activities that they are taken for granted and effectively disappear into the background. Recent progress in several areas, including the development of smaller and more powerful computing and communication devices, the connectivity in both wired and wireless networks and the emergence of accepted standards for data transfer and presentation (for example HTTP, XML and WAP),

are bringing the vision of pervasive computing closer to reality.

Context-awareness is one of the cornerstones of the pervasive computing paradigm. A context-awareness framework provides mechanisms to support context-aware applications. Satyanarayanan (2001) points out that a context-awareness framework must address a number of issues:

- How is context represented and stored?
- How is the stored context accessed?
- What are the minimum services needed to make context-awareness feasible?
- How is context acquired? Context may be part of a user's personal computing space or may have to be sensed in real-time from the environment.
- What are the relative merits of different location-sensing technologies?

A number of frameworks to support the development of context-aware applications have been proposed. The Context Toolkit (Dey, Abowd & Salber, 1999) consists of context widgets and a distributed infrastructure to host the widgets. Context widgets encapsulate context information and hide the details of context sensing. The infrastructure includes services to store, share and protect context. SOCAM (Gu, Pung & Zhang, 2005) is a service-oriented middleware to support context-aware applications. It is based on Web services and provides services for service discovery and context storage, provision and interpretation. The Java Context Awareness Framework (JCAF) (Bardram, 2005) is a service-oriented infrastructure that provided context acquisition, management and distribution through a network of cooperating context services. Context services are Java entities that provide a well-defined API.

A context management system addresses the first two issues raised by Satyanarayanan. It supports the discovery and understanding of local services, devices and environmental constraints (daCosta, Yamin & Geyer, 2008). It is typically made up of a context model and a context manager middleware that implements the model. The context model provides the overall structure of the framework, and specifies how interactions take place between devices. The context manager middleware is the software that implements the interaction specified by the model.

Strang and Linnhoff-Popien (2004) present a survey of context models. They identify several main types of models:

- **Key-value models** represent context values as (variable, value) pairs and are frequently used in distributed services frameworks.
- **Markup scheme models** integrate the model schema and values using markup languages such as XML (Bray, Paoli, Sperberg-McQueen, Maler, & Yergeau, 2006).
- **Graphical models** have been derived from generic modeling methods such as UML and ORM.
- **Object-oriented models** exploit the encapsulation and reusability present in an object-oriented approach. The details of context processing are encapsulated at the object level and access to context information is only through specified interfaces.
- **Logic-based models** formulate the context as a set of facts, expressions and rules.
- **Ontology-based models** provide a uniform way of specifying a model's core concepts as well as an arbitrary amount of subconcepts and facts, which facilitates sharing and reuse of contextual knowledge.

The survey evaluates models from these classes with respect to criteria including distributed composition, partial validation, quality of information, incomplete information, and level of formality. The authors conclude that object-oriented and ontology-based models best meet the criteria and that ontology-based models are the most promising for context modeling.

CoBrA (Chen, Finin & Joshi, 2004) is a context management system that uses a centralized approach to managing context and incorporates a collection of intelligent software agents as its context manager middleware. A principal component of CoBrA is the "context broker" agent that acts as a hub, providing a shared context model and disseminating context information among all devices and agents in its environment. While the broker approach provides a consistent context model, it also creates a server-centric architecture, where devices in the environment must rely on a centralized server in order to achieve pervasive functionality. Our context management system uses a distributed approach that avoids the central server issue.

CoBrA agents follow the Foundation for Intelligent Physical Agents (FIPA) Agent Management Specification (FIPA, 2004) as a standardized means of communication. CoBrA uses Web Ontology Language (OWL) (McGuiness & van Harmelen, 2004) to define its ontologies for representing context and modeling. The main ontology associated with CoBrA is SOUPA (Standard Ontology for Ubiquitous and Pervasive Applications) which is made up of vocabularies that represent intelligent agents with associated beliefs, desires, and intentions, time, space, actions and events, user profiles, and policies for security and privacy (Chen, Perich, Finin & Joshi, 2004).

Anagnostopoulos, Tsounis and Hadjiefthymiades (2005) focus on the use of ontologies for describing the communication schemes between entities in pervasive computing environments. They are similar to our approach in that entities exchange data and semantics to allow the interactions. Their model is, however, not implemented.

Christopoulou, Goumopoulos and Kameas (2005) describe an ontology-based system for context modeling, management and reasoning. It is intended to be used in building context-aware applications. Their work focuses on the rule engine used in the system. Our work differs in that we concentrate on providing a robust middleware to discover, store and exchange contexts.

da Rocha and Endler (2005) are concerned with the efficient evolution of the context model and dealing with the heterogeneity of pervasive computing environments. Their approach, like our own, identifies roles (context provider, context consumer and context service) in their model. It also uses event-based communication which is similar to the WSDM notifications employed in our implementation. The key difference is that our work is based on accepted standards while da Rocha and Endler implement their context management on a non-standard research prototype.

PersonisAD is a framework for constructing context aware applications (Assad, Carmichael, Kay & Kummerfeld, 2007). It is built on a consistent mechanism for scrutable modeling of people, sensors, devices and places. A scrutable model is designed such that a person can control their personal information and how it is used in a pervasive environment. The framework includes a context model and a set of operations to facilitate application-model interaction. The context model is organized as a tree containing context attributes of the entities being represented. PersonisAD collects evidence for the value of the context attributes. When a value is requested, the framework examines the available evidence and derives a value based on the evidence at the time of the request,

PersonisAD applications interact with the context model trees using a set of simple operations including "tell", "ask" and "notify". The "tell" operation is used to supply a model with evidence for a component. Applications use the "ask" operation to retrieve component values which are generated by a resolver function using available component evidence. The "notify" operation serves to notify applications when new component evidence is added.

PersonisAD has the same general goal as our ACMF, namely context management. Its focus,

however, is different. PersonisAD focuses on the timeliness of context information and uses a rule-based approach. It also models a wider range of entities including people and locations. ACMF, on the other hand, focuses on providing a flexible and adaptable context management scheme based on appropriate standards.

ADAPTABLE CONTEXT MANAGEMENT

Context management systems for pervasive computing environments, as explained earlier, must be both adaptable and robust. An adaptable context management system is able to deal with the frequent changes occurring in a pervasive environment. More specifically, the system is able to continue to provide its management functionality by automatically reacting to events such as devices moving within the environment or devices entering and leaving the environment. We ensure this adaptive property with a novel management framework that allows devices to store context information locally or on proxy context servers and that automatically transfers context information in response to changes in the environment.

A robust context management system is able to deal with the heterogeneity present in a pervasive computing environment and with the occurrence of unanticipated events or circumstances. We ensure this property is present in a context management system by implementing our framework with accepted industry standards, namely Web Services Distributed Management (WSDM). We chose Web services in general and WSDM in particular, as the basis for our implementation for several reasons. First, Web services are a popular application level communication model for the Internet environment. They are a good model for pervasive computing environments because they support discovery and loosely-coupled interactions. Second, WSDM is a widely accepted standard in the Web services area. Third, WSDM provides the facilities to support the discovery, retrieval and exchange of context information.

Adaptable Context Management Framework (ACMF)

We model a pervasive computing environment as a collection of *domains* where each domain contains a set of *regions* and a set of *device types*. Conceptually, a domain corresponds to some physical space while regions correspond to discrete smaller spaces within that space. Various context-aware devices may move about freely and interact with one-another in useful ways while requiring minimal conscious human effort. We assume that devices have some means of storing and sharing context information.

Our framework, which is shown in Figure 1, consists of an entity specification which provides a logical representation of physical spaces and devices, a context model which provides a specification for storing context information, and context-exchange protocols which specify how context information is exchanged between devices.

Figure 2 illustrates how ACMF's components fit together. Two physical devices are shown that have context profiles corresponding to a common

Figure 1. Adaptable context-management framework

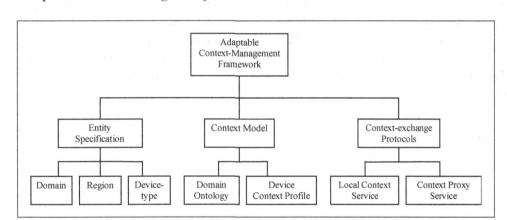

Figure 2. Organization of ACMF's components

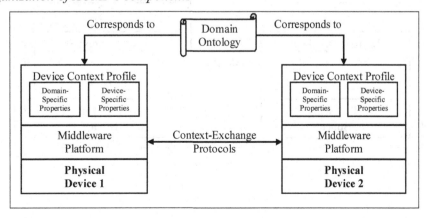

domain ontology. A middleware platform serves as the mechanism for implementing context-exchange protocols.

A pervasive computing environment consists of exactly one domain, a set of one or more regions and a set of one or more device types. A domain is a logical representation of a physical space, such as a building or campus, containing regions and device-types. Each region represents a discrete physical space that exists within a domain, such as a room in a building, and device-types represent the kinds of devices that can reside within a domain.

We illustrate the features of our framework in the remainder of the chapter with an example based on a Computer Science Building domain. The building's regions correspond to rooms such as a conference room, lecture hall, main office or lab. The building's device-types include a data projector, laser printer, PDA and smart thermostat. The context maintained for the building domain could be used to support context-aware applications such as a smart lecture hall or smart meeting room.

Context Model

The context model, which is shown in Figure 3, consists of a domain ontology specification and a device context profile specification. A domain ontology specifies a single domain in terms of its regions and device-types. A device context profile is a collection of properties that describe a particular device's contextual state. Devices within a domain use context profiles to share their context information with one another. Each device must have a device schema from which it generates its context profile. Each device schema must in turn be based on a domain ontology.

Domain ontologies, which are defined as XML instance documents, provide a common vocabulary and semantic structure. Domains and regions are specified as simpleType XML Elements of type "string". Device-types are more complex, each having a unique name and a set of properties. The framework's master domain ontology schema is illustrated in Figure 4 using Altova XMLSpy Content Model View (Altova GmbH, 2007).

Figure 3. Context model

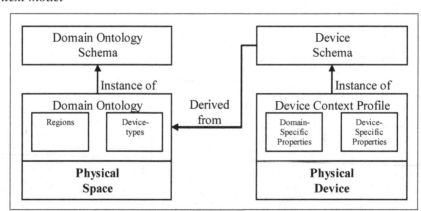

Figure 4. Master domain ontology schema

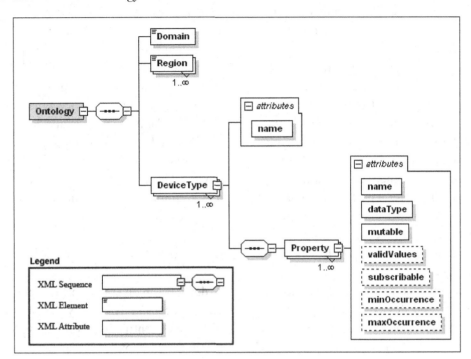

The "Domain" element specifies the domain being described, and should be given a name that appropriately reflects it (e.g. "ComputerScience-Building"). The "Region" element specifies the region(s) that exist within the domain being described. The "DeviceType" element represents the possible device-type(s) that may exist within the domain being described. It contains an XML "name" attribute representing the device-type's name and a set of additional "Property" elements representing its properties. Each "Property" element is in turn qualified by a set of attributes which contain property-specific parameters. Each "Property" must include a "name", "dataType", and "mutable" parameter. The remaining parameters are optional (as shown by the dotted outline).

Every domain ontology must include the "PervasiveDevice" device-type, which contains domain-specific properties that are common to all devices within a domain. Furthermore, this device-type must include a "Location" property that is constrained to the domain's regions using the "ValidValues" parameter. All other device-types should contain device-specific properties, which are properties unique to a specific device-type. Each device-type other than "PervasiveDevice" is a collection of the properties necessary to represent one specific type of physical device. The ontology XML instance document for our Computer Science building example is included in Appendix A.

Each ontology document should be accompanied by a prose description document in order to help clarify domain-specific semantics. For example, the "ComputerScienceBuilding" ontology includes a "Location" property constrained by the "ValidValues" parameter. The ontology itself does not describe the semantics behind each valid "Location" value (nor would it be appropriate). In this case the prose description document should include a floor plan of the building depicting the room locations and their corresponding "Location" values. Appendix A includes a prose description document to accompany the "ComputerScienceBuilding" ontology.

A device schema is used to generate a context profile that describes a device's contextual state. A device schema corresponds to a domain ontology and can only be used within the domain defined by that ontology. Devices may have schemas for multiple domains and upon moving between domains must switch schemas accordingly. If a device has no schema for a particular domain, it simply disables its context-management features. Domain determination occurs through some implementation-specific means, for example RFID room tags.

A device schema defines a collection of domain-specific and device-specific properties grouped by device-type. Each device schema forms a class hierarchy. The root level is a type defining the entity being described and must be named "Device". The "Device" node contains a

set of types including the required "PervasiveDevice" type that defines domain-specific properties. Device-specific properties are defined within additional types that are included depending on the device. All device types and property definitions must be derived from corresponding domain ontology definitions. "Device-types" are declared as XML Schema Sequences and device properties as XML Schema Elements. Figure 5 illustrates an example device schema for a "LaserPrinter" device. The complete device schema document and a sample corresponding instance document are given in Appendix A.

Context Exchange Protocols

A device's involvement in the context management process is defined by the roles the device plays. We identify four roles in ACMF namely, client, server, proxy provider and proxied device. Each device must support a *server* role, a *client* role or both. The server role allows a device to

Figure 5. Laser printer device schema

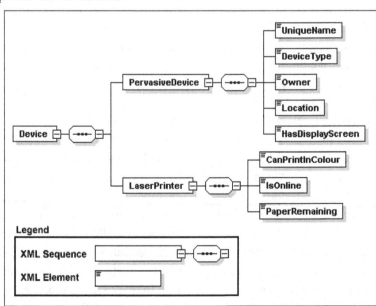

share its context information. The client role allows a device to access the context information of other devices.

ACMF also provides a context proxy service that enables a device to host and share the context information of other devices. It is used in situations where devices are limited in terms of resources such as storage, processing, bandwidth or battery power. A limited device can submit a copy of its context profile to a more robust device which will in turn relay it to other devices. The context proxy service works as an extension to the local context service and any device supporting the former must also support the latter.

We introduce two additional device roles, namely the *proxy provider* role and the *proxied device* role, in order to specify the context proxy service. A device is a proxy provider if it supports the context proxy service. All proxy providers are also servers because they must support both the context proxy and local context services. A device is a proxied device if it uses a proxy provider to host its context information. A proxied device

must still support the local context service, but is able to conserve resources by ignoring other devices' discovery requests.

Client – Server Roles

A device supporting the server role must provide a device schema and must advertise its *endpoint-reference (EPR)* using whatever network implementation the environment supports. The EPR is a unique identifier used to locate a specific device or service on the network. All device interactions are client-initiated with the exception of notifications, which are server-initiated.

From the client role perspective, devices move through a four-state "Interaction" sequence. These states are "Initialized", "Device Aware", "Context Aware" and "Interacting" which are illustrated in Figure 6.

In addition to the "Interaction" state sequence, devices concurrently maintain a "Subscription" state sequence corresponding to whether they are actively listening for property change notification

Figure 6. Device interaction state sequence diagram

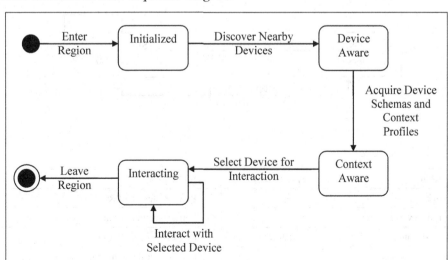

messages, which are described below. The two subscription states are "Subscribed" and "Not Subscribed" and are illustrated in Figure 7.

The state transitions shown in Figure 6 are caused by the execution of the functions provided by the server role, which enables a device to share its context information. The functions, which are summarized in Table 1, are as follows:

1. **Discover Device:** A client retrieves the EPRs of all devices within its wireless range using the device discovery function. Devices not supporting the server role may also be detected but will not provide an EPR and are thus ignored.

2. **Request Device Schema:** Once a device supporting the server role is discovered, a client retrieves its device schema in order to see the properties available in its context profile. This function means a client does not have to have any prior knowledge of another device in order to interact with it.

3. **Request Context Properties:** Using the device schema information, a client can retrieve the values of all or some of the properties that comprise the device's context profile.

4. **Subscribe to Properties:** A client can choose to receive notification messages from a device whenever a specific property value on that device changes. This is particularly useful when used with the "Location" property since it enables a client to become aware of another device's movements between regions. Properties that support notification events are identified by the "subscribed" parameter. When subscribing to a property, a client provides an EPR specifying where the notification messages should be sent.

Our protocols specify the operations to exchange device schema and context profile information but the mechanism for device selection is left as an application. This allows the greatest amount of flexibility as device selection criteria

Figure 7. Device subscription state diagram

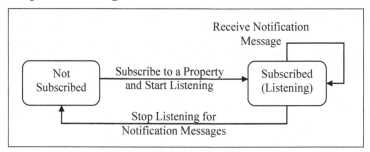

Table 1. Server role functions

Function	Parameters	Description
Discover Device	None	Retrieve device EPR
Request Device Schema	None	Retrieve device schema
Request Context Properties	Property name(s)	Retrieve property value(s)
Subscribe To Properties	Property name	Receive notifications when property value(s) change

Table 2. Laser printer context profile

Property Name	Value
UniqueName	Conference Room Printer
DeviceType	Laser Printer
Owner	IT Department
Location	Conference Room
HasDisplayScreen	True
CanPrintInColour	False
IsOnline	True
PaperRemaining	506

vary depending on the device and the application. For example, the needs of a stationary desktop PC differ significantly from those of a PDA. In some cases an application may choose to leave device selection to the user.

Considering our "ComputerScienceBuilding" scenario described earlier, a client PDA can be programmed to interact only with devices located in the same region, and to alert the user when new devices become available, such as when entering a new room. When the user enters a new region of the building, say the Conference Room, the PDA issues a request to discover the devices in that region. The local devices supporting the server role, which say includes a laser printer, respond with their EPRs. The client PDA then retrieves the device schemas and context profiles for the local devices. The context profile for the laser printer is given in Table 2. The PDA alerts the user that a new device is available and hides any devices that may have been present in the user's previous location. The user may now proceed to interact with the laser printer and say print a document on the PDA.

Context Proxy Roles

The context proxy service enables a device to host and share the context information of another device in situations where the second device has limited resources or power. The device in the proxy provider role hosts the context and the device in the proxied device role gives its context to the provider. State sequences representing the proxy provider and the proxied device roles are shown in Figures 8 and 9, respectively.

The context proxy service uses an extended version of the device schema specification which allows a proxy provider to piggyback/host the context profiles of other devices alongside its own. The extension is specified as a device-type called "ProxyProvider". This device-type represents a logical/virtual entity (as opposed to a physical device) which acts as a container for other devices' context profiles. Any device that acts as a proxy provider must include the "ProxyProvider" device-type in its schema. Since device schemas must correspond to a domain ontology, all domains allowing the use of proxy providers must include the "ProxyProvider" device-type in their ontology. The device schema for the "LaserPrinter" introduced in the "ComputerScienceBuilding" scenario extended to include the "ProxyProvider" device-type is illustrated in Figure 10.

As with all other device-types, "ProxyProvider" is declared as an XML sequence. It contains two XML Element declarations ("LeaseMinutes" and "AvailableSlots") that represent device properties and an XML Sequence declaration ("ProxiedProfile") that represents the container that is used to manage the context profiles of proxied devices.

The "LeaseMinutes" property represents the minimum amount of time in minutes that the proxy provider guarantees to retain a proxied profile. If a proxied device does not renew its lease within this time period, the proxy provider may delete its copy of that device's profile. The "AvailableSlots" property represents the number of profiles that the proxy provider is currently willing to accept for hosting. A value of zero indicates that the proxy provider is not accepting profiles.

Figure 8. Proxy provider state sequence

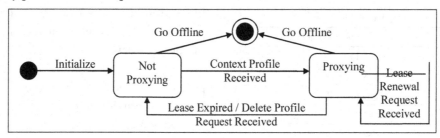

Figure 9. Proxied device state sequence

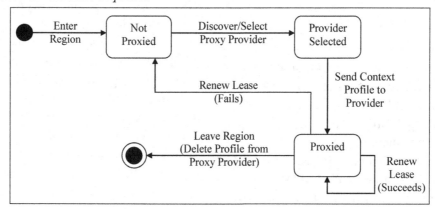

Figure 10. Laser printer device schema with ProxyProvider

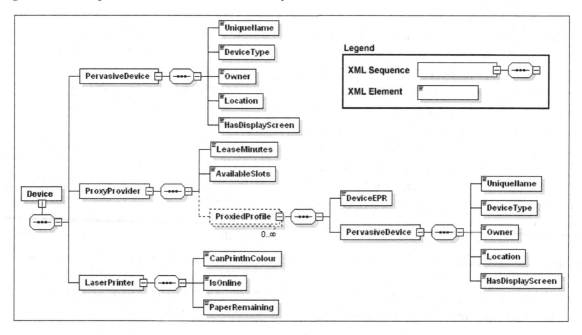

Table 3. Context proxy service functions

Function	Parameters	Description
Send Profile	DeviceEPR, {ContextProfile}	Transfer EPR and profile to proxy provider
Renew Lease	DeviceEPR	Request renewal of proxied profile lease
Delete Profile	DeviceEPR	Remove profile from proxy provider

Each instance of the "ProxiedProfile" sequence contains a single proxied context profile. The sequence has a lower cardinality of zero and an unbounded upper cardinality which means in schema terms that "ProxyProvider" may contain zero or more instances of "ProxiedProfile" at any given time. "ProxiedProfile" in turn contains one property declaration, "DeviceEPR", and one XML sequence declaration, "DeviceProperties". "DeviceProperties" represents the proxied profile itself, and "DeviceEPR" represents the EPR of the device to which the profile belongs.

"DeviceProperties" contains a set of domain-specific properties which must match those found in the proxy provider's "PervasiveDevice" device-type declaration. These properties are ultimately derived from the domain ontology as with all devices. Device-specific properties are not included because they typically change more frequently and are intended to be accessed directly rather than via proxy. Domain-specific properties provide client devices with sufficient information to facilitate device selection. Since domain-specific properties are not proxied, there is no need to proxy device schemas.

A proxied device must implement some means of discovering and selecting a suitable proxy provider in order to satisfy cases where there is more than one proxy provider available on the network. This is left as an implementation decision at the device level. Typically the proxied device will use a selection algorithm to choose a proxy provider after discovering all available devices and retrieving their schemas in order to identify which ones support the "ProxyProvider"

device-type. An example of a simple algorithm is to select the first available proxy provider.

The process of discovering and acquiring the context profiles of proxied devices is somewhat different than that of normal devices. For each discovered device that includes the "ProxyProvider" device-type in its schema, the client retrieves the "ProxiedProfile" sequence using the Request Properties function. This proxy provider responds by returning any proxied context profiles it is hosting as well as their associated device EPRs.

The state transitions shown in Figures 8 and 9 are the result of the execution of functions provided by the proxy provider role. The functions, which are summarized in Table 3, are as follows:

1. **Send Profile:** After a proxy provider is selected and its "LeaseMinutes" and "AvailableSlots" properties are determined using the server role functions, a device can use the Send Profile operation to transfer its EPR and context profile to the proxy provider.

2. **Renew Lease:** A proxied device must periodically renew its lease with a proxy provider in order to keep its context profile at the provider. Failure to renew a lease results in the eventual removal of the profile.

3. **Delete Profile:** A proxied device can explicitly remove its profile from a Proxy provider by sending its EPR.

Under normal circumstances, a proxied device will request its proxied context profile to be deleted before leaving a region or becoming unavailable. However, in the event of a communication error or device failure, the proxy provider may never receive a deletion request. The profile retention policy resolves this situation using a timed lease technique. A proxy provider retains a proxied profile as long as it continues to receive renewal requests from the proxied device within the amount of time specified by the "LeaseMinutes" property. If a proxy provider does not receive an update request within the specified time then it assumes that the proxied device has either become unavailable or no longer requires its services. In the event that a proxy provider becomes unavailable, any associated proxied devices detect the situation with their next lease renewal and then select a new proxy provider.

IMPLEMENTATION

In order to implement our framework, we define a set of mappings between ACMF and the Web Services Distributed Management Standard (WSDM) (Bullard & Vambenepe, 2006), which allows our framework to be implemented using an existing WSDM-based middleware platform.

We use Apache Muse (Apache Software Foundation, 2007) in this work. We therefore begin this section of the chapter with a brief introduction to WSDM. We then outline the mappings from ACMF to WSDM and finally discuss a proof-of-concept simulation of our framework.

WSDM

WSDM supports remote manageability for networked resources by providing a universal management interface for any type of resource. It is built around the concept of a "Manageable Resource" (MR), which is a logical entity that represents a real-world resource in a standardized form that can be exposed to external entities (Bullard & Vambenepe, 2006). The WS-Resource specification (Graham, Karmarker, Mischkinsky, Robinson & Sedukhin, 2006) composes a resource and a basic Web service. WSDM in turn adds a manageability interface, resulting in a Manageable Resource which is accessed through a WSDM endpoint. Figure 11 illustrates how a typical real-world resource such as a laser printer can be represented as a Manageable Resource which is

Figure 11. Laser printer represented as a manageable resource

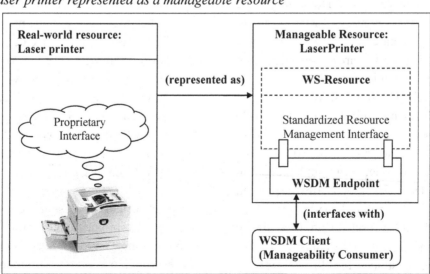

in turn accessed by a WSDM client (also referred to as a "Manageability Consumer").

WSDM Manageable Resources support a high-level facility called Manageability Capabilities which are composed of Resource Properties, Operations, and Management Events. Resource Properties are abstracted representations of attributes typically belonging to whatever real-world resource is being managed. Operations are commands that invoke specific functions on the resource. Management Events are asynchronous notifications that resources can generate on their own, as opposed to relying on Manageability Consumers to request the information. They are defined using Topics, which associate resource state changes to the generation of notification messages.

All of the above elements are defined for a Manageable Resource using four XML-based document types, namely the WSDL (Web Services Description Language) document, the Resource Properties Schema document, the Resource Metadata Descriptor document and the TopicSpace document. The WSDL document is an XML instance document that describes the services offered by a WSDM Manageable Resource. It is the top-level document and includes references to the Resource Properties Schema document and Resource Metadata Descriptor document. A Manageable Resource's Operations are also declared in the WSDL document. The Resource Properties Schema document is an XML Schema document (XSD) that provides the Resource Property declarations for a Manageable Resource. The Resource Metadata Descriptor document is an XML instance document that is used to declare static metadata information that Manageability Consumers can use to determine the semantics of a Manageable Resource's capabilities. The Topic-Space document is an XML instance document that is used to declare a Manageable Resource's available Topics.

Manageability Capabilities are sets of Resource Properties, Operations and Management Events (specified as Topics, and hereafter referred to as "Events"). They are used to define grouped representations of related functions. WSDM includes predefined Manageability Capabilities, such as the "Identity" capability, which is required for all manageable resources. Developers can also create their own custom Manageability Capabilities. Resource Properties primarily reflect the state of the real-world resource being managed. Operations are used to invoke functions on the real-world resource being managed. Operations are defined as MEPs including an input message (request), output message (response) and fault message (in case the Operation does not complete as expected). Events, which provide notification of specific occurrences taking place on a Manageable Resource, are defined in terms of Topics, Operations and MEPs. Events provide a "push" style information exchange that is not available directly via Resource Properties or Operations.

Mapping ACMF to WSDM

In order to map ACMF to WSDM we define two sets of mappings. One set maps our context model to the WSDM Manageable Resource (MR). The other set maps our context-exchange protocols to WSDM Operations. Domain ontologies are not directly mapped because there is no suitable corresponding WSDM component. The framework does not generally require domain ontologies to be accessible as they are only needed when creating new devices and can be made available to designers through application-specific means.

A WSDM MR is specified using a WSDL document, a Resource Properties Schema (RPS) document, a Resource Metadata Descriptor (RMD) document and a TopicSpace document. WSDM Resource Properties are declared in the RPS document, and Topics are declared in the TopicSpace document. Manageability Capabilities are associated with Resource Properties in the RMD document. The WSDL document specifies the Web service interface used to access the MR and includes several standard definitions as well as references which tie in the other three WSDM MR documents.

These documents can be derived from an ACMF device schema using templates we describe elsewhere (Zebedee, 2008). The ACMF device schema is used to specify a WSDM MR by mapping to the four MR documents. Specifically,

1. Each ACMF device-type is mapped to a WSDM Manageability Capability CMW. MC's are defined through a series of steps described in Section 2.8 of the WSDM MUWS Primer (Oasis, 2006). The principal steps in this process that are relevant for this chapter are:

    a. The MC is given a URI so that it can be identified. The URI is then added as an instance value of the MR's Manageability Capability Resource Property.

    b. All Resource Properties to be associated with the MC are declared as elements in a schema document (our schema documents containing related properties are used here)

    c. A topic must be created in the Topics Topic for events related to the MC.

    d. Entries are added to the RMD document to associate each Resource Property with the MC.

2. Each ACMF device property maps to a WSDM Resource Property. If a device property is subscribable, it maps to a WSDM Topic as well.

ACMF device properties are grouped by device-type when mapped to WSDM Resource Properties. Before being referenced in the RPS document, each group of properties is first mapped to its own separate XML Schema document having a namespace which reflects the corresponding device-type name (step 1.b above). For example, the "LaserPrinter" contains two device-types ("PervasiveDevice" and "LaserPrinter") and

thus has two groups of properties which map to two separate Schema documents. We preserve our Resource Property groupings by defining a Manageability Capability for each group.

The RPS document contains a single Resource Property declaration which references all of the device properties declared in the other schema documents, thereby consolidating them into a single document. The namespace of the RPS document matches the namespace of the MR itself.

The documents produced by the mapping for the "LaserPrinter" device from our "ComputerScienceBuilding" example are given in Appendix B.

Device context profiles (device schema instances) are represented in WSDM using the Resource Properties document that is produced by instantiating the resource properties schema document. A sample "LaserPrinter" Resource Properties document is included in Appendix B.

The mapping of local context service functions to WSDM operations is summarized in Table 4. The "Discover Device" operation is implemented using the facilities of the underlying network and so is not mapped to a WSDM operation. The "Request Device Schema" operation is implemented by simply accessing schemas directly via their URIs. The other two local context service functions map directly to WSDM operations. The functions provided by the context proxy service do

Table 4. Mappings between local context service functions and WSDM Operations

Local Context Service Function	WSDM Operation
Discover Device	n/a
Request Device Schema	n/a
Request Properties	GetMultipleResourceProperties
Subscribe To Properties	Subscribe

not map to any corresponding WSDM operations and so must also be implemented separately.

Simulation

We developed a simulation of an Adaptable Context Management Environment (ACME) as a proof-of-concept implementation of our framework. The structure of the simulated ACME is illustrated in Figure 12. The context management system is implemented within the simulation using WSDM and the mappings discussed above. The simulation is includes a MANET network environment simulator and pervasive device simulators for both the server and client roles. Details of the ACME simulation and its evaluation are provided elsewhere (Zebedee, 2008).

Our ACMF is designed to work with any MANET implementation (such as Zeroconf) that provides a self-configuring TCP/IP network. It is also possible to use the framework with a simulated MANET environment. This can be accomplished by using a TCP/IP network and a DHCP server combined with some means of managing the WSDM EPRs of devices available on the network. We specifically use a Web service with a predetermined EPR to maintain a database of EPRs for all connected devices.

Each simulated server is a WSDM MR implemented using Apache Muse Version 2.2.0. These MRs respond to requests from clients, behaving as if they were implemented on actual physical devices. Each MR has a GUI interface that provides real-time information about its current state. The ACME simulation includes three simulated servers: "DataProjector", "LaserPrinter" and "SmartThermostat". The "LaserPrinter" simulated server supports the "ProxyProvider" role and is thus able to manage other devices' context profiles.

The simulated client is a Java program that interacts with the simulated servers. It is meant to represent a PDA featuring an interactive GUI interface that demonstrates device discovery and context information retrieval. The simulated client also has the ability to make changes to the property values on other devices. For example, the client can operate the data projector's lamp by modifying its "LampActive" Resource Property value.

Figure 12. Structure of ACME simulation

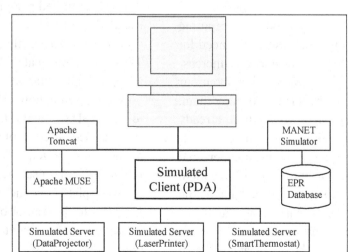

FUTURE TRENDS

As the trend toward ubiquitous computing continues context models and management frameworks will continue to advance and improve. Eventually we expect to see the convergence of these designs to a small number of universally accepted standards, much like what has happened with other technologies such as the Internet and World Wide Web. Only then will it be possible to fully enable context management on a larger scale across disparate systems and environments.

The notion of context has up till now been limited in scope and has focused on simple properties like location. As more sophisticated facilities for context management are developed we expect to see context encompass a wider range of concepts and data. Context will become more structured and context models will have to be expanded to accommodate the added complexity. Context will be viewed on the same level as application data and data queries will encompass both types of data.

Devices need to fade into the background in a pervasive computing environment. We therefore expect the autonomic computing paradigm to play an increasingly important role in these environments. Autonomic devices will have the ability to act on their own given high level guidance from their users. They will also be able to detect and adapt to changes in their environment.

The progression of embedding computing into our daily lives will necessitate the need for systems to actively handle and share ever-increasing amounts of sensitive information about our environments and the people that occupy them. As issues of security and privacy have already begun to surface in environments where computing systems are empowered with our personal data, ubiquitous systems will further the notion. Standards will need to be established that define strict parameters governing how personal data is processed and exactly what information is considered "public" or "free". The importance of such standards will increase as data-sharing scopes widen among the technologies rapidly becoming embedded into our environments.

SUMMARY

Pervasive computing environments that are made up of hundreds of devices and within which intelligent devices interact in the background on behalf of their users will soon become commonplace. Context-awareness is a key property that differentiates pervasive computing applications from the more traditional applications. A device is context-aware if it is able to adapt its behaviour to the current context.

In this chapter we argue that a context management system that is able to support the automatic discovery, retrieval and exchange of context information by devices while accommodating the variation and heterogeneity present in a pervasive computing environment is needed to provide context-awareness. An adaptable and robust context management framework, called the Adaptable Context Management Framework (ACMF), is presented.

ACMF employs a novel approach to context management that allows a device to store its context information locally or to use another device as a proxy for maintaining its context when the device has limited resources. We define context exchange protocols to accommodate the variety of changes possible in the pervasive environment. These protocols enable ACMF to automatically adapt to changes in the environment.

We describe how ACMF can be mapped to the WSDM standard in order to produce a Web service based implementation of a context management system. This prototype is robust in that it can be used across disparate devices, software platforms and physical environments. It is also, to the best of our knowledge, the first implementation of a context management system based on standards.

ACMF enhances the usability of context-aware applications in two ways. First, the automatic adaptation of ACMF insulates users from the frequent changes in context experienced by pervasive devices. Second, the standards-based implementation of ACMF allows it to be used across heterogeneous platforms.

Some possible directions for future research on ACMF include the following. First, we plan to look at extending our context model to incorporate entities beyond devices. The context model in PersonisAD, for example, explores the modeling of people and places in addition to devices. Second, while ACMF provides a solid foundation for context management, practical applications require inclusion of security standards. Future work will investigate the use of policies or other mechanisms for security integration. Third, our current prototype implementation of ACMF is in a simulated environment using a proven standard (WSDM) and middleware platform (Muse). The next logical step is to move this implementation outside the laboratory and into the real world. Future work will involve creating an ontology to represent a real-world environment and programming devices with WSDM-capable middleware to support our current prototype.

REFERENCES

Altova GmbH (2007). *Altova XMLSpy 2008 Enterprise Edition Content Model View.* Altova GmbH. Retrieved September 1, 2007 from http://www.altova.com/manual2008/XMLSpy/SpyEnterprise/index.html?contentmodelview.htm.

Anagnostopoulos, C., Tsounis, A., & Hadjiefthymiades, S. (2005). Context management in pervasive computing environments. In *Proc of International Conference on Pervasive Services* (pp. 421-424). Santorini, Greece.

Apache Software Foundation (2007). *Apache Muse - A java-based implementation of WSRF 1.2, WSN 1.3, and WSDM 1.1.* Apache Software Foundation. Retrieved May 1, 2007 from http://ws.apache.org/muse/

Assad, M., Carmichael, D.J., Kay, J. & Kummerfeld, B. (2007). PersonisAD: Distributed, active, scrutable model framework for context-aware services. In A. LaMarca et al. (Eds.): *Pervasive 2007, LNCS 4480* (pp. 55-72) Springer-Verlag, Berlin.

Bardram, J. (2005). The java context awareness framework (JCAF) – A service infrastructure and programming framework for context-aware applications. In *Proceedings of 3rd International Conference on Pervasive Computing (Pervasive 2005)* (pp. 98-115), Munich, Germany.

Bray, T., Paoli, J., Sperberg-McQueen, C., Maler, E. & Yergeau, F. (2006). *XML 1.1, (Second Edition).* World Wide Web Consortium. Retrieved March 11, 2008 from http://www.w3.org/TR/2006/REC-xml11-20060816/.

Bullard, V., & Vambenepe, W. (2006). *Web services distributed management: management using web services (MUWS 1.1) Part 1.* OASIS. Retrieved June 1, 2007 from http://docs.oasis-open.org/wsdm/wsdm-muws1-1.1-spec-os-01.pdf.

Chen, H., Finin, T., & Joshi, A. (2004). An ontology for context-aware pervasive computing devices. *Special Issue on Ontologies for Distributed Systems, Knowledge Engineering Review, 3*(18), 197-204. .

Chen, H., Perich, F., Finin, T., & Joshi A. (2004). SOUPA: standard ontology for ubiquitous and pervasive applications. In *Proceedings of the First Annual International Conference on Mobile and Ubiquitous Systems: Networking and Services* (pp. 258-267). Boston, MA.

Christopoulou, E., Goumopoulos, C., & Kameas, A. (2005). An ontology-based context management and reasoning process for UbiComp applications. In *Proceedings of the 2005 Joint Confer-*

ence on Smart Objects and Ambient Intelligence (265-270). Grenoble, France.

da Costa, C., Yamin, A., & Geyer, C. (2008). Toward a general software infrastucture for ubiquitous computing. *IEEE Pervasive Computing, 7*(1), 64-73.

da Rocha, R., & Endler, M. (2005). Evolutionary and efficient context management in heterogeneous environments. In *Proceedings of the 3rd International Workshop on Middleware for Pervasive and Ad-hoc Computing* (1-7). Grenoble, France.

Dey, A. (2001). Understanding and using context. *Personal and Ubiquitous Computing, 7*, 4-7.

Dey, A., Abowd, G., & Salber, D. (1999). A context-based infrastructure for smart environments. In *Proceedings of 1ˢᵗ International Workshop on Managing Interactions in Smart Environments* (pp. 114 -128).

FIPA (2004). *FIPA agent management specification*. Foundation for Intelligent Physical Agents. Retrieved March 3, 2008 from http://www.fipa.org/specs/fipa00023/SC00023K.pdf.

Frodigh, M., Johansson, P., & Larsson, P. (2000). *Wireless ad hoc networking -- The art of networking without a network*. Ericsson Inc. Retrieved May 1, 2007 from http://www.ericsson.com/ericsson/corpinfo/publications/review/2000_04/files/2000046.pdf.

Graham, S., Karmarker, A., Mischkinsky, J., Robinson, I., & Sedukhin, I. (2006) *Web services resource 1.2.* OASIS. Retrieved June 1, 2007 from http://docs.oasis-open.org/wsrf/wsrf-ws_resource-1.2-spec-os.pdf

Gu, T., Pung, H., & Zhang, D. (2005). A service-oriented middleware for building context-aware services. *Journal Network Computing Applications, 28*(1), 1-18.

McGuiness, D., & van Harmelen, F. (2004). *OWL web ontology language overview*. World Wide Web Consortium. Retrieved March 3, 2008 from http://www.w3.org/TR/owl-features/.

OASIS (2006). *Web services distributed management: MUWS primer*. Retrieved March 3, 2008 from http://docs.oasis-open.org/wsdm/wsdm-1.0-muws-primer-cd-01.pdf

Satyanarayanan, M. (2001). Pervasive computing: vision and challenges. *IEEE Personal Communications, 8*(4), 10-17.

Strang, T., & Linnhoff-Popien, C. (2004). A context modeling survey. In J. Indulska & D. De Roure (Eds.), *Proc of first international workshop on context modeling, reasoning and management (UbiComp 2004)*. Nottingham England.

Weiser, M. (1991). The computer for the twenty-first century. *Scientific American*, 94-104.

Zebedee, J. (2008). *An adaptable context management framework for pervasive computing*. MSc thesis, School of Computing, Queen's University.

APPENDIX A

Master Domain Ontology Schema Document

```
<xs:schema xmlns:xs="http://www.w3.org/2001/XMLSchema"
    xmlns="http://www.cs.queensu.ca/OntologySchema"
    targetNamespace="http://www.cs.queensu.ca/OntologySchema"
    xmlns:meta="http://www.cs.queensu.ca/MetadataSchema"
    elementFormDefault="qualified" attributeFormDefault="unqualified">

    <xs:annotation>
        <xs:documentation xml:lang="en">
                Schema for Creating Context-Managed Environment Ontologies
                Created by Jared A. Zebedee (2007)
        </xs:documentation>
    </xs:annotation>

    <xs:import namespace="http://www.w3.org/2001/XMLSchema"
    schemaLocation="http://www.w3.org/2001/XMLSchema.xsd"/>

    <xs:import namespace="http://www.cs.queensu.ca/MetadataSchema"
    schemaLocation="http://www.cs.queensu.ca/MetadataSchema.xsd"/>

    <xs:simpleType name=»propertyType»>
        <xs:restriction base=»xs:string»>
                <xs:enumeration value=»boolean»/>
                <xs:enumeration value=»integer»/>
                <xs:enumeration value=»string»/>
        </xs:restriction>
    </xs:simpleType>

    <xs:element name=»Ontology»>
        <xs:complexType>
                <xs:sequence>
                        <xs:element name=»Domain» type=»xs:string»/>
                        <xs:element name=»Region» type=»xs:string» maxOccurs=»unbounded»/>
                        <xs:element name=»DeviceType» maxOccurs=»unbounded»>
                                <xs:complexType>
                                        <xs:sequence>
                                                <xs:element name=»Property»
maxOccurs=»unbounded»>
                                                        <xs:complexType>
                                                                <xs:attribute name=»name» type=»xs:
string» use=»required»/>
```

```
                                                      <xs:attribute name=»dataType»
type=»propertyType» use=»required»/>
<xs:attribute name="mutable" type="xs:boolean" use="required"/>
    <xs:attribute name=»subscribable» type=»xs:boolean» use=»optional»
        default=»false»/>
    <xs:attribute name=»ValidStringValues» type=»meta:stringList»
        use=»optional»/>
    <xs:attribute name=»ValidIntegerValues» type=»meta:integerList»
        use=»optional»/>
    <xs:attribute name=»minOccurrence» type=»xs:nonNegativeInteger»
        use=»optional» default=»1»/>
    <xs:attribute name=»maxOccurrence» type=»xs:allNNI» use=»optional»
        default=»1»/>
                                                    </xs:complexType>
                                                </xs:element>
                                            </xs:sequence>
                                    <xs:attribute name=»name» type=»xs:string» use=»required»/>
                                    </xs:complexType>
                                </xs:element>
                        </xs:sequence>
                </xs:complexType>
        </xs:element>
</xs:schema>
ComputerScienceBuilding Ontology XML Instance Document


<Ontology xmlns:xsi=»http://www.w3.org/2001/XMLSchema-instance»
xsi:schemaLocation=»http://www.cs.queensu.ca/OntologySchema http://www.cs.queensu.ca/OntologySchema.
xsd»
xmlns=»http://www.cs.queensu.ca/OntologySchema»
elementFormDefault=»qualified» attributeFormDefault=»unqualified»>

    <!-- Domain Definition -->
    <Domain>ComputerScienceBuilding</Domain>

    <!-- Region Definitions -->
    <Region>Conference Room</Region>
    <Region>Lecture Hall</Region>
    <Region>Main Office</Region>
    <Region>Lab</Region>

    <!-- PervasiveDevice DeviceType Definition -->
    <DeviceType name=»PervasiveDevice»>
        <Property name=»UniqueName» dataType=»string» mutable=»false»/>
        <Property name=»DeviceType» dataType=»string» mutable=»false» ValidStringValues=»Data_Projec-
```

```
tor Laser_Printer PDA Smart_Thermostat»/>
        <Property name=»Owner» dataType=»string» mutable=»true»/>
        <Property name=»Location» dataType=»string» subscribable=»true» mutable=»true» ValidStringValue
s=»Conference_Room Lecture_Hall Main_Office Lab»/>
        <Property name=»HasDisplayScreen» dataType=»boolean» mutable=»false»/>
    </DeviceType>

    <!-- DataProjector DeviceType Definition -->
    <DeviceType name=»DataProjector»>
        <Property name=»LampActive» dataType=»boolean» mutable=»true»/>
        <Property name=»SlidesLoaded» dataType=»boolean» mutable=»false»/>
        <Property name=»SlideNumber» dataType=»integer» mutable=»false»/>
    </DeviceType>

    <!-- LaserPrinter DeviceType Definition -->
    <DeviceType name=»LaserPrinter»>
        <Property name=»CanPrintInColour» dataType=»boolean» mutable=»false»/>
        <Property name=»IsOnline» dataType=»boolean» mutable=»true»/>
        <Property name=»PaperRemaining» dataType=»integer» mutable=»true»/>
    </DeviceType>

    <!-- PDA DeviceType Definition -->
    <DeviceType name="PDA">
        <Property name=»BacklightActive» dataType=»boolean» mutable=»true»/>
        <Property name=»BatteryLevel» dataType=»integer» mutable=»true»/>
        <Property name=»LowBattery» dataType=»boolean» mutable=»true»/>
    </DeviceType>

    <!-- SmartThermostat DeviceType Definition -->
    <DeviceType name=»SmartThermostat»>
        <Property name=»CurrentTemperature» dataType=»integer» mutable=»true»/>
        <Property name=»TemperatureSetting» dataType=»integer» mutable=»true»/>
        <Property name=»IsCelcius» dataType=»boolean» mutable=»true»/>
    </DeviceType>
</Ontology>
```

Metadata Schema Document
(Used by Ontology and Device Schemas)

```
<xsd:schema xmlns:xsd="http://www.w3.org/2001/XMLSchema"
    xmlns="http://www.cs.queensu.ca/MetadataSchema"
    targetNamespace="http://www.cs.queensu.ca/MetadataSchema"
    elementFormDefault="qualified" attributeFormDefault="unqualified">>
```

```
    <xsd:simpleType name="stringList">
        <xsd:list itemType="xsd:string"/>
    </xsd:simpleType>

    <xsd:simpleType name="integerList">
        <xsd:list itemType="xsd:integer"/>
    </xsd:simpleType>

    <xsd:attribute name="mutable" type="xsd:boolean"/>
    <xsd:attribute name="subscribable" type="xsd:boolean"/>
    <xsd:attribute name="ValidStringValues" type="stringList"/>
    <xsd:attribute name="ValidIntegerValues" type="integerList"/>
</xsd:schema>
```

ComputerScienceBuilding Prose Description Document

The ComputerScienceBuilding domain represents a hypothetical university computer science building comprised of one floor containing four device-types and four regions (rooms). The device types are Data Projector, Laser Printer, PDA and Smart Thermostat. The regions are Conference Room, Lecture Hall, Main Office and Lab. The building floor plan is illustrated in Figure A.1.

Figure A.1 ComputerScienceBuilding floor plan

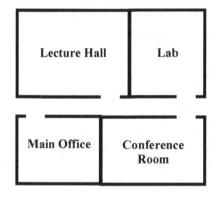

Laser Printer Device Schema Document

```
<xs:schema xmlns:xs="http://www.w3.org/2001/XMLSchema"
xmlns:meta="http://www.cs.queensu.ca/MetadataSchema"
xmlns="http://www.cs.queensu.ca/ComputerScienceBuilding/LaserPrinterDevice"
targetNamespace="http://www.cs.queensu.ca/ComputerScienceBuilding/LaserPrinterDevice"
elementFormDefault="qualified" attributeFormDefault="unqualified">
```

```
<xs:annotation>
    <xs:documentation xml:lang="en">
            Laser Printer Device Schema
            Created by Jared A. Zebedee (2007)
    </xs:documentation>
</xs:annotation>

<xs:import namespace="http://www.cs.queensu.ca/MetadataSchema" schemaLocation="http://www.
cs.queensu.ca/MetadataSchema.xsd"/>

<!-- Top-level Pervasive Device Definition -->
<xs:element name=»Device»>
    <xs:complexType>
            <xs:sequence>

                    <!-- PervasiveDevice device-type (required) -->
                    <xs:element name=»PervasiveDevice»>
                            <xs:complexType>
                                    <xs:sequence>
                                            <xs:element name=»UniqueName» type=»xs:string»
meta:mutable=»false»/>
                                            <xs:element name=»DeviceType» type=»xs:string» meta:
mutable=»false» meta:ValidStringValues=»Laser_Printer»/>
                                            <xs:element name=»Owner» type=»xs:string» meta:
mutable=»true»/>
                                            <xs:element name=»Location» type=»xs:string» meta:
mutable=»true» meta:subscribable=»true» meta:ValidStringValues=»Conference_Room Lecture_Hall Main_Of-
fice Lab»/>
                                            <xs:element name=»HasDisplayScreen» type=»xs:bool-
ean» meta:mutable=»false»/>
                                    </xs:sequence>
                            </xs:complexType>
                    </xs:element>
                    <!-- /PervasiveDevice -->

                    <!-- LaserPrinter Device Definition -->
                    <xs:element name="LaserPrinter">
                            <xs:complexType>
                                    <xs:sequence>
                                            <xs:element name="CanPrintInColour" type="xs:boolean"
meta:mutable="false"/>
                                            <xs:element name=»IsOnline» type=»xs:boolean» meta:
mutable=»true»/>
                                            <xs:element name=»PaperRemaining» type=»xs:integer»
```

```
meta:mutable=»true»/>
                                    </xs:sequence>
                          </xs:complexType>
                    </xs:element>
                    <!-- /LaserPrinter -->
             </xs:sequence>
       </xs:complexType>
    </xs:element>
    <!-- /Device -->
</xs:schema>
```

Laser Printer Context Profile XML Instance Document

```
<Device xmlns:xsi=»http://www.w3.org/2001/XMLSchema-instance»
xsi:schemaLocation=»http://www.cs.queensu.ca/ComputerScienceBuilding/LaserPrinterDevice http://www.
cs.queensu.ca/ComputerScienceBuilding/LaserPrinterDevice.xsd»
xmlns=»http://www.cs.queensu.ca/ComputerScienceBuilding/LaserPrinterDevice»
elementFormDefault=»qualified» attributeFormDefault=»unqualified»>

    <PervasiveDevice>
        <UniqueName>Conference Room Printer</UniqueName>
        <DeviceType>Laser Printer</DeviceType>
        <Owner>Conference Room Manager</Owner>
        <Location>Conference Room</Location>
        <HasDisplayScreen>true</HasDisplayScreen>
    </PervasiveDevice>

    <LaserPrinter>
        <CanPrintInColour>true</CanPrintInColour>
        <IsOnline>true</IsOnline>
        <PaperRemaining>500</PaperRemaining>
    </LaserPrinter>

</Device>
```

APPENDIX B

ComputerScienceBuilding WSDM MR Documents

LaserPrinter WSDL Document

Note: In order to conserve space, we have included only the resource-specific schema references here. The complete specification is given elsewhere [17].

```
LaserPrinterDevice.wsdl:
<wsdl:definitions targetNamespace="{domain namespace}/{device name}"
xmlns:tns="{domain namespace}/{device name}"
xmlns="http://schemas.xmlsoap.org/wsdl/"
xmlns:wsa="http://www.w3.org/2005/08/addressing"
xmlns:wsdl="http://schemas.xmlsoap.org/wsdl/"
xmlns:wsdl-soap="http://schemas.xmlsoap.org/wsdl/soap/"
xmlns:xsd="http://www.w3.org/2001/XMLSchema"
xmlns:wsx="http://schemas.xmlsoap.org/ws/2004/09/mex"
xmlns:wsrf-rp="http://docs.oasis-open.org/wsrf/rp-2"
xmlns:wsrmd="http://docs.oasis-open.org/wsrf/rmd-1"
xmlns:muws1="http://docs.oasis-open.org/wsdm/muws1-2.xsd"
xmlns:muws2="http://docs.oasis-open.org/wsdm/muws2-2.xsd"


xmlns:wsnt="http://docs.oasis-open.org/wsn/b-2"
xmlns:wsntw="http://docs.oasis-open.org/wsn/bw-2"
xmlns:wst="http://docs.oasis-open.org/wsn/t-1"


name=»{device name}»>

    <wsdl:types>
        {...} (refer to WSDL template)

<!-- Include Resource-Specific Schemas -->

        <xsd:schema elementFormDefault="qualified" targetNamespace="http://www.cs.queensu.ca/Compu-
terScienceBuilding/LaserPrinterDeviceTopicSpace">
                <xsd:include schemaLocation="LaserPrinterDevice_TopicSpace.xsd" />
        </xsd:schema>
        <xsd:schema elementFormDefault="qualified" targetNamespace="http://www.cs.queensu.ca/Compu-
terScienceBuilding/PervasiveDevice">
                <xsd:include schemaLocation="PervasiveDevice.xsd" />
        </xsd:schema>
        <xsd:schema elementFormDefault="qualified" targetNamespace="http://www.cs.queensu.ca/Compu-
terScienceBuilding/LaserPrinter">
```

```
            <xsd:include schemaLocation="LaserPrinter.xsd" />
      </xsd:schema>
      <xsd:schema elementFormDefault="qualified" targetNamespace="http://www.cs.queensu.ca/Compu-
terScienceBuilding/LaserPrinterDevice">
              <xsd:include schemaLocation="LaserPrinterDevice_RPS.xsd" />
      </xsd:schema>
   </wsdl:types>
```

{...}

```
</wsdl:definitions>
```

LaserPrinter Schema Documents

Note : The LaserPrinter device has a total of three schema documents as shown.

PervasiveDevice.xsd :

```
<schema targetNamespace="http://www.cs.queensu.ca/ComputerScienceBuilding/PervasiveDevice"
xmlns="http://www.w3.org/2001/XMLSchema">
    <element name="UniqueName" type="string"/>
    <element name="DeviceType" type="string"/>
    <element name="Owner" type="string"/>
    <element name="Location" type="string"/>
    <element name="HasDisplayScreen" type="boolean"/>
</schema>
```

LaserPrinter.xsd:

```
<schema targetNamespace="http://www.cs.queensu.ca/ComputerScienceBuilding/LaserPrinter" xmlns="http://
www.w3.org/2001/XMLSchema">
    <element name="CanPrintInColour" type="xs:boolean"/>
    <element name="IsOnline" type="xs:boolean"/>
    <element name="PaperRemaining" type="xs:int"/>
</schema>
```

LaserPrinterDevice_RPS.xsd :

```
<xsd:schema targetNamespace="http://www.cs.queensu.ca/ComputerScienceBuilding/LaserPrinterDevice"
    xmlns:tns="http://www.cs.queensu.ca/ComputerScienceBuilding/LaserPrinterDevice"
    xmlns:xsd="http://www.w3.org/2001/XMLSchema"
    xmlns:wsrf-rp="http://docs.oasis-open.org/wsrf/rp-2"
    xmlns:muws1="http://docs.oasis-open.org/wsdm/muws1-2.xsd"
    xmlns:muws2="http://docs.oasis-open.org/wsdm/muws2-2.xsd"
```

```
xmlns:context="http://www.cs.queensu.ca/ComputerScienceBuilding/PervasiveDevice"
xmlns:laserprinter="http://www.cs.queensu.ca/ComputerScienceBuilding/LaserPrinter"

xmlns:wsnt="http://docs.oasis-open.org/wsn/b-2"
xmlns:wsntw="http://docs.oasis-open.org/wsn/bw-2"
xmlns:wst="http://docs.oasis-open.org/wsn/t-1">

<!-- Import schemas for PervasiveDevice and LaserPrinter device-types -->

<!-- Resource Properties Document Element Declarations -->
<xsd:element name=»LaserPrinterDeviceResourceProperties»>
      <xsd:complexType>
            <xsd:sequence>
                  <!-- Must be specified for all MRs -->
                  <xsd:element ref=»wsrf-rp:QueryExpressionDialect» minOccurs=»0»
maxOccurs=»unbounded» />
                  <xsd:element ref=»muws1:ResourceId»/>
                  <xsd:element ref=»muws1:ManageabilityCapability» minOccurs=»0»
maxOccurs=»unbounded» />
                  <xsd:element ref=»muws2:OperationalStatus»/>

                  <!-- Must be specified if topics are supported -->
                  <xsd:element ref=»wsnt:FixedTopicSet»/>
                  <xsd:element ref=»wst:TopicSet» minOccurs=»0»/>
                  <xsd:element ref=»wsnt:TopicExpression» minOccurs=»0»
maxOccurs=»unbounded»/>
                  <xsd:element ref=»wsnt:TopicExpressionDialect» minOccurs=»0»
maxOccurs=»unbounded»/>

                  <!-- PervasiveDevice Capability Properties -->
                  <xsd:element ref=»context:UniqueName»/>
                  <xsd:element ref=»context:DeviceType»/>
                  <xsd:element ref=»context:Owner»/>
                  <xsd:element ref=»context:Location»/>
                  <xsd:element ref=»context:HasDisplayScreen»/>

                  <!-- LaserPrinter Capability Properties -->
                  <xsd:element ref=»laserprinter:CanPrintInColour»/>
                  <xsd:element ref=»laserprinter:IsOnline»/>
                  <xsd:element ref=»laserprinter:PaperRemaining»/>
            </xsd:sequence>
      </xsd:complexType>
</xsd:element>
</xsd:schema>
```

LaserPrinter RMD Document

```
<Definitions xmlns="http://docs.oasis-open.org/wsrf/rmd-1">
    <MetadataDescriptor xmlns:wsrl="http://docs.oasis-open.org/wsrf/rl-2"
    xmlns:muws1="http://docs.oasis-open.org/wsdm/muws1-2.xsd"
    xmlns:muws2="http://docs.oasis-open.org/wsdm/muws2-2.xsd"
    xmlns:wsnt="http://docs.oasis-open.org/wsn/b-2"
    xmlns:wst="http://docs.oasis-open.org/wsn/t-1"
    xmlns:xsd="http://www.w3.org/2001/XMLSchema"
            xmlns:myns="http://www.cs.queensu.ca/ComputerScienceBuilding/LaserPrin
terDevice"
            xmlns:pervasive="http://www.cs.queensu.ca/ComputerScienceBuilding/Perv
asiveDevice"
            xmlns:laserprinter="http://www.cs.queensu.ca/ComputerScienceBuilding/LaserPrinter"

    name="LaserPrinterMetadataDescriptor"
interface="myns:LaserPrinterPortType"
            wsdlLocation="http://www.cs.queensu.ca/ComputerScienceBuilding/LaserPrinterDevice
http://www.cs.queensu.ca/ComputerScienceBuilding/LaserPrinterDevice/LaserPrinterDevice.wsdl" >

    <!-- PervasiveDevice Capability Resource Property Metadata Declarations -->
    <Property name=»pervasive:UniqueName» mutability=»mutable» modifiability=»read-only»>
            <muws2:Capability>
                    http://www.cs.queensu.ca/ComputerScienceBuilding/
                    PervasiveDeviceCapability
            </muws2:Capability>
    </Property>

    <Property name=»pervasive:DeviceType» mutability=»constant»                    modifiability=»read-
only»>
            <ValidValues>
                    <pervasive:DeviceType>Laser Printer</pervasive:DeviceType>
                    <pervasive:DeviceType>Smart Thermostat</pervasive:DeviceType>
                    <pervasive:DeviceType>PDA</pervasive:DeviceType>
            </ValidValues>

            <muws2:Capability>
                    http://www.cs.queensu.ca/ComputerScienceBuilding/
                    PervasiveDeviceCapability
            </muws2:Capability>
    </Property>

    <Property name=»pervasive:Owner» mutability=»mutable»
            modifiability=»read-only»>
```

```
        <muws2:Capability>
                http://www.cs.queensu.ca/ComputerScienceBuilding/
                PervasiveDeviceCapability
        </muws2:Capability>
    </Property>

    <Property name=»pervasive:Location» mutability=»mutable»
modifiability=»read-only»>
        <ValidValues>
                <pervasive:Location>Boardroom</pervasive:Location>
                <pervasive:Location>Conference Room</pervasive:Location>
        </ValidValues>
        <muws2:Capability>
                http://www.cs.queensu.ca/ComputerScienceBuilding/
                PervasiveDeviceCapability
        </muws2:Capability>
    </Property>

    <Property name=»pervasive:HasDisplayScreen» mutability=»constant»
modifiability=»read-only»>
        <muws2:Capability>
                http://www.cs.queensu.ca/ComputerScienceBuilding/
                PervasiveDeviceCapability
        </muws2:Capability>
    </Property>

    <!-- LaserPrinter Capability Resource Property Metadata Declarations -->

    <Property name=»laserprinter:CanPrintInColour» mutability=»mutable»
modifiability=»read-write»>
        <muws2:Capability>
                http://www.cs.queensu.ca/ComputerScienceBuilding/
                LaserPrinterCapability
        </muws2:Capability>
    </Property>

    <Property name=»laserprinter:IsOnline» mutability=»mutable»
modifiability=»read-only»>
        <muws2:Capability>
                http://www.cs.queensu.ca/ComputerScienceBuilding/
                LaserPrinterCapability
        </muws2:Capability>
    </Property>
```

```
        <Property name=»laserprinter:PaperRemaining» mutability=»mutable»
modifiability=»read-write»>
                <muws2:Capability>
                        http://www.cs.queensu.ca/ComputerScienceBuilding/
                        LaserPrinterCapability
                </muws2:Capability>
        </Property>


        <Property name=»wsnt:TopicExpression» modifiability=»read-only»
mutability=»constant»>
                <StaticValues>
                        <wsnt:TopicExpression>pervasive:Location</wsnt:TopicExpression>
                </StaticValues>
        </Property>


        </MetadataDescriptor>
</Definitions>
LaserPrinter TopicSpace Document
<wst:definitions   targetNamespace=»http://www.cs.queensu.ca/ComputerScienceBuilding/LaserPrinterDevice-
TopicSpace»
        xmlns:tns=»http://www.cs.queensu.ca/ComputerScienceBuilding/LaserPrinterDeviceTopicSpace»
        xmlns:wsrf-rp=»http://docs.oasis-open.org/wsrf/rp-2»
        xmlns:wst=»http://docs.oasis-open.org/wsn/t-1»>
        <wst:TopicSpace name=»PervasiveDeviceTopics» targetNamespace=»http://www.cs.queensu.ca/Comput-
erScienceBuilding/PervasiveDeviceTopicSpace»>
                <wst:Topic name=»Location» messageTypes=»wsrf-rp:ResourcePropertyValueChangeNotification» />
        </wst:TopicSpace>
</wst:definitions>
```

Chapter VI
Context–Aware Database Querying:
Recent Progress and Challenges

Yuanping Li
Tsinghua University, China

Ling Feng
Tsinghua University, China

Lizhu Zhou
Tsinghua University, China

ABSTRACT

Context is an essential element in mobile and ubiquitous computing. Users' information needs can be better understood and supplied by means of context-awareness. Context data may be sensed, inferred, or directly input by users, and so forth, which calls for specific query mechanisms to acquire context information. On the other hand, traditional non-context-aware database querying techniques need to be re-examined, taking query context into account. In order to design effective context-aware database query processing mechanism, the authors survey the latest developed context-aware querying techniques in the data management field. They outline six ways to query context directly, and provide a categorization about how to use context in querying traditional databases. The approaches of handling imperfect context in context-aware database querying are also described. They discuss some potential research issues to be addressed at the end of the chapter.

INTRODUCTION

Mobile and ubiquitous computing refers to a computing environment, where computers can be moved and are more adaptable, personalized, and unobtrusive in human's lives. To make applications in such an environment more usable and more effective, context has been introduced. Context can be any information that can be used to characterize the situation of an entity. An entity can be a person, place, or object that is considered relevant to the interaction between a user and an application, including the user and applications themselves (Dey & Abowd, 2000). According to Dey and Abowd, a system is *context-aware* if it uses context to provide relevant information and/or services to the user, where such relevancy depends on the users' task. Context-awareness constitutes a prominent feature in mobile and ubiquitous computing. The applications of context-awareness include tour guide, monitoring, mobile device manipulations, etc. Such applications often entail acquiring and processing a large mount of (possibly imperfect) context data, and leveraging context in decision making. Towards this goal, effective context-aware data management support is needed. As querying is one of the most fundamental functionalities in data management, an understanding of how to process a context-aware database request enables database designers to choose appropriate design schemes. The aim of this chapter is to survey some latest developed techniques involved in context-aware database querying, and outline some research topics that merit further investigation.

It is obvious that context can enhance the power of database querying in various ways. Meanwhile, context also influences the traditional architecture of database querying mechanism in many aspects. A *context-aware database query* is generally regarded as a database query, whose query results are influenced by the context under which the query is issued (Stefanidis, Pitoura, & Vassiliadis, 2007b). In order to deliver a context-aware querying solution, we need to answer a number of questions as follows.

Question 1: *How to acquire context information, in particular, which mechanism will be used to get context information?*

Question 2: *How to use the obtained context to process a database query? What influence does context impose on traditional database querying?*

Question 3: *How to deal with imperfection of context information in context-aware database query processing?*

In this chapter, we will survey some recently developed techniques to tackle the above questions, including context query mechanisms, context-aware database querying techniques, as well as methods to deal with imperfect context. We also present some research questions and challenges that are worth further exploration.

BACKGROUND

To start the discussion, let us first look at two scenarios, which may occur in a mobile and ubiquitous computing environment.

Scenario 1. John is on a vocational trip and come to a city for the first time. He has a tour guide in his PDA, and the main function of this tour guide is to tell John where he is. When he wants to visit the museum, he uses the PDA to guide his way to museum. When he is visiting the museum, the PDA can provide the information of an exhibit when he comes close to the exhibit. Such a function needs to request location context information from a GPS provider or a RFID system.

The scenario involves querying context information. In many context-aware applications, context information acquisition is essential and should be considered before using context information. It is always necessary to provide sufficient support for context querying in context-aware applications because many operations and functions of the applications would be based on it.

To query context data, we should first examine the characteristics of context data. There are many different kinds of context coming from diverse sources. Some context data are gathered from sensors which are often dynamic and uncertain; some context data are static like users' profile information; and some context data are derived from basic data sources, e.g., to infer whether a person is sitting on a seat through camera and other sensors. Here, one particular difficulty for context querying lies in handling heterogeneous context information. Setting an effective representation for context query requests and query results are thus very important, where context reasoning element shall also be incorporated in context querying. Another difficulty for querying context lies in the selection and synthesis of different context data since there may be several providers for the same context information.

Scenario 2. It is an afternoon where Mary and her friends are in a new place. They want to find a restaurant to have dinner. They submit a query *"find a restaurant nearby"* via her PDA. There may be many restaurants in the database and some of them may not suit Mary and her friends, e.g., the restaurant is full or the restaurant provides food that Mary and her friends do not like. Here, several kinds of context information will be used, such as the location of Mary and her friends, their food preferences, and the busy state of the restaurant, etc. Obviously, to help them find suitable restaurants for Mary and her friends, there needs a mechanism to integrate all these context data into this restaurant query.

The second situation depicts a database query by leveraging context information. With the growth of Internet and proliferation of information

systems, it is desirable to conceive approaches to facilitate database query processing, and to provide really useful information to users. Nowadays, mobile devices such as PDAs and smart phones are used widely by more and more people, and sensors become cheaper than before. These imply that context information could be easier to obtain and could play a role in serving users' information needs. For example, query mechanisms could be designed to proactively provide information based on context change, or rank query results under different contexts. To do a good job, the query processor must know the associations between context information and users' requested information by means of semantic analysis and reasoning. The performance of such analysis and reasoning in accuracy, efficiency, and effectiveness will eventually influence people's experiences in using context-aware database systems.

Scenario 3. Reverting to scenario 1 and 2 where both John and Mary rely on mobile devices to provide their locations. But this time, they are in a place where their location information that the devices provide are rather rough. That is, the devices can only identify the city where they are in, but cannot provide the street or the building they are located in. How do mobile devices fulfill the functions described in the previous two scenarios?

In a mobile and ubiquitous environment, a lot of context information can be exploited to enhance applications' usability. For example, mobile devices equipped with GPS can be used as a collector of the location context information of the user. Various sensors and computing facilities in the environment can provide such context information as temperature, intensity of light etc. However, sometimes data imperfection incurs difficulties in context-aware applications, as described in scenario 3. In addition, the mobile devices also have some unfavorable aspects. For example, the screens of the mobile devices are always small; network bandwidth of the mobile devices are subject to variability; many mobile devices rely heavily on batteries' energy, so the power is relatively limited (Barbará, 1999).

To take advantage of mobile and ubiquitous environments, and meanwhile overcome the difficulties that arise in processing context-aware database queries in such environments, researchers have contributed to propose many pragmatic approaches, which will be overviewed in the following sections.

CONTEXT-AWARE DATABASE QUERYING TECHNIQUES

Context Querying Mechanisms

Querying context information is more straightforward than using context information in database querying. The context information are collected and stored in a context database and managed by a context management system (CMS). The CMS takes care of data formats in which the underlying context data is captured, stored, and manipulated. One characteristic of CMSs in literature is that context information itself can be represented in different types of traditional databases, such as relational, object-oriented, and XML database, so that the CMS can be implemented upon a traditional database management system. Another characteristic of CMSs is that when the logic model of context information is specified, the underlying database management system can be transparent to the users. For example, a context data modeled by ontology can be stored in an OWL XML file or transformed into a relational database.

The support of the CMS lays down a foundation for context querying with various querying mechanisms being developed to cope with different context data and their properties. Haghighi *et al.* made a good categorization of context query languages (Haghighi, Zaslavsky, & Krishnaswamy, 2006), where they argued that context query languages are "*pivotal for querying con-*

text and determining the way in which queries are expressed and what information needs to be obtained". Five kinds of context query languages were listed in their description, including SQL-based, graphical, XML-based, RDF-based, and programming-based context query language. We agree with the importance of context query languages in the whole process of context-aware database querying, and agree with their categorization but making some extensions. We change RDF-based to *Ontology-based* languages for generality, and add a category of *API-based* context query language. By such categorization, we can distinguish the input from the output more clearly. In the following, we describe the six types of context querying languages, namely, SQL-based, XML-based, ontology-based, programming-based, graphical, API-based context query language.

SQL-Based Context Query Mechanism

SOL is widely recognized as an effective language to access relational databases, and many computer users and programmers are familiar with the SQL language. It is natural to formulate context queries in an SQL-like format with little learning time required. Judd and Steenkiste (2003) gave an SQL-based solution for querying context. First, they modeled the context into four classes: device, access point, people, and space. Then, they identified the relationships among these context entities to create a relational model. Besides, they annotated context information with four meta-attributes: accuracy, confidence, update time, and sample interval so as to model some quality attributes of context information. Box 1 illustrates a location context query example in an SQL-like style.

PersonLocation is a relation denoting the relationship between people and space. *PersonID* is the ID of a person in the relation *PersonLocation*. A special function of this query is to explicitly require the query execution time to be less than

1 minute. The update time and accuracy requirement of the location data can be proposed as well. To improve the performance of query execution, Judd and Steenkiste stored the intermediate query results and used a query synthesizer to synthesize them.

Madden and Franklin (2002) presented a pioneering method of querying context data from sensor networks. They differentiated between two kinds of queries: push query and pull query. For push query, *"results are pushed from the sensors out toward the user, and are delivered as soon as they become available."* The sensor data received is put into an input queue, and then the data will pass through a filter, and will be put in the output queue only when they satisfy certain query conditions. Yet, pull query requests data to the system and the system responses the request with results. When querying sensor data, push queries can be used, because the sensors transmit data back in a specified interval continuously. When querying people's profiles, pull queries can be used since the context information is static. An example of a push query is in Box 2, in which the average speed of people in cars in specified road segments is requested.

In Box 2 w stands for the window size when calculating the average people's car speed (Madden and Franklin, 2002).

Beyond that, the authors combined push and pull modes in one query to make a join operation. For example, when discovering the average speed of some road segment is lower than a threshold value, one may want to query the incident that

Box 1.

Select	Location
From	PersonLocation
Where	PersonID = John's UID
Require	location.updateTime within 2 minutes of present time location.accuracy within 500 meters of actual location
TimeLimit	1 minute

Box 2.

Select	avg(speed, w)
From	sensorReadings as s
Where	s.segment $\in$ knownSegments

Box 3.

Select	avg(s.speed, w), i.description
From	incidents as I sensorReadings as s
Where	i.time >= now − timeWindow
group by	i.description
having	speedThreshold > (select avg(s.speed, w) from sensorReadings as s where i.segment = s.segment and s.segment $\in$ knownSegments)

happened, as shown by the following query, where relation *incidents* takes the records of incidents that happened in the district.

To improve query performance, the Framework in Java for operators on remote data streams (Fjords) had been exploited for multiple query execution. The experiments have validated this approach.

Here, one big concern with querying sensor data is power consumption of sensor nodes in communication. A mechanism was proposed where some computation such as information aggregation can be done on the sensor nodes, i.e., transmitting less data in the sensor network. Madden *et al.* (2005) studied the mechanism to querying sensor network, resulting in an Acquisitional Query Processing (ACQP) system called *TinyDB*. In ACQP, a semantic routing tree is built to effectively manage the routing and processing queries in wireless sensor networks. Acquisitional issues of communication scheduling, prioritizing data delivery, and adapting transmission rate are considered. ACQP techniques can further decrease the energy consumption in sensor networks.

McFadden and Henricksen (2004) further presented a method called CML to model context. They designed a tool which can map such a model to relational databases automatically. For example, the following is the context model written in CML.

```
CREATE PROFILED TEMPORAL FACT TYPE Per-
sonEngagedInActivity
DEPENDS(PersonLocatedAt)
(
person          personID KEY,
activity        ActivityName
)
```

The above code snippet creates a profiled temporal context type *PersonEngagedInActivity*, which has two attributes *personID* and *Activity-Name*. This snippet in CML is mapped into SQL DDL language as follows.

```
CREATE TABLE          DSTC_PAGE_COMM.
PersonEngagedInActivity
(
person          DSTC_PACE_COMM.PersonID,
activity        DSTC_PACE_COMM.Activity-
Name,
fStartTime              TIMESTAMP,
fEndTime                TIMESTAMP,
PRIMARY                 KEY(person, fstartTime)
)
```

We see that a special characteristic of such a mapping lies in the meta-data generated according to the type of context. It specifies corresponding meta-data with respect to the type of context information. Since *PersonEngagedInActivity* is a temporal context, its start-time *fStartTime* and end-time *fEndTime* are generated. It is difficult to unify all the meta-data that different contexts may have. For this reason, such a mechanism in CML might be useful in modeling different contexts, which do not have the same meta-data.

XML-Based Context Query Mechanism

This kind of context query mechanism is often associated with specific XML schema designed by system designers. Since there are tools for XML parsing, XML-based context queries are more flexible in its schema definition.

Buchholz *et al.* (2004) proposed a context-aware computing architecture, in which CIS (Context-aware Information Services) provides context information for CAS (Context-Aware Services). The context queries are written in an XML format called *CoColanguage*. The underlying model of *CoColanguage* is *CoCoGraph*, which is a subclass of Petri nets. One virtue of the model is that it can represent parallel query processing. In the *CoColanguage*, some basic concepts are defined, including *CI-object* and *CI-factory*. *CI-object* is a context information object, which for each entity describes one specific aspect of the entire context. *CI-factory* is used to request a *CI-object*. *Factory-Node* is the core node of any *CoCoGraph* to represent queries. *Operator-Node* can adapt, select, or aggregate data. *InnerGraph-Node* capsules a part of the *CoCograph*, i.e. *InnerGraph-Node* can contain multiple other nodes to form a combined node. For example, if we want to query the location of a user, whose telephone number is +491789127256, the *Factory-Node* can be written as follows.

```
<factory_node id = "getUserLocation" class = "location">
    <entity class = "user">
        <identity class = "phone_number">+491789127256</identity>
    </entity>
</factory_node>
```

The execution of this query will return a *CI-object* with requested context information in any of the allowed scales. It is constructed as follows.

```
<context_information class = "location">
<entity class="user">
<identity class = "phone_number">+491789127256</identity>
</entity>
<scale class="postal_address">
<street> Oettingentrasse </street>
<number> 67 </number>
<zipcode> 80538 </zipcode>
<city> Munich </city>
<country> Germany </country>
    </scale>
</context_information>
```

Heer *et al.* (2003) leveraged XML to represent both queries and query results. They built a context-aware distributed query execution engine called *liquid*, where they explicitly addressed the way to handle distributed and continuous query processing of context data. An operator tree was also designed to support the query execution logic. Hönle *et al.* (2005) used XML as the query

format to analyze the mechanism of incorporating meta-data of context in query processing.

Ontology-Based Context Query Mechanism

Ontology is suitable for concept definition and interoperation. Some existing ontology languages can be used to query context, such as RDF, DAML+OIL, and OWL. Ontology web language (OWL) is an extension of Resource Description Framework (RDF), and is a revision of DAML+OIL web ontology language. Description Logics (DL) form the formal foundation of OWL, and OWL DL is correspondent to Description Logics. Because of the direct and close relationships among RDF, DAML+OIL, DL, and OWL, they are all regarded as ontology-based here. Originally, Haghighi *et al.* (2006) singled out a kind of context query language named RDF-based language. Since OWL and DL are not limited to RDF, we coin this type of query representation to be ontology-based for generality.

Gu *et al.* (2004a; 2004c) gave an infrastructure for context-aware applications grounded on Open Service Gateway initiative (OSGi), which is an open architecture that deploys different services in local networks. The context information is denoted in first order predicate calculus. For instance, *Location* (*John, bathroom*) denote that John's location is bathroom. They designed a set of procedures and Application Programming Interfaces (APIs) to support context querying and context event subscription. In addition, Service-Oriented Context-Aware Middleware (SOCAM) architecture was also constructed to query both external and internal context information. External context information is obtained from the local system, e.g., weather information from a server on the internet, while internal contexts are obtained directly from local sensors.

The query (*locatedIn John ?x*) to find John's location will be sent to service-locating service (SLS), which will first load the context ontology stored in the database, and then find out the appropriate context service provider that can provide John's location. Query results are returned in OWL language. For example, a query result for John's posture is

```
<socam:Person rdf:about = "john">
    <socam::hasPosture
rdf:resource = "http://lucan.ddns.comp.nus.edu.
sg/octopus
/posture#LIEDOWN">
</socam:Person>
```

Because context information can be either low-level (e.g., raw sensor data) or high-level (e.g., location and activity of a person), and high-level context information can be inferred from low-level context information, Gu *et al.* emphasized the context reasoning function within their infrastructure, where context reasoning can be fulfilled in such two ways as ontology-based reasoning and user-defined rule-based reasoning.

An ontology reasoning rule example is:

(?a rdfs:subClassOf ?b),(?b rdfs:subClassOf ?c)→(?a rdfs:subClassOf ?c)

A user-defined rule example is:

(?user rdf:type Elderly) ∧ (?user locatedIn Bedroom) ∧ (?user hasPosture LieDown) ∧ (Bedroom doorStatus Closed) ∧ (Bedroom lightLevel low) → (?user status Sleeping)

Perich *et al.* (2005) used DAML+OIL to express context queries. A context query is modeled as: query = $(O, \sigma, \theta, \sum, \tau)$, where O is a set of used ontologies, σ is a selection list, θ is a filtering statement, $\sum$ is the cardinality, and τ is temporal constraints. User profiles can be incorporated to improve the effectiveness of caching in query processing.

Furthermore, Description Logics can also be used as a presentation language for context to describe context-aware database queries under the specified grammar and semantics (van Bunningen, 2006b), and can be easily transformed into other context presentation methods.

Programming-Based Context Query Mechanism

Some researchers designed new programming languages to support context queries. Cohen *et al.* (2002) proposed a programming language called *iQL* to compose context data. It can realize the querying of context information, and directly write program to derive high-level context information from low-level context data. In addition, it can define data types, and compose context data into high-level information. In *iQL*, context data sources can include active context sources and passive context sources. Passive context sources supply context data only upon request. Active context sources get an initiative signal and then push the context data in a stream to the subscriber. Hybrid data sources are those that not only supply context data upon request, but also push context data stream. For example, the following programming segment is to query nearby employees whose physical distances are not greater than a threshold.

```
type Point { double x; double y; }
type EmployeeID
schema("http://acmebadges.com/empID");
type BadgeAd
schema("http://acmebadges.com/badgeAd");

boolean function withinDistance
(Point p1, Point p2, double distance) {
double dx is p2.x - p1.x;
double dy is p2.y - p1.y;
output dx*dx + dy*dy <= distance*distance;
}
```

```
list(EmployeeID) composer function AllNearbyEm-
ployees
(EmployeeID myID, double threshold) {

tagged(EmployeeID) myTaggedID is
input(BadgeAd ba:
ba.empID=myID && ba.tagged="yes");

BadgeAd myAd is myTaggedID.source;
Point myPoint is myAd.coordinates;

list(EmployeeID) nearbyIDs is
input every
( BadgeAd ba:
withinDistance
(ba.coordinates, myPoint, threshold) );

output nearbyIDs;
}
```

The data type *Point* is defined in the program, while data type *EmployeeID* and *BadgeAd* are defined in external schemas. A context composer function *AllNearbyEmployees* is implemented to return a list of *EmployeeID,* whose distance to *myID* is within the threshold, as measured by function *withinDistance.*

Graphical Context Query Mechanism

Another type of context query language is graphical-based. To query information in location-based applications, Rahman and Bhalla (2005) added a *spatial condition* entry to the traditional Query-by-Example (QBE) language. It looks like relational tables, where users fill in a blank cell with what they know, and the program will supply the required information satisfying users' query conditions. The *spatial condition* cell is used for the entry of geographic conditions. For instance, a user may query the buildings that are less than 100 meters from the building where the user is located by entering their *spatial condition.* Polyviou *et al.* (2004) also proposed a graphical context query-ing mechanism called *query-by-browsing.* The context information is organized in a folder-like hierarchy. Users can browse context information by clicking on the folders. The folders' attributes stand for the meta-data of the context. Graphical representation of query and query results is more suitable for the users who are not system designer or technical person, as this kind of query languages may be easier for them to learn.

API-Based Context Query Mechanism

The last mechanism for context querying is to directly develop some specific APIs. These APIs can be used as libraries by existing programming languages, such as Java. Context information can be queried through prepared APIs. In SQL-based context queries, we know that McFadden and Henricksen (2004) used CML to define the schema of context data. They in fact also used APIs to query context information and provided APIs in their context management tools.

Comparison of Different Context Query Mechanisms

Before comparing different context query mechanisms, we need first look at what is needed by a system that queries context information in a mobile and ubiquitous environment. According to the context properties - "dynamic vs. static, continuous data streams, metadata of context (i.e. QoC, temporal), and spatial situations", Haghighi *et al.* (2006) compared different context-aware systems in context modeling. Beyond that, we provide some other aspects that are important for executing a context query. The first is the support for context reasoning. The context information provided by sensors is often low-level raw information, and could not satisfy a user's need for high-level context information. For example, the sensors may only sense the number of people at a meeting room and the state of the projector, but the user may want to know whether a meeting is being held at the meeting room. The second is the support for handling heterogeneity of context data. The context information provided by the provider may be different from what is requested by the target system. For example, the context provider may supply the context information through web services, say in the SOAP protocol, while the application may query the context in the format of an ontology instance stored in a context database. More important, suitable users should be considered for each query mechanism when building a query system. As a result, we evaluate different context querying mechanisms based on such criteria as *support for context reasoning, support for handling context heterogeneity,* and *suitable user* (Table 1).

The SQL-based context query mechanism is close to SQL language, and many techniques used here are analogues to the techniques in relational databases. However, little work has been done in the SQL-based context query mechanism to support context reasoning and handling context heterogeneity. The SQL-based mechanism is suitable for both system developers and end users.

XML is a useful data format to store and exchange context information. So the XML-based mechanism can help handle the heterogeneity caused by network transmission. However, existing work so far provides no specific support for context reasoning. This mechanism is primarily used by system developers. To implement the XML-based context querying mechanism, it is often required to define context XML schema by system designers. Thus, different system designers might design different schemas, hindering the reuse of context schemas.

Ontology can easily be shared by users, and can effectively support context reasoning. The heterogeneity among different ontologies can be handled through ontology mapping, but little work has been done to handle the heterogeneity between ontology and other context formats. This mechanism may be appropriate for system developers and end users.

The programming-based context querying mechanism language is efficient to express context composition logic. It can be primarily used by system developers who are mastery of programming. The context reasoning and context heterogeneity handling can be achieved by the user program if the language is expressive enough.

The graphical-based context query mechanism is not expressive enough for technical professionals in some aspects, but it can give non-pro-

Table 1. Comparisons of different context querying mechanisms

Context Querying Mechanism	Support for Context Reasoning	Support for Handling Heterogeneity	Suitable User
SQL-based	No specific support	No specific support	System developer, end user
XML-based	No specific support	Decrease heterogeneity caused by network transmission	System developer
Ontology-based	Good reasoning support	Handle heterogeneity among different ontologies through ontology mapping	System developer, end user
Programming-based	Through User program	Through User program	System developer
Graphical	No specific support	No specific support	End user
API-based	No specific support	No specific support	System developer

fessionals an easy-to-use interface. No specific support has been provided for context reasoning and context heterogeneity handling.

The API-based context query mechanism is flexible and ad-hoc, and can be invoked in an embedded way. It is easier to be integrated into existing programs. This method may be primarily used by system developers. Also no specific work has been done within this mechanism to support context reasoning and context heterogeneity handling.

In addition, some critical techniques are to be considered in representing and processing context queries. These techniques include representing meta-data of the context, discriminating push query and pull query, managing internal and external context sources, distributed query execution, and caching intermediary query results. Although not all of these context querying techniques are implemented in one single research work described previously, it would be helpful to extend a certain context querying mechanism with corresponding techniques when necessary. Many query execution mechanisms in context querying are generally based on existing database techniques. For space reason, the chapter introduces each kind of context query only in a brief manner. As for the specific implementation details, interested readers may refer to the corresponding literature.

Effect of Context upon Traditional Database Query Processing

After acquiring context information, another important job for context-aware database querying is to examine the context's influence upon traditional database query processing. An investigation of the effect of context on the traditional database querying will help application designers uncover the most effective way to use context in their applications. According to different functionalities of context, Feng *et al.* presented five strategies to take context into account (Feng, Apers, &

Jonker, 2004). They are: 1) context as present on-the-spot query condition; 2) context as past recall-based query condition/target; 3) context as query constraint; 4) context as criteria for query result measurement; and 5) context as guide to query result delivery. Although these strategies well reflect the functions of contexts in a query, their discussions still remained at a high abstract level. Later, van Bunningen (2004) categorized the ways of using context into three groups, i.e., query augmentation; placing triggers on context; and using the context for retrieval purpose.

By taking into account the recent research advances in context-aware querying, we provide a more comprehensive categorization which includes: 1) *query reformulation*, 2) *query augmentation with query meta-data*, 3) *query trigger*, and 4) *result delivery guide*.

Query Reformulation

Query reformulation works in structured, semi-structured or unstructured query domains, where context is interpreted and mapped to a query request. Some researchers (Feng *et al.*, 2004; Iftikhar, *et al.*, 2006) proposed approaches of query reformulation by instantiating context variables and integrating them into context-aware queries. This is formulated as $CQ(db; [Context]) \rightarrow A$, where CQ denotes a context-aware query, db denotes the database, and A denotes the query result. In contrast, a non-context-aware database query is in the form of $NCQ(db) \rightarrow A$, where NCQ denotes a non-context-aware database query. For example, given a relation *Flight* in Table 2, suppose that we want to query the earliest departure time of the flight from AMS to ADP which is at least 3 hours from now. The query can be represented as follows.

SELECT   MIN(departureTime) FROM Flight
WHERE   origin= 'AMS' AND destination= 'ADP'
        AND departureTime $>_{time}$ ($time $+_{time}$ 3:00)

Table 2. The relation Flight

oid	flightNumber	Origin	destination	departureTime	price
5	91	BRU	ADP	8:00	180
4	89	AMS	ADP	21:00	200
3	88	AMS	ADP	13:00	280
2	87	AMS	ADP	10:00	280
1	86	AMS	ADP	7:00	234

where $time is the context variable to be instantiated at run-time, representing the current time when the query is issued.

Iftikhar *et al.* (2006) presented another method for query reformulation using domain ontology. Suppose Mary wants to find a place for lunch. The original query in SQL is:

```
SELECT          *
FROM    restaurant r, facility f, offer o
WHERE   f.lable = 'lunch' AND r.restaurantid =
o.restaurantid
AND o.facilityid =f.facilityid;
```

The context data is obtained from sensors and user's profile, and combined to retain only the relevant context information, which is "Mary is hosting a business lunch at Greendam, Down Town; consisting of 5 persons; on Monday; at 14:00:00" in this example. Based on it, the original query will be reformulated into a new query as follows:

```
SELECT *
FROM    restaurant r, businessfacility f, offer o, ad-
dress a,
lunchperiod p, seating s
WHERE   f.lable = 'businesslunch'  AND  p.stophour
> 14:0:0
AND s.availableseating = 5         AND  a.street=
'Down Town'
AND a.city = 'Greendam'            AND  p.day  =
'Monday'
AND f. businessfacilitytid = o.businessfacilityid
AND o.restaurantid = r.restaurantid
AND r.restaurantid = a.restaurantid
AND a.restaurantid = p.restaurantid
AND p.restaurantid = s.restaurantid;
```

Along with the database field, context-aware retrieval technologies developed in the information retrieval field (Bhogal, *et al.*, 2007; Hattori, *et al.*, 2006; Hattori, 2007; Jones & Brown, 2003) might also be used to database querying. Liaqaut *et al.* (2006) gave an ontology-based context mapping strategy, which can map properties from user's role to query schema. For instance, a lessee wants to search for some information of rental properties with an initial query for accommodation. Through the role ontology of lessee, we know there is an attribute "location" of accommodation. There is also a linkage between "location" and lessee. Then we can map the location of the lessee to the location of the accommodation he wants to rend. Suppose his location is New York, then the query can be reformulated to "accommodation in New York". The query reformulation can also be done by means of an SQL query. With the same example, the initial query can be written as: SELECT * FROM ACCOMMODATION, which is reformulated into: SELECT * FROM ACCOMMODATION WHERE LOCATION='New York'.

Although using context information can make the query system more usable, identifying which context to be augmented in a query and how to automatically augment this context is not trivial, except that all are fixed in very limited domains. Further studies on ontology mapping might give promising approaches to solve this problem.

Query Augmentation with Query Meta-Data

Another impact on database querying is that context can be used to express some meta-data that the query users are concerned about the underlying databases, e.g., users' query preferences about database data in the most recent research. van Bunningen *et al.* (2007) described approaches of ranking database query results according to context-aware preferences. The context-aware preference of a user is generated by the context and the user's query history. For example, "when the user is relaxing in the morning, which TV program would he prefer?" This question can be answered by calculating the preference for each TV program. First, TV program data is annotated with a preference score of a value in [0,1], and this score is associated with some specific context. Suppose that under the context "relax in the morning", the preference score for Channel 5 TV program is 0.9 and the preference score for Channel 9 is 0.2. Then Channel 5 TV program will be ranked higher than Channel 9 for the TV program query. Based on this principle, van Bunningen *et al.* extended the traditional statistical model of information retrieval by adding the effect of context, denoting the probability that a database tuple d satisfying a query Q for user u_{sit} in a certain context as $P(D{=}d \mid Q{=}q \wedge U{=}u_{sit})$.

In the same line, Stefanidis *et al.* (2005; 2006; 2007a; 2007b) added context to query preferences, where the associations between context-dependent preferences and database relations are stored explicitly. Let c_i denote a context parameter, and A_i denote a set of non-context parameters. Preference is represented as a quantity within [0,1] named *interest_score*. Then *basic preference*, i.e. the preference with only one context parameter can be represented in the form of *preference* $(c_i, A_{k+1}, \dots, A_n) = interest\_score_i$, denoting that preference for non-context parameters $A_{k+1}, \dots, A_n$ under context c_i is *interest_score*$_i$. For example, suppose location is a context parameter, and Mary's preference for restaurant R at location L is 0.8. This can be denoted as *preference* (R, L, Mary) = 0.8. When there is a set of context parameters $\{c_1, \dots, c_k\}$, the preference can be represented as *preference* $(c_1, \dots, c_k, A_{k+1}, \dots, A_n) = interest\_score_i$, indicating the preference for non-context parameters $A_{k+1}, \dots, A_n$ under contexts $c_1, \dots, c_k$ is *interest_score*$_i$. This kind of preference is called aggregate preference. For storage reduction reason, only basic preferences need to be stored; leaving aggregate preferences calculated by a function of basic preferences. The calculation function is actually a sum of basic preferences, multiplied by weights, and the weight values are input by users. Their formula for calculating aggregate is *interest score* = $w_1 \times$ *interest score*$_1$ + ... + $w_k \times$ *interest_score*$_k$. For example, if *preference* (L, R, Mary) = 0.8 and *preference*(*warm*, R, Mary) = 0.9 for Mary, weight of location will be 0.6 and weight of weather is 0.4. The interest score of R is $0.6 \times 0.8 + 0.4 \times 0.9 = 0.84$. That is, *preference*($L$, *warm*, R, Mary) = 0.84.

When preference is obtained, it can be used when users access the databases. The system looks for the values of context parameters when the query is issued, and then ranks the requested data according to the preferences. Moreover, context can be organized in a hierarchy. For example, location can be represented in country, city, or region, with country at the highest level, city the next, and region the lowest level, because a country has multiple cities, and a city has multiple regions. Regarding the hierarchical structure of context, Stefanidis *et al.* suggested to express the preferences in multiple dimensions, modeled by data cube, where operations such as Slice, Dice,

Roll-up, and Drill-down can be easily implemented (Stefanidis *et al.* 2007a; 2007b).

Note that it is necessary to calculate the aggregate preferences during query execution, but this will definitely incur some extra computing. To speed up query processing, Stefanidis *et al.* proposed to cache the results of former executed queries, including the aggregate preference values and already ordered query results. Suppose a user has executed a query to select restaurants with the context parameters "location = *L*" and "weather = *warm*". Next time when the user wants to find the same information under the same context, the system will fetch the results directly from a cache of a *context tree* structure. Even if there is no exactly the same context path that the current query demands, similar context path can be used for approximation. Apart from that, Stefanidis *et al.* suggested that context parameters with small domain cardinality should be put at a high level closer to the root in the context tree, as this can decrease the size of the context tree which has to be maintained.

In EdFest system, Norrie *et al.* (2007) built a content publishing framework called XCM (eXtensible Context Management System). XCM tags content information (data to be queried) with metadata called "format characteristic". Then a match algorithm is used to select the best content variant according to the current context and deliver the content variant to the client.

In fact, some other meta-data can also be conveyed through context, such as the confidentiality level of data. While the company's news information is open to the public, its financial information may not be allowed to be queried, as the confidential level of financial information is higher than that of company's news information in a public space context domain.

Query Trigger

Context can be used as a trigger of certain database queries. For example, when someone enters the room, the computing environment will detect this context event and trigger a query to find the user's profile. It can also trigger other actions like turning on the light or starting an alarm. van Bunningen *et al.* (2006b) demonstrated that the trigger itself can be a query upon context conditions, and its activation depends on whether the query result is empty or not. Through Description Logics, triggering a signal when Mary is in *room_a* could be

$$Trigger = \exists hasLocation.\{room\_a\} \sqcap \{Mary\}$$

This trigger can be transformed into a query request over the context database. For instance, we can store a relation hasLocation(person, location) in the context database, and the content of the relation is refreshed when Mary enters *room_a*. If the query result of "SELECT * from hasLocation where person = 'Mary' and location = 'room_a'" is empty, a record insertion operation will be automatically executed.

Result Delivery Guide

The fourth influence of context is on query result delivery. Query results can be delivered through different output modalities with different formats and contents, depending on the specific context (Feng *et al.*, 2004). For example, when a user is driving a car, the query results can be delivered in an audio format rather than on screen. A user with a small PDA often prefers to see query results of large size. According to the screen size of the display, we can consider to output the most important result items to users, since in many cases users can get most value from a subpart of information. For example, suppose a user wants to query the information of a downloadable game via a cell phone. Let the relation of game information be *Game_info(game_name, charge_fee, producer, version, type, figure_in_game)* and the order of the importance degree to the user is *game_name > charge_fee > type > producer >*

figure_in_game > version. Here, $A > B$ means A is more important than B to the user. When the user requests the information, only the highly-ranked attributes and their values will be transferred and displayed on the screen. If the user also wants to see some other information, s/he may either scroll the window or go to a new window for the rest of information (Qiao, Feng, & Zhou, 2008).

Not only the screen size, but also other factors like network bandwidth can influence the query result presentation. For example, in a wireless network where the network condition is more unstable than the wired network, adapting the information contents to the network condition will help users obtain part of important information with acceptable waiting time. In a context-aware service demo named POIsmart, Agostini, Bettini & Riboni (2005) used the context of network bandwidth to adapt the query delivery manner. For example, when the network bandwidth is low, only text and small images are shown on the mobile device. Mechanisms like this will facilitate information acquisition process across different hardware devices and network conditions.

Discussion

In this section, the criteria we used for comparing the four kinds of effects of context on traditional database querying is actually the position of such effect. As shown in Figure 1, in traditional database querying, the query is processed and delivered directly as the upper part of the figure. Query reformulation and meta-data generation take place in the query processing. And the former is to prepare the adaptive query and the latter is to prepare the adaptive data source. Guide of query result delivery takes place between query processing and final result delivery. Trigger gives the bridge between context data and actions.

Context-Aware Querying under Imperfect Context

Context information obtained is likely imperfect due to several possible reasons.

(1) *Context aging.* Some context possess temporal-spatial feature, and may be valid within a limited period, e.g., the location information

Figure 1. Effects of context on traditional database querying

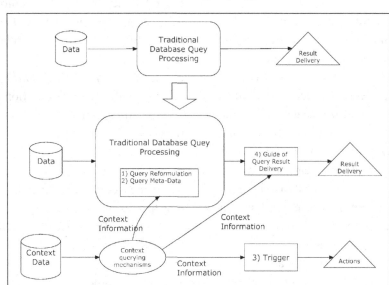

provided by mobile device when the user is moving, the dynamically changing temperature data and light data from sensors. Of course there are also some types of context data that are relatively stable, e.g., one's birthday and birthplace.

(2) *Uncertain context.* Sensed context information is often inaccurate or unavailable as a result of noise or sensor failures, and user-supplied information is subject to problems such as human error and staleness (Henricksen & Indulska, 2004). For derived context information, the inference may be inaccurate, e.g., sometimes we can only say it has the probability of 0.9 that Mary is at a certain room. All these factors contribute to context uncertainty in the end.

Hunter (1996) identified four types of information in a database in terms of uncertainty, and these types are also suitable for context data as well. 1) The context information is accurate when all incorrect information is absent and all expected information is present; 2) the context information is incomplete when all incorrect information is absent and some expected information is absent; 3) the context information is incompatible when some incorrect information is present and all expected information is present; and 4) the context information is approximate when some incorrect information is present and some expected information is absent.

(3) *Imprecise context.* Imprecise context is closely related to uncertain context, and may be regarded as incompleteness of the user's expected information. Here, we take imprecise context as a separate type of imperfection, because sometimes imprecise context does not mean that we lack some parts of the information. It might be correct at a given scale, but lack of precision. For example, if a GPS system can provide the location within 10 meters, it would be sufficient to locate a university, but insufficient to locate more specific location of the object in the scope of a small room, such as whether the cup is on the table.

When querying context information, context imperfection often makes users confused

whether such information can be used and how it can be used. Context imperfection will make it more difficult to leverage context information to achieve context-awareness when querying database information. In the following, we report some research that has been done in context-aware querying under imperfect context.

Querying Imperfect Context Information

One typical method of handling imperfect context information is to improve it by cleaning or filtering the context data (Bai, *et al.*, 2006; Elnahrawy & Nath, 2003; Jeffery, *et al.*, 2006a; Jeffery, *et al.*, 2006b), or making data fusion (Pfeifer, 2004). Another method is to model the imperfection and notify such information to the query issuer. To dispose aging context information, Schmidt (2004; 2006) suggested using aging function to annotate context data as additional schema-level information. If c is a context fact; f is a context feature; t is the time the context fact is added; α is the probability of validity of context feature f at the point of time t; and t^* is the time when the query is issued, then the confidence for c at t^* can be calculated as: $confidence(c, t^*) := [A(f)](t^* - t) \cdot \alpha$ with $A(f)$ denoting the aging function associated with the context feature. Gu *et al.* (2004b) extended the ontology-based model of context to express uncertainty, where *Prob*(*Status*(Mary. *Sleeping*)) = 0.8 means the probability that John is currently sleeping is 0.8. They defined two classes *PriorProb* and *CondProb* in OWL: the prior probability and conditional probability of context information. For example, $P(A)=0.7$ is represented as follows.

```
<prob.PriorProb rdf:ID = "P(A)">
    <prob:hasVariable><rdf:value>A</rdf:value></prob:hasVariable>
    <prob:hasProbValue>0.7</prob:hasProbValue>
</prob:PriorProb>
```

$P(A|B)=0.5$ is represented as follows:

```
<prob:CondProb rdf:ID="P(A|B)">
    <prob:hasCond><rdf:value>B</rdf:value></
prob:hasCond>
    <prob:hasVariable><rdf:value>A</rdf:value></
prob:hasVariable>
    <prob:hasProbValue>0.5</prob:hasProbValue>
</prob:CondProb>
```

Such a representation in ontology also facilitates the reasoning of uncertain context. Gu *et al.* exploited the use of Bayesian Network to do reasoning. In a similar way, Ranganathan *et al.* (2004) modeled the probability of context in predicate and presented them in DAML+OIL. They conducted context reasoning using probabilistic logic, fuzzy logic, and Bayesian Networks. van Bunningen *et al.* (2006a) modeled uncertain context in Description Logics with event probabilities, and introduced the operations upon event probabilities.

Antifakos *et al.* (2004) evaluated the effect of context uncertainty via a feedback mechanism for context-aware systems. They conducted two user studies to mimic memory aid. In the first experiment, they let users see some numbers, and then let them remember those numbers. The memory aid will give some clues, but the clues are not all correct. Therefore, the uncertainty of the clues is displayed in the meantime. In the second experiment, they replaced the numbers with real objects. By varying the uncertainty of the clues, they found that human performance in a memory task is increased by explicitly displaying uncertainty information.

Querying Database Information under Imperfect Context

As mentioned previously, context can influence reformulation of query, augment of query with some meta-data like query preferences, trigger placement on query, and delivery manner of query results. A kind of interesting problems is to query traditional databases with imperfect context in-

formation. By analyzing users' preferences over traditional databases under specified context, van Bunningen *et al.* (2007) discussed the effect of the uncertainty of context, and calculated users' preferences and database records' ranking when context is annotated with a certain probability.

Discussion

The imperfection of context data is a frequently encountered problem in a mobile and ubiquitous computing environment. Generally, to handle data imperfection, more semantics need to be added to context data model. By coming up with a better mathematical model of imperfect context, we can then utilize the context information more effectively. However, sometimes if we want to make the context information more perfect, more sensors, more computing resources and more network bandwidth are needed. So, a balance should be considered between cost and benefit at this situation.

FUTURE TRENDS

We identify some potential research questions to be addressed in order to deliver context-aware database querying solutions. Some of them have already been tackled by the academic community, but still need further investigation in depth. Some questions are at the starting stage with limited literature, and may become future research topics.

Context-Aware Database Querying Platform

The context-aware applications need the data management support. Although many context-aware systems embed the context query function, the work on constructing a platform that is specially for context-aware database querying is inadequate. Constructing such a platform to examine the effect and performance of the above context-aware querying strategies is desirable and important. Apparently, context acquisition, context reasoning, query reformulation, query processing, and query output are indispensable components of such a platform. This is especially useful for outdoor work or in the situation where users need to move around, e.g., querying with mobile devices in a restaurant, querying in a tour guide application, and guide maintenance applications.

In addition, adding the function of managing context history may make context-aware querying more effective. We are now building such a component, which models the context history like the memories of human brains. It is our hope to make the platform know the context, think and behave like humans. In this way, we will not communicate with a dull computing program any more, instead of a system that responds like a professional expert who knows the needs of people. Some of our design principles are proposed here.

First, the architecture of the component can be analogous to a human brain. There are short term memories, long term memory, explicit memory, and implicit memory (Dubin, 2002) in the database management system.

Second, the data access strategy can be an integration of a direct access and a priming access. When the system is idle, previous less-precisely or unanswered queries can still be executed in a "roaming" way.

Third, the computer can have "attentions" and "emotions" to select information to store and retrieve. The aim is to let the platform focus on the most useful context information when hardware resources are limited.

Fourth, the encoding mechanism can be used in the platform to compress the context information received, such as visionary and auditory information. Current neuroscience is uncovering the mystery of memory encoding mechanism in the human brain. Recently, the biologist Tsien (2007) and his research team have found out that memory impulse is in a "neural cliques" form and the memory is organized in an abstract hierarchy; and the memory features in such a hierarchy can be coded in a certain way. Such a mechanism may be used for organization of context information on this context-aware querying platform.

Measurement of Context's Effect on Querying Results

Recent research focuses on query reformulation or preference inference under a given context. However, does the information returned really satisfy users' needs under the acquired context? When context is used to reformulate the query to provide more personalized query results, we might be eager to know the following questions: How many kinds of context information do we need to get the information we are concerned about? How much precision should the context information have in order to deliver useful query results to the user? The quantitative analysis should be done to answer these questions based on the context's effect on query results, e.g., the size of query results. Answering these questions will not only decrease the intense of computing by eliminating the context information that unrelated to the user's need, but also make query results more accurate.

Querying Result Presentation

Selection of appropriate device, presentation style and content for query output according to context are also important for users (Feng *et al.*, 2004). So far there is some literature to explore this aspect. This could be an interesting issue to pursue.

CONCLUSION

In a mobile and ubiquitous computing environment, database querying must be context-aware. In this chapter, we have provided a survey of context-aware database querying techniques. Three aspects of context-aware database querying have been discussed: querying mechanisms upon context data, the effects of context on traditional database querying, context-aware querying under imperfect context. The ways to query context data are classified into six categories: SQL-based, XML-based, ontology-based, programming-based, graphical, and API-based context querying. The effects of context on database querying are expounded in four classes: query reformulation, query augment with meta-data, trigger placement on query, and guide of query result delivery. We also discuss some potential research trends at the end of the chapter.

ACKNOWLEDGMENT

We thank the National Natural Science Foundation of China (60773156) for supporting this work.

REFERENCES

Agostini, A., Bettini, C., & Riboni, D. (2005). Demo: Ontology-based context-aware delivery of extended points of interest. *The 6th International Conference on Mobile Data Management,* (pp. 322-323).

Antifakos, S., Schwaninger, A., & Schiele, B. (2004). Evaluating the effects of displaying uncertainty in context-aware applications. *The Sixth International Conference on Ubiquitous Computing (Ubicomp),* (pp. 54-69).

Barbará, D. (1999). Mobile Computing and Database-A Survey. *IEEE Transactions on Knowledge and Data Engineering, 11*(1), 108-117.

Bai, Y., Wang, F., & Liu, P. (2006). Efficiently filtering RFID data streams. *CleanDB Workshop,* (pp. 50-57).

Bhogal, J., Macfarlane, A., & Smith, P. (2007). A review of ontology based query expansion. *Information Processing & Management, 43*(4), 866-886.

Buchholz, T., Krause, M., Linnhoff-Popien, C., & Schiffers, M. (2004). CoCo: Dynamic composition of context information. *The First Annual International Conference on Mobile and Ubiquitous Systems: Networking and Services (MOBIQUITOUS 2004),* (pp. 335-343).

Cohen, N. H., Lei, H., Castro, P., Davis II, J. S., & Purakayastha, A. (2002). Composing pervasive data using iQL. *The Fourth IEEE Workshop on Mobile Computing Systems and Applications,* (pp. 94-104).

Dey, A. K., & Abowd, G. D. (2000). *Towards a better understanding of context and context-awareness.* Paper presented at the CHI 2000 Workshop on the What, Who, Where, When, Why and How of Context-Awareness.

Dubin, M. W. (2002). *How the brain works.* Blackwell Science, Inc.

Elnahrawy, E., & Nath, B. (2003). Cleaning and querying noisy sensors. *The 2nd ACM International Conference on Wireless Sensor Networks and Applications,* (pp. 78-87).

Feng, L., Apers, P., & Jonker, W. (2004). Towards context-aware data management for ambient intelligence. *The 15th International Conference on Database and Expert Systems Applications (DEXA),* (pp. 422-431).

Gu, T., Pung, H. K., & Zhang, D. Q. (2004a). Toward an OSGi-based infrastructure for context-aware applications. *Pervasive Computing, IEEE, 3*(4), 66-74.

Gu, T., Pung, H. K., & Zhang, D. Q. (2004b). A Bayesian approach for dealing with uncertain contexts. Paper presented at the Second International Conference on Pervasive Computing.

Gu, T., Pung, H. K., & Zhang, D. Q. (2004c). A middleware for building context-aware mobile services. The *59th Vehicular Technology Conference, IEEE,* (pp. 2656-2660).

Haghighi, P. D., Zaslavsky, A. B., & Krishnaswamy, S. (2006). An evaluation of query languages for context-aware computing. *The 17th International Conference on Database and Expert Systems Applications (DEXA),* (pp. 455-462).

Hattori, S., Tezuka, T., & Tanaka, K. (2007). Context-aware query refinement for mobile web search. *The 2007 International Symposium on Applications and the Internet Workshops (SAINTW),* (pp. 15-15).

Hattori, S., Tezuka, T., & Tanaka, K. (2006). Activity-based query refinement for context-aware information retrieval. *ICADL 2006, LNCS 4312,* (pp. 474-477).

Heer, J., Newberger, A., Beckmann, C., & Hong, J. I. (2003). Liquid: Context-aware distributed queries. *Proceedings of 5th International Conference on Ubiquitous Computing (Ubicomp 2003),* (pp. 140-148).

Henricksen, K., & Indulska, J. (2004). Modelling and using imperfect context information. *The Second IEEE Annual Conference on Pervasive Computing and Communications Workshops (PERCOMW),* (pp. 33-37).

Hönle, N., Kappeler, U. P., Nicklas, D., Schwarz, T., & Grossmann, M. (2005). Benefits of integrating meta data into a context model. *The 2nd IEEE PerCom Workshop on Context Modeling and Reasoning (CoMoRea)(at PerCom'05),* (pp. 25-29).

Hunter, A. (1996). *Uncertainty in information systems: An introduction to techniques and applications.* The McGraw-Hill Companies.

Iftikhar, N., Liaquat, H., & Qadir, M. A. (2006). Profile based context-aware query processing architecture. *Multitopic Conference, 2006. INMIC '06.* (pp. 250-254).

Jeffery, S. R., Alonso, G., Franklin, M. J., Hong, W., & Widom, J. (2006a). Declarative support for sensor data cleaning. *The 4th International Conference on Pervasive Computing,* Dublin, Ireland. (pp. 83-100).

Jeffery, S. R., Alonso, G., Franklin, M. J., Hong, W., & Widom, J. (2006b). A pipelined framework for online cleaning of sensor data streams. *The 22nd International Conference on Data Engineering (ICDE'06),* (pp. 140-140).

Jones, G. J. F., & Brown, P. J. (2003). Context-aware retrieval for ubiquitous computing environments. *Mobile HCI Workshop on Mobile and Ubiquitous Information,* (pp. 227-243).

Judd, G., & Steenkiste, P. (2003). Providing contextual information to pervasive computing applications. *The First IEEE International Conference on Pervasive Computing and Communications (PerCom 2003).* (pp. 133-142).

Liaqaut, H., Iftikhar, N., & Qadir, M. A. (2006). Context aware information retrieval using role ontology and query schemas. *Multitopic Conference, 2006. INMIC '06.* (pp. 244-249).

Madden, S., & Franklin, M. J. (2002). Fjording the stream: An architecture for queries over streaming sensor data. *The 18th International Conference on Data Engineering.* (pp. 555-566).

Madden, S. R., Franklin, M. J., Hellerstein, J. M., & Hong, W. (2005). TinyDB: An acquisitional query processing system for sensor networks. *ACM Transactions on Database Systems (TODS), 30*(1), 122-173.

McFadden, T., Henricksen, K., & Indulska, J. (2004). Automating context-aware application development. *UbiComp 1st International Workshop on Advanced Context Modelling, Reasoning and Management,* (pp. 90-95).

Norrie, M. C., Signer, B., Grossniklaus, M., Belotti, R., Decurtins, C., & Weibel, N. (2007). Context-aware platform for mobile data management. *Wireless Networks, 13*(6), 855-870.

Perich, F., Joshi, A., Finin, T., & Yesha, Y. (2004). On data management in pervasive computing environments. *IEEE Transactions on Knowledge and Data Engineering, 16*(5), 621-634.

Perich, F., Joshi, A., Yesha, Y., & Finin, T. (2005). Collaborative joins in a pervasive computing environment. *The International Journal on Very Large Data Bases, 14*(2), 182-196.

Pfeifer, T. (2004). Redundancy vs. imperfect positioning for context-dependent services. Paper presented at the 1st International Workshop on Advanced Context Modeling, Reasoning, and Management (UbiComp 2004).

Polyviou, S., Evripidou, P., & Samaras, G. (2004). Context-aware queries using query by browsing and chiromancer. Paper presented at the Second International Conference on Pervasive Computing.

Qiao, L., Feng, L., & Zhou, L. (2008). Information presentation on mobile devices: Techniques and practices. Paper presented at the 10th Asia-Pacific Web Conference (APWeb 2008).

Rahman, S. A., & Bhalla, S. (2005). Supporting spatial data queries for mobile services. *The 2005 IEEE/WIC/ACM International Conference on Web Intelligence (WI'05P),* (pp. 696-699).

Ranganathan, A., Al-Muhtadi, J., & Campbell, R. (2004). Reasoning about uncertain contexts in pervasive computing environments. *Pervasive Computing, IEEE, 3*(2), 62-70.

Schmidt, A. (2004). Management of dynamic and imperfect user context information. *On the Move to Meaningful Internet Systems 2004: OTM 2004 Workshops,* (pp. 779-786).

Schmidt, A. (2006). Ontology-based user context management: The challenges of imperfection and time-dependence. *On the Move to Meaningful Internet Systems,* (pp. 995-1011).

Stefanidis, K., Pitoura, E., & Vassiliadis, P. (2005). On supporting context-aware preferences in relational database systems. Paper presented at the First International Workshop on Managing Context Information in Mobile and Pervasive Environments.

Stefanidis, K., Pitoura, E., & Vassiliadis, P. (2006). Modeling and storing context-aware preferences. *10th East European Conference on Advances in Databases and Information Systems (ADBIS 2006). Thessaloniki, Greece,* (pp. 124-140).

Stefanidis, K., Pitoura, E., & Vassiliadis, P. (2007a). Adding context to preferences. The 23rd International Conference on Data Engineering(ICDE), (pp. 846-855).

Stefanidis, K., Pitoura, E. & Vassiliadis, P. (2007b). A context-aware preference database system. *International Journal of Pervasive Computing and Communications*, 3(4), 439-460.

Tsien, J. (2007). The memory code. *Scientific American Magazine, 297*(1), 52-59.

van Bunningen, A. H. (2004). *Context aware querying: Challenges for data management in ambient intelligence.* (Tech. Rep. No. TR-CTIT-04-51). The Netherlands: University of Twente.

van Bunningen, A. H., Feng, L., & Apers, P. M. G. (2006a). Modeling uncertain context information via event probabilities. *The Second Twente Data Management Workshop TDM'06,* (pp. 25-32).

van Bunningen, A. H., Feng, L., & Apers, P. M. G. (2006b). A context-aware preference model for database querying in an ambient intelligent environment. *The 17th International Conference on Database and Expert Systems Applications (DEXA)*, (pp. 33-43).

van Bunningen, A. H., Fokkinga, M. M., Apers, P. M. G., & Feng, L. (2007). Ranking query results using context-aware preferences. *First International Workshop on Ranking in Databases,* (pp. 269-276).

KEY TERMS

Context: The context is any information that can be used to characterize the situation of an entity. An entity is a person, place, or object that is considered relevant to the interaction between a user and an application, including the user and applications themselves (Dey *et al.*, 2000).

Context-Awareness: A system is context-aware if it uses context to provide relevant information and/or services to the user, where relevancy depends on the user's task (Dey *et al.*, 2000).

Context-Aware Database Query: A database query whose query results are influenced by the context under which the query is issued.

Imperfect Context: Imperfect context is the context information which is aging, uncertain, or imprecise.

Preference: Preference is an interest degree on which the user's data choice is based among different data. Preference can be represented in either a qualitative or a quantitative way.

Pull Query: Pull query is the query which requests data from the source, and the source responses to the request with the query result.

Push Query: Push query is the query which sets an initial condition and the query result is returned to the user without being requested as soon as the condition holds.

Query Reformulation: A transformation from user's original query into a more specific one in order to elaborate the user's information need more precisely, taking the context into account.

Query Result Delivery: Query result delivery is the process in which the query result is transferred from the querying system to the user, including the format, transfer, and display of query results.

Query Trigger: An activation of query execution when a specified context condition is reached.

Section III
Context–Aware Mobile Services and Service–Oriented Architectures

Chapter VII
Employing Context Information and Semantics to Advance Responsiveness in Service Composition

Carsten Jacob
Fraunhofer Institute for Open Communication Systems (FOKUS), Germany

Heiko Pfeffer
Fraunhofer Institute for Open Communication Systems (FOKUS), Germany

Stephan Steglich
Technische Universität Berlin, Germany

ABSTRACT

The idea of context-aware services has been around for a long time. The rise of user mobility enabled by well-equipped mobile devices, increasing interconnectedness and available service platforms such as the mobile Web offers new possibilities for context-aware computing, but, at the same time, produces a number of novel challenges. In this chapter, the authors observe current approaches in this active research area, and identify the respective challenges, achievements, and trends. The authors also extend the notion of context-aware services by considering service composition approaches, and present a middleware aiming at the autonomic and context-aware provision of services in mobile peer-to-peer networks. In this regard special attention is paid to a semantic blackboard concept to cache and disseminate context data and a context-aware service composition approach in terms of the identified trends and challenges.

INTRODUCTION

The growing number of well-equipped handheld devices and the increasing mobility of users influence the way today's available services can be used. In this respect context information is one of the key enablers for improving service quality and, at the same time, minimizing complexity for the user. For instance, location-based services automatically utilize the user's location make corresponding adjustments in results. However, apart from location information in infrastructure-based networks, the easy and pervasive use of context data for service provision is still difficult given the lack of sensor interfaces, the limited availability of context sources, and the need for predefined complex descriptions, e.g., specifying user preferences. Indeed, despite the many challenges raised by the consideration of context, such as the need for appropriate sensors and the harmonization of heterogeneous data, the increasing use of context information in the service provision domain clearly shows its importance and high user acceptance. The challenges of context-aware computing in mobile environments can be categorized in two complementary groups. The first group comprises challenges that pertain to the meaning and provision of context information itself in the service provision process, e.g., access, quality of information, and propagation. The second group contains aspects affecting the use of context information in the various stages of the service provision process in an active or passive manner, e.g., enhanced service discovery or composition. Indeed, both groups cannot be considered in isolation, but strongly influence each other, i.e., the quality of available information directly affects the result of provided services.

In particular mobile service composition approaches combining functionality provided by multiple different services in a coherent manner can dramatically profit from additional context information. This is no trivial task given the multiple aspects that need to be considered and multiple services that need to be integrated into one process especially when aiming at a general and flexible application of context data. Hence, in this chapter we illustrate current trends in mobile service composition in peer-to-peer environments with a particular emphasis on the role of context information.

In the light of the broad and multifaceted nature of the research area, this article focuses solely on the utilization of high level context information in user-centric service environments, leaving other aspects such as privacy and security out of consideration. The focal point is on the interplay of context information, mobile peer-to-peer environments, and service composition, which implies particular requirements that need to be addressed.

To introduce the topic, the general role of context information in mobile service environments is dealt with in Section "Background". Three trends in this area are identified and transferred to current research in mobile service composition. In Section "Mobile Service Communities" we propose middleware ideas aiming at the context-aware execution and combination of services in peer-to-peer environments as an approach to the aspects identified. The special role of context information is highlighted and future research issues are identified which are further described in Section "Future Trends". Finally, Section "Conclusion" presents our conclusions.

BACKGROUND

Increasing user mobility, availability of services, and capabilities of mobile devices all offer new opportunities for the provision of services, but also introduce substantial new requirements and challenges.

Chen and Kotz (2000) examined the status of context-aware mobile computing in 2000 and named the key examples and achievements in this area at that time. Starting from general definitions of context and context-awareness, four possible categories for context are depicted that extend the three categories proposed by Schilit et al. (1994): computing context, user context, physical context, and time the extra category. Their survey also lists a number of context-aware applications developed at that time, concluding that the type of context information mostly applied was location information (1). It is not clear to the authors whether other kinds of context information are more difficult to sense or simply not that useful. Their representation of context information gives six categories: location model, key-value pairs, tagged encoding, object-oriented model, logic-based model, and others (2). In terms of system infrastructure two kinds were identified: those with a centralized structure and those with a decentralized one (3).

The Role of Context Information in Mobile Service Environments

With this survey as its point of departure this section will particularly focus on the use of context information in mobile environments identifying those key challenges in context-aware mobile computing that are relevant for an understanding of the remaining chapters. For this purpose three of the most relevant aspects numbered 1 to 3 are selected from the survey and discussed in the following sections that focus on current approaches in this area. First, current trends in mobile context-aware services are discussed in Section "Context-Aware Mobile Services" Second, Section "Semantics in Context-Aware Applications" depicts current means of representing context data. Third, current approaches and developments that key in mobility aspects are illustrated in Section "Context on the Move".

Context-Aware Mobile Services

There is now an exponential increase in the number of approaches applying some kind of context information in areas ranging from mobile tourist guides to pervasive gaming. This is also fueled by the emergence of mobile web applications that make more and more services pervasively available and enable the creation of new kinds of services.

For example, the Context Watcher (Koolwaaij, 2006) is an application that can be downloaded and installed on the mobile phone to gather context data from users, e.g., location, share information with other users, and adapt applications accordingly. It is built on top of a management platform developed by the MobiLife (Klemettinen, 2007) project.

A server-based approach for providing services in a context-aware manner to mobile clients is described by Han et al. (2004). This web-based AnyServer platform uses device, network, and application-specific information to forward requests to particular proxies and make corresponding adjustments in multimedia content. A first prototype was realized on a Pocket PC using XML to represent context information.

In the DYNAMOS project (Riva, 2007) a system platform and application prototype is proposed supporting a hybrid approach to provide context-aware services to mobile users. This considers not only service-generated content, but also user-generated and user-annotated content which allow users to share data within the community. Besides the reactive means of user interaction, a proactive way is also proposed, i.e., providing services to users according to their profiles and contexts. A matcher component is used to find suitable services, e.g., based on a category- and taxonomy- based matching algorithm. Riva et al. also describe a field trial where yacht crews on a lake could share photos and comments, and also retrieve information based on their context, e.g., location. Many of the problems depicted have a particular bearing on very practical issues such as 2G/3G handover problems.

One approach striving to integrate context-aware features in a mobile phone is Sen-

Say (Siewiorek, 2003). A separate sensor box carried by the user and connected to the mobile phone is utilized to measure context information such as the noise level or temperature. The behavior of the mobile phone can be adapted according to available context information, e.g., it sends an SMS to the caller or switches off the vibration. The decision is based on defined states such as "uninterruptable" depending on a particular sensed context. Experiments were carried out to identify distinct user states and map them to actions.

ContextPhone (Raento, 2005) is another approach, describing a software platform for Nokia Series 60 Smartphones running Symbian OS for the provision of context-aware services. Raento et al. define four interconnected modules: sensors, communications to connect to external services, customizable applications, and system services. The software can be downloaded and installed to use ContextPhone based applications such as viewing the current context of contacts or sharing mobile media.

However, context awareness is still not yet applied in a more general and essential way to exploit the increased capabilities of today's mobile devices in terms of computing capabilities, advanced communication facilities, and integrated sensors. Most of the examples given above are service-specific usages of context information or rely on the availability of additional servers, whereas most applications apply location information as one of the most important concepts in context-aware mobile computing (Anagnostopoulos, 2007). The potential of enhanced device capabilities is not yet fully exploited especially when it comes to context-aware seamless combination of functionalities from different devices to offer a new generation of services to users.

Semantics in Context-Aware Applications

As shown in the introduction to Section "Background" Chen and Kotz (2000) identify six differ-

ent categories for modeling context information: location model, key-value pairs, tagged encoding, object-oriented model, logic-based model, and others. In 2004 the study on available means for modeling context was further enhanced by Strang et al. (2004) who evaluated six similar categories in terms of specific criteria: key-value, markup scheme, graphical, object oriented, logic based, and ontology based models. Model criteria comprised level of formality or distributed composition. Strang et al. came to the conclusion that the ontology-based model best meets requirements and thus offered a promising means for modeling context.

Gruber (1993) defines an ontology as "an explicit specification of a conceptualization". In the context of the Semantic Web (Lee, 1998) it can be described as a hierarchy of concepts that also defines relationships and properties. One of the most popular and widely used languages to describe ontologies is the Web Ontology Language (OWL) based on the Resource Description Framework (RDF). The wide availability of tools for defining, processing, querying, or interpreting OWL, have made it a popular language for describing not only web resources and service interfaces, but also context information.

For example, Korpipää et al. (2003) define a context ontology for sensor values of mobile devices geared to various design principles such as simplicity, practical access, or flexibility. They apply RDF as a formal syntax and define a context object as a set of six properties: context type, context value, confidence, source, timestamp, and free attributes.

Specht et al. (2006) describe a relational database-driven approach for reasoning with ontological knowledge that is distributed on mobile clients and a server with special account taken of the restrictions of mobile devices. There are also a number of other context-aware frameworks focusing on different domains, e.g., smart spaces (Chen, 2004) or context-aware mobile services (Gu, 2004), that apply ontologies and enable the inference of additional facts. These approaches typically support multiple stages in the context-aware service provision process such as gathering and administering context data, but often assume centralized components that can be queried for desired information.

Although the number of approaches utilizing ontologies for context modeling is constantly increasing, the application of semantic technologies in mobile environments can still be considered as ambivalent. On the one hand, the defined concepts provide a valid way of accurately describing a particular situation, and the implicit knowledge residing in ontologies can be used by inference engines to derive additional facts, and, with agreement on a common data schema, context data stemming from different sources can be harmonized or related. On the other hand, semantic descriptions can become exceedingly complex if capturing too many aspects or details, agreement on common concepts or vocabulary is not always possible, and the twofold nature of describing context and processing it in terms of inference may not be flexible enough to cope with dynamic environments of multiple and fast context changes. These problems are especially intensified in mobile environments of multiple different nodes with different capabilities and interfaces.

Even so, the increasing number of approaches applying semantic descriptions for context-aware computing shows the importance such technologies have gained. Indeed, assigning results to mobile environments brings up new sets of challenges that need to be addressed.

Context on the Move

According to the survey by Chen and Kotz (2000) context provision in terms of general frameworks can be approached in two ways: centralized and decentralized. Similarly, from the context provisioning perspective, Riva et al. (2006) distinguish three types of context-awareness support: internal context provisioning, external centralized context provisioning, and external distributed context provisioning. Internal support for context-awareness is restricted to the device responsible for processing respective sensed information. The external and centralized approach assumes a suitable processing infrastructure, with guaranteed access from the context-aware mobile device for reasonable provision of services. The external and distributed approach incorporates devices that are able to share particular context information with each other, exploiting the mobility aspects. Riva et al. suggest a middleware supporting all three types of provisioning principles and making context information accessible by means of a SQL-based query language. This is used in the DYNAMOS architecture approach (Riva, 2007), depicted in Section "Context-Aware Mobile Services" for context provision on smart phones.

The distinction proposed by Riva et al. is a clear indicator of the direction taken by ongoing developments in the area of context-aware frameworks that place increasing importance on context information in mobile environments. This can also be shown by the huge number of approaches specifically addressing particular aspects of mobile context-aware computing such as varying quality of information or potential unavailability of context sources.

For example, Scagnetto et al. (2005) consider tagging particular context information with probability values to take account of the possibility that some values may not be definite. This kind of approach may be applied in heterogeneous environments to provide context-aware services in a best-effort manner.

Mobility of both context producers in terms of sensors and context consumers, e.g., context-aware applications, can also be an essential requirement when approaching the varying availability and quality of context information in mobile environments. The directed diffusion approach (Intanagonwiwat, 2003) considers context requests in terms of key-value pairs that are automatically propagated in a peer-to-peer network to enable context-awareness in networks without a centralized server. In this area, gossiping (Datta, 2004; Williamson, 2006) is another possibility for randomly propagating information in such a network as a particular piece of information, e.g., context information, may be available for a context-aware application although the original context sensor is not.

The context relay approach (Jacob, 2007) introduces intermediate components that are, on the one hand, able to gather context information from sensors, and, on the other, to provide this information to interested applications. The assumed mobility of nodes benefits the dissemination of context information in the network and may make particular data available to them that is not directly connected to a corresponding sensor. Indeed, the quality of context is especially important for estimating the value of a particular piece of information. Buchholz et al. (2003) identify five aspects as essential: precision, probability of correctness, trust-worthiness, resolution, and up-to-dateness.

The approaches available illustrate the increasing efforts being made in this area to specifically address need imposed by the growing mobility of users and their devices to target decentralized systems in particular. Taking the unstable and heterogeneous nature of these environments into account also allows for a best-effort delivery of context-aware mobile services.

Context-Aware Service Composition

In Section "The Role of Context Information in Mobile Service Environments" three basic trends were identified in the area of mobile context-aware service provision. First, today's mobile devices are on the right track for making context an essential component of service provision as the emergence of location based services indicates. Second, semantics are increasingly used to describe high-level context information as they have a number of advantages in this area like being able

to infer additional knowledge or harmonize data from different sources. Third, many approaches also factor in specific characteristics of mobile environments such as heterogeneous devices or incomplete knowledge due to the lack of context sources.

Combining these three trends in mobile environments, this section expands the view from single interacting applications to the process of composing services from different devices in a context-aware manner for optimal exploitation of the functionality of available services and to offer a completely new functionality. In this context semantics play a vital role in enabling a flexible and general approach in terms of describing crucial information such as service interfaces, user requests, and user preferences. The specifics of mobile environments strongly influence the outcome of the service composition process and call for dynamic adaptation, e.g., in terms of service recovery going beyond traditional systems with central controlling instances.

Against this backdrop this section discusses the procedures of service composition and their possible enhancement through context information. We first outline the general principles of service composition and their current implementation in different systems and then discuss the integration of context information within the service composition flow. These considerations provide the background for the context-aware composition approach presented in Section "Mobile Service Communities".

Service Composition in Mobile Environments

Service Composition became widely known with the emergence of Service Oriented Architecture (SOA), an architectural style based on the composition of loosely coupled services. With SOA a new request does not necessarily need to be met with a newly developed application, but may be answered by a composition of services already on hand.

We can distinguish between three basic steps in the service composition procedure as illustrated in Figure 1:

1. *Creation*—In the Creation phase, a service composition is created on a structural level, referred to as *abstract service composition* in the following. The service composition is expressed by a higher-level language specifying the execution order of single services, their respective data flow and message exchange. Single services are represented by *blueprints*, i.e. placeholders for actual service implementations that contain a description of the service's functionality and (possibly) its non-functional properties.

2. *Binding*—Service Composition binding addresses the selection of appropriate service implementations for the service blueprints within the abstract service composition. An abstract service composition that is fully bound up with actual service implementations is an *instance* of the abstract service composition and for simplicity's sake is referred to as *service composition*.

3. *Execution and Runtime Control*—A service composition can be executed within a runtime environment capable of interpreting the corresponding control structures. Control of the service composition can operate on all three phases of the service composition procedure. First, it may adjust certain parameters to observed changes during runtime. Second, a service implementation can be replaced with another, i.e. another service implementation can be bound to a service blueprint during runtime, either because the current service is no longer available and thus has to be replaced or because a service with a better quality has become available. Third, adjustment of the service composition may reach the structural level where adaptation of the service composition can no longer be compensated by the exchange of a single service implementation, and the structure of the abstract service composition has to be modified. The latter case also entails a subsequent binding phase where the new service blueprints have to be bound to actual service implementations.

Various approaches for service composition rely either on central control or fixed infrastructures (Mokhtar, 2005; Ponnekanti, 2001; Roman, 2003) and thus do not address our need for a completely distributed and mobile computing environment. In general, we must distinguish between automatic procedures for service compo-

Figure 1. Three major steps of a service composition procedure

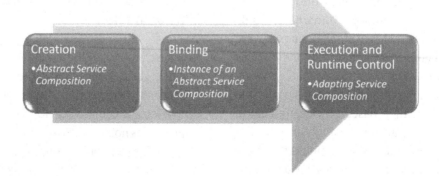

sition that aim at easing the development of service compositions during their design phase, i.e., supporting the application developer (Chakraborty, 2004; Grimm, 2004; Kiciman, 2000), and those providing the user with the means to create requests and service compositions during runtime (Edwards, 2002; Garlan, 2002).

Bottaro et al. (2007) introduce a Web Service based approach to enable context-aware service composition for home applications. Their proposed solution aims at autonomically controlling today's home devices such as screens, loud speakers and PDAs. Restrictively, automatic device discovery and communication relies on a central gateway holding the business logic and container for context-aware and autonomic management.

Vallée et al. (2005) describe a context-aware service composition approach that utilizes context information to turn abstract composition plans into concrete realizations based on SOA principles. A service infrastructure administers the available services that can be used by a composition system to adapt service compositions according to current sensor values.

All these approaches to service composition for mobile environments show limitations due to one or more restricting assumptions:

- Assumption of central control
- Reliance on fixed infrastructure elements
- Need for lengthy descriptions and resource-intensive reasoning techniques
- Restriction to special sets of scenarios.

In general, the assumptions outlined are made in order to limit the complexity of the automating parts of the service composition procedure. We argue that a large part of such complexity is due to a lack of additional information that could be used to restrict the large search space; context data could constitute such missing information. For instance, service binding procedures do not scale well or they must rely on central repositories since the loosely coupled exploitation of services does not scale well. Context information may help to restrict the search space by eliminating larger sets of services that do not match a required context. In the following section we discuss how context information can be integrated at various points within the service composition procedure and how such integration will affect procedure performance. We also discuss how context information can not only be used for performance amelioration, but also as means for providing value-added services.

Service Composition Enhanced by Context Information

In service composition procedures as discussed in Section "Service Composition in Mobile Environments", context data can either be considered as additional information enhancing service selection mechanisms or as a trigger for adjusting and optimizing service composition performance. Based on these two elementary principles, the integration of context information affects the following three aspects of the service composition procedure:

1. Service Composition and Service Discovery
2. Service Composition Recovery
3. Service Composition Adaptation

When given a user's request, the system has to select an abstract service composition that can meet it. Should multiple appropriate abstract service compositions be available, the system has to select one. This selection may either be performed at random or based on heuristics to increase the chances of selecting a service with better quality than the others. At this point of service composition, context information can be a valuable asset. For instance, if the user has initiated a request from a mobile device whose connection to other devices, i.e. potential service providers, was unstable in the latest time span, a service composition containing fewer services is beneficial as it reduces the chances of a device hosting a service leaving the requester's connection range during service composition execution. In the same way, context information can facilitate the selection of service implementations bound to the blueprints of the abstract service composition. Selection of a service can depend on the user's preferences or current active profile, and physical parameters such as time and location or the service's surrounding, e.g. the number and type of devices and services within connection range. The same mechanism is applied for service recovery. Thus, if a device leaves the connection range, entailing the loss of one or more services, the service discovery process re-starts in order to reallocate the free blueprints to the services.

Unlike service discovery and recovery, service composition adaptation also uses context information for triggering replacement of single services. Thus, if the user's context changes, i.e. his or her location, service composition may react to such environmental variations and select a service more appropriate to the new context.

We conclude this section with an example which is often considered in the area of context-aware spaces (Chen, 2004; Román, 2002), and demonstrates integration of context information during the service composition procedure as discussed above. Consider a group of business people having a meeting. Since a key member of the group was unable to travel, he can only join the group spontaneously by a call.

Assume a user requests the invitation of the missing college to the meeting; as a response to this request, multiple service compositions may become available, providing the set-up of a simple audio call or a video conference. Given that the devices surrounding the requester haven't changed over a considerable amount of time, the group of devices may be considered as stable. Moreover, a WLAN connection is detected, enabling the transmission of videos. Accordingly the service composition providing a video conference is selected based on the context of the user device. As many services are capable of displaying the video or the audio stream, selection can depend on the capabilities of the devices that host the services. For instance, a big Plasma TV is rated as more appropriate for the video playback than the screen of a PDA. Since no external speakers are available, the audio is streamed over a service running on a laptop. Should this laptop drops out as the user has to leave for another meeting, the service composition recovers by streaming the audio file through another device.

Perhaps the absent colleague wants to show some slides during the talk, another screen may be required to display them. Based on the preferences of the users, a decision is made that displaying the slides in a readable size is more important than transmitting the colleague himself. The service composition is then adapted in such a way that the slides are now shown on the big Plasma TV while the video-stream is relocated to the screen of a user's laptop.

Especially for the execution and adaption of service compositions during runtime, joint state management of all the devices hosting a service composition is essential. We therefore introduce a middleware for collaborative task processing in the next section. Special emphasis is placed on a context-aware service composition approach using the middleware concepts for dynamic service binding and execution. Section "Mobile Service Communities" will thus describe the basic middleware ideas, show how they relate to the field of context-aware mobile composition, and offer an approach for the dynamic incorporation of context information in service composition processes.

MOBILE SERVICE COMMUNITIES

Inspired by the recent success of Web2.0 communities, we define a Universal Service Terminal (UST) middleware layer supported by context information that directly addresses the trends discussed in Section "Background" for mobile peer-to-peer networks and provides an execution environment for service compositions. In this respect a Universal Service Terminal (UST) is defined as a combination of functionality provided by multiple services on one or more devices - so-called "UST nodes" - to fulfill a particular user request. These services are managed and composed by means of the middleware including functions such as service discovery or recovery. A service community embraces all services at a moment offered by UST devices that are able to communicate, i.e., exchange information, with each other by means of the UST middleware layer (Jacob, 2008).

The community-like behavior of the services is defined by the four following characteristics supported by the middleware. First, services aim at joint work with respect to a particular user-defined goal. This goal may be a simple service request directly addressed or equally a long-term task running in the background. Second, the middleware supports active and open sharing of information, e.g., the proactive dissemination of particular data. Third, a service community consists of complementary functionalities and data that can be combined to offer new and context-aware service compositions. Fourth, devices hosting the services are able to group and interact in an ad hoc and loosely coupled manner.

The three trends described in Section "Background" can be directly related to this notion of service communities and, thus context-aware composition of services. First, the exploitation of the service and device capabilities is addressed by the interaction of services, the combination of complementary functionalities, and the loosely coupled grouping. These aspects necessitate the definition of a distributed state management for signaling messages, a appropriate semantic description language, and a suitable means for service discovery. Second, semantics have to be applied for the description of a user goal in terms

of a request, service interfaces, and context information to enable dynamic reaction to changing environment variables and user-specific demands. These aspects call for a service matching mechanism that is able to interpret and relate semantic descriptions, as well as a recovery module that can replace a service by a similar one if required. To prevent reliance on a central ontology or extensive reasoning technologies, rather light-weight descriptions that apply a reduced number of concepts and constructs are targeted (Pfeffer, 2007). Third, special consideration of mobility aspects is particularly addressed by active and open sharing of information to enhance middleware functions by additional information, e.g., service discovery, and flexible management a distributed state and recover disappearing services. These aspects additionally require a component for caching, evaluating, and propagating data that applies semantic descriptions to enable the automatic interpretation by respective components.

SmartWare and the Semantic Data Space (SDS)

As a base for the realization of the UST middleware components, we defined a software framework for the autonomic management of software, called *SmartWare*. The SmartWare model considers each computing entity as a node that is able to exchange data with other nodes according to the REST architectural style (Fielding, 2000). On top of the data exchange layer, two complementary frameworks are defined: the *Service Framework* and the *Interaction Framework*.

The service framework consists of application-related components called *Services,* and management-related components, called *Mediators*. Services are described by appropriate dynamic descriptions and fulfill respective application functionalities. Mediators are responsible for administering and organizing the life-cycles of node-specific services, e.g., discovery and execution.

The interaction framework defines node interaction models utilized by the mediators for a controlled data exchange. One common example for an interaction model is Publish/Subscribe. For our realization of the SmartWare interaction framework we use the Semantic Data Space (SDS) as an interaction model directly addressing the loosely coupled communication (Linner, 2006). Service requesters use the SDS to publish appropriate semantic descriptions. Suitably subscribed service providers are notified accordingly and use the SDS to publish results or acknowledge the execution of services. Basically, from the conceptual point of view there are two differences to a traditional Publish/Subscribe interaction model. First, service requests are cached by the SDS if no appropriate service provider is currently subscribed for a defined life-time. This means that suitable service providers can be notified even if the request was published beforehand. Second, the SDS can be queried by all mediators for available requests or responses. The semantic descriptions allow for subscription to particular service classes and, thus, for the monitoring of the respective requests and responses.

UST Middleware and Context Information

The UST middleware uses the general concepts introduced by the SmartWare approach to define particular functionality that is essential to mobile and distributed service environments, i.e., environments with multiple mobile devices offering distinct services, which should be combined in a reasonable manner according to user demands. Definition is given to the Universal Service Layer (USL) which can be conceptually embedded in the management part of the SmartWare service framework. Respective mediators are grouped into *USL Modules* according to their functionality. Hence, a USL module is a functional entity of the UST middleware that is a combination of one or more SmartWare mediators commonly serving a particular purpose in service invocation or administration processes. The given level of functionality depends on multiple factors, e.g., the node's capabilities. An USL module can use functions provided by other USL modules and can control UST node specific services. They are active

Table 1. USL module and general purpose

Module	Description
Request Processing	The request processing module provides an interface that can be used to publish new semantically described requests. Current request data can also be retrieved.
Description& Discovery	This module is used for the simple discovery of services providing a listing of available local and remote services. Local service descriptions are also provided.
Composition	The composition module creates service compositions according to the request and available services.
State Management	The state management module executes services and administers currently running services. It provides methods for adding new service tasks, updating running tasks, or stopping tasks. It is also possible to retrieve the current state of a node or services.
Recovery	The recovery node is responsible for finding a compatible service to replace one no longer available.
Event Notification	The event notification module provides an interface for publishing events which are then forwarded to the appropriate modules according to the subscriptions. The event notification module should use the supported interaction model.
Security& Privacy	The security&privacy module covers mediators administering access restrictions in the form of rules that can be applied. Trust relationships can also be managed for identification of trusted nodes.
Data Dissemination	The data dissemination module utilizes an appropriate dissemination model to propagate data stored in the UST blackboard (see Section "UST Distributed Blackboard") in the UST service community. The dissemination model contains a method for evaluating the relative importance of a particular piece of information.

Table 2. USL modules and module enablers

Aspect	USL module	USL module enabler
Executes USL module services	yes	no
Uses USL module enablers	yes	no
Controls UST services	yes	no
Purpose	specific	determined by the available USL modules

components that serve a well-defined purpose in the service community administration process. A USL module can comprise multiple mediators, but one mediator may also belong to multiple modules. Currently, there are nine different modules defined: description&discovery, request processing, recovery, composition, security&privacy, configuration, state management, event notification, and data dissemination. Table 1 lists these modules and their general purposes.

Furthermore, the USL enhances the Smart-Ware service framework with additional components used by modules, the *USL Module Enablers.* USL module enablers are also components of the Universal Service Layer and provide functionality that is exclusively used by USL modules. They are conceptually different from modules in terms of various aspects listed in the table below.

A USL module enabler can be considered as a component or a combination of components that is able to process and interpret inputted data, but does not actively execute actions depending on the respective results. USL module enablers only serve a particular purpose if controlled by one or more USL modules. Hence, the enabler function can change in accordance with the current task and the responsible USL module(s). With the help of USL module enablers respective USL modules are able to influence the behavior of a service not only before its execution, but also during run-time, e.g., available context information can be used for this purpose. As an example of a USL module enabler the so-called *UST Distributed Blackboard*

(UDB) is introduced. In the following section the UDB is specified with special attention on its application as a component enabling context-aware services in a best-effort manner.

UST Distributed Blackboard

In a UST blackboard approach, the UST distributed blackboard (UDB), is used to allow service community members to proactively cache and exchange information. Pieces of data cached in a node-specific blackboard and marked as public can be read and changed by all service community members. Furthermore, new data can be added. Thus service community members can use their own UDB or that of other members to enhance the functionality of the USL modules provided. Depending on the given level of functionality, the UDB may also be able to infer additional knowledge from the cached facts by means of sophisticated reasoning processes. For instance, a service matching mechanism could use the cached information to relate services of similar classes. Hence, the matching process may not only attempt to consider service A, but also the similar service composition combining service B and C that provides the same functionality. The assumed mobility of the addressed peer-to-peer networks also facilitates the autonomous dissemination of data. Here, context information is an important factor since disseminating annotated context data may replace missing context sources (Jacob, 2007). For example, a service that relies on location information but is currently not able to find a suitable sensor may use the dissemination cache to retrieve the location of a user reported by a GPS sensor in another community some minutes ago. Although the proactive dissemination of information cannot guarantee the availability of the requisite data, it does allow for a best-effort approach.

Following the REST architectural style, the blackboard of a node can be simply accessed by a suitable URL and provides methods for adding, deleting, updating, and retrieving semantically enhanced data. For instance, for retrieving potentially existing GPS sensor data a requesting node would use the GET method with the *GPSData* concept as a parameter. Semantic concepts are defined in appropriate semantic languages, such as OWL/RDF (OWL).

As an example for the use of the UDB in mobile service environments we defined and realized the *Public Jukebox showcase*. According to the UST notion the user's home stereo system should provide UST middleware functionality and thus is capable of using the UDB of the user's UST enabled mobile device to store simple music profiles. For instance, an anonymous profile may contain the fact that the user likes music of the *Jazz* genre, but dislikes *Hard Rock*. Once more, semantic description languages are used to define these facts, which are proactively stored in the respective UDB. This storage process may be triggered by a suitable mediator provided by the stereo vendor or on behalf of the data dissemination module because of similar facts in the UDB or previous music profile requests. A configuration interface permits the administration of this kind of functionality which also allows the user to read and delete current data from the UDB. The profile stored in the user's UDB can now be accessed by other UST devices, e.g., by a device hosting a jukebox service. This service simply uses a number of available music files to create a play

list and plays the next song accordingly. Hence, this service can be utilized in a public place to provide suitable background music. This service can now be enhanced with UST functionality to create a context-aware play list utilizing user profiles. Shortly before a song ends the available semantic music profiles of all UST devices near-by are gathered by the jukebox device and merged to adapt the play list accordingly. For instance, if most of the users like Jazz jazz-related music files are preferred. Given the semantic description, subclass relationships can be considered, too. If no suitable profile is found the music files are selected randomly.

With the semantic descriptions utilized in the blackboard, the approach is very flexible and can be used in a number of applications. The jukebox example described above can be easily extended to cover any kind of context information. Indeed, the current solution is only a best-effort approach which also requires a default value should no suitable data be available. Furthermore, the size and capabilities of the blackboard strongly depend on the device hosting it. To date four distinct blackboard versions are worth considering and are detailed in Table 3.

According to the UST device the respective version of the blackboard is to be supported. A tiny node such as a sensor may have no blackboard or only a simple one. A requesting node may need to retrieve all available data, but is not able to select facts belonging to a particular concept. A mobile node may support an enhanced semantic model, but full reasoning support can only be provided by more capable nodes, such as a desktop PC. For instance, the mobile devices utilized in the Public Jukebox showcase illustrated above use a J2ME implementation based on the CDC framework and Foundation Profile and a tiny version of the blackboard.

Table 3. Blackboard versions

Version	Support
None	No blackboard supported
Tiny	Plain semantic model (e.g., RDFS) and simplified interface to add and retrieve data
Basic	Enhanced model (e.g., OWL Lite or DL) and basic operations are supported
Full	Enhanced model (e.g., OWL DL) and full reasoning support

Context-Aware Service Composition in UST

In addition to the blackboard, which can be applied to provide services in a context-aware manner, context-aware service composition features are also supported. In this section, we discuss integration of context information during the runtime phase of such a service composition.

In (Pfeffer, 2008), we introduced a representation of service compositions by a bipartite graph concept. A *workflow graph* defines the execution order of services while a *dataflow* graph specifies the passing of I/O data between the single services of the service composition. We used timed automata (Clarke, 1999) to define workflows of services; for simplicity's sake, we abstracted the real-time behavior of these automata and regarded

them as simple finite automata (Alur, 1990) (Dill, 1989). In general, a finite automaton consists of a finite set of *locations* and a finite set of *transitions* connecting those locations. A transition is labeled with *annotations* that contain *guards* and *actions*. Guards, which are expressed by a propositional logic formula evaluated by Boolean logic, restrict the passage of a transition. When a transition guard g evaluates to `true` and the transition is passed, the annotated action α is performed. In our workflow graph, the execution of an action α corresponds to a service invocation. The left-hand side of Figure 2 shows the classic transition of a workflow graph represented by a finite automaton labeled by a guard g and an action α.

In the rest of this section, we discuss the extension of the classic workflow by context sensitive transitions. A transition is expanded to multiple transitions that are candidates for execution. The right-hand side of Figure 2 shows an extension of the classic transition on the left, whereby the single transition is extended to four transitions on the right.

The new guards g_1, g_2, g_3 contain the original guard g and a constraint operating on context information. Guard g_d is the default guard that is evaluated to `true` should the requested context information not be available. Thus, depending on context data, different services α_1, α_2 or α_3, can be executed. Since the transition relation of automata selects non-deterministically between multiple enabled transitions, the context sensitive guards g_1, g_2 and g_3 have to ensure that the domain space of the context variable is disjunctively covered.

Figure 2. Classic transition (left) and context sensitive transition (right) of a workflow graph

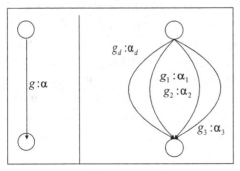

Figure 3. Example of a complete workflow graph featuring context sensitive transitions

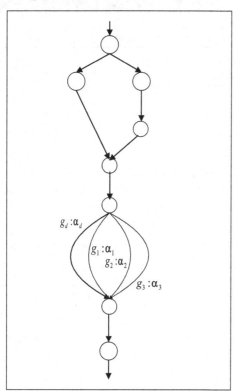

As introduced in Section "Service Composition in Mobile Environments", we assume three elementary steps in a service composition procedure, i.e. creation of the abstract service composition, binding of suitable service implementations, and execution of the service composition. Context sensitive transitions play a special role during the binding procedure. The workflow graph gives the structural representation of the service composition, i.e. the abstract composition. Here, the actions α correspond to a service description or service interface description of a service. During the binding procedure, appropriate service implementations for these descriptions are discovered. This binding procedure has to be finalized before execution of the service composition is started

in order to ensure that an appropriate service composition is available. If the execution were started before the binding was finished, a considerable part of the service composition might have already been executed before it is noticed that no services for a specific service blueprint can be discovered. Hence, all resources consumed by the previously executed services would have been wasted. Context sensitive transitions constitute an exception since they express context-dependent alternatives. In the binding procedure only the default action α_d has to be bound; the context dependent actions α_i remain unbound. Figure 3 illustrates a model workflow featuring a set of context sensitive transitions; the bold transitions indicate transitions whose actions have to be bound to concrete service implementations before execution of the service composition.

Context sensitive transitions are not bound directly, but rather during service composition execution for two reasons. First, multiple services would be bound although only one is required; this increases the time for service discovery and reserves resources of the bound services. Second and more importantly, the context for service discovery would have been determined during the binding instead of the actual execution, thus neglecting the fact that context can change rapidly over time and services can influence the context itself. Assume that the context information describes the location of a user. Thus, g_1 may mean that the user is at home, g_2 that he or she is in a 2 kilometer range from home and g_3 that his/her distance to home is greater than 2 kilometers. The user may be 3 kilometers away from home when he or she starts to execute the service composition, thus, α_3 would be bound if the context sensitive transitions were also bound during the binding phase. However, it may happen that the user has reached home before the execution of the service composition has entered the location that entails the execution of a context-dependent service. Thus, when the location containing the outgoing context sensitive transitions is entered, the *cur-*

rent context is determined. In this example, the user would already be at home, so an appropriate service matching α_1 would be discovered. In case no matching service can be found, the context-independent transition entailing execution of α_d is passed, ensuring termination of the holistic service composition.

Such securing of the executability of a service composition must also be ensured when context sensitive transitions are nested within the workflow graph. Figure 4 depicts such a nested set of transitions.

The binding of α_d secures the executability of the composition. However, to ensure that α_3 can be executed if found, g_{3_d} must also be bound during the binding phase, i.e. before service execution.

The depicted context-aware composition approach can be directly embedded in the UST middleware utilizing respective components and given functionality. The UDB can be used to cache and disseminate appropriate composition blueprints specifying such automata as depicted above. The representation format needs to be capable of defining the used concepts and needs to be interpreted by the composition module as part of the UST layer which finally binds and executes service composition. The request processing module can be used to map a user request in terms of a task for a suitable blueprint. During the binding process the services needed are requested by the composition module through the Semantic Data Space (SDS). This is where suitable service requests are published (Linner, 2006) and acknowledging services bound to the respective blueprint. During execution the composition module is also responsible for caching the current state within the composition execution process.

Whenever context information is needed to decide on an optional action in the graph, the UDB is requested for this kind of information by the composition module. Hence, sensors may use the UDB to publish and update their information accordingly using an appropriate semantic concept,

e.g., *GPSData*. Alternatively, the composition module may also publish appropriate context requests via the Semantic Data Space (SDS) and subscribe for respective providers accordingly. Whenever a request is unsuccessful the default action is triggered. This best-effort approach can be compared to a search service whose result quality can be considerably enhanced by providing the location of the user. Indeed, if no user location is available, the search service can still be executed, but usually returns worse results.

The depicted approach can, of course, be extended to support more sophisticated composition models, but such extensions also introduce new requirements and challenges making the process even more complex. For example, the assumption of multiple alternative services as part of a service composition whose results quality is heavily context-dependent requires an evaluation component to decide on the most appropriate service.

The presented composition approach using UST middleware strives to take particular account of the characteristics of context-aware service composition in mobile environments to allow for the consideration of context information.. Semantics are an essential requirement for this kind of functionality as they can harmonize

Figure 4. Nested context sensitive transitions

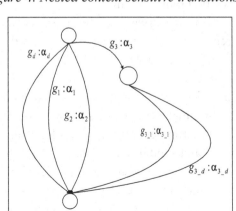

heterogeneous data for automatic processing. Indeed, this approach can only be a first step towards a flexible and general context-aware service composition framework for peer-to-peer environments. Multiple challenges still remain in this area, which are especially related to the three trends identified in Section "The Role of Context Information in Mobile Service Environments".

FUTURE TRENDS

The issues considered in the previous sections indicate that context information will increasingly penetrate everyday life as multiple location-based services become more widely available and benefit from the steady development of mobile web applications and services. More enhanced applications will follow that integrate context information and make new services possible. For example, pervasive gaming may be one potential and increasingly economically relevant application domain.

Service composition in a flexible and general way is still very much a research topic due to the large number of not yet satisfactorily solved questions related to very practical problems such as seamless incorporation of multiple technological approaches, as well as other aspects like security. Even in terms of the three trends of context-aware mobile computing identified in Section "Background", the challenges in the area of service composition remain daunting.

In terms of service capability exploitation, the trend towards one device used for multiple purposes is making steady headway not only by integrating more and more functionality into a single device, e.g., a camera into a mobile phone, but by proving more seamless remote services for the environment. Approaches focusing on wrapping and combining key functionality from multiple devices (Schuster, 2007) or providing a common interface for services in the personal area network and managing the sharing of resources

(Jønvik, 2003) already point in this direction. Indeed, a general and user-centric way of service provision can only be achieved by considering the context, especially the user's location and his or her preferences.

In the area of utilizing semantics for the description of service interfaces, context or general knowledge, and user preferences, it is especially important to further reduce the overheads introduced by these descriptions. The benefits are twofold. First, reducing complexity can be considered as a crucial requirement for leveraging the use of semantics in service provision processes as the effort for both service provider and requester can be reduced. This can be further supported by automatic processes for creating or disseminating semantic information. Second, the software for interpreting and deducing knowledge can be optimized to incorporate the reduction of processing time, along with development of distributed reasoners and processing of incomplete knowledge. The latter would directly address requirements as presented in mobile environments. In short, some of the most critical challenges are:

- To make reasonable use of semantic context descriptions and matching algorithms in distributed service environments without the availability of a global ontology,
- To strike the right balance between accurate context description and reduction of the amount of necessary information,
- To free up the user or service provider from having to define extensive and complex descriptions before being able to provide and use a service,
- To make semantic context descriptions an integral part of mobile service composition and recovery processes.

To support these mobility aspects will mean a greater need for dynamic composition principles and service binding mechanisms. Semantic descriptions are one possible way of going beyond static plans and consideration of autonomic characteristics, e.g., self-recovery or self-learning. Context data are a crucial enabler to facilitate the reaction to environmental changes. The ad hoc interworking of services also assumes the presence of loosely coupled interaction models to dynamically discover, execute, and replace heterogeneous services.

CONCLUSION

In this document we have discussed some of the basic developments in the area of context-aware mobile service composition. We based our considerations on the identification of three trends with respect to context-aware service provision in mobile environments. First, the enhanced service and device capabilities offered today are increasingly exploited, but their full potential still remains untapped. Second, semantics are increasingly applied for description purposes providing multiple benefits such as the inference of implicit knowledge. Third, mobility aspects are especially incorporated not only to deal with particular requirements, but also to take explicit advantage of the characteristics. By addressing these three trends we have extended the view from single services to the process of combining services from different devices. We started from the general definition of service composition processes to reach a description of ideas for a middleware approach that particularly allows for the use of context information. The focus was put on a best-effort approach of selecting and executing services in a context-aware manner. Finally, our depiction of future trends and challenges in this area highlights the need for further research to make the vision of pervasive and seamless context-aware service composition real.

However, the ultimate success of mobile context-aware service composition processes, as assumed here, strongly depends on the economic benefits which call for appropriate business mod-

els and a broadly comprehensive approach that directly addresses and adapts to user community needs. Apart from this, regard for privacy aspects is a crucial factor in gaining widespread user acceptance as users should not lose control over applications of their own data.

REFERENCES

Alur, R., Courcoubetis, C., & Dill, D. (1990). Model-checking for real-time systems. In *Proceedings of of the 5th Annual Symposium on Logic in Computer Science.*

Anagnostopoulos, C. B., Tsounis A., & Hadjiefthymiades, S. (2007). *Context Awareness in Mobile Computing Environments.* Wireless Personal Communications, Springer.

Bottaro, A., Bourcier, J., Escoffier, C., & Lalanda, P. (2007). Context-Aware Service Composition in a Home Control Gateway. *4th IEEE International Conference on Pervasive Services (ICPS'07),* Istanbul, Turkey.

Buchholz, T., Küpper, A., & Schiffers, M. (2003). Quality of Context: What It Is And Why We Need It. *Workshop of the HP OpenView University Association 2003 (HPOVUA2003),* Geneva.

Chakraborty, D., Joshi, A., Finin, T., & Yesha, Y. (2005). Service composition for mobile environment. *Mobile Networks and Applications, 4*(10), 435-451.

Chen, G., & Kotz, D. (2000). *A survey of context-aware mobile computing research.* Technical Report TR2000-381, Dartmouth College.

Chen, H., Finin, T., & Joshi, A. (2004). Semantic Web in the Context Broker Architecture. In *Proceedings of PerCom 2004,* Orlando FL.

Clarke, E. M. J., Grumberg, O., & Peled, D. A. (1999). *Model Checking.* MIT Press

Datta, A., Quarteroni, S., & Aberer, K. (2004). Autonomous Gossiping: A self-organizing epidemic algorithm for selective information dissemination in wireless mobile ad-hoc networks. In *Proceedings of the International Conference on Semantics of a Networked World (IC-SNW04)*, Paris, France.

Dill, D. (1989). Timing assumptions and verification of finite-state concurrent systems. In J. Sifakis, (Ed.), *Proceedings of the International Workshop on Automatic Verification Methods for Finite State Systems*.

Edwards, W. K., Newman, M. W., Sedivy, J., & Izadi, S. (2002). Challenge: Recombinant computing and the speakeasy approach. In *Proceedings of ACM MobiCom*, ACM Press, (pp. 279-286), New York, USA.

Fielding, R. T., & Taylor, R. N. (2000). *Principled design of the modern Web architecture In Proceedings of the 22nd International Conference on Software Engineering*, Limerick, Ireland, (pp. 407-416).

Garlan, D., Siewiorek, D., Smailagic, A., & Steenkiste, P. (2002). Project Aura: toward distraction-free pervasive computing. *Pervasive Computing, IEEE 1*(2), 22-31.

Grimm, R. (2004). One. world: Experiences with a Pervasive Computing Architecture. *IEEE Pervasive Computing, 3*(3), 22-30.

Gruber, T. R. (1993). *Toward principles of the design of ontologies used for knowledge sharing.* Presented at the Padua workshop on Formal Ontology, March 1993, later published in International Journal of Human-Computer Studies, Vol. 43, Issues 4-5, November 1995, pp. 907-928.

Gu, T., Pung, H. K., and Zhang, D. Q. (2004). A Middleware for Building Context-Aware Mobile Services. In Proceedings of IEEE Vehicular Technology Conference (VTC2004), Milan, Italy.

Han, B., Jia, W., Shen, J., and Yuen, M.-C. (2004). Context-Awareness in Mobile Web Services. J. Cao et al. (Eds.): ISPA 2004, LNCS 3358, pp. 519-528.

Intanagonwiwat, C., Govindan, R., Estrin, D., Heidemann, J. S., and Silva, F. (2003). Directed diffusion for wireless sensor networking. IEEE/ACM Transactions on Networking, vol. 11, no. 1, pp. 2-16.

Jacob, C., Linner, D., Steglich, S., and Radusch, I. (2007). Autonomous Context Data Dissemination in Heterogeneous and Dynamic Environments. In Proceedings of the 4th Consumer Communications and Networking Conference (CCNC) 2007, CD-ROM, Las Vegas, NV, USA, IEEE Catalogue Number: 07EX1539C, ISBN: 1-4244-0667-6.

Jacob, C., Pfeffer, H., Zhang, L., and Steglich, S. (2008). Establishing Service Communities in Peer-to-Peer Networks, 1st IEEE International Peer-to-Peer for Handheld Devices Workshop CCNC 2008, Las Vegas, NV, USA.

Jønvik, T. E., Engelstad, P., and van Tanh, D.. (2003). Building a Virtual Device on Personal Area Network. In Proceedings of the 2nd International Conference on Communications, Internet & Information Technology, Scottsdale, Arizona.

Kiciman, E., and Fox, A. (2000). Using dynamic mediation to integrate COTS entities in a ubiquitous computing environment. In Proceedings of HUC2000, no. 1927 in LNCS, pp. 211-226.

Klemettinen, M. (editor). (2007). Enabling Technologies for Mobile Services: The MobiLife Book, John Wiley & Sons Ltd., England.

Koolwaaij, J., Tarlano, A., Luther, M., Nurmi, P., Mrohs, B., Battestini, A., and Vaidya, R. (2006). Context Watcher—Sharing context information in everyday life. In Proceedings of the IASTED International Conference on Web Technologies, Applications, and Services (WTAS'06).

Korpipää, P., and Mäntyjärvi, J. (2003). An Ontology for Mobile Device Sensor-Based Context Awareness. In Proc. of the 4th International and Interdisciplinary Conference on Modeling and Using Context 2003, LNAI 2680, Springer-Verlag, pp.451-459.

Lee, T. B.. (1998). Semantic Web roadmap. [Online]. Available: http://www.w3.org/DesignIssues/Semantic.html. [Accessed: March 17, 2008].

Linner, D., Radusch, I., Steglich, S., and Jacob, C. (2006). Loosely Coupled Service Provisioning in Dynamic Computing Environments. In Proceedings of ChinaCom 2006. First International Conference on Communications and Networking in China, Beijing, China, IEEE Catalog Number: 06EX1414C, ISBN: 1-4244-0463-0, Library of Congress: 2006926274.

Mokhtar, S., Liu, J., Georgantas, N., and Issarny, V. (2005). QoS-aware dynamic service composition in ambient intelligence environments. In Proceedings of IEEE ASE 2005, pp. 317-320, ACM Press New York, NY, USA.

OWL Web Ontology Language Overview. (2004). [Online]. Available: http://www.w3.org/TR/owl-features/. [Accessed: March 17, 2008].

Pfeffer, H., Linner, D., Jacob, C., and Steglich, S. (2007). Towards Light-weight Semantic Descriptions for Decentralized Service-oriented Systems. In Proceedings of the 1st IEEE International Conference on Semantic Computing (ICSC 2007), volume CD-ROM, Irvine, California, USA.

Pfeffer, H., Linner, D., and Steglich, S. (2008). Modeling and Controlling Dynamic Service Compositions, Third International Multi-Conference on Computing in the Global Information Technology (ICCGI 2008)

Ponnekanti, S., Lee, B., Fox, A., Hanrahan, P., and Winograd, T. ICrafter. (2001). A Service Framework for Ubiquitous Computing Environments. Proceedings of Ubicomp 1.

Raento, M., Oulasvirta, A., Petit, R., Toivonen, H.. (2005). ContextPhone: a prototyping platform for context-aware mobile applications. IEEE Pervasive Computing 4 (2).

Resource Description Framework (RDF) / W3C Semantic Web Activity. [Online]. Available: http://www.w3.org/RDF/. [Accessed: March 17, 2008].

Riva, O., and di Flora, C. (2006). Contory: A Smart Phone Middleware Supporting Multiple Context Provisioning Strategies. In Proceedings of the 26th IEEE International Conference on Distributed Computing Systems Workshops (ICDCSW06).

Riva, O., Toivonen, S. (2007). The DYNAMOS approach to support context-aware service provisioning in mobile environments. Journal of Systems and Software 80(12): 1956-1972.

Román, M., Hess, C., Cerqueira, R., Ranganathan, A., Campbell, R. H. & Nahrstedt, K. (2002). Gaia: a middleware platform for active spaces. SIGMOBILE Mob. Comput. Commun. Rev., ACM, 6, pp. 65-67.

Roman, M., et al. (2003). Dynamic application composition: Customizing the behavior of an active space. In Proceedings of IEEE PERCOM, IEEE Computer Society, p. 169, Washington, DC, USA.

Scagnetto, I., Selva, A., Vassena, L., and Rizio, P.Z. (2005). Mobe: Context-aware mobile applications on mobile devices for mobile users. 1st International Workshop on Exploiting Context Histories in Smart Environments, pp.49–54.

Schilit, B., Adams, N., and Want, R. (1994) Context-aware computing applications. In Proceedings of IEEE Workshop on Mobile Computing Systems and Applications, pp. 85-90, Santa Cruz, California. IEEE Computer Society Press.

Schuster, M., Domene, A., Vaidya, R., Arbanowski, S., Kim, S. M., Lee, J. W., and Lim, H.

(2007). Virtual Device Composition. In Proceedings of the Eighth International Symposium on Autonomous Decentralized Systems (ISADS07), Sedona, Arizona.

Siewiorek, D., Smailagic, A., Furukawa, J., Krause, A., Moraveji, N., Reiger, K., Shaffer, J., and Wong, F. L. (2003). SenSay: A Contect-Aware Mobile Phone. In Proceedings of the 7th IEEE International Symposium on Wearable Computers (ISWC03).

Specht, G., and Weithoner, T. (2006). Context-Aware Processing of Ontologies in Mobile Environments. In Proceedings of the 7th International Conference on Mobile Data Management (MDM'06).

Strang, T., and Linnhoff-Popien, C. (2004). A Context Modeling Survey. Workshop on Advanced Context Modelling, Reasoning and Management, UbiComp 2004.

Vallée, M., Ramparany, F., and Vercouter, L. (2005). Flexible Composition of Smart Device Services. In Proc. of the 2005 International Conference on Pervasive Systems and Computing (PSC'05), Las Vegas, USA.

Williamson, G., Stevenson, G., Neely, S., Coyle, L., and Nixon, P. (2006). Scalable information dissemination for pervasive systems: implementation and evaluation. In Proceedings of the 4th international workshop on Middleware for Pervasive and Ad-Hoc Computing (MPAC 2006), Melbourne, Australia, ISBN:1-59593-421-9.

Chapter VIII
A Methodology for the Design, Development and Validation of Adaptive and Context–Aware Mobile Services

Heinz-Josef Eikerling
Siemens AG SIS C-LAB, Germany

Pietro Mazzoleni
IBM Watson Research, USA

ABSTRACT

The authors present a holistic approach for the efficient design, implementation, and validation of context-aware mobile services. The according concepts have been developed within the PLASTIC project which devises a methodology based on model-to-model transformations to be applied at different stages of the service lifecycle. Starting from a conceptual model, these models reflect characteristic properties of the mobile service under development such as context information. For the implementation of the service, a middleware suite then is used which comprises a set of constituents which significantly simplify and shorten the mobile services development cycle. The authors focus on demonstrating the concepts in terms of mobile business-to-business field services as opposed to business-to-consumer services. Here through the methodology and tools the dynamicity can be significantly enhanced. By using the contained adaptation mechanism, service specifications (static by nature) can be qualified to deal with additional information (e.g., context) needed for achieving a better quality of service and usability.

INTRODUCTION

During the last few years, many companies started (or envisioned to start) a slow but radical transformation in the way they conduct businesses. There are two important factors which, among others, help explaining such trend: the widespread need for *Mobility* and *Service-oriented Computing*.

Mobility of humans and objects has become a characteristic and perhaps, more than that, an essential requirement of daily life. Basic functions like for instance telephony, data exchange, as well as more advanced functions like conducting / tracking / steering businesses, sampling and transmission of critical data etc. are required to be accessed *anywhere*, *anytime* and *anyhow*.

On the other hand, *Service Computing* is becoming a paradigm more and more popular within enterprises because it proposes an architecture which can promote IT agility through modularity and to align transformation to business priorities. Service Oriented Architectures (SOA) help in fact to cost-efficiently create IT solutions composed by loosely coupled web services which can be reused and seamlessly integrated with others promoting business alignment as well as cross-enterprise collaborations.

In this chapter we recognize and address some of the challenges of combining mobility and service computing. In our work, we focus on *context-aware "mobile web services"* which are going to be offered to users in varying situations, adapting service provisioning to the environment so as to offer the best quality of service in the most cost-effective way. Such quality is assumed to be specified through functional and/or non-functional attributes (like average service response time, availability, ...) which can be observed at the service interface.

Note that while there is a W3C standard definition of web service ("*a software system designed to support interoperable machine to machine interaction over a network*") there is no widely accepted definition for mobile web service. The notion of mobile web service is less clear since it suggests that (i) either the web service can be consumed from within a mobile setting or (ii) that the service can be deployed on (and made available by) mobile devices. In either case, one of the key problems is handling adaptation for service consumer or service provider (or both) to a changing environment like the one offered in a B3G (*Beyond 3G*) network setting. The goal of B3G is in fact to exploit the integration of different connectivity standards (WiFi, Bluetooth, GRPS/UMTS, Ethernet, IrDA, etc.) while preserving the heterogeneity of the various networking systems and their qualitative and quantitative characteristic.

The work presented in this chapter is part of an initiative carried out in PLASTIC[1] (*Providing Lightweight & Adaptable Service Technology for pervasive Information & Communication*). PLASTIC is a project funded by the European Union to address several challenges pertaining to the development of adaptable and context-aware mobile services. In order to validate the broad applicability of the approach, the real-world usage in the e-Health, e-Voting, e-Learning and e-Business domains is demonstrated. The project devises a methodology and a platform comprising:

- **A development environment** enabling the thorough design and modeling of context- and resource-aware adaptive services, which may be deployed on the various networked nodes, including mobile terminals and handheld devices.

- **A middleware** enabling B3G networking through the comprehensive integration of multi-radio networks and further context-aware, discovery, and access to networked services.

- **A validation framework** enabling off-line and on-line validation of networked services regarding functional and non-functional properties.

After reviewing the state-of-the art in the area, we will introduce the complete methodology developed within PLASTIC and we explain how it has been applied to a realistic e-Business application from the *Field Service Management* (FSM) domain and how it improves particularly the development practice currently in place. As some aspects of the project are beyond the scope of this book, in the following we focus on the aspect directly related to collecting, managing, and consuming context information.

BACKGROUND

The two research areas, context-aware computing and service computing, are quite active. We refer to the classical notions of both, i.e., a *software service* as an entity which wraps data and functions operating on it through well-defined interfaces (Erl, 2008) and *context* as any information used to characterize the situation of an entity (Abowd, 2001). Such entity can be a person (*user domain context*), a site (*physical domain context*), or an object (*system domain context*) that is considered to be relevant to the interaction. Several general purpose approaches to context modeling exist (Strang, 2004). Since we focus on a specific class of service, i.e., services which are mobile with respect to the service host and/or with the users using them, we can limit the scope of modeling significantly. Note that due to the convergence of the conventional and the mobile web we use the terms *mobile service* and *mobile web service* interchangeably. With respect to advanced mobile networks exploiting the availability of different connectivity standards, context-awareness facilitates the integration of such standards while preserving the heterogeneity of the various networking systems in the user's environment including their qualitative and quantitative characteristics. Thus, service-oriented applications must be context-aware and adapt to the variations of context data lying in the system domain.

Sensing and retrieving contextual data is done with a certain purpose. Such purpose is frequently referred to as *adaptation* which we understand as an '*adjustment of an object to environmental conditions*' where environmental conditions are given by the context. This adaptation requires the acquisition of extensive context information. Henricksen (2003) interprets context as an enabling mechanism for applications to perform tasks on behalf of users in an *autonomous* and *flexible* manner. This is especially relevant to our targeted application domain as will be seen below. A lot of work exists on how to apply context under rather special conditions (Brown, 1997 and Mitchell, 2002). Hence, such approaches are mostly limited to a special scenario and do not feature a more capable overall framework for context-awareness . They often consider a fixed set of context information which is not extensible. Especially, there have been several efforts to address location-aware systems (Baldauf, 2007). Espinoza (2001) describes a system which enables users to access information in relation to their position in geographical space. This idea was also followed in a work by Ryan (1999) where users can attach e-notes to geographic positions such that the information is accessible by other users whenever they approach that position. A presence aware system is presented by Kerer (2004).

In this work, we are focusing on services as the to be adapted objects. In this regard, Pauty (2006) through COWSPOTS describes how web service-based context-awareness is used to provide enriched services to medical professionals. The system consists of a central server and several mobile devices that run so called SPOTlets. While several approaches present good solutions for context processing and/or management, they fail to constitute a mechanism that considers traditional web services when it comes to context-aware service invocation. Keidl (2004) presents a framework that facilitates the development and deployment of context-aware adaptable web services. The framework features *context plug-*

ins that pre- and post-process service requests based on available context information. There is one set of context information belonging to each web service. The data set is recursively appended to the exchanged messages whenever a service sends a message to another service. On the invoked side the appended context can be processed and used either by the invoked service or through the context plug-ins. There is one plug-in for each type of context.

In summary, currently the *notion of context* is quite well introduced and elaborated but a consistent, model-driven methodology to rapidly develop context-aware and adaptive mobile services is not available. We will now lay out our approach to devising such methodology by introducing a realistic scenario settled in the e-Business domain and explaining the considerations that will have to be taken into account.

APPLICATION SCENARIO

Basics

In order to illustrate the concepts, we will use a real mobile e-Business scenario from the domain of *Field Service Management* (FSM) solutions. FSM is identified as the attempt to optimize processes and information defined by large manufacturing companies who send technicians or staff out of the office / into the field in order to fix problems regarding products on behalf of the respective company. In the concrete example, FSM allows to dispatch car dealer alerts to field workers issued by the service division of a car manufacturer which is in charge to resolve complex vehicle issues. The engineer can search and download all the relevant information concerning the site where the alert was raised (e.g., relevant service bulletins, parts information, and dealer profile information) before leaving to reach the dealership location. Once at the dealership, the engineer can access new information if needed through the dealer's

communication resources and can devise the best possible strategy to fix the problem searching for the available services available in the dealer's vicinity (e.g., the closest spare parts depot that has the appropriate part).

The mobile users targeted in our scenario are therefore expert users who have to access mobile applications for their work routinely. The scenario already sketches how contextual information plays an important role in our scenario.

Rationale

While in the past companies relied on an in-house workforce, we perceive an increasing number of situations (for instance in facility management a workforce consisting of plumbers and carpenters) in which the workforce is outsourced to small and medium enterprises (SMEs), as well as one-man companies.

This change poses several business and technological challenges to next-generation field worker applications. One business challenge is that each field worker might have *unique and potentially private information* and *business requirements* he or she wants to apply as part of the solution. In other words, there is no a central authority deciding how field workers and manufacturer should collaborate. In addition, other business challenges to be addressed by next generation field worker applications are the following:

- *Higher mobility* and *data accessibility* for the field sales representatives to manage customer information and interactions.
- Improved mobile solutions to allow field technicians to *improve effectiveness* in customer support through mobile access to real time job information such as schedule changes and parts pricing and availability, as well as providing instant information updates from field for quicker customer billing and service.

- Decreased cost - tools to optimize the workforce management of field technicians by providing *added flexibility* in dispatching jobs to workers.

On the technical side, the main challenge is to build a flexible service-oriented architecture for handling context data and interaction across multiple field workers in B3G networks. In more detail, we identified the following technical challenges to be addressed in our solution:

- An increasing number of networked legacy services expose potentially useful *context information*. There is the need to facilitate easy to use (and low-cost) service composition taking into account context.
- There is no a central entity but rather *multiple autonomous entities* sharing only certain amounts of their data.
- Field Workers are mobile by nature. There is a strong need to enable communication across heterogeneous *networking environments*, e.g. B3G.
- Field Workers may implement different architectures. There is a strong need for *adaptability* in this regard.

Scenario Focus

There are different challenges in creating a mobile application addressing our scenario. Among those, in this book we focus on building a complete approach to efficiently dispatch issues across autonomous mobile field workers roaming inside B3G networks. Instead of proposing a one-fits-all approach, the overall task is split into three elementary solutions featuring different functions and services in a complementary way. All solutions can be addressed under a common solution approach as we will show later on, once the methodology and the tools supporting this methodology have been introduced.

The scenario sketched here is only one of many which require the combination of advanced mobility (and resulting issues related to B3G networking) and service computing. Within PLASTIC, similar requirements for applications in e-Voting, e-Health, and e-Learning domains have been identified and solutions have been devised.

REQUIREMENTS FOR METHODOLOGY AND PLATFORM

Nowadays, one of the key issues of creating mobile web services is the lack of a methodology which could help the developer in designing, deploying, interacting with, and testing services in a B3G network.

In this chapter we address this limitation presenting an end-to-end methodology built in PLASTIC to facilitate the exploitation of existing and upcoming mobility technologies to implement services with the adequate quality of service. The methodology relies on three main constituents:

- A *conceptual model* to be used throughout the whole services development life cycle. The conceptual model reflects key require-

Box 1. Requirements for methodology and platform

ments for easing the design, implementation and testing of mobile services.

- A *middleware suite* to support basic and advanced functionalities on the application layer.
- A *service validation and testing framework*, which both could simulate B3G environment for off-line testing and monitor services after deployed.

Prior to entering the details of the solution, in what follows we describe the detailed list of requirements motivating our methodology.

Support for Context-Awareness and Location-Awareness

Mobile web services have to take into account information about the targeted execution environment(s) for making choices and adjustments. In some cases, the code to be executed in different contexts may change substantially according to the device that is being used, the network and the web services available at that particular moment, and even the time of the day or – as the core aspect of mobility - geographical location. To take such decisions, services need to have quantitative and qualitative information at their disposal. Moreover, such context information might be provided by other services either deployed on a mobile device or elsewhere.

Context-awareness becomes then a key feature necessary to provide adaptable services, for instance when selecting the best suited service according to the relevant context information or when adapting the service during its execution according to context changes. In a model-based approach to mobile services design and implementation the support for defining context attributes will have to be ensured.

Support for Service Mobility

User mobility and connectivity changes lead to the necessity of considering features like automatic handover and service reconfiguration to ensure services quality across B3G networks. Automatic handover is required; for instance, when in the above scenario a Field Worker leaves a WLAN zone on his or her way to the Dealer and thus needs to switch to a GPRS network. Though this is usually handled on lower networks layers, there might also be an impact on the service logic. Therefore the middleware should propagate such contextual changes to the service layer. The challenge then lies in ensuring the proper service execution without loosing data or having to starting all over again a transaction. In case of loosing connection, dynamic service reconfiguration is needed to automatically continue the transaction through a new equivalent service without loosing the state reached with the previous connection.

The challenge to dynamically handle changes in the underlying connection leads us to the discussion of the next item: dynamic binding.

Support for Dynamic Binding

A mobile application may employ various services, some of which may be used complementary whereas others may only exist locally (e.g., while being on the Dealer's site). Thus, the binding of services to applications must be resolved dynamically at run time as the location of the user and the quality of his connection cannot be known beforehand. Moreover, it is not possible to predict which service will have the best "offer", in terms of quality of service. Finally, even a strategy of static binding with all available services would be wrong, because services are often provided by third parties and they might change following their own patterns. Hence, dynamic binding is a must for runtime services composition, and in a changing context.

Support for Multi-Radio Networking and Advanced Routing

Another basic issue for mobile web services is given by networking and routing over heterogeneous and evolving networks. Communication between services must automatically take into account multiple kinds of networks (WLAN, Bluetooth, GPRS, etc.) which can potentially be used and selected indistinctly. New routing mechanisms, such as content-based routing, are needed to support mobile communication over evolving B3G networks.

Support for Dependability

Dependability requirements, such as security and reliability, plus quantitative requirements such as performance and scalability, are part of the quality of service (QoS) requirements. They are called non-functional requirements or sometimes "-ilities". In order to guarantee QoS, each service must count with clear information from the commitments assumed by every service to be invoked. In some cases, QoS is the main parameter to choose among available services for dynamic binding. If this information is not available in a way that can be analyzed during runtime, and if it is not monitored effectively, it is not possible to take informed decisions.

The need to assess QoS automatically requires the specification of Service Level Agreements (SLAs) that must be monitored and supervised. The permanent monitoring of QoS also poses a challenge, because of the impact it may have on performance, due to the overhead needed.

We will now describe how the above requirements can be turned into a consistent design methodology for the design and implementation of context-aware adaptive services.

SERVICE DEFINITION AND DESIGN METHODOLOGY

In the proposed methodology, the first element is a *conceptual model for context-aware adaptive mobile services*. The conceptual model focuses on the following key concepts:

- *Context-awareness* and *adaptation* as the context is a key feature distinguishing services in the vast B3G networking environment. Starting with the conceptual model a developer can define a mobile service which will be easily transformed into a running instance by mapping generic functionalities for accessing and processing context to middleware components. Concerning contextual information, the conceptual model distinguishes *context providers* and *context consumers* as shown in the fragment in Figure 2.
- *Service Level Agreements (SLAs)* can be viewed as commitments between *service*

Box 2. Service definition and design methodology

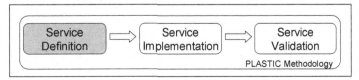

Figure 1. Context-related concepts in the PLASTIC conceptual model

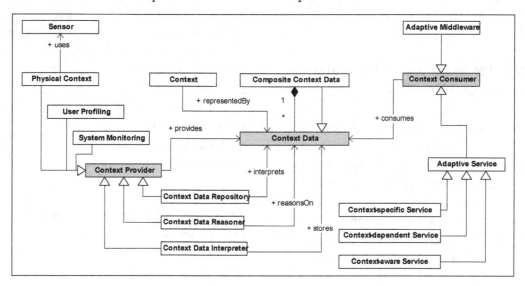

Figure 2. PLASTIC service design process model.

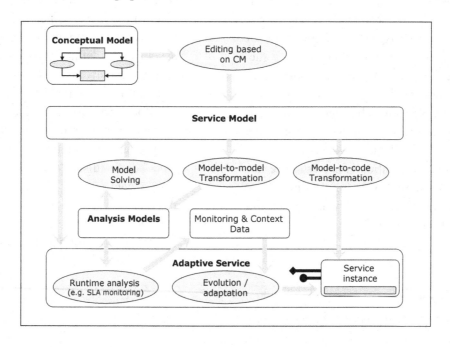

consumers and *service providers*. *SLAs* are built on service descriptions that are characterized functionally, via a service interface, and non-functionally via Service Level Specifications (SLS) which involve parameters exactly from the same domains (physical, user, system) as the context data. For instance, an SLS may specify bandwidth as Quality of Service attribute to be preserved. In order to preserve the bandwidth in case of a contextual change and thus to maintain the SLA, a handover has to be performed.

According to the PLASTIC approach to service design, a definition of a service consists of a functional description and of a Service Level Specification which defines the Quality of Service characteristics of the service. The overall service description is obtained by means of an iterative analysis specification phase that makes use of behavioral models. These models iteratively refined with information from the implementation chain are then made available as artifacts accompanying the service specification.

The elements defined in the conceptual model serve as the basis for a set of model-to-model transformations generating artifacts to be used in following phases of the methodology. The main novelty of this PLASTIC process model is to consider non-functional properties such as SLS as *part of a Service Model*, as opposed to existing approaches where such properties consist, in best cases, of additional annotations reported on a (service) functional model (Skene, 2003).

Figure 3 describes such transformations. This characteristic of the proposed procedure brings several advantages:

- As the whole service model is driven by the conceptual model, less consistency errors can be introduced in its functional and non-functional specification.
- SLS embedded within a service model better supports the model-to-model transformations towards analysis models.
- The path to code generation, the SLS will drive the adaptation strategies.

SERVICE IMPLEMENTATION AND MIDDLEWARE

Overview

As part of the methodology, a set of integrated middleware constituents have been designed to effectively enable the fast implementation and deployment of services on B3G-enabled mobile, resource-constrained devices. In order to address the related issues, the project devised a platform comprising: tools for the *implementation of services*, a *middleware suite* designed as a set of cooperating components, and *testing methods* and tools to validate the dependability of mobile, adaptive services.

The middleware supports services developed following the PLASTIC methodology as well as it enables the execution of, and/or interaction with, networked legacy services.

Box 3. Service implementation and middleware

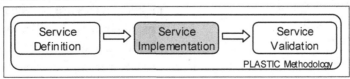

Figure 3. Layered view of adaptive, context-aware middleware advanced communication

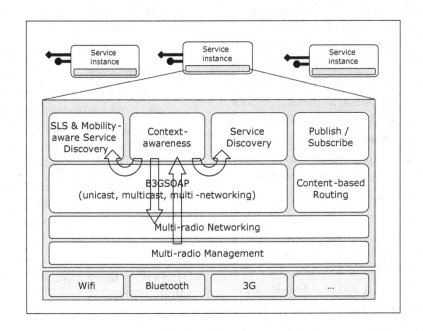

The middleware is structured into two layers:

- At the lower layer, the *Communication Middleware* offers abstractions for the B3G networking environment together with advanced communication protocols supporting interactions in such an environment. The Communication Middleware specifically offers an adaptation of SOAP for B3G (*B3G-SOAP*) and advanced routing protocols over multi-radio networking.
- At the upper layer, the *Middleware Services* offer advanced generic functionalities for the application layer. Middleware Services are built on the Communication Middleware and enable:
  - i. Service management (discovery, access and composition),
  - ii. Context-awareness,
  - iii. Security and trust,
  - iv. Content-based routing.

The middleware suite can be deployed in a distributed way over a wide range of hardware devices, including:

- *Resource-limited devices* on which specific services or client applications are deployed. Such devices primarily access the middleware services through libraries bound to the service or client application.
- *Multi-radio devices* on which the middleware B3G communication components can support dynamic composition of independent networks and creation of multi-networks and overlay networks.
- *Powerful devices* (may have multiple radio interfaces) on which all the middleware components can be deployed and activated.

However, while the hardware platforms of mobile devices are advanced enough, their runtime environments still impose many limitations (e.g., limited access to system information, less capable protocol stacks, no controlled access to network configuration). Therefore the used platform constitutes a certain context that will have to be taken into account when deploying services to a device as well as when accessing remote services from a specific device.

We will now describe middleware starting from the bottom in more detail.

Communication Middleware

The communication middleware targets the creation of a consistent networking environment composed of heterogeneous IP-based networks (Bluetooth, WiFi, GPRS, etc.) by providing proper abstractions and tools which autonomously adapt an application to the underlying networks. Therefore, middleware-aware devices are able to roam throughout such a networking environment by sensing the different wireless radio links available and switching between them (*multi-radio network handover*) according to the application requirements and the networks characteristics. Towards achieving this objective, the communication middleware is composed of several modules illustrated in Figure 4 which also shows the interdependencies of the context-awareness component with the other components of the middleware.

Multi-radio Networking. The Multi-radio Networking module is in charge of (a) selecting the best available network(s) (with respect to both the application requirements and networks characteristics) and switching among networks, (b) managing the communication between devices by means of multi-interfaces addressing scheme and packet routing.

Hence, multi-radio networking defines:

1. An *Addressing Scheme,* referred to as *PLASTIC Address,* that uniquely identifies a PLASTIC-enabled device (and consequently the services hosted by it), and translates into a set of IP addresses.

2. A *routing* scheme to deliver packets in B3G networks by properly choosing one of the available networks and by adopting the corresponding communication protocol.

Multi-Radio Management. The Multi-Radio Management module manages the lower-level characteristics of the networks by means of functionalities and QoS properties. That is, the module is in charge of:

1. Sensing the available networks and retrieving their characteristics (attributes and offered services).
2. Monitoring the status of the networks.
3. Accessing the networks to exploit the offered services.

B3GSOAP. This module features the WS-oriented communication in B3G networks and includes the following functionalities:

- *SOAP interactions over B3G networks* to exchange SOAP messages over the most effective network, considering enforcement of QoS.
- *Multi-network routing* to access services in remote networks as long as there is a path bridging the (heterogeneous) networks between service consumer and producer.
- *Seamless mobility* to maintain active sessions with WSs despite the mobility of nodes.

Protocols. The Advanced Communication Protocols module implements a number of value-added communication services on top of one or more primitive link-level or network-level communication mechanisms. The advanced communication protocol module does not implement any low-level data transport mechanism for wired and/or wireless links and networks, but rather relies on the ones that are available on each device. These low-level communication mechanisms are accessed either directly through the operating system (e.g., in the case of traditional network services such as stable wired IP service) or through the multi-radio network management module. It devises content-based routing as a content-driven communication primitive. This primitive supports a mode of communication where the flow of information, from senders to receivers, is determined by the content of messages together with the declared interests of receivers, rather than by a traditional addressing scheme. Content-based routing realizes a form of communication that is very similar to the publish / subscribe paradigm. Through the PLASTIC middleware, content-based routing protocols are devised that are suitable for deployment over a network of heterogeneous, resource-constrained devices. I.e., the deployment environment consists of for instance mobile terminals and handsets rather than the large, resource-unconstrained routers which are found in the core of fixed communication infrastructures (Carzaniga, 2004).

Middleware Services

In addition to core functionalities, the PLASTIC middleware comes with services of general utility to applications. The set of middleware services provided by the PLASTIC middleware are:

1. Service discovery, and access
2. Context-awareness
3. Security and trust
4. Content sharing and dissemination

We will now introduce all components of the middleware layer putting a focus on the context-awareness module.

Service discovery and access. These middleware elements are mainly intended to enable service discovery of services and access in the B3G networking environment. According to the PLASTIC objective to adhere as much as possible to standard specifications, those elements build upon relevant WS standards like for instance WS-Discovery.

Figure 4. Interfaces of context engine

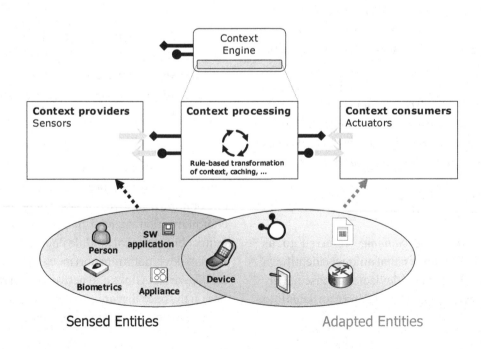

The key contributions of the service discovery, access and composition elements are the following:

- A service discovery for B3G networks that accounts for context, mobility and QoS of service provisioning.
- A Service composition for B3G networks that accounts for the inherent mobility of nodes, introducing advanced capabilities for the dynamic reconfiguration of composite services together with associated consistency management.

Context-awareness and adaptation. The context-awareness and adaptation module features concepts for integrating contextual information into advanced services for the support of mobile processes. Due to the emergence of a variety of location-based legacy services, the middleware primarily focused on *spatio-temporal* context data, which is generated by a configurable set of different sensing systems providing positioning and proximity data.

For the detection, provision, storage, retrieval and application of context data the accurate modeling of the data is quite important. Currently there are several means for context modeling, mainly they are:

1. Key-value models
2. Mark-up scheme models
3. Graphical models
4. Object oriented models
5. Logic based models
6. Ontology based models

Key-Value-Pairs Models constitute the simplest category of models, which is not very efficient for sophisticated structuring and reasoning purposes. Mark-up Scheme Models are typically represented as profiles, for example, CC/PP (Indulska 2003). Graphical Models are particularly useful for structuring, but usually not used on an instance level. Object Oriented Models use general object oriented mechanisms to represent contextual knowledge about temporal, goal, spatial etc. properties. Logic Based Models use logic to define conditions under which a concluding expression or fact may be derived from a set of other expressions or facts. This provides a high degree of formality. Ontology Based Models are used as explicit specification of a shared conceptualization; since most recently OWL is widely used in pervasive computing, it allows for consistency checking and contextual reasoning using inference engines. Within the core component, the so called *context engine*, we feature logic based models since they supports distributed composition and a high level of formality which permits to precisely control the usage of context.

As opposed to other architectural approaches to context management (widget-based or blackboard, see Winograd 2001), the context engine is implemented as a service offering a flexible service interface to process the acquired raw data and making it accessible to other services and applications through various interaction modes. The service-oriented wrapping of the context engine results in the key advantage that the underlying context-sensing (i.e., tracking) technology can be easily exchanged without affecting the rest of the system or – even worse – the process.

The context engine contains means to dynamically register any networked legacy web service as context sensing systems (context producers); through complying with a prescribed context provider adapter (CPA) these sensing systems can be easily changed without affecting the business logic the engine is part of. A high-level of customization is achieved by implementing the processing (transformations, reasoning) of context data through a rule engine which works on an editable hierarchical rule set.

We devise an inner component for the management of the entire lifecycle of the rules contained in the engine:

- *Organise* rules depending on the involved data sets, their respective purposes and priorities; for instance with respect to the featuring of context-awareness in a scenario as the one described here, rules for the *transformation* of location contexts and rules for triggering changes as a consequence of *executing a rule* (when a user enters the vicinity of a maintenance object, the procedure should pop up) have to be distinguished.
- *Manage rules*, i.e.,
  ○ The *creation* of new rules
  ○ The *deletion* of existing rules
  ○ Updating and *modifications* of rules should be possible at runtime
- *Enter rules* in different formats (external representation in XML, spreadsheets) and to interface with state-of-the-art programming languages; within the current implementation, the Java programming language has a prominent place.
- *Administer* access to rules concerning authentication and authorization, either for changing the rule database or for applying the rules contained therein.

In order to support this, the rules are represented in a storable format / language which depends on the underlying rule engine used to execute them. We use the Open Source Rule Engine Drools (Drools) which comes with a rather proprietary but nevertheless very intuitive set of input formats.

The rule data base follows a specific schema. In principal, the following rules can be distinguished (Eikerling 2007):

- *System rules*: these are kind of default rules applied to context data entering or leaving the engine. These rules can be only changed through the administrator and refer e.g. to the management of the context cache (management of cache size, data replacement strategies etc.).

- *Producer rules*: these rules refer to the production of context data. Informally rules of this type can look like this: if an object moves from one location to another, remove location data and transform & store new data set.
- *Consumer rules*: potential consumers of context information provide the format in which they expect to receive the context data (Required Context Syntax) and subscribe for context through the according rules.

These rules are persistently stored in a database which is administrated through a thin ORM layer.

Security. Security is an important aspect of mobile web services. The PLASTIC security module is designed and developed in a service-oriented way. Caution has in particular been taken in order to be able to expose services as Web services. The two main classes of the security services support: (i) standard security functionality (cryptographic operations) and (ii) WS-Security standards. Considering usage by the PLASTIC middleware, the former will aid mostly the service discovery process by ensuring the desired security level and the latter will guide the service composition process in order to assess the security interoperability of the different services.

Content sharing. The set of content sharing services provided by the middleware decompose into: (i) a content-based event notification and data dissemination facility, and (ii) a distributed shared data storage facility. These services are built directly on top of the Communication Middleware. The following are the value-added functionalities implemented by the content sharing and dissemination services:

- *Publish / subscribe* data dissemination is a content-based communication service implemented on top of the content-based routing primitive described above.

• *Distributed, shared data storage* is a collection of algorithms that implement a content-addressable, shared data storage system. This service consists in storing resources (e.g., files, simple tuples, or even service interfaces) in a distributed storage realized through a decentralized community of cooperating but loosely-coupled hosts.

The peer-to-peer overlay management component of the advanced communication module is the basis for this service. In terms of its functional interface, the main feature of this storage facility is typical of many well-established peer-to-peer systems, in that it allows participants to store and access resources by their content or by short content-specific identifiers. In terms of its extra-functional features, this data store is intended to support dynamically networked entities, offering high reliability and minimal access latency overcoming problems caused by temporary disconnections and other adverse network dynamics.

SERVICE VALIDATION AND TESTING

The validation of mobile web services demands for novel technologies to face the high complexity of the systems considered in terms of distribution, mobility, heterogeneity, dynamics, and context-awareness. Considering the plethora of functional and non-functional properties that need to be validated, PLASTIC aims at a holistic approach to testing; the approach includes analytical and empirical techniques to be employed both during development and at runtime.

The testing framework has been organized around two modes of testing referred to as *off-line* and *on-line testing*. The main distinction between the two concerns whether a service is tested in a mock-up environment prior to deployment, or after deployment, by validating its behavior while operating in the real environment.

In order to get a rather complete view on the compliance of a service with the previously established definition and behavior, validation of PLASTIC services should ideally combine both kinds of testing. In particular, in addition to off-line testing, PLASTIC offers on-line testing because the high run-time dynamics of service-oriented systems makes it impossible to foresee and model (as part of the mock-up environment) all possible contexts in which a service will be used. Both off-line and on-line validation should consider the functional and the non-functional properties.

With respect to off-line validation, PLASTIC proposes advanced techniques such as simulation-based testing (Rutherford 2006), model-based testing on symbolic state machine (Frantzen 2007), and support for distributed experimentation and automated test harness generation (Bertolino 2007).

On the other hand, the on-line validation can be further classified into (i) on-line testing before publication, by which a service undergoes a sort of qualification exam, called *Audition*, before it can be "officially" recognized as having adequate quality for being deployed in the platform, and (ii) online monitoring of the service behavior during real usage (Bianculli 2007), in which case we offer an aspect-oriented approach for monitoring service compositions, as well as verification that

Box 4. Service validation and testing

Figure 5. PLASTIC service testing methodology

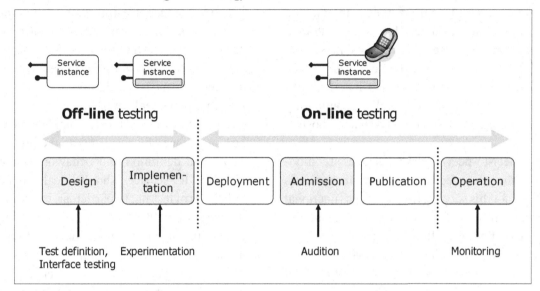

the contractually agreed extra-functional specifications are fulfilled.

As a consequence of the rich variety of challenges, the testing framework features a set of technologies. The combination of the various techniques provides a powerful multilateral approach to the validation of mobile web services.

APPLYING PLATFORM AND METHODOLOGY

Having introduced the model-driven methodology to the design of context-aware mobile services and the supporting software platform in terms of middleware and tools building on it, we now describe the usage with respect to a scenario (dispatching issues to Field Workers across B3G networks) from the e-Business domain.

To achieve IT flexibility and business agility, our solution exploit two SOA principles (Erl 2008, Artus 2006): *Decoupling* and *Ease of Process Implementation.*

Decoupling technologies such as asynchronous message delivery and machine-readable interfaces (e.g. WSDL, see Christensen 2001) enable web service consumers to make choices of implementation and availability independently of the web service provider and vice-versa. Both Manufacturer' and Field Workers' architectures are built on web services. In other words, mobile devices not only consume web services made available by the Manufacturer (or generally available on the Web) but they can also provide services for others to use. This is an important step towards integrating mobility and service computing technologies. However, at the time of writing many mobile devices do not support de-facto service container standards like Axis2[2] available for stationary devices. To cope with such limitation, on mobile devices services are deployed to CSOAP (Sacchetti 2005), a SOAP container specifically built for wireless, resource-constrained devices. Nevertheless, the methodology presented in the paper is generic and can be adapted for other light-weight web services types such as REST (*Representational State Transfer*) or JSON (*JavaScript Object Notation*).

Ease of process implementation is the other key principle we adopted in our solution. We simplified and reduced the implementation cost by adopting the model-to-model transformation functions and the middleware components built in PLASTIC. Complexity and cost of implementation is particularly important for small companies (i.e. Field Workers) which do not have time and resources to invest into an expensive service environment. However, even medium and large companies (i.e. Manufacturer) can benefit from our approach as their IT investments can be used for core business activities rather than generic IT functionalities.

Instead of proposing a monolithic approach, the overall task is split into three elementary solutions featuring different functions and services in a complementary and modular way:

1. **Task Assigner:** the Manufacturer directly dispatches issues to Field Workers as soon as he receives them.

2. **Task Planner:** the Manufacturer plans Field Worker activities by accessing the Field Workers' calendars.

3. **Task Advertiser:** the Manufacturer advertises the issue among the Field Workers interested to solve it.

In the rest of the section, we present some details of the three solutions. For each of them, we present the main challenges, the system architecture, and the impact of PLASTIC methodology and middleware.

Task Assigner

The first approach we built for dispatching issues to Field Workers is quite straightforward: the Manufacturer receives a request and directly assigns it to the Field Worker he or she considers more apt in solving it. At first sight, the solution seems straightforward. However, in our solution the Field Worker receiving the issue might not be

Figure 6. E-business scenario—task assignment

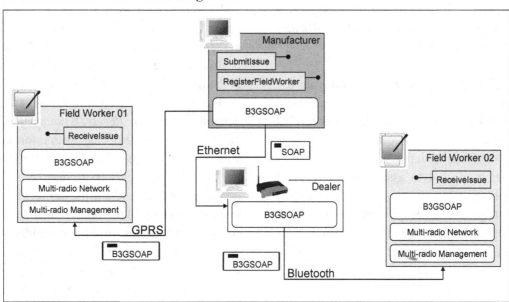

connected to a fixed network but through a B3G network. Consider for example the scenario illustrated in Figure 7. At the time the Manufacturer dispatches an issue, *Field Worker1* has GPRS connectivity to the Internet while *Field Worker2* only has the Bluetooth connectivity offered by the Dealer in which he or she is currently working. Note that Field Workers might choose a B3G network not only because wide area cellular networks (e.g. GPRS / EDGE) are not available, but also to achieve better quality of service (e.g. larger bandwidth) or to reduce connection costs.

In such environment, the main challenge for the Task Assigner solution is therefore discovering the network the Field Worker is currently connected to and to transmit the message across multiple protocols.

Without PLASTIC, the implementation of the solution would have been rather cumbersome as the developers would have to directly manage communication in B3G. On the contrary, by adopting PLASTIC Design Methdology and PLASTIC Communication Middleware, we have been able to rapidly implement a solution which can now be used by a large number of Field Workers being situated in different communication contexts.

Our solution is composed of three core web services, all developed starting from the PLASTIC conceptual model: *RegisterFieldWorker, SubmitIssue,* and *ReceiveIssue.*

1. *RegisterFieldWorker* is running at the Manufacturer side and is invoked each time a new Field Worker subscribes for receiving issues.
2. *SubmitIssue* is deployed at Manufacturer side; it is used to assign issues to Field Workers.
3. Finally, *ReceiveIssue* is deployed to the Field Worker's mobile devices and it is used to receive new issues sent by the Manufacturer.

The use of the conceptual model is especially valuable for the design and implementation of *SubmitIssue* and *ReceiveIssue* service. Specifically, following the methodology proposed in PLASTIC, we

1. first modeled the interface of the Services by specifying its messages (IO data types) and operations.
2. For each operation, we represented the relation between services and context information. In the model, services can be described as *Context providers* (if they provide contextual information from other to use), *Context consumers* (if they need some contextual information as part of their behavior) or both.
3. Finally, we defined if the service was expected to run on B3G networks.

As a result of the modeling process, we had richer service interfaces which can be used by the model-to-model methodology presented in Figure 2. The *model-to-code* transformation has been used to generate the Service stub. Deviating from existing solutions (such as Axis2 wsdl2java), our solution automatically implements both SOAP and CSOAP stub for running on mobile web application servers. To support communication across B3G networks, a unique PLASTIC address is also generated and associated with the service at the time it is deployed or a server.

For instance, a unique PLASTIC address is generated for each *ReceiveIssue* service to be deployed to a mobile device. Such information is communicated to the Manufacturer the first time the Field Worker registers to receive issues (by invoking the *RegisterFieldWorker* service) and it is used by the PLASTIC middleware to seamlessly communicate across different networks.

Not only, the code for connecting service and Context Engine is automatically generated to be able to retrieve (advertise) the context information as defined in the model. With such pre-generated code, the developer can now focus on implementing the core logic which is strictly related to the service. Context information can be retrieved by simply specifying the URL hosting the Context Engine and invoking by the automatically generated class. Similarly, services acting as service providers will automatically publish their information to the Context Engine following the user profiling rules defined in the model (e.g. push context information every hour or for each service invocation).

In our solution, we reduced the burden of managing B3G communication as part of the solution development process by installing PLASTIC Multi-radio Communication and B3G SOAP components in both the Field Workers' mobile devices and at the Manufacturer premises. A similar installation has been also deployed to Dealers offering B3G communication to Field Workers working on their site. An example for this is sketched in Figure 7.

To dispatch an issue to a Field Worker, the Manufacturer invokes the *SubmitIssue* service specifying the Id of the Field Worker who should handle the problem plus information concerning the issue itself. The behavior of *SubmitIssue* is such that it first retrieves (from a local registry) the PLASTIC address of the *ReceiveIssue* service deployed in the Field Worker mobile device. Knowing such information, the multi-radio network automatically discovers the path bridging the heterogeneous networks between *SubmitIssue* and *ReceiveIssue* services. Once the path has been discovered, the request can be routed. B3GSOAP is used to establish connections across different protocols as well as to resolve scenarios in which the Field Worker switches the network before the message is routed to him or her.

The behavior of *ReceiveIssue* is decided by each Field Worker. Some Field Workers might in fact immediately accept the issue while some others might simply generate an alert on the mobile device. However, this is independent of our solution because Field Workers can implement

the behavior they think more appropriate for their business as long as the machine-readable interface of *ReceiveIssue* service doesn't change.

Task Planner

The second solution we built for dispatching issues to Field Workers is called *Planner* as the Manufacturer plans appointments (times and dates) when an issue will be solved by accessing Field Workers' personal calendars.

Existing calendar applications expose calendar information as web services for others to use. While sharing his or her calendar, a user has the possibility to choose to either share the details of each calendar entry or the busy/free status only as context information. While such option is considered sufficient for most applications, it is not enough for our Field Worker scenario. As discussed in the introduction, it is in fact likely that autonomous Field Workers want to apply their own business rules prior to sharing their calendars to others. Rules might be:

- *Public* (e.g., 'on Monday morning, don't accept issues from Dealers located more than 10 miles away from my office') or
- *Private* (e.g., 'on Friday afternoon, show free time-slots only to Dealers with good credit history').

Existing calendar applications do not support such feature as it requires the integration of a context management system flexible enough to handle all information users might be interested to adopt in their rules. Such limitation is even more evident when calendars are managed directly in the mobile device while context information is contained in web services deployed to his or her mobile device (e.g., Field Worker's GPS coordinates) or on the Internet (e.g., Dealer's credit history).

The Task Planner solution we built using PLASTIC is composed of two basic web services: *ShareCalendar* and *CombineCalendars*.

- *ShareCalendar* is deployed to the Field Workers mobile devices and it is used to share calendar information with the Manufacturer. Given each Field Worker might be familiar with a different calendar application, we created adapters to convert data from a common data model to the data model adopted by a specific calendar application and vice-versa.
- *CombineCalendar* is deployed at the Manufacturer side and it is used to access multiple Field Workers' calendars and to directly assign issues into them.

In addition to those, the solution uses the *RegisterFieldWorker* service described in the Task Assigner solution. Like before, *RegisterFieldWorker* is used by the Field Worker to inform the Manufacturer he or she is interested to accept issues and to communicate the PLASTIC address of his or her *ShareCalendar* service.

For editing an issue, the Manufacturer invokes the *CombineCalendar* Service. As part of its implementation, *CombineCalendar* service invokes the *ShareCalendar* services of one or more Field Workers among the ones registered to handle issues. *CombineCalendar* and *ShareCalendar* services communicate across B3G networks using the same methodology as described in the previous section.

The request is transmitted to *ShareCalendar* which does more than sharing calendar information. As part of its behavior, it interacts with the PLASTIC Context Engine to retrieve the information needed to evaluate the rules Field Workers wish to enforce when sharing their calendar.

With our solution, when the Manufacturer requests to access a calendar, the agent at the Manufacturer side does not get access to the actual Field Worker calendar but to a new, *contextualized calendar* which includes the business rule the calendar owner wants to enforce on that specific request. Thus, the PLASTIC middleware enables to federate data (like personal calendars) and helps to avoid data diffusion. Moreover, the sharing of data can be changed at runtime. By adopting the PLASTIC Context Engine, each Field Worker can decide which context information to use in their

Figure 7. E-business scenario—task planner

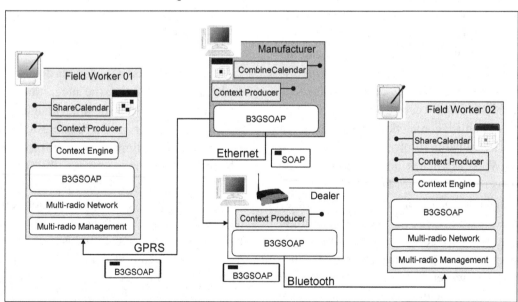

rules by dynamically registering context sensing systems (context producers). Using PLASTIC methodology, we are able to study SLS between *ShareCalendar* services and *CombineCalendar*. For instance, we used PLASTIC Validation and Testing techniques to understand the overall latency of retrieving Calendars from Field Workers in B3G network. In the model, we defined the expected latency of the service (when executed in different mobile devices) along with typical B3G network performances. We then run experiment simulating *CombineCalendar* Service retrieving multiple Calendars from different networks and in different traffic conditions.

Figure 8 depicts the Task Planner behavior. The scenario is the one described for the Task Assigner solution where Field Worker 01 is connected to the Internet via GPRS and Field Worker 02 is connected using Bluetooth. Both Field Workers host the *ShareCalendar* service. In addition, they do host a Context Engine to retrieve and use contextual information for creating ad-hoc customization on their calendar. Any web service (represented in light-gray in Figure 7) can be used as context producer independently from who is hosting the service and the network in which it is currently available.

The main advantage of our solution is that Field Workers can flexibly integrate any context information. Users which are already familiar with a specific calendar application don't have to change their habits as the management of rules is decoupled from the calendar applications.

Task Advertiser

The third and last solution we built to dispatch issues to Field Workers takes a slightly different approach. While in the previous solutions the Manufacturer directly elicits the Field Worker solving an issue, here the Manufacturer advertises issues among all Field Workers interested in handling it. The first Field Worker answering to the offer takes the job.[3] Each Field Worker can either

receive all issues advertised by the Manufacturer or specify rules to filter the issues he or she will receive. For example, a Field Worker might be interested to receive issues from Dealers located in New York or only if they are related to specific problems (e.g. engine failure).

Once again, at first glance the solution resembles a typical publish/subscribe application. However, there are two main challenges in building a publish/subscribe application for dispatching issues to Field Workers in an advanced mobile network environment.

The first challenge is to efficiently advertise issues in absence of a centralized node routing all messages. Thus a distributed approach is required in which each Field Worker can route messages to others. To achieve such behavior, we used the Content-based Routing (CBR) developed in PLASTIC. Built on top of B3GSOAP and Multi-radio Communication components, the PLASTIC CBR comprises algorithms that implement a content-addressable, shared data store. This store is implemented via a decentralized community of loosely-coupled but nevertheless cooperating hosts. Both parties, Field Workers and Manufacturers, are nodes in this community. When a message is routed to a node, the PLASTIC CBR uses the PLASTIC Service discovery to identify other nodes in the proximity. For each of those nodes, PLASTIC Multi-radio Communication is used to route the message across the available B3G network. The CBR is also in charge of evaluating the rules each node specifies against the information (e.g. name and address of the Dealer, type of problem,...) associated to the issue.

The second challenge of implementing the Task Planner is to support Field Workers (subscribers) specifying rules using contextual information which are different from the ones defined by the Manufacturer (publisher). For instance, when advertising an issue, the Manufacturer might specify the name and the address of the Dealer submitting the issue. On the other hand, the Field Worker might be interested to use additional data like the credit history of the Dealer or the physical distance from his or her current positions. Such context information might be private for a single Field Workers or accessible only to a restricted community of Field Workers. The challenge is therefore to implement a flexible solution for each Field Worker participating in the community.

To achieve such objective, we leveraged PLASTIC by integrating Content Based Routing and Context Engine components. Specifically, we extended the routing process implemented by the PLASTIC CBR to consider information retrieved by the PLASTIC Context Engine. When a request is routed to a node, the information associated with the message is treated as a context producer for the Context Engine. The Context Engine can now compute additional context information (e.g. given the address, the context engine can derive the distance between the Dealer and the Field Worker's current position) and use it for evaluating the rules defined by the node. Not only, the information generated by the context engine can

be added to the message and routed to other nodes in the network.

In Figure 9, we give a sketch of how the Task Assigner works. In the example, the Manufacturer advertises an issue to Field Worker 02. The Dealer bridges (and transforms the protocol from SOAP to B3GSOAP) the message and routes it to the Field Worker 02. After receiving the message, Field Worker 02 invokes his or her context engine to derive context information needed to evaluate if the message is relevant. Then, the PLASTIC discovery service component is used to identify the Field Workers in the network to whom to send the message. In this case, Field Worker 01 is found and the message containing the issue advertised by the Manufacturer is transmitted to his or her mobile device via Infrared.

By integrating Content Based Routing and Context Engine we have been able to build a solution in which Field Workers can decide which information (and rules) should be used when filtering for the messages advertised by the Manufacturer.

Figure 8. E-business scenario—task advertiser

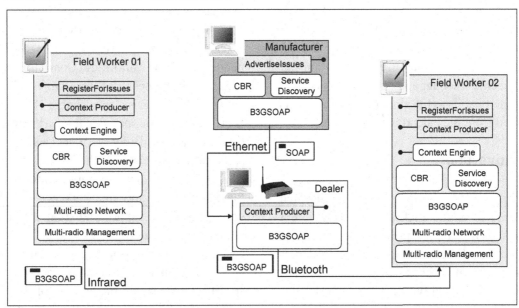

INTENDED IMPACT

The methodology and tools developed in PLASTIC adopt and revisit service-oriented computing for advanced mobile networks such as B3G. The intended impact of the technology is as follows:

Accelerating Mobile B3G Service Development

PLASTIC simplifies the creation of robust, lightweight, context-aware services for open wireless environments, through integrated software engineering methods and tools, from design to validation and testing. Through the PLASTIC platform, developers can now focus on the business logic of their services rather than worrying about subordinated technical requirements such as handling of network heterogeneity, contextual changes, and required adaptations resulting from it or device capabilities.

Particularly, MNOs (mobile network operators) can use PLASTIC to boost the rapid design, deployment and configuration of new revenue generating value-added services with the adequate capabilities for the network they have at their disposal. Alternatively, businesses (like for instance the manufacturing industries) can exploit PLASTIC to embed context-aware adaptive services into their assets. Thus, computational tasks can be installed as services on the devices far beyond data containment and delivery as is done by state-of-the art sensors and RFID tags.

Aligning Business Processes to B3G Services

While the market demonstrated interest in investing in mobility, mobility projects still raise concerns about costs and reliability, especially as they start to interface with enterprise applications like inventory management, field service, and sales force automation across enterprises. PLASTIC, with its modular middleware, consents

a gradual adaptation of existing business processes to support service applications on B3G networks. Service Level Agreements, uniform access to Services independently from their environments, and QoS monitoring of both functional and not functional criteria are only some of the features which simplify the creation of a mobility project. With PLASTIC, mobile projects can start small, be validated over offline and online testing environments and then evolve over time.

Supporting Key Application Areas

In general, PLASTIC impacts organizations willing to introduce mobile services either as final users or as providers. As part of the project, the assessment of PLASTIC is certified through advanced prototype applications with mobile solutions.

We explained the use of the methodology in terms of an e-Business application which straightforwardly can be casted into the manufacturing sector where pending issues are to be dispatched to mobile field workers according to multiple alternatives. Additional to the e-Business domain represented through the Field Service Management application described above, the following application areas are envisaged:

e-Health: the services target the provision of medical care to patients at home and everywhere via B3G networking. SLAs are defined and monitored to check process data among the involved stakeholders (patient, health care provider, insurance company, patient's relatives). Contextual information is constituted by handling the mobility of the users (patients), by multiple user devices to be handled and varying networking parameters. For example, alerts and information accompanying the alert (i.e., patient record) can be routed to a health professional that better fits the demand in terms of qualification or location.

e-Learning: in this scenario, mobile services are used to enable cooperation between students and teachers. Feedback concerning the learning process and the involved material can be given from within a mobile environment. Moreover, the services can be used to establish and maintain online learning communities. For example, the PLASTIC platform can be used to enable and control the diffusion of learning material.

e-Voting: the focus of this scenario is on establishing a high-level of security for a configurable "election" procedure. The key aspect is to ensure universal result verifiability as demanded by market-research and opinion-research companies. The impact of PLASTIC on such application is mainly in ensuring the required security, confidentiality, data integrity attributes on B3G networks readily in place.

FUTURE TRENDS

The focus of this contribution was on introducing a methodology to more efficiently implement mobile services with the primary goal of relieving service developers from handling aspects subordinate to the development of the core service logic. With respect to the currently foreseen trends: (i) the next generation Web will evolve into an Internet of services (ii) the mobility of involved actors (users, devices/terminals, software artifacts) will increase, a next step in developing such services would consist of pulling out certain aspects of handling mobility out of the development process to be handled at runtime. The idea would be to exploit some *emergent behavior* for tuning the services' operations.

As the methodology specifically addresses the support for context-awareness and adaptation, in the future we foresee to describe and model self-adaptations techniques for services. With respect to the context-awareness module, this could be implemented for instance by permitting to enter and modify adaptation rules handled by the Context Engine at runtime.

CONCLUSION

The vision of PLASTIC is that users in the B3G era should be provided with a variety of application services exploiting the network's diversity and richness, without requiring systematic availability of an integrated network infrastructure. In order to significantly ease the development, deployment, on-the-fly adaptation and testing of such services, the PLASTIC platform contributes three core ingredients for this, namely a model-to-model transformations based design approach covering nearly the entire service lifecycle, a configurable middleware suite comprising communication primitives and advanced services and techniques for on-line and off-line testing of services. The chapter presented the complete methodology and its application on a real e-business scenario in the area of Field Service Management (FSM) solutions. Specifically, we demonstrated how PLASTIC can be used to implement multiple techniques for dispatching issues to field workers across B3G networks.

ACKNOWLEDGMENT

This work is partially supported by the PLASTIC Project (EU FP6 STREP n.26955): Providing Lightweight and Adaptable Service Technology for pervasive Information and Communication. http://www.ist-plastic.org.

REFERENCES

Abowd, G. D., Dey, A. K., Brown, P. J., Davies, N., Smith, M., & Steggles, P. (2001). Towards a Better Understanding of Context and Context-Awareness. Lecture notes in computer science: Vol. 1707. *Handheld and ubiquitous computing Proceedings* (pp. 304–307). Berlin: Springer.

Abowd, G. D., Dey, A. K., Brown, P. J., Davies, N., Smith, M., & Steggles, P. (2001). Towards a Better Understanding of Context and Context-Awareness. Lecture notes in computer science: Vol. 1707. *Handheld and ubiquitous computing. Proceedings* (pp. 304–307). Berlin: Springer.

Artus, David J. N. (2006). *SOA realization: Service design principles.* IBM DevelopmentWorks. Available at http://www.ibm.com/developer-works/webservices/library/ws-soa-design/

Baldauf, M., Dustdar, S., & Rosenberg, F. (2007). A survey on context aware systems. *IJAHUC, 2*(4), 263–277.

Bertolino, A., De Angelis, G., & Polini, A. (2007). A QoS Test-bed Generator for Web Services. *Proceedings of ICWE 2007,* Como, Italy, July 16 - 20.

Bianculli, D., & Ghezzi, C. (2007). Monitoring conversational web services. In *Proceedings of the 2nd International Workshop on Service-Oriented Software Engineering* (IW-SOSWE'07), collocated with ESEC/FSE 2007.

Brown, P. J., Bovey, J. D., & Chen, X. (1997). Context-aware Applications: from the Laboratory to the Marketplace. *IEEE Personal Communications, 4*(5), 58–64.

Carzaniga, A., Rutherford, M. J., & Wolf, A. L. (2004). A Routing Scheme for Content-Based Networking. *Proceedings of IEEE INFOCOM 2004.* Hong Kong, China. March, 2004.

Christensen, E., Curbera, F., Meredith, G., & Weerawarana. S. (2001). *Web Services Description Language (WSDL) 1.1.* W3C standard.

Drools, website: http://www.drools.org

Erl, T. (2008). *SOA Principles of Service Design.* 1st ed. Prentice Hall PTR, Upper Saddle River.

Eikerling, H.-J., Benesch, M., & Berger, F. (2007). Using Proximity Relations for the Adaptation of Mobile Field Services. *Proceedings of the International Workshop on the Engineering of Software Services for Pervasive Environments* (ESSPE '07) at ESEC/FSE 2007, September 4, 2007, Dubrovnik, Croatia

Espinoza, F., Persson, P., Sandin, A., Nyström, H., Cacciatore, E., & Bylund, M. (2001). GeoNotes: social and navigational aspects of location-based information systems. *Proceedings of the 3rd International Conference on Ubiquitous Computing* (pp. 2–17). Atlanta, Georgia, USA.

Frantzen, L., & Tretmans, J. (2007), Model-Based Testing of Environmental Conformance of Components. *Proceedings at Formal Methods of Components and Objects* -- FMCO 2006, LNCS 4709, (pp. 1-25). Springer-Verlag.

Henricksen, K. (2003a). *A Framework for Context-Aware Pervasive Computing Applications.* Ph.D. Thesis, University of Queensland, Queensland, Queensland.

Indulska, J., Robinson, R., Rakotonirainy, A., & Henricksen (2003). Experiences in using CC/PP in context-aware systems. *Proceedings of the 4th International Conference on Mobile Data Management* (MDM2003) (Melbourne/Australia, January 2003), M.-S. Chen, P. K. Chrysanthis, M. Sloman, and A. Zaslavsky, Eds., Lecture Notes in Computer Science (LNCS 2574), Springer, (pp. 247–261).

Keidl, M., & Kemper, A. (2004). Towards context-aware adaptable web services. *Proceedings of the 13th International World Wide Web Conference.* Alternate track papers & posters (pp. 55–65). New York: Association for Computing Machinery.

Kerer, C., Schahram, D., Jazayeri, M., Szego, A., Gomes, D., & Caja, J. A. B. (2004). Presence-Aware Infrastructure using Web services and RFID technologies. *Proceedings of the 2nd European Workshop on Object Orientation and Web Services.* Oslo, Norway.

Mitchell, K. (2002). *A Survey of Context-Awareness*. University of Lancaster, Lancaster, UK

Pauty, J., Preuveneers, D., Rigole, P., & Berbers, Y. (2006). *Research Challenges in Mobile and Context-Aware Service Development*.

Rutherford, M., Carzaniga, A., & Wolf, A. L. (2006). Simulation-Based Test Adequacy Criteria for Distributed Systems. *Proceedings of the 14ᵗʰ FSE*, Portland, Oregon, November 2006.

Ryan, N., Pascoe, J., & Morse, D. (1999). Enhanced Reality Fieldwork: the Context Aware Archaeological Assistant. *BAR International Series, 1999*(750), 269–274.

Sacchetti, D., Talamona, A., Cerisara, C., Chibout, R., Ben Atallah, S., & Van Raemdonck. W. (2005). Seamless Access to Mobile Services for the Mobile User. Video at the *3rd International Conference on Pervasive Computing* (Pervasive 2005).

Skene, J., & Emmerich, W. (2003). A Model Driven Architecture Approach to Analysis of Non-Functional Properties of Software Architectures. *Proceedings of the 18th IEEE Conference on Automated Software Engineering*, October 2003, Montreal, Canada. (pp. 236-239). IEEE Computer Society Press.

Strang, T., & Linnhoff-Popien, C. (2004). A Context Modeling Survey. *Proceedings of the Workshop on Advanced Context Modeling, Reasoning and Management* as part of UbiComp 2004, Nottingham.

Winograd, T. (2001). Architectures for Context. *Human-Computer-Interaction, Special Issue on Context-Aware Computing*, 16(2-4).

ENDNOTES

[1] PLASTIC web site, http://www.ist-plastic.org/

[2] http://ws.apache.org/axis/

[3] More complex approaches (e.g. choose the cheapest Field Worker or the one with most experience) can be also applied.

Chapter IX
Bridging the Gap between Mobile Application Contexts and Semantic Web Resources

Stefan Dietze
Open University, UK

Alessio Gugliotta
Open University, UK

John Domingue
Open University, UK

ABSTRACT

Context-awareness is highly desired, particularly in highly dynamic mobile environments. Semantic Web Services (SWS) address context-adaptation by enabling the automatic discovery of distributed Web services based on comprehensive semantic capability descriptions. Even though the appropriateness of resources in mobile settings is strongly dependent on the current situation, SWS technology does not explicitly encourage the representation of situational contexts. Therefore, whereas SWS technology supports the allocation of resources, it does not entail the discovery of appropriate SWS representations for a given situational context. Moreover, describing the complex notion of a specific situation by utilizing symbolic SWS representation facilities is costly, prone to ambiguity issues and may never reach semantic completeness. In fact, since not any real-world situation completely equals another, a potentially infinite set of situation parameters has to be matched to a finite set of semantically defined SWS resource descriptions to enable context-adaptability. To overcome these issues, the authors propose Mobile Situation Spaces (MSS) which enable the description of situation characteristics as members in geometrical vector spaces following the idea of Conceptual Spaces (CS). Semantic similarity between situational contexts is calculated in terms of their Euclidean distance within a MSS. Extending merely symbolic SWS descriptions with context information on a conceptual level through MSS enables similarity-based matchmaking between real-world situation characteristics and predefined resource representations as part of SWS descriptions. To prove the feasibility, the authors provide a proof-of-concept prototype which applies MSS to support context-adaptation across distinct mobile situations.

INTRODUCTION

Current and next generation wireless communication technologies will encourage a widespread use of available resources—data and services—via a broad range of mobile devices resulting in the demand for a rather context-adaptive resource retrieval. Context-adaptation is a highly important feature across a wide variety of application domains and subject to intensive research throughout the last decade (Dietze, Gugliotta & Domingue, 2007; Schmidt & Winterhalter, 2004; Gellersen, Schmidt & Beigl, 2002). Whereas the context is defined as the entire set of surrounding situation characteristics, each individual situation represents a specific state of the world, and more precisely, a particular state of the actual context (Weißenberg, Gartmann & Voisard, 2006). Particularly, a situation description defines the context of a specific situation, and it is described by a combination of situation parameters, each representing a particular situation characteristic. Following this definition, context-adaptation can be defined as the ability of Information Systems (IS) to adapt to distinct possible situations.

To achieve this, we base on a promising technology for distributed and highly dynamic service oriented applications: Semantic Web Services (SWS). SWS technology (Fensel et al., 2006) addresses context-adaptation by means of automatic discovery of distributed Web services as well as underlying data for a given task based on comprehensive semantic descriptions. First results of SWS research are available in terms of reference ontologies—e.g. OWL-S (Joint US/EU ad hoc Agent Markup Language Committee, 2004)

and WSMO (WSMO Working Group, 2004)—as well as comprehensive frameworks (e.g. DIP project[1] results). However, whereas SWS technology supports the allocation of appropriate services for a given goal based on semantic representations, it does not entail the discovery of appropriate SWS goal representations for a given situation. Particularly in mobile settings, the current situation of a user heavily determines the intentional scope behind a user goal and consequently, the appropriateness of particular resources. For instance, when attempting to retrieve localized geographical information, the achievement of a respective goal has to consider the location and device of the user.

Despite the strong impact of a (mobile) context on the semantic meaning and intention behind a user goal, current SWS technology does not explicitly encourage the representation of domain situations. Furthermore, the symbolic approach—describing symbols by using other symbols without a grounding in the real world—of established SWS and Semantic Web (SW) representation standards in general, such as RDF (World Wide Web Consortium, W3C, 2004a), OWL (World Wide Web Consortium, W3C, 2004b), OWL-S (Joint US/EU ad hoc Agent Markup Language Committee, 2004), or WSMO (WSMO Working Group, 2004), leads to ambiguity issues and does not entail semantic meaningfulness, since meaning requires both the definition of a terminology in terms of a logical structure (using symbols) and grounding of symbols to a conceptual level (Cregan, 2007; Nosofsky, 1992). Moreover, while not any situation or situation parameter completely equals another, the description of the complex notion of a specific situation in all its facets is a costly task and may never reach semantic completeness. Apart from that, to enable context-adaptability, a potential infinite set of (real-world) situation characteristics has to be matched to a finite set of semantically defined parameter representations. Therefore, we claim, that fuzzy classification and matchmaking techniques are required to extend and exploit the current functionalities provided by SWS and match the specific requirements of context-aware mobile applications.

Conceptual Spaces (CS), introduced by Gärdenfors (Gärdenfors, 2000; Gärdenfors, 2004) follow a theory of describing entities at the conceptual level in terms of their natural characteristics similar to natural human cognition in order to avoid the symbol grounding issue. CS enable representation of objects as vector spaces within a geometrical space which is defined through a set of quality dimensions. For instance, a particular color may be defined as point described by vectors measuring the quality dimensions hue, saturation, and brightness. Describing instances as vector spaces where each vector follows a specific metric enables the automatic calculation of their semantic similarity, in terms of their Euclidean distance, in contrast to the costly representation of such knowledge through symbolic SW representations. Even though several criticisms have to be taken into account when utilizing CS (Section 0) they are considered to be a viable option for knowledge representation.

In this chapter, we propose Mobile Situation Spaces (MSS) as a specific derivation of Conceptual Situation Spaces (CSS). MSS utilize CS to represent situations and are mapped to standardized SWS representations to enable first, the situation-aware discovery of appropriate SWS descriptions and finally, the automatic discovery and invocation of appropriate Web services to achieve a given task within a particular situation. Extending merely symbolic SWS descriptions with context information on a conceptual level through MSS enables a fuzzy, similarity-based matchmaking methodology between real-world situation characteristics and predefined SWS representations within mobile environments. Since semantic similarity between situation parameters within a MSS is indicated by the Euclidean distance between them, real-world situation parameters are classified in terms of their distance to predefined prototypical parameters,

which are implicit elements of a SWS description. Whereas current SWS technology addresses the issue of allocating services for a given task, our approach supports the discovery of SWS task representations within a given mobile situation. Consequently, the expressiveness of current SWS standards is extended and fuzzy matchmaking mechanisms are supported.

To prove the feasibility of our approach, a proof-of-concept prototype is provided which uses MSS to support context-adaptation by taking into account context parameters such as the current location and desired knowledge subject.

The paper is organized as follows. The following Section 2 provides background information on SWS, whereas Section 3 introduces our approach of Conceptual Situation Spaces which are aligned to current SWS representations. Section 4 illustrates the application of CSS to mobile settings by introducing MSS. Utilizing MSS, we introduce a context-adaptive prototype in Section 5. Finally, we conclude our work in Section 6 and provide an outlook to future research.

SEMANTIC WEB SERVICES AND WSMO

SWS technology aims at the automatic discovery, orchestration and invocation of distributed services for a given user goal on the basis of comprehensive semantic descriptions. SWS are supported through representation standards such as *WSMO* and *OWL-S*. We refer to the *Web Service Modelling Ontology (WSMO)*, a well established SWS reference ontology and framework. The conceptual model of WSMO defines the following four main entities:

- *Domain Ontologies* provide the foundation for describing domains semantically. They are used by the three other WSMO elements. WSMO domain ontologies not only support Web service related knowledge representation but semantic knowledge representation in general.

- *Goals* define the tasks that a service requester expects a Web service to fulfill. In this sense they express the requester's intent.
- *Web service* descriptions represent the functional behavior of an existing deployed Web service. The description also outlines how Web services communicate (*choreography*) and how they are composed (*orchestration*).
- *Mediators* handle data and process interoperability issues that arise when handling heterogeneous systems.

WSMO is currently supported through several software tools and runtime environments, such as the *Internet Reasoning Service IRS-III* (Cabral et al., 2006) and WSMX (WSMX Working Group, 2007). IRS-III is a *Semantic Execution Environment (SEE)* that also provides a development and broker environment for SWS following WSMO. IRS-III mediates between a service requester and one or more service providers. Based on a client request capturing a desired outcome, the goal, IRS-III proceeds through the following steps utilizing the set of SWS capability descriptions:

1. Discovery of potentially relevant Web services.
2. Selection of set of Web services which best fit the incoming request.
3. Invocation of selected Web services whilst adhering to any data, control flow and Web service invocation constraints defined in the SWS capabilities.
4. Mediation of mismatches at the data or process level.

In particular, IRS-III incorporates and extends WSMO as core epistemological framework of the IRS-III service ontology which provides semantic links between the knowledge level components

describing the capabilities of a service and the restrictions applied to its use.

However, even though SWS technologies enable the dynamic allocation of Web services for a given goal, it does not consider the adaptation to different user contexts. In order to fully enable context-aware discovery of resources as required by mobile settings (Section 1), the following shortcomings have to be considered:

I1. *Lack of explicit notion of context*: current SWS technology does not entirely specify how to represent domain contexts. For example, WSMO addresses the idea of context: Goal and web service represent the user and provider local views, respectively; the domain ontologies define the terminologies used in each view; and the mediators are the semantic bridges among such distinct views. However, WSMO does not specify what a context description should define and how the context elements should be used.

I2. *Symbolic Semantic Web representations lack grounding to conceptual level*: the symbolic approach, i.e. describing symbols by using other symbols, without a grounding in the real world, of established SWS, and Semantic Web representation standards in general, leads to ambiguity issues and does not entail semantic meaningfulness, since meaning requires both the definition of a terminology in terms of a logical structure (using symbols) and grounding of symbols to a conceptual level (Cregan, 2007; Nosofsky, 1992).

I3. *Lack of fuzzy matchmaking methodologies*: Describing the complex notion of a specific situation in all its facets is a costly task and may never reach semantic completeness. Whereas not any situation and situation parameter completely equals another, the number of (predefined) semantic representations of situations and situation parameters is finite. Therefore, a possibly infinite set of given (real-world) situation characteristics has to be matched to a finite set of predefined parameter instance representations which are described within an IS. Consequently, fuzzy classification and matchmaking techniques are required to classify a real-world situation based on a limited set of predefined parameter descriptions.

CONCEPTUAL SITUATION SPACES

To address the issues I1—I3 introduced in Section 0, we propose *Mobile Situation Spaces (MSS)* as a setting-specific realisation of our metamodel for *Conceptual Situation Spaces (CSS)* (Dietze, Gugliotta & Domingue, 2008).

CSS Formalisation

CSS enable the description of a particular situation as a member of a dedicated CS. As defined in (Weißenberg et al., 2006) a situation is defined as:

$$S^n = \left\{ (t_1, t_2, cp_1, cp_2, ..., cp_n) \middle| cp_i \in CP \right\}$$

Where t_1 is the starting time of a situation, t_2 represents the end time of a situation and cp_i being situation parameters which are invariant throughout the time interval defined through t_1 and t_2. Referring to (Gärdenfors, 2004; Raubal, 2004), we define a CSS (*css:Conceptual Situation Space* in Figure 1) as a vector space:

$$C^n = \left\{ (c_1, c_2, ..., c_n) \middle| c_i \in C \right\}$$

with c_i being the quality dimensions *(css:Quality Dimension)* of C. In that, a CSS C represents a particular situation S whereas its situation parameters cp_i are represented through certain quality dimensions c_i. Please note, that we do not distinguish between dimensions and domains—beings sets

of integral dimensions (Gärdenfors, 2004)—but enable dimensions to be detailed further in terms of subspaces. Hence, a dimension within one space may be defined through another conceptual space by using further dimensions (Raubal, 2004). In such a case, the particular quality dimension c_j is described by a set of further quality dimensions with

$$c_j = D^n = \left\{ (d_1, d_2, ..., d_n) \middle| d_k \in D \right\}$$

In this way, a CSS may be composed of several subspaces and consequently, the description granularity of a specific situation can be refined gradually. To reflect the impact of a specific quality dimension on the entire CSS, we consider a prominence value p *(css:Prominence)* for each dimension. Therefore, a CSS is defined by

$$C^n = \left\{ (p_1 c_1, p_2 c_2, ..., p_n c_n) \middle| c_i \in C, p_i \in P \right\}$$

where P is the set of real numbers. However, the usage context, purpose and domain of a particular CSS strongly influence the ranking of its quality dimensions. This clearly supports our position of describing distinct CSS explicitly for specific domains only.

Particular members *(css:Member)* in the CSS are described through a set of valued dimension vectors *(css:Valued Dimension Vectors)*. Symbolic representations of domain situations and parameters, such as *css:Situation Description* and *css:Situation Parameter*, refer to particular CSS *(css:Conceptual Situation Space)* whereas parameter instances are represented as members *(css:Member)*.

Moreover, referring to Gärdenfors (2004) we consider prototypical members *(css:Prototypical Member)* within a particular space. Prototypical members enable the classification of any arbitrary member m within the a specific CSS, by simply calculating the Euclidean distances between m and all prototypical members in the same space to identify the closest neighbours of m. For instance,

Figure 1. The CSS metamodel

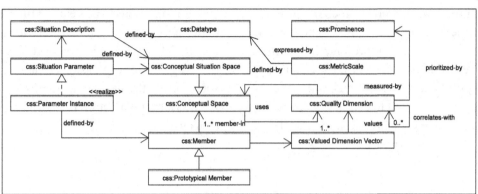

given a CS to describe apples based on their shape, taste and colour, a green apple with a strong and fruity taste may be close to a prototypical member representing the typical characteristics of the Granny Smith species. Figure 1 depicts the CSS metamodel.

The metamodel introduced above has been formalized into a *Conceptual Situation Space Ontology (CSSO)*, utilizing OCML (Motta, 1998). In particular, each of the depicted entities is represented as a concept within CSSO whereas associations are reflected as their properties in most cases. The correlation relationship indicates whether two dimensions are correlated or not. For instance, when describing an apple the quality dimension describing its sugar content may be correlated with the taste dimension. Information about correlation is expressed within the CSSO through axioms related to a specific quality dimension instance. CSSO is aligned to a well-known foundational ontology: the Descriptive Ontology for Linguistic and Cognitive Engineering (DOLCE) (Gangemi, Guarino, Masolo, Oltramari, Schneider, 2002) and, in particular, its module Descriptions and Situations (D&S) (Gangemi, Mika, 2003). The aspect of gradually refining a CSS through subspaces corresponds to the approach of DOLCE D&S to gradually refine a particular description

by using parameters where each parameter can be described by an additional description.

With respect to (Raubal, 2004), we define the semantic similarity between two members of a space as a function of the Euclidean distance between the points representing each of the members. However, we would like to point out, that distinct distance metrics, such as the Taxicab or Manhattan distance (Krause, 1987), could be considered, even though the nature of the space and its possible metrics suggests the Euclidean distance as a useful metric to calculate similarities. Applying a formalization of CS proposed in Raubal (2004) to our definition of a CSS, we formalize the Euclidean distance between two members in a CSS as follows. Given a CSS definition C and two members represented by two vector sets V and U, defined by vectors $v_0, v_1, ...,v_n$ and $u_1, u_2,...,u_n$ within C, the distance between V and U can be calculated as:

$$\left|d(u,v)\right|^2 = \sum_{i=1}^{n}(z(u_i) - z(v_i))^2$$

where $z(u_i)$ is the so-called Z-transformation or standardization (Devore, Peck, 2001) from u_i. Z-transformation facilitates the standardization of distinct measurement scales which are utilized by different quality dimensions in order to enable the calculation of distances in a multi-dimensional and multi-metric space. The z-score of a particular observation u_i in a dataset is calculated as follows:

$$z(u_i) = \frac{u_i - \bar{u}}{s_u}$$

where $\bar{u}$ is the mean of a dataset U and s_u is the standard deviation from U. Considering prominence values p_i for each quality dimension i, the Euclidean distance $d(u,v)$ indicating the semantic similarity between two members described by vector sets V and U can be calculated as follows:

$$d(u,v) = \sqrt{\sum_{i=1}^{n} p_i \left(\left(\frac{u_i - \bar{u}}{s_u} \right) - \left(\frac{v_i - \bar{v}}{s_v} \right) \right)^2}$$

Utilizing CSS for SWS Selection

Whereas the discovery of distributed Web services for a given user goal is addressed by current SWS technology, such as WSMO, and corresponding reasoners, the context-aware selection of a specific SWS goal representation for a given situation is a challenging task to be tackled when developing SWS-driven applications. By providing an alignment of CSS and SWS, we address this issue by enabling the classification of an individual situation along predefined situation descriptions—used within SWS descriptions—based on semantic similarity calculation. Therefore, CSS are aligned to WSMO to support the automatic discovery of the most appropriate goal representation for a specific situation. Since both metamodels, WSMO as well as CSS, are represented based on the OCML representation language (Motta, 1998), the alignment was accomplished by defining relations between concepts of both ontologies as depicted in Figure 2.

Grey colored concepts in Figure 2 represent concepts of WSMO. A goal description (*wsmo: Goal*) utilizes particular situation parameters (*css:Situation Parameters*) to semantically describe its capabilities, i.e. its assumptions, effects, preconditions and postconditions in terms of semantic situation descriptions *(css:Situation Description)*. A WSMO runtime reasoning engine utilizes capability descriptions to identify SWS (*wsmo:Web Service*) which suit a given Goal. In contrast, the preliminary selection of the most appropriate goal description for a given situation is addressed by classification of situation parameters through CSS. For instance, given a set of real-world situation parameters, described as members in a CSS, their semantic similarity with predefined prototypical parameters *(css: Prototypical Member)* is calculated. Given such a classification of a particular real-world situation, a goal representation which assumes matching

Figure 2. Alignment of CSS and WSMO

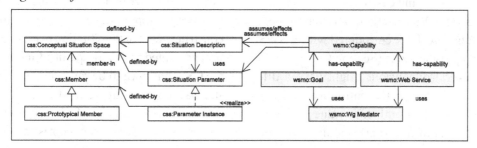

prototypical parameter instances is selected and achieved through the reasoning engine.

Deriving CSS for certain Application Contexts

As stated in Gärdenfors (2000), the definition and prioritization of quality dimensions within a CS is highly dependent on the purpose and context of the space. For instance, when describing an apple, dimensions may be differently weighted, dependent on whether the apple is subject to visual cognition exclusively or to full sensory perception, what would be the case if the apple is supposed to be eaten. Whereas in the first case, dimensions such as color and shape are highly ranked, taste and texture may additionally be important in the latter case.

Consequently, the derivation of an appropriate space for a certain purpose is considered an important task which usually should be carried out by a qualified individual such as an application designer. We particularly foresee a procedure consisting of the following steps:

S1. Identification of situation parameters eligible for representation as quality dimension c_i.
S2. Assignment of prominence values p_i to each quality dimension c_i.
S3. Assignment of metrics to each quality dimension c_i.

With respect to *S1*, one has to take into account which aspects of a situation are relevant from an application perspective, i.e. which characteristics have an impact on the applied context adaptation strategy or rules. In the case of our intended usage of CSS for SWS selection, only parameters are important, which are considered within SWS capability representations (Section 0).

Since several dimensions might have a different impact factor on the entire space, *S2* is aimed at assigning a prominence value p_i to each dimension c_i. Prominence values should usually be chosen from a predefined value range, such as 0...1. However, since the assignment of prominences to quality dimensions is of major importance for the semantic meaning of calculated distances within a space, this step is not straightforward and most probably requires ex post re-adjustment.

During the final step *S3*, a quantitative metric has to be assigned to each previously defined dimension. Whereas certain dimensions naturally are described using qualitative measurements, such as a size or a weight, other dimensions are usually described using rather qualitative values. The latter applies for instance to the notion of a color. In case no quantitative metric can be assigned to a certain quality dimension c_i, a subspace has to be defined which refines the particular dimension through further dimensions. For instance, in the case of the color dimension, a subspace could be defined using the quantitative dimensions hue, saturation and brightness. Hence, the proposed procedure has to be repeated iteratively until a sufficient description depth has been achieved leading to the definition of a CSS C of the form (Section 0):

$$C^n = \left\{ \left(p_1 c_1, p_2 c_2, ..., p_n c_n \right) \middle| c_i \in C, p_i \in P \right\}$$

A MOBILE SITUATION SPACE

Following the steps introduced in Section 0, we derive a CSS aimed at representing situations in mobile settings. A mobile situation is defined by parameters such as the technical environment used by a user, his/her current objectives and particularly the current location. Since each of these parameters apparently is a complex theoretical construct, most of the situation parameters cannot be represented as a single quality dimension within the CSS, but have to be represented as dedicated subspaces which are defined by their very own dimensions (Section 0). Moreover, applying CSS to represent a particular concept is only reasonable in cases where similarity calculation is possible and semantically meaningful, i.e. a particular measurement can be applied to each quality dimension. For instance, the native language of a user is a crucial important situation parameter, but in this case, only a direct match is reasonable in order to provide appropriate information resources in the correct language to the user.

Therefore, this section focuses exemplarily on the representation of two parameters through a CSS subspace, which are of particular interest: the *location* and the *subject* a user is interested in. Due to the complex and diverse nature of a particular subject or spatial location, traditional symbolic representation approaches of the Semantic Web are supposed to fail since it is nearly impossible to define either a subject or a location in a non-ambiguous and comprehensive way by just following a symbolic approach.

Moreover, a one-to-one matchmaking between different locations and subjects is hard to achieve, since fairly not any instance of these parameters completely equals another one. Therefore, fuzzy similarity detections, as enabled through MSS, have to be utilized.

To represent spatial locations, we define a CSS subspace L with 2 quality dimensions l_i

representing the latitude and longitude of a particular location

$$L^2 = \left\{ \left(l_1, l_2\right) \middle| l_i \in L \right\}$$

In order to represent a particular subject, we currently consider 4 dimensions (history, geography, culture, languages) which are used to describe the semantic meaning of a particular subject within subspace S:

$$S^4 = \left\{ \left(s_1, s_2, s_3, s_4\right) \middle| s_i \in L \right\}$$

Figure 3 depicts the key concepts of the ontology describing L and S as subspaces (*css:Location Space, css:Subject Space*) within the mobile space (*css:Mobile Situation Space*).

Moreover, Figure 3 depicts the relation of the subspace L (*css:Location Space*) and subspace S (*css:Subject Space*) with WSMO-based SWS descriptions, represented via grey-colored concepts (Section 0).

Instances of a situation parameter representing a subject are defined by particular members within the space S (*css:Subject Space*), which itself uses 4 quality dimension c_i, whereas instances

Figure 3. Key concepts representing mobile situation subspaces

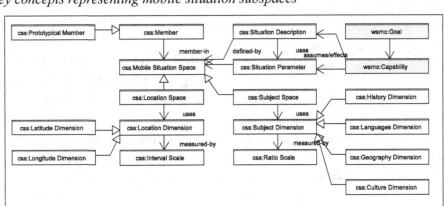

of a parameter representing a spatial location are defined by members within the space L (*css: Location Space*), which itself uses 4 quality dimension l_i. The metric scale, datatype and value range for each dimension s_i and l_i are presented in Table 1.

As depicted in Table 1, each quality dimension l_i is ranked on an interval scale with value ranges being float numbers between -90 and +90 in case of the latitude and between -180 and +180 in case of the longitude. Furthermore, each quality dimension c_i is ranked on a ratio scale with value ranges being float numbers between 0 and 100. The authors would like to highlight, that no prominence values have been assigned since each dimension has an equal impact to define a particular member. It is obvious, that the assignment of prominence values is a highly subjective process, strongly dependent on the purpose, context and individual preferences. Therefore, future work is aimed at enabling users to assign rankings of quality dimensions themselves in order to represent their individual priorities regarding the service retrieval process.

To classify an individual mobile situation, we define prototypical members (*css:Prototypical Member*) in the Mobile Situation Space. For instance, to describe particular cities as members within L, we utilized geodata, retrieved from GoogleMaps[2], to describe a prototypical member for each location which is targeted by a particular SWS. A few examples of prototypical location members used in the current prototype application are represented in Table 2:

An example of how such parameters are represented in a formal knowledge modeling language is given in Section 0. Moreover, we predefined several prototypical subjects in S, each representing the maximum value of a particular quality dimension s_i what resulted in the following 4 prototypical subjects.

Apart from the depicted subjects, each subject which is described as part of a symbolic SWS

Table 1. Metric scale, range, and data type of quality dimensions l_i and s_i

	Quality Dimension	Metric Scale	Data-type	Range
l_1	Latitude	Interval	Float	-90..+90
l_2	Longitude	Interval	Float	-180..+180
s_1	History	Ratio	Float	0..100
s_2	Culture	Ratio	Float	0..100
s_3	Geography	Ratio	Float	0..100
s_4	Language	Ratio	Float	0..100

Table 2. Prototypical members within L

Prototype	l_1 (Latitude)	l_2 (Longitude)
L1: Milton Keynes (UK)	52.044041	-0.699569
L2: London (UK)	51.500152	-0.126236
L3: Brighton (UK)	50.820931	-0.139846
L4: Paris (FR)	48.85667	2.350987
L5: Toulouse (FR)	43.604363	1.442951

Table 3. Prototypical members within S

Prototype	s_1	s_2	s_3	s_4
S1: History	100	0	0	0
S2: Culture	0	100	0	0
S3: Geography	0	0	100	0
S4: Languages	0	0	0	100

capability representation had been referred to an individual member in S.

SIMILARITY-BASED SWS SELECTION AND ACHIEVEMENT IN A MOBILE SETTING

To prove the feasibility of our approach, we provide a proof-of-concept prototype application, which utilizes MSS (Section 4)—based on the CSS metamodel introduced in Sections 0—and supports context-adaptation in a mobile environment based on SWS and CSS.

Runtime Support for CSS and SWS

The following Figure 4 depicts the general architecture adopted to support reasoning on MSS and SWS in distinct domain settings through a Semantic Execution Environment (SEE), which in our case is IRS-III (Section 0).

Multiple mobile devices—such as PDAs, mobiles or any other portable device hosting a Web browser—can serve as user interface of the SEE, enabling the user (and the device itself) to provide information about his/her goal and the current real-world situation.

The SEE makes use of semantic representations of the CSS formalisation (CSS ontology, CSSO), specifically derived for mobile settings, and of SWS annotations based on WSMO in order to discover and allocate the most appropriate resource for a given user goal within a current situation. Ontologies had been represented us-

ing the OCML knowledge modeling language (Motta, 1998).

WSMO capabilities are represented by defining the assumptions and effects of available SWS and goals in terms of certain situation description or situation parameter instances (Section 0). Such situation descriptions are refined as particular prototypical members of an associated CSS, such as prototypical members of the MSS S and L introduced in Section 4.

As mentioned in Section 3, CSSO allows us to describe a specific mobile situation description instance in terms of a collection of situation parameter instances. Mobile situation description instances are automatically and gradually defined at runtime by the SEE as the result of the user interaction with the mobile device. On the basis of the detected context parameters, the SEE performs the following steps:

1. Computation of similarities between the detected real-world context parameters— obtained from the user and its device—and

Figure 4. Architecture to support runtime reasoning on CSS and SWS

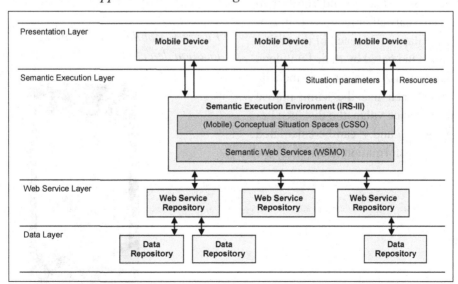

symbolic representation of prototypical situation parameters;

2. Progressive update of the current mobile situation description with the closest prototypical situations parameters;

3. Determination of (WSMO) goal matching the refined situation description;

4. Achievement of selected goals by means of discovery and orchestration of available web services.

Consequently, we enable the classification of real-world context parameters along available predefined parameters in order to enable a similarity-based selection and orchestration WSMO goals.

Context Classification and Adaptation

As outlined in the previous section, the SEE automatically detects the semantic similarity of specific situation parameters with a set of predefined prototypical parameters to enable the allocation of context-appropriate resources. In this section, we further detail these aspects, since they are central in the contribution of this chapter. In particular, we specify the concepts of classification and adaptation.

Referring to CSS subspaces L and S described in Section 0, given a particular member U in L or S, its semantic similarity with each of the prototypical members is indicated by their Euclidean distance. Since we utilize spaces described by dimensions which each use the same metric scale and no prominence value, the distance between two members U and V can be calculated disregarding a Z-transformation (Section 0) for each vector:

$$d(u,v) = \sqrt{\sum_{i=1}^{n}(u_i - v_i)^2}$$

Please note, that it would be possible to calculate distances either between entire situations (members within *css:Mobile Situation Space*) or between particular parameter (members in subspaces such as L and S). Since individual semantic similarities between instances of parameters such as the current location or the desired subject are usually important knowledge when deciding about the appropriateness of resources for a given context, the current application calculates distances between each parameter, i.e. between members within each individual subspace.

The calculation of Euclidean distances using the formula shown above is performed by a standard Web service, which is annotated as SWS and invoked through IRS-III at runtime. Given a particular CSS description, a member (representing a specific parameter instance) as well as a set of prototypical member descriptions (representing prototypical parameter instances), similarities are calculated by the Web service at runtime in order to classify a given situation parameter.

For instance, a user is currently located in Eastbourne (UK) and is interested in historical information about the surrounding area. Consequently, the particular situation description (*css:*

Figure 5. Mobile device showing semi-automatic location detection

MobileSituationDesccription) includes a location parameter which is defined by a member E in the specific location space (*css:Location Space*) with the following vectors describing latitude and longitude of Eastbourne:

$$E = \left\{ (e_1 = 50.766868, e_2 = 0.284804) \middle| e_i \in L \right\}$$

To represent the current aim of the user, a user selects one of the subject prototypes (Section 0), in this case *S1* (Table 3), which is added to the situation description.

Figure 5 depicts a screenshot of a mobile device showing the application web-interface while supporting a user to semi-automatically locate him-/herself utilizing geodata dynamically retrieved from GoogleMaps. By providing incomplete knowledge about the current location, for instance the current city, full geospatial

datasets, including the latitude and longitude of a location, are retrieved dynamically to enable similarity-based location matchmaking.

Based on the current situation description, SWS are selected which are able to address the situation. Whereas parameters which are not defined by members in a specific CSS require a direct match with a corresponding SWS description, a similarity-based match is computed for parameters which are described in a CSS, e.g. the location or the subject. Hence, distance calculation was utilized to identify similarities between current context parameters—such as E and *S1*—and prototypical parameters which had been defined as part of SWS capability descriptions in order to represent the parameters targeted by available SWS. In order to illustrate the representation of prototypical CSS members, the following OCML code defines a location parameter instance rep-

Listing 1. Partial OCML code defining location parameter instance and respective MSS member

```
(def-instance brighton-location location
      ((has-instance-title "Brighton")
      (defined-by p2-location-brighton)))


(def-instance p2-location-brighton location-prototypical-member
      ((has-title "Location-Brighton ")
      (has-description "Prototype describing Brighton")
      (member-in location-space)
(has-valued-dimension (brighton-valued-lat-vector brighton-valued-long-vector))))


(def-instance brighton-valued-lat-vector location-valued-dimension-vector
      ((values latitude-dimension)
       (has-value 50.820931)))


(def-instance brighton-valued-long-vector location-valued-dimension-vector
      ((values longitude-dimension)
       (has-value -0.139846)))
```

Table 4. Distances between E and targeted locations

Prototype	Euclidean Distance
L1: Milton Keynes (UK)	1.6125014961413195
L2: London	0.8406303029608179
L3: Brighton	0.42807759865356176

Table 5. Distances between S1 and targeted subjects

Subject	Euclidean Distance
S5 (50,0,50,0)	70.71067811865476
S6 (65,0,0,35)	49.49747468305833
S7 (70, 30,0, 0)	35.35533905932738

resenting the geospatial location Brighton, as well as the respective prototypical member (*L3*) in the MSS *L*.

Calculating distances between *E* and targeted locations—represented as prototypical MSS members—led to the identification of the following distances to the three closest matches:

Since not any SWS targets historical interests (*S1*) exclusively—as desired by the user—no direct match between the situation and subjects targeted by available SWS was achieved. However, similarity calculation identified related subject

areas, which partially target historical information. Table 5 indicates their vectors and distances to the required subject *S1*.

The subjects *S5*, *S6* and *S7* as well as the locations *L1*, *L2*, and *L3* shown in Table 4 and Table 5 had been described as prototypical members in the MSS (Section 0) during the development of SWS representations targeting certain subjects and locations. By following our alignment from Section 0, this task could be performed by either the Web service provider or any SWS expert who is providing and publishing a semantic representation of available Web services.

As indicated by the Euclidean distances depicted in Tables 4 and 5, the closest matching SWS provides historical and cultural (*S7*) resources for the Brighton (*L3*) area, as these show the lowest distances. Provided these similarities, a user is able to select predefined parameters that best suit his/her specific preferences within the current situation. In that, the use of similarity-based classification enables the gradual refinement of a situation description and fuzzy matchmaking between real-world situations, and prototypical parameters predefined within a SWS description. For example, the following OCML code defines the partial capability description of a Web service that provides historic and cultural information for the area of Brighton (Listing 2).

In fact, the assumption expression presented above describes that situation description representing the current situation (*has-situation*)

Listing 2. Partial OCML code representing SWS capability in terms of assumed MSS members

```
(def-class lpmo-get-brighton-his-and-cult-LOs-ws-capability (capability) ?capability
((used-mediator :value lpmo-get-brighton-his-and-cult-LOs-mediator)
    (has-assumption :value
        (KAPPA (?web-service)
(and (= (get-location (wsmo-role-value ?web-service 'has-situation)) " Brighton"))
(= (get-subject (wsmo-role-value ?web-service 'has-situation)) "S7")))))
```

consider the location *Brighton* and the subject *S7*.

As a result, in our approach, the actual mobile situation description (i.e. the actual context) is the result of an iterative process that involves several distance calculations to map symbolic representations and real world characteristics. Notice that this process actively involves the end users in providing observables and validating the distance calculations. According to the obtained situation parameters and the selected user goal, the SEE discovers and orchestrates annotated Web services, which show the capabilities to suit the given situation representation. Whereas discovery and orchestration are addressed by existing SWS technology, the context-aware selection of a specific SWS goal representation is addressed through CSS by enabling similarity-based classifications of individual situations as described in the previous sections.

RELATED WORK

Since our work relates to several different but related research areas, we report here related work on (i) Semantic Web Services, (ii) Context-adaptive systems, and (iii) Context-adaptation in mobile environments. Moreover, by comparing our approach with related work in (iii) we describe our contribution to the current state of the art in context-adaptive mobile and ubiquitous computing.

SWS: OWL-S (OWL-S Coalition. 2004) is a comparatively narrow framework and ontology for adding semantics to Web service descriptions. In order to identify problematic aspects of OWL-S and suggest possible enhancements, a contextualized core ontology of services has been described in Mika et al. (2004). Such an ontology is based on DOLCE (Gangemi et al., 2002) and its specific module D&S (Gangemi, Mika, 2003). Even though we followed a similar approach, we adopt WSMO (WSMO Working Group, 2004) instead of OWL-

S as reference ontology for SWS. Moreover, the aim of our resulting ontology is not proposing changes to WSMO, but creating domain-specific models which incorporate WSMO-based SWS representations.

Context-adaptive systems: in Bouquet et al. (2003) the authors define contexts as the local models that encode a party's view of a domain. They distinguish contexts from ontologies, since the latter are shared models of some domain that encode a view which is common to a set of different parties. Contexts are best used in those applications where the core problem is the use and management of local and autonomous representations with a need for a lack of centralized control. For example, the notion of contexts is used in some applications of distributed knowledge management Bonifacio et al. (2003), pervasive computing environments (Chen, Finin & Joshi, 2003) and peer-to-peer applications (Serafini et al., 2003). According to the definition introduced in Bouquet et al. (2003), we propose a novel use of contexts. The local models encode party's view of SWS-based process descriptions.

Context-adaptation in mobile environments: Weissenberg et al. (2006) adopt an approach to context-adaptation in mobile settings which shows some similarities to ours: given a set of context parameters—based on sensor data—first a context is identified and then a matching situation. However, they rely on manually predefined axioms which enable such a reasoning compared to the automatic detection as proposed in this paper. Korpipaa et al. (2003) propose a related framework but firstly, require client-side applications to be installed and, secondly, relies on Bayesian reasoning for matching between measured lower-level contexts and higher-level context abstractions represented within an ontology. Hence, as a major lack, it is required to provide information about contexts and their relations within a Bayesian Network in order to perform the proposed reasoning. Gu, Wang, Pung & Zang (2004) propose a context-aware middleware which also distinguishes between lower-level and higher-level contexts. However, there is no mechanism to automatically identify relationships between certain contexts or context parameters. The same criticism applies to the approaches to a semantic representation of user contexts described in Toivinen, Kolari & Laako (2003) and Sathish, Pavel & Trossen (2006).

Finally, it can be highlighted, that current approaches to context-adaptation in mobile settings usually rely on the manual representation of mappings between a given set of real-world context data and predefined context representations. Since this approach is costly and time-consuming, our approach could contribute there significantly by providing a similarity-based and rather fuzzy method for automatically identifying appropriate symbolic context representations given a set of detected context parameters.

CONCLUSION

In this paper, we proposed an approach to support fuzzy, similarity-based matchmaking between real-world situation parameters in mobile settings and predefined semantic situation descriptions by incorporating semantic context information on a conceptual level into symbolic SWS descriptions based on Conceptual Situation Spaces. Given a particular mobile situation, defined by parameters such as the location and device of the user, the most appropriate resources, whether data or services, are discovered based on the semantic similarity, calculated in terms of the Euclidean distance, between the real-world situation and predefined resource descriptions as part of SWS representations. Even though we refer to the SWS framework WSMO in this paper, we would like to highlight, that our approach could be applied to other SWS reference ontologies such as OWL-S (OWL-S Coalition. 2004). Consequently, by aligning CSS to established SWS technologies, the expressiveness of symbolic SWS standards is

extended with context information on a conceptual level described in terms of natural quality dimensions to enable fuzzy context-aware delivery of information resources at runtime. Whereas current SWS frameworks address the allocation of distributed services for a given (semantically) well-described task, Mobile Situation Spaces particularly address the similarity-based discovery of the most appropriate SWS task representation for a given situation. To prove the feasibility of our approach, a proof-of-concept prototype application was presented, which applies the MSS to enable context-adaptive resource discovery in a mobile setting.

However, although our approach applies CS to solve SWS-related issues such as the symbol grounding problem, several criticisms still have to be taken into account. Whereas defining situational contexts, respectively members within a given MSS, appears to be a straightforward process of assigning specific values to each quality dimension, the definition of the MSS itself is not trivial at all and strongly dependent on individual perspectives and subjective appraisals. Whereas the semantics of an object are grounded to metrics in geometrical vector spaces within a MSS, the quality dimensions itself are subject to ones perspective and interpretation what may lead to ambiguity issues. With regard to this, MSS do not appear to solve the symbol grounding issue but to shift it from the process of describing instances to the definition of a MSS. Moreover, distinct semantic interpretations and conceptual groundings of each dimension may be applied by different individuals. Apart from that, whereas the size and resolution of a MSS is indefinite, defining a reasonable space for a specific domain and purpose may become a challenging task. Nevertheless, distance calculation as major contribution of the MSS approach, not only makes sense for quantifiable parameters but also relies on the fact, that parameters are described in the same geometrical space.

Consequently, CS-based approaches, such as MSS, may be perceived as step forward but do not fully solve the issues related to symbolic Semantic Web (Services)-based knowledge representations. Hence, future work has to deal with the aforementioned issues. For instance, we foresee to enable adjustment of prominence values to quality dimensions of a specific space to be accomplished by a user him/herself, in order to most appropriately suit his/her specific priorities and preferences regarding the resource allocation process, since the prioritization of dimensions is a highly individual and subjective process. Nevertheless, further research will be concerned with the application of our approach to further domain-specific situation settings.

REFERENCES

Bouquet, P., Giunchiglia, F., van Harmelen, F., Serafini, L., & Stuckenschmidt, H. (2003). C-OWL: Contextualizing Ontologies. *ISWC-2003, LNCS 2870*, 164-179. Springer Verlag.

Bonifacio, M., Bouquet, P., Mameli, G., & Nori, M. (2003). Peer-mediated knowledge management. In *AAAI-03 Spring Symposium on Agent-Mediated Knowledge Management (AMKM-03)*.

Cabral, L., Domingue, J., Galizia, S., Gugliotta, A., Norton, B., Tanasescu, V., & Pedrinaci, C. (2006). IRS-III: A Broker for Semantic Web Services based Applications. *Proceedings of the 5th International Semantic Web Conference (ISWC)*, Athens, USA.

Chen, H., Finin, T., & Joshi, A. (2003). An Ontology for Context Aware Pervasive Computing Environments. The Knowledge Engineering Review, *18*, 197-207.

Cregan, A. (2007). Symbol Grounding for the Semantic Web. *4th European Semantic Web Conference 2007*, Innsbruck, Austria.

Devore, J., & Peck, R. (2001). *Statistics—The Exploration and Analysis of Data*. 4th ed. Pacific Grove, CA: Duxbury.

Dietze, S., Gugliotta, A., & Domingue, J., (2007). A Semantic Web Services-based Infrastructure for Context-Adaptive Process Support. *Proceedings of IEEE 2007 International Conference on Web Services (ICWS)*, Salt Lake City, Utah, USA.

Dietze, S., Gugliotta, A., & Domingue, J., (2008). Towards Context-aware Semantic Web Service Discovery through Conceptual Situation Spaces. *Workshop: International Workshop on Context enabled Source and Service Selection, Integration and Adaptation (CSSSIA), 17th International World Wide Web Conference (WWW2008)*, Beijing, China.

Fensel, D., Lausen, H., Polleres, A., de Bruijn, J., Stollberg, M., Roman, D., & Domingue, J. (2006). *Enabling Semantic Web Services—The Web service Modelling Ontology*. Springer.

Gangemi, A., & Mika, P. (2003). Understanding the Semantic Web through Descriptions and Situations. In R. Meersman, Z. Tari, & et al. (Eds.), *Proceedings of the On The Move Federated Conferences (OTM'03)*, LNCS. Springer Verlag.

Gangemi, A., Guarino, N., Masolo, C., Oltramari, A., & Schneider, L. (2002). Sweetening Ontologies with DOLCE. In A. Gómez-Pérez , V. Richard Benjamins (Eds.), *Knowledge Engineering and Knowledge Management. Ontologies and the Semantic Web: 13th International Conference*, EKAW 2002, Siguenza, Spain, October 1-4.

Gärdenfors, P. (2000). *Conceptual Spaces—The Geometry of Thought*. MIT Press.

Gärdenfors, P. (2004). How to make the semantic web more semantic. In A. C. Vieu & L. Varzi, (Eds.), *Formal Ontology in Information Systems*, (pp. 19–36). IOS Press.

Gellersen, H-W., Schmidt, A., & Beigl, M. (2002). Multi-Sensor Context-Awareness in Mobile Devices and Smart Artefacts. *ACM Journal Mobile Networks and Applications (MONET), 7*(5).

Gu, T., Wang, X. H., Pung, H. K., & Zhang, D. Q. (2004). A middleware for context-aware mobile services. In IEEE Vehicular Technology Conference (VT)C. Los Alamitos, CA: IEEE Computer Society Press.

Joint US/EU ad hoc Agent Markup Language Committee (2004). OWL-S 1.1 Release. http://www.daml.org/services/owl-s/1.1/.

Krause, E. F. (1987). *Taxicab Geometry.* Dover.

Korpipaa, P., Mantyjarvi, J., Kela, J., Keranen, H., & Malm, E. (2003). Managing Context Information in Mobile Devices. *IEEE Pervasive Computing, 2*(3), 42-51, Jul-Sept, 2003.

Mika, P., Oberle, D., Gangemi, A., & Sabou, M. (2004). *Foundations for Service Ontologies: Aligning OWL-S to DOLCE, WWW04.*

Motta, E. (1998). An Overview of the OCML Modelling Language.*The 8th Workshop on Methods and Languages.*

Nosofsky, R. (1992). Similarity, scaling and cognitive process models. *Annual Review of Psychology, 43*, 25- 53.

OWL-S Coalition: OWL-S 1.1 release. (2004). http://www.daml.org/services/owl-s/1.1/

Raubal, M. (2004). Formalizing Conceptual Spaces. In A. Varzi & L. Vieu (Eds.), *Formal Ontology in Information Systems, Proceedings of the Third International Conference (FOIS 2004).Frontiers in Artificial Intelligence and Applications, 114*, 153-164., Amsterdam, The Netherlands: IOS Press.

Sailesh, S., Pavel, D., & Trossen, D. (2006). Context Service Framework for Mobile Internet. *International Worskshop on System Support for Future Mobile Computing Applications (FUMCA 2006)*, September 2006, Irvine, California, USA.

Serafini, L., Giunchiglia, F., Mylopoulos, J., & ernstein, P. (2003). Local relational model: a logical formalization of database coordination. In P. Blackburn, C. Ghidini, & R. Turner (Eds.), *Context'03.*

Schmidt, A., & Winterhalter, C. (2004). User Context Aware Delivery of E-Learning Material: Approach and Architecture. *Journal of Universal Computer Science (JUCS), 10*(1), January 2004.

Toivonen, S., Kolari, J., & Laakko, T. (2003). Facilitating mobile users with contextualized content. *In Proc. Workshop Artificial Intelligence in Mobile Systems.*

Weißenberg, N., Gartmann, R., & Voisard, A. (2006). An Ontology-Based Approach to Personalized Situation-Aware Mobile Service Supply. *Geoinformatica 10*, 1 (Mar. 2006), 55-90. DOI= http://dx.doi.org/10.1007/s10707-005-4886-9.

World Wide Web Consortium, W3C (2004a): Resource Description Framework, W3C Recommendation 10 February 2004, http://www.w3.org/RDF/.

World Wide Web Consortium, W3C (2004b): Web Ontology Language Reference, W3C Recommendation 10 February 2004, http://www.w3.org/TR/owl-ref/.

WSMO Working Group (2004), D2v1.0: Web service Modeling Ontology (WSMO). WSMO Working Draft, (2004). (http://www.wsmo.org/2004/d2/v1.0/).

WSMX Working Group (2007), The Web Service Modelling eXecution environment, http://www.wsmx.org/.

ENDNOTES

[1]   DIP Project: http://dip.semanticweb.org

[2]   http://maps.google.com/

234

Chapter X
Adaptive Resource and Service Management in a Mobile–Enabled Environment

Claudia Raibulet
Universitá degli Studi di Milano-Bicocca, Italy

ABSTRACT

Due to its nature, a mobile-enabled environment is very dynamic: reachable resources and services change very often. Users hardly know which resources they can exploit and which services they may require. In such a context, a technical support which identifies the available resources and services and indicates which resource is the best one to execute a service would be very helpful. This chapter proposes an adaptive solution to achieve these issues. Adaptivity is related to the fact that besides searching for the reachable resources or services, this approach proposes the most appropriate one for the current request by exploiting additional information about users, resources and services. Moreover, it ensures that services are delivered with the qualities requested and expected by the users. In the scientific literature adaptivity is exploited for functionality reasons (i.e., a system is not able to do what it was supposed to do) or for performance reasons (i.e., a system is not able to ensure the qualities of the services expected by the users or there is a better configuration for a given task). A challenging issue of adaptivity is the identification and design of the knowledge useful for the adaptation process and how this knowledge is exploited at run-time especially in a highly dynamic environment. This chapter proposes an approach which models the adaptation knowledge through reflective entities, qualities and properties, the management of the adaptation knowledge through views, the decision support through strategies, and the management of the functional and non-functional elements through managers.

INTRODUCTION

Today information systems are built of various types of devices (i.e., PCs, laptops, PDAs, mobile phones) and communication networks (i.e., LAN, WI-FI, Bluetooth, ZigBee). One of the main features of such systems is their mobility nature. Devices can change their location and hence may connect to different types of other devices providing different services through various types of networks.

From the architectural point of view a software system is built of components and connections among them (Garlan & Shaw, 1994). Generally, *mobility* is defined as *the quality of moving freely* (Merriam-Webster, 2008). Mobile-enabled systems are usually very dynamic in that components may join and leave a system anytime. This implies that such systems define communication mechanisms (i.e., discover, connect, disconnect), which enable their components to interact among them independent of their current location. Furthermore, the dynamic nature of mobile-enabled systems may lead to the modification of their performance features (i.e., in a client-server approach with a significant number of clients) or of their functionalities (i.e., in a P2P approach where peers may provide different functionalities). In this context, adaptivity plays an important role and it is closely related to the execution environment of a system.

Service Oriented Architectures (SOA) (Erl, 2005) aim to provide a solution to the ever growing complexity of today's information systems. The idea behind SOA is to define independent components which provide autonomous and atomic functionalities. The interaction among these components is based on the loose-coupling paradigm: components offering services (called providers) and requiring services (called consumers) are not tightly linked among them. They discover each other and interact among them through a well-established protocol and using well-defined high-level interfaces. Implementa-

tion or functional details are not visible outside of a component.

A challenging issue to address in SOA is related to the high number of components providing identical or similar services. The problem of consumers is how to decide which provider to choose for the requested service. Hence, their decision should be based on additional information about services. This information is related to the quality of the provided services (QoS – Quality of Service (Aagedat, 2001; Chalmers & Sloman, 1999; OMG, 2004)) which may include aspects regarding availability, reliability, costs, delivery time and many other significant non-functional aspects.

In this context, adaptivity becomes one of the most challenging issues to be addressed (Cheng Garlan & Schmerl, 2006; Kon Costa Blair & Champbell, 2002; McKinley Sadjadi Kasten & Cheng, 2004; Poladian Sousa Garlan & Shaw, 2004). It is achieved by exploiting information at run-time which is not usually modelled in a software representation of a system. Thus, it needs appropriate abstractions to represent this information and efficient mechanisms to implement activities usually performed by humans based on their own knowledge and experience.

Adaptive Resource and Service Management (ARSM) (Ceriani Raibulet & Ubezio, 2007; Raibulet Arcelli Mussino Riva Tisato & Ubezio, 2006) represents the solution proposed in this chapter for the design of service-oriented mobile-enabled adaptive systems. The idea behind ARSM has arisen from case studies which are common in the context of universities or companies. For example, a person wants to exploit the services offered by a company without knowing exactly which are the available services, which are their related qualities and where are the resources providing services (i.e., an IT consultant wants to print the slides prepared for a meeting with a given resolution, colour and on an A3 format on the nearest printer). ARSM is able to identify the most appropriate resource based on the name of the service (i.e., print) and on additional information (i.e., colour, A3 format, nearest) and to ensure that the required qualities are satisfied at run-time.

The aim of ARSM is to provide an example on how to design flexible systems predisposed to adaptation. Adaptation in ARSM regards various aspects ranging from the selection of the most appropriate system component to execute a service based on aspects behind its functionality (i.e., performance, quality, cost) to the observation of execution of services to check if the non-functional aspects are ensured at run-time.

ARSM exploits reflection (Maes, 1987) to observe and control various aspects of the underlying system. Reflection introduces meta-representations of the system's components and a causal connection mechanism to maintain them up-to-date with the status and the non-functional features of the system's components. This mechanism is also used to apply the changes required by the adaptation process after the observation of the meta-representations. Reflection may introduce several disadvantages (i.e., increased number of entities in the system, modifications at the reflective level may cause overall damage if reflection is not properly exploited), but it provides significant advantages too: separation of concerns, modularity, reusability, and an easier overall maintainability and evolution of the software system.

The rest of the chapter is organized as following. The Background Section provides an overview on the most important aspects related to the mobile-enabled architecture presented in this chapter: adaptivity, context-awareness, and reflection. The Related Work Section introduces the key aspects of the approaches addressing the concepts presented in the Background Section. The Motivating Example Section describes two scenarios which have lead to the development of the solution presented in this chapter. Such scenarios play an important role in the understanding of the problems addressed by ARSM, The ARSM Architecture Section focuses on the

main components of this approach, as well as on their role in the adaptation process: reflection, QoS and properties to model the adaptive knowledge, views to organize the adaptive knowledge and to improve its usage at run-time, strategies to implement decision support, and managers to handle the domain, functional and non-functional knowledge. Furthermore, it describes how services are defined in the context of ARMS. The Discussion Section presents how ARSM is applied in a healthcare context together with the advantages it provides. The chapter ends with the Conclusions and Further Work related to ARSM. This section addresses also open issues for adaptive mobile systems related to interoperability, security and development support (i.e., including an adaptation description language, the definition of appropriate concepts, and tools for their development).

BACKGROUND

Mobility, service-orientation, quality of services, adaptivity, reflection, and context-awareness represent key features of today's information systems. Users expect to be able to perform every day tasks whenever they have time and wherever they are. This means they should be able to access services through mobile devices they usually carry with them. Moreover, users expect to be allowed to choose a service based on the quality it offers (i.e., financial news provided in real time or a summary of news provided once a day), the price it has associated (i.e., the cost of an international phone call may vary from operator company to operator company) or the location it has (i.e., the choice of the nearest restaurant). In the same time, they expect systems to adapt to their preferences, requirements, and current context. To address these issues, a system should be aware both of its surrounding environment and its own structure and behavior in order to take decisions and to improve its functionalities at run-time.

This section aims to provide a background on adaptivity, context-awareness and reflection.

Adaptivity and Context-Awareness

Adaptivity is a complex topic. It regards the changes which should be performed in a system at run-time as a result of changes occurred internally to the system or externally in its execution environment.

A key role in the previous sentence is played by the *at run-time* phrase. There are changes which should be done before running a system, which are mainly related to installation and configuration steps. For example, a user may download and install one of the Java Virtual Machine (JVM) versions for Windows, Mac OS or Solaris. The user may also indicate the preferred language for the requested JVM. Sun Microsystems has already implemented those versions for various operating systems and languages, and based on the two criteria (operating system and language) it provides the appropriate solution. In this case adaptivity is considered *off-line*, being limited to the parameterized choice of the requested version of the JVM. Sun does not modify the JVM after the request has been made in order to personalize it for the current request. It has already implemented various versions *off-line* by exploiting static information about the possible types of operating systems and human languages.

Online adaptivity deals with changes performed in a system while the system is running.

Why is Online Adaptivity Needed?

There are various reasons of different natures claiming for adaptivity. They derive mostly from the ever growing complexity of today's information systems as well as from the need to improve productivity. (Seceleanu & Garlan, 2005) identifies three of the most important reasons why adaptivity is needed: (1) systems should run continuously in the presence of component-level faults, variability in resources or users' needs, (2) administrative overheads should be reduced allowing smooth operation with minimal human oversight, and (3) systems should provide various levels of services to different users depending on their current needs and context.

(McKinley Sadjadi Kasten & Cheng, 2004) underlines the role of ubiquitous and autonomic computing in the growing interest in run-time adaptivity. These two areas have different overall objectives and strategies: ubiquitous computing aims to remove the boundaries on how, when, and where humans and computer interact, while autonomic computing regards self-managing systems which require only high-level human guidance. Despite these differences, they share several common requirements regarding adaptivity such as survival of components failure or security attacks.

(McHugh, 2007) provides an organizational point of view on adaptivity by identifying its role in an enterprise network infrastructure: strengthening of security aspects, increase of productivity, and reduction of the complexity.

An additional reason which may claim for adaptivity is mobility (Malek, 2005). Mobility enables users to change their location and context, hence their execution environment. Adaptivity aims either to overcome the differences generated by these modifications or to exploit them properly in order to improve performance-related issues.

Where is Online Adaptivity Used?

Primarily, adaptivity has been used in the context of control engineering (Landau Lozano & M'Saad, 1998). Currently, its advantages are exploited in various types of systems and in various domains where self-management (Cheng Huang Garlan Schmerl & Steenkiste, 2004), self-organization (Wermelinger, 1998), self-healing (Shaw, 2002) or self-optimization (Ganak & Corbi, 2003) aspects are necessary.

Among the most common research areas where adaptivity is exploited there can be mentioned robotics, intelligent, multimedia, e-learning, web services, and healthcare systems (Miller & Page, 2007).

In robotics, adaptivity is requested to address the dynamic behaviour, situations and environmental modifications at run-time (Kim Park Jin Chang Park Ko Lee Lee Park & Lee, 2006). Typically, robot systems are characterized by unknown a priori behaviour or execution environment (Tzafestas, 1997). Hence, they should observe their environment and their current status and make changes in their behaviour according to the current situation in order to achieve their goal. Intelligent systems (Sterling & Juan, 2005; Oudeyer & Kaplan, 2004) may be considered a step further according to robotics. In this context, systems should not only observe, but also learn by acquiring new information and reason about it in order to be able to recognize new situations and to address them properly in the future. Hence, adaptivity may improve or extend the functionalities offered by an intelligent system.

Multimedia systems exploit adaptivity to manage properly text, audio and video information according to the available computational and communication resources (Basu Cheng Mun & Rao, 2007; Gecsei, 1997; Jones, 2004). Today's multimedia systems are built of various types of networks (e.g., LAN, wireless) and devices (e.g., laptops, PDAs, mobile phones) which are characterized by significantly different features. For example, networks have different bandwidth and latency specifications, while devices have different data processing and physical resources for delivering multimedia information. Moreover, users of multimedia information work in different environments. Hence, for this type of systems adaptivity should be performed based on the networks, devices, and users environments.

In the context of e-learning (Chorfi & Jemni, 2004; Sasakura & Yamasaki, 2007) adaptivity is exploited to improve the efficiency of the edu-cational systems in heterogeneous environments where students have different backgrounds and different abilities to assimilate and comprehend knowledge. An adaptive e-learning system provides a personalized mechanism for students with the final objective of achieving a similar level of knowledge.

Web services have the characteristic of being loosely coupled with their consumers (Erl, 2005). Hence, the same web service can be required in various contexts and with different characteristics. Adaptivity consists in the ability of the provider to offer a service in the most appropriate way for the current customer and its current context (Nagarajan Verma Sheth Miller & Lathem, 2006). Usually, this may be achieved by defining various levels of quality for the same service and, based on the current service request, offering the appropriate quality level.

Healthcare systems represent the most used application domain to present the advantages offered by adaptive systems (Bardram, 2003; Favela Rodriguez Preciado & Gonzalez, 2004; Kumar Shirazi Das Sung Levine & Singhal, 2003). Case studies range from an adaptive visualization of medical information to the recognition and management of emergency situations. Furthermore, they consider the heterogeneity and diversity of available devices and networks, as well as the efficient usage of the available resource and services in critical situations.

How is Online Adaptivity Achieved?

To achieve adaptivity a system should consider various internal and external aspects. Internal information may regard structural or behavioral aspects related to its components and to the services they provide. External aspects may be related to the role of users, their preferences, their current location and needs. The last type of information is part of the context of the user, being external to the system. Hence, it is known as context-aware information. An important role is played by location. Location-aware system may deduce further information about the current context of a user: for example, if a user is in a meeting room, he wants to receive only meaningful information for the current meeting, or in a video-surveillance system the location of the video cameras determine the location of users.

Independent of why and where on-line adaptivity is used, there are three main steps which should be considered during its design (Garlan Cheng Huang An-Cheng Schmerl & Steenkiste, 2004; Kielmann van Nieuwpoort & Maassen, 2003; Karsai Ledeczi Sztipanovits Peceli Simon & Kovacshazy, 2000) (see Figure 1):

- **Monitoring**, through which the meaningful information for adaptation is collected; the challenging issue in this step is to identify what should be monitored;
- **Analyzing**, which analyzes the collected information according to a reference information to decide if the current behavior of the system meets the defined requirements; based on this analysis, there are identified the changes to be performed;
- **Changing** or **adapting**, which applies the most appropriate changes identified during the analysis phase.

A good practice in developing adaptive systems is to apply the separation of concerns (Karsai Ledeczi Sztipanovits Peceli Simon & Kovacshazy, 2000; Maes, 1987) paradigm and to maintain separately the functional part of the system from the adaptive mechanisms. The adaptive part may be considered a supervisor of the functional one because it observes and controls the last when functional or performance problems occur. Usually, functional entities are not aware of the adaptive entities. However, they should be designed to be easily observable and controllable by the adaptive ones. This separation between the functional and adaptive parts has both advantages and disadvantages. Advantages are related to an easy maintenance, reuse, modification and evolution of each of the two parts. For example, functionalities can be added to the system without modifying the adaptive part. Or, adaptation can be performed by considering different issues or criteria without any modification of the functional entities. Disadvantages are related to an overhead communication between the two parts.

Note that this approach should be used also for the monitoring, analysis and adaptation of the external information related to the execution context of an adaptive system.

Figure 1. Adaptation fundamental loop

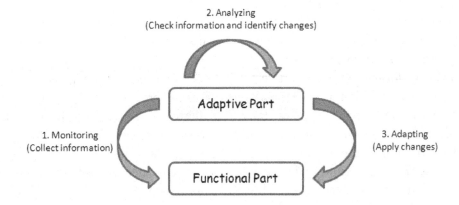

Monitoring mechanisms are responsible to collect information, which is used to analyze the current state of a component or an entire system by focusing on the adaptation objective. During this step it is important to:

- Collect the meaningful information focusing on the objectives of the adaptation process;
- Collect information fast enough in order to avoid delays in the adaptation process.

These two aspects are highly bound to the system under development, as well as to the application domain. Essentially, the techniques to collect information for adaptation can be divided in two main categories (Kielmann van Nieuwpoort & Maassen, 2003):

- **Active:** monitoring components are implemented as active entities (i.e., threads), which have their own execution flow. Transparently to the components in a system, they collect information periodically. This solution satisfies the separation of concerns concept: the functional part of a system is not aware of the tasks performed by the active entities.
- **Passive:** monitoring components are implemented as simple containers. The functional part of the system updates the containers with the current values of the meaningful information.

The tasks of the analyzing mechanisms are to access the information collected by the monitoring entities, to analyze it and to decide whether adaptation is needed or not. Similarly to the monitoring mechanisms, analysis may be:

- **Active:** analyzing mechanisms have their own execution flow and are synchronized with the collecting mechanisms of information. Thus, they analyze available information immediately after it is collected and decides if adaptation is required.
- **Passive:** analyzing mechanisms are implemented as a library of functions. The functional part of a system calls periodically these functions. In this way delays may be introduced in the adaptation process.

The analysis of the current state of a component or a system is implemented through strategies which model the human experience (i. e., premises and solutions) in a computable form (Garlan Cheng Huang An-Cheng Schmerl & Steenkiste, 2004). Thus, strategies have two main parts: (1) a set of possible inconsistencies, which may be defined as differences between the current values of collected information and their related predefined values, and (2) a set of actions to be performed to solve each inconsistency.

This step is the most complex one for two different reasons. First, all possible inconsistencies should be considered. Second, the action proposed should leave the entire system in a functional state which maintains its functionalities. Adaptation should not have undesirable collateral effects (i.e., affect security aspects or change functionalities).

Adaptation mechanisms should apply the changes proposed during analysis and to make actually modifications in a system. During the design of a system, all possible situations should be considered and each of them should be addressed through at least one configuration. Modifications in a system may be performed in two ways:

- Developing different components which perform the same task in different ways in order to be able to switch among these components based on the current situation.
- Developing one parameterized component which may perform a task in different ways. Depending on the values of its parameters, the component changes the way it does its task.

Reflection

Reflection (Maes, 1987) is defined as the activity performed by a system when doing computation about itself. Essentially, reflection enables a system to observe and control itself through appropriate metadata. This is particularly useful in adaptive systems which should modify their own features and behaviour at run-time as a result of the changes occurred internally (i.e., modifications in their own structure) or externally (i.e., modifications in their running environment).

Primarily, reflection has been successfully used by the programming language community (Maes, 1987; Smith, 1982). Today, its benefits are exploited also within the software architecture domain (Ancona & Cazzola, 2004; Cazzola Sosio Savigni & Tisato, 2000; Elianssen Andersen Blair Costa Coulson Goebel Hansen Kristensen Plagemann Rafaelsen Saikoski & Weihai, 1999). At the architectural level, reflection may introduce additional components (Lemos, 2000; Taiani Fabre & Killijian, 2002), or additional layers (Blair Coulson Andersen Blair Clarke Costa Duran Parlavantzas & Saikoski, 2000; Capra Emmerich & Mascolo, 2003). Architectural reflection (Cazzola Sosio Savigni & Tisato, 2000) represents explicitly architectural aspects of a system, and moreover, exploits these aspects. It enables a system to inspect its internal structure and behaviour.

The scientific literature provides a reflection architectural pattern (Demesticha Gergic Kleindienst Mast Polymenakos Schulz & Seredi, 2001; Suzuki & Yamamoto, 1999) which aims to establish general guidelines for the design of reflective architectures. The pattern focuses on the separation of concerns, which is the fundamental principle of reflection. Architecture is divided into two main parts: the *base* level, which implements the application logic, should be separated from the *meta*-level, which provides information about system's properties enabling software to become self-aware. Hence, architectural reflection intro-

duces an additional layer which plays an intermediary role between the system representation and applications. This layer enables applications to adapt to system features, and vice-versa, systems to adapt (whenever is possible) to applications' requirements. A reflective layer should capture only information that is related to the system representation and that is meaningful at run-time. This information consists of non-functional aspects. A reflective layer is *causally connected* to the base layer, which models system's components and functionalities.

Essentially, reflection exploits the causal connection mechanism to observe and control the underlying components of a system through appropriate *metadata*. Metadata models non-functional information (i.e., QoS) of the systems' components which is used at run-time in the adaptation process. This information represents the reflective knowledge. The causal connection mechanism ensures that any modification in a system component is propagated to its corresponding meta-representation, and vice-versa, any modification at the meta level is reflected on the corresponding system component (whenever this is possible).

RELATED WORK

There are various approaches which address adaptivity in mobile-enabled systems. In this section, there are introduced four examples of those which exploit reflection mechanisms to achieve run-time adaptivity: Odyssey, ReMMoC (A Reflective Middleware to support Mobile Client Interoperability), MobiPADS (Mobile Platform for Actively Deployable Service) and CARISMA (Context-Aware Reflective mIddleware System for Mobile Applications).

Odyssey (Noble Satyanarayanan Narayanan Tilton Flinn & Walker, 1997; Noble, 2000) is the first system which addresses simultaneously the problems of adaptation related to mobility, application, context diversity and concurrency among applications exploiting common resources. It proposes and implements an architecture for application-aware adaptation in the context of mobile systems. Odyssey achieves these goals through a reflective middleware which monitors the resources of a systems such as bandwidth, CPU usage or battery level. The middleware interacts with the applications to understand their requirements and to improve the resources' monitoring based on the applications' needs. For example, when connectivity is missing the Odyssey middleware becomes immediately aware and notifies the applications. On the other hand, when connectivity is available again it notifies applications. Each application exploiting Odyssey decides independently how to react to the notified changes based on their execution contexts. Concurrency among applications is addressed by the middleware which monitors the systems' resources and manages their allocation in the most appropriate way.

The main advantages offered by Odyssey are given by the speed and the accuracy of identification and adaptation to changes related to the availability of resources. Hence, agility (Noble Satyanarayanan Narayanan Tilton Flinn & Walker, 1997) plays a key role in the context of Odyssey. This is due to the straight collaboration between the reflective middleware and applications. Developers of Odyssey provide also quantitative information and measures for agility.

The ReMMoC (Grace Blair & Samuel, 2003) project investigates the use of reflection as a solution to overcome the problems generated by heterogeneous middleware approaches in mobile-enabled environments. Attention is focused on the service concept: applications discover and exploit the services available at a given location. The solution defines two key components for binding and service discovery, whose behaviour can be dynamically altered using reflection mechanisms (Capra Blair Mascolo Emmerich Grace, 2002). The binding framework can be re-configured

among different types of interaction protocols (e.g., SOAP, CORBA), while the service discovery framework can change among different technologies (e.g., SLP, Jini, UpnP). Reflection is used as a mechanism to observe and adapt dynamically the components of the middleware. Reflection is used recursively in that a component at a given level may use the meta-interface of a component at a lower level to interact with the last. In this way, ReMMoC defines various meta-levels above the base one. The meta-levels introduce different points of views on the reflective knowledge. This concept is present also in ARSM. The difference is related to the fact that ReMMoC does not consider QoS. Moreover, its application domains regard real-time and multimedia systems.

MobiPADS (Chan & Chuang, 2003) is a reflective middleware designed to support context-aware processing by providing an execution platform which enables service deployment and configuration in response to a variable environment. In this context services are intended as system components which are highly configurable and robust enough to enable the system itself to respond to varying conditions in the execution environment. MobiPADS provides support for run-time adaptation at the application and middleware levels. Actually, there are three types of adaptation: interservice (which regards the reconfiguration of the composition of the services), intraservice (which allows a service to react to a set of composite events) and application (which enables applications to react to a change in a context information). This leads to a flexible configuration of resources in order to optimize the operations of mobile applications. MobiPADS defines three types of meta-level objects which abstract the contextual information and the service adaptation. Through these meta-objects, mobile applications can subscribe to the contextual changes. This makes MobiPADS highly flexible in selecting and adjusting the adaptation policy.

CARISMA (Capra Emmerich Mascolo, 2003) exploits the principle of reflection to enhance the development of adaptive and context-aware mobile systems. In this solution, a middleware must implement context-aware mechanisms in order to enable applications which run on mobile devices to adapt to frequent and unannounced changes in their execution environment. To achieve these goals, it defines mechanisms to describe how context changes should be managed at run-time through the use of policies. There may occur conflicts among the defined policies. Conflicts are solved at run-time by the middleware.

The main contributions offered by CARISMA are related to the design and evaluation of novel abstractions and mechanisms in a middleware which aims to offer support for the development of context-aware mobile applications. These novel concepts exploit both structural and behavioral reflection (Kon Costa Blair & Champbell, 2002).

The main differences between these approaches and ARSM are related to the variety of the types of knowledge considered for adaptation (i.e., network as well as device features, context, domain specific information) as well as on the management of the reflective part of ARSM through views and strategies.

MOTIVATING EXAMPLE: THE H-ARSM CASE STUDY

The meaningful scenarios motivating the idea behind the solution presented in this chapter describe the requests of different services with various QoS from different types of devices and networks in the context of healthcare systems. The H-ARSM (Healthcare ARSM) case study aims to integrate ARSM with applications already available in the healthcare system (Raibulet Mussino & Ubezio, 2007). The advantages offered by this integration are mostly related to the fact that ARSM exploits at run-time information about the system structure and may improve the quality of the services provided usually by healthcare systems. To sustain this affirmation two different types of situations in

which ARSM may provide an enhanced solution are described: access of information in clinical records and requests of medical tests which should be booked or executed immediately.

Access of Medical Information

Patients require the visualization of information of their personal medical records, while the medical staff members access and modify the information of any patient record. Both types of users may access information from various locations through various devices with different visualization characteristics: PC, PDA, mobile phones. For example, a member of the medical staff asks for information (i.e., using a mobile phone) specifying only his current location (i.e., revealed by a sensor). The system identifies the component which can display the information in a clinical record including images (i.e., wall monitor, PC) and which is the nearest one to the user. Or, the user asks for the information specifying the QoS the displayed information should be characterized by. The system identifies a component with the required QoS. In both cases the system sends all the information in the clinical record of the patient and notifies the user where the information is displayed.

There can be adapted also the information in the clinical record to the device used for visualization. For example, when using a PDA, a user receives only textual information, while when using a wall monitor also images can be displayed. Furthermore, a user asks only for partial information related to a particular disease of a patient and the current cures. Or, a doctor wants to receive only the information of a patient regarding his specialization. In this case, only domain specific knowledge is involved in the decision process. There are also cases in which both domain and system knowledge are required for adaptation. For example, a doctor claims the clinical record of a patient specifying his specialization and current location. The system should identify the nearest display device and extract the requested information from the clinical record.

Bookings of Services

Patients or medical personnel request a medical test which should be performed immediately or within a specified period of time. For immediate execution requests, the system verifies who is the available doctor able to perform the test and if required, the available medical equipment. If there are no immediate solutions it checks who will finish first the current activity and uses him as soon as possible. For non-immediate execution requests, ARSM books them in a specified period of time (i.e., after 48 hours and before 72 hours) or within a time limit (i.e., within fifteen days). The system books the first available resource meeting the time constraint.

This type of requests raises two issues which are closely related to each other: the first regards the time dimension and the second the allocation of resources. There are requests in which a service should be provided immediately, or as soon as possible, while there are requests that claim for a service reservation. In both cases of this scenario (service execution or booking) the adaptation process exploits only domain specific knowledge (i.e., doctors, medical equipment). However, the same operations can be done also for the system physical components: for example, a high-quality monitor is booked for a videoconference for a given day.

In this particular example there is no information about the quality of the devices used to perform the required test. Generally, there may be more types of devices which do the same type of test, but with different levels of qualities, precision and response time. Currently, the system groups together the same type of tests to improve the resource allocation and usage.

ARSM ARCHITECTURE

ARSM defines a service oriented based architecture which exploits reflection at the architectural level to achieve adaptivity at run-time.

In ARSM, the reflective knowledge is modeled through four elements: *reflective objects*, *reflective services*, *QoS*, and *properties* (see Figure 2). Reflective objects are the meta-representations of the system objects modeling their current status, while reflective services are meta-representations of the services offered by the system objects. *Low-level* QoS (representing measurable values) model the non-functional features of services which may be used to achieve adaptivity (i.e., bandwidth, availability, cost). Properties represent additional information about the system's components which are not strictly related to the services they provide, but which may be meaningful for the adaptation process (i.e., location of a user or a resource).

To improve the organization and the management of the reflective knowledge two additional elements have been introduced: *views* and *strategies*. A view is defined as an organizational structure on the reflective objects which has its own semantic and its own computational strategies to evaluate the elements under its control (Mussino, 2005). A reflective object may be used in various views, but it has only one representation in the system. Views contain references to the reflective objects they manage.

Strategies implement the logic necessary to take decisions. A view has associated a best-effort strategy which assigns scores to the reflective objects it manages based on its own semantic. A score indicates the distance between the requested QoS and those offered by the reflective objects. The lower the score is, the better suits the object to the current service request. In this way, a view is able to indicate the most appropriate object or a classification of the most appropriate objects able to fulfill a request.

Figure 2. ARSM Main components

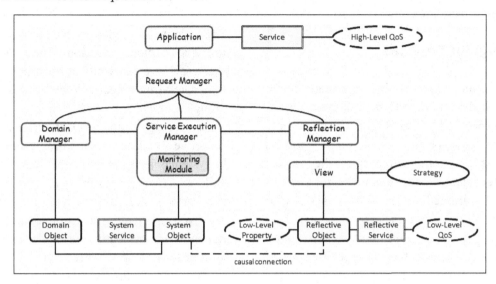

When applying ARSM to an actual case study three types of knowledge should be managed: *domain knowledge* (i.e., defining objects specific to the current application domain), *system knowledge* (i.e., defining objects specific to the underlying physical components of the system), and *reflective knowledge* (i.e., defining objects which influence the performances of the system). Each of the three types of knowledge is manipulated through a manager: domain, service execution and reflection. For example, in the H-ARSM case study the domain manager deals with patients, doctors, nurses, medical records, medical tests and equipment information. Managers can interact among them to exchange information related to the services' requests. As views, also managers have associated strategies. For example, the *reflection manager* has associated a strategy which decides the views to be used to solve each service request.

The *request manager* receives the services' requests from applications and chooses, based on the information available in each request, the types of knowledge to exploit to solve it. Whenever a request claims for adaptivity, the reflection

manager is asked to identify the most appropriate resource offering the requested service based on its related QoS and properties.

At the application level services are characterized by *high-level* QoS, which may be either qualitative (i.e., high resolution) or quantitative (i.e., 1600 x 1200 resolution). The high-level QoS include both QoS and properties. For example, a user may claim for a printing service with a *high quality* on the *nearest printer* to his current location. These high-level QoS are translated into resolution, color depth, and printing speed as *low-level* QoS of a reflective service and into the location property of its corresponding reflective object. These mappings between high-level and low-level QoS and properties are performed by mapping strategies associated to views (Mussino, 2005; Riva, 2006).

The service execution manager (Cammareri & Raibulet, 2007) has a monitoring module which verifies if the QoS claimed in a request are guaranteed during the execution of the service. Currently, two solutions are considered in case QoS become out of an expected range. The first regards the specification of the two most appropriate system objects able to execute a service. If the first system object fails to ensure the promised QoS or a failure occurs, the second one is asked to execute the service. In an alternative solution, the service execution manager asks the reflection manager to choose another solution for the current request. In both cases the request manager (and implicitly the application or user) is not aware of the problems occurred.

Adaptation Level of Service Requests

In ARMS requests of services may claim for various levels of adaptivity:

- **High-level**: A user specifies only the type of service and a set of high-level QoS. ARMS maps the high-level QoS into quantitative values and tries to identify, among the resources providing the requested service, the one which may offer QoS as close as possible to the requested ones (Raibulet Arcelli & Mussino, 2006).
- **Low-level:** A user specifies the type of service, the resource he wants to execute the service and a set of QoS. In this case, ARMS has to set only the QoS of the indicated resource on the requested values.
- **No adaptivity:** A user specifies the type of service and the resource he wants to execute the service. In this case the reflective part of the system is not exploited.
- **Inspection request:** A user specifies a service and the underlying architecture should provide a list of the resources able to provide the service with their related QoS.

Definition of Services

In ARMS a service is considered as the basic functionality provided by a resource (Cammareri & Raibulet, 2007).

From the structural point of view services can be divided in:

- **Simple**: requires a single execution on a single resource.
- **Complex**: requires multiple executions on one or more resources; it is composed of two or more simple services.

From the functional point of view services can be divided in:

- **Sequential**: it is a complex service in which the execution of its simple services is done sequentially: the execution of a simple service starts only when the previous one is completed.
- **Parallel**: it is a complex service in which the execution of its simple services may be done in parallel: the order of their execution is not relevant.

From the execution point of view services can be divided in:

- **Atomic:** it is a complex service for which a fail of execution of one of its simple services causes the fail of the complex one;
- **Not atomic:** it is a complex service for which a fail of execution of one of its simple services does not cause the fail of the complex one; the simple service which failed can be re-executed on another resource without affecting the execution of the other simple services.

The execution part of ARMS receives in input the request token shown in Figure 3. From the execution point of view, the requested service may be composed of several simple services.

The token contains all the information necessary to execute the request: the type of service, the input data (i.e., usually it is related to the domain specific knowledge), the QoS specified by the user, and a list of resources which will execute the service(s). For each request it is specified a minimum and a maximum time, modelling the time interval when the service should be executed. If the maximum time is zero, than the request should be immediately executed. Otherwise, the request may be executed not before the minimum time and not after the maximum time. This allows users not only to require an immediate execution of a service but also to book a service.

Reflective Objects

Reflective objects represent the basic elements of the reflective part of ARSM. They are modelled independently of the other components of the architecture. The causal connection between them and the system objects (see Figure 2) allows reflective objects to automatically adapt themselves to the modifications occurred at the system objects, and vice versa, allows system objects to adapt themselves to the reflective objects.

The causal connection is modelled through the Observer design pattern (Gamma Helm Johnson & Vlissides, 1994). This pattern provides an effi-

cient mechanism for the synchronization between objects, or more precisely, for the synchronization of the state of objects. Reflective objects define two main methods: *update()*, which allows them to adapt according to their corresponding system objects, and *force()*, which tries to constrain system objects to adapt to the reflective objects (Raibulet Arcelli Mussino Riva Tisato & Ubezio, 2006).

Views and Strategies

Views represent the fundamental mechanism to exploit reflective objects. Views offer at least three advantages: a uniform and common mechanism to organize reflective objects based on various criteria, the possibility to extend the number of views on the reflective objects, and to not include external information in the representation of the reflective objects (i.e., location, structure, topology). The main view is the services one. It is used in every request that claims for adaptivity, while other views (i.e., structural, topological) may not be always exploited (Raibulet Arcelli Mussino Riva Tisato & Ubezio, 2006). The implementation of the services view is based on the Chain

Figure 3. Request token received in input by the execution part of ARMS

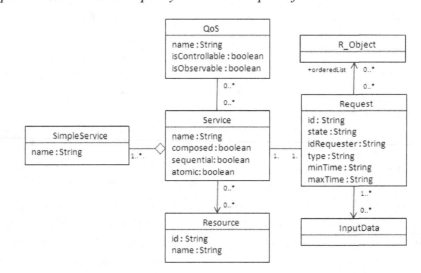

of Responsibility design pattern (Gamma Helm Johnson & Vlissides, 1994), which addresses two main problems: the dynamic control of a collection of service views, and the execution of composed services (Mussino, 2005; Raibulet Arcelli Mussino Riva Tisato & Ubezio, 2006).

Another view which is used very often especially in mobile-enabled environments is the location one. In ARSM, three types of locations have been considered: geographical location provided by GPS systems at run-time, (2) location within buildings based on building maps and access points where the current location of users is provided by badge-based systems at run-time, and (3) static location known at configuration time (Arcelli Raibulet Tisato & Ubezio, 2005). The type of location is strongly related to the application domain.

In the context of ARSM, decisions are modelled through strategies. Each view has associated one or more strategies that implement the logic necessary to take decisions. For example, each reflective view uses two types of strategies: (1) *adaptive strategies* through which the most appropriate resources to execute an actual service are chosen, and (2) *mapping strategies,* which translate high-level QoS into low level QoS and viceversa. Mapping strategies define two methods: *mapUp()*, which maps the low-level QoS or properties of the resources on the high-level QoS of the services, and *mapDown()*, which maps the high-level QoS of services on the low-level QoS or properties of the resources. For example, the high-quality QoS of a display service is obtained through the combination of the dimension, resolution, and colour depth QoS of a monitor.

Strategies depend strongly on the application domain. Hence, various applications may use various implementations of the same strategy. To increase the modularity, extensibility and reuse of the ARSM's architecture components, it is necessary that both managers and views exploit strategies in order to separate decisional policies from the underlying managed data. To define a

common interface of strategies in ARSM, the Strategy design pattern (Gamma Helm Johnson & Vlissides, 1994) has been used.

Strategies may have complex structures. Furthermore, they cannot be defined exhaustively until the implementation phase. To address their complexity the Composite design pattern (Gamma Helm Johnson & Vlissides, 1994) has been used to define their structure. The strategy that analysis a complex service is actually a composition of strategies related to the sub-services of the required one. This improves significantly the implementation of strategies, by requiring the definition of the simple strategies and the definition of the complex ones as composition of the already defined simple strategies. Furthermore, modifications of the simple strategies are automatically propagated to the complex ones that exploit them (Raibulet Arcelli Mussino Riva Tisato & Ubezio, 2006).

The Reflection Manager

The reflection manager supervises the reflective part of the architecture. Its main objective is to identify the most appropriate system's objects which may execute the requested service through their corresponding reflective objects.

Based on the types of the QoS specified in the request token, the reflection manager selects the reflective views which are used to search for the most appropriate system resource. Each view performs two tasks. The first is related to the translation of the high-level QoS (indicated in the request and related to its semantics) into low-level QoS. During the second task, each view assigns a score to its reflective objects. This score indicates how close are the QoS or properties of a resource to the QoS specified in the service request. In this case all the available values related to a resource are considered, not just the current value. For example, in the case of a display service all the supported resolutions are interrogated. The final score of a reflective object belonging to two or more views is calculated as the sum of the partial scores. After each view has assigned its score to its related objects, the reflection manager extracts the most appropriate one or makes a classification of the resources for the current request. This result is added to the request token and used by the service execution manager for the actual execution of services.

The Service Execution Manager

The execution manager supervises the functional part of a system. It receives the requests claiming for the execution of services and it communicates the results to the request manager. The aim of the functional part of ARMS is to execute services and in the same time to guarantee their QoS claimed and expected by the users. Moreover, ARMS aims to execute services in the time interval specified in the service request.

In ARMS, the three steps for the adaptation are translated into:

- **Monitoring** the QoS of the resources which are executing services, the actual execution time, and the expected execution time of the services' requests.
- **Analyzing** the monitored QoS with respect to the values specified in the requests, and the remaining time until the expected execution of the services' requests (a service cannot be executed before the minimum time and not after its maximum time associated).
- **Adapting** may consists in various solutions: reconfiguration of the QoS of a resource, abort of the execution on a resource and start the execution of the same service on another resource.

In ARMS all requests are considered independent of each other, hence, each resource is monitored and analyzed separately. When a request arrives to the execution manager, the last creates a *request handler* and delegates the execution of

the requested service to this handler. The handler is responsible of executing the service on one of the indicated resources (through its corresponding reflective objects R_Object (see Figure 3) - if it is the reflective part to choose the resources, or through the Resource entity if it is the user to indicate the desired resource).

From the adaptation point of view the request handler monitors the minimum and the maximum execution time, changes the priority of the request if the maximum time is approaching (if more than one request claims the usage of the same resource), or changes the resource which executes a service.

Every time a request handler chooses a resource to execute a simple service, ARMS creates a *resource handler*. This handler is responsible to execute a service on the indicated resource and to communicate the execution result. Whenever a resource handler fails to execute a service or the execution time becomes too long, its corresponding request handler checks if in the service request are indicated other resources on which this service can be executed. In the affirmative case, it stops the execution of the service on the current resource and creates another resource handler for the alternative resource.

From the adaptation point of view each resource handler sets the QoS of the chosen resource on the values specified in the request and checks for QoS inconsistencies during the execution of a service.

DISCUSSION

ARSM defines a reflective architecture for adaptive systems. It identifies the meaningful concepts for on-line adaptivity. It proposes a model to represent the significant knowledge for adaptivity in terms of reflective objects, QoS and properties. ARSM defines also the mechanisms necessary to exploit efficiently this knowledge at run-time: the causal connection, views and strategies concepts.

The approach provided by ARSM can be extended to the representation and management of any application domain. In the case of H-ARSM the domain knowledge includes patients, doctors, nurses, medical records, medical tests and equipment. The first scenario presented in the Motivating Examples Section is related to the access of clinical records information. The request manager asks the domain manager to provide this information. Through domain specific strategies which filter the information based on the user type and on the access device of the user, the requested information is extracted. Then, the service manager is asked to execute the service, hence to display the requested information. When the user does not specify the device on which information should be displayed, the reflection manager is asked to identify the most appropriate one. This identification takes into consideration the location of the user and the types of the information which should be displayed (i.e., text, images).

In the second scenario adaptation regards only the domain knowledge. Though the ARSM approach also domain aspects, which are not usually considered, are explicitly represented and exploited at run-time. Generally, this information is the property of the actors of the system and they use it implicitly when making requests or offering solutions. For example, the actors know the QoS of the medical tests hence they make specific request. This may be considered subjective in that two actors with similar characteristics may ask for different tests in identical situations. Therefore, ARSM aims to represent explicitly this knowledge and to exploit it properly in order to provide adaptivity support at run-time.

It is well known that adaptivity requires additional software elements. Using reflection to achieve adaptivity leads to an increased number of the components in the system. Moreover, modifications at the reflective components may cause overall damage if reflection is not properly used.

Hence, the advantages offered by adaptivity should overcome these problems. Advantages include: separation of concerns, modularity, reusability and maintainability. The main feature of the reflection is separation of concerns (Maes, 1987). In ARSM, this feature has lead to significant advantages: the separation between the representation of the functional and non-functional aspects of the system's resources and services, as well as the separation among domain, system and reflective knowledge. A further feature of ARSM is modularity. A first level of modularity is given by the reflection itself through the separation of concerns. A further modularity is obtained by separating the representation of the reflective entities (reflective objects, services, QoS, and properties) from their management mechanisms (views and strategies). Modularity enables implicitly maintainability and reusability. Each component of the reflective architecture performs a well-defined and standalone task. Each component can be changed independently of the others. For example, the implementation of a service may change, although its abstraction at the reflective level remains unchanged. Or, the mapping strategies between the low-level and high-level QoS may differ from application domain to application domain without affecting the representation of the other components in the systems. Or, the adaptive strategies may be implemented based on the best-effort or first in - first out principles.

The aim of ARSM has been to define the main concepts to be applied when designing adaptive systems. Performance and optimization aspects are strongly related to the application domains.

CONCLUSION AND FURTHER WORK

Sterling and Juan assert that *future software systems will be adaptive* (Sterling & Juan, 2005). From the works available in the scientific literature this affirmation seems to be true. More and more software engineers focus their attention on addressing adaptivity in the systems they are developing. Moreover, adaptivity is requested in a wide range of application domains which regard delivery of services in heterogeneous mobile-enabled environments built of various types of devices, networks, users, preferences and contexts.

Currently, there is no common and well-established definition of adaptivity (Zadeh, 1963). This may be considered a consequence of the generality feature of adaptivity, as well as to its emerging status. Essentially, adaptivity consists in performing structural and behavioral changes in a system as a result of other changes occurred inside or outside a system. There is no further specification about these changes: what type of changes should be done, when should be done, how to do them at run-time, or who or what decides what to change, which is the trigger of adaptation. Moreover, there is no design support for adaptivity (e.g., tools, models, verification and validation criteria).

These affirmations are sustained also by the various types of possible adaptation: structure, architecture and behavior (Gorton Liu & Trivedi, 2007). Structure adaptation regards the changes made in the application components (e.g., a method signature). Architecture adaptation deals with the changes in the structure of components and their interaction. Behavioral adaptation focuses on the changes in the execution of existing components in a non-intrusive way (e.g., change of the configuration of a component). This leads to the conclusion that adaptivity is a complex task which regards various aspects of a system including architectural, structural and functional information. Furthermore, adaptivity addresses both for functional and non-functional aspects.

Adaptivity is an open research issues. Currently, scientists are trying to identify its possible usages and specifications. In this chapter, attention has been focused on the representation and

management of the knowledge exploited in the adaptation process in a mobile-enabled environment. Reflection plays an important role in the observation and control of the knowledge exploited at run-time to achieve adaptivity. To improve the management of the reflective knowledge, views have been introduced. Decision support is implemented through strategies. Separation of concerns is a fundamental aspect in adaptive systems: adaptive knowledge should be separated from the functional and domain specific knowledge, as well as the adaptive process should be separated from the application business process.

The issues raised by service-oriented mobile-enabled systems are complex because they claim for architectural, behavioural as well as context adaptation. Architectural adaptation is needed because of the intrinsic nature of the mobility feature. Users and devices change their location hence the architecture of a system changes. Behavioural adaptation may be required when users change location and the reachable services change. Due to the modification of the users' location also the context may change. Hence, context adaptation is needed.

Adaptivity requires additional software for the representation of its related meaningful information and for the run-time decision support. This increases not only the size of the software but also its complexity. Hence, the advantages offered by adaptivity should overcome these problems. Software engineers have focused their attention on how to exploit adaptivity to improve the systems functionalities in terms of automating tasks previously done off-line and to minimize the interaction between a system and its administrator at run-time. Further, research should focus also on the performances of an adaptive system in that the overhead introduced by adaptivity should be overcome by its benefits.

As mentioned in (McKinley Sadjadi Kasten & Cheng, 2004), further work related to the assurance, security, interoperability and decision making in adaptive systems is required. Assurance regards the correctness of the changes needed by adaptivity. This is tightly related to the conflicts which may occur and to the priority of the issues addressed through adaptivity. While assurance addresses the integrity of a system, security regards its protection from malicious entities. Changes should not alter the security characteristics of a system. Adaptive distributed systems allow the adaptivity of components, as well as of its layers and platforms. Attention should be focused on maintaining the interoperability among the components and inside the entire system. Decision making is a complex task due to the fact that adaptive systems work in heterogeneous environments where context changes may occur very often. Systems must act autonomously, performing modifications to better fit the current context while preventing damage or loss of services.

REFERENCES

Aagedal, J.O. (2001). *Quality of Service Support in Development of Distributed Systems*. PhD Thesis, University of Oslo, Norway.

Ancona, M., & Cazzola, W. (2004). Implementing the Essence of Reflection: a Reflective Run-Time Environment. In *Proceedings of the 2004 ACM Symposium on Applied Computing* (pp. 1503-1507). New York: ACM Press.

Arcelli, F., Raibulet, C., Tisato, F., & Ubezio, L. (2005). Designing and Exploiting the Location Concept in a Reflective Architecture". In *Proceedings of the 14th International Conference on Intelligent and Adaptive Systems and Software Engineering* (pp. 134-139).

Blair, G. S., Coulson, G., Andersen, A., Blair, L., Clarke, M., Costa, F., Duran, H., Parlavantzas, N., & Saikoski, K. A (2000). Principled Approach to Supporting Adaptation in Distributed Mobile Environments. In *Proceedings of the International Symposium on Software Engineering for Parallel and Distributed Systems* (pp. 3-12)

Bardram, J. E. (2003). Hospitals of the Future – Ubiquitous Computing support for Medical Work in Hospitals. In *Proceedings of the 2nd International Workshop on Ubiquitous Computing for Pervasive Healthcare Applications*, from http://www. healthcare.pervasive.dk/ubicomp2003/papers/ Final_Papers/13.pdf

Basu, A., Cheng, I., Mun, P., & Rao, G. (2007). Multimedia Adaptive Computer based Testing: An Overview. In Proceedings *of the International Conference on Multimedia and Expo* (pp. 1850-1853) IEEE Press.

Cammareri, D. & Raibulet, C. (2007). Self-Adaptive Execution Mechanisms in ARMS. In *Journal of System and Information Sciences Notes*, 2(1), 58-63.

Capra, L., Blair, G. S., Mascolo, C., Emmerich, W., & Grace, P. (2002). Exploiting Reflection in Mobile Computing Middleware. In *ACM SIGMOBILE Mobile Computing and Communications Review*, 6(4), 33-44.

Capra, L., Emmerich, W., & Mascolo, C. (2003). CARISMA: Context-Aware Reflective mIddleware System for Mobile Applications. In *IEEE Transactions on Software Engineering*, 29(10), 929-945.

Cazzola, W., Sosio, A., Savigni, A., & Tisato, F. (2000). Architectural Reflection. Realizing Software Architectures via Reflective Activities. In *Proceedings of the International Workshop on Engineering Distributed Objects. LNCS*, (pp. 102-115). Springer Verlag.

Ceriani, S., Raibulet, C., & Ubezio, L. (2007). A Java Mobile-Enabled Environment to Access Adaptive Services", In *Proceedings of the 5th Principles and Practice of Programming in Java Conference* (pp. 249-254). ACM Press.

Chalmers, D., & Sloman, M. (1999). A Survey of Quality of Service in Mobile Computing Environments. *IEEE Communications Surveys*, 2-10.

Chan, A. T. S, & Chuang, S. N. (2003). MobiPADS: A Reflective Middleware for Context-Aware Mobile Computing. In *IEEE Transactions on Software Engineering, 29*(12), 1072-1085.

Cheng S. W, Huang, A. C., Garlan, D., Schmerl, B., & Steenkiste, P., (2004). An Architecture for Coordinating Multiple Self-Management Modules. In *Proceedings of the 4th Working IEEE/IFIP Conference on Software Architecture*, (pp. 243-252).

Cheng, S. W., Garlan, D., & Schmerl, B. (2006). Architecture-based Self-Adaptation in the Presence of Multiple Objectives. In *Proceedings of the ICSE Workshop on Software Engineering for Adaptive and Self-Managing Systems*, (pp. 2-8).

Chorfi, H., & Jemni, M. (2004). PERSO: Towards an Adaptive E-Learning System. In *Journal of Interactive Learning Research*, 15(4), 433-447.

de Lemos, R. (2000). A Co-operative Object-Oriented Architecture for Adaptive Systems. In *Proceedings of the 7th IEEE International Conference and Workshop on the Engineering of Computer Based Systems*, (pp. 120-128).

Demesticha, V., Gergic, J., Kleindienst, J., Mast, M., Polymenakos, L. Schulz, H. & Seredi, L. (2001). Aspects of Design and Implementation of a Multi-channel and Multi-modal Information System. In *Proceedings of the IEEE International Conference on Software Maintenance.* (pp. 312-319).

Elianssen, F., Andersen, A., Blair, G. S., Costa, F., Coulson, G., Goebel, V., Hansen, O., Kristensen, T., Plagemann, T., Rafaelsen, H. O., Saikoski, K. B., & Weihai Y. (1999). Next Generation Middleware: Requirements, Architecture, and Prototypes. In *Proceedings of the 7th IEEE Workshop on Future Trends of Distributed Computing Systems*, (pp. 60-65).

Erl, T. (2005) *Service-Oriented Architecture: Concepts, Technology and Design.* USA: Prentice Hall PTR, USA

Favela, J., Rodriguez, M., Preciado, A., & Gonzalez, V. M. (2004). Integrating Context-Aware Public Displays Into a Mobile Hospital Information System. In *IEEE Transactions on Information Technology in Biomedicine, 8*(3), 279-286.

Gamma, E., Helm, R., Johnson, R., & Vlissides, J. (1994). *Design Patterns: Elements of Reusable Object-Oriented Software*, USA: Addison Wesley, Reading MA.

Ganak, A. G., & Corbi, T. A. (2003). The Dawning of the Autonomic Computing Era. In *IBM Systems Journal. 42*(1), 518.

Garlan, D. & Shaw M. (1994). An Introduction to Software Architecture. *Technical Report*, Carnegie Mellon University, CMU-CS-94-166.

Garlan, D., Cheng, S., W., Huang, An-Cheng, Schmerl, B., & Steenkiste, P. (2004). Rainbow: Architecture-based Self-Adaptation with Reusable Infrastructure. In *IEEE Computer, 37*(10), 46-54.

Gecsei, J. (1997). Adaptation in Distributed Multimedia Systems. In *IEEE Computer*, (pp. 58-66)

Gorton, I., Liu, Y., & Trivedi, N. (2007). An extensible and lightweight architecture for adaptive server applications. In *Software – Practice and Experience Journal*, (pp. 853-883). Wiley InterScience.

Grace, P., Blair, G. S., & Samuel, S. (2003). ReMMoC: A reflective Middleware to Support Mobile Client Interoperability. In *Proceedings of International Symposium on Distributed Objects and Applications, LNCS 2888,* (pp. 1170-1187).

Jones, G. F. G. (2004). Adaptive Systems for Multimedia Information Retrieval. In *Adaptive Multimedia Retrieval, LNCS 3094*, (pp. 1-18).

Karsai, G., Ledeczi, A., Sztipanovits, J., Peceli, G., Simon, G., & Kovacshazy, T. (2000). An Approach to Self-Adaptive Software based on Supervisory Control. In *Self-Adaptive Software Applications, LNCS, 2614,* (pp. 77-92).

Kielmann, T., van Nieuwpoort, R., & Maassen, J. (2003). Gridlab - A Grid Application Toolkit and Testbet. Design of Adaptive Components, Vrije University, The Netherlands.

Kim, D., Park, S., Jin, Y., Chang, H., Park, Y.-S., Ko, I.-Y., Lee, K., Lee, J., Park, Y.-C., & Lee, S. (2006). SHAGE: A Framework for Self-managed Robot Software. In *Proceedings of the ICSE Workshop on Software Engineering for Adaptive and Self-Managing Systems,* (pp. 79-85).

Kon, F., Costa, F., Blair, G., & Champbell, R. H. (2002). Adaptive Middleware: The Case for Reflective Middleware. In *Communications of the ACM, 45*(6), 33-38.

Kumar, M., Shirazi, B. A., Das, S. K., Sung, B. Y., Levine, D., & Singhal, M. (2003). PICO: A Middleware Framework for Pervasive Computing. In *IEEE Pervasive Computing Mobile and Ubiquitous Systems, 2*(3), 72-79.

Landau, I. D., Lozano, R., & M'Saad, M. (1998). *Adaptive Control,* London: Springer.

Maes, P. (1987). Concepts and experiments in computational reflection. In *Proceedings of the Object-Oriented Programming Systems Languages and Applications,* (pp. 147-155).

Malek, M. (2005). The NOMADS Republic – A Case for Ambient Service Oriented Computing. In *Proceedings of the 2005 IEEE International Workshop on Service Oriented System Engineering,* (pp. 9-11)

McHugh. J. (2007). *Adaptive Networks Vision – White Paper.* ProCurve Networking, HP Innovation. - http://www.hp.com/rnd/pdfs/Adaptive_Networks_Vision_White_Paper.pdf

McKinley, P. K., Sadjadi, S. M., Kasten, E. P., & Cheng, B. H. C. (2004). Composing Adaptive Software. In *IEEE Computer, 37*(7), 56-64.

Merriam-Webster Dictionary (2008). – http://www.m-w.com

Miller, J. H., & Page, S. E. (2007). *Complex Adaptive Systems: An Introduction to Computational Models of Social Life.* Princeton University Press.

Mussino, S. (2005). *ARM (Adaptive Resource Management): Design and Development of Adaptive Applications.* BSc Thesis, University of Milano-Bicocca. DISCo, Milan, Italy.

Nagarajan, M., Verma, K,, Sheth, A. P., Miller, J. A., & Lathem, J. (2006). Semantic Interoperability of Web Services – Challenges and Experiences. In *Proceedings of the 4th IEEE International Conference on Web Services,* (pp. 373-382).

Noble, B. D., Satyanarayanan, M., Narayanan, D., Tilton, J. E., Flinn, J., & Walker, K. R. (1997). Agile Application-Aware Adaptation for Mobility. In *Proceedings of the 16th ACM Symposium on Operating Systems Principles,* (pp. 276-287).

Noble, B. (2000). System Support for Mobile, Adaptive Applications. In *IEEE Personal Communications.* (pp. 44-49).

OMG Adopted Specification (2004). *UML Profile for Modeling Quality of Service and Fault Tolerance Characteristics and Mechanisms.* ptc/2004-06-01, http://www. omg.org

Oudeyer, P. Y., & Kaplan, F. (2004). Intelligent Adaptive Curiosity: a source of Self-Development. In *Proceedings of the 4th International Workshop on Epigenetic Robotics.* (pp. 127-130).

Poladian, V., Sousa, J. P., Garlan, D., & Shaw, M. (2004). Dynamic Configuration of Resource-Aware Services. In *Proceedings of the 26th International Conference on Software Engineering,* (pp. 604-613).

Raibulet, C., Arcelli, F., Mussino, S., Riva, M., Tisato, F., & Ubezio, L. (2006) Components in an Adaptive and QoS-based Architecture. In *Proceedings of the ICSE 2006 Workshop on Software Engineering for Adaptive and Self-Managing Systems*, (pp. 65-71).

Raibulet, C., Arcelli, F., & Mussino, S. (2006). Mapping the QoS of Services on the QoS of the Systems Resources in an Adaptive Resource Management System. In *Proceedings of the 2006 IEEE International Conference on Services Computing*, (pp. 529-530).

Raibulet, C., Mussino, S., & Ubezio, L. (2007). An Adaptive Resource Management Approach for a Healthcare System. In *Proceedings of the 19th International Conference on Software Engineering & Knowledge Engineering*, (pp. 286-291).

Riva, M. (2006). *Exploiting Architectural Reflection to Achieve Adaptivity in Context-Aware Environments.* MSc Thesis, University of Milano-Bicocca, DISCo, Milan, Italy.

Sasakura, M, & Yamasaki, S. (2007). A Framework for Adaptive e-Learning Systems in Higher Education with Information Visualization. In *Proceedings of the 11th International Conference on Information Visualization*, (pp. 819-824).

Seceleanu, T. & Garlan. D. (2005). Synchronized Architectures for Adaptive Systems. In *Proceedings of the 29th Annual International Computer Software and Applications Conference.* (pp. 146-151).

Shaw, M. (2002). Self-Healing Softening Precision to Avoid Brittleness. In *Proceedings of the Workshop on Self-Healing Systems*, (pp. 111-113).

Smith, B. (1982). *Reflection and Semantics in a Procedural Language.* PhD Thesis, MIT Laboratory for Computer Science, Cambridge, MA, USA.

Sterling, L. & Juan, T. (2005). The Software Engineering of Agent-Based Intelligent Adaptive Systems. In *Proceedings of the International Conference on Software Engineering.* (pp. 704-705).

Suzuki, J. & Yamamoto, Y. (1999). OpenWebServer: An Adaptive Web Server Using Software Patterns. In *IEEE Communications Magazine, 37*(4), (pp.46-52).

Taiani, F., Fabre, J. C., & Killijian, M. O. (2002). Principles of Multi-Level Reflection for Fault Tolerant Architectures. In *Proceedings on the Pacific Rim International Symposium on Dependable Computing*, (pp. 59-66)

Tzafestas, S. G., (1997). Editorial: Robot Adaptive and Robust Control. In *Journal of Intelligent and Robotic Systems, 20*, 87-91.

Wermelinger, M. (1998). Towards a Chemical Model for Software Architecture Reconfiguration. In *IEE Proc Software, 145*(5), 130-136.

Zadeh, L.A. (1963). On the Definition of Adaptivity. In *Proceedings of the IEEE*, (pp. 469-470).

Section IV
Context–Aware Communication, Security and Privacy

Chapter XI
Kindergarten:
A Novel Communication Mechanism for Mobile Context–Aware Applications

Nahuel Lofeudo
LIFIA. Facultad de Informática, UNLP, La Plata, Argentina

Andrés Fortier
LIFIA. Facultad de Informática, UNLP, La Plata, Argentina
DSIC. Universidad Politécnica de Valencia, Valencia, Spain
CONICET, Argentina

Gustavo Rossi
LIFIA. Facultad de Informática, UNLP, La Plata, Argentina
CONICET, Argentina

Silvia E. Gordillo
LIFIA. Facultad de Informática, UNLP, La Plata, Argentina
CICPBA, Argentina

ABSTRACT

Mobile context-aware applications have specific needs regarding data communications and position sensing, that current standard hardware is still not able to fulfill. Current mechanisms are inadequate for applications that need constant communications because of their high power needs and low precision when used to measure the physical indoor position of a mobile device. For this reason the authors have created a new, flexible and inexpensive technology that aims to solve both the needs of communication and position estimation on mobile platforms. This new network type uses recently developed technology to minimize power consumption, leading to a longer battery life and maximizing the precision of the position sensing of the device. Finally, on top of their hardware platform they have devised a software layer, named Kindergarten, which allows high-level languages to interact with the underlying hardware.

INTRODUCTION

During the last decade, mobile context-aware (CA) applications have been gaining importance and are slowly weaving into everyday life. In a conscious and seamless fashion, we start to get used to incorporate new technologies, appliances and applications that where almost unthinkable ten years ago. The penetration of this kind of applications in the society is mainly due to improvements in hardware and communication areas.

However we are still far from having solved all these issues in these areas. Even tough there are different hardware devices and protocols for wireless communication and position estimation, we still need one that is small enough to be integrated into a wide range of appliances, not only PDAs and Smartphones, but also in active badges or key rings. This device must also have very low power consumption, so that the mobile appliance's battery life is not significantly shortened. Most current wireless communication standards have successfully accomplished the size constraint, being effectively embedded in mobile devices. However, low power consumption is still an unresolved issue which leads us to the necessity of conceiving a new kind of hardware.

During our research we tested existing technologies for suitability in our project, including Wi-Fi (O'Hara & Petrick, 1999) and Bluetooth (Morrow, 2002) which, despite their presence in nearly all current PDAs and Smartphones, we found to be too power-hungry. We also tested GPS (Hofmann-Wellenhof, Lichtenegger & Collins, 2004), whose location sensing capabilities only work outdoors making it unusable inside buildings. Unfortunately we arrived to the conclusion that there is no standard hardware device that can be added to any mobile system and that can be used for both communication and position sensing in a practical manner. For this reason we decided to build our own hardware and software platform to communicate and position mobile devices in an efficient way. In this chapter we will describe the design and implementation of our software/hardware combination, which is designed to provide a balance between network bandwidth, power consumption and roaming capabilities. To complement this work, at the end of the chapter we present an example showing how the hardware is combined with our sensing layer to develop context-aware applications. In particular we will show how to use Kindergarten to provide location-based services (Rao, Minakakis, 2003).

PREVIOUS WORK

In order to understand our needs for new hardware and sensing architectures, we have to consider previous approaches and analyze their weaknesses and strengths. In the next subsections we will discuss some of the most pervasive communication and location mechanisms available today. In particular we will describe Infrared, Bluetooth, Wi-Fi and GPS technologies and examine their characteristics from the point of view of a CA application.

Infrared Port

Maybe the most basic device at the hardware level is the infrared (IR) port, which is primarily considered as a communications interface for small devices such as PDAs or cell phones (Knutson & Brown, 2004). In its most pure form, as defined by the IrDA association (IrDA, n.d.), an infrared port sends and receives data between two devices coding it as a stream of infrared pulses. Each device has a small infrared emitter (an infrared LED) to send the light pulses to the other device and an infrared detector to receive the ones sent to it.

This mechanism leaves to software stacks the responsibility of assembling and disassembling the higher-level data structures to allow applications in both sides of the infrared link to exchange data in a reliable and structured way.

This lack of sophistication at the lowest levels of the communications mechanism can be an advantage to adapt this port to serve other functions. In particular, we can make it act not as a communications mechanism but as a location sensing device. To do this, an infrared emitter is configured to continuously send a fixed stream of infrared data, such as a numeric identifier or a position identifier. These devices could be attached to specific objects or locations in the environment to broadcast their data to any infrared-receiving handheld device that passes by, effectively acting as a beacon in its vicinity. When a user carrying one of these infrared-receiving devices (which could be a Smartphone, a PDA or a specifically designed device) approaches the beacon, it will receive the beacon's signal. Then the software running in the device will be able to decode the information present in the beacon and infer its position.

The approach of using infrared light to tag a position in space has all the intrinsic advantages and disadvantages of this transmission medium. An important advantage is its high spatial accuracy: since the infrared beam can be focused to cover a specific area, only devices within this area will be able to receive the IR signal and thus interpret the data it carries. As a downside, the only event that this kind of position sensing mechanism is capable of detecting is the actual approach of the handheld (receiver) device to the beacon emitter. However a second event, which can be related to the user taking away the handheld device or turning away from the beacon emitter, can be inferred when the receiver ceases to detect the beacon.

Summing up, a location system as the one described above is a good choice when there is a need to tag a precise location, as it provides an acceptable response time and relatively good spatial resolution. It cannot, however, be used to detect the physical position of the handheld device (and thus the position of its user) in wide areas, due to its generally narrow field of view, or in places where no beacon can be received at all. Finally, other disadvantage of a solution employing infrared beacons is its limited bandwidth when used to transfer data. The standard IrDA specification reaches only up to 115.2 Kbps, and although a high-speed standard exists for data rates of up to 4 Mbps, it is not supported by all devices.

Bluetooth

Bluetooth is a communications mechanism that, only in recent years, has found its way into the market mainstream. Developed in 1999 as a wireless link between low-power mobile devices, its primary goal was to provide reliable data-transmission services without significantly reducing battery life (Morrow, 2002). Even though the bandwidth achieved by Bluetooth is not high enough to compete with other communication methods standards such as Wi-Fi, it is not a problem for applications when no important amounts of data must be transferred, which is the case in most mobile context-aware systems.

Similarly to infrared technology, Bluetooth can also be used to estimate the device position, based on other Bluetooth devices acting as beacons to mark a specific position. The use of radio signals improves on the use of light by employing a communications medium immune to interference by the mere presence of any objects between transmitter and receiver.

To apply this method a desktop computer or an autonomous transmitter must be set up to constantly broadcast its Bluetooth identification, which would be received by the mobile device. The mobile device would then relate the beacon's ID to its physical position in a similar manner to the one used in the infrared approach. A second approach to infer the user's position is to use a triangulation mechanism. In this procedure the relative signal strength (RSSI) of a received frame is used, which can be roughly correlated to the distance from the mobile device to the device sending it.

As a data communications mechanism, Bluetooth works in a master-slave connection (Tanenbaum, 2002) oriented network. A Bluetooth master device can connect with up to other seven slave devices for data transfer and a slave device can connect to only **one** master device, the only exception being a few very specialized devices that can sustain simultaneous connections to different masters. This makes it impossible for a roaming device to hold a data transfer while moving, because in order for a slave (mobile) device to connect to a different master device, it first has to break all connections to the old Bluetooth master to be able to connect to a new one. This problem cannot be bypassed because the closed nature of the Bluetooth stack makes it impossible to access the hardware directly in a standard and portable manner.

In our tests we found that the process of detecting Bluetooth beacons is slow, taking several seconds to complete this process. Also the most common API exposed to the developer by Bluetooth only allows detecting if a certain beacon is present or not. Some Bluetooth stack vendors (notably IVT Corporation (IVT, n.d.), makers of the BlueSoleil Bluetooth stack) provide ad-hoc API calls to obtain the relative signal strength of a received frame, which can be roughly correlated to the distance from the mobile device to the device sending it. By using this signal strength indicator, we can use triangulation mechanisms to estimate the device's physical distance to fixed beacons, and thus infer the device's physical position. Regrettably, this feature is by no means standard in all implementations of the stack, especially for mobile devices such as PocketPC handhelds.

As a side effect, having the Bluetooth adapter constantly scanning the network for new devices makes it unavailable for data communications and can severely reduce the battery lifetime of the mobile device.

Wi-Fi (IEEE standard 802.11b/g)

Wi-Fi is a communication standard first developed to be used in laptop and portable computers (O'Hara & Petrick, 1999). With data speeds of up to 54Mbps (IEEE 802.11g), nothing in the mobile communications hardware market compares with the transfer speeds achievable with 802.11g, making it an excellent wireless communications tool.

In the same way as Bluetooth, a mechanism based on Wi-Fi can be devised to infer the presence of the device within the coverage area of a certain wireless access point by detecting the beacon frames it emits at regular intervals. In addition to this feature, most wireless adapters have the ability to report the signal strength of the beacons received by the various access points. Since this can be done in a standard and relatively portable way, it allows us to roughly estimate the distance between mobile device and access points, and thus estimate its position.

However, even though it was designed with power-saving features in mind, the energy consumption is still too high to use for more than a few minutes in a highly portable device, such as a Smartphone or a PDA. When active, the battery life of a typical PDA decreases to less than an hour and a half, rendering it unacceptable for real-world context-aware applications, where autonomy of at least eight hours is needed.

GPS

Finally, even though it cannot be used as a communication medium, we must consider the Global Positioning System (GPS) (Hofmann-Wellenhof, Lichtenegger & Collins, 2004), which is the de-facto standard for location sensing mechanisms. Even if it remains the only reliable choice whenever the spatial position of the system is needed, it only works in outdoor environments (Kaplan & Hagerty, 2005) making it unsuitable for our needs. Thus we decided to discard this technology in favor of a more suitable one.

INTRODUCTION TO KINDERGARTEN

From the discussion in the previous section we can infer a very clear set of requirements for the new hardware. In particular we need to:

- Build a location estimation mechanism to provide a means for measuring the physical position of a portable device, and thus the position of the user.
- Build a communication service to provide a reliable message-passing mechanism for data interchange between two different mobile devices.
- Update the physical position estimation at a regular time interval, regardless of the mobile system CPU load and data traffic across the wireless network.
- Complete any data interchange operation in a deterministic time. Also no station should be able to flood the network and prevent other stations to make use of it.
- Use as efficiently as possible the available bandwidth provided by the physical communications medium.
- Make the implementation of the protocol small enough to fit in memory-constrained devices, and simple enough to execute quickly even in low-power CPUs.

Since none of the previously mentioned communications and location estimation mechanisms met all the above requirements, we set out to build a completely new communications architecture exactly tailored to our needs. Consequently, we began to evaluate several hardware alternatives to base our design on.

The Hardware Platform

The first step in the construction of Kindergarten was to decide the wireless communications mechanism on which all services would depend. This step is not a simple one since there are many wireless communication standards (Cooklev, 2004), each one of them incompatible with all the others, operating at different radio frequencies, and with completely different modulation schemes and link level protocols. As Andrew Tanenbaum wrote: "The good thing about standards is that there are so many to choose from" (Tanenbaum, 2002), and of course, for each standard there are sometimes several different implementations in silicon, by different vendors, with different software interfaces, every one of them incompatible with all the others.

It is not our purpose to describe in detail all the available technologies currently being offered in the electronics market. A simple search in any of the major portals on the subject can do it better than this chapter. We will, however, briefly describe the ones we evaluated and the reason for discarding them in favor of the chosen alternative.

The first approach was to use the hardware already present in devices already at our disposal. These devices had Bluetooth and Wi-Fi interfaces and the plan was to use these interfaces bypassing the whole built-in radio stacks and writing a more lightweight software for the same hardware.

It was soon apparent that the problem of lack of freely available documentation for the controller chips for both Bluetooth and Wi-Fi was an insurmountable obstacle. In both cases the manufacturers provided no documentation on the hardware interfaces for the baseband controllers.

The next step was to look for other standards and radio communication devices that, even if they required a separate external controller, would give the advantage of complete flexibility over the implementation. Understandably, not all requirements outlined above had equal weight in the election of the final hardware. We decided to privilege flexibility and simplicity of the solution over more performing but complex alternatives. For this purpose, a relatively new microcontroller (the CC2431) was selected. CC2431 is being manufactured by ChipCon, which has recently been acquired by Texas Instruments (TI, n.d.). This microcontroller integrates a radio transceiver for the IEEE 802.15.4 wireless standard, an 8051 CPU, 128KB of flash memory and 8KB of static RAM in the same chip. On top of that, what really made the CC2431 stand out is that it also integrates a location estimation unit, acting as a hardware co-processor operating independently of the software. Each time a data packet is received by the CC2431's radio interface, the hardware also records the strength of the radio signal that carried the data packet. This signal strength is appended to the data itself, and made available to the application software.

The location estimation unit takes as its input the signal strength of received data of between three and eight other radio stations and their corresponding coordinates in space, and produces the best estimation of its own position. The processing takes a few microseconds and is done in parallel with the execution of the program by the CPU (Figure 1).

Figure 1. Position estimation in a mobile device

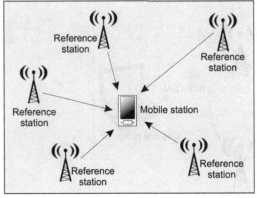

A Few Words about IEEE 802.15.4

IEEE standard 802.15.4 (IEEE, n.d.) defines the first two layers (Physical and Link) for a low-cost, low-power personal area network. This standard focuses on ubiquitous communication between wireless devices with no extra infrastructure (besides the stations themselves) for several physical layers in the 870 MHz, 900 MHz and 2400 MHz bands, providing data transfer speeds of 20, 40, 100 and 250 Kilobits per second. For low-power embedded devices, the standard provides a tradeoff between speed or coverage range and power consumption to lower even more the needs of the device. Special care has been put forth to ensure the lowest possible manufacturing costs for the controllers, and technological simplicity while maintaining flexibility in the design.

Other important features of IEEE 802.15.4 include real-time suitability by reservation of guaranteed time slots, collision avoidance and integrated support for secure communications. Devices also include power management functions such as link quality and energy detection.

IEEE 802.15.4 is mostly known as the two lowest layers for the ZigBee protocol standard, which aims to create networks of low-power connected devices mainly for home automation and remote sensing (ZigBee, n.d.). An interesting ZigBee feature is the possibility to create "mesh" networks, where all nodes in the network are equally responsible for routing data to and from any other node. Other operating modes of a ZigBee network are a tree and star-shaped topologies, with one or more "router" nodes coordinating the data flow between "leaf" or low-power, low-performance nodes.

Even though ZigBee could seem as a good starting point for development, given that it already support low-power wireless networks, ZigBee lacks a deterministic timing behavior needed by base stations when sending beacons to update the location estimation in mobile stations. As ZigBee is an inherently asynchronous network, and at the time when the project began there was no free implementation of the stack that supported mesh topology, it was decided that it was a simpler solution to create a new kind of network specifically for our purposes than to re-implement and adapt ZigBee to suit our needs. In recent days Texas Instruments has released a royalty-free ZigBee stack that can be downloaded from their web site. Even so, in our opinion the complexity of the protocol still justifies the development of our proposed solution.

The Bird's Eye View of the Network

With the selection of the CC2431 as the network controller the first required task was to create the overall communications architecture. Since the CC2431 can calculate its position relative to other reference stations, we decided to create two different sets of devices based on this controller. One set of devices are base stations, fixed in the environment, which know their physical position. The other set is composed of mobile stations, attached to the mobile device (PDA or Smartphone), or acting autonomously.

As stated earlier, since the position estimation should be refreshed at regular intervals, it was clear from the beginning that a purely asynchronous network (such as CSMA (Tanenbaum, 2002)) would not work. A mechanism was needed to ensure that every controller attached to a portable device would receive a steady supply of packets from the base stations to refresh its position estimation. For this reason we decided to create a slotted globally-synchronous network, where the base stations would coordinate the network access by the mobile stations and transmit the necessary information for them to be aware of their position. The basic premises of the design were:

- The whole network operates synchronously, with no two stations (regardless of being base stations or mobile stations) transmitting at the same time.
- If the physical space covered by a network exceeds the coverage of at least one radio station, the network can be split in multiple sub-networks. It is important that **any** mobile station in a network can receive the data transmitted by **all** base stations belong-

Figure 2. Bird's eye view of Kindergarten

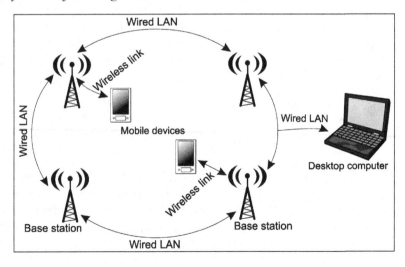

ing to that network. We will discuss this requirement in more detail in the following pages.

- There has to be at least three and at most eight base stations in a network, since these are the absolute minimum and maximum number of references that the location engine of the CC2431 can handle.

In this network, each mobile station receives the signals sent by all base stations in order to update its calculated position, but only communicates with one base station. Thus it acts as a Wi-Fi client, associating itself to a base station and routing all its communications through it. The base stations are wired to an Ethernet network which allows them to receive and send data to each other and to desktop computers (Figure 2).

KINDERGARTEN'S IMPLEMENTATION

In this section we will show a detailed description of the network protocol, the principles behind its operation and the different types of frames that stations exchange. We will also address the issue of communication between the CC2431 acting as a mobile station controller and the PDA or smartphone to which it is attached. At the end of the section we compare our approach with other related technologies.

Operation of the Network

The stations exchange data through the use of frames, much like any other network in existence. In our case the frames conform to the IEEE 802.15.4 standard, although we use the "packet type" field in the 802.15.4 header to mark our own set of packet types.

As we stated earlier, the whole network operates synchronously. Every base station has a time slot during which it can use the communications

channel. The time slot is itself divided in a number of frame slots of fixed size, large enough to accommodate a frame of up to 64 bytes of payload. We have named the time slot of the base station a **superframe** to stress the fact that it encompasses the set of data frames sent and received by a base station.

At the start of a superframe, a base station transmits the data frames for the mobile stations. Then it broadcasts to its mobile stations a special frame named "Order Of Transmission" (OOT) which is simply a list of station addresses, in the order they should transmit their data to the base station. Thus, each station knows exactly when to send its data. Since the frame slots are of a fixed size, there will be no collisions with any other transmission from another station.

Once the time for all the data slots has passed, whether or not the data frames had actually been used, the base station sends a second type of special frame, called "Point Of Entry" (POE). This frame serves two functions: firstly it signals the start of a contention period during which new mobile stations can join the network by sending an association request to the mobile station. Secondly, since the POE is transmitted by every base station in every superframe, we use it for piggybacking the location information for that base station so that all mobile stations in range can update their position.

The number of data frames in each superframe is fixed, to ensure that all base stations start and end their superframe in the same time period. Also every station transmits and receives its superframe in its allocated time slot until all stations have done so, and the cycle begins again in an endless loop. We call this cycle **network heartbeat** (Figure 3).

At a first glance, Kindergarten may seem similar to Token Ring (Love, Siegel, Wilson, 1998), because both networks give each station (base station, in the case of Kindergarten) a time slot to use the communications channel. In this time they can send and receive data, arranged in a

Figure 3. Operation cycle of Kindergarten

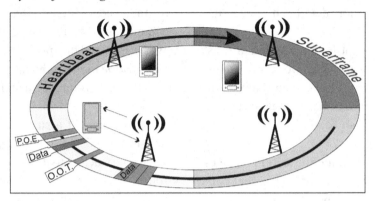

sort of ring. However, the similarity between both systems ends there, since in Kindergarten there is no concept of "Token", and both the sequence of the base stations and the length of the time slots remains fixed regardless of the amount of data to be sent or received by a station. Also, Kindergarten is much simpler than Token Ring, both in its design and operation, so that it can be implemented in devices with limited capabilities.

This never ending cycle is what gives Kindergarten its name. The analogy can be seen as follows: imagine a group of small children, running around in the playground, shouting at each other while they play. In a sense, wireless stations are like small children: they roam free, shouting (through the wireless channel) when they feel like it, and overlapping (interfering with) each other. Our goal in designing Kindergarten was to create a setting in which children (mobile stations) are supervised by teachers (base stations) who make them take turns to play.

In case the volume of space to cover is larger than the coverage range of a base station (e.g. when deploying the network in a large hall) we need to scale up the network. Since the location mechanism depends on the mobile station receiving beacons from all base stations in the network, in large spaces it is necessary to split the network

in sub-networks operating independently. This is where the synchronous nature of Kindergarten comes into play. The fact that all superframes have the same length in time allows us to create several sub-networks where the base stations are synchronized in a way that ensures they will never interfere with each other.

As an example let us suppose the following setup of two sub-networks with four base stations each (see Figure 4).

Figure 4 represents the heartbeat with a ring, and the stations with the same position in the superframe (i.e. stations whose superframes are simultaneous) with the same grey level. The coverage area of the stations currently transmitting is shown as a circle around the station.

As this example show, even if both stations S2 and S6 are using the channel in the same instant, since they are outside each other's coverage area their signals will not interfere inside the space occupied by the network (depicted as the grey rectangle). And even if S2 and S5 are inside each other's coverage area they use the channel at different times, thus ensuring that no collision will occur.

Moreover, all base stations are kept synchronized by wiring a second data line through all of them. This data line, the *heartbeat line*, has as its

Figure 4. Non-overlapping simultaneous transmissions

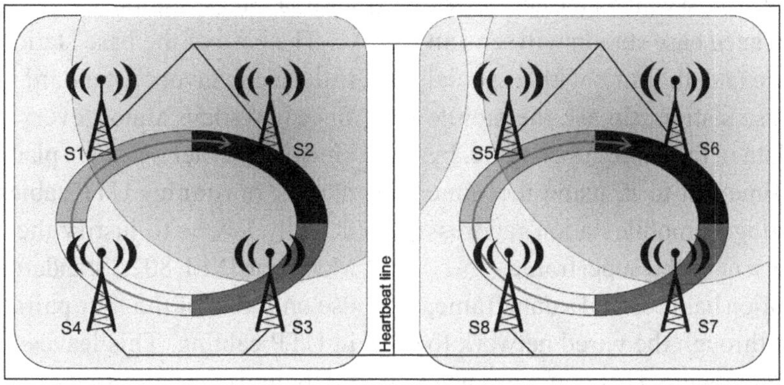

only purpose to signal the start of a heartbeat by transitioning from a logic HIGH (1) to a logic LOW (0). The rate at which the heartbeat line toggles is determined by the amount of time needed to transmit a single frame times the number of frames per superframe, times the number of superframes in a heartbeat.

Communications Architecture

The life cycle of a mobile station begins when it is initialized. At this moment the mobile station waits for a POE (Point Of Entry) frame from any base station and sends an association request to that base station. Then, the mobile station must wait until the next network heartbeat, when the base station to which it sent the request can send a response. If the mobile station receives a rejection frame, it must wait for the POE frame from a different base station and retry the procedure. If the mobile station receives an acceptance response it becomes associated to the base station, routing all data frames through it.

All base stations are wired together to a common communications channel, usually a wired LAN (such as Fast Ethernet), to exchange data frames routed through them. Since all stations in the Kindergarten network operate under very

strict timing constraints, it is the responsibility of a base station to enforce the format and timing of its superframe. On the other hand, every mobile station must only transmit when asked to by its base station. Failure of any station to meet these requirements will create interference, forcing retransmission of data frames or mobile stations not receiving OOT or POE frames as long as the interference persists. The stateless nature of Kindergarten makes it possible for the network to recover at the start of the next network heartbeat, when the sequence begins again.

When a mobile station needs to transmit data, it must wait for an OOT with its own address in it. Once the mobile station receives an OOT frame with its own address as part of the frame data, the station must check to which one of the data slots it has been assigned.

A mobile station can only transmit data in a time slot assigned to it by its associated base station, thus once the mobile station has found its time slot it must wait until this time arrives. And since the time slot for a data frame is of fixed length, the amount of data that a station can send is limited to a maximum value. In Kindergarten it is 64 bytes due to limitations in the various buffer sizes in the radio transceiver and the memory space available in the CC2431 microcontroller.

Once the mobile station has sent to the base station a data frame, it must wait for the next heartbeat when its associated base station will send an acknowledge frame (a data frame with a special *type* field). The base station can ask the mobile station for more data in the same superframe, by assigning a new time slot to it, using the same procedure of inserting the mobile station's address to the OOT frame sent in the superframe.

Once a base station has received a data frame, it sends the frame through the wired network to a central desktop computer. This computer acts as a router for all communications, storing the associations between the mobile stations and base stations, and routing the data frames to any mobile station through the appropriate base station. The routing is done using the addressing scheme of the wired interconnection between base stations. In our case, it is done addressing the base stations by their MAC (Ethernet) addresses.

When a mobile station is taken away from the base station through which it sends and receives data, its signal starts to fade. The mobile station, then, requests the central router to switch the data communications to a closer base station through a special data frame addressed to the router. Thus data frames keep being able to travel to and from the mobile station as it moves.

Hardware Platform and Basic Software Abstractions

The next step after the design and implementation of a new communications architecture like Kindergarten is the physical construction of the devices, which are the ones to actually carry out the processing. In our case, a large part of the hardware design and implementation work was already done by the makers of CC2431 by creating a chip that could carry out the processing and communication stages in a single package. However, we still have to connect the controller to either the PDA or Smartphone, in the case of

a mobile station, or to the wired network, in the case of a base station.

The case of the base station was the quickest to decide in favor of standard LAN technologies, since nowadays almost every building has some kind of Ethernet wiring in place or, in its absence, the cost of running UTP cables through it is sufficiently low as to justify the decision to use it. Moreover, IEEE 802.3 standards (IEEE 802.3, n.d.) use only two of the four pairs of wires available in UTP cabling. This leaves the other two (normally unused) pairs free to run the power lines for the base stations and the heartbeat line. We chose to use a relatively new controller to interface the CC2431 and the Ethernet network: the ENC28J60 made by Microchip Corp (MCP, n.d.). This integrated circuit is a complete IEEE 802.3 MAC and PHY controller designed specifically to be used in micro controlled projects through an SPI (Serial Port Interface) interface. SPI is a synchronous serial bus created for data exchange between micro controlled devices (SPI, n.d.). It only needs three data lines (*Clock, Master Input Slave Output* and *Master Output Slave Input*) to transfer data at the maximum data rate supported by both endpoints of the bus. This means that there is no need of complex connections between the CC2431 and the ENC28J60. All in all, we use just six data lines between both circuits:

- Clock, Master Input Slave Output and Master Output Slave Input (SPI bus)
- Slave Select line, for the CC2431 to specifically address the ENC28J60
- Interrupt line, for the ENC28J60 to signal an event to the CC2431
- RESET line, to initialize the ENC28J60 once the software in the CC2431 has begun its execution.

If we add two other lines for power supply, this makes a total of eight electrical connections between the CC2431 running the Kindergarten protocol and the ENC28J60 working as Ethernet adapter, enormously simplifying the task of electronics design. As an added value, Microchip Corp. has created a free TCP/IP stack to be used with its ENC28J60. We have used this stack to allow the Kindergarten router (running on a standard PC computer) to exchange data with all base stations through UDP packets.

In the case of mobile devices the choice was not so easy. After surveying the communication mechanisms available in our devices and others available in the market, it was evident that the only common expansion mechanisms for all devices were either wireless (Bluetooth or WiFi), USB (USB, n.d.) or the SD/MMC (SDMMC, n.d.) slot.

We quickly discarded the wireless protocols because that would force the design of the mobile station to include a second radio interface just to communicate with the PDA, raising significantly both the cost and the complexity of the solution.

USB was discarded due to hardware constraints. The basic rate for the USB serial line is 1,5 Mbps, much higher than the data rates achievable with either software or hardware serial ports in the CC2431 and beyond the processing capabilities of the CC2431's 33MHz CPU. We also discarded adding a separate USB controller to the design since it would have made the design more complex and costly.

Consequently we settled in using the SD/MMC slot. On the hardware level, it is a serial communications bus 1 or 4 bit wide, depending on the device's capabilities, operating in a command-response scheme. The same physical bus is used for three separate standards: MMC, SD and SDIO, the first two being purely for data storage, and the third one supporting non-storage devices and I/O operations. We chose SDIO mostly because its basic data rate is 400 Kbps., that can easily be handled by the CC2431's hardware serial ports. The command-response times are also more lax

than in the case of USB, allowing sufficiently long times for the CC2431's CPU to do all the necessary processing. In this way, the CC2431 could emulate a SDIO card inserted in the SD/MMC slot of the PocketPC or Smartphone and be detected as such by the operating system.

The implementation of a SDIO card emulator for the CC2431 was based on information publicly available on the Internet: the lower-level SD bus specification is downloadable directly from the SD Card Association (SDCARD, n.d.) and the higher-level functions are described in great detail in the Linux SDIO Stack source code (LNXSD, n.d.).

For the PocketPC / Smartphone side, we developed a SDIO client driver (MSDN, n.d.) to be loaded by the operating system upon the insertion of the card carrying the CC2431. This driver creates a pseudo-file which constitutes the interface to higher-level software functions, and it is through reads and writes to this file that the application software (in our case written in VisualWorks Smalltalk) and the lower-level functions communicate.

At the Smalltalk level we leverage the user of having to think in terms of packets and pseudo files and use a mailbox-based approach to communicate the different hosts in the network. Each host can use three classes to interact with the network:

- A KindergartenConnection class, that is used to manage the connection of the host to the network. This class allows the host to get information about the network (e.g. knowing if the host is connected, its address or asking for the available hosts in the network).
- A KindergartenOutbox class, that is used to send synchronous or asynchronous messages to other hosts in the network. Asynchronous messages are supported by Kindergarten's hardware, while synchronous messages are emulated. This class takes care of splitting

the message in packets of 64 bytes and sending the corresponding commands to the pseudo-file.

- A KindergartenInbox class, that is used to queue received messages. The programmer can poll this class for new messages or use it through a publish-subscribe mechanism.

As a result we are able to use high level abstractions to control the proposed hardware, both at the communication and location level.

In the next subsection we will compare Kindergarten with other similar technologies.

Comparison with Other Protocols and Communications Hardware

In section 2 we analyzed the advantages and drawbacks of existing hardware technologies for position estimation and data communication. In short, we have found that most "off the shelf" hardware has severe limitations when employed in context-aware applications, the most significant ones being high power needs and low spatial resolution, thus leading us to create Kindergarten.

The hardware employed in Kindergarten (the CC2431 microcontroller) has significantly lower power needs, especially in low-power mode, where most of the chip is shut down and only the basic functions remain active, awaiting an external event. Kindergarten is designed for mobile stations

to maximize the time where the microcontroller is in low power mode, thus reducing power consumption to a minimum.

In comparison, when used as a location detection mechanism both Bluetooth and Wi-Fi have to scan all available channels for beacons. This forces them to spend a significant time in active mode hopping from channel to channel just to receive said beacons.

Table 1 summarizes the main points of section 2.

In section 3 we introduced Kindergarten as a globally-synchronous network. We have chosen this approach to simplify the protocol and keep its implementation in the CC2431 as lean as possible. By assigning each station (either base or mobile) a fixed slot to send and receive data, we avoid problems and complexity created by collisions in accessing the shared medium.

This approach is similar in spirit to that of Token Ring, where a station can only transmit while it holds a special "token", but is much simpler since there is no token to pass around and is more adequate to the shared medium of wireless networks.

Approaches with "carrier sense multiple access"(CSMA) algorithms like CSMA/CD (Ethernet) or CSMA/CA (Wi-Fi) were discarded because of their nondeterministic nature: each mobile station needs beacons emitted from each of the base stations at a regular rate to update its own

Table 1. Summary of the different wireless technologies discussed in this chapter

Technology	Data Bandwidth	Location precision	Power consumption (min/max)
Wi-Fi	11 / 54 Mbps	0.5 Meters	50 uA / 90 mA
Bluetooth	720 Kbps / 2.1 Mbps	20 Meters	15 mA / 60 mA
Infrared	115 kbps / 1.5 Mbps	N/A	0 / 15 mA
GPS	N/A	3 – 5 Meters	90 mA
Kindergarten	250 Kbps	0.5 – 1 Meter (estimated)	0.9 uA / 25 mA

estimated position, and CSMA algorithms cannot guarantee their transmission under conditions of heavy network load (Tanenbaum, 2002).

Finally, even though Kindergarten shares similarities with ZigBee, it lacks Kindergarten's deterministic timing and simplicity.

Although no formal Kindergarten network is fully functional at this time, initial measurements of wireless performance on the CC2431 have yielded excellent results.

As for throughput alone, we have achieved speeds of more than 200 frames with a 64 bytes payload per second, with a packet error rate of below 2% over medium distances. With these data it is possible to obtain a rate of 3 superframes per second when each superframe includes 32 slots for data frames, yielding up to 98 Kbps of raw data throughput. Another possible configuration would be to reduce the data slots to 2, which would give us a rate of 20 superframes per second, reaching 41 Kbps of data speed. This allows the implementer of the network to balance the raw data throughput versus the frequency of location updates.

The design and implementation of a new communications infrastructure is not something to be taken lightly. We have struggled to keep the hardware and software design as simple as possible. Early results show promise for this technology although further work is needed to ensure its correct implementation and operation. We have confidence that the low cost (less than five dollars in the case of CC2431) and low complexity of the hardware will encourage others to build their own units and contribute to the development of Kindergarten.

CASE STUDY: USING KINDERGARTEN TO PROVIDE LBS

In this section we will show how to use Kindergarten combined with our sensing architecture to monitor the user's location and provide Location Based Services (LBSs) (Rao & Minakakis, 2003).

For the sake of simplicity we will use a minimal context model that just takes into an account the user's location. Also, since location modeling is not a trivial task and it is out of the scope of this paper to discuss the different approaches (the interested reader can see (Bauer, Becker & Rothermel, 2002; Haibo Hu & Dik-Lun Lee, 2004; Hightower & Borriello, 2001) for further references) we will represent the user's position with a symbolic location model (Leonhardt, 1998). In this model areas are represented as symbols and the relationships between them with graphs and trees (e.g. a tree to establish the containment between areas and a graph to represent adjacency). All these relationships are encapsulated inside a *symbolic map*.

Finally, to provide location-based services we use a set of mappings that associate symbolic areas with a collection of available services. Thus, each time the user's location changes (i.e. he enters a new area) the system must recalculate the available services.

Context Model Overview

To build context aware applications we devised a layered architecture, where the context model resides in a lower layer and the context-dependent behavior sits on an upper layer. Since it is not the purpose of this chapter to discuss our context model or how to provide context-dependent behavior we will just define the basic abstractions used in our context model. The interested reader can obtain more information in (Challiol, Fortier, Gordillo & Rossi, 2007; Fortier, Cañibano, Grigera, Rossi & Gordillo, 2006; Rossi, Gordillo, & Fortier, 2005).

The context model layer contains two main abstractions: the *aware objects* and the *context features*. An aware object is any object whose context is relevant to decide the application's behavior, like a user to provide location based services (LBSs) or a room to provide smart home facilities. Also, since we do not conceive context

Figure 5. Object diagram of a user with a location context feature

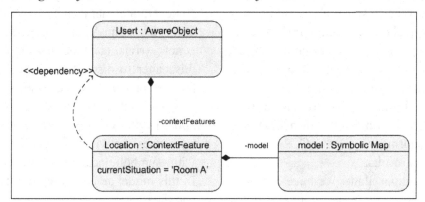

as a whole, closed object, we split the context into a collection of context features. As a result, in our LBSs example, we represent the user as an aware object and his location as a context feature. Figure 5 shows an object diagram of this situation.

As explained before, we will use a symbolic map of a building, assuming that we already have the required classes for managing symbolic maps (i.e. finding adjacent locations, testing for inclusion and so on). This management can be achieved because the context feature holds a reference to the symbolic map (its model), which gives meaning to the symbol that represents his location.

Sensing Layer Outline

In order to ease the process of gathering sensor data to update the context model we have built a set of abstractions, grouped in a specific layer. As in the previous section, we will give a short description of this layer so that the main concepts are understood. The interested reader can get more detailed information in (Grigera, Fortier, Rossi & Gordillo, 2007).

The purpose of the sensing layer is to help in a set of tasks that are common to most context-aware applications that need to access sensor data. In particular the process of sensing data and feeding the derived information to the context model involves:

- Using a (generally low-level) API. This API is commonly wrapped in an object that represents the physical sensor.
- Configuring sensors acquisition policies. While some may provide a notification mechanism others require constant polling for new data.
- Filtering signals gathered by sensors. In some cases a signal may not fit the required standards (e.g. a measure's error is greater that a certain threshold) while in other cases the data may be corrupted. Also, like in the case of Kindergarten, we may want to avoid processing multiple consecutive times the same information.
- Converting sensor data to match the context model domain. This step generally involves some sort of abstraction, since most sensors operate with low-level data (bytes, numbers, strings, tuples) and context models composed of semantically-rich objects. It is worth to mention that this transformation can vary in its complexity, ranging from a simple table lookup (e.g. matching a beacon id to a specific area) to complex algorithms

(e.g. using machine learning techniques to infer the user's activity).

- Updating the context model. After the signal is converted to the context domain, it must be used to update the corresponding context feature. Once this is done the application can perform its context-dependent behavior (e.g. providing new services).

We show a class diagram with the main components of this layer in Figure 6.

The entry point of this layer is the SensingConcern class, which coordinates the actions of its three collaborators:

- SensingPolicy. This class is in charge of abstracting whether the sensor must be polled

Figure 6. Class diagram of the sensing layer

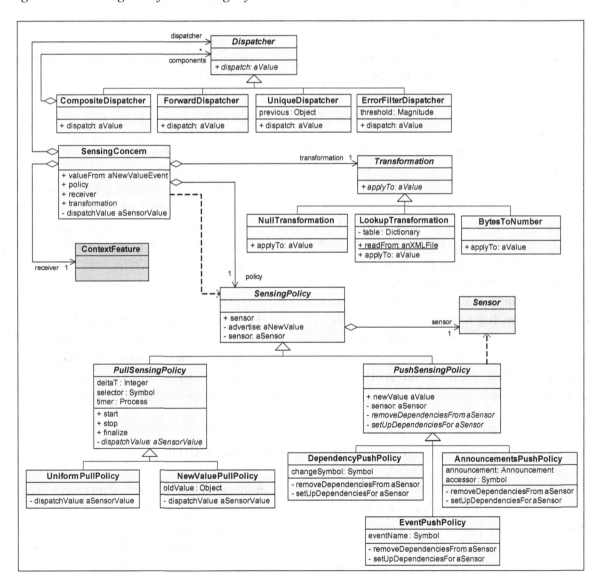

for data or not, adding a level of indirection between the sensor and the SensingConcern. This allows the SensingConcern to treat sensors as if all of them used a push policy (i.e. triggering an event each time a new value is sensed).

- Dispatcher. Its responsibility is to decide whether a signal should reach the context model or not, acting like a filter. Multiple dispatchers can be combined by means of the CompositeDispatcher class, allowing the reuse of already implemented ones.

- Transformation. This class is used to map low level data to context information. In case no transformation is needed (e.g. a temperature value is directly used by the context model) a NullTransformation is used, according to the Null Object pattern (Woolf, 1997). Other common transformations are already provided by our toolkit, like lookup tables or simple conversions (e.g. interpreting a byte array as an integer or converting a string to a floating point).

After the transformation has been applied, the new object is sent to the context model by the SensingConcern class. This step is performed by sending the #currentSituation: message to the context feature. Thus, the SensingConcern class can be seen as a "big brother", always watching over sensors and deciding when and how a new sensed value will be passed to the context model.

Using Kindergarten to Sense the User's Position

Having introduced our context model and the sensing layer we can now show how Kindergarten can be used to obtain the user's position while he is moving indoors and translate it to a symbolic location. To obtain the user's coordinates in an indoor space the KindergartenConnection class (discussed at the end of section 3) is used. Thus, from the sensing layer point of view, an instance of

KindergartenConnection acts like a sensor, providing information about the user's location. We next enumerate how the sensing layer is configured to update the context model:

- In Kindergarten we can configure a callback to be executed every time a superframe finishes, retrieving the mobile location according to the chip's location module. This location is retrieved in 2D coordinates, according to the position of the static bases. Thus a simple push policy is created to notify the sensing concern each time the callback is triggered.

- In most of the cases we expect many superframes to be completed without the user changing his position. Thus, to avoid unnecessary recalculations, the location should be only allowed to reach the context model if it is different than the previous one. To achieve this behavior a UniqueDispatcher is used, only propagating the signal if a new position is detected.

- Finally we must map the 2-dimensional coordinates provided by Kindergarten, to the symbolic areas used in the context model. This is achieved by using a custom Transformation subclass (2DToSymbolic, that uses an RTree to provide fast geometric lookups).

Having set up the context model and the sensing layer to keep it updated, establishing what services should be available for the user at a given time is just a matter of performing a lookup in the set of associations between areas and services.

FUTURE TRENDS

Even though we have a set of prototypes built, we consider our work to be in an early stage. Regarding Kindergarten, we hope to be able to build a prototype network with all its services in place. This network will support mobile devices such as PDAs and Smartphones, and smaller more limited devices packaged in badges or key chains, designed to just report their position to an external system running in a standard computer. This prototype network will let us acquire hard data on the true reliability and throughput of the design, and to make changes in the location estimation mechanism if needed.

At this moment we have yet to tune and test the software that will run on the base stations and in the Kindergarten controller in the mobile station (the previously described CC2431). We are also finishing the device driver that will run in the Windows Mobile powered devices, where the CA application will reside, and allow these applications to interact with other CA applications and the Kindergarten controller.

Our next task will be to create a prototype network using the prototype nodes mentioned above. The aim of this network will be to create a realistic environment upon which we will be able to do real-life measurements of location estimation precision. One of our concerns is the effect that furniture, people and walls will have in the radio signal, and thus the amount of post-processing necessary to sanitize the estimated physical coordinates.

We also wish to test data throughput of the network under real-life load scenarios and to stress test the implementation of the Kindergarten stack.

Regarding the sensing layer we still have a couple of areas that require improvements and different enhancements. Improvements include solving the case of having multiple sensors for the same context feature with different values. An example of this situation could be gathering weather from a web service and from a weather station in a smart home. In this case, the sensing concerns are marked as conflicting and a marshaler decides which of the values will be sent to the context feature (or maybe a new value, derived from the previous ones). In order to choose one value over the other we could use different indica-

tors, like the quality of service, the cost of it or the sampling ratio.

CONCLUSION

In this chapter we have tackled the problem of communication and location estimation for mobile devices, which is a must in any context-aware application. Since our aim is to provide a complete solution for handling external data we also showed how, by means of our sensing layer, Kindergarten can be used to develop very simple location-based services.

As we discussed in the chapter, the implementation of Kindergarten meets the following design requirements:

- Build a location estimation mechanism for a small portable device.
- Build a communication service to communicate such devices.
- Use the transmission medium as efficiently as possible.
- Make the implementation of the protocol small and simple to fit in small CPUs.

Kindergarten is a globally-synchronous network that arranges all stations in an endless sequence called network heartbeat. Each station (be it a base station or a mobile station) has a specific time slot allocated to transmit its information, and all mobile stations refresh their position by triangulating the signal level received from the base stations.

The location estimation mechanism has been designed to be easily integrated to context-aware applications thanks to an event-based mailbox interface. The communications mechanism is fast enough to allow applications to send and receive simple messages, and simple enough to be easily used by other programs. It also allows the user to roam freely while maintaining all communications uninterrupted.

ACKNOWLEDGMENT

Partially supported by the SeCyT under the project PICT-2005, Nro 32536.

REFERENCES

Bauer, M., Becker, C., & Rothermel, K (2002). *Location Models from the Perspective of Context-Aware Applications and Mobile Ad Hoc Networks.* Personal Ubiquitous Comput., *6*(5-6), 322-328.

Challiol, C., Fortier, A., Gordillo, S., & Rossi, G. (2007). A Flexible Architecture for Context-Aware Physical Hypermedia, *dexa*, (pp. 590-594) *In the 18th International Conference on Database and Expert Systems Applications (DEXA 2007).*

Cooklev, T. (2004). *Wireless Communication Standards: A Study of IEEE 802.11, 802.15, and 802.16.* Standards Information Network/ IEEE Press

Dey, A. K. (2000). *Providing architectural support for building context-aware applications.* PhD thesis.

Fahy, P., & Clarke, S. (2004). CASS: Middleware for Mobile, Context-Aware Applications. In *Workshop on Context Awareness at MobiSys 2004.* Boston, MA, USA.

Fortier, A., Cañibano, N., Grigera, J., Rossi, G., & Gordillo, S. (2006). An Object-Oriented Approach for Context-Aware Applications. *In Proceedings of the 2006 Smalltalk research Conference*, Also Springer Verlag, 2006, LNCS.

Gamma, E., Helm, R., Johnson, R., & Vlissides, J. (1995). *Design Patterns.* Addison-Wesley Professional.

Grigera, J., Fortier, A., Rossi, G., & Gordillo, S. (2007). A Modular Architecture for Context Sensing. In *Proceedings of PCAC-07, IEEE Computer Society*, (pp. 147-152).

Haibo, H., & Dik-Lun, L. (2004). Semantic location modeling for location navigation in mobile environment Mobile Data Management, 2004. *Proceedings of 2004 IEEE International Conference*, (pp. 52-61).

Harter, A., Hopper, A., Steggles, P., Ward, A., & Webster, P. (2002). The anatomy of a context-aware application. *Wireless Networks, 8*(2 - 3), 187-197.

Hightower, J., & Borriello, G. (2001). *Location systems for ubiquitous computing.* IEEE Computer, *34*(8), 57–66.

Hofmann-Wellenhof, B., Lichtenegger, H., & Collins, J. (2004). *Global Positioning System: Theory and Practice.* Springer.

IEEE (n.d.). *IEEE 802.15.4 task group*, from http://www.ieee802.org/15/pub/TG4.html

IEEE802.3 (n.d.), *IEEE 802.3 (Ethernet) Standard*, from http://standards.ieee.org/getieee802/

IrDA (n.d.), *Infrared Data Association*, from http://irda.org/

IVT (n.d.), *IVT Corporation*, from http://www.ivtcorporation.com

Knutson, C. D., & Brown, J. M. (2004). *IrDA Principles and Protocols: The IrDA Library, Vol. 1.* MCL Press.

Leonhardt, U. (1998). *Supporting Location-Awareness in Open Distributed Systems.* PhD thesis, University of London.

LNXSD, (n.d.). *SDIO Linux Stack*, from http://sourceforge.net/projects/sdio-linux/

Love, R. D., Siegel, M., & Wilson, K. T. (1998). *Understanding Token Ring Protocols and Standards.* Artech House Publishers

MCP, (n.d.). *ENC28J60 product page*, from http://www.microchip.com/stellent/idcplg?

IdcService=SS_GET_PAGE&nodeId=1335&d DocName=en022889

Morrow, R (2002). *Bluetooth: Operation and Use*. McGraw-Hill.

MSDN, (n.d.). Microsoft Developers Network, Secure Digital Card Drivers, from http://msdn2. microsoft.com/en-us/library/ms923739.aspx

O'Hara, R., & Petrick, A. (2005). *802.11 Wireless Networks: The Definitive Guide, Second Edition*. IEEE Computer Society.

Rao, B., & Minakakis, L. (2003). Evolution of mobile location-based services. *Communications of the ACM, 46*(12), 61-65.

Rossi, G., Gordillo, S., & Fortier, A. (2005). Seamless Engineering of Location Aware Services. *International Workshop on Context-Aware Mobile Systems, Lecture Notes in Computer Science*.

Schmidt, A., Beigl, M., & Hans-W, H. (1999). There is more to context than location. *Computers and Graphics, 23*(6), 893-901.

Schmidt, A., & Van Laerhoven, K. (2001). How to build smart appliances? *Personal Communications, IEEE, 8*(4), 66-71.

SDCARD, (n.d.). *Secure Digital simplified Physical Layer Specification*, from http://www.sdcard. org/about/memory_card/pls/

SDMMC, (n.d.). *SD Card Association*, from http://www.sdcard.org

SPI, (n.d.). *SPI reference*, from http://en.wikipedia. org/wiki/Serial_Peripheral_Interface_Bus

Strang, T., & Popien, C. L. (2004). A context modeling survey. In *Workshop on Advanced Context Modelling, Reasoning and Management, UbiComp 2004 - The Sixth International Conference on Ubiquitous Computing*.

Tanenbaum, A. S. (2002). *Computer Networks*. Prentice Hall PTR

TI, (n.d.). *CC2431 product page*, from http://focus. ti.com/docs/ prod/folders/print/cc2431.html

USB, (n.d.). *USB Developers page*, from http:// www.usb.org/developers

Wang, X. H., Zhang, D. Q., Gu, T., & Pung, H. K. (2004). Ontology based context modeling and reasoning using owl. In *Proceedings of the Second IEEE Annual Conference on Pervasive Computing and Communications Workshops* (March 14 - 17, 2004). PERCOMW. IEEE Computer Society, Washington, DC, 18.

Woolf, B. (1997). Null object. *Pattern languages of program design 3*, (pp. 5–18).

ZigBee (n.d.). *Zigbee Alliance*, from http://www. zigbee.org

Chapter XII
Access Control in Mobile and Ubiquitous Environments

Laurent Gomez
SAP Research, France

Annett Laube
SAP Research, France

Alessandro Sorniotti
SAP Research, France

ABSTRACT

Access control is the process of granting permissions in accordance to an authorization policy. Mobile and ubiquitous environments challenge classical access control solutions like Role-Based Access Control. The use of context-information during policy definition and access control enforcement offers more adaptability and flexibility needed for these environments. When it comes to low-power devices, such as wireless sensor networks, access control enforcement is normally too heavy for such resource-constrained devices. Lightweight cryptography allows encrypting the data right from its production and the access is therefore intrinsically restricted. In addition, all access control mechanisms require an authenticated user. Traditionally, user authentication is performed by means of a combination of authentication factors, statically specified in the access control policy of the authorization service. Within ubiquitous and mobile environment, there is a clear need for a flexible user authentication using the available authentication factors. In this chapter, different new techniques to ensure access control are discussed and compared to the state-of-the-art.

INTRODUCTION

Ubiquitous computing is the computing paradigm that refers to scenarios in which computing is omnipresent, and particularly in which devices that are traditionally perceived as dumb are endowed with computing capability (Stajano, 2002). The use of context information represents a significant benefit for applications in the highly dynamic environments addressed by ubiquitous computing. The deployment of collaborative mobile applications in ubiquitous environments is accompanied by an increasing demand on security. In addition to technical challenges, ubiquitous environments raise security issues such as access control for resources shared between mobile applications. Access control represents a real challenge due to the highly dynamic nature of communications, where former unknown partners communicate in an ad-hoc way.

Access control is a standard security technique to control the access to resources in a system. It consists of a set of mechanisms and processes that allow the definition of access control rules - the authorization policy - and the enforcement of these rules (Samarati, 2001). Access control is the process of granting permissions in accordance with an authorization policy. An authorization policy states "who can do what to what". The "who" is a subject, the first "what" is an action, and the other "what" is a resource. In a context-aware authorization policy the context is taken into account as additional constraint. The statement can be extended as follows: "who can do what to what under which circumstances". The circumstances correspond to the context of the application.

The availability of context information allows reconfiguration and enhancement of a system and application security, depending on the changing context. Context-aware security is defined as a dynamic adaptation of security policies according to the context. For instance, context information can be used to automatically reconfigure security mechanisms in order to provide a predefined level of security and, at the same time, to optimize the use of resources. As a concrete example, email messages sent by mobile workers using a public WLAN hotspot as an access point for their PDA can be automatically encrypted, whereas the same messages could be sent in plain text when they connect to a secured access point in his office.

SCENARIOS

In the following section, the challenges of access control in ubiquitous and mobile environments are highlighted in 2 different scenarios.

Scenario 1: Remote Healthcare Monitoring

The use of context-aware security techniques is illustrated in the following e-health scenario: an application constantly monitors the health and well-being of elderly at home. The elderly are wearing body sensors, which register several measurements related to the physical condition, like heart rate, oximetry (SpO2), blood glucose level and body temperature. The homes of aged people are equipped with ambient sensors, delivering additional information about the activities of the monitored subject and of the environment. All measurements are forwarded to a backend application and stored permanently there as part of the personal medical records. Since these medical records contain sensitive data, access to the data has to be controlled.

In the e-health example, medical records can be accessed by people in different roles such as: general practitioners, gerontologists (specialist for diseases and problems specific to old people), and nurses. But often the role concept alone is not sufficient to control access to the medical data. Additional criteria, like the relationship between patient and doctor or context information, e.g. the health status or location, have to be considered.

Normally, only family doctors can access the entire personal medical record of a patient. But in an emergency situation, any physician, who is close to the patient, can get access to the data. An emergency situation can be described as a complex type of context information derived from the body sensor readings. The proximity of two individuals also represents complex context information, calculated out of the position gained, for example, by GPS sensors.

The personal medical record of a person contains in general more than the recorded sensors readings from body and ambient sensors. Medical data may include the clinical history, medication history, hospital stays, activity records, and personal data. Looking on the variety of roles defined in the e-health scenario, it is not always necessary to disclose the entire medical record: a nurse needs not to know all the information that a doctor in turn needs to access to perform a task. In most situations, it is sufficient to grant access to the smallest subset of information needed.

In addition a doctor should have the rights to book a room for a patient in a hospital or to plan a surgery only when he is physically in the hospital or in his office and not on vacation. An emergency team member can get access to all medical information about a victim, only if he is close to the patient and the patient is unconscious, whereas access to the private medical information is normally restricted to the assigned doctors (general practitioner, specialists, etc.).

An additional concept is represented by context-aware delegation of rights. For example, when a manager is out of office, he can delegate some of his rights to his secretary until he is back. Depending on the urgency of certain tasks, the context-aware system can decide whether delegation is allowed or not.

Scenario 2: E-Insurance

The use of context-aware security techniques is not restricted to e-health business domain. Car accident management is an e-Insurance scenario from the automotive business domain. In this scenario, a car is uniquely identified with a car ID. This information allows authorized third party (e.g. police, insurance) to authenticate a car and to map it to any information such as the car owner driving licenses, vehicle registration. In addition to the car ID, speed information, fuel consumption, brakes usage information can be distributed.

Nevertheless, the broadcast of such information raises a major security issue: information confidentiality. In a car accident for example, all involved cars send information such as GPS position, insurance contract ID to their insurance company. This information is used to automatically fill the accident report and supports insurance companies to find an agreement. In the case of car theft, the car ID and GPS location of car is sent to the police in order to track the car.

In the same way as in the e-health scenario, an access control to the exchanged data within this ubiquitous environment is required, in the case of the car accident scenario: one of the security threats is the interception of the GPS location by fake garage owner. Pretending to be certified garage owner, they could steal the damaged car.

CONTEXT-AWARE ACCESS CONTROL

State-of-the-Art

A classical approach to tackle the challenge of protecting data access is role-based access control (RBAC), introduced in (Sandhu, 1996). RBAC associates to each user one or more roles. Permissions to objects (resources) are defined for each role. However powerful, simple RBAC reaches its limits when the access control policy becomes more complex. Additional information has to be integrated in the policy enforcement process. Organization-based access control (OrBAC)

(Kalam et al., 2003) is a solution for this kind of access control policies. As the name suggests, OR-BAC uses contextual rules related to specific organizational structures. Other extensions of the RBAC model, like generalized RBAC (GRBAC) or dynamic role-based access control (DRBAC), also consider the use of context information to extend the standard RBAC model.

Table 1 provides a set of approaches for access control. Extended with contextual information, several architectures have been developed for context-aware access control.

Proximity-based access control defines a set of security rules based on the proximity of entities or groups (Gupta, 2006). Temporal-RBAC (Bertino, 2001) supports periodic role enabling and disabling and temporal dependencies among permissions by introducing time into the access control infrastructure. Encounter-based access control (Thomas, 2004) is used to define special policies related to the occurrence of defined situations or events. Covington et al (Covington, 2002) propose a uniform access control framework for environmental roles, named generalized RBAC (GRBAC), which is an extension of the role-based access control model. In an administrative domain, a role can be, for example, an employee or a manager. A role determines the user's position or ability in an administrative domain. An environmental role is a role that captures environmental conditions. Unlikely in the RBAC model which is only subject-oriented, GRBAC allows the definition of access control policies based on subject, object or environment. Dynamic Role Based Access Control (DRBAC) (Zhang, 2004) extends the traditional RBAC to use dynamic context information during the decision process. DRBAC addresses two key requirements: (1) A user's access privileges must change when the user's context changes. (2) A resource must adjust its access permissions when its system information changes. (Roman, 2002) defines generic context-based software architecture for physical spaces, so-called Gaia. A physical space is a geographic region with limited and well defined boundaries, containing physical objects, heterogeneous networked devices, and users performing a range of activities. Derived from the physical

Table 1. Access control families

Model name	Description	Example
Mandatory access control	*Subject* permissions on *target* are defined and enforced by the operating system itself	Biba (Biba, 1975),
Discretionary access control	Each *owner* of a *resource* defines the triple (*Subject*, *Object*, *Permission*). A matrix therefore maps *Object* to *Subject's permissions*.	BLP (Bell, 1973)
Role-based access control	A set of rules are defined as (*Subject*, *Resource*, *Action*), where a *Subject* can perform an *Action* on a *Resource*.	XACML (OASIS, 2007)
Task-based access control	A task is considered as a logical unit of work in an application and may consist of subtasks. At each task within a workflow process, the security model will evaluate and check dynamically the user authorization in order to perform this task.	TBAC (Thomas, 2004)
Context-aware access control	An extension of RBAC model which includes contextual information (e.g. *Subject's* GPS location), in addition to *Subject's* role.	OrBAC (El Kalam, 2003), GRBAC (Covington,2000), proximity-based access control (Gutpa, 2006), encounter-based access control (Thomas, 2004), DRBAC (Zhang, 2004)

space concept, the Active Space system provides the user a computing representation of physical space. Active Space helps the user to interact with the physical space. Cerberus is a framework for context-aware identification, authentication and access control and reasoning about context, based on Kerberos (Neuman, 1994) authentication and Gaia. Cerberus focuses on user's identification via user's context information such as fingerprint, voice and face recognition. The context-aware authorization architecture proposed in (Wullems, 2004) is based on the Kerberos authentication and enables to activate or deactivate roles assigned to a user depending on the context. In (Hu, 2004), the authors propose a dynamic, context-aware access control especially suited for distributed healthcare application. Permissions are associated with context-related constraints that are dynamically evaluated.

Challenges

Context-aware access control can be seen from two different perspectives:

- Adaptation of security policies based on the context: As defined in (Dey, 1999), context is any kind of information, which can be used to characterize the state of an entity. An entity might be any kind of asset of a system such as user, software, hardware, media storage or data. Context aware access control can be then seen as an extension of common access control, that takes context information into account to perform the decision.
- Secure acquisition of context: In order to be used, context information must be acquired in the system: this additional acquisition potentially opens up new threats and creates new challenges.

The first refers to the use of context information within the definition and enforcement of security policies. A system is considered as context-aware if it uses context information before or during service provisioning. The smart floor infrastructure is a good illustration of a context-aware system (Orr, 2000). The smart floor is a device equipped with force measuring sensors, so that it can detect users walking on it. The smart floor is connected to a backend application which maps users' identity to their walking pattern. The backend system in charge of users' authentication is the context-aware system; the context information is the pressure measured by the smart floor; and the latter acts as the context information provider.

In order to enforce context-aware security policies, context information have to be securely integrated in the system. Since clearly any forgery or modification of contextual information could compromise the enforcement of security policies.

Solutions

A context-aware authorization service must enforce authorization policies featuring rules based on contextual information. Raw contextual data, such as location or heart rate, is gathered from sensors and further processed in order to derive complex information such as proximity or health status. The authorization process thus relies on actual circumstances in addition to the common role-based access control model.

Figure 1 outlines an approach for context-aware access control presented in (Laube, 2007). This architecture has been designed and implemented in the scope of the MOSQUITO project (MOSQUITO, 2006). It provides a security framework for mobile applications based on web services.

All SOAP messages between the application (web service client) and the web service itself have to pass intermediaries, to enforce the configured security policies on message (SOAP) level. Intermediaries are a pipeline of message filters (proxy) which support WS-Security (OASIS, 2006).

Figure 1. Context-aware access control

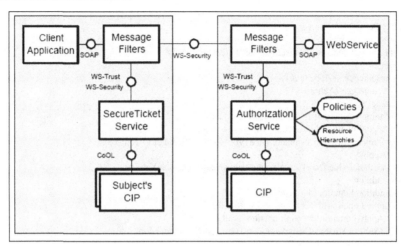

The client-side intermediary adds encryption, integrity checks and credentials. The server-side intermediary decrypts, verifies the integrity and checks the credentials validity. It offers the same interface as the web service plugged behind it and is therefore completely transparent. The Security Token Service (STS) (OASIS, 2005) on the client device generates signed context information retrieved from the client's Context Information Providers (CIP). The CIP is in charge of collecting contextual information, such as the patient pulse, which characterizes his health condition. The server-side authorization filter extracts the credentials from the incoming SOAP request. The filter verifies the signature. The credentials and the target are provided to the STS. The STS provides the credentials to the Authorization Service that is in charge of authorizing or denying access based on the credentials, the SOAP message and the defined authorization policies. The Policy Decision Point (PDP) then enforces the access control policy. If access is granted, the original request from the web service client is passed to the web service and processed there. Otherwise, an exception is sent to the client application. The response of the web service is as well passed through the security proxy with its message pipeline to take care of encryption/decryption and integrity.

The access control policies are defined in XACML that supports RBAC authorization policies as well as context-aware access control (see an example in Figure 2). The policy enforcement relies on verifying attribute values distributed in four categories, related to the subject, the resource, the action and the environment. To support evaluation of context information, the existing implementation was extended by defining new primitive attributes types that offer a higher level of abstraction for data representation.

The architecture to enforce context-aware access control policies for web service based application, is highly applicable to mobile and ubiquitous environments. Following the service oriented approach (SOA), based on the loose coupling of services provided by different parties, the enforcement of flexible access control policies is highly demanded. The approach proves how standard role-based access control can be made more flexible by using any kind of context information available in the system. Access control can now dynamically adapt to the current situation.

Figure 2. Authorization policy example

```
<Policy PolicyId="EmergencyPolicy">
 <Target>...</Target>
 <Rule RuleId="MixedLocalisationRule" Effect="Permit">
  <Target>
   <Resources>...</Resources>
    <Actions>...</Actions>
  </Target>
  <Condition FunctionId="function:string-equal">
   <Apply FunctionId="function:string-one-and-only">
    <SubjectAttributeDesignator DataType=string AttributeId="role"/>
   </Apply>
   <AttributeValue DataType="string">physician</AttributeValue>
  </Condition>
  <Condition FunctionId="function:and">
   <Apply FunctionId="coolFunction#CloseTo">
    <Apply FunctionId="coolFunction#findLocation">
     <SubjectAttributeDesignator DataType=cool#GPSLocation
          AttributeId="SubjectLocation"/>
    </Apply>
    <Apply FunctionId="coolFunction#findLocation">
     <SubjectAttributeDesignator DataType="cool#GPSLocation"
         AttributeId="ObjectLocation"/>
    </Apply>
    <AttributeValue DataType="integer">50</AttributeValue>
   </Apply>
   <Apply FunctionId="coolFunction#IsEmergency">
    <Apply FunctionId="coolFunction#findEmergency">
     <SubjectAttributeDesignator DataType="cool#Emergency"
AttributeId="ObjectEmergency"/>
    </Apply>
   </Apply>
  </Condition>
 </Rule>
</Policy>
```

In a SOA based system, web service operations are considered as resources for which permission is granted or denied. Web services, especially enterprise services which expose business objects to the outside world, can return complex results. In not all cases, like depicted in e-health scenario, it is desirable to grant access to the entire returned object. A solution is the use of resource hierarchies in combination with context-aware access control, like proposed in (Laube, 2007).

The granularity used during the access control should not only be defined by the (web) services but should also be more abstract and in relation to the service using application. Resource hierarchies allow the definition of the resource granularity outside of the service itself. The authorization policy can then contain access control rules for parts of the resources.

A resource hierarchy can be described as directed acyclic graph over a finite set of nodes, built from a resource and all its direct descendants at any depth. The definition of the node set in the hierarchy and the relations between the nodes are highly dependent on the application and the authorization policy.

An example is a business application that exposes a service to access an object Business-Partner. This object maintains the information of partners of the company, such as its personnel or external companies like customers or suppliers. Several concrete classes are derived from the abstract class BusinessPartner, see the class diagram in Figure 3. Each derivation adds specific attributes that are only relevant for this type of object. For example, an employee has a salary grade, a private bank account, a private and a business address. A customer has marketing data, a shipping address and an invoice address.

The use of the object BusinessPartner as interface for the application allows an identical manipulation of the different classes in the hierarchy. The following authorization rules shall, for instance, be applied to the retrieve method of the Employee object:

- Only a member of HR can access all data of an employee.
- An employee has access to the business address of all employees and to his own private address and bank account. He has no write access to his salary.

- A manager has access to the data of his/her employees, except for the sensible personal data, like private address or bank account.

RBAC roles would be powerful enough to differentiate between a HR accountant and a normal employee. However, RBAC gives either permission to a resource or denies it completely (all or nothing paradigm). In order to implement the authorization rules described above, it would be necessary to implement a much more detailed and fine-grained service interface. In this case, there are two possibilities: the first is to implement an interface specialized for each role, which creates a very high dependency to the authorization policy.

The second option is to have many smaller services that allow retrieving parts (sub resources) of the BusinessPartner, like the name or bank

Figure 3. BusinessPartner class diagram

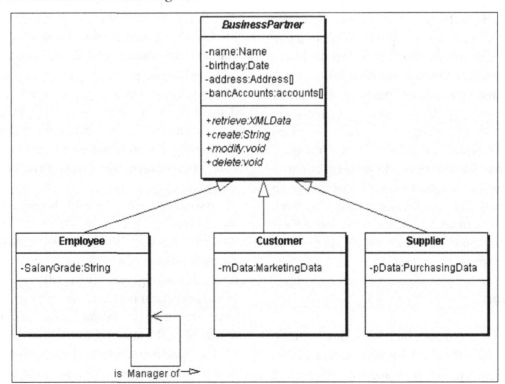

account. This would create a big impact on performance. Instead of having only one service call to get all data, multiple calls are necessary.

With the use of resource hierarchies, there is no change of the service interface according to the need of the authorization policy necessary. The originally defined interface (BusinessPartner in our previous example) can be used and, at the same time, it is possible to enforce access control with a finer granularity. On the other hand, the concept facilitates the integration of all kind of context information into the policy enforcement process and also in the process of defining the resource hierarchy. This result is highly fined grained, dynamically adaptable authorization policies needed for mobile applications in ubiquitous environments.

ACCESS CONTROL TO WIRELESS SENSOR DATA

Challenges

Under a standard access control scenario, entities that wish to benefit from the produced information, have to authenticate themselves, receive a credential, produce the credential to the data source and receive a specialized stream of information that contains just the information the requester received an authorization for. Many solutions exist for this problem however most of them are unsuitable for low-power ubiquitous environments such as wireless sensor networks, given the technological constraints of the nodes. Such devices with limited capacities on memory, CPU and battery power are rarely capable to evaluate complex access control policies.

Solution

Sensor nodes produce, on a broadcast medium, highly diverse data, which is often very sensitive. Sensor listeners may be numerous, diverse and

have different access rights to sensor data. The problem of multiple-resources/multiple-accesses is usually solved using access control. Under a standard access control scenario, entities that wish to benefit from the produced information, have to authenticate themselves, receive a credential, produce the credential to the data source and receive a specialized stream of information that contains just the information the requester received an authorization for. Many solutions exist for this problem; however most of them are unsuitable for WSN scenarios, given the technological constraints of the nodes. In addition, nodes produce data in real-time, hence the generation of multiple streams is difficult.

In (Sorniotti, 2008), the authors present a possible solution to the problem of access control to data produced by wireless sensor network, relying on cryptography: right from its production, data can be encrypted, and therefore its access is intrinsically restricted. This way, sensors can encrypt data and publish it regardless of the present consumer(s). In a centralized authorization module, the related access control policies are enforced. If a user or application provides sufficient credentials to get access to a certain authorization class, he gets the associated key to decrypt the data: the knowledge of the cryptographic key used to encrypt data, belonging to a given level in the defined hierarchy, allows proper decryption – and therefore access – to data belonging to that level. Conversely, it is impossible to access encrypted data for consumers who do not have the proper decryption key.

In scenarios such as the e-health one, the sensed data is often highly sensitive. Moreover, the sensed data often has very different levels of sensitivity: the mere information on the room occupancy of a hospital is not highly sensitive, whereas the ECG of a given patient is indeed very private information, since it could possibly reveal information about the health status of the person.

There can also be several consumers of wireless sensor data, belonging to a heterogeneous population, and having intrinsically different data access rights: within a healthcare scenario, patients, social workers, nurses, relatives, generic physicians and specialists naturally form a hierarchy of entities that are interested in the data delivered by a healthcare WSN. Data consumers can be therefore conveniently organized in hierarchies. Low levels in the hierarchy can just access data with low level of sensitivity whilst higher levels can also access more sensitive data.

To satisfy the hierarchical requirement, the idea is to map each distinct sensor data type to an authorization level. Data, whose disclosure does not rise high privacy issues, is mapped to low authorization levels. Similarly, highly private data will be mapped to high authorization levels. The resulting mapping expresses the security preferences of a central access control policy point. The hierarchy of authorization levels is then mapped to keys in a hierarchical structure, whereby low-level keys can be derived from high-level ones.

The hierarchy of authorization levels can be modeled as a tree. The adoption of encryption as a way to enforce access control reduces the problem of granting, denying and revoking access rights to a problem of key management. The scheme assumes the presence of a central access control manager (ACM) which – after evaluation of data consumers' (from now on also referred to as users) credentials – takes care of granting, denying and revoking access rights. Granting a user to a given authorization level means giving her the key to decrypt all data units mapped to that level and to descendant ones. Denying access simply implies not providing the decryption key(s). Finally, revocation of access rights is based on rekeying: changing the keys used at a given point, forces data consumers to re-contact the ACM in order to receive the new keys. Consumers whose access rights have been revoked do not receive the new keys, which accomplish the revocation. This approach achieves the desirable property of no specific interactions between data producers (the sensor nodes) and data consumers, other than data publishing.

State-of-the-Art

The seminal work of Akl and Taylor (Akl, 1983) first proposes a solution for data access control based on cryptography. Access controlled resources (data), users and cryptographic keys are mapped to a hierarchy of classes, represented by a directed acyclic graph. Data belonging to a given class is encrypted with the key associated to that class. The key generation scheme uses the homomorphic properties of modular exponentiation. It assures that a user, who is given the decrypting key of a class, can generate the keys of that class' descendants, and therefore access data mapped to descendant classes as well. On the contrary, the inverse – generating the key of a parent class – is unfeasible. However, the expensive operations used in the scheme (modular exponentiation) make this scheme unsuitable for a WSN environment.

In (Chien, 2004), Chien proposes a much lighter key generation scheme, based on one way hash functions instead of modular exponentiation. In addition, the author places a time bound on keys, introducing time periods: during each time period, a new key for each class of data is derived. However, this scheme suffers from a few drawbacks: first of all it requires tamper resistant devices, in order to store secret material used to derive keys. Second, similarly to Akl's scheme, it is impossible to revoke a user's access right to a lower class in the hierarchy. Finally, in (Yi, 2005), Yi showed an attack where, despite the tamper resistance requirement, a coalition of three user can access some secret class keys that they should not know according to Chien's scheme.

In (Tzeng, 2002), Tzeng proposes a time-bounded key assignment scheme for hierarchies. The computation of the keys however, involves particularly expensive Lucas function computation. This scheme is not suitable for resource-constrained WSN nodes due to the high cost operations required for the computation of keys.

In (Shehab, 2005), Shehab et al. propose a mechanism to generate and distribute hierarchical keys. Although efficient and very well suited for WSN, this scheme has no time bound on keys, and therefore it is not ready to represent a fully flourished access control solution.

In (Atallah, 2007), Atallah and colleagues propose a general and efficient scheme to incorporate time bounds in existing management scheme. In addition, they show how to create a full-fledged hierarchical access control scheme with time capabilities. The scheme is elegant and efficient, relies just on one way hash functions, but – seen from a WSN viewpoint – requires a too elevated amount of public information in order to allow for efficient key derivation.

USER AUTHENTICATION

Access control mechanisms require the access requester to authenticate himself. After establishing a more flexible access control framework better responding to the challenges of mobile and ubiquitous environments, additional flexibility is needed also for the authentication phase of the access control model. Users of a ubiquitous computing system should be able to authenticate themselves with the means at their disposal. For instance a physician should be able to authenticate with a login-password mechanism, with a certificate stored on his private smart card or PDA, with biometric information like fingerprints, or with a combination of two mechanisms.

Challenges

In order to gain access to a resource protected by an authorization service, users are required to authenticate. User authentication is traditionally performed by producing a combination of authentication factors (e.g. two-factor authentication) statically specified in the access control policy of the authorization service. An authentication factor is any piece of information used to assess the identity of a user. Depending on the context, the user may have access to different authentication services. The flexibility of user's authentication can be enhanced by allowing users to authenticate using different authentication factors at his disposal. In order to achieve that, the authorization service specifies an authentication level to be reached in order to get access to a resource. Resource owner's authentication preferences are thus comprised in an authentication level policy. The user is bound to reach a pre-defined authentication level with the factor he owns. The problem is to weigh the different factors, assigning a metric to each of them.

State-of-the-Art

In the literature, several researchers have already proposed models for authentication factor metric. In (Reither, 1999), the authors propose a set of principles for designing a metric for authentication factors. Nevertheless, they only focus on issuers of authentication factors and not on supported authentication mechanisms. In (Burr, 2006), an assurance level on authentication factors is defined in an arbitrary manner. It consists basically of a categorization of authentication mechanisms. Moreover, the authors do not propose any solution for combining authentication factors in order to achieve a better authentication level. (Al-Muhtadi, 2005) is closer to the authentication-level approach by introducing the notion of confidence values for authentication mechanisms. The authors use the Gaia authentication framework, which calculates the net confidence value of available Gaia authentication modules. It implies that the user has to authenticate by means of all available authentication mechanisms. Moreover the authors do not consider the use of heuristics for combining authentication mechanisms. In addition, the confidence in the service implementing the authentication mechanisms is not considered as criteria on authentication mechanisms. To combine confidence values, the authors finally suggest using the consensus operator from subjective logic. In (M. Covington, 2004), the authors still propose to abstract authentication factors to subjective logic opinions. In order to calculate the confidence in a combination of authentication factors, the author also uses the consensus operator from subjective logic. Liberty Alliance (Liberty Alliance, 2005) introduces the notion of identity provider which is in charge of federating user identities. When users want to consume a service, they authenticate to their identity provider by means of an authentication context encapsulated in SAML assertions where the circumstance of the authentication (e.g. mechanism used, service) are described. With this additional information, the service provider can evaluate its trust during user's authentication. Moreover, the identity provider can still combine different authentication context. Nevertheless, the service provider still imposes the user to authenticate by using statistically defined authentication factors.

Solution

In (Gomez, 2007), the following authentication process (see Figure 4) is introduced:

- A user wants to gain access to a resource protected by an authorization service. The authorization service responds to the user with an obligation stating an authentication level to be reached.

- The user attempts to reach the expected authentication level by combining authentication factors, using available authentication services at his disposal.

- Then, the user forwards the chosen combination of authentication factors to the authorization service, which then checks if they meet the required authentication level.

In order to simplify user's authentication, three objectives are defined:

- The authentication level specification is done by resource owners.
- The authentication level specified is met by legitimate users.
- The enforcement of access control can be done based on a specified authentication level, reached by combining different authentication factors.

The approach defines a metric for authentication levels based on subjective logic. The definition of confidence values for authentication mechanism on a fined grained level enables to distinguish between, for example, a password of length of 4 characters and another of length of 10 characters.

Figure 4. User Authentication Flexibility

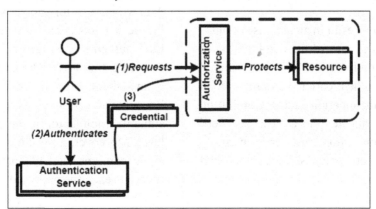

Figure 5. Evolution of combine operator

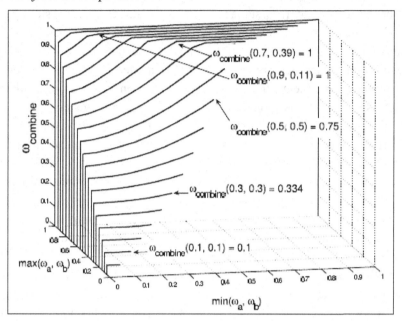

The confidence values assigned to authentication factors and their combinations allow going beyond the models described in the literature (Schneier, 2005). The approach capitalizes on subjective logic in order to define a trust metric for authentication level. A new operator on subjective logic for mitigating opinions on combination of authentication factors was defined. Figure 5 depicts the evolution of opinion combination. This combination of two opinions, ω_a and ω_b fulfills the two following requirements:

- It must always result in an increase of opinion: it tends to reward the combination of authentication factors, which is considered as stronger authentication factor rather than a single authentication factor. Combining an X509 certificate, plus a basic password authentication, is more trustworthy than only X509 certificate, or a password authentication.

- It must be proportional to the $| \omega_a - \omega_b |$ and to the $\max(\omega_a, \omega_b)$: it tends to reward the combination of strong opinions on authentication factors rather than weak opinions. The goal is to avoid the combination of multiple weak authentication factors in order to reach a high level of confidence.

Numerous operators are already available in the subjective logic framework. Nevertheless none of them fulfills those two requirements. A new operator for subjective logic, $\omega_{combine}$ (see Figure 5), has been defined in (Gomez, 2007). Each authentication factor is associated with an authentication level. The latter is an abstraction of an authentication factor to a confidence value. Resource owners may specify their preferences in authentication factor by means of authentication level. Moreover, a resource requester should be able to combine available authentication factors in order to reach the expected authentication level.

FUTURE TRENDS

In ubiquitous environments, compromised context providers (e.g. a malicious sensor node within a wireless sensor network) represent a big threat for the context-aware security approaches previously discussed. The challenge arises from the fact that sensor nodes often need to be low-cost to justify their deployment, which makes it very hard to satisfy tamper-resistance requirements. An attacker could take control of a sensor node in a fraudulent way in order to maliciously craft data or to alter the data processing. Once a node is compromised, the key material contained within is completely exposed and usable by the attacker. In order to cope with such threats, a few trust frameworks have been proposed in the literature to detect bogus sensor data. This implies a trust evaluation of sensor data at acquisition and aggregation time: trust refers to the reliability and accuracy of sensed information and it is related to the quality of the delivered sensor data. Computing the distance between the delivered context information and the real context and evaluating the trustworthiness of delivered context information may be approached in several ways: (i) context provider failure detection, (ii) reputation systems, or (iii) trust based framework. (i) refers to the failure detection (e.g. crash, omission, timing, value and arbitrary (Tanenbaum, 2001) of context providers such as sensor nodes. (ii) aims at determining the reputation of context providers (Ganeriwal, 2004). Reputation is defined as the perception that an entity has of another's intentions, based on past experiences with a given entity. At the contrary, (iii) enables trust to encompass objective and subjective characteristic of an entity. The goal of (iii) the trust based framework proposed in (Zhang, 2006) for wireless sensor networks is to establish trust in all sensor nodes based on the expectation that they will deliver non-compromised data.

From the access control to sensor data viewpoint, the increasing interest in the subject of lightweight access control schemes for WSNs is showing how the problem is important for the both academic and enterprise environment. (Atallah, 2007) represents the state-of-the-art approach to hierarchical data access control with time capabilities. It is foreseeable in the near future that new schemes will improve the latter to make it suitable in resource constrained environments such as WSN's.

CONCLUSION

Access control in ubiquitous and mobile environments is a challenging task. The use of the context information related to the communicating partners or the technical infrastructure used as communication channels offers new possibilities towards adaptable security mechanisms. A first step is the use of (static) context information in the access control policies to define fine-grained rules to access the available resources. Context information can extend the wide spread RBAC and make it more flexible. The dynamic enforcement of context-aware access control policies is the next step towards adaptive security. During the enforcement process, context information is retrieved and processed. Raw data obtained from physical or logical sensors is aggregated to high-level context information. Thereby, many questions related to trust and dependability of context information are still subject of research.

The use of context information in the access control policies and the dynamic enforcement facilitate the definition of a flexible access control that can adapt automatically to the current situation. Context-aware access control is often combined with the concept of separation of security and application logic. Based on the SOA principle and implemented with web services, access control policies are defined and enforced in a security framework instead in the (web) service exposing resources. This increases the reusability of the services and avoids the complexity of security and application logic during development and implementation.

Based on the concept of separation of security, the use of resource filters to define the granularity of resources also outside the implementing service is another step towards more flexible and adaptable security mechanisms.

Access control is only one part of the chain of security means needed to protect resources. Access to resources is in general only granted to authenticated users. Authentication in ubiquitous and mobile environment has to fulfill the same requirements regarding flexibility and adaptability as the access control. In mobile applications, users use different technical devices and communication infrastructures. The combination of authentication factors assigned to the different means, which a user has at his disposal, requires a metric of authentication level. The approach based on subjective logic is a very promising as it combines not only the authentication factors but also the authentication services and allows a fined grained characterization of authentication factors and means. In addition, subjective logic allows the distinction between subjective aspect (e.g. reputation of the authentication service) from concrete aspects (e.g. type of authentication mechanism, quality of service). The subjective aspects are based on the past experience with a given authentication mechanism, while the concrete aspects are derived from measurable elements which characterize an authentication mean. Additionally, combination of authentication means benefits from subjective logic operators for combining opinions on them. Beside, the subjective logic framework provides a set of logical operators for the combination opinions, and allows the definition of new operators.

Especially in ubiquitous environments, where all kind of devices can produce context information, it is often difficult to enforce access control. On resource-restricted or ubiquitous devices, the use of standard access control mechanism like RBAC or the use of context-aware access control is often not possible. An approach for access control based on lightweight cryptography can easily be extended for ubiquitous devices. The sensors or devices produce encrypted context information and only authenticated users with a sufficient authorization level are able to obtain the key to decrypt the data. The calculation of the authorization level is in a simple case based on user's credential but can also include the evaluation of any kind of context information.

The use of context information for authentication and access control in ubiquitous and mobile environments is a way to reach a higher level of flexibility and adaptability of the systems' security. But the process of obtaining trusted and reliable context information introduces new challenges which have to be addressed in the near future.

REFERENCES

Akl, S. G., & Taylor, P. D. (1983). Cryptographic solution to a problem of access control in a hierarchy. *ACM Transaction Computing Systems.*, *1*(3),239–248.

Al-Muhtadi, J. (2005). *An Intelligent Authentication Infrastructure for Ubiquitous Computing Environments.*

Atallah, M. J., Blanton, M., & Frikken, K. B. (2007). Incorporating temporal capabilities in existing key management schemes. *Cryptology ePrint Archive, Report.*

Bell, D., & La Padula, L. (1973). Secure Computer Systems: Mathematical Foundations. *Technical Report MTR 254, 1.* MITRE Corporation.

Bertino, E., Bonatti, P. A., Ferrari, E. (2001). TRBAC: A Temporal Role-Based Access Control Model. *ACM Transactions on Information and System Security, 4*(3), 191-223.

Biba, K. (1975). Integrity Considerations for Secure Computer Systems. *Technical Report MTR-3153*, Mitre Corporation.

Burr, W. E., Dodson, D. F., Polk, W. T. (2006). Electronic authentication guideline. *NIST Special Publication 800 63*. National Institue of Standards and Technology.

Chien, M.-H.-Y. (2004). Efficient time-bound hierarchical key assignment scheme. *IEEE Transactions on Knowledge and Data Engineering*, *16*(10), 1301–1304.

Chris, W., Looi, M., & Clark, A. (2004). Toward context-aware security: an authorization architecture for intranet environments. *Second IEEE Annual COnference on Pervasive Computing and Communication Workshops (PERCOMM'04)*

Covington, M. J., Moyer, M. J., & Ahamad, M. (2000). Generalized role-based access control for securing future applications. *23rd National Information Systems Security Conference*.

Covington, M. J., Fogla, P., & Ahamad, M. (2002). A context-aware security architecture for emerging applications. *Annual Computer Security Applications Conference (ACSAC)*.

Dey, A. K., Abowd, G. D., & Saber, D. (1999). Context-Based Infrastructure for Smart Environments. *1st International Workshop on Managing Interactions in Smart Environments (MANSE '99)* (pp. 114-128).

Dey, A. K. (2001). Understanding and using context. *Personal and Ubiquitous Computing Journal*, *5*(1), 4–7.

El Kalam, A. A., Benferhat, S., Miege, A., El Baida, R., Cuppens, C., Saurel, C., Balbiani, P., Deswarte, Y., & Trouessin, G. (2003). Organization based access control. *IEEE International Workshop on Policies for Distributed Systems and Networks*. IEEE Computer Society.

Ganeriwal, S., & Srivastava, M. B. (2004). Reputation-based framework for high integrity sensor networks. *ACM Workshop on Security of Ad Hoc and Sensor Networks* (pp. 66–77).

Gomez, L., & Thomas, I. (2007). Towards User Authentication Flexibility. *IEEE and ACM International Conference of Security and Cryptography*.

Gupta, S. K. S., Mukherjee, T., Venkatasubramanian, K., & Taylor, T. B. (2006). Proximity Based Access Control in Smart-Emergency Departments. *4th annual IEEE international conference on Pervasive Computing and Communications Workshops*. (p. 512).

Hu, J., & Weaver, A. C. (2004). Dynamic, Context-Aware Access Control for Distributed Healthcare Applications. *Pervasive Security, Privacy and Trust (PSPT2004)*.

Kim, Y.-G., Mon, C.-J., Jeong, D., Lee, J.-O., Song, C.-Y., & Baik, D.-K. (2005). Context-Aware Access Control Mechanism for Ubiquitous Applications. *Advances in Web Intelligence, Lecture Notes in Computer Science, Springer 2005*, (p. 236-242).

Laube, A., & Gomez, L. (2007). Dynamic context-aware access control. *IEEE and ACM International Conference of Security and Cryptography*.

MOSQUITO. (2006). IST 004636 MOSQUITO Project, from http://www.mosquito-online.org.

Moyer, M., Covington, M., & Ahamad, M. (2000). Generalized role-based access control for securing future applications. *23rd National Infromation Systems Security Conference*.

Neuman, B. C., & Ts'o, T. (1994). Kerberos: An authentication service for computer networks. *IEEE Communication Magazine*.

OASIS. (2007). *eXtended Access Control Markup Language* (XACML) 2.0.

OASIS. (2005). *Web Service Trust Language (WS-Trust) 1.3.*

OASIS. (2006). *Web Service Security: SOAP Message Security 1.1* (WS-Security 2004).

Orr, R. J., & Abowd, G. D. (2000). The Smart Floor: A Mechanism for Natural User Identification and Tracking. *Conference on Human Factors in Computing Systems (CHI 2000).*

Reither, M. K., & Stubblebine, S. G. (n.d). Authentication metric analysis and design. *ACM Transactions on Information and System Security.* ACM Press.

Roman, M., Hess, C., Cerqueira, R., Ranganathan, A., Campbell, R., & Nahrstedt, K. (2002). Gaia: A middleware infrastructure to enable active spaces. *IEEE Pervasive Computing, 1*(4), 74-83.

Samarati, P., & Vimercati, S. (2001). Access Control: Policies, Models and Mechanisms. *Foundations of Security Analysis and Design,* (pp. 137–196).

Sandhu, R., Coyne, E., Feinstein, H., & Youman, C. (1996). Role-based access control models. *IEEE Computer, 2,* 38-47.

Schneier, B. (2005). Two-Factor Authentication: Too Little, Too Late. *Communication of the ACM, 48*(4).

Shehab, M., Bertino, E., & Ghafoor, A. (2005). Efficient hierarchical key generation and key diffusion for sensor networks. *Second Annual IEEE Communications Society Conference on Sensor and AdHoc Communications and Networks*

Sorniotti, A., Molva, R., & Gomez, L. (2008). Efficient access control for wireless sensor data.

IEEE International Symposium on Personal, Indoor and Mobile Radio Communications. 15-18 September, 2008, Cannes, France.

Stajano, F. (2002). *Security for Ubiquitous Computing.* John Wiley and Sons.

Tanenbaum, A. S., & Steen, M. V. (2001). Distributed Systems: Principles and Paradigms. *Prentice Hall PTR.*

Thomas, R. K., & Sandhu, R. (2004). Proximity based access control in smart-emergency departments. *Pervasive Computing and Communications Workshops, 5.*

Tzeng, W. G. (2002). A time-bound cryptographic key assignment scheme for access control in a hierarchy. *IEEE Transactions on Knowledge and Data Engineering, 14*(1), 182–188.

Wullems, C., Looi, M., & Clark, A. (2004). Toward context-aware security: An authorization architecture for intranet environments. *Pervasive Communication and Communication Workshops.*

Yi, X. (2005). Security of chien's efficient time-bound hierarchical key assignment scheme. *IEEE Transactions on Knowledge and Data Engineering, 17*(9), 1298–1299.

Zhang, G., Parashar, M. (2004). Context-aware Dynamic Access Control for Pervasive Applications. *Proceedings of the Communication Networks and Distributed Systems.*

Zhang, W., Das, S., & Liu, Y. (2006). A trust based framework for secure data aggregation on wireless sensor networks. *IEEE Communications Society Conference on Sensor, Mesh and Ad Hoc Communications and Networks.*

Chapter XIII
Privacy Automation in Context–Aware Services

Amr Ali Eldin
Accenture, The Netherlands

Semir Daskapan
Delft University of Technology, The Netherlands

Jan van den Berg
Delft University of Technology, The Netherlands

ABSTRACT

With the growing interest in context-aware services, attention has been given to privacy and trust issues. Context-aware privacy architectures are usually proposed and developed without taking into account the trustworthiness of a service provider. Therefore, this chapter deals with two challenges in context-aware services. The first one is to improve privacy architectures with a trust functionality and the second one is to integrate this refined privacy architecture in larger service-oriented architectures (SOAs).

INTRODUCTION AND BACKGROUND

With the rapid developments of mobile telecommunications technology over the last two decades, a new computing paradigm known as anywhere and anytime or *ubiquitous* computing has evolved. Consequently, attention has been given not only to extending current (mobile) web services models, but increasingly also to make these services context-aware. Despite the expected benefits behind this new technology and the need for developing more and more context-aware applications, we enunciate that privacy and trust represent challenges for the success and widespread adoption of these services (Amr Ali Eldin & Stojanovic, 2007).

Privacy has always been of the utmost importance to people since Warren and Brandeis (1890) who wrote *"The Right to Privacy"* in response to an article that contained personal information about the Warren family. There has been an intensive concern about privacy threats and ways of protecting user privacy in the literature. Privacy threats arise from the linkage between users' identity and their private information. Simply, it can be seen that breaking this link helps protecting users' privacy. This can be achieved by either protecting user identity as in most anonymity and pseudonymity solutions (Beresford & Stajano, 2003; Chaum, 1985; Lysyanskayal, Rivest, Sahai, & Wolf, 1999; Wang, 2004) or by controlling private information collection. Most literature focused on the assumption that *unknown* service providers are simply non-trustworthy and the traditional approach to privacy was always to block all un-authorized requests to private information using access control mechanisms and anonymity solutions (Clifton , Kantarcioglu, Vaidya, Lin, & Zhu, 2002; Linn, 2005; Park & Sandhu, 2002 ; Sandhu, Coyne, Feinstein, & Youman, 1996 ; Tolone, Ahn, Pai, & Hong, 2005). Therefore, cryptographic solutions such as public key and symmetric key encryption mechanisms were always positioned as means of privacy protection. For example, a watermarking algorithm is proposed in (Agrawal & Kiernan, 2002) to encrypt database records by a user's private keys. To make these records usable by others, a user's private key has to be communicated so again an assumption has to be made on trustworthiness. Further, real identities can be leaked still when engaged in an online transaction by traffic analyzers (Christian Hauser, 2002; Christian Hauser & Kabatnik, 2001; Linn, 2005).

In analogous to the previous efforts, we cannot guarantee an ultimate privacy. In daily life interactions we need to make assumptions of a service provider (SP) trustworthiness to some degree. Based on this trustworthiness degree, an SP might be given a certain type of access

to sensitive information. This is called the authorization or informed consent decision. The tolerance of non-trustworthy service providers seems, however, to be non-realistic in daily life interactions with increasing mobile services (Daskapan, Vree, & Ali Eldin, 2003). Given the fact that many proposed privacy architectures are developed without the clearance of this trust issue, the purpose of this chapter is to propose an integrated solution to privacy that automates trustworthiness assessment as well.

The chapter is organized as follows. In the next section we elaborate in details on the research problem and related work. Then, we introduce the extended *ShEM* architecture concepts and components where we extend its architecture to introduce a trust valuation mechanism and its high level architecture showing how it is integrated in *ShEM* overall architecture. Then we develop the high level design of the overall architecture and apply it in a case using the service-oriented architecture (SOA) approach. Finally, we conclude the chapter highlighting potential future work.

PROBLEM DESCRIPTION AND RELATED WORK

In this section, we discuss the motivation behind this work and the type of research problem we are addressing. The research problem investigated in this work can be seen as a multidisciplinary problem where legal, social and technical domains are concerned with providing solutions. In this work, we focus on the technological perspective taking into consideration requirements set by the other domains.

There is a trade-off between users' privacy needs and their motivation behind giving private information away. Complete privacy is impossible in a society where a user would have to interact with other members of the society such as colleagues, friends, or family members. Each flow of user information would reveal some private information about him/her at least to the other destination. Since this flow of information is needed and maybe initiated by the user himself, a user would have to make sure that the other party (the destination) is going to keep his/her privacy requirements. Privacy policies and legal contracts help users and service providers to reach an agreement on the type of privacy users would have. However, these contracts do not provide enough flexibility for users on choosing the type of privacy they need. It also does not guarantee that their privacy will not be violated but it guarantees that the user would have the rights to sew them if these agreed upon contracts were violated.

Informed consent is considered one of the requirements of the European directives (European-Directive, 2002). Accordingly, an SP should ask for a user's informed consent before any information collection and a user will in turn have to make a decision on that consent. From a usability point of view, it will be difficult to let each user enter his or her response each time his or her location is collected for instance. Increasingly, the type of requested data will highly influence his or her privacy concerns. The problem becomes even more complex when more than one SP gets involved in collecting user information, for example third parties. Third parties of a certain SP represent unknown parties to the user. Despite that the first party (SP) might list in his privacy policy that user information is being given to those third parties in one way or another, it is not possible yet in the literature to provide a means for the user to know which party collects which information (Christian Hauser & Kabatnik, 2001). Further, the issue that this party is trustworthy - whether he will keep his promises - adds more challenges to the consent decision-making process and thus new approaches are needed to help overcome these challenges and facilitate users with means to make the right consent decisions. Trustworthiness of SPs plays a major role in users' willingness to give up or to continue the SP's service (A. Ali Eldin, van den Berg, & Wagenaar, 2004). Trustworthiness of an

SP can be influenced by a number of factors such as quality of the service offered to the users, user need of the service, and user expectations of the SP with regard to their information collection. Besides, the user's former experience with an SP will also impact the user's trust in that SP. Trust analysis and measurement have been of major interest in the literature (Currall & Judge, 1995; Gambetta, 1988). However, users' cognition of trust is still not efficiently mapped onto physical measurements. Before we are able to make consent decisions, we need to make a decision on trustworthiness of SPs. As a consequence, we need to define at the first place trust and trustworthiness and argue for an appropriate trust model that we will adopt in this chapter.

Privacy-enhancing technologies (PET) are assumed to help reducing privacy threats. Privacy threats emerge as a result of the linkage between identities and users contextual data. Therefore, most literature has focused on the separation between both types of information: whether to control users´ identities, by deterring identity capturing through anonymity solutions (Camenisch & Herreweghen, 2002; Chaum, 1985; Lysyanskayal et al., 1999), or to control private information perception such as water marking techniques as in (Agrawal & Kiernan, 2002), distributing and encrypting of data packets in Clifton et al.(2002) and physical security through limiting data access within a specified area (Langheinrich, 2001). Most of the previous efforts lack the involvement of users. Stated differently, user control of their privacy has not been taken seriously as a requirement for the design of context-aware services in previous efforts. Instead, a lot of efforts have been concentrated on developing sophisticated encryption mechanisms that prohibit unauthorized access to private information when stored locally on a database server managed by the information collector or by a trusted third party. We argue that not only user identity information but also other information with different degrees of confidentiality can represent a private matter as well especially when user context is associated with them. Therefore, controlling user contextual information collection could represent a more realistic approach in such context-aware systems. Controlling users' contextual information perception implies taking decisions of whether to allow contextual entities to be collected by a certain party or not in what is known as user consent decisions.

The Platform for Privacy Preferences (P3P), developed by the World Wide Web Consortium (W3C), has made a significant effort on providing an approach that maps legal requirements onto machine readable policies (L. Cranor, Langheinrich, & Marchiori, 2002) and gives users more awareness of their data collection through defining what is known as a privacy policy and a privacy preference. In their model, a privacy policy consists of a number of specifications written in *XML* tags, which web sites publish at a known location (L. Cranor et al., 2002; L. F. Cranor, Guduru, & Arjula, 2006). A privacy preference describes users' allowed data practices-what they allow the service providers to do with their information. Privacy preferences description and evaluation is done by APPEL, a machine-readable specification of privacy preferences (L. Cranor et al., 2002).

In (A. Ali Eldin & Wagenaar, 2004a, 2004b, 2007), *ShEM, Sharing Evaluation Model*, a privacy control architecture is proposed as an extension of P3P specifications to context-aware environments. ShEM provides users with manual and automatic ways of dynamically controlling their informed consent decisions. The authors assume the existence of a number of factors that together influence users consent decisions. Among these factors, trustworthiness is assumed to be assessed manually by users. They modelled the influence of these factors which they call *privacy attributes* using a Mamdani fuzzy inference system (A. Ali Eldin et al., 2004). In their work they made manual assessment of trust by users. However, this might not guarantee a good consent decision all the time because of users' limited knowledge.

Further, user experience if combined with other factors such as service provider reputation can help better assess the SP's trustworthiness and hence a better consent decision can be made. In the following section, we propose an extended ShEM architecture by providing a trust valuation method that assesses SPs' trustworthiness.

THE EXTENDED SHARING EVALUATOR MODEL (SHEM)

The *sharing evaluator model* (*ShEM*), proposed by (A. Ali Eldin & Wagenaar, 2007) provides users with ways to make informed consent decisions complying with the requirements of privacy support in context-aware systems (Ackerman, Darrell, & Weitzner, 2001; Amr Ali Eldin & Stojanovic, 2007; Langheinrich, 2001; Nilsson et al., 2001). In their work, trust valuation of the individual SPs was assumed to be done manually by users. However, in reality this assumption will burden users with a lot of complexity. In this section, we introduce the extended *ShEM* architecture concepts and features where we introduce a trust valuation method and integrate it with the ShEM consent decision procedure.

The *ShEM* approach adopts letting users have control capabilities of their contextual information and recommend users automatic consent decisions based on a fuzzy logic engine, taking into consideration a number of influencing factors, which are called *privacy attributes* (A. Ali Eldin et al., 2004). The values of these attributes and their effect on the estimated permission cannot be crisply measured and differ from one user to another (A. Ali Eldin & Wagenaar, 2004a). Therefore, Ali Eldin et al (2004) make the assumption that these attributes can be represented by fuzzy sets. The *ShEM* model architecture is shown in Figure 1 .

The *sharing evaluator model* (ShEM) provides the user final consent decision on a three-step process (A. Ali Eldin & Wagenaar, 2004b):

Figure 1. The extended ShEM architecture

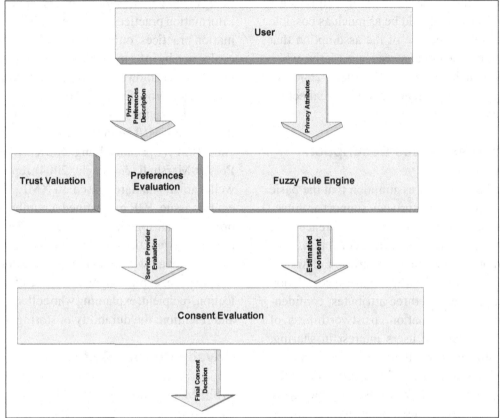

Firstly, user privacy preferences are described in a machine readable way based on an extension of the platform of privacy preferences (P3P) specifications in a dynamic privacy preferences model. They adopted three data practices from P3P. These are: purpose of data collection, recipients of the data and retention of the collected data. In *ShEM*, a user context is defined as the situation the user finds himself in. Each privacy level is linked to a certain situation on the one hand and to a set of the above mentioned P3P data practices on the other hand. When the situation changes, the P3P set of preferences are loaded automatically to meet the new privacy level. Service providers' ways of dealing with collected data from users, also known as asked information practices, are usually stored in a privacy policy. These practices are compared to users' P3P preferences and the comparison output is fed to the consent evaluation stage (see Figure 1).

In parallel, privacy-influencing factors consist of the privacy attributes, which are represented by information confidentiality, user interest in sharing, and the trustworthiness of the SP. These attributes are evaluated in the fuzzy system which develops an estimated consent permission based on a Mamdani fuzzy inference engine (A. Ali Eldin et al., 2004). In this stage of the evaluation, trustworthiness of a service provider is assumed to highly influence users' willingness to share their information and is manually fed by users. Finally, a consent decision is made based on the outputs of the above-mentioned two stages. The evaluation rules are based on the assumption that consent decisions should be as much as possible carefully given because of the assumption that people tend to be rather more conservative when it comes to their privacy (A. Ali Eldin, 2006). In the following, we present the ShEM architecture processes in details.

Privacy Preferences Description

ShEM is based on the assumption that the basic control element of any privacy support architecture consists of users' predefined preferences that govern the process of their data collection. The depicted preferences in *ShEM* are as follows:

ShEM assumes that there exists a correlation between privacy and three attributes; confidentiality of the information, trustworthiness of service provider and users interest in sharing. Privacy attributes are attributes that evaluate users' willingness to share their information with service providers. They are used by the fuzzy rule engine to develop autonomously an estimated permission decision.

The following properties are associated with each of them:

* Value: this is the value of each attribute.
* Mode: mode represents how these values are updated. There are three modes of updating:
  ○ Self: where the user chooses to self update his/her preferences.
  ○ Group: where the user chooses to update his/her preferences based on other users experiences or voting.
  ○ System: where the *ShEM* updates users' preferences autonomously based on default preferences.

Information Practices

Information practices, as a part of users' privacy preferences model, control the way the service provider should deal with users' information after being received. The service provider publishes its information practices, which we call asked information practices, online so that it is available for evaluation by information owners. A user defines his/her own allowed practices. However, both the service providers and the information owners should use the same semantics in describing these practices. The platform of privacy preferences (P3P) (L. Cranor, Langheinrich, Marchiori, Presler-Marshall, & Reagle, 2004) represents a well-known standard, based on XML, that covers this issue. P3P has defined a number of data practices that together constitute a P3P privacy policy. Data practices describe the ways users' data would be dealt with. Examples of such practices are purpose: explaining the purpose of data collection, recipient: explaining who collects the data and retention: the durability of storing data.

Privacy Control Modes

In ShEM, users are able to switch among a combination of three control modes regarding evaluating access to their private information. The ShEM then takes those modes into consideration in the consent evaluation part:

Manual mode: In this mode, the user is capable of manually controlling his/her information submission to service providers. S/he decides completely whether to give information to a service provider or not. The ShEM directly gets a response from the user without passing through the evaluation process. Users' interactions are also stored in their profile so that the system learns from the users' preferences and makes use of it later in future requests.

Automatic mode: In this mode, the user is only capable of controlling his/her data through valuating the privacy attributes that govern the autonomous decision making process. S/he defines also allowed information practices. Evaluation of service provider requests is then performed autonomously by the *ShEM* and based on the results; the system recommends a decision without the need for users' interaction. However, there might be a case where *ShEM* cannot sharply define a decision. In this case, the system would switch to the manual mode and get user response manually.

Preferences Evaluation

In this step, users' preferences on how their collected information should be used are compared to service providers' privacy policies. ShEM adopts the platform of privacy preferences (P3P) specifications in modeling both information types. In (L. Cranor et al., 2002), a P3P preference exchange language (APPEL) was proposed as the language for expressing users' preferences. APPEL is a machine-readable specification of user's preferences that can be programmatically compared against a privacy policy. A P3P privacy policy is a step towards automating and simplifying user assessments of an service provider through the use of user agents and APPEL. When a service provider issues a request for user data, users' preferences would be automatically compared against users privacy preferences expressed as a set of APPEL rules. Depending on rules evaluation, three types of consent would be issued: *request*, *limited* and *block*. *Request* results in all asked user data to be transmitted. When *limited*, only identity information is being blocked while a *block* consent blocks all information from being transmitted.

The Fuzzy Rule Engine

The use of fuzzy logic helps in supporting reasoning under uncertainty (Dubois & Prade, 1995). Since fuzzy inference systems are linguistically interpretable, they provide a useful way of combining collected data with expert knowledge. The notation of fuzzy sets was used in ShEM to help better understand the effect of privacy attributes on consent decisions. For example, information confidentiality and interest in sharing highly depend on the user perception and could vary from one user to another. However, trustworthiness of the service provider represents a different type of factors, which could be highly affected by other users' experiences or by the service provider reputation (Daskapan et al., 2003).

The concept of fuzzy logic was first introduced by Zadeh (1973). Fuzzy logic employs fuzzy sets to deal with imprecise and incomplete phenomena (Bojadziev & Bojadziev, 1997). A fuzzy set is defined by a so-called membership function. A fuzzy set is a set without a crisp boundary, which qualifies it to represent human brain concepts and cognitive process (Konar, 2000). The fuzzy rule engine (see Figure 2) implements a mapping $X \rightarrow S$ where, for every context element, an L-dimensional input vector $x = (x_1, x_2, \ldots, x_L)$ of privacy attribute values is mapped into a calculated consent value S. The fuzzy logic engine uses a Mamdani type (Mamdani, 1976) of fuzzy system architecture, so its kernel consists of a Mamdani reasoning engine together with a fuzzy rule base.

Consent Evaluation

Consent evaluation can be summarized as follows:

- The evaluator checks first whether automatic control mode is set.

Figure 2. ShEM fuzzy logic engine

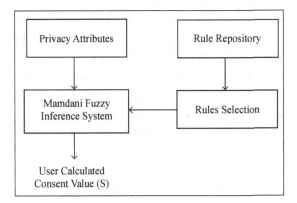

- If the automatic control mode is set to false, then the consent decision will be made by manual interference of the user.
- If the automatic control mode is set to true, then the consent decision process will go through the preference evaluation and the fuzzy logic engine steps.
- Then both values are aggregated into one final consent decision.

Trust Valuation as an Extension to ShEM

According to the ISO/IEC 10181-1, trust is a relationship between two elements, a set of operations, and a security policy in which element X trusts element Y if and only if X has confidence that Y behaves in a well-defined way (with respect to the operations) that does not violate the given security policy. *Trustworthiness* is the degree of trust of a system or component. In a direct trust relationship there are at least two entities involved in which at least one of them is to be judged (by another judging entity) about its trustworthiness. As the word trust implies reliance on others, in open networks there is no trust without intermediates to refer to or to be recommended by. Since trust is relative and intangible, in the virtual world it is addressed indirectly by recommendations between unknown entities, like X trusts Y, because X trusts Z and Z trusts Y. Z is then called a point of trust reference (POR) or trust intermediate. Trust is considered to propagate better when the PORs are more recognized. Such recognition is for example achieved when the POR has a higher status (acceptance of authority) in the considered space (LAN, WAN, nation or world).

Several trust models exist to include such a POR. One of the common trust model classes is represented by a single central institutionalised authority. According to this *hierarchical authority* trust principle, one or more superior entities grant credentials to the computing peers. A typical instance of this class is the public key

infrastructure (PKI) (Adams & Lloyd, 2002). PKI is the process and structure of using X.509 digital certificates with digital signatures to verify the use of asymmetric keys (Adams & Lloyd, 2002; Housley, Ford, Polk, & Solo, 1999).

Another trust model, the *central peer* trust model relies on a central entity. In this case, the POR is also centralized, but in contrast with the previous model, the POR has globally a low status, i.e. recognition; it has only a high status in a local environment (local networks, etc). Examples of such systems are KeyNote/PolicyMaker (Blaze, Feigenbaum, Ioannidis, & Keromytis, 1999), Kerberos (Steiner, Neuman, & Schiller, 1988) and KryptoKnight (Bird et al., 1995). In the *decentralized peer* model, a third trust model, the POR has also a low status, but this time not one, but all entities can function as a POR. This is an easy anarchistic and simple model, but also the least reliable, since none of the consulted peer PORs needs to have an irrefutable proof of its own trustworthiness. Examples are PGP and Poblano (Chen, 2002; Zimmermann, 1994). A fourth trust model would consist of models representing trust by a few joined decentralized PORs with a high status. These inter-hierarchy models or *meshed hierarchical models* grant high trust values. Some initiatives and tests have been carried out with bridge certification authorities (BCA) (NationalSecurityAgency, 2001) and cross certification authorities (CCA) (Polk & Hastings, 2000).

Basically, all trust models can be tailored to context-aware architectures. However, given the ad-hoc behaviour of SPs and users we assume that the *central peer* trust principle, where a prior subscription by an administrator is required, is the least appropriate in such an open space. A *peer-to-peer* trust model is also less appropriate, since it relies on other peers. The shortcoming of this model is that it requires many peers to make their recommendations reliable. Unfortunately, it is not always sure that many peers know all SPs to provide the user with their recommendation. As such this model is also not preferred. Conclusively, we consider the hierarchical and meshed hierarchical models appropriate for context-aware architectures.

Trustworthiness of an SP needs to be assessed before allowing the SP to collect any sensitive data from the user or before accepting any code from that SP (A. Ali Eldin et al., 2004). The challenge is how to formalize trust that is based on the trust models discussed above and to calculate trustworthiness of an SP autonomously. Previous works (Beth, Borcherding, & Klein, 1994; Marsh, 1994; Marti, 2005; Reiter & Stubblebine, 1999; Shi, Bochmann, & Adams, 2004; Winsborough & Li., 2002) base trust, T_{xy}, between two Computing Entities x (*CEx*) and y (*CEy*) at least on the next variables:

- $n_{x,y}$, number of (positive-negative) *experiences* of *CEx* with *CEy*; effect on T_{xy} is positive/ negative,
- $0 \leq p_{x,y} \leq 1$, a priori *probability of distrusting CEy* by *CEx*; effect on T_{xy} is negative.
- $ql_{x,y}$, *quality,* refers to the trust value of *CEy* as perceived by the assessor *CEx*.
- $qn_{x,y}$, *quantity,* refers to the number of entities (*CEx*) that vouch for *CEy*.

Given that hierarchical and meshed models are most appropriate for our context-aware architecture, we can apply the following calculus from (Daskapan and Costa, 2008):

$$T_{x,y} =$$

$$\frac{\arctan(n_{x,y} \cdot qn_{TA,y} \cdot \prod (ql_{TA,y} \cdot q\ l_{x,TA}))}{\pi / 2} \cdot (1 - p_{x,y})$$

and

$$n = \sum_{a=-1,0,1} \alpha \cdot a \text{ with } \alpha \in N$$

The notation $(n)_{x,y}$ or $n_{x,y}$, indicates an assertion n by CEx about CEy, where x = user, y = SP and TA = trust authority or POR. Since certain

events can damage the SP's reputation radically, positive and negative experiences cannot simply be summed up. Each experience can therefore additionally be amplified by a weight α. As for example, the default values for α could be: α = 1 for each positive experience and α = 2 for each negative experience.

The previous trust calculus can be incorporated in the trust valuator component of the *ShEM* architecture (see Figure 3). Assume that the users have embedded updated lists of the TA's they trust. This list contains at least the identity of the TA, its public key PK and the trust value of the TA according to the user. The users also keep track of the identity, number n of interactions with the different SPs and a default $p_{x,y}$, a priori *probability of distrust*. The TAs on their turn issue certificates for the SPs and have as such to maintain a list with the identity, keys, issue date, trust value, etc. of the SPs.

The service provider has to register himself first at a recognized TA, where he requests for a certificate, according to a X.509v.3 specification for example.

The SP provides the TA with his credential information to prove his identity and the trustworthiness of his service (steps 1a and 1b). This certificate states then that the SP is trusted for a certain service to a certain extent. This "certain extent" is formalized by a trust value $ql_{TA,y}$ and valid date that is attached to the certificate. The TA checks this credentials and service and if the SP passes this check successfully then it is granted the certificate (step 2). Armed with this certificate the SP request the user for consent (steps 3a and 3b). After that the user has verified the SP's certificate (steps 4 and 5) it calculates its trust value and sends it to the fuzzy rule engine (step 6). This engine uses this trust value together with other privacy attributes to estimate a consent value. This estimated value together with privacy policy evaluation output, contribute to a consent decision (step 7).

Figure 3. Trust valuation functional architecture

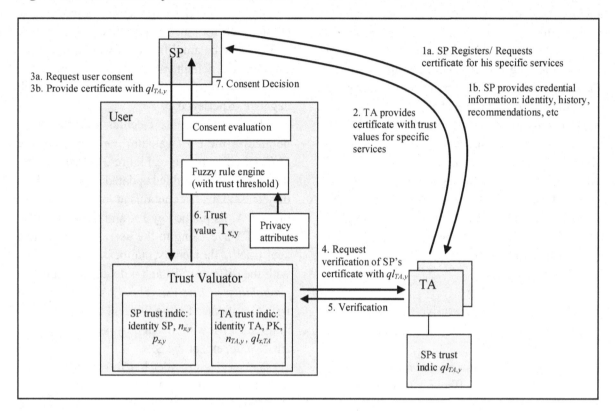

TECHNICAL IMPLEMENTATION

A next step will be to prototype the functional architecture into a technical one using state of the arts of technology. In daily life applications, an organization infrastructure highly influences the choices of the implementation architecture and technological components. However, recently, we have noticed the growing interest of organizations in service-oriented architectures (SOA) and the evolution of the Internet in the form of Web services (Kaye, 2003). Web service technology depends highly on the adoption of the following standards: XML, WSDL, SOAP and UDDI. The Internet, once solely a repository of various kinds of information, is now evolving into a provider of a variety of business services and applications. In

this manner, Web services technology and SOA are increasingly becoming a business issue based on the new technology's ability to deliver strategic business value (Barry, 2003).

The basic elements of a SOA architecture here are a service provider, a service consumer and a service broker. The *service provider* makes the service available and advertises it on the *service broker* by issuing the *service contract*. The *service consumer* finds the *service that matches its needs* in a service repository of the *service broker* using the published service contract. The *service consumer* and the *service provider* then interact in terms of providing/using the service. It is important to note that the communication between a service provider, a service consumer and a service broker is performed using the same set of interoperable, technology independent standards for communication, such as XML, SOAP and WSDL.

Implementation Scenario

Two service providers, SP1 and SP2 provide different types of entertaining services to users with SP1 providing mobile TV broadcasts and SP2 providing mobile books and learning material. Both service providers decided to make it possible to exchange both user profiles at both organizations to learn more about users and to reach users with better services. This will bring more revenues to both of them and will help them face the business challenges in the field of mobile entertainment. Furthermore, both companies thought of doing the exchange with keeping users' privacy issues and giving users the ability to control access to their location and to opt in/out when it's needed. Therefore, they decided to integrate the *ShEM* solution into their business to provide users with complete control over their privacy aspects.

Integration Architecture

In order to be able to provide users with control capabilities and to integrate with both service providers' architectures, the ShEM functional architecture will be realized using the service-oriented architecture and web services. The reason for the adoption of SOA is that SOA facilitates a smooth and loosely coupled integration without the need to do many changes in the internal structure and processes of integrating parties. In this scenario, we can present the basic high level architecture as shown by Figure 4.

SPs Service Requestors represent the service requestors at each SP which communicate using SOAP messages with the ShEM application via the ShEM Service Broker asking for user profiles. ShEM Service Broker communicates with Profile Exchange Service to get copies of the requested profiles including users' current GPS locations.

Since users' locations are changing, their preferences on authorization might change as well and hence the ShEM approach is useful in this case to provide a recommendation on user consent autonomously. In this scenario, we assume that both SPs decided to outsource the exchange of user profiles process to ShEM. The Profile Exchange Service communicates with the ShEM Authorization Service to determine the profile information allowed to be propagated to the SP Service Requestor. The ShEM Authorization Service gets the needed authorization based on the consent decision-making engines stand-alone application on the ShEM web application server (WAS) environment.

Preferences can be maintained in encrypted XML files or in databases depending on the business case and will be accessed/edited from a user's mobile device using mobile access portals. These preferences consist mainly of trust and privacy preferences. Privacy preferences represent ShEM preferences as discussed above. These include P3P related preferences and privacy attribute values. Trust preferences are maintained by the user via the Trust Authority (TA), which is implemented as a plug in to the ShEM Internet Information Service (IIS). Each user maintains a list of TA's he or she trusts in his or her profile. This list contains at least the name of the TA, its public key and the trustworthiness of the TA as perceived by the user. The user device keeps track of the number of interactions with the different SPs. We assume that the TA's on their turn issue certificates for the SPs and have as such to maintain a list with the names, address, keys, issue date, trust value, etc. of the SPs.[1]

CONCLUSION AND FUTURE WORK

In this chapter, we showed how a trust component can be integrated in a context-aware privacy architecture. The presented approach in this chapter is mainly based on users (data subject) involvements

Figure 4. ShEM solution integration example

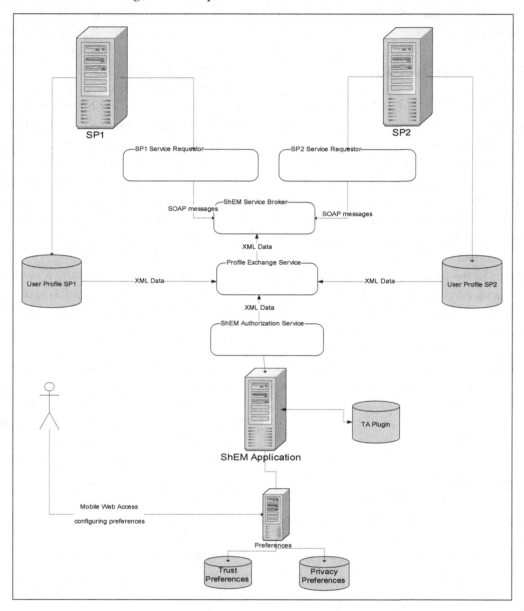

concerning the authorized access to their private context by external service providers. The trust valuation method is simple and practical, since it relies on existing trust models and technologies, like Pubic Key Infrastructure (PKI) and X.509 v3 certificates. Further, we provided a high level technical architecture, which shows how the *pri-*

vacy architecture *ShEM* can be integrated with other applications. In the implementation, we showed the importance of adopting the service-oriented architecture concepts and web services in the integration. We further intend to extend the concepts of the *ShEM* architecture into a running SOA environment defining an integration services bus to support consent decisions enforcement. Besides, we intend to refine and optimize the trust valuator functionality. A more thorough research into the exact behaviour of trust is needed to capture the real function. Another limitation of this approach is the assumption of user's awareness of setting their preferences on trust and privacy. We intend to further research this limitation by investigating possible default recommendations on preferences allowing users to make fewer configurations.

ACKNOWLEDGMENT

The authors would like to acknowledge the support of the late Professor René Wagenaar.

REFERENCES

Ackerman, M., Darrell, T., & Weitzner, D. J. (2001). Privacy in context. *HCI, 16*(2), 167-179.

Adams, C., & Lloyd, S. (2002). *Understanding PKI: Concepts, Standards, and Deployment Considerations* (Second Edition ed.): Addison-Wesley.

Agrawal, R., & Kiernan, J. (2002). *Watermarking relational databases.* Paper presented at the 28th VLDB Conference, Hong Kong, China.

Ali Eldin, A. (2006). *Private Information Sharing Under Uncertainty.* Delft: Amr Ali Eldin.

Ali Eldin, A., & Stojanovic, Z. (2007). Privacy control requirements for context-aware mobile services. In R. Gonzalez, N. Chen & A. Dahanayake (Eds.), *Personalized Information Retrieval and Access: Concepts, Methods and Practices*: IGI.

Ali Eldin, A., van den Berg, J., & Wagenaar, R. (2004). *A Fuzzy reasoning scheme for context sharing decision making.* Paper presented at the 6th International Conference on Electronic Commerce, Delft, The Netherlands.

Ali Eldin, A., & Wagenaar, R. (2004a). *A Fuzzy Logic based Approach to support users self-control of their private contextual data retrieval.* Paper presented at the 12th European Conference on Information Systems (ECIS04), Turku, Finland.

Ali Eldin, A., & Wagenaar, R. (2004b). *Towards a users driven privacy control.* Paper presented at the IEEE conference on Systems, Man, and Cybernetics (SMC 2004), The Hague.

Ali Eldin, A., & Wagenaar, R. (2007). Towards Autonomous User Privacy Control. *International Journal of Information Security and Privacy, 1*(4), 24-46.

Barry, D. K. (2003). Web Services and Service-Oriented Architectures. In M. Kaufmann (Ed.), *Savvy Manager's Guide.*

Beresford, A. R., & Stajano, F. (2003). Location privacy in pervasive computing. *Pervasive Computing, IEEE, 2*(1), 46 - 55.

Beth, T., Borcherding, M., & Klein, B. (1994). *Valuation of Trust in Open Networks.* Paper presented at the Third European Symposium on Research in Computer Security, Brighton.

Bird, R., Gopal, I., Herzberg, A., Janson, P., Kutten, S., Molva, R., et al. (1995). The KryptoKnight Family of Light-Weight Protocols for Authentication and Key Distribution. *IEEE/ACM Transactions on Networking, 3*(1), 31-41.

Blaze, M., Feigenbaum, J., Ioannidis, J., & Keromytis, A. D. (1999). The Role of Trust Management in Distributed Systems Security. In J. Vitek & C. Jensen (Eds.), *Secure Internet Programming* (pp. 185-210): Springer-Verlag.

Bojadziev, G., & Bojadziev, M. (1997). *Fuzzy Logic for Business, Finance, and Management*: World Scientific.

Camenisch, J., & Herreweghen, E. V. (2002). *Design and Implementation of Idemix Anonymous Credential System*: IBM Zurich Research Laboratory.

Chaum, D. (1985). Security without Identification Card Computers to make Big Brother Obsolete. *Communications of ACM, 28*(10), 1034-1044.

Chen, R. (2002). Poblano-A Distributed Trust Model for Peer-to-Peer Networks. *Sun.*

Clifton , C., Kantarcioglu, M., Vaidya, J., Lin, X., & Zhu, M. Y. (2002). Tools for Privacy Preserving Distributed Data Mining. *ACM SIGKDD Explorations, 4*(2), 28 - 34.

Cranor, L., Langheinrich, M., & Marchiori, M. (2002). *A P3P Preference Exchange Language 1.0 (APPEL1.0) W3C Working Draft.*

Cranor, L., Langheinrich, M., Marchiori, M., Presler-Marshall, M., & Reagle, J. (2004). *The Platform for Privacy Preferences 1.1 (P3P1.1) Specification W3C Working Draft.*

Cranor, L. F., Guduru, P., & Arjula, M. (2006). User Interfaces for Privacy Agents. *ACM Transactions on Human Computer Interactions.*

Currall, S. C., & Judge, T. A. (1995). Measuring Trust between Organizational Boundary Role Persons. *Organizational Behavior and Human Decision Processes, 64*(2), 151-170.

Daskapan, S., Vree, W. G., & Ali Eldin, A. (2003). *Trust metrics for survivable security systems.* Paper presented at the IEEE International Conference on Systems, Man & Cybernetics,, Washington.

Daskapan, Semir, Costa, Ana Cristina, "Reengineering Trust in Global Information Systems", in *Trust and New Technologies: Marketing and Management on the Internet and Mobile Media.* Cheltenham, UK and Lyme, US: Edward Elgar, Edited by Kautonen, T. and H. Karjaluoto (Eds), 2008

Dubois, D., & Prade, H. (1995). What does fuzzy logic bring to AI? *ACM Computing Surveys (CSUR), 27*(3).

EuropeanDirective. (2002). Directive 2002/58/EC of the European Parliament and of the Council of 12 July 2002, electronic communications sector (Directive on privacy and electronic communications). *Official Journal of European Communities, L,* 201-237.

Gambetta, D. G. (1988). *Can we trust trust?* New York: Basil Blackwell.

Hauser, C. (2002). *Privacy and Security in Location-Based Systems With Spatial Models.* Paper presented at the PAMPAS'02 Workshop on Requirements for Mobile Privacy and Security.

Hauser, C., & Kabatnik, M. (2001). *Towards Privacy Support in a Global Location Service.* Paper presented at the IFIP Workshop on IP and ATM Traffic Management (WATM/EUNICE 2001), Paris.

Housley, R., Ford, W., Polk, W., & Solo, D. (1999). Internet X.509 Public Key Infrastructure--Certificate and CRL Profile. *IETF RFC 2459.*

Kaye, D. (2003). *Loosely Coupled: The Missing Pieces of Web Services* (1st edition ed.): Rds Associates.

Konar, A. (2000). *Artificial Intelligence and Soft Computing: Behavioral and Cognitive Modeling of the Human Brain.* New York: CRC Press.

Langheinrich, M. (2001). *Privacy by Design- Principles of Privacy-Aware Ubiquitous Systems.* Paper presented at the 3rd International Conference on Ubiquitous Computing (Ubicomp2001).

Linn, J. (2005). Technology and web user data privacy - a survey of risks and countermeasures. *Security & Privacy Magazine, IEEE, 3*(1), 52-58.

Lysyanskayal, A., Rivest, R. L., Sahai, A., & Wolf, S. (1999). *Pseudonym Systems.* Paper presented at the Sixth Annual Workshop on Selected Areas in Cryptography (SAC, 99).

Mamdani, E. H. (1976). Advances in the Linguistic Synthesis of Fuzzy Controllers. *Journal of Man-Machine Studies, 8*, 669-678.

Marsh, S. P. (1994). *Formalizing Trust as a Computational Concept.*

Marti, S. (2005). *Trust and reputation in peer-to-peer networks.* Stanford University, USA.

NationalSecurityAgency. (2001). *Phase II Bridge Certification Authority Interoperability Demonstration Final Report*: A&N Associates.

Nilsson, M., Lindskog, H., & Fischer-Hübner, S. (2001). *Privacy Enhancements in the Mobile Internet.* Paper presented at the IFIP WG 9.6/11.7 working conference on Security and Control of IT in Society, Bratislava.

Park, J., & Sandhu, R. (2002). Towards usage control models: beyond traditional access control. In *Proceedings of seventh ACM symposium on Access control models and technologies* (pp. 57-64). Monterey, California, USA ACM Press.

Polk, W. T., & Hastings, N. E. (2000). *Bridge Certification Authorities: Connecting B2B Public Key Infrastructures*: National Institute of Standards and Technology.

Reiter, M., & Stubblebine, S. (1999). Authentication metric analysis and design. *ACM Transactions on Information and System Security, 2*(2).

Sandhu, R. S., Coyne, E. J., Feinstein, H. L., & Youman, C. E. (1996). Role-Based Access Control Models *Computer 29*(2), 38-47.

Shi, J., Bochmann, G., & Adams, C. (2004). *A Trust Model with Statistical Foundation.* Paper presented at the Workshop on Formal Aspects in Security and Trust, Toulouse, France.

Steiner, J. G., Neuman, B. C., & Schiller, J. I. (1988). *Kerberos: An Authentication Service for Open Network Systems.* Paper presented at the Usenix, Dallas, Texas.

Tolone, W., Ahn, G.-J., Pai, T., & Hong, S.-P. (2005). Access control in collaborative systems *ACM Comput. Surv., 37*(1), 29-41.

Wang, S.-J. (2004). Anonymous wireless authentication on a portable cellular mobile system. *Computers, IEEE Transactions on, 53*(10), 1317-1329.

Warren, S. D., & Brandeis, L. D. (1890). The Right to Privacy. *Harvard Law Review, IV*(5).

Winsborough, W. H., & Li, N. (2002). *Towards Practical Automated Trust Negotiation.* Paper presented at the IEEE Workshop on Policies for Distributed Systems and Networks.

Zadeh, L. A. (1973). Outline of a new approach to the analysis of complex systems and decision processes. *IEEE Trans. on Systems, Man and Cybernetics, 3*(1), 28-44.

Zimmermann, P. (1994). *PGP User's Guide.* Cambridge, USA: MIT Press.

ENDNOTE

[1]   For the sake of simplicity, security requirements such as authentication and data transmission encryption protocols are included in the architecture, but considered out of the scope of this chapter.

Section V
Context–Awareness for Enhanced Usability and Personalization

Chapter XIV
Leveraging Semantic Technologies towards Social Ambient Intelligence

Adrien Joly
Alcatel-Lucent Bell Labs, France
Université de Lyon, LIRIS / INSA, France

Pierre Maret
Université de Lyon, France
Université de Saint Etienne, France

Fabien Bataille
Alcatel-Lucent Bell Labs, France

ABSTRACT

These times, when the amount of information exponentially grows on the Internet, when most people can be connected at all times with powerful personal devices, we need to enhance, adapt, and simplify access to information and communication with other people. The vision of ambient intelligence which is a relevant response to this need brings many challenges in different areas such as context-awareness, adaptive human-system interaction, privacy enforcement, and social communications. The authors believe that ontologies and other semantic technologies can help meeting most of these challenges in a unified manner, as they are a bridge between meaningful (but fuzzy by nature) human knowledge and digital information systems. In this chapter, the authors will depict their vision of "Social Ambient Intelligence" based on the review of several uses of semantic technologies for context management, adaptive human-system interaction, privacy enforcement and social communications. Based on identified benefits and lacks, and on their experience, they will propose several research leads towards the realization of this vision.

INTRODUCTION

These times, when the amount of information exponentially grows on the Internet, when most people can be connected at all times with powerful personal devices, users suffer from the growing complexity of the information society. Our use of technology is moving towards the vision of "Ambient Intelligence", derived from the vision of "Ubiquitous computing" in which "the most profound technologies are those that disappear" (Weiser, 1991) . Thus, access to information is no longer limited to personal computers and the web browsing paradigm. This vision brings many technological and psychological challenges (Streitz & Nixon, 2005) that are considered in several research domains, including:

- Context-awareness: how to take one's context into account to improve his communication ?
- Multimodality: how to span user interfaces from a terminal into separate modal interfaces ? (e.g. various screens, input controllers, microphones, phones)
- Social networking: how to enhance and leverage social communication ?
- Privacy & Trust: how to ease one's life without delegating human control to machines ?

There is one transversal question yet to answer: is there a unified approach that could answer these challenges in a global way and that makes sense? Actually, a common approach exists that is considered in all these research domains, and in most corresponding works and has been shown as very promising. This approach is the use of semantic technologies.

In this chapter, we propose a review of research works relying on semantic technologies towards what we call "Social Ambient Intelligence", a social extension of ambient intelligence. The intention here is to identify the key technologies, approaches and issues that may be blended in order to build an optimal platform for a widescaled ubiquitous system that can support social applications. After defining the foundational terms of this chapter in the Background section, we will review several research works to identify their key technologies, approaches and issues in the State-of-the-Art section, then we will propose several research leads towards our vision of "Social Ambient Intelligence" in the Future Trends section, to finally conclude this chapter.

In this section, we propose and discuss the underlying definitions needed to set the foundations of this chapter: ubiquitous computing, context-awareness and semantic technologies.

Ubiquitous Computing, Ambient Intelligence and Context-Awareness

The phrase "ubiquitous computing" was proposed by Mark Weiser while working for the Xerox Palo Alto Research Center (PARC), to qualify a possible evolution of computers. "The Computer for the 21st century" (Weiser, 1991) has become a foundational paper for following works in this area. Indeed, it introduced a vision, in which "ubiquitous computers" are simple communicative devices and appliances that are suited for a particular task and are aware of their surrounding environment while fading into the background. For example, paper sheets could be replaced with flexible screens, bringing any information of the web as an independent element of a real desktop, an element that one could stack into piles, stick on a wall, lend to a colleague or take for lunch.

As depicted on Figure 1, the generation of ubiquitous computers has already arrived, as powerful and communicative computers are spread in many devices like watches, mobile phones, portable media players, game consoles, PDAs (Personal Digital Assistants), ticket machines, bike renting beacons and kids toys. Even though Mark Weiser's vision of interoperable and shared ubiquitous computers has not been reached yet,

Figure 1. The evolution of computing, adapted from "Nano computing & Ambient intelligence" (Waldner, 2007), © 2007 Hermes Science Publishing. Used with permission.

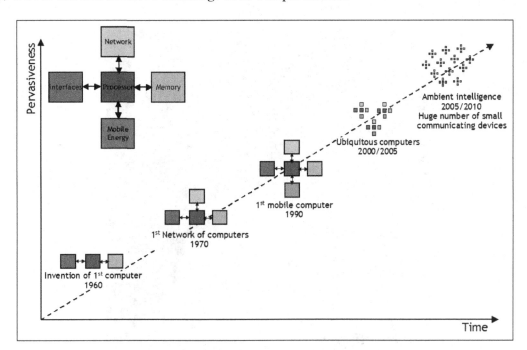

a significant research effort is done towards the vision of "Ambient intelligence" . As such, "Ambient Intelligence" is considered as an evolution of "ubiquitous computing" in which networked devices can also be integrated in the environment (and thus not expecting any user intervention), can sense the environmental, personal and social situation to adapt the experience, and can anticipate forthcoming situations or actions in order to ease and enhance people lives.

Firstly defined by (Schilit, Adams, & Want, 1994), context-awareness is a key research domain towards the vision of Ambient Intelligence. It consists in acquiring low-level context data (e.g. from sensors), inferring high-level knowledge from this data, and predicting context changes in order to clearly improve the user experience. As depicted on Figure 2, the low level of context contains current raw sensor data like GPS coordinates, IP address, surrounding Bluetooth

MAC addresses or temperature. By combining and inferring on this knowledge, a meaningful position or activity like "in a meeting" or "watching TV" can be deduced to form a higher level of context. Then, after having learnt the habits of the user, predictions can be made about the actions that are probably going to happen next or about the exceptional cases that have occurred (e.g. the user is going to arrive late at work because he has not left home yet) in order to undertake relevant actions pro-actively (e.g. inform the colleagues that the meeting is delayed).

Context-awareness aims to make user interfaces automatically adapt to the user's environment and intents. It can enhance user inputs without requiring additional efforts from the user (Leong, Kobayashi, Koshizuka, & Sakamura, 2005) and also adapt outputs (Sadi & Maes, 2005). Although several works have been focusing on the implementation of context-awareness on mobile

Figure 2. Levels of context (© Bell Labs. Used with permission.)

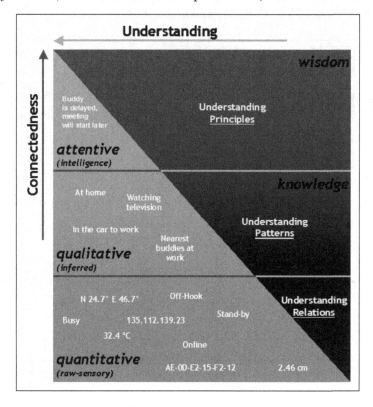

devices (Christopoulou, 2008; Korpipää, Häkkilä, Kela, Ronkainen, & Känsälä, 2004; Häkkilä & Mäntyjärvi, 2005), we will not specifically address mobile-based context-aware platforms in this paper.

Semantic Technologies: Ontologies, Knowledge Representation and Reasoning

In their study, (Strassner, O'Sullivan, & Lewis, 2007) define ontologies as « a formal, explicit specification of a shared, machine-readable vocabulary and meanings, in the form of various entities and relationships between them, to describe knowledge about the contents of one or more related subject domains throughout the life cycle of its existence ». Semantic technologies, including ontologies and semantic description languages, are quite similar to human thinking and memorization: they allow the definition of concepts and instances (of these concepts) that are related with each other using semantically qualified links. They also allow to develop an inferred knowledge from the reasoning on this knowledge (Gruber, 1993). Applying such approach to information technologies enable machines to understand the actual meaning of data which is formulated using a distributed and evolving vocabulary. That way, ontologies fill the gap between ambiguous/fuzzy human thinking (e.g. in natural languages, a word can have different meanings) and formalized digital data (i.e. stored using specific formats and interpreted by specific applications for a specific purpose).

One of the benefits of using semantic languages is to allow progressive/incremental modeling of a system, reflecting the natural progression of conceptual understanding of domains. Ontologies can ease the communication between heterogeneous entities (i.e. using different languages/protocols) by matching similar portions of the semantic graph of the sender's knowledge with the recipient's knowledge.

On the other hand, we would like to prevent the reader to make the naïve assumption that semantic technologies are a magic solution to empower machines with autonomic intelligence. It may seem possible to model our universe as an ontology, allowing computers to understand the human world, but it is actually impossible. Indeed, modeling is always relative to a point of view, and integrating ontologies from experts of several domains would necessarily lead to inconsistencies. There is also a usual confusion about the so-called "Semantic Web" (Berners-Lee, Hendler, & Lassila, 2001). This expression does not mean that internet users will have to deal with semantic languages to communicate on the web, but it refers to a set of languages and tools that would allow web resources (i.e. web pages and services) to be described semantically in order to allow seamless processing of knowledge distributed among heterogeneous sites. Today, with the rise of the "Web 2.0" (O'Reilly, 2005), users are already able to create "mash-ups" relying on several components and data streams hosted on different sites. However, the next step is possibly to automatize (or, at least, to ease) the development of such mash-ups, assuming that web data and components are semantically described.

In the next section, we will investigate the use of semantic technologies in ubiquitous context-aware systems in order to identify the existing blocks that we will rely on to build our vision of "Social Ambient Intelligence".

STATE-OF-THE-ART

Previous studies (Strang & Linnhoff-Popien, 2004; Baldauf, Dustdar, & Rosenberg, 2007; O. Lassila & Khushraj, 2005) have identified ontologies as the most promising enabler for ubiquitous context-aware systems because they are heterogeneous and extensible by nature, and semantic technology enables « future-proof » interoperability. In this section, we will study the use of semantic technologies in four aspects of ambient intelligence: context management, human-system interactions, privacy enforcement, and social communications.

Semantic Context Management

According to (Dey, 2001), "a system is context-aware if it uses context to provide relevant information and/or services to the user, where relevancy depends on the user's task". By context, Dey means "any information that can be used to characterize the situation of an entity. An entity is a person, place, or object that is considered relevant to the interaction between a user and an application, including the user and applications themselves".

(Gu, Wang, Pung, & Zhang, 2004) gave an introduction to context-awareness by proposing the following requirements: « An appropriate infrastructure for context-aware systems should provide support for most of the tasks involved in dealing with contexts - acquiring context from various sources such as physical sensors, databases and agents; performing context interpretation; carrying out dissemination of context to interested parties in a distributed and timely fashion; and providing programming models for constructing of context-aware services. »

The use of ontologies to store and manipulate context have an impact on other aspects of the underlying system: context knowledge exchange, learning, user interactions, security and applications. In this section we will review several semantic-based approaches for context management platforms and identify the most successful approaches and current lacks.

Review of Major Context-Aware Platforms

One of the first semantic context modeling approaches was the **Aspect-Scale-Context (ASC)** model proposed by (Strang, Linnhoff-Popien, & Frank, 2003). Compared to non-semantic models, ASC enabled contextual interoperability during service discovery and execution in a distributed system. Indeed, this model consists of three concepts:

- Aspects are measurable properties of an entity (e.g. the current temperature of a room)

- Scales are metrics used to express the measure of these properties (e.g. Celsius temperature)
- Context qualifies the measure itself by describing the sensor, the timestamp and quality data

Contexts can be converted from a scale to another using Operations, also described semantically, and can be mapped to an implemented service. This model has been implemented as the CoOL Context Ontology Language. The CoOL core ontology can be formulated in OWL-DL (Dean & Schreiber, 2004) and F-Logic (object-oriented). The CoOL integration is an extension of the core to inter-operate with web services. OntoBroker (Decker, Erdmann, Fensel, & Studer, 1999) was chosen for semantic inference and reasoning, supporting F-Logic as knowledge representation and query language.

Figure 3. Overview of CoBrA, © 2003-2008 Harry Chen. Used with permission.

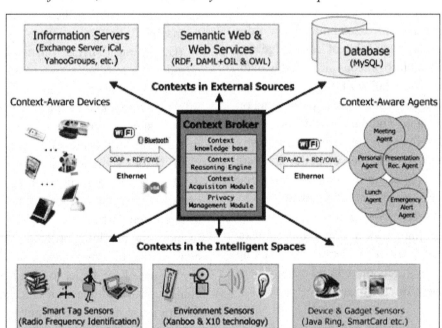

With EasyMeeting, (Chen et al., 2004) proposed a pragmatic application to demonstrate the benefits of their semantic context-aware system called **CoBrA**, for Context Broker Architecture. This application assists a speaker and its audience in a meeting situation by welcoming them in the room, dimming the lights, and displaying the presentation slides, either by vocal commands or automatically. The underlying prototype that they developed is a multi-agent system based on JADE (Java Agent DEvelopment Framework) [http://sharon.cselt.it/projects/jade/] in which a broker maintains a shared context model for all computing entities by acquiring context knowledge from various sensors and by reasoning on this knowledge to make decisions, as depicted on Figure 3. In the EasyMeeting application, this broker can deduce the list of expected participants and their role in the meeting by accessing their schedule, and can sense their actual presence when the bluetooth-enabled mobile phone declared in their profile is detected in the room. That way, the system can notify the speaker about their presence, decide to dim the lights and turn off the music when he arrives. These decisions are made possible by reasoning on the context knowledge using rules defined by the EasyMeeting application. The context knowledge is represented as RDF triples relying on the COBRA-ONT OWL ontology that includes vocabularies from the SOUPA ontology (Chen, Perich, Finin, & A. Joshi, 2004) covering time, space, policy, social networks, actions, location context, documents, and events, as depicted on Figure 4. Inferencing on the OWL ontology is handled by JENA's API [http://jena.sourceforge.net] whereas the JESS rule-based engine [http://herzberg.ca.sandia.gov/] is used for domain-specific reasoning. The execution of rules (when results cannot be inferred from ontology axioms alone) uses the forward-chaining inference procedure of JESS to reason about contextual information. Note that, in this case, essential supporting facts must be extracted from RDF to JESS representation and the eventual results have to be injected in RDF to the knowledge base, which implies additional overhead in the process.

CoBrA's broker enforces privacy policies to define rules of behavior and restrict context communication. The enforcement of user-defined policies relies on the Rei role-based policy-reasoning engine (Kagal & T. A. Joshi, 2003) which does description logic inference over OWL. CoBrA also implements a meta-policy reasoning mechanism so that users can override some aspects of a global policy to define specific constraints at their desired level of granularity. However, they do not provide a tool for the user to express his/her privacy policy.

The **SOUPA** ontology proposed by (Chen et al., 2004) and used in CoBrA was a collaborative effort to build a generic context ontology for ubiquitous systems. Since 2003 it has been maintained by the "Semantic Web in Ubiquitous Comp Special Interest Group". The design of this ontology is driven by use cases and relies on FOAF, DAML-Time, OpenCyc (symbolic) + OpenGIS (geospatial) spatial ontology, COBRA-ONT, MoGATU BDI (human beliefs, desires and intentions) and Rei policy ontology (rights, prohibitions, obligations, dispensations). SOUPA defines its own vocabulary, but most classes and properties are mapped to foreign ontology terms using the standard OWL ontology mapping constructs (equivalentClass and equivalentProperty), which allows interoperability. In the core ontology in which both computational entities and human users can be modeled as agents, the following extensions are added: meeting & schedule, document & digital document, image capture and location (sensed location context of things).

Like CoBrA, **MOGATU** (Perich, Avancha, Chakraborty, A. Joshi, & Yesha, 2005) is a context-aware system based on the SOUPA ontology. However, this decentralized peer-to-peer multi-agent system implements several use cases covering automatic and adaptive itinerary computation based on real-time traffic knowledge, and commercial recommendation. In this approach,

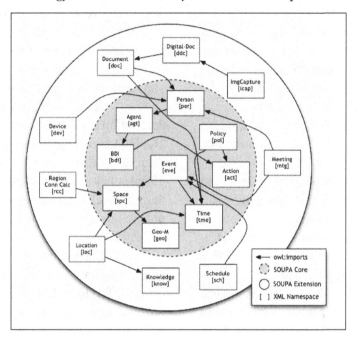

Figure 4. The SOUPA ontology, © 2003-2008 Harry Chen. Used with permission.

each device is a semi autonomous entity driven by the user's profile and context, relying on a contract-based transaction model. This entity is called InforMa and acts as a personal broker that handles exchanges with other peers. The user profile semantically defines his beliefs, desires and intentions, following the BDI model that is part of the SOUPA ontology. Beliefs are weighted facts depicting user's knowledge and preferences such as his schedule and food preferences, whereas desires express the user's goals. Intentions are defined as a set of intended tasks that can be inferred from desires or explicitly provided. However no clues are given by the authors about how these beliefs and intentions are defined by the user or the system, which let us assume that this is still a manual process yet to be enriched with profiling mechanisms and a graphical user interface to edit the profile. Moreover, this work being apparently focused on trusted peer-to-peer exchange of information according to the BDI user profile, details on the actual reasoning process on context knowledge are not given. InforMa is able

to process queries that can possibly involve other peers and advertise information to these peers in vicinity, relying on graph search and caching techniques. However no details were given on how pro-activity is made possible. Another lack identified in the underlying BDI model is that the representation of pre-conditions and effects of intentions are left to the applications, but we have found no clues on how applications fill this issue. Facing an important cost of network transmissions in the exchange process, it seems that this research group is focusing on peer-to-peer networking optimization and trusted exchanges more than on the actual context management. However, they suggested that preparing purpose-driven queries in advance and caching intermediate query results could improve the performance of their system, which is an interesting approach that should be considered in distributed context-aware systems.

The CORBA-based **GAIA** platform proposed by (Ranganathan, Al-Muhtadi, & Campbell, 2004) focuses on hybrid reasoning about uncertain context, relying on probabilistic logic, fuzzy logic and Bayesian networks. In their approach, context knowledge is expressed using predicates which classes and properties are defined in a DAML+OIL ontology (Horrocks, 2002). Predicates can be plugged directly into rules and other reasoning and learning mechanisms for handling uncertainty. This choice reduces the overhead of the CoBrA system relying on RDF triples. Rules are processed by the XSB engine [http://xsb.sourceforge.net/], which is described as a kind of optimized Prolog that also supports HiLog, allowing unification on the predicate symbols themselves as well as on their arguments. HiLog's sound and complete proof procedure in first-order logic is needed to write rules about the probabilities of context.

GAIA's authentication mechanism demonstrates the usefulness of fuzzy/uncertain context reasoning. It allows users to authenticate with various means such as passwords, fingerprint sensor or bluetooth phone proximity. Each of these means have different levels of confidence, and some user roles may require that the user authenticates himself on two of them to cumulate their confidence level up to the required level.

Although GAIA proposes a common reasoning framework, application developers have to define the expected context inputs and specify the reasoning mechanism to be used by providing Prolog/HiLog rules (for probabilistic/fuzzy logic) or Bayesian networks. A graphical user interface is provided to help developers construct rules, whereas MSBN (Microsoft's Belief Network) can be used to create Bayesian nets. Although Bayesian networks are a powerful way to perform probabilistic sensor fusion and higher-level context derivation, they need to be trained. Moreover, inference with large networks (more than 50 nodes) becomes very costly in terms of processing and can result in scalability problems.

Based on previous works, (Gu et al., 2004) propose **SOCAM** (Service-Oriented Context-Aware Middleware), another OWL-based context-aware framework with the aim to address more general

use cases by adding more qualitative information on acquired context. The classifiedAs property allows the categorization of context facts as Sensed, Defined, Aggregated or Deduced. The dependsOn property allows the justification of a deduced context based on other context facts. Another contribution is the possibility to qualify context information with parameters such as accuracy, resolution, certainty and freshness. The SOCAM framework was proven (Gu, Pung, & Zhang, 2004) to reason successfully on uncertain contexts using Bayesian Networks, but no performance results were given. The same group of authors have also carried out a performance experiment of the **CONON** ontology (Wang, Zhang, Gu, & Pung, 2004) depicted on Figure 5, which is the name that was given to SOCAM's context ontology. Their results show that the duration of the reasoning process exponentially increases with the number of RDF triples stored in the context knowledge base, which reveals that this approach is not scalable for a widespread context-aware system. Therefore two leads were proposed to increase performance:

- To perform static, complex reasoning tasks (e.g., description logic reasoning for checking inconsistencies) in an off-line manner.
- To separate context processing from context usage, so that context reasoning can be performed by resource-rich devices (such as a server) while the terminals can acquire high-level context from a centralized service, instead of performing excessive computation themselves.

Later works of that team were focused on the peer-to-peer architecture for context information systems.

Basing on the CONON ontology, (Truong, Y. Lee, & S. Y. Lee, 2005) proposed the PROWL language ("Probabilistic annotated OWL") to generalize fuzzy/probabilistic reasoning from applications to domains by mapping Bayesian

Networks to ontology classes and properties. This approach must be experimented with various context-aware applications to prove its feasibility.

The FP6 IST project **SPICE** (Service Platform for Innovative Communication Environment) brought a fresh approach to ubiquitous system, considering them in a wider scope centered on semantic knowledge management for improved ubiquitous end-user services (SPICE, 2006) (SPICE, 2007). On its Knowledge Management Layer, SPICE proposes two different implementations of the context provisioning subsystem: the IMS Context Enabler (ICE) (M. Strohbach, Bauer, E. Kovacs, C. Villalonga, & Richter, 2007) and the Knowledge Management Framework (KMF). In ICE, the SIP protocol (Session Initiation Protocol) is leveraged to control the parameters of the exchange sessions (e.g. data sets to communicate, update trigger, update frequency) and to flexibly adjust the communication path based on the changes in network structure and available

context information. Both KMF and ICE rely on a shared ontology called the Mobile Ontology which is freely downloadable on the Internet [http://ontology.ist-spice.org/], the most important difference being the interfaces: ICE uses SIP whereas KMF uses OWL over SOAP Web Services for exchanging context information. However, gateways are also provided so that context data can be converted from a format to the other. Therefore we will abstract these implementations and focus on the common knowledge model. Embracing the recommendations of the W3C, SPICE Mobile Ontology is defined in OWL and the context data is expressed in RDF. Inspired from the Dutch project Freeband Awareness, SPICE's Physical Space ontology has a finer granularity than any previous context ontology: it notably defines properties for connections between rooms and floors. Following the approach of the « Doppelgänger User Modeling System » (Orwant, 1995), SPICE's User Profile ontology supports domain-specific

Figure 5. Partial definition of the CONON ontology extended with the home domain (Wang, Zhang, Gu, & Pung, 2004), © 2004 IEEE. Used with permission.

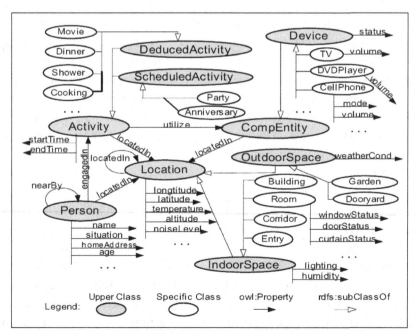

and conditional (situation-specific) submodels. In this approach, the profile contains subsets which are considered on certain conditions expressed with the form: Context Type, Operator, Value. This allows variations of the profile, depending on the user's context and/or the targeted application/service.

The Knowledge Management Layer also contains a Knowledge Storage module, a Profile Manager, a Service and Knowledge Push and Notification module and three kinds of Reasoners: a Predictor, a Learner and a Recommender. The reasoners can request past knowledge directly from context sources or from an external knowledge storage source. Both feedback-based and observation-based learning are supported, generating LearntRule and LearntRuleSet instances in OWL. The results can be leveraged to propose Recommendations to the user. Experimental results on the use of different learning techniques are to be published. Another interesting contribution

of SPICE in the context-awareness domain is the use of a KnowledgeParameter class that is used to qualify context information with values defining their probability, confidence, timestamp, temporal validity and accuracy. However we have not found any mechanism that is similar to the "dependsOn" property supported by SOCAM to justify high-level context with lower-level facts from which it was inferred.

Another part of the SPICE project called the Distributed Communication Sphere (Kernchen et al., 2007) allows dynamic discovery of users' surrounding devices, networks and services. This part includes components that leverage context knowledge to enable multimodal interaction, content delivery, data synchronization and dynamic widgets on terminals, requiring a lightweight rule engine to be deployed on every terminal. SPICE also provides the End User Studio, an Eclipse-based GUI (Graphical User Interface) shown on Figure 6 that allows end users to create custom trigger-action rules visually.

Figure 6. Creating a rule-based service using SPICE's End User Studio (SPICE 2007) © 2008 SPICE. Used with permission.

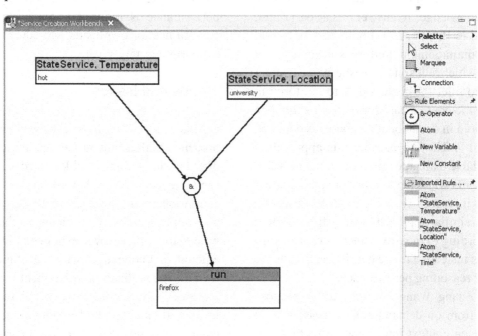

Figure 7. HCoM: Hybrid Context Management and reasoning system (Ejigu et al. 2007), © 2007 IEEE. Used with permission.

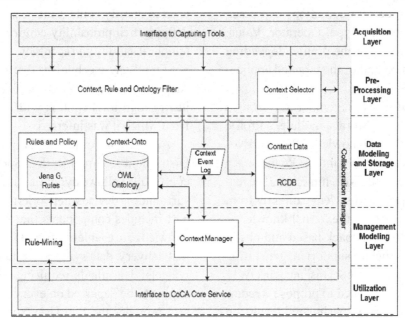

One of the biggest identified issues in previously reviewed semantic context-aware systems is the processing time required for reasoning on context knowledge. To answer this issue, (Ejigu, Scuturici, & Brunie, 2007) proposed an hybrid context management and reasoning system (HCoM) which relies on a heuristic-based context selector to filter the context data to be stored in the semantic context base for reasoning, the rest being stored in a relational database, as depicted on Figure 7. They report that this approach is more scalable than pure semantic context-awareness systems when the number of static context instances increases. (Lin, Li, Yang, & Shi, 2005) propose a similar approach but they filter context data according to their relevance to running applications instead of usage heuristics, in order to boost the reasoning performance.

(Tan, Zhang, Wang, & Cheng, 2005) propose to move from on-demand context reasoning to event-driven context interpretation so that rea-

soning on context data is processed as soon as it is received by the context management framework. However, in their distributed system, the performance is reduced because of increased communication overheads. Moreover, it does not support uncertainty yet.

Trends and Issues

In this section, we have reviewed several approaches addressing modeling, reasoning and distribution of contextual knowledge. Although semantic technologies have been shown as powerful tools to empower context-awareness, they also imply scalability problems, as the required processing time grows exponentially with the amount of knowledge, which is a major issue towards the realization of Ambient Intelligence. However, hybrid context management approaches leverage the assets of both relational and semantic context management, therefore they should be considered in the aim of building a powerful and scalable context-awareness system. Nevertheless, the selection/filtering of context data to be merged in the semantic database is not trivial and may need further research. Another track to consider is closer coupling or integration of rule engines with knowledge bases in order to reduce processing overheads.

Semantics for Adapted Human-System Interactions

After context-awareness, another key aspect of Ambient Intelligence is how the user interacts with the digital world. Today, most internet-based interactions rely on the use of computers (i.e. a screen, a keyboard and a mouse). Whereas most people carry their own powerful mobile phone with them, most of the popular content and services are not adapted to general mobile devices with their constraints (small screen, no keyboard). Of course some of those have been adapted specifically to some popular platforms like the iPhone, but the vision of Ambient Intelligence is not only (i) to bring most of them to virtually any terminal according to its capabilities, but also (ii) to span various modalities of interaction over multiple interfaces (i.e. displays, inputs, speakers and other objects). Therefore, ambient services need to know the capabilities of every platform and interface they are used with, and they need to adapt the interaction to the user according to these capabilities. In this section we will review existing technologies for the discovery of devices and the description of their capabilities in order to enable rich user interactions and multimodality.

Semantic Discovery and Description of Interfaces

CC/PP (Composite Capabilities / Preferences Profile) (Klyne et al., 2004) is a recommendation from the W3C based on the Resource Description Framework (RDF) to create profiles that describe device capabilities and user preferences. It provides a syntax and tools to create terminal profiles and preference vocabularies, and thus can not be used as is. Indeed, the vocabulary of capabilities used for defining profiles is not in the scope of this recommendation and only structural rules and guidelines for interoperability are provided. However, the recommendation includes a pointer to the UAProf vocabulary as a referred example; we will review this vocabulary below. Among the features of the CC/PP syntax, allowed value types are listed, and the definition of default values is explained. The state-of-the-art of (SPICE, 2006) pointed out that conditional constraints are not supported in CC/PP. Moreover, the recommendation clearly informs that a CC/PP profile may include sensitive data, and delegates the enforcement of privacy to the application/system.

UAProf (User Agent Profile) (WAP Forum, 2001) is a CC/PP vocabulary for WAP (Wireless Application Protocol) enabled cell phones developed by the Open Mobile Alliance (OMA). The idea is that compliant cell phones have their capabilities described in a profile stored on a web repository so that adaptive services can gather this information in order to tailor content for embedded web browsers. This vocabulary is focused on software and hardware capabilities, and thus does not cover preferences.

WURFL (Wireless Universal Resource File) [http://wurfl.sourceforge.net/uaprof.php] is a collaborative effort to build an open XML file that describes device profiles based on fixes of their UAProf profiles. This promising initiative addresses several shortcomings of the original UAProf approach in which profiles can be inconsistent across providers, not up to date, or even do not exist.

The Foundation for Intelligent Physical Agents (**FIPA**) also proposed a device description ontology (FIPA, 2002) that can be used to reason and make decisions on the best device and modalities to create a user interface in multi-agent systems. Due to the nature of multi-agent systems, this approach differs from CC/PP in the manner of transmitting the profile. Instead of providing its complete profile on-demand, the terminal returns profile subsets adaptively to requests, allowing to set the granularity and scope of the required profile content in a gradual negotiation between agents. Whereas a CC/PP profile defines the capabilities for the software, hardware and the browser, FIPA Device Description supports the description of agent-related capabilities instead of the browser's. However, it is possible to use this ontology in a CC/PP profile, similarly to UAProf.

Even though this approach is not based on semantic technologies, the **UPnP** (Universal Plug and Play) discovery protocol (UPnP Forum, 2003) defines a XML language that can describe a physical device into a hierarchy of logical devices which map every hardware component of the device and thus its corresponding capability. A deeper study of UPnP is not in the scope of this chapter, but the modularity of this approach is interesting and should be considered in order to improve the re-usability of profiles, according to the fact that common hardware components are part of many devices.

Semantics for Multimodality

When devices and their capabilities are discovered, their use for multimodal interaction requires additional negotiation and synchronization so that user interaction constraints and preferences are respected for a rich user experience. The constraints to validate cover the quality of rendering/sampling, the robustness of the connectivity, the privacy of exchanges (e.g. displaying emails on a public screen should be avoided), and also the environmental context and user preferences.

The members of the W3C Multimodal Interaction Working Group propose their specifications of a **Multimodal Interaction Framework** (W3C, 2003) based on a central Interaction Manager that connects user inputs (e.g. audio, speech, handwriting, keyboard...) and outputs (e.g. speech, text,

graphics, motion...) to applications and on two other components, as shown on Figure 8:

- The Session Component, which handles the state management for application sessions that may involve multiple steps, multiple modality modes, multiple devices and/or multiple users.
- The System and Environment component, which handles the changes of device capabilities, user preferences and contextual/environmental conditions.

The Interaction Manager coordinates data and manages the execution flow from various input and output modality components. It combines various user inputs for submitting meaningful actions to applications (multimodal fusion) and dispatches responses to the user through various output interfaces (multimodal fission).

Also proposed by the W3C Multimodal Interaction Working Group, the EMMA (Extensible MultiModal Annotation) markup language (W3C, 2007) is a XML markup language for describing the interpretation of user inputs. An example of input interpretation is the transcription of a raw signal into words, for instance derived from speech, pen or keystroke input, or a set of attribute/value pairs describing a gesture. The interpretations of user's input are expected to be generated by signal interpretation processors, such as speech and ink recognition, semantic interpreters, and other types of processors for use by components that act on the user's inputs such as interaction managers. As shown on Figure 8, user inputs are processed in two layers to generate EMMA data which is integrated for submission to the Interaction Manager. The two layers of input processing consist of:

- Recognition components, which capture natural input from the user and translate them into a form useful for later processing. (e.g. speech to text, handwritten symbols

Figure 8. The input process of the Multimodal Interaction Framework (W3C 2003), © 2003 World Wide Web Consortium

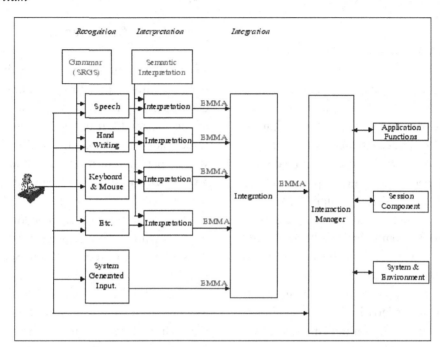

and messages to text, mouse movements to x-y coordinates on a two-dimensional surface…)

- Interpretation components, which further process the results of recognition components by identifying the meaning/semantics intended by the user. (e.g. pointing somewhere on a map would result in knowing the name of the corresponding country, nodding or saying "I agree" would both mean acceptation from the user…)

Recommended by the W3C, EMMA is probably going to become a standard for annotation of multimodal inputs. It has shown its usefulness especially for speech-based dialog in extensible multimodal applications (Reithinger & Sonntag, 2005; Manchón, del Solar, de Amores, & Pérez, 2006; Oberle et al., 2006).

The IST project **Mobilife** proposed a solution (Kernchen, Boussard, Moessner, & Mrohs, 2006)

to describe devices and modality services to form context-aware multimodal user interfaces. Their identified requirements include the deployment of a fission component implementing a rule-based algorithm on the device in order to adapt the user's mobile multimodal interface best to the current situation. In the SPICE project (Kernchen et al., 2007), the « Multimedia Delivery and Control System » depicted on Figure 9 has been developed as a part of the « Distributed Communication Sphere », is a multimodal platform relying on the W3C-recommended Synchronized Multimedia Integration Language (SMIL) (Ayars et al., 2000), that supports multimodal fusion and fission. First, the « resource discovery system » of the **MDCS** finds appropriate interfaces, then modalities are selected according to user preferences, context (e.g. Walking, driving), available resources in user's DCS and provision constraints. Modality, device and network recommendations are proposed by the knowledge management framework. This implementation is available as an open source project [https://sourceforge.net/projects/mdcs].

Trends and Issues

In this section, we have identified that semantic technologies have shown their usefulness to improve the discovery, description and exploitation of multimodal interfaces. Several collaborative efforts have been carried out to describe device capabilities. Besides, multimodal platforms are emerging with standardization support from the W3C. This progress leads to the interface-agnostic aspect of ubiquitous computing, but the state of the art of multimodality has still not been transferred from researchers to end-users.

The vision of ubiquitous computing, in which any screen can be used to display personal information, requires privacy enforcement mechanisms, especially if public screens are expected to be shared as well for this matter. In the next

part, we will study how semantic technologies can help enforcing privacy in such systems.

Semantics for Privacy

The vision of ubiquitous computing in which personal information flows in a highly networked ecosystem requires privacy enforcement mechanisms, especially if public screens are expected to be shared for displaying such information as well as personal terminals. Although privacy is a very rich and specific research domain, in this part, we will study how semantic technologies can help to enforce privacy in ubiquitous systems by reviewing a few approaches that must be considered to enforce privacy in Social Ambient Intelligence systems.

According to (Damianou, Dulay, Lupu, & Sloman, 2001), the use of policies is an emerging technique for controlling and adjusting the low-level system behaviors by specifying high-level rules. Policies enforced using semantic rule

Figure 9. SPICE Multimedia Delivery and Control System (Kernchen et al. 2007), © 2007 Ralf Kernchen. Used with permission.

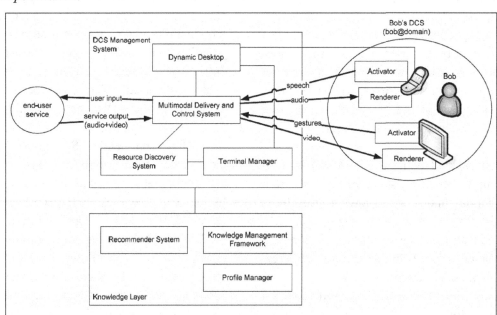

engines are implemented in most secure semantic context-aware platforms studied earlier in this chapter. In their review of semantic web languages for policy representation and reasoning, (Tonti et al., 2003) explain that "the use of policies allows administrators to modify system behavior without changing source code or requiring the consent or cooperation of the components being governed". **KAoS and Rei** are both semantic policy languages: KAoS is an OWL-based language and uses Java Theorem Prover to support reasoning whereas Rei uses Prolog and RDF-S. They also propose different enforcement mechanisms: KAoS requires the enforcers to be implemented and integrated in the system entities to control, whereas the Rei's actions are to be executed outside the Rei's engine.

(Shankar & Campbell, 2005) propose an extension to the ECA (Event-Condition-Action) rule framework, called Event-Condition-PreCondition-Action-PostCondition (**ECPAP**). In this framework, actions are annotated with axiomatic specifications that enable powerful reasoning to detect conflicts and cycles in policies.

(Brar & Kay, 2004) propose "secure persona exchange" (SPE), a framework based on W3C's Platform for Privacy Preferences (P3P) for secure anonymous/pseudonymous personal data exchange. This framework allows users to negotiate agreements with services that declare their privacy practices and request personal data. The P3P defines such a semantic service description format whereas privacy preferences are described using the APPEL language (A P3P Preference Exchange Language). SPE addresses the following identified end-user requirements: purpose specification, openness, simple and appropriate controls, limited data retention, pseudonymous interaction and decentralized control.

Trends and Issues

We have identified three semantic models that can be used to enforce privacy in ubiquitous systems: rule-based policies, ECA-based policies and secure exchange negotiation according to privacy preferences. Although the last one is the only one to address the issue of secure exchange of personal information, these approaches are complementary and promising to enforce privacy in Social Ambient Intelligence systems.

Semantics for the Social Communications and Activities

In the era of social networking and the participative web, of always-connected chat messengers and virtual worlds, people communicate and exchange more and more over the Internet. If computers are expected to disappear, the communication and exchange paradigms must be adapted to take the context of the users into account and to leverage the social knowledge held in web platforms in order to improve the awareness (and thus, intelligence) of Social Ambient Intelligence systems. One of the key points of such communications is user presence, because being online does not mean paying attention to any discussion at anytime. The second point that we will discuss covers user profiling techniques and the expression of the social graph. Finally, promising technologies for augmenting social activities with the Internet in an interoperable way will be discussed.

User Presence and Communication

The major context information in a synchronous communication network is presence, which is information on reachability, availability, and status across all communication channels (e.g., networks, applications, transports over Internet, wireless and wireline).

Two major presence exchange formats are considered here. The first one is **SIMPLE** (Session Initiation Protocol for Instant Messaging and Presence Leveraging Extensions), an extension of the SIP protocol recommended by the Open Mobile Alliance (OMA) that supports new features such as: voice, video, application sharing, and messaging. Leveraging the communication and security of the IMS (IP Multimedia Subsystem) platform, SIMPLE extends the user's presence to take into account the user's willingness, ability and desire to communicate across all different kinds of media types, devices, and places. Even though it is not a semantic language, the Dutch project Freeband Awareness (Bargh et al., 2005) chose the SIP/SIMPLE protocol for realizing a context-aware network infrastructure with the focus on secure and privacy-sensitive context exchange between a core network owner (e.g. a cell carrier) and external entities. In other projects, the use of SIP can be limited to exchanges that imply an interaction with the user: notifications, confirmations... In the SPICE project (M. Strohbach, E. Kovacs, & Goix, 2007), SIP is used to share presence information with the IMS platform and exchange data with the communicating user. On another hand, SPICE's Mobile Ontology includes a presence ontology based on **PIDF** (Presence Information Data Format) which allows definitions of the user's input, mood, contact relationship, place characteristics, current activity, and service. Transformation templates are provided to switch from the internal semantic representation in RDF into PIDF, and the other way round.

SIP has a wide range of possible uses but is not an optimal solution for all kinds of exchange. (Houri, 2007) criticized the weakness of SIP/SIMPLE in domain scaling. Furthermore it appears (Saint-Andre, 2005) that SIP/SIMPLE does not support advanced messaging mechanisms like workflow forms, multiple recipients, reliable delivery and publish-subscribe which are useful for context-aware systems. PIDF has shown to be suitable for the SPICE project.

Profiling and Social Graph

Considering the user's profile and social graph is important to personalize access to information and communication means. At a time when silo web-based social networking sites rapidly spread, many initiatives try to free our social data from these platforms using interoperable formats.

FOAF (Friend-of-a-Friend) (Brickley & Miller, 2007) is a RDF vocabulary based on an OWL ontology to describe people profiles, friends, affiliations, creations and other metadata related to people. FOAF's vision is a decentralized and extensible machine-readable social network based on personal profiles. The profile contains descriptions of personal user data, possibly his/her work history, and links to his/her contacts and affiliated services. Each person has a unique identifier, usually a hash of the email address. The community of FOAF users being principally made of researchers and semantic web enthusiasts, it does not compete with popular social networks like LinkedIn [http://www.linkedin.com], Myspace [http://www.myspace.com] or Facebook [http://www.facebook.com]. Many tools have appeared, including FOAFexplorer [http://xml.mfd-consult.dk/foaf/explorer/] which can be used to visualize FOAF profiles. However, there is a potential privacy issue with this language because selective privacy-aware views of a FOAF file are not addressed. It may be interesting to evaluate a mechanism similar to the conditional profiles proposed in the SPICE project or to enforce selective distribution of content using a policy-based system.

SIOC (Semantically-Interlinked Online Communities, http://sioc-project.org) represented on Figure 10 is an ontology-based framework aimed at interconnecting online community sites and internet-based discussions. The idea is to enable cross-platform interoperability so that conversation spanning over multiple online media (e.g. blogs, forums, mailing lists) can be unified into one open format. The interchange format expresses the information contained both explicitly and implicitly in internet discussion methods, in a machine-readable manner. A similar approach is proposed by the OPSN (Open Portable Social Network, http://www.opsn.net/) initiative which also covers notification and synchronization of contacts across platforms. However there is no existing implementation, and privacy control for personal published information seems not to have been addressed yet. DISO (distributed social networking, http://diso-project.org/), is yet another collaborative work to follow.

These initiatives would be a promising way to leverage consistent social relations, discussions and exchanges from various web platforms in order to build a more precise profile of user's interests, like with the **APML** language (Attention Profiling Mark-up Language, http://www.apml.org/), and qualify the types of relations in order to improve the social communication experience.

Social Interactivity

Social networking sites (SNSs) have become very popular communication platforms on the Internet, enabling new ways for people to interact with each other. Although the proposed interactions are similar on most SNSs, each of these sites were developed as silos, and thus their social graph (i.e. the list of "friends") and applications are not portable. We believe that consolidating SNS-based interactions is a key towards our vision of Social Ambient Intelligence, and that semantic technologies can help to solve this interoperability issue.

With its open application platform, the social networking site **Facebook** became a huge Internet player in a few months, attracting many service providers and increasing their population of users significantly. Indeed, Facebook made it easy for application developers to leverage the user's profile and social graph of the underlying platform, and thus bring user-friendly services with a social dimension. For example, as shown on Figure 11, the "Movies" application allows the user to rate movies so that his/her favorite movies are shown

Figure 10. Overview of SIOC: Semantically-Interlinked Online Communities [http://sioc-project.org]. © *2006 John Breslin. Used with permission.*

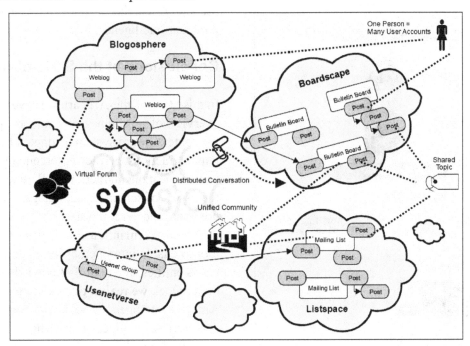

on his profile page. But the most interesting aspect of this application is the possibility for friends to compare their movie tastes to evaluate their compatibility.

Because there are many existing social networking sites on the Internet that are adopting the application platform approach à la Facebook, Google initiated the **OpenSocial** project, an interoperable framework to build applications on any compliant social networking site. However this framework implements basic contact management actions only and don't have access to all the information and capabilities of all social networking sites. For example, some of them are capable of exchanging "pokes", "gifts" and comments, but there is no interoperable way of invoking these capabilities from OpenSocial so far. This could be the opportunity to develop an

ontology of social interaction which could be enriched by the platforms and gradually supported by applications without preventing them to work in degraded mode (e.g. by sending a comment instead of a gift, if this capability is not supported by the platform).

Trends and Issues

Despite the exponential popularity and value of Social Networking Websites (SNSs) on the Internet, the possible links between ubiquitous context-aware platforms and existing "Web 2.0" platforms (O'Reilly, 2005) have been neglected by academia, while Internet players are working together to build controlled interoperability. Although extraction of consistent knowledge from the Web 2.0 is not trivial (Gruber, 2006), there is a huge value in social networks sites (and user-generated content) that should be leveraged to extend the awareness of Social Ambient Intelligence systems, as we will explain in the next section. We believe that proposing a common SNS interaction ontology in current collaborative efforts such as the OpenSocial project is a good track for researchers towards our vision of Social Ambient Intelligence.

Conclusions of the State-of-the-Art

In this State-of-the-Art part, we have depicted an overview of several past and current approaches for context-aware systems, adapted human-system interactions, privacy enforcement and social communications and activities. We have identified the assets of semantic technologies in all these domains, and several issues.

Whereas semantic technologies are a powerful tool to enable interoperability among heterogeneous entities, and to unify knowledge in a common model, we realise that existing research on Ambient Intelligence does not leverage the value of collective intelligence which has emerged with the Web 2.0 and its Social Networking Sites. In

Figure 11. The "Movies" application on Facebook,© 2008 Flixster, Facebook. Used with permission.

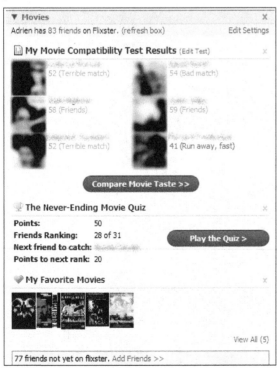

the next part of this chapter, we will respond to this paradox by defining our vision of "Social Ambient Intelligence" and proposing several research leads towards this vision.

REALIZING SOCIAL AMBIENT INTELLIGENCE

In this part, we define our vision of "Social Ambient Intelligence" and propose several research leads towards this vision, based on our previous study.

What is Social Ambient Intelligence?

As explained in the Background part of this chapter, the vision of "Ambient Intelligence" consists in leveraging new technologies and techniques (including context-awareness) to design applications that are user-centric, and thus more adapted to the user, his knowledge and his current environment/situation. As the Web 2.0 gave birth to the concept of Collective Intelligence, which consists in generating knowledge from user contributions and interactions on the Internet, it sounds like leveraging this knowledge would be extremely valuable to increase the awareness of "Ambient Intelligence" systems. Assuming that, for instance, recommendations coming from friends are necessarily given more confidence than recommendations coming from predictive statistics, adding a social dimension to "Ambient Intelligence" would result in more relevant results for users, and thus a better user-centricity, which was the rationale of "Ambient Intelligence".

Based on this analysis, we propose "Social Ambient Intelligence" (SocAmI) as an extension of "Ambient Intelligence" (AmI) that adds a social dimension in order to increase awareness, knowledge and intelligence of such systems. This social dimension would benefit from the "collective intelligence" of Web 2.0 platforms (such as Social Networking Sites), and therefore it will

bring more relevance and confidence to users. The addition of this dimension also gives the opportunity to augment the user communication experience with new kinds of social interactions inspired by Social Networking Sites, without having to sit behind a computer.

As semantic technologies have been shown as an excellent framework to model, integrate and exchange formalized knowledge in a unified manner among heterogeneous agents/entities that constitute Ambient Intelligence systems, we believe in their capability to integrate the social knowledge gathered from the Collective Intelligence of the Web users.

In the following paragraphs, we will discuss the issues and challenges implied by the realization of Social Ambient Intelligence.

Converging with the Social Web

It is time for the social web, context awareness, and multimodal interfaces to converge into a Social Ambient Intelligence platform that enforces users' privacy. We believe that semantic technologies are the best enablers for interoperability, extensibility and intelligent exploitation of user, hardware and social web knowledge, in order to improve interactions between users and information. However, leveraging web knowledge in a semantic ubiquitous system may not be a trivial task according to (Strassner et al., 2007) who claimed that: in order for ontologies to be adopted by a system, this system should have a sufficient amount of semantic knowledge and minimal legacy information to carry. Indeed, the Semantic Web still being an unachieved vision (Berners-Lee, Hendler, & O. Lassila, 2001; Cardoso, 2007), most websites don't rely on semantic technologies to maintain their data. We have presented several initiatives that intend to create interoperable standards based on semantic technologies for universal use of user-generated content and communications kept in separate web platforms. Academics should get involved in this process, in order to take into account the requirements of Social Ambient Intelligence platforms that will leverage these standards. In the mean time, web platforms APIs (Application Programming Interface) can be used to build gateways between specific web social platforms and ubiquitous systems. For example, user feeds (e.g. Facebook's mini-feed, twitter, del.icio.us) could be analyzed as an additional source of context knowledge in the aim of identifying user activities and profile. On the other hand, ubiquitous systems could also be used to push content to these platforms, e.g. automatic presence information inferred from the context.

Bringing Ubiquitous Systems to People

Another issue that we want to address here by adding a Social dimension to Ambient Intelligence is the lack of integration and public visibility of research works related to Ambient Intelligence. The growing ubiquity of networks (infrastructures and ad-hoc), screens and mobile devices brings more exciting opportunities for people to communicate and exchange content but we lack interoperability standards, preventing people from experimenting state-of-the-art research results. In the meantime, innovative ubiquitous products appear on the market, such as electronic photo frames, widget displays, toys that can give weather reports and read emails, and powerful domestic management systems but they all work on their own because we lack common standards and platforms. One promising way of making people progressively adopt ubiquitous systems is to advertise them as applications on popular social platforms (e.g. Facebook), inviting users to deploy required software on their terminal to benefit from exciting new services that could possibly leverage users' context and social graph. Some people may be reluctant to use such systems

at first, but we believe that there are solutions to make them accept them.

Gain Trust from Potential Users

Potential users of ubiquitous context-aware systems can be reluctant for the following reasons:

1. Privacy

Users will be concerned with the idea of provisioning private contextual knowledge (such as user positioning) to a "black-box" system which they may not trust, because they are afraid of loosing control of this information (Abowd & Mynatt, 2000), of being tracked or even spied (Bohn, Coroama, Langheinrich, Mattern, & Rohs, 2004). Moreover, most Internet users are already concerned with spam, and many already complain about profiling operated by web sites to improve the relevance of advertising; therefore sharing contextual knowledge can be seen as a major threat for privacy and control of personal information. We believe that advertising should be taken into account as the fair counterpart of a service, but it must be moderated by the system. E.g. a music recommendation service that advertises live performances and merchandising of one's favorite artists seems like an fair service that benefits both the user and the service provider, if the user is fond of music. Nevertheless, the user must constantly be in control of his private information, and confidentiality/security of exchanges must be enforced using mechanisms such as pseudonymity or cryptology. The transparency of the ubiquitous system's implementation and knowledge base can be a major source of trust for users, like it has been with open source software.

2. Intrusion

The subscription to many services that have access to extensive knowledge about users (e.g. their interests, their social network) and also privacy policy management can lead to digital pollution. Users could receive hundreds of recommendations, being asked hundreds of questions about their current situations and confirmations for proposed relevant actions to undertake. Research must be carried out to moderate explicit user interaction (i.e. requests and notifications) without compromising intended communications, user awareness and control. A promising approach for semi-autonomous control of user private data is the use of policies. However, as (O. Lassila, 2005) pointed out, we need a rich representation of policies so that users can define and visualize their privacy rules in a clear and easy way, and delegate their enforcement to the system.

In this section, we have sketched our vision of Social Ambient Intelligence. Main issues consist of the convergence of Ambient Intelligence with the Social web, the involvement of end-users with current research works, the definition of common standards, and the trust to be gained from users (regarding privacy and intrusion).

CONCLUSION

In this chapter, we have reviewed several uses of semantic technologies for context management, adaptive human-system interaction, privacy enforcement and social communications in the scope of Ambient Intelligence. Based on identified benefits and lacks, we defined our vision of "Social Ambient Intelligence" and proposed several research leads towards the realization of this vision based on the convergence of Ambient Intelligence, Collective Intelligence of the Social Web and Semantic Technologies. Through our involvement in several ongoing European, national and internal research projects, we will strive to focus our research on these points and to convey our position and trends to our collaborators.

ACKNOWLEDGMENT

The authors would like to thank Laure Pavlovic for her kind support to improve the quality of this chapter. We would also like to thank the authors of the figures included in this chapter for granting us permission to include them.

REFERENCES

Abowd, G., & Mynatt, E. (2000). Charting Past, Present, and Future Research in Ubiquitous Computing. *ACM Transactions on Computer-Human Interaction, 7*(1), 29-58.

Ayars, J., Bulterman, D., Cohen, A., Day, K., Hodge, E., Hoschka, P., et al. (2000). Synchronized multimedia integration language (smil) 2.0 specification, *Work in progress. W3C Working Drafts are available at http://www. w3. org/TR*, 21.

Baldauf, M., Dustdar, S., & Rosenberg, F. (2007). A survey on context-aware systems, *International Journal of Ad Hoc and Ubiquitous Computing, 2*(4), 263-277.

Bargh, M., Benz, H., Brok, J., Heijenk, G., Groot, S. H. D., Peddemors, A., et al. (2005, January 10). J. In Brok (Ed.), *Initial architecture for awareness network layer Retrieved from http://awareness. freeband.nl.*

Berners-Lee, T., Hendler, J., & Lassila, O. (2001). The semantic Web. *Scientific American, 284*(5), 28-37.

Bohn, J., Coroama, V., Langheinrich, M., Mattern, F., & Rohs, M. (2004). Social, Economic, and Ethical Implications of Ambient Intelligence and Ubiquitous Computing. *Ambient Intelligence. Springer-Verlag.*

Brar, A., & Kay, J. (2004). *Privacy and security in ubiquitous personalized applications.*

Brickley, D., & Miller, L. (2007, November 2). Foaf vocabulary specification, *Namespace Document*. Retrieved from http://xmlns.com/foaf/spec/.

Cardoso, J. (2007). The semantic web vision: where are we? *Intelligent Systems, 22*(5), 84-88.

Chen, H., Finin, T., Joshi, A., Kagal, L., Perich, F., & Chakraborty, D. (2004). Intelligent agents meet the semantic web in smart spaces. *IEEE Internet Computing, 8*(6), 69-79.

Chen, H., Perich, F., Finin, T., & Joshi, A. (2004). Soupa: standard ontology for ubiquitous and pervasive applications, *Mobile and Ubiquitous Systems: Networking and Services, 2004. MOBIQUITOUS 2004. The First Annual International Conference on*, (pp. 258-267).

Christopoulou, E. (2008). Context as a Necessity in Mobile Applications. *Handbook of Research on User Interface Design and Evaluation for Mobile Technology*.

Damianou, N., Dulay, N., Lupu, E., & Sloman, M. (2001). The ponder policy specification language. *Policies for Distributed Systems and Networks: International Workshop, Policy 2001,* Bristol, Uk, January 29-31, 2001: Proceedings.

Dean, M., & Schreiber, G. (2004). Owl web ontology language reference. *W3C Recommendation*.

Decker, S., Erdmann, M., Fensel, D., & Studer, R. (1999). Ontobroker: ontology based access to distributed and semi-structured information. *Database Semantics: Semantic Issues in Multimedia Systems*, (pp. 351–369).

Dey, A. K. (2001). Understanding and using context. *Personal and Ubiquitous Computing, 5*(1), 4-7.

Ducatel, K., Bogdanowicz, M., Scapolo, F., Leijten, J., & Burgelma, J. C. (2001). *Scenarios for ambient intelligence in 2010 (ISTAG 2001 Final Report)*.

Ejigu, D., Scuturici, V., & Brunie, L. (2007). Semantic approach to context management and reasoning in ubiquitous context-aware systems In *The Second IEEE International Conference on Digital Information Management (ICDIM 2007), Proceedings of ICDIM'07*. (pp. 500-5005). Retrieved from http://liris.cnrs.fr/publis/?id=3242.

FIPA. (2002, December 6). *Fipa device ontology specification*.

Gruber, T. R. (1993). A translation approach to portable ontology specifications. *Knowledge Acquisition, 5*(2), 199-220.

Gruber, T. (2006). Where the social web meets the semantic web. *Lecture Notes in Computer Science, 4273*(994).

Gu, T., Pung, H. K., & Zhang, D. Q. (2004). A bayesian approach for dealing with uncertain contexts, *Proceedings of the Second International Conference on Pervasive Computing*.

Gu, T., Wang, X. H., Pung, H. K., & Zhang, D. Q. (2004). An ontology-based context model in intelligent environments, *Proceedings of Communication Networks and Distributed Systems Modeling and Simulation Conference*, 2004.

Häkkilä, J., & Mäntyjärvi, J. (2005). Combining Location-Aware Mobile Phone Applications and Multimedia Messaging. *Journal of Mobile Multimedia, 1*(1), 18-32.

Horrocks, I. (2002). Daml+oil: a description logic for the semantic web. *IEEE Data Engineering Bulletin, 25*(1), 4-9.

Houri, A. (2007, October 29). Draft-ietf-simple-interdomain-scaling-analysis-02 - presence interdomain scaling analysis for sip/simple, *Presence Interdomain Scaling Analysis for SIP/SIMPLE*. Retrieved November 13, 2007, from http://tools.ietf.org/html/draft-ietf-simple-interdomain-scaling-analysis-02.

Kagal, L. F., & Joshi, T. A. (2003). A policy language for a pervasive computing environment, *Policies for Distributed Systems and Networks, 2003. Proceedings. POLICY 2003. IEEE 4th International Workshop on*, 63-74.

Kernchen, R., Boussard, M., Hesselman, C., Villalonga, C., Clavier, E., Zhdanova, A. V., et al. (2007). Managing personal communication environments in next generation service platforms, *Mobile and Wireless Communications Summit, 2007. 16th IST*, 1-5.

Kernchen, R., Boussard, M., Moessner, K., & Mrohs, B. (2006). Device description for mobile multimodal interfaces In Mykonos, Greece.

Klyne, G., Reynolds, F., Woodrow, C., Ohto, H., Hjelm, J., Butler, M. H., et al. (2004). *Composite capability/preference profiles (cc/pp): structure and vocabularies 1.0. w3c recommendation, w3c, january 2004.*

Korpipää, P., Häkkilä, J., Kela, J., Ronkainen, S., & Känsälä, I. (2004). Utilising context ontology in mobile device application personalisation. *Proceedings of the 3rd international conference on Mobile and ubiquitous multimedia*, (pp. 133-140).

Lassila, O., & Khushraj, D. (2005). Contextualizing applications via semantic middleware In , *Mobile and Ubiquitous Systems: Networking and Services, 2005* (pp. 183-189).

Lassila, O. (2005, August). *Using the semantic web in mobile and ubiquitous computing.* Jyväskylä (Finland).

Leong, L. H., Kobayashi, S., Koshizuka, N., & Sakamura, K. (2005). CASIS: a context-aware speech interface system. *Proceedings of the 10th international conference on Intelligent user interfaces*, (pp. 231-238).

Lin, X., Li, S., Yang, Z., & Shi, W. (2005). Application-oriented context modeling and reasoning in pervasive computing, *Proceedings of the The*

Fifth International Conference on Computer and Information Technology, (pp. 495-501).

Manchón, P., del Solar, C., de Amores, G., & Pérez, G. (2006). The mimus corpus In (pp. 56-59). Genoa, Italy.

Oberle, D., Ankolekar, A., Hitzler, P., Cimiano, P., Sintek, M., Kiesel, M., et al. (2006). Dolce ergo sumo: on foundational and domain models in swinto (smartweb integrated ontology), *Submission to Journal of Web Semantics (2006).*

O'Reilly, T. (2005). What is web 2.0: design patterns and business models for the next generation of software, *O'Reilly.* Retrieved from http://www.oreillynet.com/pub/a/oreilly/tim/news/2005/09/30/what-is-web-20.html.

Orwant, L. (1995). Heterogeneous learning in the doppelganger user modelling system. *User Modelling and User Adapted Interaction, 4*(2), 107-130.

Perich, F., Avancha, S., Chakraborty, D., Joshi, A., & Yesha, Y. (2005). *Profile driven data management for pervasive environments.* Springer.

Ranganathan, A., Al-Muhtadi, J., & Campbell, R. H. (2004). Reasoning about uncertain contexts in pervasive computing environments. *Pervasive Computing, IEEE, 3*(2), 62-70.

Reithinger, N., & Sonntag, D. (2005). An integration framework for a mobile multimodal dialogue system accessing the semantic web, *Ninth European Conference on Speech Communication and Technology.*

Sadi, S. H., & Maes, P. (2005). *xLink: Context Management Solution for Commodity Ubiquitous Computing Environments.* In Tokyo, Japan.

Saint-Andre, P. (2005, December 8). Xmpp-simple feature comparison, *XMPP-SIMPLE Feature Comparison.* Retrieved November 13, 2007, from http://www.jabber.org/protocol/xmpp-simple.shtml.

Schilit, B. N., Adams, N., & Want, R. (1994). *Context-Aware Computing Applications*. Santa Cruz, CA, USA.

Shankar, C., & Campbell, R. (2005). A policy-based management framework for pervasive systems using axiomatized rule-actions. *Network Computing and Applications, Fourth IEEE International Symposium on*, (pp. 255-258).

SPICE. (2006). *Spice d4.1: ontology definition of user profiles, knowledge information and services*. Retrieved February 13, 2008, from http://www.ist-spice.org/documents/D4.1-final.pdf.

SPICE. (2007). *Spice unified architecture*. Retrieved from http://www.ist-spice.org/documents/SPICE_WP1_unified_architecture_Phase%202.pdf.

Strang, T., & Linnhoff-Popien, C. (2004). A context modeling survey. *Workshop on Advanced Context Modelling, Reasoning and Management, UbiComp*, (pp. 34-41).

Strang, T., Linnhoff-Popien, C., & Frank, K. (2003). Cool: a context ontology language to enable contextual interoperability, *Distributed Applications and Interoperable Systems: 4th Ifip Wg6. 1 International Conference, Dais 2003, Paris, France, November 17-21, 2003, Proceedings*.

Strassner, J., O'Sullivan, D., & Lewis, D. (2007). Ontologies in the engineering of management and autonomic systems: a reality check. *Journal of Network and Systems Management, 15*(1), 5-11.

Streitz, N., & Nixon, P. (2005). The disappearing computer. *Communications of the ACM, 48*(3), 32-35.

Strohbach, M., Kovacs, E., & Goix, L. W. (2007). Integrating ims presence information in a service oriented architecture.

Strohbach, M., Bauer, M., Kovacs, E., Villalonga, C., & Richter, N. (2007). *Context sessions: a novel approach for scalable context management in ngn networks*. Newport Beach, California, USA.

Tan, J. G., Zhang, D., Wang, X., & Cheng, H. S. (2005). Enhancing semantic spaces with event-driven context interpretation, *Pervasive Computing: Third International Conference, Pervasive 2005, Munich, Germany, May 8-13, 2005, Proceedings*.

Tonti, G., Bradshaw, J. M., Jeffers, R., Montanari, R., Suri, N., & Uszok, A. (2003). Semantic web languages for policy representation and reasoning: a comparison of kaos, rei, and ponder. *The Semantic Web—ISWC*, (pp. 419-437).

Truong, B. A., Lee, Y., & Lee, S. Y. (2005). A unified context model: bringing probabilistic models to context ontology. *Lecture notes in computer science*, (pp. 566-575).

UPnP Forum. (2003, December 2). *Upnp device architecture 1.0*. Retrieved from http://www.upnp.org/.

W3C. (2003). W3c multimodal interaction framework. *W3C Note*. Retrieved from http://www.w3.org/TR/mmi-framework/.

W3C. (2007). Emma: extensible multimodal annotation markup language. *W3C Working Draft 14 December 2004*. Retrieved from http://www.w3.org/TR/emma/.

Wang, X., Zhang, D., Gu, T., & Pung, H. (2004). Ontology based context modeling and reasoning using owl. In *Pervasive Computing and Communications Workshops, 2004. Proceedings of the Second IEEE Annual Conference on* (pp. 18-22).

WAP Forum. (2001, October 20). Wag uaprof. Retrieved from http://www.openmobilealliance.org/tech/affiliates/wap/wap-248-uaprof-20011020-a.pdf.

Waldner, J. B. (2007). *Nano-informatique et intelligence ambiante: inventer l'ordinateur du XXIe siècle*. Lavoisier.

Weiser, M. (1991). The computer for the 21st century. *Scientific American, 265*(3).

Chapter XV
An Evaluation of Context–Aware Infomobility Systems

Federica Paganelli
National Inter-University Consortium for Telecommunications, Italy

Dino Giuli
National Inter-University Consortium for Telecommunications, Italy

ABSTRACT

The delivery of real-time, context-aware, and personalized information to end-users for mobility support is a high-priority objective in improving mobility services efficiency and effectiveness. This chapter aims at providing an analysis of existing studies in the field of context awareness research targeted to the infomobility application domain. The authors propose an evaluation framework for infomobility services based on the elicitation of context information items and high-level requirements. The framework is applied to some relevant state-of-the art research works among personal navigation systems, infomobility service integration frameworks and context-aware location-based communication platforms. Evaluation results are discussed in order to highlight open research challenges in the infomobility application domain.

INTRODUCTION

The mobility of people and goods and the efficiency of transport systems are calling for requirements which are more and more critical in our society in terms of social, economical and individual issues. Traffic congestion and related environment problems represent serious threats to citizens' quality of life and economic development. According to a study for the European Commission, it is estimated that congestion costs will represent 1% of the gross domestic product of the European Union in 2010 (European Commission, 2001).

In order to face these problems, national and local governments are promoting several efforts to make mobility more efficient and sustainable. Sustainable mobility relies on the capabilities of optimizing each transport mode with respect to safety, environmental friendliness and energy efficiency.

Obviously, proper actions for transport services and infrastructure enhancement are needed in order to improve the efficiency and effectiveness of mobility services. Nonetheless, providing valuable on-time information services to end-users can strongly contribute to more efficient mobility. Thus, the delivery of real-time and personalized information services to end users for mobility support (i.e. "infomobility services") is a high-priority objective. At present most commercially available infomobility services are conceived as static information delivery. They are usually targeted to drivers and rarely to pedestrians and often focus on a single transportation mode (e.g. either private, pedestrian or public transport) (Rehrl et al., 2007). As a consequence, the burden of managing different transportation modes when planning travel and modifying travel plans according to up-to-date information about traffic events (e.g. accidents and congestion, parking places availability, delays in public transportation) is mainly placed on end-users.

Infomobility services typically include a wide range of services: navigation, route planning and re-planning, geo-referenced content delivery (e.g. Points of Interest descriptions, localization of nearest shops, railway and bus stations, parking facilities, etc.), alerts about critical events (incidents, congestion, public transport delays, etc.), payment services and facilities booking (e.g. parking and seat reservation). Infomobility services for mobility of persons can also be named as Traveler Information Services (U. S. Department of Transportation, 1998).

Research on context-awareness can provide significant progress in the infomobility application domain with respect to the systems and applications state of the art. As a matter of fact, information delivery for user mobility support (infomobility) is a domain that is especially challenging for research activities in the field of context awareness. This is due to several reasons, but mainly because application focus is on user location, which is a first-level context attribute. Not surprisingly, initial research studies on context awareness have focused on location-aware applications, such as the Active Badge Location System (Want et al., 1992) and location-aware tour guides (Abowd et al., 1997; Cheverst et al., 2000). In the infomobility domain, location strongly influences user information and service requirements, as well as other contextual attributes (especially those related to the environment surrounding the user). User requirements for infomobility services' content and delivery channel adaptation may be influenced by context events, such as incidents, traffic congestion and public transport delays that may require assisting users with appropriate navigation services and re-planning trip schedules.

A relevant challenge is also determined by the fact that in this application domain, context knowledge should include a large amount and a variety of information (ex. user location, current transport mode, traffic and public transport events, weather conditions, etc.) to be appropriately acquired and managed in order to provide users with up-to-date, reliable and complete information for navigation and mobility assistance.

Aim of the Chapter

Our objective is to investigate how research on context-aware and mobile communication and computing might provide significant progress in the infomobility domain, with special focus on persons' mobility.

This chapter aims at providing an analysis of existing research studies and trends in the field of context awareness research targeted to the infomobility application domain. Several surveys and state-of-the-art analyses exist in the field of context-aware mobile computing and applications

(Baldauf et al., 2007; Bernard, 2006; Saha & Mukherjee, 2003; Anagnostopoulos et al., 2007; Henricksen et al., 2005). Some studies have also focused on the delivery of location-based services (D'Roza & Bilchev, 2003; Dao et al., 2002; Barnes, 2006). We argue that a special analysis should be devoted to the infomobility application domain, due to its own specific features and requirements which distinguish it from the wider "location-based services" application domain.

This paper is organized as follows: Section II clarifies what we mean with the term "context-awareness" in the infomobility domain. In Section III we discuss main high-level requirements in designing information services for more efficient mobility. The result of this analysis is a set of criteria used for evaluating some state of the art studies in Section IV and V. Section VI briefly presents related studies which have not been selected for evaluation but have provided relevant results. Section VII concludes the paper by highlighting open research issues for infomobility service design and motivating our future research activities.

CONTEXT AWARENESS FOR INFOMOBILITY

Context awareness is a concept which can be applied to several application domains (e.g. smart homes, e-health, emergency management) with the objective of designing applications which should be responsive to specific contexts and situations, helping end users in their activities and improving their quality of life. A definition that has been widely accepted in the international research community is the one provided by Abowd et al. (1999): *"Context is any information that can be used to characterize the situation of an entity. An entity is a person, place, or object that is considered relevant to the interaction between a user and an application, including the user and applications themselves."*

According to this definition, a designer can define what context is according to the target application domain requirements. As a general approach, context information should describe the "who", "what", "why", "where" and "when" attributes influencing the interaction between a user and the application.

Based on the five coordinates "who", "what", "why", "where" and "when" we try to define basic context items for context-aware infomobility services (see Figure 1).

Who? This may consist of all the information concerning the user with respect to mobility, for instance his/her preference for public or private transport means or walking, and his/her habits (e.g. going to work at the same time every day). It may also include the fact that the user is travelling alone or in a group. The value of these context items could be exploited to adapt system decisions for proposing transport means and itineraries optimized according to time, costs and other user-dependent parameters.

What? This dimension may refer to "what the user is doing" and "what mobility and transport services are available". Some examples of user activity and mobility status are: planning and/or re-planning his/her route; driving his/her own vehicle; being a passenger of public transport; walking in transfer sites; in-door visiting or staying at a specific place; controlled-gate access (highway, parking areas, tunnels, local buses, etc.). Knowledge of this kind of information should be properly exploited in order to minimize the required level of user attention with respect to what the user is doing (e.g. driving a vehicle) by choosing the appropriate interaction channel (e.g. text-based or voice based interface).

Information about available mobility and transport services may include planned mobility and transport services information (road networks, public transport itineraries), as well as unexpected events related to mobility and transport services (e.g., road incidents, traffic congestions, etc.), which may influence user mobility and planned services. Infomobility services should adapt to such information by accordingly planning and/or re-planning user itineraries in order to offer up-to-date and reliable information and assistance.

Why? The purpose of the user's journey can be exploited in order to appropriately adapt content delivery. For instance, users moving for holiday might appreciate a proactive delivery of the Points of Interests' description, while users moving for work might be more interested in information such as available network connectivity and facilities in transit places (e.g. meeting and conference rooms in airports and railway stations).

The Where and When dimensions of context information are extremely important for providing effective infomobility services. Firstly, infomobility services should provide up-to-date location-based content. Secondly, also context

items pertaining to the above-mentioned categories (who, what and why) may be enriched with geographical and time references. For instance, geographical and time references may be needed to properly exploit and correlate information about mobility and transport services (what?) and to adapt services according to user location at a certain instant of time (who?).

Where? A "location" context item may refer to user current location, as well as to intermediate locations in the user itinerary. Moreover, as mentioned above, other context items may also be associated to location information (i.e. geo-referentiation). Location may be represented in terms of physical or logical information. Physical location is represented in terms of geographical coordinates according to standard reference systems; logical location is usually represented in

Figure 1. Context Items for infomobility services

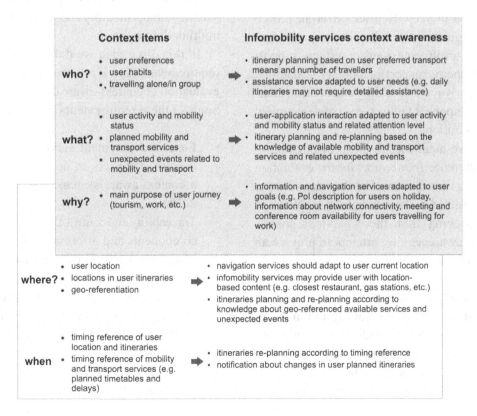

terms of symbolic information, such as "at home" or "at work" (Hightower & Borriello, 2001).

When? A timing reference can be used to characterize user current location and consequently to determine the progress with respect to a planned itinerary. Timing information can also be associated to a planned, monitored or estimated timetable of public transport vehicles and road network events.

REQUIREMENTS FOR CONTEXT-AWARE INFOMOBILITY SERVICES

Several reviews on general-purpose context-aware computing exist (Baldauf et al., 2007; Henricksen et al., 2005, Chen & Kotz, 2000; Strang & Linnhoff–Popien, 2004). The evaluation methodology proposed by Baldauf et al. (2007) is based on a conceptually layered framework that includes the following functions: architecture, sensing, context model, context processing, resource discovery, historical context data, security and privacy. Henricksen et al. (2005) have distinguished the following requirements for middleware in context-aware systems: support for heterogeneity, support for mobility, scalability, support of privacy, traceability and control, tolerance for component failures, ease of deployment and configuration.

The above-mentioned studies provide comprehensive reference frameworks for the evaluation of context-aware systems, but they are not specifically targeted to the infomobility application domain. Moving from these previous studies on context-awareness, we attempt to provide an evaluation framework targeted to the infomobility domain. In the following we describe a set of requirements that should be satisfied in planning and deploying context-aware infomobility services for tourists. The analysis is based on our previous work (Paganelli et al., 2006; Paganelli et al., 2007) and on some available studies, such as the analysis of end user needs concerning infomobility (Infopolis2 Project, 1999), expert evaluations of technological challenges (Safety Forum – Working Group RTD, 2006), as well as the above-mentioned reviews on context-aware systems.

We have elicited a set of seven requirements. Five requirements are general and could be applied to evaluate also other kinds of context-aware distributed systems: seamless service continuity, compliance with standards for interoperability and dynamic integration of information sources, personalization and user interaction adaptation, information reliability, security and privacy. Hereafter these requirements are discussed with the aim of highlighting issues specifically related to the infomobility application domain, and thus eliciting attributes which are used in evaluating state-of-the-art infomobility projects in the following sections.

We also considered two requirements that are more specific to the infomobility application domain, as they are related to managing mobility and transport information: awareness of real-time situations about mobility and support for transport multimodality.

In this discussion we did not consider other requirements, even if relevant for the design and evaluation of context-aware distributed systems. Some of these requirements are, for example:

- Ease of deployment and configuration: the easiness for users to deploy and configure a context-aware system (Henricksen et al., 2005).
- Traceability and control: the state of the system components and information flows between components should be traceable in order to provide adequate understanding and control of the system, in order to enable mechanisms for estimating the occurrence of possible system malfunctioning and/or management of system faults.
- Scalability: the system should continue to function well as it is changed in size, for

instance if the number of users increases or new mobility-related information sources (i.e. sensors, weather services, mobility servers, etc.) are used in the system.

- Dependability: a property of a computer system such that reliance can justifiably be placed on the service it delivers (Randell, 1998). Such a requirement is especially challenging for pervasive and context-aware systems, as they should dynamically adapt to changing situations, inferred on the basis of information acquired from heterogeneous distributed sources.

Such requirements have not been taken into account in this evaluation as they can be discussed in terms of architectural patterns and technological implementation details, but they do not represent specific issues of the infomobility domain.

Seamless Service Continuity

End user's access to infomobility services should be "always-on". This requirement is relevant for several application domains, but it is especially challenging for the infomobility application domain. As a matter of fact, while the user is moving, service access may be compromised, mainly due to possible changes in the communication infrastructure. End user mobility within short (e.g. urban environment) as well as long distances (e.g. driving on the highways) may strongly influence user capability in accessing infomobility services. Changeable factors that can compromise such capability may include: user device features (e.g. PC, PDA, vehicle on-board device), different access networks (e.g. Wi-Fi, WiMax, cellular networks, etc.) and heterogeneous network operators, as well as related network characteristics such as billing and available bandwidth. Providing seamless always-on access to information requires proper mechanisms to mask these discontinuities.

An extended analysis of communication requirements of the Intelligent Transport System (ITS) is provided in (Fiedler et al., 2005). In this study, ITS services are classified in five categories (i.e. public streaming service, individual messaging service, backwards streaming service, selective streaming service, personal interactive service), and their communication needs in terms of availability, performance, security and cost are represented in a format which is suitable to be matched with network parameters.

In the field of ubiquitous communication these research challenges are specifically addressed with the term "Seamless mobility". Seamless mobility can be intended as uninterrupted service access, independently from available networks and user devices, thus enabling the users to move across different access networks and change computing devices. As specified by the International Telecommunication Union (2006), seamless mobility can include:

- **Terminal mobility**: the ability of a terminal to change location and still be able to communicate.
- **Personal mobility**: the ability of a user to maintain the same user identity irrespective of the terminal used and its network point of attachment.
- **Service mobility**: the ability of a user to use the particular service irrespective of the location of the user and the terminal that is used for that purpose.

All-IP communication platforms are now seen as potential candidates for providing seamless mobility. An approach based on Mobile IP for handling terminal mobility at the IP layer is described in (Morand & Tessier, 2002). SIP is an application-layer protocol that inherently supports personal mobility and can be extended to support service and terminal mobility (Schulzrinne &

Wedlund, 2000). Multilayered approaches are also being discussed in (Wang & Abu-Rgheff, 2003; Zeadally et al., 2004).

One further aspect, which can be included in the "seamless continuity" requirement, is the capability of an infomobility system to provide assistance both in the pre-trip and on-trip phases and in different mobility statuses (e.g. walking, driving a private vehicle, being passenger in public transport means). The concept of seamlessness may also include the system's capability to continuously support user needs by providing both push- and pull-based information delivery. The proper delivery modality should be chosen according to different parameters, such user preferences, interests and current activity (e.g. "visiting a cultural heritage site" or "driving a vehicle") as well as technological requirements.

Awareness of Real-Time Situations about Mobility

Infomobility services should be managed and delivered by exploiting awareness of real-time situations about mobility in order to provide users with complete and updated information. Such awareness should include both static (e.g. cartographic data, public transport scheduled routes) and dynamic information (e.g. traffic status, public transport real-time schedules, weather forecasts). This information might be exploited in order to adapt infomobility services' content (e.g., for dynamic route re-planning), delivery paradigms and channels (e.g. push/pull, audio/text) to changing mobility conditions and traffic events. Context data sources needed to acquire information about mobility situations usually include heterogeneous sensors and monitoring applications. Moreover, different context data providers, such as traffic monitoring centers, public transport operators and municipalities may be required to interoperate. Nowadays the capability of organizing and exploiting user-generated content is being experimented (Holone et al., 2007). This approach

based on user communities can potentially enrich awareness of mobility situations, but is likely to highlight information reliability requirements (see below).

Support for Transport Multimodality

Transport multimodality (e.g. bus/railways/boat, public/private transport) is a key approach towards more sustainable and safe mobility. The objective of achieving an optimal exploitation of current transport and road infrastructure in order to decrease current congestion rates may be facilitated by delivering accurate and real-time multimodality information (Safety Forum – Working Group RTD, 2006). Nowadays, information about public transport-based itineraries can be obtained via pre-trip web-based research, while most personal and mobile navigation systems are conceived for car driving. At present, in-car navigation systems and multi-modal trip planning systems are non-interoperating domains (Rehrl et al., 2007). Completeness, freshness and validity of information delivered to end users are essential requisites to effectively support transport multimodality. Support for this requirement is thus strictly tied to the previous one, in terms of the integration of heterogeneous information for both private and public transport.

Compliance with Standards for Interoperability and the Dynamic Integration of Information Sources

Delivering real-time and reliable mobility services requires the integration of heterogeneous, geo-referenced, static and/or dynamic information coming from different and autonomous sources, such as transport operators, public institutions and traffic management centers. Interoperability and the integration of such heterogeneous information require a wide agreement on common rules and models for information exchange. At present, some standard specifications for exchange of infomobility information exist. Examples of European standards based on XML and Web Services technologies include DATEX, a specification for traffic event information exchange (European Commission - DG for Transport and Energy, 2006), SIRI, a standard specification for public transport information exchange (CEN TC 278, 2006) and TRANSMODEL, a conceptual data model for public transport operation and management (CEN TC278, 1997). The Open Geospatial Consortium (2007) has published international specifications for location-based services, such as route planning and geo-referencing. Nonetheless, most available route planners, navigation and map services do not offer open and standard interfaces for third party service integration. Semantic-based service-oriented architectural design is a promising approach towards semantic interoperability and service integration offered by heterogeneous providers, but research is still at an early stage (Vetere & Lenzerini, 2005).

Personalization and User Interaction Adaptation

Personalization concerns how information services should adapt to user profile and preferences. In the infomobility application domain this approach should be focused on user preferences and profile explicitly related to mobility (e.g. physical disabilities or preference for private transport). Service delivery and user interaction should be adapted according to several parameters, such as different user devices (e.g. mobile phones, PC, in-car navigation systems), preferences, profiles and current contexts. For instance, navigation and assistance services should adapt to a user's current mobility status, as a user's spatial behavior is different in walking or car-driving situations. Different techniques can be used for user profiling (individual or group profiling): manual input or more sophisticated techniques (learning technolo-

gies, collaborative filtering). Moreover, several techniques can be adopted for application adaptation to user profiles and contexts (e.g. rule-based adaptation, machine learning algorithms, etc.). An evaluation of existing predictive algorithms for personalizing a mobile application is proposed by Nurmi et al. (2007).

Information Reliability

Information delivered to end-users should be reliable or should at least respect specific service levels agreed upon with the end-users. Imprecise, incomplete, or wrong information could compromise attaining the final objective (supporting users in their mobility) and thus cause the users' disaffection with infomobility services. This problem may arise as infomobility services have to be based on the integration of different information sources, usually managed by different providers (for instance, user-generated content can also be exploited for updated information about mobility). Analogously, context data can be acquired by heterogeneous sensors with different precision and reliability characteristics and managed by different subjects. As a consequence, a huge amount of heterogeneous, probably redundant and incoherent information has to be properly processed and managed in order to provide reliable information to end-users. Information modeling and management techniques for assuring information quality and reliability are required to guarantee a wide acceptance of infomobility services. A method for measuring context information quality in ubiquitous environments has been proposed by Younghee & Keumsuk (2006). The method is based on the following quality dimensions: accuracy, completeness, representation consistency, access security and up-to-dateness. Furthermore, trust and reputation systems can be applied to estimate the reliability of user-generated content (Jøsang et al., 2007).

Privacy and Security

The effectiveness of context-aware infomobility services strongly depends on the continuous and distributed acquisition and processing of user-sensitive data, such as current position, activity, physical disabilities and health status. Thus, achieving a wide user acceptance of infomobility services requires the adoption of techniques for privacy protection and user perception on personal data control. Techniques for protecting privacy of the user's identity and location may include anonymity, pseudonimity, cryptography, policy-based privacy systems, etc. Cardoso and Issarny (2007) proposes a taxonomy for privacy invasion attacks and classification of existing privacy enhancing technologies according to the protection provided for those attacks.

When dealing with context-aware and pervasive systems, traditional approaches to security may be not satisfactory. This is mainly due to the strong relevance that user interaction with the physical environment and with related contextual attributes plays in context-aware applications. This scenario may require security techniques to be flexible enough for providing different levels of security services based on system policy, context information, environmental situations, temporal circumstances and available resources (Campbell et al., 2002).

INFOMOBILITY SERVICES: STATE OF THE ART SHORT ANALYSIS

This section provides an analysis of some relevant state of the art research and experimental activities in the infomobility application domain. At present, the term "infomobility" is widely adopted by European research communities and industries (European Commission, 1999), but it is not widely diffused at international level. Nonetheless, a huge amount of research projects may be related to this application domain. As already mentioned in the introductory section, infomobility deals with providing users with information useful for their mobility and may include navigation, multimodal route planning and re-planning (including services for booking transport facilities), location-based content delivery, alerts about events which can have an impact on user mobility in the pre-trip, on-trip and post-trip phases. To summarize, infomobility includes these main issues: navigation information targeted to personal user mobility plan, integration of information about multimodal transport, location-based content delivery and multi-modal communication channels.

To the state of our knowledge, research studies covering the whole infomobility domain do not exist. Nonetheless, many research activities and projects have tried addressing some of the above-mentioned issues. Hereafter we propose a categorization schema, where each category represents one or more of the above-mentioned issues. In choosing the following categories, we have also tried to represent the most diffused patterns in collected research studies.

- *Personal navigation systems*: services for navigating pedestrian routes, public transport or private vehicles (related to the issue "navigation information targeted to personal user mobility plan");
- *Infomobility integration frameworks*: systems designed to allow the integration of different information repositories about mobility (related to the issue: integration of information about multimodal transport);
- *Context-aware location-based communication platforms* towards Next Generation Networks (related to the issues: location-based content delivery and multi-modal communication channels).

We collected research studies in the area of context awareness and infomobility by searching in major electronic research databases (IEEE

Explore, ACM Digital Library, Science Direct) as well as web search engines (e.g. Google and Google Scholar). We also identified and collected studies from main international conferences in the domain. Among the rich amount of research papers that we found we chose a set of nine papers for evaluation using the following selection criteria (in order of priority): originality of methodology and novelty of research results, specific focus on one or more of the above mentioned categories, most recent publication date.

Many valuable research papers have thus not been selected, but many of them are worth mentioning. The section "Related work" provides a brief overview of relevant contributions which could no be taken into account in this study.

Personal Navigation Systems

Personal Travel Companion

Rehrl et al. (2007) have designed and implemented a prototype, named Personal Travel Companion, aiming at providing users with continuous assistance services including personalized multimodal trip planning in the pre-trip phase as well as mobile multi-modal trip management in the on-trip phase. They have realized a smart-phone based application for orientation and guidance in complex public transport buildings.

The prototype provides door-to-door multimodal route planning accessible from a desktop PC or a mobile device. The route is calculated on integrated public transport, road and pedestrian networks. User preferences (e.g. preferred transport modes, mobility requirements, options and time constraints) are taken into account by the system for calculating personalized routes. Personalized routes can be stored in order to keep a personal history of planned routes, frequent itineraries, etc.

On-trip assistance services are delivered by means of multimodal extensions to in-car navigation systems or a mobile personal travel companion

on smart phones. Continuity and seamlessness of guidance and assistance are approached by means of mobile multimodal trip management on different devices and navigation and orientation to the destination address (included pedestrian navigation inside transfer buildings). As a matter of fact, the system integrates services for both the pre-trip and on-trip phase. Moreover, navigation help is also provided in transfer buildings (e.g. a parking where travelers change from car to public transport). Real-time awareness of the mobility situation is not guaranteed and context awareness is conceived only in terms of service content adaptation according to user location, preferences and transport means. Service access relies on GPRS connectivity, thus seamless always-on access supported by converged communication platforms is not specifically addressed in this work. The prototype does not include mechanisms and techniques aiming at coping with information reliability, privacy and security requirements.

Smart Travel Information Service (STIS)

STIS is a system that offers travelers a multimodal journey planning service aimed at bridging the coordination gap between the available transport systems (Brennan & Meier, 2007). Journey plans are created based on the preferences expressed by end-users and integrate static and dynamic information about traffic and public transport.

The STIS is a middleware platform that uses transport data made available by a data layer, named iTransit Framework, and uses an HTTP interface to provide users with personalized journey plans. The service can be accessed by PCs or mobile phones and it is implemented by means of an XML message exchange over an HTTP connection. The iTransit framework (discussed below) integrates information coming from different legacy systems based on a common spatial data model. Context is here conceived in terms of updated traffic and public transport information, while user context awareness (e.g. location) is not an object of the application. Moreover, the focus of the application is on journey planning rather than on navigation help during the on-trip phase. Real-time information on mobility conditions may be acquired by integrating traffic and transport monitoring centers via the iTransit Framework, but the system does not support dynamic re-planning on user routes based on real-time information, such as public transport delays and traffic congestions.

Navitime

Navitime is a mobile navigation service that is offered in Japan and used by a large number of users (1,82 million of user were estimated in January 2007) (Arikawa et al., 2007). Navitime provides users with itinerary calculations and on-route guidance services combining several types of transportation: walking, driving and riding trains, taxis and airplanes.

Navitime is a distributed system: servers compute routes and generate maps, mobile phone clients capture location information, handle user input, download data, visualize maps, and handle interruptions through incoming email messages and phone calls. Routes are selected based on a set of criteria, including fastest route, minimized travel expense, transfer and walking distance. Contextual information which is managed by the system includes user location, acquired through GPS-enabled devices or manually specified by end users and used to adapt navigation and assistance services to current location, mobility and transport information and other geo-referenced information used to annotate maps and routes (e.g. additional weather information, amount of carbon dioxide emitted for each route).

Navitime integrates mobility information coming from heterogeneous data suppliers by converting them into four common formats: Dformat for timetable data, Mformat for road network data, Vformat for 2D map data representation and V3Dformat for 3D map data representation. Publicly available documentation does not make any explicit reference to Navitime's compliance with existing standards for mobility-related information exchange and storage.

Further considerations about personalization, real-time mobility information availability, seamless mobility access and information reliability cannot be provided due to lack of publicly available documentation.

Evaluation of Presented Personal Navigation Systems

In this paragraph we discuss how the above mentioned personal navigation systems address the set of requirements proposed for the infomobility application domain.

Seamless mobility is tackled in different ways by these systems. The Personal Travel Companion focuses on uninterrupted navigation help, even inside transfer buildings, thus addressing seamless mobility at the information level. In STIS and Navitime, seamless service access is demanded for cellular network communication, but no special focus is dedicated to terminal, service or personal mobility.

All research projects provide a minimal level of awareness of the real-time mobility situation by providing basic features in user location detection and location-based content delivery. Knowledge-based dynamic information services of real-time mobility situations (e.g. delays, congestions, etc.) are not explicitly supported by any of the analyzed studies. Nonetheless, such services would be extremely useful especially in enhancing multimodal travel planning services, as those delivered by STIS, Personal Travel Companion and Navitime, with additional features for dynamically adapting and re-planning user multimodal routes.

Personalization is realized in the Personal Travel Companion and STIS by adapting multimodal trip planning to user preferences, whereas Navitime puts more concerns on managing privacy-sensitive information. More precisely, with Navitime, privacy-protection is managed by detaching and encrypting personally identifiable information before forwarding service requests; also, stored location-search queries are not linked to user identifiers.

Differences between Navitime and the other two systems with respect to privacy and personalization are probably due to the fact that Navitime is a commercial service, with a wide user basin (almost 2 million users in Japan), and thus is more concerned with respecting regulations on user sensitive data, rather than providing advanced personalization features.

None of the analyzed personal navigation systems seem to adopt international standards for mobility data exchange.

Infomobility Integration Frameworks

iTransit

iTransit is the framework for a multi-layered Intelligent Transport System (ITS) architecture designed for integrating novel as well as legacy-intelligent transport systems (Meier et al., 2005). The framework is based on a multi-layered object data model. Interoperability is achieved by specifying this common data model as the basis of a federated architecture of heterogeneous and legacy ITS systems. The model contains spatial and temporal aspects of transport and traffic data and represents a unified mechanism for querying and processing information coming from heterogeneous ITS systems. It also includes global data layers (i.e. data of general interest), containing the physical and political geography and transport network of a region. Global layers can be extended through system view layers, which represent information generated or used by a specific system (e.g., public transport schedules, weather information, etc.). Interoperability between different data layers is ensured by a set of high-level concepts (named "context abstrac-

tions") representing main abstractions for global and system layers: Real World, System, Data, Location and Identification Objects.

An application-programming interface has been designed on this data model. Data exchange among systems composing the iTransit architecture is based on CORBA and Web Services. The data model is compliant with OpenGIS specifications (Open Geospatial Consortium, 1999), but, to the state of our knowledge, European standard specifications specifically addressing the mobility domain, such as DATEX and SIRI, have not been taken into account.

Built on the above-mentioned data model, the iTransit architecture is made of three tiers, each implementing a different interoperability layer: a legacy tier that includes legacy systems implementing their own data model; iTransit tier integrating transportation systems that natively implement the iTransit data model, and an application tier including value added services built upon the iTransit system.

Highway Traveler Information System in the Jiangsu Province of China

Xiang et al. (2007) describe guidelines and design principles that have been adopted for the implementation of the Highway Traveler Information System (HTIS) in the Jiangsu Province of China . In China, the specifications for defining a national ITS architecture have been published. Nonetheless, the Jiangsu province is one of the few Chinese provinces that have planned HTIS development within research projects promoted by the Jiangsu provincial Highway Bureau.

The HTIS architecture aims at providing a framework that enable the interaction among distributed heterogeneous systems. It is organized into seven logical levels that represent different political geographical organizations, responsibility for data sharing and network routing and legacy systems. These levels include: a provincial hub level, hosting provincial hubs which represent the central data collection and distribution points and connect to various regional hubs; a regional hub level populated by 14 regional hubs interfacing with data sources and providing users with information within each region; a hub interface level which supports integration with ITS legacy systems by converting legacy protocols and data formats into HTIS specifications; HTIS subsystem level, including all the subsystems which acquire data from field devices and connect to their regional hub (directly or through hub interfaces); a field device level including field devices (e.g. sensors, detectors, etc.) acquiring raw data for traffic monitoring; an Information service provider level including information-based agencies that connect to the provincial hub and use HTIS data for disseminating to end users (via kiosks, users' personal devices, etc.) and analysis purposes; an Internet level, which includes services providing end users with HTIS data via the internet.

The focus is on context information concerning highway monitoring and control, while context items centered on end users (e.g. location, activity, etc.) seem not to be taken into account. Emphasis is on a model for integrating heterogeneous and distributed information systems, based on a layered architecture, shared protocols and data formats.

Arktrans

Arktrans (Natvig & Westerheim, 2007) is the Norwegian national framework architecture for multimodal Intelligent Transportation Systems (ITS). Its aim is to establish a common view of the transport domain for all transport modes (road, sea, rail and air) in terms of standard functionalities and interfaces for interoperability among heterogeneous ITSes.

At present, Arktrans specifications define information needed by users travelling on public transport means, such as timetables, real-time information about delays and services provided on board and at stops. This information is defined by a conceptual model that represents concepts and logical relationships defined on UML diagrams and XML syntax. Existing European standards, such as TRANSMODEL, have been analyzed but not implemented, as they do not completely address some basic Arktrans requirements (e.g. multimodality with special emphasis on waterborne transport). Several related pilot projects are now being developed for the creating a door-to-door multimodal travel planner, combining scheduled planning (public transport via road, sea and rail) and non-scheduled (car, bike, walk) transport means. Route calculation personalization is made by considering user preferences.

According to publicly available documentation (Natvig et al. 2007), pilot implementation activities focus on supporting users in pre-trip and on-trip travel planning, whereas navigation service integration seems not to be foreseen.

Evaluation of Presented Infomobility Integration Frameworks

The above-mentioned integration frameworks do not consider seamless mobility as a primary objective, as they focus on the issue of integrating back-end systems rather than on providing information services to end-users. They provide potentially full support of real-time mobility information delivery, as they are specifically designed to integrate static and dynamic information about traffic and multimodal transport coming from different providers and sensor systems. Nonetheless, limited support is provided for dynamic adaptation with respect to real-time information about mobility and traffic status, as they are not targeted to deliver end-user information. As a consequence, also personalization, user interaction adaptation and privacy concerns do not specifically apply to these studies. The Arktrans program also includes the development of a multimodal planning service in the near future, which would consider user preferences. Presently, all these systems provide an integrated information layer on top of which advanced information services could be designed.

Interoperability among heterogeneous systems is mostly addressed through layered architecture models. As a matter of fact, a layered model approach promotes interoperability by defining layers characterized by specific functions and interfaces between layers. Compliance with existing standard specifications for data representation and exchange is not supported, or well-documented. In the Arktrans design case, existing standard specifications were judged as not appropriate for fulfilling project goals.

Information reliability is partially achieved by almost all systems by involving transport operators and public governments as authoritative information providers. However, to the state of our knowledge, no data management techniques have been systematically applied in order to manage data quality.

Context-Aware Location-Based Communication Platforms

LoL@

Lol@, the Local Location Assistant, is a UMTS tourist guide prototype that has been developed within a collaborative project between a company and a university at the ForschungsZentrum Telekommunications Wien (Umlauft et al., 2003). Lol@ is a guided tour service developed on an architecture for location-based services implementing SIP and OSA/Parlay standards. It provides tourists with a navigation service along predefined routes including Points of Interest and multimedia content delivery related to sights.

The application is based on a client/server architecture and has been implemented using Java Applets and Java Servlets together with XML-technology for content representation. Communication with the server is based on the HTTP protocol over a GPRS or UMTS connection.

Lol@ provides navigation and routing functionalities in the Wien city centre. A central concept for user interaction is the "map" metaphor. POIs and itineraries are shown over a map and users can interact with the application by clicking on icons and hypertext links and through spoken commands. Users may choose among textual, graphical and voice-based navigation and routing.

Context is modeled in terms of user location. Lol@ can use different positioning techniques: GPS, cell-based positioning, and users' manual input. A location server assures location information quality by acquiring location information from the GPS or cellular network operator infrastructure and calculating accurate location information. It has been planned to extend the context model with a date and time reference (for instance opening hours for museums).

MapWeb

MapWeb is a location-based service platform built on top of the IP Multimedia Subsystem (IMS) architecture (Huang et al., 2006). The MapWeb architecture includes three layers: the Application layer, the Control layer and the Media and End-point layer. The Application layer hosts the MapWeb server which provides location-based information and communication services by integrating different Application Servers (AS), e.g. a Location AS, Presence AS, and other external servers (e.g. map servers). The Control layer provides session and routing management. The Media and End-point layer includes terminals that initiate and terminate signaling for session establishment.

For instance, the MapWeb application can show a map-based interface on the user device. Through map-based interaction, the user can view his/her own position, locate buddies and contact them via phone call or instant messaging and locate POIs. The system can adapt services and communication channels according to user preferences and profile. Moreover, the user can specify some rules for adapting services according to context. In MapWeb, context is conceived in terms of location, current time, user presence and activity (obtained from a user calendar). MapWeb does not specifically aim at providing infomobility services; rather it provides a platform enabling the development of such services based on integrated communication, personalization and context management services.

IMS-Based Location-Aware Services

The IP Multimedia Subsystem (IMS) is an international standard for advanced multimedia service delivery in next generation converged networks. Several research studies are investigating how to extend IMS with support for location-based services. The advantage of such an approach is to enhance location-based services with value-added features provided by the IMS architecture, such as Quality of Service support, standard-based service integration over an IP-based infrastructure and charging facilities. Mosmondor et al. (2006) propose an extension of the IMS architecture by designing and implementing an IMS Location Server that provides IMS and IMS application servers with location information obtained from different positioning systems. The IMS Location Server is a generic SIP Application Server that can obtain location information from network-based positioning systems via Mobile Location Protocol (MLP) (Open Mobile Alliance, 2007). Complementary to this network-centric view, a terminal-centric location system has been proposed by Fabini et al. (2006) to provide the IMS core and IMS services with location information obtained by client devices equipped with positioning systems (e.g. GPS or Galileo receivers). The proposed technique also interoperates with network-centric location mechanisms and aims at improving location information accuracy. User

information privacy protection can be assured by SIP-based privacy mechanisms (Jennings et al., 2002; Peterson, 2002).

Evaluation of Context-Aware Location-Based Communication Platforms

The systems analyzed in this section address seamless mobility in terms of communication services. In Lol@ service access is guaranteed only if there is cellular network availability (GPRS and UMTS network). A minimal level of seamless service delivery is provided by means of a resume functionality that is provided when connection is lost (e.g. by network loss or simply because of an dead battery).

Systems relying on SIP signaling, such as MapWeb and IMS-based location services, can leverage on personal mobility features. None of the analyzed systems (Lol@, MapWeb and IMS-based location services) support multimodal planning services.

Regarding personalization, Lol@ and MapWeb implement personalization techniques for adapting interface and user interaction paradigms to user preferences, but do not implement techniques for privacy protection. Privacy-sensitive information management is addressed by IMS-based systems (Mosmondor et al., 2006; Fabini et al., 2006) and other research studies related to mobile communication (Arikawa et al., 2007; Umlauft et al., 2003).

DISCUSSION

In this section we comment on the results of the state-of-the art studies analysis shown in the previous section. Our findings are summarized in Table I, where each system is evaluated according to the context items and high-level requirements discussed in Section II and III, respectively.

Seamless service continuity is a critical aspect, partially addressed only by a few solutions with focus on different issues. Personal navigation systems focus on providing contents for uninterrupted navigation assistance aimed at managing transitions (such as outdoor/indoor, transportation means changes), whereas location-based communication platforms address the seamless service continuity requirement in terms of uninterrupted service access, or "seamless mobility". This difference is due to the fact the studies belonging to these categories usually pertain to different research areas: human computer interaction, graphical user interfaces, geographic information management and mobile application development (personal navigation systems) and communication protocols and platforms (location-based communication platforms).

Awareness of real-time situations concerning mobility and (partial) support for transport multimodality are usually guaranteed by infomobility integration platforms. This is a straightforward consequence due to the fact that these platforms provide mechanisms and models for integrating both static and dynamic data that come from different providers. These platforms could be used to develop personal navigation systems and location-based communication platforms enriched with real-time information. This has not yet happened for several reasons. First, infomobility integration platforms are not widely available. As a matter of fact, developing an infomobility integration platform requires a strong effort in terms of standardization, agreements with different transport operators, costs and resources. Usually this implies the intervention of public administrations, as in the cases of Arktrans, HTIS and iTransit. Second, these frameworks rarely present open and standard interfaces that enable the development of added value services. This is also a consequence of the poor adoption of standards for interoperability and dynamic information sources integration.

At present, limited support is provided for dynamic real-time information adaptation for mobility and traffic status. To the state of our knowledge, existing systems do not provide both dynamic planning and navigation systems integrating multimodal mobility information and automatic adaptation to context events (e.g. congestions and public transport delays).

Personalization is usually intended as adaptation of multimodal trip planning to user preferences and disabilities or adaptations of interfaces and user interaction paradigms to user preferences.

Information reliability is a requirement that has not yet been widely addressed. Only iTransit, HTIS and Arktrans partially face this issue by involving transport operators and public governments as authoritative information providers. However, to our knowledge, no data management techniques have been systematically applied in order to manage data quality in the infomobility domain.

Most analyzed works do not implement techniques for privacy protection, except for Navitime, Map-web and the IMS-based location-aware services. As already discussed, major attention for privacy protection is shown in commercial products (e.g. Navitime) and prototypes for commercial products (MapWeb).

Regarding context information management, the results in Table I show how similar patterns can be found for systems in the same category (personal navigation systems, infomobility integration frameworks, context-aware location-based communication platforms). This is due to the high-level objectives that such studies may have in common (see the description of categories' main objectives in Section IV). As a matter of fact, infomobility integration frameworks manage context information that is mainly related to planned and real-time mobility and transport services as well as to other geo-referenced content. Context-aware communication platforms focus on information characterizing the end user (e.g., preferences, activity, location and time). Personal navigation systems manage information describing planned and real-time transport services, but do not extensively manage user location and time. None of the analyzed systems manage information characterizing the trip in terms of user habits and social context (e.g. being alone/in group). Nonetheless, this contextual information could be exploited in order to properly adapt navigation and information services in order to optimize trip planning and management according to factors such as travel duration in specific day times (e.g. peak hours) and costs.

RELATED WORK

Several research systems have addressed issues related to the infomobility domain. For sake of completeness, we mention also other relevant research contributions beyond those more deeply discussed in the previous paragraphs.

A pioneer work is the GUIDE system (Cheverst et al., 2000), which provides tourists

Table I. Evaluation Results. The table shows whether state-of-the-art works address high-level requirements for infomobility: yes (y), partially (p), no (n). In some cases, required information was not publicly available (n.a.), or the requirement was not a specific design objective (-).

		Personal Travel Companion	STIS	Navitime	iTransit	HTIS	Arktrans	Lol@	MapWeb	IMS-based location – aware services
High-level Requirements										
Seamless service continuity		p	p	p	-	-	-	n	p	p
Awareness of real-time situations about mobility		n	p	p	y	y	y	p	p	-
Support for transport multimodality		y	y	y	y	n	y	n	n	-
Personalization and user interaction adaptation		y	y	n.a	-	-	p	y	y	-
Compliance with standards for Interoperability and dynamic integration of information sources		p	n.a.	n.a.	n.a.	p	p	n	-	-
Information reliability		n	n	n.a.	p	p	p	p	n.a.	n.a.
Privacy and Security		n	n.a.	y	-	-	n.a	n.a.	y	y
Context Information										
Who?	User preferences	y	y	y	n	n	y	y	y	n
	User habits	n	n	n	n	n	n	n	n	n
	Alone/in group	n	n	n	n	n	n	n	n	n
What?	User activity and mobility status	p	n	n	n	y	y	y	n	n
	Planned mobility and transport services	y	y	y	y	y	y	n	n	n
	Real-time mobility and tran sport services	n	y	y	y	y	y	n	n	n
Why?	Purpose of user journey	n	n	n	n	n	y	y	n	n
Where?	User location	n	n	y	n	n	n	y	y	y
	Geo-referenced content	y	y	y	y	y	y	y	y	n
When?	Timing reference for user location	n	n	n	n	n	n	n	y	y
	Timing reference for mobility and transport services	y	y	n	y	y	y	n	n	n

with location-based information by accessing a PDA. COMPASS (Van Setten et al., 2004) is an application providing tourists with context-aware recommendations and services. Gulliver Genie (O'Grady et al., 2004) is a prototype of a context-aware application delivering proactive information services to tourists based on their location and preferences. Another example of a city guide is Sightseeing4U (Scherp & Boll, 2004), which delivers location-based information via a multimodal user interface on a mobile device. These studies were not selected as they especially focus on tourism, a restricted area of the infomobility domain.

A more recent research trend concerns the exploitation of user-generated content to enrich navigation and geo-referenced content delivery. Some examples are CityFlocks (Bilandzic et al., 2008) and OurWay (Holone et al., 2007). The former is a mobile system enabling visitors and new residents in a city to access knowledge and experiences of local residents, thus facilitating "social navigation" in urban places. The latter is a prototype system for mobile pedestrian navigation that uses user-generated maps and annotations to provide accurate information services adapted to users' physical abilities and personal preferences. We did not analyze these studies in detail as they exploit a specific information source (end-users).

The Im@gine IT system is an agent-based service network architecture proposed for a real world applications in the infomobility sector (Spanoudakis & Moraitis, 2006). The Im@gine IT system is configured as a federation of agents distributed across different geographical areas, each of them serviced by one service integrator (named broker agent), one or more service providers (agents acting as service providers and events handlers) and other operators. Canali and Ancellotti (2006) propose a distributed architecture to support next generation infomobility services that provide interaction and collaboration among mobile users.

These systems have not been selected for evaluation as the available documentation focused more on illustrating the underlying system infrastructure rather than on describing the actual infomobility services developed, which are instead the focus of our analysis.

CONCLUSION

In this paper we have discussed high-level requirements and related technological challenges that should guide infomobility services innovation and evolution. We have also presented existing works in the field on infomobility, including personal navigation systems, infomobility service integration frameworks and context-aware location-based communication platforms. From the analysis of these works, with respect to the selected evaluation criteria, we found that at present most existing systems do not fully address infomobility requirements (i.e. seamless service continuity, awareness of real time mobility situations, multimodality support, personalization, information reliability and privacy protection) in a holistic way. Moreover, existing context models do not fully cover the information items that could be profitably exploited to improve the effectiveness of adaptive infomobility services.

Of course, it is not feasible to address the whole set of requirements through separate research and development projects, due to the amount of information bases, expertise and resources needed. Rather, it is required to adopt modular architectures based on standard interfaces in order to be able to build scalable, flexible and extensible products by combining results of different projects, maximizing reuse of existing building blocks and minimizing the need for new code. Future research activities could be profitably directed towards combining context-aware semantic-based service frameworks for dynamically adapting and orchestrating infomobility services that come from heterogeneous providers, with results of research activities in All-IP communication platforms for seamless mobility. A primary requirement for that is the adoption of standards, as already discussed in the previous sections. Research on converged communication platforms and the design of multi-protocol devices (PDA, RFID readers etc.) are paving the way towards effective seamless mobility.

An aspect that could influence future research and development activities is the support by public authorities and stakeholders (such as transport operators, highway and railways infrastructures' managers). This support is required in order to promote standardization activities and the adoption of the same standard specifications in a wide geographical area and to facilitate the collaboration among different stakeholders in terms of information sharing, communicating critical events and creating synergies for facing emergencies and abnormal conditions.

At present, our research work is oriented towards the development of a flexible and scalable service-oriented architecture, aimed at addressing infomobility requirements. This research activity is based on our results of previous research projects on the following topics:

- The development of a context-aware mobile tourist guide, providing tourists with geo-referenced and community services, such as reputation services and instant messaging (Paganelli et al., 2006: Paganelli et al., 2007). The system, developed in the framework of the KAMER research project, is a context-aware application integrating in a novel way location-based content delivery with communication and knowledge exchange services. Context awareness is conceived in terms of user location, but also in user preferences awareness, current activities, closeness to points of interest and physical proximity to other tourists, especially those with similar preferences and itineraries. The KAMER prototype includes a context man-

agement middleware that supports context data acquisition, processing, storage and delivery to applications.

- The development of an architectural framework for Semantics-Driven Integration of heterogeneous systems, implementing Service oriented Architecture principles (SOA) (OASIS, 2006). The framework is built over Sun's Java Business Integration (JBI) specification (JSR-208) and it has been enhanced with a special Knowledge-Base Module service integration framework, based on semantic web technologies that promote interoperability among heterogeneous systems. A first proof-of-concept has been developed for a specific application domain: trust intermediation for eTourism (Parlanti et al., 2006).

These previous works constitute the basis for the development of an infomobility service platform, built on the above-mentioned service integration framework enriched with context management modules. The system will also include a Java-based client side application for delivering navigation and information services to travelers and tourists via mobile devices. Thanks to its modular and standard-based architecture, the framework will ease the progressive integration of heterogeneous information providers (traffic monitoring centers, public transport operators, geo-referenced content providers, etc.) in order to provide users with complete, reliable and updated information about mobility. This work aims at directly addressing requirements for awareness in real time mobility situations, multimodality support, personalization and information reliability. The adoption of an SOA approach facilitates the integration with third-party added value services that are coping with other requirements.

Results of this research and development activities will be integrated in a test-bed for infomobility services promoted by the Regione Toscana Public Authority, also in participation with regional public transport operators, "Autostrade per l'Italia", the leading Italian Concessionaire for toll motorway management and for related transport services, and other companies specialized in vehicular technologies and mobile information services.

REFERENCES

Abowd, G. D., Atkeson, C. G., Hong, J., Long, S., Kooper, R., & Pinkerton, M. (1997). Cyberguide: a mobile context-aware tour guide. *Wireless Networks, 3*(5), 421–433.

Abowd, G. D., Dey, A. K., Brown, P. J., Davies, N., Smith, M., & Steggles, P. (1999). Towards a Better Understanding of Context and Context-Awareness. In H. Gellersen (Ed.), *Proceedings of the 1st international Symposium on Handheld and Ubiquitous Computing* (Karlsruhe, Germany, September 27 - 29, 1999). *Lecture Notes In Computer Science, 1707,* 304-307. London: Springer-Verlag

Anagnostopoulos, C. B., Tsounis, A., & Hadjiefthymiades, S. (2007). Context Awareness in Mobile Computing Environments. *Wireless Personal Communication, 42*(3), 445-464. Hingham, MA, USA: Kluwer Academic Publishers.

Arikawa, M., Konomi, S., & Ohnishi, K. (2007). Navitime: Supporting Pedestrian Navigation in the Real World. *Pervasive Computing, 6*(3), 21-29. IEEE Computer Society.

Baldauf, M., Dustdar, S., & Rosenberg, F. (2007). A survey on context-aware systems. *International Journal of Ad Hoc and Ubiquitous Computing, 2*(4), 263–277.

Barnes, S. J. (2006). Location-Based Services: The State of the Art. *E-Service Journal, 2*(3), 59-70. Indiana University Press.

Bernard, G. (2006). Middleware for Next Generation Distributed Systems: Main Challenges and Perspectives. *Proceedings of Database and Expert Systems Applications, 2006. DEXA '06. 17th International Conference on,* 237-240. IEEE Computer Society Press.

Brennan, S., & Meier, R. (2007). STIS: Smart Travel Planning Across Multiple Modes of Transportation. *Proceedings of the 10th International IEEE Conference on Intelligent Transportation Systems (IEEE ITSC 2007).* Seattle, Washington, USA: IEEE Computer Society, 2007, (pp. 666–671).

Bilandzic, M., Foth, M., & De Luca, A. (2008). CityFlocks: Designing Social Navigation for Urban Mobile Information Systems. In J. van der Schijff, G. Marsden, & P. Kotze (Eds.), *Proceedings ACM Designing Interactive Systems (DIS),* Cape Town, South Africa.

Campbell, R., Al-Muhtadi, J., Naldurg, P., Sampemanel, G., & Mickunas, M. D. (2002). Towards security and privacy for pervasive computing. In *Proceedings of International Symposium on Software Security,* Tokyo, Japan.

Canali, C., & Lancellotti, R. (2006). A distributed architecture to support infomobility services. *In Proceedings of the 2nd international Workshop on Advanced Architectures and Algorithms For internet Delivery and Applications* (Pisa, Italy, October 10 - 10, 2006). AAA-IDEA '06, 198., New York, NY: ACM.

Cardoso, R. S., & Issarny, V. (2007). Architecting Pervasive Computing Systems for Privacy: A Survey. *Proceedings of the Sixth Working IEEE/IFIP Conference on Software Architecture (WICSA'07),* (pp. 44-47). IEEE.

CEN TC278 (1997). *Road Transport and Traffic Telematics – Public Transport – Reference Data Model.* ENV 1997.

CEN TC 278 (2006). *Public transport — Service interface for real-time information relating to public transport operations — Part 1: Context and framework* (Technical Specification prCEN/TS 00278181-1). Accessed September 20, 2007, from http://www.cen.eu/cenorm/homepage.htm.

Chen, G., & Kotz, D. (2000). *A Survey of Context-Aware Mobile Computing Research*. Technical Report. Hanover, NH, USA: Dartmouth College.

Cheverst, K., Davies, N., Mitchell, K., Friday, A., & Efstratiou, C. (2000). Developing a context-aware electronic tourist guide: some issues and experiences. *Proceedings of the SIGCHI conference on Human Factors in Computing Systems*, (pp. 17-24). New York: ACM Press.

Dao, D. Rizos, C., & Wang, J. (2002). Location-based services: technical and business issues. *GPS Solutions*, 6(3), 169-178. Berlin: Springer.

D'Roza, T., & Bilchev, G. (2003). An overview of location-based services. *BT Technology Journal*, 21(1), 20-27. The Netherlands: Springer.

European Commission (1999). *Info-Mobility*. European Commission (DGXIII) Consultation Meeting on. Retrieved 16 may 2008 from ftp://ftp.cordis.europa.eu/pub/telematics/docs/tap_transport/introinfomob.pdf

European Commission Directorate General for Transport and Energy (2006). *DATEX II Exchange Platform Specific Model (version 1.0)*. Accessed September 25, 2007, from http://www.datex2.eu/?q=node/28

European Commission (2001). *European Transport Policy for 2010*. White Paper. Retrieved October 15, 2007, from http://ec.europa.eu/transport/white_paper/.

Fabini, J., Happenhofer, M., & Pailer, R. (2006). Terminal-Centric Location Services for the IP Multimedia Subsystem. *Proceedings of Vehicular Technology Conference, 2,* 881-885. IEEE.

Fiedler, M., Chevul, S., Isaksson, L., Lindberg, P., & Karlsson, J. (2005). Generic communication requirements of ITS-related mobile services as basis for seamless communications. *Next Generation Internet Networks*, (pp. 426- 433). IEEE.

Henricksen, K., Indulska, J., Mcfadden, T., & Balasubramaniam, S. (2005). Middleware for distributed context-aware systems. *On the Move to Meaningful Internet Systems 2005: CoopIS, DOA, and ODBASE, Lecture Notes in Computer Science, 3760*, 846–863. Berlin: Springer.

Hightower, J., & Borriello, G. (2001). Location systems for ubiquitous computing. *Computer, 34*(8), 57-66. IEEE Computer Society.

Holone, H., Misund, G., & Holmstedt, H. (2007). Users Are Doing It For Themselves: Pedestrian Navigation With User Generated Content. In the *Proceedings of Next Generation Mobile Applications, Services and Technologies*, (pp. 91-99).

Huang, D., Liu, F., Shi, X., Yang, G., Zheng, L., & Zhou, Z. (2006). MapWeb: A location-based converged communications platform. *Bell Labs Technical Journal, 11*(1), 159-171. Wiley Periodicals.

Infopolis2 Project (1999). *Needs of travellers and analysis based on the study of their tasks and activities*. (Infopolis2 Project Deliverable n. 3). Retrieved March 15, 2007, from http://www.ul.ie/~infopolis/pdf/info2_del3.pdf.

International Telecommunication Union (2006). *Mobility management requirements for NGN (ITU-T Recommendation* Q.1706/Y.2801). Retrieved February 20, 2007, from http://www.itu.int/rec/dologin_pub.asp?lang=e&id=T-REC-Q.1706-200611-I!!PDF-E&type=items.

Jennings, C., Peterson, J., & Watson, M. (2002). *Extensions to the Session Initiation Protocol (SIP) for Asserted Identity within Trusted Networks* (IETF Request For Comment: 3325). Retrieved April 10, 2007, from http://www.ietf.org/rfc/rfc3325.txt

Jøsang, A., Ismail, R., & Boyd, C. (2007). A survey of trust and reputation systems for online service provision. *Decision Support Systems, 43*(2), 618-644. Elsevier Science Publishers B. V.

Meier, R., Harrington, A., & Cahill, V. (2005). A Distributed Framework for Intelligent Transportation Systems. *Proceedings of 12th World Congress on Intelligent Transport Systems (ITSWC2005)*. ITS America.

Morand, L., & Tessier, S. (2002). Global mobility approach with Mobile IP in "All IP" networks. *Proceedings of IEEE International Conference on Communications ICC 2002, 4*, 2075-2079. IEEE.

Mosmondor, M., Skorin-Kapov, L., & Kovacic, M. (2006). Bringing Location Based Services to IP Multimedia Subsystem. *Proceedings of Mediterranean Electrotechnical Conference MELECON 2006*, (pp. 746-749). IEEE.

Natvig, M. K., & Westerheim, H. (2007). National multimodal travel information – a strategy based on stakeholder involvement and intelligent transportation system architecture. *Intelligent Transportation Systems, 1*(2), 102–109. IET.

Natvig, M., Westerheim, H., & Skylstad, G. F. (2007). *ARKTRANS The Norwegian system framework architecture for multimodal transport systems supporting freight and passenger transport* (Technical Report v. 4.0). Retrieved September 23, 2007, http://www.sintef.no/units/informatics/projects/arktrans/arktransweb/.

Nurmi, P., Hassinen, M., & Lee, K. C. (2007). A Comparative Analysis of Personalization Techniques for a Mobile Application. *In the Proceedings of the 21st International Conference on Advanced Information Networking and Applications Workshops, 2*, 270-275. IEEE.

OASIS (2006). *Reference Model for Service Oriented Architecture*. Committee Specification 1, 2 August 2006, version 1.0. Retrieved 10 March 10, 2008, from http://www.oasis-open.org/committees/tc_home.php?wg_abbrev=soa-rm.

Open Mobile Alliance Mobile (2007). *Location Protocol Specification* (v. 3.0). Retrieved March 2, 2007, from http://www.openmobilealliance.org/tech/affiliates/lif/lifindex.html

Open Geospatial Consortium Inc. (1999) OpenGIS Simple Features Specification for SQL (OpenGIS Project Document 99-049). Retrieved September 25, 2007, 1999, from http://www.opengeospatial.org/standards/sfs.

Open Geospatial Consortium (2007). *Location Service (OpenLS): Core Services* (Technical Specification). Retrieved January 25, 2007, from http://www.opengeospatial.org

O'Grady, M. J., & O'Hare, G. M. P. (2004). Gulliver's Genie: agency, mobility, adaptivity. *Computers & Graphics, 28*(5), 677-689.

Paganelli, F., Bianchi, G., & Melani, V. (2006). A Context-aware eTourism Application Enabling Collaboration and Knowledge Exchange among Tourists. *Exploiting the Knowledge Economy: Issues, Applications, Case Studies*. Amsterdam: IOS Press.

Paganelli, F., Bianchi, G., & Giuli, D. (2007). A Context Model for Context-aware System Design towards the Ambient Intelligence Vision: Experiences in the eTourism Domain. *Universal Access in Ambient Intelligence Environments, Lecture Notes in Computer Science, 4397*, 173-191. Springer.

Parlanti, D., Giuli, D., & Pettenati, M. C. (2006). Intermediation for trust-enabling networked decentralized exchange systems. In *Proceedings of the 13th European Conference on Cognitive Ergonomics: Trust and Control in Complex Socio-Technical Systems* (Zurich, Switzerland, September 20 - 22, 2006). *ECCE '06, 250*. New York, NY: ACM.

Peterson, J. (2002). *A Privacy Mechanism for the Session Initiation Protocol (SIP)*. (IETF Request for Comments: 3323). Retrieved April 10, 2007, from http://tools.ietf.org/html/rfc3323.

Randell, B. (1998). Dependability - A Unifying Concept. *Computer Security, Dependability, and Assurance: From Needs to Solutions*, (pp. 16-25). IEEE Computer Society.

Rehrl, K., Bruntsch, S., & Mentz, H. J. (2007). Assisting Multimodal Travelers: Design and Prototypical Implementation of a Personal Travel Companion. *IEEE Transactions on Intelligent Transportation Systems*, 8(1).

Riecken, D. (2000). Introduction: personalized views of personalization. *Communications of the ACM 43*(8), 26-28. New York, USA: ACM.

Saha, D., & Mukherjee, A. (2003). Pervasive Computing: A Paradigm for the 21st Century. *IEEE Computer*, 36(3), 25-31. IEEE Computer Society Press.

Safety Forum – Working Group RTD (2006). Strategic Research Agenda ICT for Mobility. European Commission. Retrieved February 20, 2007, from http://ec.europa.eu/information_society/activities/esafety/doc/esafety_2006/sra_ict_for_mobility_v.3_final.pdf

Scherp, A., & Boll, S. (2004). mobileMM4U - framework support for dynamic personalized multimedia content on mobile systems. In *Proceedings of Techniques and Applications for Mobile Commerce Track of Multi Conference Business Informatics*, Essen, Germany.

Schulzrinne, H., & Wedlund, E. (2000). Application-layer mobility using SIP. *Mobile Computing and Communications Review*, 4(3), 47–57. ACM SIGMOBILE.

Spanoudakis, N., & Moraitis, P. (2006). Agent Based Architecture in an Ambient Intelligence Context. *Proc. 4th European Workshop Multi-Agent Systems (EUMAS06)*, (pp. 163–174).

Strang, T., & Linnhoff–Popien, C. (2004). A Context Modeling Survey. *Proceedings of the Workshop on Advanced Context Modelling, Reasoning and Management associated with the Sixth International Conference on Ubiquitous Computing (UbiComp 2004)*. Nottingham/England.

Umlauft, M., Pospischil, G., Niklfeld, G., & Michlmayr, E. (2003). LoL@, a Mobile Tourist Guide for UMTS. *Information Technology & Tourism*, 5(3), 151-164.

U. S. Department of Transportation (1998). Developing Traveler Information Systems Using the National ITS Architecture. Retrieved February 23, 2007, from http://itsdocs.fhwa.dot.gov/jpodocs/repts_te/4163.pdf.

Van Setten, M., Pokraev, S., & Koolwaaij, S. (2004). Context-Aware Recommendations in the Mobile Tourist Application COMPASS. In *Proceedings of Adaptive Hypermedia and Adaptive Web-Based Systems Third International Conference* (pp. 235-244). Eindhoven, The Netherlands

Vetere, G., & Lenzerini, M. (2005). Models for semantic interoperability in service-oriented architectures. *IBM Systems Journal, 44*(4).

Wang, Q., & Abu-Rgheff, M. A. (2003). Next-generation mobility support. *Communications Engineer*, 1(1), 16- 19. IET.

Want, R., Hopper, A., Falcao, V., & Gibbons, J. (1992). The active badge location system. *ACM Transactions on Information Systems*, 10(1), 91–102.

Xiang, Q. J. Ma, Y. F., Lu, J., Xie, J. P., & Sha, H. Y. (2007). Framework design of highway traveller information system of Jiangsu Province of China. *Intelligent Transportation Systems*, 1(2), 110-116. IET.

Younghee, K., & Keumsuk, L. (2006). A Quality Measurement Method of Context Information in Ubiquitous Environments. *Proceedings of the*

International Conference on Hybrid Information Technology, 2, 576-581. IEEE.

Zeadally, S., Siddiqui, F., Deepak Mavatoor, N., & Randhavva, P. (2004). SIP and mobile IP integration to support seamless mobility. *Proceedings of 15th IEEE International Symposium on Personal, Indoor and Mobile Radio Communications, 3*, 1927- 1931

Chapter XVI

Incorporating Human Factors in the Development of Context–Aware Personalized Applications:
The Next Generation of Intelligent User Interfaces

Nikos Tsianos
National & Kapodistrian University of Athens, Greece

Panagiotis Germanakos
National & Kapodistrian University of Athens, Greece

Zacharias Lekkas
National & Kapodistrian University of Athens, Greece

Constantinos Mourlas
National & Kapodistrian University of Athens, Greece

George Samaras
University of Cyprus, Cyprus

ABSTRACT

The notion of context in context-aware applications is not merely an issue of external situational circumstances or device/channel properties, but it could also refer to a wide array of user characteristics that have an effect throughout users' interactions with a system. Human factors such as cognitive traits and current state, from a psychological point of view, are undoubtedly significant in the shaping of the perceived and objective quality of interactions with a system, and by defining context in that sense, personalization may as well become an essential function of context aware applications. The research that is presented in this chapter focuses on identifying human factors that relate to users' performance in Web applications that involve information processing, and a framework of personalization rules that are expected to increase users' performance is depicted. The environments that empirical results were derived from were both learning and commercial; in the case of E-Learning personalization was beneficial, while the interaction with a commercial site needs to be further investigated due to the implicit character of information processing in the Web.

INTRODUCTION

In the spectrum of all parameters that can be considered as the context of context-aware applications, users' intrinsic characteristics should not be disregarded, especially if information processing is involved. Though it seems that this approach is not the predominant in context aware systems research (Korkea-aho, 2000), human factors are by definition a crucial parameter in the shaping of human computer interaction (HCI)—as suggested by the term itself. According to Dey (2001), "context is any information that can be used to characterize the situation of an entity. An entity is a person, place, or object that is considered relevant to the interaction between a user and an application, including the user and applications themselves"; Schmidt et al (1999) depict context as a three dimensional construct, including the dimension of self (device state, physiological, cognitive).

In accordance to the aforementioned definitions, our research interests focus on extruding information about the user, which can be proven of significant importance in enhancing the quality of HCI, with emphasis placed upon cognitive and emotional characteristics. The term cognitive describes systemic functions of the mind that are involved in information perception and processing, whilst emotional parameters refer to the arousal of emotions that affect the learning (as a process) performance, combined with the moderating role of emotional intelligence and skills. The clarification and the weighting of the effect of these human factors could provide new insights to context-aware personalization systems and intelligent user interfaces. In addition, the semantic enhancement of both user profile and services content are expected to increase the effectiveness of eServices, delivered in the best qualitative manner.

This context related semantic information, which actually is the basis of user profiling, provides adequate feedback to an adaptive system that personalizes the Web environment provided to the user according to his preferences or abilities- the context at an intrinsic level that is. This approach and the proposed user model of information processing characteristics also may have a modular role in a context aware system, along with other parameters that compose the broader concept of context.

Moreover, even if such a perspective may seem theoretically viable, we nevertheless consider that its validity may be objectively and empirically measured, in the sense that users are either benefited or not by introducing their intrinsic characteristics as context related information. This empirical validation is the backbone of this chapter, in an effort to elucidate if a certain set of application design guidelines may gradually be developed. Addressing the issue of HCI design, it would be of high practical value to explore new ways of translating theories from the field of social sciences and psychology into apt design rules.

One of the key issues is nevertheless the notion of adaptivity that allows the meaningful use of context related information in the area of individual differences. The function of adaptivity may as well be considered as a level of intelligence embedded in a Web environment, regardless of whether users' or interface/technical characteristics are involved. A certain form of mapping rules and corresponding implications on the information space are required, in order for a system to alter visible to the user aspects of the environment, utilizing in our case the intrinsic context information. Therefore, a serious analysis of user requirements and characteristics has to be undertaken, documented and examined, taking into consideration their multi-application to the various delivery channels and devices- though the latter issue of delivery and device context is not part of our research at this point.

To be more specific about users' requirements (characteristics, abilities and preferences), our psychometrically based research focuses on user cognitive and emotional characteristics that have an effect on real-time information processing. We consequently approach the issue of context from the perspective of the psychology of individual differences, aiming to maximize the performance of users within information distributing Web environments, by personalizing on the basis of their needs. This is somehow related to previous work on adaptive hypermedia, mainly educational, where learners' characteristics are the motivating factor of a personalization mechanism (Papanikolaou et al, 2003; Carver, Howard, & Lane, 1999; Gilbert & Han, 2002).

Within this framework, we are in the process of building, evaluating and validating a user profiling model that could be applied in various Web-based settings, since our first efforts in the field of educational applications have been fruitful (Germanakos et al, 2007a; Germanakos et al, 2008); the generalization of this perspective of context that focuses on users regardless of application specific aims would much contribute to a coherent theory of information processing in the Web.

This chapter describes in section 2 the theoretical framework of applications' design guidelines and our proposed model as well as the resultant three-dimensional construct we propose, whereas section 3 illustrates how our adaptive system

translates context-related information to personalization rules. Sections 4 and 5 present (a) the methodology that has been applied in order to clarify whether personalization in this context contributes to a significant difference, and (b) the results from two different implementation fields of our model, an educational and a commercial Web environment respectively. Section 6, finally, is comprised of conclusions, future work considerations and discussion.

THEORETICAL BACKGROUND

Knowledge of human cognitive and perceptual capabilities has provided a solid ground for formulating principles and guidelines for designing usable and pleasing context-aware applications that will increase user performance, with regards to assimilation of the targeted information, and satisfaction during interaction time.

Usability and Visual Design Principles

According to Ottersten and Berndtsson (2002) a common mistake when developing interactive applications is to neglect interaction design. The consequence of not viewing interaction design as an important and controlled process is usually that user interfaces become a reflection of the underlying technological architecture, hence forcing the user to understand how the system works. Interaction design is sometimes confused with graphic design. Whereas graphic design involves the graphic part of interfaces, the interaction designer works mainly with the behaviour of a system, which is the part that is *not visible*. The purpose of interaction design is to describe the interaction between the application and the user. This involves designing the user interface content, behaviour and presentation in a way that pleases the user. Usability goals are central for interaction design. Norman (2002) describes the most common usability design guidelines. These are briefly related to:

a. *Visibility*: Important and frequently used functions should always be easy to find. In fact, with visible functions the user is more likely to understand what to do next when interacting with an object or a system;

b. *Feedback*: After an action, the user wants to know the effect of this action. Informing the user of this effect is feedback. Without feedback in our daily life, it would be almost impossible to carry out the simplest of tasks;

c. *Constraints*: Taking advantage of constraints in design means restricting the actions that can be executed by the user;

d. *Mapping*: Mapping refers to a relationship between a control and the effects of using that control. Norman (2002) discusses *natural mapping* which means using physical analogies and cultural standards in design.

e. *Consistency*: Consistency refers to keeping related operations for achieving related tasks.

f. *Affordances*: Affordances are the properties of an object that give an indication of its operations.

Whereas the design principles described by Norman keep focus on usability, Mullet and Sano (1995) discuss communication oriented visual principles and techniques. These techniques are based on psychological phenomena and functional aesthetics found in graphic design, industrial design and architecture. The most predominant visual principles are:

a. *Elegance and simplicity*: The meaning of elegance is to carefully select elements in a design with conscious decision. Simplicity involves solving a design problem in a clear and economical manner. Being strongly related it is no coincidence that both elegance

and simplicity are evident in practically every timeless design. In fact, the simplicity of an elegant solution is usually striking. Simplicity is also a design principle that many other principles depend on. Thus, to increase quality of design, conceptual and formal components must be reduced to a minimum. Simplicity itself depends on the principles of *unity, refinement* and *fitness*. Unity involves ensuring that elements are perceived as a coherent whole. Refinement means keeping the users attention on vital properties of the design. Fitness involves assessing the appropriateness of a specific design. Elegance cannot, as simplicity, be reduced to a set of principles, as it often involves taste. Reducing design to its essence however usually enhances elegance, regularizing elements (keeping a predictable a regular pattern) and letting elements have multiple roles.

b. *Scale, contrast and proportion*: To create harmonious designs a good relationship between scale, contrast and proportion must be accomplished. These aspects are some of the subtlest in design and they require practice. The design will always suffer if elements are too big or small, too light or dark, too prominent or indistinct. Scale refers to the size of an element relative the whole composition and other elements. Contrast is the provider of visual distinctions in the form of position, shape, texture, size, colour, orientation and movement. Both scale and contrast can be used to emphasize and differentiate elements from each other. Proportion involves balance and harmony of relations between elements. Techniques for accomplishing harmonious designs are establishing perceptual layers, sharpening visual distinctions and integrating figure and ground.

c. *Organization and visual structure*: Keeping elements in a design organized and structured help the user in finding guidance to interaction. The perception of structure happens automatically and is usually one of the first impressions of a product. Hence, the structure can either support or disrupt interaction. Without good organization the content may very well be difficult to interpret and understand. Users will however always try to find structure even where it's not obvious. Organization and structure in interfaces can be accomplished by grouping related elements followed by the establishing of a hierarchy based on importance. The composition must also be kept balanced and revealing the relationships between elements.

d. *Image and representation*: Being essential for communication, images are often an obvious element of GUI (Graphical User Interface) design. Despite this fact, imagery is one of the least understood aspects of interfaces. First, images must follow the same principles as the whole composition and second, they must be perceptually immediate to be recognized at once. Images must also be sensitive to the conceptual, physical and cultural context in which they will be displayed. Representation is used to give a GUI meaning. The analysis of representations depends on the relationship between the representamen and its object. Three forms of this relationship can be identified; an icon, which relates to the object by resemblance, an index, which is an association not based on resemblance and a symbol, which relates to the object by convention.

The Proposed Three-Dimensional Cognitive Model

Preece, Rogers and Sharp (2002) describe how usability can be broken down to a set of *usability goals*, which are: effectiveness, efficiency, safety, utility, learnability and memorability.

Our proposed perspective of context that focuses on user profiling includes cognitive and emotional processes that could be described as user "perceptual preferences"; the aim of constructing such a user model is to enhance information learning efficacy by personalizing the Web content and therefore increasing user usability and satisfaction.

User Perceptual Preferences could be described as a continuous mental process, which starts with the perception of an object in the user's attentional visual field, and involves a number of cognitive and emotional processes that lead to the actual response to that stimulus (Germanakos et al., 2005a).

This model's primary parameters formulate a three-dimensional approach to the problem (see Figure 1). The first dimension investigates the visual and cognitive processing of the users, the second their cognitive style, while the third captures their emotional processing mechanism during the interaction with the information space.

Cognitive Processing Speed Efficiency

The cognitive processing parameters (Demetriou, Efklides, & Platsidou, 1993; Demetriou & Kazi, 2001) that constitute the first dimension of our model consist of the:

a. *Actual speed of processing*, that is further composed of the, (i) Control of processing (refers to the processes that identify and register goal-relevant information and block out dominant or appealing but actually irrelevant information); (ii) Speed of processing (refers to the maximum speed at which a given mental act may be efficiently executed); and (iii) Visual attention (based on the empirically validated assumption that when a person is performing a cognitive task, while watching a display, the location of his / her gaze corresponds to the symbol cur-

Figure 1. Three dimensional model of User Perceptual Preferences

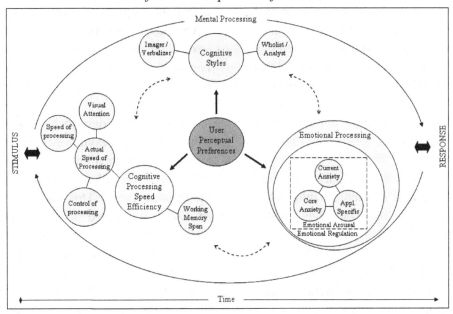

rently being processed in working memory and, moreover, that the eye naturally focuses on areas that are most likely to be informative). We measure each individual's ability to perform control/speed of processing and visual attention tasks in the shortest time possible, with a specific error tolerance, while as mentioned the working memory span test focuses on the visuospatial sketch pad sub-component, since all information in the Web is mainly visual.

b. *(Visual) working memory span (VWMS)*, which refers to the processes that enable a person to hold visual information in an active state while integrating it with other information until the current problem is solved. A brief description of the working memory system is that is consisted of the central executive that controls the two slave systems (visuo-spatial sketchpad and pho-nological loop), plus the episodic buffer that provides a temporary interface between the slave systems and the Long Term Memory

(Baddeley, 2000). We are mainly interested in the notion of the working memory span, since it can be measured and the implications on information processing are rather clear. Due to the visual form of presentation in the Web, we have focused especially on the measurement of visual working memory (Logie, Zucco, & Baddeley, 1990) in terms of psychometrics.

Cognitive Style

Cognitive styles represent an individual's typical or habitual mode of problem solving, thinking, perceiving or remembering, and "are considered to be trait-like, relatively stable characteristics of individuals, whereas learning strategies are more state-driven…" (McKay, Fischler, & Dunn, 2003). Amongst the numerous proposed cognitive style typologies (Cassidy, 2004; Kolb & Kolb 2005; MyersBriggs et al, 1998) we favour Riding's Cognitive Style Analysis (Riding, 2001), because we consider that its implications can be mapped on the information space more precisely, since it is consisted of two distinct scales that respond to different aspects of the Web. The imager/verbalizer axis affects the way information is presented, whilst the wholist/analyst dimension is relevant to the structure of the information and the navigational path of the user. Moreover, it is a very inclusive theory that is derived from a number of pre-existing theories that were recapitulated into these two axises.

We prefer the construct of cognitive rather than learning style because it is more stable (Sadler-Smith & Riding, 1999), and to the extent that there is a correlation with hemispherical preference and EEG measurements (McKay, Fischler, & Dunn, 2003; Glass & Riding, 1999), the relationship between cognitive style and actual mode of information processing is strengthened.

Emotional Processing

In our study, we are interested in the way that individuals process their emotions and how they interact with other elements of their information-processing system. Emotional processing is a pluralistic construct which is comprised of two mechanisms: *emotional arousal*, which is the capacity of a human being to sense and experience specific emotional situations, and *emotion regulation*, which is the way in which an individual is perceiving and controlling his emotions. We focus on these two sub-processes because they are easily generalized, inclusive and provide some indirect measurement of general emotional mechanisms. These sub-processes manage a number of emotional factors like anxiety boredom effects, anger, feelings of self efficacy, user satisfaction etc. Among these, our current research concerning emotional arousal emphasizes on anxiety, which is probably the most indicative, while other emotional factors are to be examined within the context of a further study.

Anxiety is an unpleasant combination of emotions that includes fear, worry and uneasiness and is often accompanied by physical reactions such as high blood pressure, increased heart rate and other body signals like shortness of breath, nausea and increased sweating. The anxious person is not able to regulate his emotional state since he feels and expects danger all the time (Kim & Gorman, 2002).

Barlow (2002) describes anxiety as a cognitive-affective process in which the individual has a sense of unpredictability, a feeling of uncertainty and a sense of lack of control over emotions, thoughts and events. This cognitive and affective situation is associated as well with physiological arousal and research has shown that an individual's perception is influenced in specific domains such as attentional span, memory, and performance in specific tasks. In relation to performance, the findings are controversial but there is a strong body of research which supports that anxiety is strongly correlated to performance and academic achievement. (Spielberger, 1972; Spielberger & Vagg, 1995)

Accordingly, in order to measure emotion regulation, we are using the cognominal construct of emotion regulation. An effort to construct a model that predicts the role of emotion, in general, is beyond the scope of our research, due to the complexity and the numerous confounding variables that would make such an attempt rather impossible. However, there is a considerable amount of references concerning the role of emotion and its implications on academic performance (or achievement), in terms of efficient learning (Kort & Reilly, 2002). Emotional intelligence seems to be an adequate predictor of the aforementioned concepts, and is surely a grounded enough construct, already supported by academic literature (Goleman, 1995; Salovey & Mayer, 1990).

Additional concepts that were used are the concepts of self-efficacy, emotional experience and emotional expression. Self-efficacy is defined as people's beliefs about their capabilities to produce and perform. Self-efficacy beliefs determine how people feel, think, motivate themselves and behave. Such beliefs produce these diverse effects through four major processes. They include cognitive, motivational, affective and selection processes. Emotional experience is the conceptualization of an emotion, the way in which the individual is dealing with it and how he perceives it. Emotional expression is the way in which the individual is reacting after an emotion triggers. It is his behaviour after an affective stimulus. It can be argued that emotional expression is the representation of an emotion (Schunk, 1989).

System Design Implications

For a better understanding of the three dimensions' implications and their relation with the information space a diagram that presents a high level correlation of these implications with selected tags of the information space (a code used in Web languages to define a format change or hypertext link) is depicted in Figure 2. These tags (images, text, information quantity, links – learner control, navigation support, additional navigation support, and aesthetics) have gone through an extensive optimization representing group of data affected after the mapping with the implications. The main reason we have selected the latter tags is due to the fact that they represent the primary subsidiaries of a Web based content. With the necessary processing and / or alteration we could provide the same content in different ways (according to a specific user's profile) but without degrading the message conveyed (see Figure 3).

The particular mapping is based on specific rules that are consistent to psychological theory, in order to filter the raw content and deliver the most personalized Web-based result to the user. As it can be observed from the diagram above

Figure 2. Data – implications correlation diagram

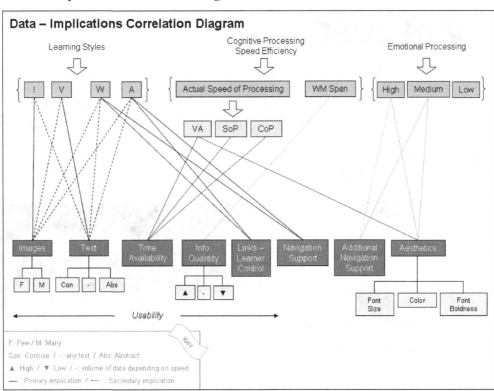

almost each profiling dimension has primary (solid line) and secondary (dashed line) implications on the information space altering dynamically the weighting of each factor on the creation of the environment.

As mentioned in section 2, Riding's Cognitive Style Analysis has been used in the Cognitive Style dimension, since the CSA applies in a greater number of information processing circumstances, since it deals rather with the broader construct of cognitive, than learning, style. According to theory (see Figure 3), for example, the number of images (few or many) to be displayed has a primary implication on imagers, while text (more concise or abstract) has a secondary implication. The analytic preference has a main effect on the links (learner control and navigation support tag), which in turn is secondary affected by high and medium levels of emotional processing. Moreover, levels of emotional processing

Figure 3. Content adaptation according to user's comprehensive profile

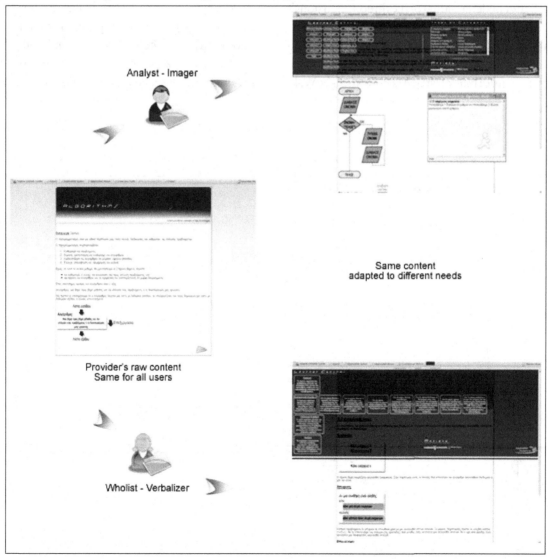

might secondary affect the number of images or the kind of text to be displayed. Actual speed of processing parameters (visual attention, speed of processing, and control of processing) as well as working memory span primarily affect information quantity. Eventually, emotional processing primarily affects the provision of additional navigation support and aesthetics (which is also the case with visual attention), while secondary affects information quantity.

A practical example of the Data – Implications Correlation Diagram could be as follows, a user might be identified that is: Verbalizer (V) – Wholist (W) with regards to the Learning Style, has an Actual Cognitive Processing Speed Efficiency of 1000 msec, and a fair Working Memory Span (weighting 5/7), with regards to his Cognitive Processing Speed Efficiency, and (s)he has a High Emotional processing. The tags affected, according to the rules created and the Data – Implications Correlation Diagram, for this particular instance are the: Images (few images displayed), Text (any text could be delivered), Info Quantity (less info since his cognitive processing speed efficiency is moderate), Links – Learner Control (less learner control because he is Wholist), Additional Navigation Support (significant because he has high emotional processing), and high aesthetics (to give more structured and well defined information, with more colors, larger fonts, more bold text, since he has high emotional processing). At this point it should be mentioned that in case of internal correlation conflicts primary implications take over secondary ones. Additionally, since emotional processing is the most dynamic parameter compared to the others, any changes occurring at any given time are directly affecting the yielded value of the adaptation and personalization rules and henceforth the format of the content delivered.

Based on the abovementioned considerations an adaptive Web-based environment is overviewed, trying to convey the essence and the peculiarities encapsulated. The current system,

AdaptiveWeb[1] is a Web application that can be ported both to desktop computer and mobile devices. It is composed of four interrelated components[2], each one representing a stand-alone Web-based system, outlined below (see Figure 4 – Germanakos et al, 2007b; Germanakos et al, 2007c).

1. The *User Profiling Construction* component. The user gives his / her traditional and Device Characteristics and further the component extracts the *User Perceptual Preference Characteristics* by completing a number of real-time tests (attention and cognitive processing efficiency grabbing psychometric tools) as well as answer some questionnaires for generating his / her cumulative profile.

2. The *Semantic Web Editor*. The provider will create his / her own content by defining the content as semantic objects and metadata for describing data and the relation between them.

3. The *Adaptation and Personalization* component. It runs the "mapping rules" process applied to the provider's content according to the user's comprehensive profile.

4. The *AdaptiveWeb User Interface,* AdaptiveInteliWeb. It provides a framework where all personalized Web sites can be navigated. Using this interface the user will navigate through the provider's content (normal and personalized mode), with the necessary learner and navigation support provided based on his / her profile.

The AdaptiveWeb system is currently at its final stage. All the components, except the Semantic Web Editor have been developed and smoothly running. For this reason, all the tests implemented so far, to prove components efficiency as well as the effect of our cognitive three-dimensional model described above into the Web, have been based on predetermined online contents in the field of eLearning and eCommerce multimedia

Figure 4. AdaptiveWeb system architecture

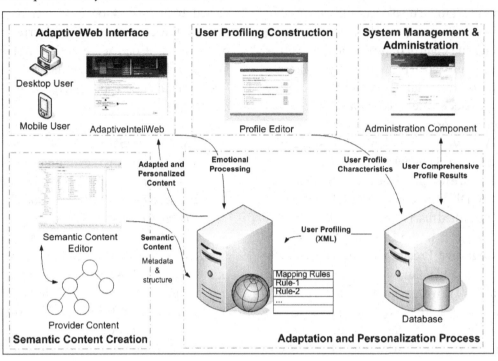

environments respectively. The current system has been evaluated both at system's response time performance and resources consumption, as well as with regards to users' learning performance and satisfaction, with really encouraging results as it is described into the following two sections.

As it concerns how the AdaptiveWeb system could support mobile applications, it should be considered that the main requirement of providing information "anytime, anywhere and anyhow" is not an easy task. Nevertheless, this adaptable provision of information may be rendered possible through personalization techniques. Such applications should be characterized by flexibility, accessibility, quality and security in a ubiquitous interoperable manner (Germanakos et al, 2005b).

Excluding the issue of security which is not at the scope of our research, user interfaces must be friendlier by a) enabling active involvement (information acquisition), b) giving the control to the user (system controllability), c) providing easy means of navigation and orientation (navigation), d) tolerating users' errors and supporting system-based and context oriented correction of users' errors, and e) finally enabling customization of multi-media and multi-modal user interfaces to particular user needs (De Bra & Nejdl, 2004).

Intelligent techniques have to be implemented in order to enable the development of an open Adaptive Mobile Web (De Bra & Nejdl, 2004), having as fundamental characteristics the directness, high connectivity speed, reliability, availability, context-awareness, broadband connection, interoperability, transparency and scalability, expandability, effectiveness, efficiency, personalization, security and privacy (Lankhorst et al, 2002; Volokh, 2000).

Specifically, our proposed three-dimensional model by definition addresses users' needs, and aims to provide a friendlier and more flexible user interface in any context-aware environment that involves interaction and information processing. Navigation support and access to information are core elements of our approach at the level of system design; consequently the overall quality of users' experience with mobile applications can be considered as interrelated with the satisfaction of their perceptional needs (UPPC model).

The experiments that are presented in the following sections demonstrate that the factors that are included in the three-dimensional model have a main effect on users' interactions with the information space. Additionally, it is possible to increase the efficiency of these interactions, which also is a key issue in mobile applications. The open architecture of the system and the intelligent techniques that are employed also make possible the integration of the AdaptiveWeb filter into a multi-modal mobile environment that would serve as an application area for future experimentation that could lead to levels of satisfaction and information assimilation similar to those of our already conducted research.

EMPIRICAL EVALUATION OF THE PROPOSED MODEL IN AN EDUCATIONAL ENVIRONMENT

Due to the fact that there is an increased interest on distant education via the Web, we have decided to implement the first phase of our experiments in an e-Learning environment, with the corresponding characteristics and constraints imposed by its nature. In this case, we were able to control factors such as previous knowledge and experience over distributed information, as well as the given interaction time of the users with the system, since learning in the context of a specific course is a far more controlled condition than Web browsing.

This section presents the results from experiments that were conducted in the context of an educational Web-setting, which support our approach in terms of optimizing users' performance in the sense of information comprehension.

Sampling and Procedure

All participants were students from the Universities of Cyprus and Athens; phase I was conducted with a sample of 138 students, whilst phase II with 82 individuals. 35% of the participants were male and 65% were female, and their age varied from 17 to 22 with a mean age of 19. The environment in which the procedure took place was an e-learning undergraduate course on algorithms. The course subject was chosen due to the fact that students of the departments where the experiment took place had absolutely no experience of computer science, and traditionally perform poorly. By controlling the factor of experience in that way, we divided our sample of the first phase in two groups: almost half of the participants were provided with information matched to their cognitive style, while the other half were taught in a mismatched way. In the second phase, the sample was divided in six, with a matched and mismatched condition for each factor. We expected that users in the matched condition, both in phase I and phase II, would outperform those in the mismatched condition.

In order to evaluate the effect of matched and mismatched conditions, participants took an online assessment test on the subject they were taught (algorithms). This exam was taken as soon as the e-learning procedure ended, in order to control for long-term memory decay effects. The dependent variable that was used to assess the effect of adaptation to users' preferences was participants' score at the online exam.

At this point, it should be clarified that matching and mismatching instructional style is a process with different implications for each dimension of our model. These are described below:

- Matched Cognitive Style: Presentation and structure of information matches user's preference
- Mismatched Cognitive Style: Presentation and structure of information does not coincide with user's preference
- Matched VWMS: Low VWMS users are provided with segmented information
- Mismatched VWMS: Low VWMS users are provided with the whole information
- Matched CPSE: Each user has in his disposal the amount of time that fits his ability
- Mismatched CPSE: Users' with low speed of processing have less time in their disposal (the same with "medium" users.
- Matched Emotional Processing: Users with moderate and high levels of anxiety receive aesthetic enhancement of the content and navigational help
- Mismatched Emotional Processing: Users with moderate and high levels of anxiety receive no additional help or aesthetics

Questionnaires

In this specific e-learning setting, Users' Perceptual Preferences were the sole parameters that comprised each user profile, since demographics and device characteristics were controlled for. In order to build each user profile according to our model, we used a number of questionnaires that address all theories involved.

- Cognitive Style: Riding's Cognitive Style Analysis, standardized in Greek and integrated in .NET platform
- Cognitive Processing Speed Efficiency: Speed and accuracy task-based tests that assess control of processing, speed of processing, visual attention and visuospatial working memory. Originally developed in the E-prime platform, we integrated them into the .NET platform.

- Core (general) Anxiety: Spielberger's State-Trait Anxiety Inventory (STAI) – 10 items (Only the trait scale was used).
- Application Specific Anxiety: Cassady's Cognitive Test Anxiety scale – 27 items (Cassady, 2004).
- Current Anxiety: Self-reported measures of state anxiety taken during the assessment phase of the experiment, in time slots of every 10 minutes – 6 Time slots.
- Emotion Regulation: This questionnaire was developed by us; cronbach's α that indicates scale reliability reaches 0.718.

Results

As expected, in both experiments the matched condition group outperformed those of the mismatched group (Tsianos et al, 2007). Table 1 shows the differences of means (one way ANOVA) and their statistical significance for the parameters of Cognitive Style (CS), Cognitive Processing Speed Efficiency (CPSE), and Emotional Processing (EM).

As hypothesized, the mean score of those that received matched to their cognitive style environments is higher than the mean score achieved by those that learned within the mismatched condition ($F_{(2,113)}=6.330$, $p=0.013$). This supports the notion that cognitive style is of importance within the context of Web-education and that this construct has a practical application in hypermedia instruction. The same applies with the case of Cognitive Processing Speed Efficiency: $F_{(2, 81)}=5.345$, $p=0.023$). It should at least be of some consideration the fact that in case designers' teaching style mismatched learners' preference, performance may be lowered.

In the case of Emotional Processing, results show that in case an individual reports high levels of anxiety either at the Core Anxiety or the Specific Anxiety questionnaire, the matched condition benefits his/her performance ($F_{(2, 81)}=4.357$, $p=0.042$).

The relatively small sample that falls into each category and its distribution hamper statistical analysis of the working memory (WM) parameter. In any case, the difference between those with high WM and those with low WM, when both categories receive non-segmented (whole) content, approaches statistical significance: 57.06% for those with High WM, 47.37% for those with Low WM, Welch statistic= 3.988, p=0.054.

This demonstrates that WM has indeed some effect on an e-learning environment. Moreover, if those with low WM receive segmented information, then the difference of means decreases and becomes non-significant (57.06% for High WM, 54.90% for those with Low WM, Welch statistic=0.165, p=0.687).

All the aforementioned differences between the matched and the mismatched condition are illustrated in Figure 5.

Correlations and Statistics of Emotional Processing Constructs

The emotional processing factor is discussed further due to the fact that it can be applied in various environments that relate to performance but do not require extended use of cognitive resources.

Table 1. Differences of means for cognitive style and cognitive processing speed efficiency

	Match Score	Match n	Mis-match Score	Mis-match n	F	Sig.
CS	66.53%	53	57.79%	61	6.330	0.013
CPSE	57.00%	41	48.93%	41	5.345	0.023
EP	57.91%	23	48.45%	29	4.357	0.042

Figure 5. Differences of matched and mismatched condition regarding each personalization parameter

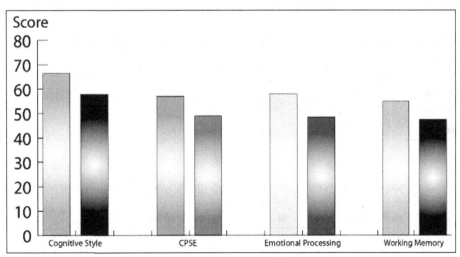

It is observed in Table 2 that all types of anxiety are positively correlated with each other and are negatively correlated with emotion regulation. These findings support our hypothesis and it can be argued that our theory concerning the relationship between anxiety and regulation has a logical meaning (Lekkas et al, 2008). In Tables 3 and 4 we can see an even stronger relationship between emotion regulation and core and specific anxiety respectively. A statistically significant analysis of variance for each anxiety type shows that if we categorize the participants according to their emotional regulation ability, then the anxiety means vary significantly with the high regulation group scoring much higher than the low one. Finally, in Table 5 we can see that the two conditions (matched aesthetics/mismatched aesthetics) are differentiating the sample significantly always in relation with performance. Participants in the matched category scored higher than the ones in the mismatched and additionally lower anxious (core or specific or both) scored higher than high anxious, always of course in relation to match/mismatch factor.

We also found that participants with low application specific anxiety perform better than participants with high specific anxiety in both matched and mismatched environments. Additionally, In categories that a certain amount of anxiety exists, match-mismatch factor is extremely important for user performance. Participants with matched environments scored highly while participants with mismatched environments had poor performance. Emotion regulation is negatively correlated with current anxiety. High emotion regulation means low current anxiety and low emotion regulation

Table 2. Correlations of types of anxiety and emotion regulation

	Core Anxiety	Application Specific Anxiety	Current Anxiety	Emotion Regulation
Core Anxiety	1	.613(**)	.288(**)	-.569(**)
Application Specific Anxiety	.613(**)	1	.501(**)	-.471(**)
Current Anxiety	.288(**)	.501(**)	1	-.094
Emotion Regulation	-.569(**)	-.471(**)	-.094	1

** Correlation is significant at the 0.01 level (2-tailed).

Table 3. Analysis of variance between emotion regulation groups and core anxiety means

	Sum of Squares	df	Mean Square	F	Sig.
Between Groups	4.316	2	2.158	18.554	.000
Within Groups	10.700	92	.116		
Total	15.015	94			

Table 4. Analysis of variance between emotion regulation groups and specific anxiety means

	Sum of Squares	df	Mean Square	F	Sig.
Between Groups	8.345	2	4.173	15.226	.000
Within Groups	25.213	92	.274		
Total	33.558	94			

Table 5. Multifactorial ANOVA (Factors—Core Anxiety, Application Specific Anxiety and Aesthetics)

Dependent Variable: Score %

Source	Type III Sum of Squares	df	Mean Square	F	Sig.
(a)					
Matched Aesthetics	1097.361	1	1097.361	4.238	.043
core_groups * specific_groups* Matched Aesthetics	983.259	1	983.259	3.797	.055

(a) R Squared = .102 (Adjusted R Squared = .017)

means high current anxiety. Finally, current anxiety is indicative of performance. High current anxiety means test scores below average while low current anxiety means high scores.

EXTENDING THE PROPOSED USER MODEL IN GENERIC WEB ENVIRONMENTS

The second phase of our research was to apply our evaluated information processing model in a setting other than educational. For the purposes of such an empirical validation, we created an adaptive version of a commercial site[3], in order to investigate users' possible responses to a personalization process as the aforementioned.

At this point we should mention that our methodology in this preliminary study is not yet concrete, since we have no objective dependent variables to indicate users' performance, but only their self-reported levels of satisfaction and a measurement of the amount of time spent for the completion of a set of simple tasks.

Sampling and Procedure

A between participants experimental design was adopted; almost half of the participants were provided with the original Website, whereas the other half navigated through a personalized version. In order to motivate them to explore the site at a satisfactory level they were asked to perform a set of simple tasks. Specifically, the Web pages they visited in each condition presented a number of laptops, and their tasks were to find information in order to answer a 7 item questionnaire concerning which laptop model is most suitable for a specific use.

The experiment was conducted with a total sample of 144 users; 19 users were excluded from the analysis process since they were considered to have spent insufficient time navigating in the environment they were allocated in. All participants were students from the University of Cyprus; their age varied from 19 to 23, with a mean of 20 years. Approximately 40% were male and 60% female. All of them were quite proficient in the use of the English language, and due to their academic status were familiar with technological issues such as those involved in our study- though since this was a comparative study between two environments, both of these factors were not expected to have a main effect.

After completing the task questionnaire, users were asked to fill in a satisfaction questionnaire.[4] The amount of time that was required for each user to complete the tasks was also measured.

Personalization Rules

For this preliminary study, the parameters that constituted each user's profile were cognitive style and visual working memory span (VWMS). According to these factors, the implications were similar to those described above for the case of the educational setting. The imager/verbalizer dimension of cognitive style affected the representation of the Web content (pure text or diagrammatical presentation), whilst the holist/analyst dimension had an effect on the structure of the environment and the number of links. Holists also had an extra navigational and tabbing tool.

For the case of users with low VWMS, instead of segmenting the content (which was already rather clear cut and susceptible to cognitive style differences in terms of structuring the navigational patterns), we provided users with an additional tool that served as an extra buffer for storing information that was considered to be relevant to the tasks involved.

Preliminary Results

The levels of satisfaction that users reported were identical in both conditions. There was absolutely no difference between the two conditions, as perceived by the users, since their overall mean in a scale from 1 to 5 was 3.2, with very little dispersion.

Even if the personalized environment was rather burdened with personalization tools and was more complicated, users didn't seem to be discouraged; this could be interpreted as positive, presuming of course that in the intrinsic level of information processing there could be some improvement. Still, since there is no objective dependent variable indicating performance in this study, we can only conclude that the extra Web-site features did not have a negative effect on perceived ergonomics and usability.

There were however differences in the amount of time that users spent navigating in the environments before they decided to fill in the task questionnaire. By dividing users in four catego-

Table 6. Post hoc analysis of differences between user groups with regards to navigating time

Dependent Variable: timeTukey HSD

(I) matched	(J) matched	Mean Difference (I-J)	Std. Error	Sig.
pers_low	pers	1.29899	.84696	.421
	raw	1.43759	.88778	.372
	raw_low	**3.01974(*)**	.95669	**.011**
pers	pers_low	-1.29899	.84696	.421
	raw	.13860	.69557	.997
	raw_low	1.72074	.78162	.129
raw	pers_low	-1.43759	.88778	.372
	pers	-.13860	.69557	.997
	raw_low	1.58214	.82567	.227
raw_low	pers_low	**-3.01974(*)**	.95669	**.011**
	pers	-1.72074	.78162	.129
	raw	-1.58214	.82567	.227

* The mean difference is significant at the .05 level.

ries, according to the level of personalization provided or not, statistically significant differences were found. The division was as follows: non-personalized environment for users with low visual working memory span (VWMS), non-personalized environment for users with normal or high VWMS, personalized environment for users with normal or high VWMS and personalized environment for users with low VWMS; there is some linearity in the sense that the degree of personalization involved increases from the first to the fourth group. Post hoc analysis of variance has shown that there was a difference in navigation time spent between users in the first and the fourth group (see Table 6).

The interpretation of this finding is somehow ambiguous. It perhaps implies that users did indeed make use of the additional tool, and were willing to spend more time navigating in the specific Web-environment. Taking into consideration the fact there were no time limits imposed and users' were free to leave the session whenever they wished to, there could be a positive interpretation of this finding. On the other hand, in the absence of an objective measurement of the quality of information processing, there cannot be any conclusive results extracted.

For the time being, we have found that restructuring a generic Web environment according to users' preferences and altering the typical methods of information representation in the Web does not have a negative effect on users' perceived satisfaction. The next experimental sessions will necessarily include a measurement of accuracy in fulfilling the tasks, in order to examine the depth of comprehension that was achieved in both conditions (personalized-raw). Moreover, a within participants experimental design seems more objective, in order to control for elusive confiding variables among different participants.

DISCUSSION

Considering the user as a vital part of what is considered as context in HCI may improve the quality of services offered, especially if the aim is learning or higher order information processing is involved. It makes sense that if one examines the characteristics of a device or the location of the user in providing context aware services, the same should be applied with the case of human factors. In the same way that a device has a certain processing ability, individuals differ in their perceptual and processing preferences and abilities. Therefore, it could be supported that an essential part of HCI context are the users themselves.

The empirical study on the field of e-learning presented above demonstrates that an "intrinsic" context aware application (in our perspective) is proven helpful for users and an actual benefit is objectively measured. All things considered, such a statistically significant effect that is consistent to the psychological theories supporting it is rather encouraging for the notion of expanding individual differences theories to various research areas.

The case of the Web-environment, on the other hand, yields rather ambiguous results. Users do not seem to distinguish between the personalized and the raw environment in terms of preference, while a specific group of users spent more time navigating within the environment in the personalized condition. That may be positive if the goal is educational or commercial, though in the event of a costly mobile access that might not be desirable.

The next step of our work, besides improving the methodology of our experiments in a commercial Web environment (introducing objective measurements of task accuracy), is the integration of the remaining parameters of our proposed model as personalization factors in the Web. With regards to emotional processing, we are setting out a research framework that involves the use of sensors and real-time monitoring of emotional arousal (Galvanic Skin Response and Heart Rate). As a matter of fact, the use of sensors is closely related to existing context aware systems research, and as mentioned in the definitions that were referred to in the introduction of this chapter, users' physiological state is also an issue of context.

Thus, describing the user as context requires a multi dimensional model of representation, which should incorporate cognitive and emotional characteristics that seem to have a main effect in interacting with applications that involve information processing. It is not argued of course that demographical and "traditional" profiling characteristics are of lesser importance; our proposed model could have a modular role in a setting that defines context in a variety of ways, by adding another dimension focused on intrinsic processes.

In the introductory section of this chapter we also mentioned the utter goal of setting a framework of guidelines that address individual differences. At this point of research, it seems that these differences are indeed important, and the way that theory was put into practice in our system did seem to be functional. There are of course many considerations regarding the generalization of this approach, and further experimental evaluation is required; still, especially within an educational environment, we have clear indications that context related information such as user's intrinsic characteristics may be used in a meaningful manner.

REFERENCES

Baddeley, A. (2000). The episodic buffer: a new component of working memory? *Trends in Cognitive Sciences, 11(*4), 417-423.

Barlow, D. H. (2002). *Anxiety and its disorders: The nature and treatment of anxiety and panic* (2nd ed.). New York: The Guilford Press.

Carver, C. A. Jr., Howard, R. A., & Lane, W. D. (1999). Enhancing student learning through hypermedia courseware and incorporation of student learning styles. *IEEE Transactions on Education, 42*(1), 33-38.

Cassady, C. C. (2004). The influence of cognitive test anxiety across the learning–testing cycle. *Learning and Instruction, 14*, 569–592.

Cassidy, S. (2004). Learning Styles: An overview of theories, models, and measures. *Educational Psychology, 24*(4), 419-444.

De Bra, P., & Nejdl, W. (2004). Adaptive Hypermedia and Adaptive Web-based Systems. *Proceedings of the Third International Conference (AH 2004)*, Springer Lecture Notes in Computer Science, 3137.

Demetriou, A., & Kazi, S. (2001). *Unity and modularity in the mind and the self: Studies on the relationships between self-awareness, personality, and intellectual development from childhood to adolescence.* London: Routledge.

Demetriou, A., Efklides, A., & Platsidou, M. (1993). The architecture and dynamics of developing mind: Experiential structuralism as a frame for unifying cognitive development theories. *Monographs of the Society for Research in Child Development, 58*(Serial No. 234), 5-6

Dey, A. K. (2001). Understanding and Using Context. *Personal and Ubiquitous Computing, 5*(1), 4-7.

Germanakos, P., Tsianos, N., Lekkas, Z., Mourlas, C., & Samaras, G. (2008). Realizing Comprehensive User Profiling as the Core Element of Adaptive and Personalized Communication Environments and Systems. *The Computer Journal*, Special Issue on Profiling Expertise and Behaviour, Oxford University Press. (accepted)

Germanakos, P., Tsianos, N., Lekkas, Z., Mourlas, C., & Samaras, G. (2007a). Capturing Essential Intrinsic User Behaviour Values for the Design of Comprehensive Web-based Personalized Environments. *Computers in Human Behavior*, doi:10.1016/j.chb.2007.07.010.

Germanakos, P., Tsianos, N., Lekkas, Z., Mourlas, C., Belk, M., & Samaras, G. (2007b). A Semantic Approach of an Adaptive and Personalized Web-based Learning Content – The case of AdaptiveWeb, *Proceedings of the 2nd International Workshop on Semantic Media Adaptation and Personalization (SMAP 2007)*, London, U.K., December 17-18, 2007, IEEE Computer Society, pp. 68-73.

Germanakos, P., Tsianos, N., Lekkas, Z., Mourlas, C., Belk, M., & Samaras, G. (2007c). Embracing Cognitive Aspects in Web Personalization Environments – The AdaptiveWeb Architecture, *Proceedings of the 7th IEEE International Conference on Advanced Learning Technologies (ICALT 2007)*, Niigata, Japan, July 18-20, 2007, IEEE. (accepted)

Germanakos, P., Tsianos, Mourlas, C., & Samaras. (2005a). New Fundamental Profiling Characteristics for Designing Adaptive Web-based Educational Systems, *Proceeding of the IADIS International Conference on Cognition and Exploratory Learning in Digital Age (CELDA2005)*, Porto, December 14-16, 2005, (pp. 10-17).

Germanakos P., Mourlas C., Isaia C., & Samaras G. (2005b). Web Personalized Intelligent User Interfaces and Processes—An Enabler of Multi-Channel eBusiness Services Sustainability. *Proceedings of the 2nd International Conference on E-business and TElecommunications Networks (ICETE2005)*, Reading, October 3-7, 2005, (pp. 177-180).

Gilbert, J. E., & Han, C. Y. (2002). Arthur: A Personalized Instructional System. *Journal of Computing in Higher Education, 14*(1), 113-129.

Glass, A., & Riding, R. J. (1999), EEG differences and cognitive style. *Biological Psychology, 51*, 23–41.

Goleman, D. (1995). *Emotional Intelligence: why it can matter more than IQ*. New York: Bantam Books.

Kim, J., & Gorman, J. (2005).The psychobiology of anxiety. *Clinical Neuroscience Research, 4*, 335-347.

Kolb, A. Y., & Kolb, D. A. (2005). The Kolb Learning Style Inventory – Version 3.1 2005 Technical Specifications, Experience Based Learning Systems, Inc. Korkea-aho, M. (2000). *Context-Aware Applications Survey*. Paper presented at the Internetworking Seminar (Tik-110.551), Spring 2000, Helsinki University of Technology, from http://www.hut.fi/~mkorkeaa/doc/context-aware.html.

Kort, B., & Reilly, R. (2002). Analytical Models of Emotions, Learning and Relationships: Towards an Affect-Sensitive Cognitive Machine. *In Proceedings of Conference on Virtual Worlds and Simulation (VWSim 2002)*, from http://affect.media.mit.edu/projectpages/lc/vworlds.pdf.

Lankhorst, M. M., Kranenburg, S, A., & Peddemors A. J. H. (2002). Enabling Technology for Personalizing Mobile Services. *Proceedings of the 35th Annual Hawaii International Conference on System Sciences* (HICSS-35'02).

Lekkas, Z., Tsianos, N., Germanakos, P., Mourlas, C., & Samaras, G. (2008). The Role of Emotions in the Design of Personalized Educational Systems. *Proceedings of the 8th IEEE International Conference on Advanced Learning Technologies (ICALT 2008)*, Santader, Cantabria, Spain, July 1-5, 2008, IEEE. (accepted)

Loggie, R. H., Zucco, G. N., & Baddeley, A. D. (1990). Interference with visual short-term memory. *Acta Psychologica, 75*(1), 55-74.

McKay, M. T., Fischler, I., & Dunn, B. R. (2003). Cognitive style and recall of text: An EEG analysis. *Learning and Individual Differences, 14*, 1–21.

Mullet, Kevin och Darrell, & Sano. (1995). *Designing visual interfaces – communicating oriented techniques.* SunSoft Press a Prentice Hall Title

MyersBriggs, I., McCaulley, M. H., Quenk, N. L., & Hammer, A. L. (1998). MBTI Manual (A guide to the development and use of the Myers Briggs type indicator), 3rd edition. Consulting Psychologists Press.

Norman, D. A. (2002). The design of everyday things, New York: Basic Books.

Ottersten, I., & Berndtsson, J. (2002). *Användbarhet i praktiken.* Studentlitteratur.

Papanikolaou, K. A., Grigoriadou, M., Kornilakis, H., & Magoulas, G. D. (2003). Personalizing the Interaction in a Web-based Educational Hypermedia System: the case of INSPIRE. *User-Modelling and User-Adapted Interaction, 13*(3), 213-267.

Preece, J., Rogers, Y., & Sharp, H. (2002). *Interaction design beyond human-computer interaction.* John Wiley & Sons, Inc.

Riding, R. (2001). Cognitive Style Analysis – Research Administration. *Learning and Training Technology.*

Sadler-Smith, E., & Riding, R. J. (1999). Cognitive style and instructional preferences. *Instructional Science, 27*(5), 355-371.

Salovey, P., & Mayer, J. D. (1990). Emotional intelligence. *Imagination, Cognition and Personality, 9,* 185-211.

Schmidt, A., Aidoo, K. A., Takaluoma, A., Tuomela, U., Van Laerhoven, K., & Van de Velde, W. (1999). Advanced Interaction in Context. *In Proceedings of the 1st international symposium on Handheld and Ubiquitous Computing, September 27-29, 1999, Karlsruhe, Germany,* (pp. 89-101).

Schunk, D. H. (1989). Self-efficacy and cognitive skill learning. In Ames, C., & Ames, R. (Eds.), *Research on motivation in education, 3: Goals and cognitions* (13-44), San Diego: Academic Press.

Spielberger, C. D. (1972). Conceptual and methodological issues in anxiety research. In Spielberger C. D. (Ed.), *Anxiety. Current trends in theory and research* (Vol. 2). New York: Academic Press.

Spielberger, C. D., & Vagg, P. R. (1995). Test anxiety: A transactional process model. In C. D. Spielberger & P. R. Vagg (Eds.), *Test anxiety: Theory, assessment, and treatment* (pp. 3-14). Washington, DC: Taylor & Francis.

Tsianos, N., Germanakos, P., Lekkas, Z., Mourlas, C., & Samaras, G. (2007). Evaluating the Significance of Cognitive and Emotional Parameters in e-Learning Adaptive Environments. *Proceedings of the IADIS International Conference on Cognition and Exploratory Learning in Digital Age (CELDA2007),* Algarve, Portugal, December 7-9, 2007, (pp. 93-98).

Volokh, E. (2000). Personalization and Privacy. *From the Communications of the Association for Computing Machinery, 43*(8), 84.

ENDNOTES

[1] http://www3.cs.ucy.ac.cy/adaptiveWeb

[2] The technology used to build each Web system's component is ASP .Net (http://asp.net)

[3] http://www.sonystyle.com/Webapp/wcs/stores/servlet/CategoryDisplay?catalogId=10551&storeId=10151&langId=-1&categoryId=8198552921644507782&parentCategoryId=16154

[4] http://www.wammi.com/questionnaire.html

Compilation of References

Aagedal, J.O. (2001). *Quality of Service Support in Development of Distributed Systems.* PhD Thesis, University of Oslo, Norway.

Abowd, G. D., Atkeson, C. G., Hong, J., Long, S., Kooper, R., & Pinkerton, M. (1997). Cyberguide: A mobile context-aware tour guide. *ACM Wireless Networks, 3*(5), 421-433.

Abowd, G. D., Dey, A. K., Brown, P. J., Davies, N., Smith, M., & Steggles, P. (1999). Towards a Better Understanding of Context and Context-Awareness. In H. Gellersen (Ed.), *Proceedings of the 1st international Symposium on Handheld and Ubiquitous Computing* (Karlsruhe, Germany, September 27 - 29, 1999). *Lecture Notes In Computer Science, 1707,* 304-307. London: Springer-Verlag

Abowd, G. D., Dey, A. K., Brown, P. J., Davies, N., Smith, M., & Steggles, P. (2001). Towards a Better Understanding of Context and Context-Awareness. Lecture notes in computer science: Vol. 1707. *Handheld and ubiquitous computing. Proceedings* (pp. 304–307). Berlin: Springer.

Abowd, G., & Mynatt, E. (2000). Charting Past, Present, and Future Research in Ubiquitous Computing. *ACM Transactions on Computer-Human Interaction, 7*(1), 29-58.

Ackerman, M., Darrell, T., & Weitzner, D. J. (2001). Privacy in context. *HCI, 16*(2), 167-179.

Adams, C., & Lloyd, S. (2002). *Understanding PKI: Concepts, Standards, and Deployment Considerations* (Second Edition ed.): Addison-Wesley.

Adomavicius, G., & Tuzhilin, A. (2005). Toward the Next Generation of Recommender Systems: A Survey of the State-of-the-Art and Possible Extensions. *IEEE Transactions on Knowledge and Data Engineering, 17*(6), 734-749.

Agostini, A., Bettini, C., & Riboni, D. (2005). Demo: Ontology-based context-aware delivery of extended points of interest. *The 6th International Conference on Mobile Data Management,* (pp. 322-323).

Agrawal, R., & Kiernan, J. (2002). *Watermarking relational databases.* Paper presented at the 28th VLDB Conference, Hong Kong, China.

Akl, S. G., & Taylor, P. D. (1983). Cryptographic solution to a problem of access control in a hierarchy. *ACM Transaction Computing Systems., 1*(3),239–248.

Aksit, M., & Choukair, Z. (2003). Dynamic Adaptive and Reconfigurable Systems. In Overview and Prospective Vision. In *Proceedings of the International Conference on Distributed Computing Systems Workshops 03,* (pp. 84-92) IEEE Computer Society Press.

Alferes, J. J., Amador, R., & May, W. (2005). A General Language for Evolution and Reactivity in the Semantic Web. In *PPSWR'05* (pp. 101–115). Dagstuhl, Germany: Springer.

Ali Eldin, A. (2006). *Private Information Sharing Under Uncertainty.* Delft: Amr Ali Eldin.

Ali Eldin, A., & Stojanovic, Z. (2007). Privacy control requirements for context-aware mobile services. In R. Gonzalez, N. Chen & A. Dahanayake (Eds.), *Personalized*

Information Retrieval and Access: Concepts, Methods and Practices: IGI.

Ali Eldin, A., & Wagenaar, R. (2004). *A Fuzzy Logic based Approach to support users self-control of their private contextual data retrieval.* Paper presented at the 12th European Conference on Information Systems (ECIS04), Turku, Finland.

Ali Eldin, A., & Wagenaar, R. (2004b). *Towards a users driven privacy control.* Paper presented at the IEEE conference on Systems, Man, and Cybernetics (SMC 2004), The Hague.

Ali Eldin, A., & Wagenaar, R. (2007). Towards Autonomous User Privacy Control. *International Journal of Information Security and Privacy, 1*(4), 24-46.

Ali Eldin, A., van den Berg, J., & Wagenaar, R. (2004). *A Fuzzy reasoning scheme for context sharing decision making.* Paper presented at the 6th International Conference on Electronic Commerce, Delft, The Netherlands.

Al-Muhtadi, J. (2005). *An Intelligent Authentication Infrastructure for Ubiquitous Computing Environments.*

Altova GmbH (2007). *Altova XMLSpy 2008 Enterprise Edition Content Model View.* Altova GmbH. Retrieved September 1, 2007 from http://www.altova.com/manual2008/XMLSpy/SpyEnterprise/index.html?contentmodelview.htm.

Alur, R., Courcoubetis, C., & Dill, D. (1990). Model-checking for real-time systems. In *Proceedings of of the 5th Annual Symposium on Logic in Computer Science.*

Anagnostopoulos, C. B., Tsounis A., & Hadjiefthymiades, S. (2007). *Context Awareness in Mobile Computing Environments.* Wireless Personal Communications, Springer.

Anagnostopoulos, C. B., Tsounis, A., & Hadjiefthymiades, S. (2007). Context Awareness in Mobile Computing Environments. *Wireless Personal Communication, 42*(3), 445-464. Hingham, MA, USA: Kluwer Academic Publishers.

Anagnostopoulos, C., Tsounis, A., & Hadjiefthymiades, S. (2005). Context management in pervasive computing environments. In *Proc of International Conference on Pervasive Services* (pp. 421-424). Santorini, Greece.

Ancona, M., & Cazzola, W. (2004). Implementing the Essence of Reflection: a Reflective Run-Time Environment. In *Proceedings of the 2004 ACM Symposium on Applied Computing* (pp. 1503-1507). New York: ACM Press.

Andrade, L-F., & Fiadeiro, J. L. (2003). Architecture Based Evolution of Software Systems. In M. Bernardo & P. Inverardi (Eds.), *Formal Methods for Software Architectures: Third International School on Formal Methods for the Design of Computer, Communication and Software Systems: Software Architectures, SFM 2003, Bertinoro, Italy, September 22-27, 2003,* (pp 148-181). Advanced Lectures Series: Lecture Notes in Computer Science 2804. Springer Verlag

Antifakos, S., Schwaninger, A., & Schiele, B. (2004). Evaluating the effects of displaying uncertainty in context-aware applications. *The Sixth International Conference on Ubiquitous Computing (Ubicomp),* (pp. 54-69).

Apache Software Foundation (2007). *Apache Muse - A java-based implementation of WSRF 1.2, WSN 1.3, and WSDM 1.1.* Apache Software Foundation. Retrieved May 1, 2007 from http://ws.apache.org/muse/

Arcelli, F., Raibulet, C., Tisato, F., & Ubezio, L. (2005). Designing and Exploiting the Location Concept in a Reflective Architecture". In *Proceedings of the 14th International Conference on Intelligent and Adaptive Systems and Software Engineering* (pp. 134-139).

Ardon, S., Gunningberg, P., Landfeldt, B., Ismailov, Y., Portmann, M. & Seneviratne, A. (2003). MARCH: A distributed content adaptation architecture. *International Journal of Communication Systems, 16* (1), 97-115.

Arikawa, M., Konomi, S., & Ohnishi, K. (2007). Navitime: Supporting Pedestrian Navigation in the Real World. *Pervasive Computing, 6*(3), 21-29. IEEE Computer Society.

Artus, David J. N. (2006). *SOA realization: Service design principles*. IBM DevelopmentWorks. Available at http://www.ibm.com/developerworks/webservices/library/ws-soa-design/

Assad, M., Carmichael, D.J., Kay, J. & Kummerfeld, B. (2007). PersonisAD: Distributed, active, scrutable model framework for context-aware services. In A. LaMarca et al. (Eds.): *Pervasive 2007, LNCS 4480* (pp. 55-72) Springer-Verlag, Berlin.

Atallah, M. J., Blanton, M., & Frikken, K. B. (2007). Incorporating temporal capabilities in existing key management schemes. *Cryptology ePrint Archive, Report*.

Austin, D., Barbir, A., Ferris, C., & Garg, S. (2002). *Web Services Architecture Requirements*. W3C Working Draft, retrieved July 2, 2007 from http://www.w3.org/TR/2002/WD-wsa-regs20020819

Ayars, J., Bulterman, D., Cohen, A., Day, K., Hodge, E., Hoschka, P., et al. (2000). Synchronized multimedia integration language (smil) 2.0 specification, *Work in progress. W3C Working Drafts are available at http://www. w3. org/TR*, 21.

Baddeley, A. (2000). The episodic buffer: a new component of working memory? *Trends in Cognitive Sciences, 11*(4), 417-423.

Bai, Y., Wang, F., & Liu, P. (2006). Efficiently filtering RFID data streams. *CleanDB Workshop*, (pp. 50-57).

Bailey, J., Poulovassilis, A., & Wood, P. T. (2002). An Event-condition-action Language for XML. In *WWW'02* (pp. 486–495). Honolulu, Hawaii: ACM.

Baldauf, M., Dustdar, M. S., & Rosenberg, F. (2007). A survey on context-aware systems. *International Journal of Ad Hoc and Ubiquitous Computing, 2*(4), 263-277. Inderscience

Baldauf, M., Dustdar, S., & Rosenberg, F. (2007). A survey on context-aware systems. *International Journal of Ad Hoc and Ubiquitous Computing, 2*(4), 263–277.

Barbará, D. (1999). Mobile Computing and Database-A Survey. *IEEE Transactions on Knowledge and Data Engineering, 11*(1), 108-117.

Bardram, J. (2005). The java context awareness framework (JCAF) – A service infrastructure and programming framework for context-aware applications. In *Proceedings of 3rd International Conference on Pervasive Computing (Pervasive 2005)* (pp. 98-115), Munich, Germany.

Bardram, J. E. (2003). Hospitals of the Future – Ubiquitous Computing support for Medical Work in Hospitals. In *Proceedings of the 2nd International Workshop on Ubiquitous Computing for Pervasive Healthcare Applications*, from http://www. healthcare.pervasive.dk/ubicomp2003/papers/ Final_Papers/13.pdf

Baresi, L., Guinea, S., & Tamburrelli, G. (2008). Towards decentralized self-adaptive component-based systems. In *Proceedings of the 2008 international Workshop on Software Engineering For Adaptive and Self-Managing Systems*. (pp 57-64) ACM Press

Bargh, M., Benz, H., Brok, J., Heijenk, G., Groot, S. H. D., Peddemors, A., et al. (2005, January 10). J. In Brok (Ed.), *Initial architecture for awareness network layer Retrieved from http://awareness.freeband.nl*.

Barlow, D. H. (2002). *Anxiety and its disorders: The nature and treatment of anxiety and panic* (2nd ed.). New York: The Guilford Press.

Barnes, S. J. (2006). Location-Based Services: The State of the Art. *E-Service Journal, 2*(3), 59-70. Indiana University Press.

Barry, D. K. (2003). Web Services and Service-Oriented Architectures. In M. Kaufmann (Ed.), *Savvy Manager's Guide*.

Basu, A., Cheng, I., Mun, P., & Rao, G. (2007). Multimedia Adaptive Computer based Testing: An Overview. In *Proceedings of the International Conference on Multimedia and Expo* (pp. 1850-1853) IEEE Press.

Bauer, M., Becker, C., & Rothermel, K (2002). *Location Models from the Perspective of Context-Aware Applications and Mobile Ad Hoc Networks*. Personal Ubiquitous Comput., *6*(5-6), 322-328.

Bauer, M., Heiber, T., Kortuem G., & Segall, Z. (1998). A collaborative wearable system with remote sensing. In *Second International Symposium on Wearable Computers (*ISWC 1998), 19-20 October 1998, Pittsburgh, Pennsylvania, USA (pp. 10-17) IEEE Computer Society Press

Baumeister, H., Knapp, A., Koch, N., & Zhang, G. (2005). Modelling Adaptivity with Aspects. In *ICWE'05* (pp. 406-416). Sydney, Australia: Springer.

Baumgartner, N., Retschitzegger, W., & Schwinger, W. (2008). A software architecture for ontology-driven situation awareness. In *Proceedings of the 2008 ACM Symposium on Applied Computing* (pp 2326-2330) ACM Press

Bechhofer, S., Van Harmelen, F., Hendler, J., Horrocks, I., McGuinness, D. L., Patel-Schneider, P. F. & Stein, L. A. (2004). *OWL Web Ontology Language Reference* 10 february 2004 edition, retrieved june 17, 2008 from http://www.w3.org/TR/owl-ref/

Beigl, M., Gellersen, H. W., & Schmidt, A. (2001). Mediacups: Experience with design and use of computer-augmented everyday objects. *Computer Networks*, *35*(4), 401-409.

Belhanafi Behlouli, N., Taconet, C., & Bernard, G. (2006). An Architecture for supporting Development and Execution of Context-Aware Component applications. In *International Conference on Pervasive Services*, (pp. 57-66). IEEE Computer Society Press.

Bell, D., & La Padula, L. (1973). Secure Computer Systems: Mathematical Foundations. *Technical Report MTR 254, 1.* MITRE Corporation.

Benatallah, B., Casati, F., Grigori, D., Nezhad, H. R., & Toumani, F. (2005). Developing adapters for Web services integration. In *CAiSE Conference,* (pp. 415–429) Lecture Notes in Computer Science 3520. Springer Verlag

Beresford, A. R., & Stajano, F. (2003). Location privacy in pervasive computing. *Pervasive Computing, IEEE, 2*(1), 46 - 55.

Berhe, G., Brunie, L., & Pierson, J. M. (2005). Distributed Content Adaptation for Pervasive Systems. *International Conference on Information Technology* ITCC 2005 (pp. 234-241). IEEE Computer Society Press

Bernard, G. (2006). Middleware for Next Generation Distributed Systems: Main Challenges and Perspectives. *Proceedings of Database and Expert Systems Applications, 2006. DEXA '06. 17th International Conference on*, 237-240. IEEE Computer Society Press.

Berners-Lee, T., Hendler, J., & Lassila, O. (2001). The semantic Web. *Scientific American, 284*(5), 28-37.

Bertino, E., Bonatti, P. A., Ferrari, E. (2001). TRBAC: A Temporal Role-Based Access Control Model. *ACM Transactions on Information and System Security, 4*(3), 191-223.

Bertolino, A., De Angelis, G., & Polini, A. (2007). A QoS Test-bed Generator for Web Services. *Proceedings of ICWE 2007*, Como, Italy, July 16 - 20.

Beth, T., Borcherding, M., & Klein, B. (1994). *Valuation of Trust in Open Networks.* Paper presented at the Third European Symposium on Research in Computer Security, Brighton.

Bhogal, J., Macfarlane, A., & Smith, P. (2007). A review of ontology based query expansion. *Information Processing & Management, 43*(4), 866-886.

Bianculli, D., & Ghezzi, C. (2007). Monitoring conversational web services. In *Proceedings of the 2nd International Workshop on Service-Oriented Software Engineering* (IW-SOSWE'07), collocated with ESEC/FSE 2007.

Biba, K. (1975). Integrity Considerations for Secure Computer Systems. *Technical Report MTR-3153*, Mitre Corporation.

Biegel, G., & Cahill, V. (2004)/ A Framework for Developing Mobile, Context-aware Applications. *2nd IEEE Conference on Pervasive Computing and Communications*, Orlando, FL, USA.

Bilandzic, M., Foth, M., & De Luca, A. (2008). City-Flocks: Designing Social Navigation for Urban Mobile Information Systems. In J. van der Schijff, G. Marsden, & P. Kotze (Eds.), *Proceedings ACM Designing Interactive Systems (DIS),* Cape Town, South Africa.

Bird, R., Gopal, I., Herzberg, A., Janson, P., Kutten, S., Molva, R., et al. (1995). The KryptoKnight Family of Light-Weight Protocols for Authentication and Key Distribution. *IEEE/ACM Transactions on Networking, 3*(1), 31-41.

Blair, G. S., Coulson, G., Andersen, A., Blair, L., Clarke, M., Costa, F., Duran, H., Parlavantzas, N., & Saikoski, K. A (2000). Principled Approach to Supporting Adaptation in Distributed Mobile Environments. In *Proceedings of the International Symposium on Software Engineering for Parallel and Distributed Systems* (pp. 3-12)

Blaze, M., Feigenbaum, J., Ioannidis, J., & Keromytis, A. D. (1999). The Role of Trust Management in Distributed Systems Security. In J.Vitek & C. Jensen (Eds.), *Secure Internet Programming* (pp. 185-210): Springer-Verlag.

Bohn, J., Coroama, V., Langheinrich, M., Mattern, F., & Rohs, M. (2004). Social, Economic, and Ethical Implications of Ambient Intelligence and Ubiquitous Computing. *Ambient Intelligence. Springer-Verlag.*

Bojadziev, G., & Bojadziev, M. (1997). *Fuzzy Logic for Business, Finance, and Management*: World Scientific.

Bonifacio, M., Bouquet, P., Mameli, G., & Nori, M. (2003). Peer-mediated knowledge management. In *AAAI-03 Spring Symposium on Agent-Mediated Knowledge Management (AMKM-03).*

Bonifati, A., Braga, D., Campi, A., & Ceri, S. (2002). Active XQuery. In *ICDE'02* (pp. 403-412). San Jose, California: IEEE.

Bottaro, A., Bourcier, J., Escoffier, C., & Lalanda, P. (2007). Context-Aware Service Composition in a Home Control Gateway. *4th IEEE International Conference on Pervasive Services (ICPS'07)*, Istanbul, Turkey.

Bouquet, P., Giunchiglia, F., van Harmelen, F., Serafini, L., & Stuckenschmidt, H. (2003). C-OWL: Contextualizing Ontologies. *ISWC-2003, LNCS 2870,* 164-179. Springer Verlag.

Boussard, M. et al. (2008). *Service Adaptation over Heterogeneous Infrastructures.* Plastic IST project white paper. retrieved June 16, 2008 from ftp://ftp.cordis.europa.eu/pub/ist/docs/ct/whitepaper3-service-adaptation-e2r-final_en.pdf

Brambilla, M., Ceri, S., Comai, S., Fraternali, P., & Manolescu, I. (2003). Specification and Design of Workflow-Driven Hypertexts. *Journal of Web Engineering, 1*(2), 163-182.

Brar, A., & Kay, J. (2004). *Privacy and security in ubiquitous personalized applications.*

Bray, T., Paoli, J., Sperberg-McQueen, C., Maler, E. & Yergeau, F. (2006). *XML 1.1, (Second Edition).* World Wide Web Consortium. Retrieved March 11, 2008 from http://www.w3.org/TR/2006/REC-xml11-20060816/.

Brennan, S., & Meier, R. (2007). STIS: Smart Travel Planning Across Multiple Modes of Transportation. *Proceedings of the 10th International IEEE Conference on Intelligent Transportation Systems (IEEE ITSC 2007).* Seattle, Washington, USA: IEEE Computer Society, 2007, (pp. 666–671).

Brickley, D., & Miller, L. (2007, November 2). Foaf vocabulary specification, *Namespace Document.* Retrieved from http://xmlns.com/foaf/spec/.

Brown, P. J., Bovey, J. D., & Chen, X. (1997). Context-aware Applications: from the Laboratory to the Marketplace. *IEEE Personal Communications, 4*(5), 58–64.

Brusilovsky, P. (1996). Methods and Techniques of Adaptive Hypermedia. *User Modeling and User-Adapted Interaction, 6*(2-3), 87-129.

Buchholz, T., Krause, M., Linnhoff-Popien, C., & Schiffers, M. (2004). CoCo: Dynamic composition of context information. *The First Annual International Conference on Mobile and Ubiquitous Systems: Networking and Services (MOBIQUITOUS 2004),* (pp. 335-343).

Buchholz, T., Küpper, A., & Schiffers, M. (2003). Quality of Context: What It Is And Why We Need It. *Workshop of the HP OpenView University Association 2003 (HP-OVUA2003),* Geneva.

Bullard, V., & Vambenepe, W. (2006). *Web services distributed management: management using web services (MUWS 1.1) Part 1.* OASIS. Retrieved June 1, 2007 from http://docs.oasis-open.org/wsdm/wsdm-muws1-1.1-spec-os-01.pdf.

Burr, W. E., Dodson, D. F., Polk, W. T. (2006). Electronic authentication guideline. *NIST Special Publication 800 63.* National Institue of Standards and Technology.

Cabral, L., Domingue, J., Galizia, S., Gugliotta, A., Norton, B., Tanasescu, V., & Pedrinaci, C. (2006). IRS-III: A Broker for Semantic Web Services based Applications. *Proceedings of the 5ᵗʰ International Semantic Web Conference (ISWC),* Athens, USA.

Camenisch, J., & Herreweghen, E. V. (2002). *Design and Implementation of Idemix Anonymous Credential System:* IBM Zurich Research Laboratory.

Cammareri, D. & Raibulet, C. (2007). Self-Adaptive Execution Mechanisms in ARMS. In *Journal of System and Information Sciences Notes,* 2(1), 58-63.

Campbell, R., Al-Muhtadi, J., Naldurg, P., Sampemane1, G., & Mickunas, M. D. (2002). Towards security and privacy for pervasive computing. In *Proceedings of International Symposium on Software Security,* Tokyo, Japan.

Canali, C., & Lancellotti, R. (2006). A distributed architecture to support infomobility services. *In Proceedings of the 2nd international Workshop on Advanced Architectures and Algorithms For internet Delivery and Applications* (Pisa, Italy, October 10 - 10, 2006). AAA-IDEA '06, 198., New York, NY: ACM.

Capra, L., Blair, G. S., Mascolo, C., Emmerich, W., & Grace, P. (2002). Exploiting Reflection in Mobile Computing Middleware. In *ACM SIGMOBILE Mobile Computing and Communications Review,* 6(4), 33-44.

Capra, L., Emmerich, W., & Mascolo, C. (2003). CARISMA: Context-Aware Reflective mIddleware System for Mobile Applications. In *IEEE Transactions on Software Engineering,* 29(10), 929-945.

Cardoso, J. (2007). The semantic web vision: where are we? *Intelligent Systems,* 22(5), 84-88.

Cardoso, R. S., & Issarny, V. (2007). Architecting Pervasive Computing Systems for Privacy: A Survey. *Proceedings of the Sixth Working IEEE/IFIP Conference on Software Architecture (WICSA'07),* (pp. 44-47). IEEE.

Carver, C. A. Jr., Howard, R. A., & Lane, W. D. (1999). Enhancing student learning through hypermedia courseware and incorporation of student learning styles. *IEEE Transactions on Education,* 42(1), 33-38.

Carzaniga, A., Rutherford, M. J., & Wolf, A. L. (2004). A Routing Scheme for Content-Based Networking. *Proceedings of IEEE INFOCOM 2004.* Hong Kong, China. March, 2004.

Cassady, C. C. (2004). The influence of cognitive test anxiety across the learning–testing cycle. *Learning and Instruction,* 14, 569–592.

Cassidy, S. (2004). Learning Styles: An overview of theories, models, and measures. *Educational Psychology,* 24(4), 419-444.

Casteleyn, S., De Troyer, O., & Brockmans, S. (2003). Design Time Support for Adaptive Behavior in Web Sites. In *SAC'03* (pp. 1222-1228). Melbourne, Florida: ACM.

Cazzola, W., Savigni, A., Sosio, A., & Tisato, F. (1999). *Architectural Reflection: Concepts, Design, and Evaluation.* Technical Report RI-DSI 234-99. DSI. University degli Studi di Milano

Cazzola, W., Sosio, A., Savigni, A., & Tisato, F. (2000). Architectural Reflection. Realizing Software Architectures via Reflective Activities. In *Proceedings of the International Workshop on Engineering Distributed Objects. LNCS,* (pp. 102-115). Springer Verlag.

CEN TC278 (2006). *Public transport — Service interface for real-time information relating to public transport operations — Part 1: Context and framework* (Technical Specification prCEN/TS 00278181-1). Accessed September 20, 2007, from http://www.cen.eu/cenorm/homepage.htm.

CEN TC278 (1997). *Road Transport and Traffic Telematics – Public Transport – Reference Data Model.* ENV 1997.

Ceri, S., Daniel, F., Matera, M., & Facca, F. M. (2007). Model-driven development of context-aware Web applications. *ACM Transactions on Internet Technologies, 7*(1).

Ceri, S., Fraternali, P., Bongio, A., Brambilla, M., Comai, S., & Matera, M. (2002). *Designing Data-Intensive Web Applications.* San Francisco, CA: Morgan Kauffmann.

Ceri. S., Daniel, F., Matera, M., & Facca, F. M. (2007). Model-driven Development of Context-aware Web Applications. *ACM Transactions on Internet Technologies, 7*(1), article no. 2.

Ceriani, S., Raibulet, C., & Ubezio, L. (2007). A Java Mobile-Enabled Environment to Access Adaptive Services", In *Proceedings of the 5th Principles and Practice of Programming in Java Conference* (pp. 249-254). ACM Press.

Chaari, T., & Laforest, F. (2005). SEFAGI: Simple Environment for Adaptable Graphical Interfaces - Generating User Interfaces for Different Kinds of Terminals. In *7th International Conference on Entreprise Information Systems* (pp. 232-237).

Chaari, T., Dejene, E., Laforest, F. & Scuturici, V.-M. (2006). Modeling and Using Context in Adapting Applications to Pervasive Environments. In *ICPS'06 : IEEE International Conference on Pervasive Services 2006.*

Chaari, T., Ejigu, D., Laforest, F., & Scuturici, V. M. (2007). A Comprehensive Approach to Model and Use Context for Adapting Applications in Pervasive Environments. *Int. Journal of Systems and software 80*(12), 1973-1992. Elsevier.

Chaari, T., Laforest, F., & Celentano, A. (2007) Adaptation in Context-Aware Pervasive Information Systems: The SECAS Project. *Int. Journal on Pervasive Computing and Communications, 3*(4), 400-425. Emerald Group Publishing Limited.

Chakraborty, D., Joshi, A., Finin, T., & Yesha, Y. (2005). Service composition for mobile environment. *Mobile Networks and Applications, 4*(10), 435-451.

Challiol, C., Fortier, A., Gordillo, S., & Rossi, G. (2007). A Flexible Architecture for Context-Aware Physical Hypermedia, *dexa*, (pp. 590-594) *In the 18th International Conference on Database and Expert Systems Applications (DEXA 2007).*

Chalmers, D., & Sloman, M. (1999). A Survey of Quality of Service in Mobile Computing Environments. *IEEE Communications Surveys*, 2-10.

Chan, A. T. S, & Chuang, S. N. (2003). MobiPADS: A Reflective Middleware for Context-Aware Mobile Computing. In *IEEE Transactions on Software Engineering, 29*(12), 1072-1085.

Chaum, D. (1985). Security without Identification Card Computers to make Big Brother Obsolete. *Communications of ACM, 28*(10), 1034-1044.

Chefrour, D., & André, F. (2002). ACEEL: modèle de composants auto-adaptatifs. Application aux environnements mobiles. In *Colloque Systèmes à composants adaptables et extensibles.* October 2002, Grenoble, France.

Chen, G., & Kotz, D. (2000). *A survey of context-aware mobile computing research.* Technical Report TR2000-381, Dartmouth College.

Chen, H. (2004). *An Intelligent Broker Architecture for Pervasive Context-Aware Systems.* Unpublished doctoral dissertation, Baltimore County: Department of CSEE, University of Maryland.

Chen, H., Finin, T., & Joshi, A. (2003). An Ontology for Context-Aware Pervasive Computing Environments. In *Workshop on Ontologies and Distributed Systems, International Joint Conference on Artificial Intelligence,* Mexico.

Chen, H., Finin, T., & Joshi, A. (2004). An ontology for context-aware pervasive computing environments. *Special Issue on Ontologies for Distributed Systems, Knowledge Engineering Review, 18*(3), 197-207.

Chen, H., Finin, T., & Joshi, A. (2004). Semantic Web in the Context Broker Architecture. In *Proceedings of PerCom 2004*, Orlando FL.

Chen, H., Finin, T., Joshi, A., Kagal, L., Perich, F., & Chakraborty, D. (2004). Intelligent agents meet the semantic web in smart spaces. *IEEE Internet Computing, 8*(6), 69-79.

Chen, H., Perich, F., Finin, T., & Joshi A. (2004). SOUPA: standard ontology for ubiquitous and pervasive applications. In *Proceedings of the First Annual International Conference on Mobile and Ubiquitous Systems: Networking and Services* (pp. 258-267). Boston, MA.

Chen, R. (2002). Poblano-A Distributed Trust Model for Peer-to-Peer Networks. *Sun.*

Cheng S. W, Huang, A. C., Garlan, D., Schmerl, B., & Steenkiste, P., (2004). An Architecture for Coordinating Multiple Self-Management Modules. In *Proceedings of the 4th Working IEEE/IFIP Conference on Software Architecture*, (pp. 243-252).

Cheng, S. W., Garlan, D., & Schmerl, B. (2006). Architecture-based Self-Adaptation in the Presence of Multiple Objectives. In *Proceedings of the ICSE Workshop on Software Engineering for Adaptive and Self-Managing Systems*, (pp. 2-8).

Cheung-Foo-Wo, D., Tigli, J. Y., Lavirotte S., & Riveill, M. (2007). Self-adaptation of event-driven component-oriented Middleware using Aspects of Assembly. In *5th International Workshop on Middleware for Pervasive and Ad-Hoc Computing*, California, USA.

Cheverst, K., Davies, N., Mitchell, K., Friday, A., & Efstratiou, C. (2000). Developing a context-aware electronic tourist guide: some issues and experiences. *Proceedings of the SIGCHI conference on Human Factors in Computing Systems*, (pp. 17-24). New York: ACM Press.

Chien, M.-H.-Y. (2004). Efficient time-bound hierarchical key assignment scheme. *IEEE Transactions on Knowledge and Data Engineering, 16*(10), 1301-1304.

Cho, J., & Garcia-Molina, H. (2003). Effective page refresh policies for web crawlers. *ACM Transactions on Database Systems, 28*, 390-426.

Cho, J., & Garcia-Molina, H. (2003B). Estimating frequency of change. *ACM Transactions on Internet Technology, 3*, 256-290.

Chorfi, H., & Jemni, M. (2004). PERSO: Towards an Adaptive E-Learning System. In *Journal of Interactive Learning Research, 15*(4), 433-447.

Chris, W., Looi, M., & Clark, A. (2004). Toward context-aware security: an authorization architecture for intranet environments. *Second IEEE Annual COnference on Pervasive Computing and Communication Workshops (PERCOMM'04)*

Christensen, E., Curbera, F., Meredith, G., & Weerawarana. S. (2001). *Web Services Description Language (WSDL) 1.1*. W3C standard.

Christopoulou, E. (2008). Context as a Necessity in Mobile Applications. *Handbook of Research on User Interface Design and Evaluation for Mobile Technology.*

Christopoulou, E., Goumopoulos, C., & Kameas, A. (2005). An ontology-based context management and reasoning process for UbiComp applications. In *Proceedings of the 2005 Joint Conference on Smart Objects and Ambient Intelligence* (265-270). Grenoble, France.

Clarke, E. M. J., Grumberg, O., & Peled, D. A. (1999). *Model Checking*. MIT Press

Clifton , C., Kantarcioglu, M., Vaidya, J., Lin, X., & Zhu, M. Y. (2002). Tools for Privacy Preserving Distributed Data Mining. *ACM SIGKDD Explorations, 4*(2), 28 - 34.

Cohen, N. H., Lei, H., Castro, P., Davis II, J. S., & Purakayastha, A. (2002). Composing pervasive data using iQL. *The Fourth IEEE Workshop on Mobile Computing Systems and Applications*, (pp. 94-104).

Colajanni, M. & Lancellotti, R. (2004). System Architectures for Web Content Adaptation Services. *IEEE Distributed Systems On-Line*, Invited paper on Web Systems. Retrieved Mars 12 2008 from http://dsonline. computer.org/portal/pages/dsonline/topics/was/adaptation.xml.

Cooklev, T. (2004). *Wireless Communication Standards: A Study of IEEE 802.11, 802.15, and 802.16*. Standards Information Network/ IEEE Press

Coutaz, J., Crowley, J. L., Dobson, S., & Garlan, D. (2005). Context is key. *Communications of the ACM, 48*(3), 49-53

Covington, M. J., Fogla, P., & Ahamad, M. (2002). A context-aware security architecture for emerging applications. *Annual Computer Security Applications Conference (ACSAC)*.

Covington, M. J., Moyer, M. J., & Ahamad, M. (2000). Generalized role-based access control for securing future applications. *23rd National Information Systems Security Conference*.

Cranor, L. F., Guduru, P., & Arjula, M. (2006). User Interfaces for Privacy Agents. *ACM Transactions on Human Computer Interactions*.

Cranor, L., Langheinrich, M., & Marchiori, M. (2002). *A P3P Preference Exchange Language 1.0 (APPEL1.0) W3C Working Draft*.

Cranor, L., Langheinrich, M., Marchiori, M., Presler-Marshall, M., & Reagle, J. (2004). *The Platform for Privacy Preferences 1.1 (P3P1.1) Specification W3C Working Draft*.

Cregan, A. (2007). Symbol Grounding for the Semantic Web. *4th European Semantic Web Conference 2007*, Innsbruck, Austria.

Cuppens, F., & Miege, A. (2002). Alert correlation in a cooperative intrusion detection framework. *IEEE Symposium on Security and Privacy*, (pp. 202-215).

Currall, S. C., & Judge, T. A. (1995). Measuring Trust between Organizational Boundary Role Persons. *Organizational Behavior and Human Decision Processes, 64*(2), 151-170.

D'Roza, T., & Bilchev, G. (2003). An overview of location-based services. *BT Technology Journal, 21*(1), 20-27. The Netherlands: Springer.

da Costa, C., Yamin, A., & Geyer, C. (2008). Toward a general software infrastucture for ubiquitous computing. *IEEE Pervasive Computing, 7*(1), 64-73.

da Rocha, R., & Endler, M. (2005). Evolutionary and efficient context management in heterogeneous environments. In *Proceedings of the 3rd International Workshop on Middleware for Pervasive and Ad-hoc Computing* (1-7). Grenoble, France.

Damianou, N., Dulay, N., Lupu, E., & Sloman, M. (2001). The ponder policy specification language. *Policies for Distributed Systems and Networks: International Workshop, Policy 2001*, Bristol, Uk, January 29-31, 2001: Proceedings.

Daniel, F., Matera, M., & Pozzi, G. (2008). Managing Runtime Adaptivity through Active Rules: the Bellerofonte Framework. *Journal of Web Engineering, 7*(3), 179-199.

Dao, D. Rizos, C., & Wang, J. (2002). Location-based services: technical and business issues. *GPS Solutions, 6*(3), 169-178. Berlin: Springer.

Daoud, M., Tamine, L., Boughanem, M., & Chabaro, B. (2007). Learning Implicit User Interests Using Ontology and Search History for Personalization. In Mathias Weske, Mohand-Said Hacid, Claude Godart (Eds.): *Personalized Access to Web Information (PAWI 2007), Workshop of the 8th International Web Information Systems Engineering (WISE 2007), Lecture Notes In Computer Science, Vol. 4832* (pp. 325-336). Springer-Verlag.

Daskapan, S., Vree, W. G., & Ali Eldin, A. (2003). *Trust metrics for survivable security systems*. Paper presented at the IEEE International Conference on Systems, Man & Cybernetics,, Washington.

Daskapan, Semir, Costa, Ana Cristina, "Reengineering Trust in Global Information Systems", in *Trust and*

New Technologies: Marketing and Management on the Internet and Mobile Media. Cheltenham, UK and Lyme, US: Edward Elgar, Edited by Kautonen, T. and H. Karjaluoto (Eds), 2008

Datta, A., Quarteroni, S., & Aberer, K. (2004). Autonomous Gossiping: A self-organizing epidemic algorithm for selective information dissemination in wireless mobile ad-hoc networks. In *Proceedings of the International Conference on Semantics of a Networked World (IC-SNW04)*, Paris, France.

De Bra, P., & Nejdl, W. (2004). Adaptive Hypermedia and Adaptive Web-based Systems. *Proceedings of the Third International Conference (AH 2004)*, Springer Lecture Notes in Computer Science, 3137.

De Bra, P., Aerts, A. T. M., Berden, B., de Lange, B., Rousseau, B., Santic, T., Smits, D., & Stash, N. (2003). AHA! The Adaptive Hypermedia Architecture. In *Hypertext'03* (pp 81-84). Nottingham, UK: ACM.

de Lemos, R. (2000). A Co-operative Object-Oriented Architecture for Adaptive Systems. In *Proceedings of the 7th IEEE International Conference and Workshop on the Engineering of Computer Based Systems*, (pp. 120-128).

De Troyer, O., & Leune, C. J. (1998). WSDM: A User Centered Design Method for Web Sites. *Computer Networks, 30*(1-7), 85-94.

De Virgilio, R., & Torlone, R. (2006). Modeling heterogeneous context information in adaptive web based applications. In *6th international Conference on Web Engineering, 263*, 56-63. ACM Press

Dean, M., & Schreiber, G. (2004). Owl web ontology language reference. *W3C Recommendation.*

Decker, S., Erdmann, M., Fensel, D., & Studer, R. (1999). Ontobroker: ontology based access to distributed and semi-structured information. *Database Semantics: Semantic Issues in Multimedia Systems*, (pp. 351–369).

Demesticha, V., Gergic, J., Kleindienst, J., Mast, M., Polymenakos, L. Schulz, H. & Seredi, L. (2001). Aspects of Design and Implementation of a Multi-channel and Multi-modal Information System. In *Proceedings of the IEEE International Conference on Software Maintenance.* (pp. 312-319).

Demetriou, A., & Kazi, S. (2001). *Unity and modularity in the mind and the self: Studies on the relationships between self-awareness, personality, and intellectual development from childhood to adolescence.* London: Routledge.

Demetriou, A., Efklides, A., & Platsidou, M. (1993). The architecture and dynamics of developing mind: Experiential structuralism as a frame for unifying cognitive development theories. *Monographs of the Society for Research in Child Development, 58*(Serial No. 234), 5-6

DeVaul, R., & Pentland, A. (2000). The Ektara Architecture: The Right Framework for Context-Aware Wearable and Ubiquitous Computing Applications. *The Media Laboratory*, MIT.

Devlic, A. & Klintskog, E. (2007). Context retrieval and distribution in a mobile distributed environment, In *Third Workshop on Context Awareness for Proactive Systems (CAPS 2007).*

Devore, J., & Peck, R. (2001). *Statistics—The Exploration and Analysis of Data.* 4th ed. Pacific Grove, CA: Duxbury.

Dey, A. (2000). *Providing Architectural Support for Building Context-Aware Applications.* PhD Thesis, College of Computing, GA Institute of Technology, Georgia, USA.

Dey, A. K. (2001). Understanding and Using Context. *Personal and Ubiquitous Computing, 5*(1), 4-7.

Dey, A. K., & Abowd, G. D. (2000). *Towards a better understanding of context and context-awareness.* Paper presented at the CHI 2000 Workshop on the What, Who, Where, When, Why and How of Context-Awareness.

Dey, A. K., & Abowd, G.D. (2000). Towards a Better Understanding of Context and Context-Awareness. In *CHI'00 Workshop Proceedings*, The Hague, The Netherlands.

Dey, A. K., Abowd, G. D., & Saber, D. (1999). Context-Based Infrastructure for Smart Environments. *1st International Workshop on Managing Interactions in Smart Environments (MANSE '99)* (pp. 114-128).

Dey, A. K., Abowd, G. D., & Wood, A. (1998). CyberDesk: A framework for providing self– integrating context–aware services. *Knowledge Based Systems, 11*(1), 3-13.

Dey, A. K., Salber, D., & Abowd, G. D. (2001). A conceptual framework and a toolkit for supporting the rapid prototyping of context-aware applications. *Special issue on context-aware computing Human Computer Interaction Journal, 16*(2-4), 97–116.

Dey, A. K. (2000). *Providing architectural support for building context-aware applications.* PhD thesis.

Dey, A., Abowd, G., & Salber, D. (1999). A context-based infrastructure for smart environments. In *Proceedings of 1ˢᵗ International Workshop on Managing Interactions in Smart Environments* (pp. 114 -128).

Dey, A., Abowd, G., & Wood, A. (1998). CyberDesk: A Framework for Providing Self–Integrating Context–Aware Services. *Knowledge Based Systems, 11*(1), 3-13.

Dietze, S., Gugliotta, A., & Domingue, J., (2007). A Semantic Web Services-based Infrastructure for Context-Adaptive Process Support. *Proceedings of IEEE 2007 International Conference on Web Services (ICWS),* Salt Lake City, Utah, USA.

Dietze, S., Gugliotta, A., & Domingue, J., (2008). Towards Context-aware Semantic Web Service Discovery through Conceptual Situation Spaces. *Workshop: International Workshop on Context enabled Source and Service Selection, Integration and Adaptation (CSSSIA), 17th International World Wide Web Conference (WWW2008),* Beijing, China.

Dill, D. (1989). Timing assumptions and verification of finite-state concurrent systems. In J. Sifakis, (Ed.), *Proceedings of the International Workshop on Automatic Verification Methods for Finite State Systems.*

Dowling, J., & Cahill, V. (2001). The K-Component Architecture Meta-Model for Self-Adaptive Software. In *Third International Conference on Metalevel Architectures and Separation of Crosscutting Concerns,* Reflection 2001, Kyoto, Japan (pp. 81-88).

Drools, website: http://www.drools.org

Dubin, M. W. (2002). *How the brain works.* Blackwell Science, Inc.

Dubois, D., & Prade, H. (1995). What does fuzzy logic bring to AI? *ACM Computing Surveys (CSUR), 27*(3).

Ducatel, K., Bogdanowicz, M., Scapolo, F., Leijten, J., & Burgelma, J. C. (2001). *Scenarios for ambient intelligence in 2010 (ISTAG 2001 Final Report).*

Edwards, J., McCurley, K., & Tomlin, J. (2001). An Adaptive Model for Optimizing Performance of an Incremental Web Crawler. *WWW Conference 2001,* Hong Kong, China.

Edwards, W. K., Newman, M. W., Sedivy, J., & Izadi, S. (2002). Challenge: Recombinant computing and the speakeasy approach. In *Proceedings of ACM MobiCom,* ACM Press, (pp. 279-286), New York, USA.

Eikerling, H.-J., Benesch, M., & Berger, F. (2007). Using Proximity Relations for the Adaptation of Mobile Field Services. *Proceedings of the International Workshop on the Engineering of Software Services for Pervasive Environments* (ESSPE '07) at ESEC/FSE 2007, September 4, 2007, Dubrovnik, Croatia

Ejigu, D., Scuturici, M., & Brunie, L. (2007). An Ontology-Based Approach to Context Modeling and Reasoning in Pervasive Computing. In *Proceedings of the Fifth IEEE international Conference on Pervasive Computing and Communications Workshops* (pp. 14-19). IEEE Computer Society Press.

Ejigu, D., Scuturici, V., & Brunie, L. (2007). Semantic approach to context management and reasoning in ubiquitous context-aware systems In *The Second IEEE International Conference on Digital Information Management (ICDIM 2007), Proceedings of ICDIM '07.* (pp. 500-5005). Retrieved from http://liris.cnrs.fr/publis/?id=3242

El Kalam, A. A., Benferhat, S., Miege, A., El Baida, R., Cuppens, C., Saurel, C., Balbiani, P., Deswarte, Y., & Trouessin, G. (2003). Organization based access control. *IEEE International Workshop on Policies for Distributed Systems and Networks*. IEEE Computer Society.

Elianssen, F., Andersen, A., Blair, G. S., Costa, F., Coulson, G., Goebel, V., Hansen, O., Kristensen, T., Plagemann, T., Rafaelsen, H. O., Saikoski, K. B., & Weihai Y. (1999). Next Generation Middleware: Requirements, Architecture, and Prototypes. In *Proceedings of the 7th IEEE Workshop on Future Trends of Distributed Computing Systems*, (pp. 60-65).

Elnahrawy, E., & Nath, B. (2003). Cleaning and querying noisy sensors. *The 2nd ACM International Conference on Wireless Sensor Networks and Applications,* (pp. 78-87).

Erl, T. (2005) *Service-Oriented Architecture: Concepts, Technology and Design.* USA: Prentice Hall PTR, USA

Erl, T. (2008). *SOA Principles of Service Design.* 1st ed. Prentice Hall PTR, Upper Saddle River.

Espinoza, F., Persson, P., Sandin, A., Nyström, H., Cacciatore, E., & Bylund, M. (2001). GeoNotes: social and navigational aspects of location-based information systems. *Proceedings of the 3rd International Conference on Ubiquitous Computing* (pp. 2–17). Atlanta, Georgia, USA.

European Commission (1999). *Info-Mobility.* European Commission (DGXIII) Consultation Meeting on. Retrieved 16 may 2008 from ftp://ftp.cordis.europa.eu/pub/telematics/docs/tap_transport/introinfomob.pdf

European Commission (2001). *European Transport Policy for 2010.* White Paper. Retrieved October 15, 2007, from http://ec.europa.eu/transport/white_paper/.

European Commission Directorate General for Transport and Energy (2006). *DATEX II Exchange Platform Specific Model (version 1.0).* Accessed September 25, 2007, from http://www.datex2.eu/?q=node/28

European Directive. (2002). Directive 2002/58/EC of the European Parliament and of the Council of 12 July 2002, electronic communications sector (Directive on privacy and electronic communications). *Official Journal of European Communities, L,* 201-237.

Fabini, J., Happenhofer, M., & Pailer, R. (2006). Terminal-Centric Location Services for the IP Multimedia Subsystem. *Proceedings of Vehicular Technology Conference, 2,* 881-885. IEEE.

Fahy, P., & Clarke, S. (2004). CASS: Middleware for Mobile Context-Aware Applications. *ACM MobiSys Workshop on Context Awareness*, Boston, USA.

Favela, J., Rodriguez, M., Preciado, A., & Gonzalez, V. M. (2004). Integrating Context-Aware Public Displays Into a Mobile Hospital Information System. In *IEEE Transactions on Information Technology in Biomedicine, 8*(3), 279-286.

Feng, L., Apers, P., & Jonker, W. (2004). Towards context-aware data management for ambient intelligence. *The 15th International Conference on Database and Expert Systems Applications (DEXA),* (pp. 422-431).

Fensel, D., Lausen, H., Polleres, A., de Bruijn, J., Stollberg, M., Roman, D., & Domingue, J. (2006). *Enabling Semantic Web Services—The Web service Modelling Ontology.* Springer.

Fiala, Z., & Houben, G.-J. (2005). A generic transcoding tool for making web applications adaptive. In *CAiSE'05 Short Paper Proceedings*, volume 161 of CEUR Workshop Proceedings. CEUR-WS.org.

Fiedler, M., Chevul, S., Isaksson, L., Lindberg, P., & Karlsson, J. (2005). Generic communication requirements of ITS-related mobile services as basis for seamless communications. *Next Generation Internet Networks*, (pp. 426- 433). IEEE.

Fielding, R. T., & Taylor, R. N. (2000). *Principled design of the modern Web architecture In Proceedings of the 22nd International Conference on Software Engineering,* Limerick, Ireland, (pp. 407-416).

FIPA (2004). *FIPA agent management specification.* Foundation for Intelligent Physical Agents. Retrieved March 3, 2008 from http://www.fipa.org/specs/fipa00023/SC00023K.pdf.

FIPA. (2002, December 6). *Fipa device ontology specification.*

Fortier, A., Cañibano, N., Grigera, J., Rossi, G., & Gordillo, S. (2006). An Object-Oriented Approach for Context-Aware Applications. *In Proceedings of the 2006 Smalltalk research Conference*, Also Springer Verlag, 2006, LNCS.

Fox, A., Goldberg, I., Gribble, S. et al. (1998). Experience with TopGun Wingman: A Proxy-Based Web Browser for the 3Com PalmPilot. In *Proceedings of the IFIP International Conference on Distributed Systems Platforms and Open Distributed Processing - Middleware 98* (pp. 407-426) Lake District, England.

Frantzen, L., & Tretmans, J. (2007), Model-Based Testing of Environmental Conformance of Components. *Proceedings at Formal Methods of Components and Objects* -- FMCO 2006, LNCS 4709, (pp. 1-25). Springer-Verlag.

Frasincar, F., & Houben, G.-J. (2002). Hypermedia Presentation Adaptation on the Semantic Web. In *AH'02* (pp. 133-142). Málaga, Spain: Springer.

Frodigh, M., Johansson, P., & Larsson, P. (2000). *Wireless ad hoc networking -- The art of networking without a network.* Ericsson Inc. Retrieved May 1, 2007 from http://www.ericsson.com/ericsson/corpinfo/publications/review/2000_04/files/2000046.pdf.

Gambetta, D. G. (1988). *Can we trust trust?* New York: Basil Blackwell.

Gamma, E., Helm, R., Johnson, R., & Vlissides, J. (1994). *Design Patterns: Elements of Reusable Object-Oriented Software*, USA: Addison Wesley, Reading MA.

Gamma, E., Helm, R., Johnson, R., & Vlissides, J. (1995). *Design Patterns.* Addison-Wesley Professional.

Ganak, A. G., & Corbi, T. A. (2003). The Dawning of the Autonomic Computing Era. In *IBM Systems Journal. 42*(1), 518.

Ganeriwal, S., & Srivastava, M. B. (2004). Reputation-based framework for high integrity sensor networks. *ACM Workshop on Security of Ad Hoc and Sensor Networks* (pp. 66–77).

Gangemi, A., & Mika, P. (2003). Understanding the Semantic Web through Descriptions and Situations. In R. Meersman, Z. Tari, & et al. (Eds.), *Proceedings of the On The Move Federated Conferences (OTM'03)*, LNCS. Springer Verlag.

Gangemi, A., Guarino, N., Masolo, C., Oltramari, A., & Schneider, L. (2002). Sweetening Ontologies with DOLCE. In A. Gómez-Pérez, V. Richard Benjamins (Eds.), *Knowledge Engineering and Knowledge Management. Ontologies and the Semantic Web: 13th International Conference*, EKAW 2002, Siguenza, Spain, October 1-4.

Gärdenfors, P. (2000). *Conceptual Spaces—The Geometry of Thought.* MIT Press.

Gärdenfors, P. (2004). How to make the semantic web more semantic. In A. C. Vieu & L. Varzi, (Eds.), *Formal Ontology in Information Systems*, (pp. 19–36). IOS Press.

Garlan, D. & Shaw M. (1994). An Introduction to Software Architecture. *Technical Report*, Carnegie Mellon University, CMU-CS-94-166.

Garlan, D., Cheng, S., W., Huang, An-Cheng, Schmerl, B., & Steenkiste, P. (2004). Rainbow: Architecture-based Self-Adaptation with Reusable Infrastructure. In *IEEE Computer, 37*(10), 46-54.

Garlan, D., Siewiorek, D., Smailagic, A., & Steenkiste, P., (2002). Project Aura: Towards Distraction-Free Pervasive Computing. *IEEE Pervasive Computing, 1*(2), 22-31.

Garrigós, I., Casteleyn, S., & Gómez, J. (2005). A Structured Approach to Personalize Websites Using the OO-H Personalization Framework. In *APWeb'05* (pp. 695-706). Shanghai, China: Springer.

Garrigós, I., Gómez, J., Barna, P., & Houben, G.-J. (2005b). A Reusable Personalization Model in Web Application Design. In WISM'05 (pp. 40-49). Sydney, Australia.

Gecsei, J. (1997). Adaptation in Distributed Multimedia Systems. In *IEEE Computer*, (pp. 58-66)

Geihs, K., Khan, M.U., Reichle, R., Solberg, A. & Hallsteinsen, S. (2006). Modeling of component-based self-adapting context-aware applications for mobile devices. *IFIP International Federation for Information Processing - Software Engineering Techniques: Design for Quality*, Vol. 227 (pp. 85-96). Springer.

Geihs, K., Ullah Khan, M., Reichle, R., Solberg, A., Hallsteinsen, S. O., & Merral, S. (2006). Modeling of component-based adaptive distributed applications. In *SAC 2006*: (pp. 718-722), ACM Press.

Gellersen, H-W., Schmidt, A., & Beigl, M. (2002). Multi-Sensor Context-Awareness in Mobile Devices and Smart Artefacts. *ACM Journal Mobile Networks and Applications (MONET), 7*(5).

Germanakos P., Mourlas C., Isaia C., & Samaras G. (2005b). Web Personalized Intelligent User Interfaces and Processes—An Enabler of Multi-Channel eBusiness Services Sustainability. *Proceedings of the 2nd International Conference on E-business and TElecommunications Networks (ICETE2005)*, Reading, October 3-7, 2005, (pp. 177-180).

Germanakos, P., Tsianos, Mourlas, C., & Samaras. (2005). New Fundamental Profiling Characteristics for Designing Adaptive Web-based Educational Systems, *Proceeding of the IADIS International Conference on Cognition and Exploratory Learning in Digital Age (CELDA2005)*, Porto, December 14-16, 2005, (pp. 10-17).

Germanakos, P., Tsianos, N., Lekkas, Z., Mourlas, C., & Samaras, G. (2008). Realizing Comprehensive User Profiling as the Core Element of Adaptive and Personalized Communication Environments and Systems. *The Computer Journal*, Special Issue on Profiling Expertise and Behaviour, Oxford University Press. (accepted)

Germanakos, P., Tsianos, N., Lekkas, Z., Mourlas, C., & Samaras, G. (2007). Capturing Essential Intrinsic User Behaviour Values for the Design of Comprehensive Web-based Personalized Environments. *Computers in Human Behavior*, doi:10.1016/j.chb.2007.07.010.

Germanakos, P., Tsianos, N., Lekkas, Z., Mourlas, C., Belk, M., & Samaras, G. (2007b). A Semantic Approach of an Adaptive and Personalized Web-based Learning Content – The case of AdaptiveWeb, *Proceedings of the 2nd International Workshop on Semantic Media Adaptation and Personalization (SMAP 2007)*, London, U.K., December 17-18, 2007, IEEE Computer Society, pp. 68-73.

Germanakos, P., Tsianos, N., Lekkas, Z., Mourlas, C., Belk, M., & Samaras, G. (2007c). Embracing Cognitive Aspects in Web Personalization Environments – The AdaptiveWeb Architecture, *Proceedings of the 7th IEEE International Conference on Advanced Learning Technologies (ICALT 2007)*, Niigata, Japan, July 18-20, 2007, IEEE. (accepted)

Gilbert, J. E., & Han, C. Y. (2002). Arthur: A Personalized Instructional System. *Journal of Computing in Higher Education, 14*(1), 113-129.

Glass, A., & Riding, R. J. (1999), EEG differences and cognitive style. *Biological Psychology, 51*, 23–41.

Goleman, D. (1995). *Emotional Intelligence: why it can matter more than IQ*. New York: Bantam Books.

Gomez, L., & Thomas, I. (2007). Towards User Authentication Flexibility. *IEEE and ACM International Conference of Security and Cryptography.*

Gorton, I., Liu, Y., & Trivedi, N. (2007). An extensible and lightweight architecture for adaptive server applications. In *Software – Practice and Experience Journal*, (pp. 853-883). Wiley InterScience,

Grace, P., Blair, G. S., & Samuel, S. (2003). ReMMoC: A reflective Middleware to Support Mobile Client Interoperability. In *Proceedings of International Symposium on Distributed Objects and Applications, LNCS 2888*, (pp. 1170-1187).

Graham, S., Karmarker, A., Mischkinsky, J., Robinson, I., & Sedukhin, I. (2006) *Web services resource 1.2.* OASIS. Retrieved June 1, 2007 from http://docs.oasis-open.org/wsrf/wsrf-ws_resource-1.2-spec-os.pdf

Grigera, J., Fortier, A., Rossi, G., & Gordillo, S. (2007). A Modular Architecture for Context Sensing. In *Proceedings of PCAC-07, IEEE Computer Society*, (pp. 147-152).

Grimm, R. (2004). One. world: Experiences with a Pervasive Computing Architecture. *IEEE Pervasive Computing, 3*(3), 22-30.

Grossmann, M., Bauer, M., Hönle, N, Käppeler, U.P., Nicklas, D., & Schwarz, T. (2005). Efficiently Managing Context Information for Large-scale Scenarios., *3rd IEEE Conference on Pervasive Computing and Communications*, Kauai, Hawaii, USA.

Gruber, T. (2006). Where the social web meets the semantic web. *Lecture Notes in Computer Science, 4273*(994).

Gruber, T. R. (1993). A translation approach to portable ontology specifications. *Knowledge Acquisition, 5*(2), 199-220.

Gruber, T. R. (1993). *Toward principles of the design of ontologies used for knowledge sharing.* Presented at the Padua workshop on Formal Ontology, March 1993, later published in International Journal of Human-Computer Studies, Vol. 43, Issues 4-5, November 1995, pp. 907-928.

Gu, T., Pung, H. K., & Zhang, D. Q. (2004). A bayesian approach for dealing with uncertain contexts, *Proceedings of the Second International Conference on Pervasive Computing.*

Gu, T., Pung, H. K., & Zhang, D. Q. (2004). Toward an OSGi-based infrastructure for context-aware applications. *Pervasive Computing, IEEE, 3*(4), 66-74.

Gu, T., Pung, H. K., & Zhang, D. Q. (2004c). A middleware for building context-aware mobile services. The *59th Vehicular Technology Conference, IEEE,* (pp. 2656-2660).

Gu, T., Pung, H. K., & Zhang, D. Q. (2005). A Service-Oriented Middleware for Building Context-Aware Services. *Journal of Network and Computer Applications, 28*(1), 1-18.

Gu, T., Pung, H. K., and Zhang, D. Q. (2004). A Middleware for Building Context-Aware Mobile Services. In Proceedings of IEEE Vehicular Technology Conference (VTC2004), Milan, Italy.

Gu, T., Pung, H., & Zhang, D. (2005). A service-oriented middleware for building context-aware services. *Journal Network Computing Applications, 28*(1), 1-18.

Gu, T., Wang, X. H., Pung, H. K., & Zhang, D. Q. (2004). A middleware for context-aware mobile services. In IEEE Vehicular Technology Conference (VT)C. Los Alamitos, CA: IEEE Computer Society Press.

Gu, T., Wang, X. H., Pung, H. K., & Zhang, D. Q. (2004). An ontology-based context model in intelligent environments, *Proceedings of Communication Networks and Distributed Systems Modeling and Simulation Conference*, 2004.

Gupta, S. K. S., Mukherjee, T., Venkatasubramanian, K., & Taylor, T. B. (2006). Proximity Based Access Control in Smart-Emergency Departments. *4th annual IEEE international conference on Pervasive Computing and Communications Workshops.* (p. 512).

Guttman, E. (1999). Service Location Protocol: Automatic Discovery of IP Network Services. *IEEE Internet Computing, 3*(4), 71-80.

Haghighi, P. D., Zaslavsky, A. B., & Krishnaswamy, S. (2006). An evaluation of query languages for context-aware computing. *The 17th International Conference on Database and Expert Systems Applications (DEXA),* (pp. 455-462).

Haibo, H., & Dik-Lun, L. (2004). Semantic location modeling for location navigation in mobile environment Mobile Data Management, 2004. *Proceedings of 2004 IEEE International Conference,* (pp. 52-61).

Häkkilä, J., & Mäntyjärvi, J. (2005). Combining Location-Aware Mobile Phone Applications and Multimedia Messaging. *Journal of Mobile Multimedia, 1*(1), 18-32.

Hallsteinsen, S., Floch, J., & Stav, E. (2004). A Middleware Centric Approach to Building Self-Adapting Systems. In Software Engineering. and Middleware, Lecture Notes in Computer Science 3437 (pp. 107-122) Springer Verlag

Han, B., Jia, W., Shen, J., and Yuen, M.-C. (2004). Context-Awareness in Mobile Web Services. J. Cao et al. (Eds.): ISPA 2004, LNCS 3358, pp. 519-528.

Hanson, N. E., & Widom, J. (1992). *An Overview of Production Rules in Database Systems.* Technical report, University of Florida (CIS)

Harmonia Inc. (2008). LiquidUI. Retrieved march 19, 2008 from http://www.harmonia.com/products/index. php

Harter, A., Hopper, A., Steggles, P., Ward, A., & Webster, P. (2002). The anatomy of a context-aware application. *Wireless Networks, 8*(2 - 3), 187-197.

Hattori, S., Tezuka, T., & Tanaka, K. (2006). Activity-based query refinement for context-aware information retrieval. *ICADL 2006, LNCS 4312,* (pp. 474-477).

Hattori, S., Tezuka, T., & Tanaka, K. (2007). Context-aware query refinement for mobile web search. *The 2007 International Symposium on Applications and the Internet Workshops (SAINTW),* (pp. 15-15).

Hauser, C. (2002). *Privacy and Security in Location-Based Systems With Spatial Models.* Paper presented at the PAMPAS'02 Workshop on Requirements for Mobile Privacy and Security.

Hauser, C., & Kabatnik, M. (2001). *Towards Privacy Support in a Global Location Service.* Paper presented at the IFIP Workshop on IP and ATM Traffic Management (WATM/EUNICE 2001), Paris.

Heer, J., Newberger, A., Beckmann, C., & Hong, J. I. (2003). Liquid: Context-aware distributed queries. *Proceedings of 5th International Conference on Ubiquitous Computing (Ubicomp 2003),* (pp. 140-148).

Henricksen, K. & Indulska, J. (2006). Developing Context-Aware Pervasive Computing Applications: Models and Approach. *Journal of Pervasive and Mobile Computing, 2*(1), 37-64.

Henricksen, K. (2003). *A Framework for Context-Aware Pervasive Computing Applications.* Ph.D. Thesis, University of Queensland, Queensland, Queensland.

Henricksen, K., & Indulska, J. (2004). Modelling and using imperfect context information. *The Second IEEE Annual Conference on Pervasive Computing and Communications Workshops (PERCOMW),* (pp. 33-37).

Henricksen, K., & Indulska, J. (2006). Developing context-aware pervasive computing applications: Models and approach. *Journal of Pervasive and Mobile Computing, 2*(1), 37-64.

Henricksen, K., Indulska, J., & Rakotonirainy, A. (2002). Modeling Context Information in Pervasive Computing Systems. In *Pervasive'02* (pp. 167-180). London, UK: Springer.

Henricksen, K., Indulska, J., Mcfadden, T., & Balasubramaniam, S. (2005). Middleware for distributed context-aware systems. *On the Move to Meaningful Internet Systems 2005: CoopIS, DOA, and ODBASE, Lecture Notes in Computer Science, 3760,* 846–863. Berlin: Springer.

Hightower, J., & Borriello, G. (2001). Location systems for ubiquitous computing. *Computer, 34*(8), 57-66. IEEE Computer Society.

Hillerson, G. (2001). *Web Clipping Developer's Guide.* Santa Clara, California: Palm Inc.

Hinz, M., Pietschmann, S., Fiala, Z.A (2007). Framework for Context Modeling in Adaptive Web Applications. *IADIS International Journal of WWW/Internet, 5*(1)

Hinz, M., Pietschmann, S., Umbach, M., & Meißner, K. (2007). Adaptation and Distribution of Pipeline-Based Context-Aware Web Architectures. In *Sixth Working IEEE/IFIP Conference on Software Architecture* (p. 15). IEEE Computer Society Press

Hofmann-Wellenhof, B., Lichtenegger, H., & Collins, J. (2004). *Global Positioning System: Theory and Practice*. Springer.

Holone, H., Misund, G., & Holmstedt, H. (2007). Users Are Doing It For Themselves: Pedestrian Navigation With User Generated Content. In the *Proceedings of Next Generation Mobile Applications, Services and Technologies*, (pp. 91-99).

Hong, J., & Landay, J. (2001). An Infrastructure Approach to Context-Aware Computing. *Human Computer Interaction Journal, 16*(2), 287-303.

Hönle, N., Kappeler, U. P., Nicklas, D., Schwarz, T., & Grossmann, M. (2005). Benefits of integrating meta data into a context model. *The 2nd IEEE PerCom Workshop on Context Modeling and Reasoning (CoMoRea)(at PerCom'05)*, (pp. 25-29).

Hori, M., Kondoh, G., Ono, K., Hirose, S., & Singhal, S. K. (2000). Annotation based Web Content Transcoding. *Computer Networks, 33*(1-6), 197-211.

Horrocks, I. (2002). Daml+oil: a description logic for the semantic web. *IEEE Data Engineering Bulletin, 25*(1), 4-9.

Houri, A. (2007, October 29). Draft-ietf-simple-interdomain-scaling-analysis-02 - presence interdomain scaling analysis for sip/simple, *Presence Interdomain Scaling Analysis for SIP/SIMPLE*. Retrieved November 13, 2007, from http://tools.ietf.org/html/draft-ietf-simple-interdomain-scaling-analysis-02.

Housley, R., Ford, W., Polk, W., & Solo, D. (1999). Internet X.509 Public Key Infrastructure--Certificate and CRL Profile. *IETF RFC 2459*.

Hu, J., & Weaver, A. C. (2004). Dynamic, Context-Aware Access Control for Distributed Healthcare Applications. *Pervasive Security, Privacy and Trust (PSPT2004)*.

Huang, D., Liu, F., Shi, X., Yang, G., Zheng, L., & Zhou, Z. (2006). MapWeb: A location-based converged communications platform. *Bell Labs Technical Journal, 11*(1), 159-171. Wiley Periodicals.

Hunter, A. (1996). *Uncertainty in information systems: An introduction to techniques and applications*. The McGraw-Hill Companies.

IBM research (2000). LiquidUI. Retrieved June 1, 2007 from http://www.research.ibm.com/networked_data_systems/transcoding/index.html

IEEE (n.d.). *IEEE 802.15.4 task group*, from http://www.ieee802.org/15/pub/TG4.html

IEEE802.3 (n.d.), *IEEE 802.3 (Ethernet) Standard*, from http://standards.ieee.org/getieee802/

Iftikhar, N., Liaquat, H., & Qadir, M. A. (2006). Profile based context-aware query processing architecture. *Multitopic Conference, 2006. INMIC '06.* (pp. 250-254).

Indulska, J., Robinson, R., Rakotonirainy, A., & Henricksen (2003). Experiences in using CC/PP in context-aware systems. *Proceedings of the 4th International Conference on Mobile Data Management* (MDM2003) (Melbourne/Australia, January 2003), M.-S. Chen, P. K. Chrysanthis, M. Sloman, and A. Zaslavsky, Eds., Lecture Notes in Computer Science (LNCS 2574), Springer, (pp. 247–261).

Infopolis2 Project (1999). *Needs of travellers and analysis based on the study of their tasks and activities*. (Infopolis2 Project Deliverable n. 3). Retrieved March 15, 2007, from http://www.ul.ie/~infopolis/pdf/info2_del3.pdf.

Intanagonwiwat, C., Govindan, R., Estrin, D., Heidemann, J. S., and Silva, F. (2003). Directed diffusion for wireless sensor networking. IEEE/ACM Transactions on Networking, vol. 11, no. 1, pp. 2-16.

International Telecommunication Union (2006). *Mobility management requirements for NGN (ITU-T Recommendation Q.1706/Y.2801)*. Retrieved February 20, 2007, from http://www.itu.int/rec/dologin_pub.asp?lang=e&id=T-REC-Q.1706-200611-I!!PDF-E&type=items.

IrDA (n.d.), *Infrared Data Association*, from http://irda.org/

Islam, N. & Fayad, M. (2003). Toward ubiquitous acceptance of ubiquitous computing. *Communication of ACM, 46* (2), 89-92.

IVT (n.d.), *IVT Corporation*, from http://www.ivtcorporation.com

Jacob, C., Linner, D., Steglich, S., and Radusch, I. (2007). Autonomous Context Data Dissemination in Heterogeneous and Dynamic Environments. In Proceedings of the 4th Consumer Communications and Networking Conference (CCNC) 2007, CD-ROM, Las Vegas, NV, USA, IEEE Catalogue Number: 07EX1539C, ISBN: 1-4244-0667-6.

Jacob, C., Pfeffer, H., Zhang, L., and Steglich, S. (2008). Establishing Service Communities in Peer-to-Peer Networks, 1st IEEE International Peer-to-Peer for Handheld Devices Workshop CCNC 2008, Las Vegas, NV, USA.

Java Community Process (2007). Mobile Information Device Profile (JSR 37) Java 2 Platform Micro Edition, Sun Microsystems. retrieved june 1, 2007 from http://java.sun.com/products/midp/

Jeffery, S. R., Alonso, G., Franklin, M. J., Hong, W., & Widom, J. (2006). Declarative support for sensor data cleaning. *The 4th International Conference on Pervasive Computing,* Dublin, Ireland. (pp. 83-100).

Jeffery, S. R., Alonso, G., Franklin, M. J., Hong, W., & Widom, J. (2006b). A pipelined framework for online cleaning of sensor data streams. *The 22nd International Conference on Data Engineering (ICDE'06),* (pp. 140-140).

Jennings, C., Peterson, J., & Watson, M. (2002). *Extensions to the Session Initiation Protocol (SIP) for Asserted Identity within Trusted Networks* (IETF Request For Comment: 3325). Retrieved April 10, 2007, from http://www.ietf.org/rfc/rfc3325.txt

Joint US/EU ad hoc Agent Markup Language Committee (2004). OWL-S 1.1 Release. http://www.daml.org/services/owl-s/1.1/.

Jones, G. F. G. (2004). Adaptive Systems for Multimedia Information Retrieval. In *Adaptive Multimedia Retrieval, LNCS 3094,* (pp. 1-18).

Jones, G. J. F., & Brown, P. J. (2003). Context-aware retrieval for ubiquitous computing environments. *Mobile*

HCI Workshop on Mobile and Ubiquitous Information, (pp. 227-243).

Jønvik, T. E., Engelstad, P., and van Tanh, D.. (2003). Building a Virtual Device on Personal Area Network. In Proceedings of the 2nd International Conference on Communications, Internet & Information Technology, Scottsdale, Arizona.

Jøsang, A., Ismail, R., & Boyd, C. (2007). A survey of trust and reputation systems for online service provision. *Decision Support Systems, 43*(2), 618-644. Elsevier Science Publishers B. V.

Judd, G., & Steenkiste, P. (2003). Providing contextual information to pervasive computing applications. *The First IEEE International Conference on Pervasive Computing and Communications (PerCom 2003).* (pp. 133-142).

Kagal, L. F., & Joshi, T. A. (2003). A policy language for a pervasive computing environment, *Policies for Distributed Systems and Networks, 2003. Proceedings. POLICY 2003. IEEE 4th International Workshop on,* 63-74.

Kalatzis, N., Roussaki, I., Liampotis, N., Strimpakou, M., Pils, C., & Anagnostou, M. (2008). Exploiting History of Context Data for Lightweight Inference of User Status. *ICT Mobile Summit 2008,* Stockholm, Sweden.

Kanter, T. (2003). Attaching Context-Aware Services to Moving Locations. *IEEE Internet Computing, 7*(2), 43-51.

Kappel, G., Pröll, B., Retschitzegger, W., & Schwinger, W. (2001). Modelling Ubiquitous Web Applications - The WUML Approach. In *ER'01 Workshops* (pp. 183-197). Yokohama, Japan: Springer.

Karsai, G., Ledeczi, A., Sztipanovits, J., Peceli, G., Simon, G., & Kovacshazy, T. (2000). An Approach to Self-Adaptive Software based on Supervisory Control. In *Self-Adaptive Software Applications, LNCS, 2614,* (pp. 77-92).

Kassab, R. & Lamirel, J.C. (2006) An innovative approach to intelligent information filtering. In Haddad,

H (ed.), *ACM Symposium on Applied Computing 2006 (SAC 2006)* (pp. 1089-1093). ACM Press.

Kaye, D. (2003). *Loosely Coupled: The Missing Pieces of Web Services* (1st edition ed.): Rds Associates.

Keeney, J., & Cahill, V. (2003). Chisel: A Policy-Driven, Context-Aware, Dynamic Adaptation Framework. In *Fourth IEEE International Workshop on Policies for Distributed Systems and Networks POLICY 2003*, Italy. IEEE Computer Society Press

Keidl, M., & Kemper, A. (2004). Towards context-aware adaptable web services. *Proceedings of the 13th International World Wide Web Conference*. Alternate track papers & posters (pp. 55–65). New York: Association for Computing Machinery.

Kerer, C., Schahram, D., Jazayeri, M., Szego, A., Gomes, D., & Caja, J. A. B. (2004). Presence-Aware Infrastructure using Web services and RFID technologies. *Proceedings of the 2nd European Workshop on Object Orientation and Web Services*. Oslo, Norway.

Kernchen, R., Boussard, M., Hesselman, C., Villalonga, C., Clavier, E., Zhdanova, A. V., et al. (2007). Managing personal communication environments in next generation service platforms, *Mobile and Wireless Communications Summit, 2007. 16th IST*, 1-5.

Kernchen, R., Boussard, M., Moessner, K., & Mrohs, B. (2006). Device description for mobile multimodal interfaces In Mykonos, Greece.

Ketfi, A., Belkhatir, N., & Cunin, P. Y. (2002). Adaptation Dynamique, concepts et expérimentations. In *15th International Conference on Software & Systems Engineering and their Applications ICSSEA02*, Paris, France

Khedr, M., & Karmouch, A. (2005). ACAI: Agent-Based Context-aware Infrastructure for Spontaneous Applications. *Journal of Network and Computer Applications*, *28*(1), 19-44.

Kiciman, E., & Fox, A (2000). Using dynamic mediation to integrate COTS entities in a ubiquitous computing environment. In *2nd International Symposium on Hand-*

held and Ubiquitious Computing (HUC2K). Heidelberg, Germany: Springer London

Kiciman, E., and Fox, A. (2000). Using dynamic mediation to integrate COTS entities in a ubiquitous computing environment. In Proceedings of HUC2000, no. 1927 in LNCS, pp. 211-226.

Kickzales, G., Lamping, J., Mendhekar, A. et al. (1997). Aspect-Oriented Programming. In *ECOOP'97*, (pp. 220-242) Lecture Notes in Computer Science 1241, Springer Verlag

Kielmann, T., van Nieuwpoort, R., & Maassen, J. (2003). Gridlab - A Grid Application Toolkit and Testbet. Design of Adaptive Components, Vrije University, The Netherlands.

Kim, D., Park, S., Jin, Y., Chang, H., Park, Y.-S., Ko, I.-Y., Lee, K., Lee, J., Park, Y.-C., & Lee, S. (2006). SHAGE: A Framework for Self-managed Robot Software. In *Proceedings of the ICSE Workshop on Software Engineering for Adaptive and Self-Managing Systems*, (pp. 79-85).

Kim, J., & Gorman, J. (2005).The psychobiology of anxiety. *Clinical Neuroscience Research, 4*, 335-347.

Kim, Y.-G., Mon, C.-J., Jeong, D., Lee, J.-O., Song, C.-Y., & Baik, D.-K. (2005). Context-Aware Access Control Mechanism for Ubiquitous Applications. *Advances in Web Intelligence, Lecture Notes in Computer Science, Springer 2005*, (p. 236-242).

Kindberg, T, Barton, J., Morgan, J., Becker, G., Caswell, D., Debaty, P., Gopal, G., Frid, M., Krishnan, V., Morris, H., Schettino, J., Serra, & Spasojevic, M.(2002). People, Places, Things: Web Presence for the Real World. *ACM Mobile Networks & Applications Journal (MONET)*, *7*(5), 365-376.

Kirsch-Pinheiro, M., Gensel, J. & Martin, H. (2004). Awareness on Mobile Groupware Systems. In: Karmouch, A., Korba, L. & Madeira, E.R.M. (Eds.), *1st International Workshop on Mobility Aware Technologies and Applications (MATA 2004), Lecture Notes in Computer Science*, Vol. 3284 (pp. 78-87). Springer.

Kirsch-Pinheiro, M., Villanova-Oliver, M.; Gensel, J. & Martin, H. (2006). A Personalized and Context-Aware Adaptation Process for Web-Based Groupware Systems. *4th Int. Workshop on Ubiquitous Mobile Information and Collaboration Systems (UMICS'06), CAiSE'06 Workshop* (pp. 884-898).

Kjaer, K. E. (2007). A survey of context-aware middleware. In W. Hasselbring (Ed.) 25th Conference on IASTED international Multi-Conference: Software Engineering (pp. 148-155). ACTA Press

Klemettinen, M. (editor). (2007). Enabling Technologies for Mobile Services: The MobiLife Book, John Wiley & Sons Ltd., England.

Klyne, G., Reynolds, F., Woodrow, C., Ohto, H., Hjelm, J., Butler, M. H., et al. (2004). *Composite capability/preference profiles (cc/pp): structure and vocabularies 1.0. w3c recommendation, w3c, january 2004.*

Knutson, C. D., & Brown, J. M. (2004). *IrDA Principles and Protocols: The IrDA Library, Vol. 1.* MCL Press.

Kolb, A. Y., & Kolb, D. A. (2005). The Kolb Learning Style Inventory – Version 3.1 2005 Technical Specifications, Experience Based Learning Systems, Inc. Korkea-aho, M. (2000). *Context-Aware Applications Survey.* Paper presented at the Internetworking Seminar (Tik-110.551), Spring 2000, Helsinki University of Technology, from http://www.hut.fi/~mkorkeaa/doc/context-aware.html.

Kon, F., Costa, F., Blair, G., & Champbell, R. H. (2002). Adaptive Middleware: The Case for Reflective Middleware. In *Communications of the ACM, 45*(6), 33-38.

Konar, A. (2000). *Artificial Intelligence and Soft Computing: Behavioral and Cognitive Modeling of the Human Brain.* New York: CRC Press.

Koolwaaij, J., Tarlano, A., Luther, M., Nurmi, P., Mrohs, B., Battestini, A., and Vaidya, R. (2006). Context Watcher—Sharing context information in everyday life. In Proceedings of the IASTED International Conference on Web Technologies, Applications, and Services (WTAS'06).

Korpipää, P., and Mäntyjärvi, J. (2003). An Ontology for Mobile Device Sensor-Based Context Awareness. In Proc. of the 4th International and Interdisciplinary Conference on Modeling and Using Context 2003, LNAI 2680, Springer-Verlag, pp.451-459.

Korpipää, P., Häkkilä, J., Kela, J., Ronkainen, S., & Känsälä, I. (2004). Utilising context ontology in mobile device application personalisation. *Proceedings of the 3rd international conference on Mobile and ubiquitous multimedia,* (pp. 133-140).

Korpipaa, P., Mantyjarvi, J., Kela, J. et al. (2004). Managing context information in mobile devices. *IEEE Pervasive Computing, 19*(6), 21-29

Korpipaa, P., Mantyjarvi, J., Kela, J., Keranen, H., & Malm, E.J. (2003). Managing Context Information in Mobile Devices, *IEEE Pervasive Computing, 2*(3), 42-51.

Kort, B., & Reilly, R. (2002). Analytical Models of Emotions, Learning and Relationships: Towards an Affect-Sensitive Cognitive Machine. *In Proceedings of Conference on Virtual Worlds and Simulation (VWSim 2002),* from http://affect.media.mit.edu/projectpages/lc/vworlds.pdf.

Krasner, G. & Pope, S. (1981). A cookbook for using the model-view controller user interface paradigm in Smalltalk-80, *Journal of Object-Oriented Programming* (3), 26-49.

Krause, E. F. (1987). *Taxicab Geometry.* Dover.

Kumar, M., Shirazi, B. A., Das, S. K., Sung, B. Y., Levine, D., & Singhal, M. (2003). PICO: A Middleware Framework for Pervasive Computing. In *IEEE Pervasive Computing Mobile and Ubiquitous Systems, 2*(3), 72-79.

Landau, I. D., Lozano, R., & M'Saad, M. (1998). *Adaptive Control,* London: Springer.

Langheinrich, M. (2001). *Privacy by Design- Principles of Privacy-Aware Ubiquitous Systems.* Paper presented at the 3rd International Conference on Ubiquitous Computing (Ubicomp2001).

Lankhorst, M. M., Kranenburg, S, A., & Peddemors A. J. H. (2002). Enabling Technology for Personalizing Mobile Services. *Proceedings of the 35th Annual Hawaii International Conference on System Sciences* (HICSS-35'02).

Lassila, O. (2005, August). *Using the semantic web in mobile and ubiquitous computing.* Jyväskylä (Finland).

Lassila, O., & Khushraj, D. (2005). Contextualizing applications via semantic middleware In , *Mobile and Ubiquitous Systems: Networking and Services, 2005* (pp. 183-189).

Laube, A., & Gomez, L. (2007). Dynamic context-aware access control. *IEEE and ACM International Conference of Security and Cryptography.*

Laurent, S.S., Dumbill, E.& Johnston, J. (2001). *Programming Web Services with XML-RPC.* O'Reilly & Associates, Inc.

Le Mouël, F., André, F. & Segarra, M.T. (2002). AeDEn: An Adaptive Framework for Dynamic Distribution over Mobile Environments. *Annals of Telecommunications,* 57(11-12), 1124-1148

Lee, T. B.. (1998). Semantic Web roadmap. [Online]. Available: http://www.w3.org/DesignIssues/Semantic. html. [Accessed: March 17, 2008].

Lei, H., Sow, D. M., Davis, J. S. II, Banavar, G., & Ebling, M. R. (2002). The design and applications of a context service. *SIGMOBILE Mobile Computing and Communications Review,* 6(4), 45-55.

Lekkas, Z., Tsianos, N., Germanakos, P., Mourlas, C., & Samaras, G. (2008). The Role of Emotions in the Design of Personalized Educational Systems. *Proceedings of the 8th IEEE International Conference on Advanced Learning Technologies (ICALT 2008),* Santader, Cantabria, Spain, July 1-5, 2008, IEEE. (accepted)

Lemlouma, T. & Layaïda, N. (2004). Context-Aware Adaptation for Mobile Devices. *IEEE International Conference on Mobile Data Management* (pp.106-111). IEEE Computer Society.

Leong, L. H., Kobayashi, S., Koshizuka, N., & Sakamura, K. (2005). CASIS: a context-aware speech interface system. *Proceedings of the 10th international conference on Intelligent user interfaces,* (pp. 231-238).

Leonhardt, U. (1998). *Supporting Location-Awareness in Open Distributed Systems.* PhD thesis, University of London.

Liaqaut, H., Iftikhar, N., & Qadir, M. A. (2006). Context aware information retrieval using role ontology and query schemas. *Multitopic Conference, 2006. INMIC '06.* (pp. 244-249).

Lin, X., Li, S., Yang, Z., & Shi, W. (2005). Application-oriented context modeling and reasoning in pervasive computing, *Proceedings of the The Fifth International Conference on Computer and Information Technology,* (pp. 495-501).

Linn, J. (2005). Technology and web user data privacy - a survey of risks and countermeasures. *Security & Privacy Magazine, IEEE,* 3(1), 52 - 58.

Linner, D., Radusch, I., Steglich, S., and Jacob, C. (2006). Loosely Coupled Service Provisioning in Dynamic Computing Environments. In Proceedings of ChinaCom 2006. First International Conference on Communications and Networking in China, Beijing, China, IEEE Catalog Number: 06EX1414C, ISBN: 1-4244-0463-0, Library of Congress: 2006926274.

LNXSD, (n.d.). *SDIO Linux Stack,* from http://sourceforge.net/projects/sdio-linux/

Loggie, R. H., Zucco, G. N., & Baddeley, A. D. (1990). Interference with visual short-term memory. *Acta Psychologica,* 75(1), 55-74.

Loke, S. W., Padovitz, A. & Zaslavsky, A. (2003). Context-based addressing: The concept and an implementation for large-scale mobile agent systems using publish-subscribe event notification. In Stefani, J.-B., Demeure, I. & Hagimont, D. (eds.), *4th IFIP WG 6.1 International Conference on Distributed Applications and Interoperable Systems (DAIS 2003), Lecture Notes in Computer Science,* Vol. 2893 (pp. 274-284). Springer.

Love, R. D., Siegel, M., & Wilson, K. T. (1998). *Understanding Token Ring Protocols and Standards*. Artech House Publishers

Lu, H., & Ooi, B.C. (1993). Spatial Indexing: Past and Future. *IEEE Data Engineering Bulletin, 16*(3), 16-21.

Lysyanskayal, A., Rivest, R. L., Sahai, A., & Wolf, S. (1999). *Pseudonym Systems.* Paper presented at the Sixth Annual Workshop on Selected Areas in Cryptography (SAC ,99).

Madden, S. R., Franklin, M. J., Hellerstein, J. M., & Hong, W. (2005). TinyDB: An acquisitional query processing system for sensor networks. *ACM Transactions on Database Systems (TODS), 30*(1), 122-173.

Madden, S., & Franklin, M. J. (2002). Fjording the stream: An architecture for queries over streaming sensor data. *The 18th International Conference on Data Engineering.* (pp. 555-566).

Maes, P. (1987). Concepts and experiments in computational reflection. In *Proceedings of the Object-Oriented Programming Systems Languages and Applications*, (pp. 147-155).

Malek, M. (2005). The NOMADS Republic – A Case for Ambient Service Oriented Computing. In *Proceedings of the 2005 IEEE International Workshop on Service Oriented System Engineering*, (pp. 9-11)

Mamdani, E. H. (1976). Advances in the Linguistic Synthesis of Fuzzy Controllers. *Journal of Man-Machine Studies, 8*, 669-678.

Manchón, P., del Solar, C., de Amores, G., & Pérez, G. (2006). The mimus corpus In (pp. 56-59). Genoa, Italy.

Marsh, S. P. (1994). *Formalizing Trust as a Computational Concept.*

Marti, S. (2005). *Trust and reputation in peer-to-peer networks.* Stanford University, USA.

McFadden, T., Henricksen, K., & Indulska, J. (2004). Automating context-aware application development. *UbiComp 1st International Workshop on Advanced Context Modelling, Reasoning and Management*, (pp. 90-95).

McGuiness, D., & van Harmelen, F. (2004). *OWL web ontology language overview.* World Wide Web Consortium. Retrieved March 3, 2008 from http://www.w3.org/TR/owl-features/.

McHugh. J. (2007). *Adaptive Networks Vision* – White Paper. ProCurve Networking, HP Innovation. - http://www.hp.com/rnd/pdfs/Adaptive_Networks_Vision_White_Paper.pdf

McKay, M. T., Fischler, I., & Dunn, B. R. (2003). Cognitive style and recall of text: An EEG analysis. *Learning and Individual Differences, 14*, 1–21.

McKinley, P. K., Sadjadi, S. M., Kasten, E. P., & Cheng, B. H. C. (2004). Composing Adaptive Software. In *IEEE Computer, 37*(7), 56-64.

MCP, (n.d.). *ENC28J60 product page*, from http://www.microchip.com/stellent/idcplg? IdcService=SS_GET_PAGE&nodeId=1335&dDocName=en022889

Mehrotra, A. (1997). *GSM System Engineering*. Mobile Communications Series, Artech House Publishers.

Meier, R., Harrington, A., & Cahill, V. (2005). A Distributed Framework for Intelligent Transportation Systems. *Proceedings of 12th World Congress on Intelligent Transport Systems (ITSWC2005)*. ITS America.

Meneses, E., & Torres-Rojas, F. J. (2005). Time and Order Considerations in Consistency Models for Web Caching. *PDPTA Conference 2005*, Las Vegas, Nevada, USA.

Merriam-Webster Dictionary (2008). – http://www.m-w.com

Mika, P., Oberle, D., Gangemi, A., & Sabou, M. (2004). *Foundations for Service Ontologies: Aligning OWL-S to DOLCE, WWW04.*

Mikic-Rakic, M. & Medvidovic, N. (2002). Architecture-Level Support for Software Component Deployment in Resource Constrained Environments. In *Proceedings of the First International IFIP/ACM Working Conference on Component Deployment (CD'02).*

Miller, J. H., & Page, S. E. (2007). *Complex Adaptive Systems: An Introduction to Computational Models of Social Life*. Princeton University Press.

Mitchell, K. (2002). *A Survey of Context-Awareness*. University of Lancaster, Lancaster, UK

Mokhtar, S., Liu, J., Georgantas, N., and Issarny, V. (2005). QoS-aware dynamic service composition in ambient intelligence environments. In Proceedings of IEEE ASE 2005, pp. 317-320, ACM Press New York, NY, USA.

Mondal, A.S. (2003). *Mobile IP: Present State and Future*. Series in Computer Science, Springer Publisher.

Moran, T. & Dourish, P. (2001). Introduction to this special issue on context-aware computing. *Human-Computer Interaction, 16* (2-3).

Morand, L., & Tessier, S. (2002). Global mobility approach with Mobile IP in "All IP" networks. *Proceedings of IEEE International Conference on Communications ICC 2002, 4,* 2075-2079. IEEE.

Morrow, R (2002). *Bluetooth: Operation and Use*. McGraw-Hill.

Mosmondor, M., Skorin-Kapov, L., & Kovacic, M. (2006). Bringing Location Based Services to IP Multimedia Subsystem. *Proceedings of Mediterranean Electrotechnical Conference MELECON 2006*, (pp. 746-749). IEEE.

MOSQUITO. (2006). IST 004636 MOSQUITO Project, from http://www.mosquito-online.org.

Motta, E. (1998). An Overview of the OCML Modelling Language. *The 8th Workshop on Methods and Languages*.

Moyer, M., Covington, M., & Ahamad, M. (2000). Generalized role-based access control for securing future applications. *23rd National Infromation Systems Security Conference*.

Mrissa, M., Ghedira, C., Benslimane, D., Maamar, Z., Rosenberg, F. & Dustdar S. (2007). A Context-based Mediation Approach to Compose Semantic Web Services.

ACM Transactions on Internet Technology 8(1), ACM Association for Computing Machinery.

MSDN, (n.d.). Microsoft Developers Network, Secure Digital Card Drivers, from http://msdn2.microsoft.com/en-us/library/ms923739.aspx

Mullet, Kevin och Darrell, & Sano. (1995). *Designing visual interfaces – communicating oriented techniques*. SunSoft Press a Prentice Hall Title

Mussino, S. (2005). *ARM (Adaptive Resource Management): Design and Development of Adaptive Applications*. BSc Thesis, University of Milano-Bicocca. DISCo, Milan, Italy.

MyersBriggs, I., McCaulley, M. H., Quenk, N. L., & Hammer, A. L. (1998). MBTI Manual (A guide to the development and use of the Myers Briggs type indicator), 3rd edition. Consulting Psychologists Press.

Nagarajan, M., Verma, K,, Sheth, A. P., Miller, J. A., & Lathem, J. (2006). Semantic Interoperability of Web Services – Challenges and Experiences. In *Proceedings of the 4th IEEE International Conference on Web Services*, (pp. 373-382).

NationalSecurityAgency. (2001). *Phase II Bridge Certification Authority Interoperability Demonstration Final Report*: A&N Associates.

Natvig, M. K., & Westerheim, H. (2007). National multimodal travel information – a strategy based on stakeholder involvement and intelligent transportation system architecture. *Intelligent Transportation Systems, 1*(2), 102–109. IET.

Natvig, M., Westerheim, H., & Skylstad, G. F. (2007). *ARKTRANS The Norwegian system framework architecture for multimodal transport systems supporting freight and passenger transport* (Technical Report v. 4.0). Retrieved September 23, 2007, http://www.sintef.no/units/informatics/projects/arktrans/arktransweb/.

Neuman, B. C., & Ts'o, T. (1994). Kerberos: An authentication service for computer networks. *IEEE Communication Magazine*.

Nilsson, M., Lindskog, H., & Fischer-Hübner, S. (2001). *Privacy Enhancements in the Mobile Internet.* Paper presented at the IFIP WG 9.6/11.7 working conference on Security and Control of IT in Society, Bratislava.

Noble, B. (2000). System Support for Mobile, Adaptive Applications. *IEEE Personal Communications, 7*(1), 44-49

Noble, B. D., Satyanarayanan, M., Narayanan, D., Tilton, J. E., Flinn, J., & Walker, K. R. (1997). Agile Application-Aware Adaptation for Mobility. In *Proceedings of the 16th ACM Symposium on Operating Systems Principles,* (pp. 276-287).

Norman, D. A. (2002). The design of everyday things, New York: Basic Books.

Norrie, M. C., Signer, B., Grossniklaus, M., Belotti, R., Decurtins, C., & Weibel, N. (2007). Context-aware platform for mobile data management. *Wireless Networks, 13*(6), 855-870.

Nosofsky, R. (1992). Similarity, scaling and cognitive process models. *Annual Review of Psychology, 43,* 25- 53.

Nurmi, P., Hassinen, M., & Lee, K. C. (2007). A Comparative Analysis of Personalization Techniques for a Mobile Application. *In the Proceedings of the 21st International Conference on Advanced Information Networking and Applications Workshops, 2,* 270-275. IEEE.

O'Grady, M. J., & O'Hare, G. M. P. (2004). Gulliver's Genie: agency, mobility, adaptivity. *Computers & Graphics, 28*(5), 677-689.

O'Hara, R., & Petrick, A. (2005). *802.11 Wireless Networks: The Definitive Guide, Second Edition.* IEEE Computer Society.

O'Reilly, T. (2005). What is web 2.0: design patterns and business models for the next generation of software, *O'Reilly.* Retrieved from http://www.oreillynet.com/pub/a/oreilly/tim/news/2005/09/30/what-is-web-20.html.

OASIS (2006). *Reference Model for Service Oriented Architecture.* Committee Specification 1, 2 August

2006, version 1.0. Retrieved 10 March 10, 2008, from http://www.oasis-open.org/committees/tc_home.php?wg_abbrev=soa-rm.

OASIS (2006). *Web services distributed management: MUWS primer.* Retrieved March 3, 2008 from http://docs.oasis-open.org/wsdm/wsdm-1.0-muws-primer-cd-01.pdf

OASIS. (2005). *Web Service Trust Language* (WS-Trust) 1.3.

OASIS. (2006). *Web Service Security: SOAP Message Security 1.1* (WS-Security 2004).

OASIS. (2007). *eXtended Access Control Markup Language* (XACML) 2.0.

Oberle, D., Ankolekar, A., Hitzler, P., Cimiano, P., Sintek, M., Kiesel, M., et al. (2006). Dolce ergo sumo: on foundational and domain models in swinto (smartweb integrated ontology), *Submission to Journal of Web Semantics (2006).*

Olston, C., & Widom, J. (2005). Efficient Monitoring and Querying of Distributed, Dynamic Data via Approximate Replication. *IEEE Data Engineering Bulletin, 28,* 11-18.

OMG Adopted Specification (2004). *UML Profile for Modeling Quality of Service and Fault Tolerance Characteristics and Mechanisms.* ptc/2004-06-01, http://www. omg.org

Open Geospatial Consortium (2007). *Location Service (OpenLS): Core Services* (Technical Specification). Retrieved January 25, 2007, from http://www.opengeospatial.org

Open Geospatial Consortium Inc. (1999) OpenGIS Simple Features Specification for SQL (OpenGIS Project Document 99-049). Retrieved September 25, 2007, 1999, from http://www.opengeospatial.org/standards/sfs.

Open Geospatial Consortium Inc. (2005). *Simple Feature access-Part 2: SQL Option.* v.1.1.0.

Open Mobile Alliance (2007). WAP Forum. Retrieved june 1, 2007 from http://www.wapforum.org

Open Mobile Alliance Mobile (2007). *Location Protocol Specification* (v. 3.0). Retrieved March 2, 2007, from http://www.openmobilealliance.org/tech/affiliates/lif/lifindex.html

Orr, R. J., & Abowd, G. D. (2000). The Smart Floor: A Mechanism for Natural User Identification and Tracking. *Conference on Human Factors in Computing Systems (CHI 2000).*

Orwant, L. (1995). Heterogeneous learning in the doppelganger user modelling system. *User Modelling and User Adapted Interaction, 4*(2), 107-130.

OSGi Alliance (2003). *OSGi Service Platform*, Release 3. Amsterdam : IOS Press

Ottersten, I., & Berndtsson, J. (2002). *Användbarhet i praktiken.* Studentlitteratur.

Oudeyer, P. Y., & Kaplan, F. (2004). Intelligent Adaptive Curiosity: a source of Self-Development. In *Proceedings of the 4th International Workshop on Epigenetic Robotics.* (pp. 127-130).

OWL Web Ontology Language Overview. (2004). [Online]. Available: http://www.w3.org/TR/owl-features/. [Accessed: March 17, 2008].

OWL-S Coalition: OWL-S 1.1 release. (2004). http://www.daml.org/services/owl-s/1.1/

Paganelli, F., Bianchi, G., & Giuli, D. (2007). A Context Model for Context-aware System Design towards the Ambient Intelligence Vision: Experiences in the eTourism Domain. *Universal Access in Ambient Intelligence Environments, Lecture Notes in Computer Science, 4397,* 173-191. Springer.

Paganelli, F., Bianchi, G., & Melani, V. (2006). A Context-aware eTourism Application Enabling Collaboration and Knowledge Exchange among Tourists. *Exploiting the Knowledge Economy: Issues, Applications, Case Studies.* Amsterdam: IOS Press.

Papanikolaou, K. A., Grigoriadou, M., Kornilakis, H., & Magoulas, G. D. (2003). Personalizing the Interaction in a Web-based Educational Hypermedia System: the case of INSPIRE. *User-Modelling and User-Adapted Interaction, 13*(3), 213-267.

Papazoglou, M. P. and Heuvel, W. (2007). Service oriented architectures: approaches, technologies and research issues. *The VLDB Journal* 16(3), 389-415

Park, J., & Sandhu, R. (2002). Towards usage control models: beyond traditional access control. In *Proceedings of seventh ACM symposium on Access control models and technologies* (pp. 57-64). Monterey, California, USA ACM Press.

Parlanti, D., Giuli, D., & Pettenati, M. C. (2006). Intermediation for trust-enabling networked decentralized exchange systems. In *Proceedings of the 13th European Conference on Cognitive Ergonomics: Trust and Control in Complex Socio-Technical Systems* (Zurich, Switzerland, September 20 - 22, 2006). *ECCE '06, 250.* New York, NY: ACM.

Paspallis, N., Eliassen, F., Hallsteinsen, S. & Papadopoulos G.A. (2008). Developing self-adaptive mobile applications and services with Separation-of-Concerns In: Di Nitto, R., Traverso, P., Sassen, A.M., Zwegers, A., Mylopoulos, J. & Papazoglou, M. (Eds) *At your service: Service Engineering in the Information Society Technologies Program,.* MIT Press

Pauty, J., Preuveneers, D., Rigole, P., & Berbers, Y. (2006). *Research Challenges in Mobile and Context-Aware Service Development.*

Pawlak, R., Seinturier, L., Duchien, L. et al. (2001). JAC: A Flexible Solution for Aspect-Oriented Programming in Java. (pp 1-24) Lecture Notes in Computer Science 2192. Springer Verlag

Perich, F., Avancha, S., Chakraborty, D., Joshi, A., & Yesha, Y. (2005). *Profile driven data management for pervasive environments.* Springer.

Perich, F., Joshi, A., Finin, T., & Yesha, Y. (2004). On data management in pervasive computing environments. *IEEE Transactions on Knowledge and Data Engineering, 16*(5), 621-634.

Perich, F., Joshi, A., Yesha, Y., & Finin, T. (2005). Collaborative joins in a pervasive computing environment. *The International Journal on Very Large Data Bases, 14*(2), 182-196.

Peterson, J. (2002). *A Privacy Mechanism for the Session Initiation Protocol (SIP)*. (IETF Request for Comments: 3323). Retrieved April 10, 2007, from http://tools.ietf.org/html/rfc3323.

Pfeffer, H., Linner, D., and Steglich, S. (2008). Modeling and Controlling Dynamic Service Compositions, Third International Multi-Conference on Computing in the Global Information Technology (ICCGI 2008)

Pfeffer, H., Linner, D., Jacob, C., and Steglich, S. (2007). Towards Light-weight Semantic Descriptions for Decentralized Service-oriented Systems. In Proceedings of the 1st IEEE International Conference on Semantic Computing (ICSC 2007), volume CD-ROM, Irvine, California, USA.

Pfeifer, T. (2004). Redundancy vs. imperfect positioning for context-dependent services. Paper presented at the 1st International Workshop on Advanced Context Modeling, Reasoning, and Management (UbiComp 2004).

Pils, C., Roussaki, I., & Strimpakou, M. (2006). Location-Based Context Retrieval and Filtering. *Lecture Notes in Computer Science, 3987*, 256-273.

Pils, C., Roussaki, I., & Strimpakou, M. (2007). Distributed Spatial Database Management for Context Aware Computing Systems. *16th IST Mobile and Wireless Communications Summit*, Budapest, Hungary.

Poladian, V., Sousa, J. P., Garlan, D., & Shaw, M. (2004). Dynamic Configuration of Resource-Aware Services. In *Proceedings of the 26th International Conference on Software Engineering*, (pp. 604-613).

Polk, W. T., & Hastings, N. E. (2000). *Bridge Certification Authorities: Connecting B2B Public Key Infrastructures*: National Institute of Standards and Technology.

Polyviou, S., Evripidou, P., & Samaras, G. (2004). Context-aware queries using query by browsing and

chiromancer. Paper presented at the Second International Conference on Pervasive Computing.

Ponnekanti, S., Lee, B., Fox, A., Hanrahan, P., and Winograd, T. ICrafter. (2001). A Service Framework for Ubiquitous Computing Environments. Proceedings of Ubicomp 1.

Preece, J., Rogers, Y., & Sharp, H. (2002). *Interaction design beyond human-computer interaction*. John Wiley & Sons, Inc.

Preuveneers, D. & Berbers, Y. (2007). Towards Context-Aware and Resource-Driven Self-Adaptation for Mobile Handheld Applications. In *Proceedings of the 2007 ACM Symposium on Applied Computing* (pp. 1165-1170). ACM Press.

Preuveneers, D. & Berbers, Y. Adaptive context management using a component-based approach. In Kutvonen, L. & Alonistioti, N. (ed.), *5th IFIP WG 6.1 International Conference Distributed Applications and Interoperable Systems (DAIS2005), Lecture Notes in Computer Science*, Vol. 3543 (pp. 14-26). Springer.

Preuveneers, D., den Bergh, J. V., Wagelaar, D., Georges, A., Rigole, P., Clerckx, T., Berbers, Y., Coninx, K., Jonckers, V. & Bosschere, K. D. (2004). Towards an Extensible Context Ontology for Ambient Intelligence. In Markopoulos, P., Eggen, B., Aarts, E. & Crowley, J. (ed.), *Second European Symposium on Ambient Intelligence (EUSAI 2004), Lecture Notes in Computer Science*, Vol. 3295 (pp. 148-159). Springer.

Protégé Community (2005). The Protégé Ontology Editor and Knowledge Acquisition System. retrieved June 16, 2005 from http://protege.stanford.edu/

Qiao, L., Feng, L., & Zhou, L. (2008). Information presentation on mobile devices: Techniques and practices. Paper presented at the 10th Asia-Pacific Web Conference (APWeb 2008).

Raento, M., Oulasvirta, A., Petit, R., Toivonen, H.. (2005). ContextPhone: a prototyping platform for context-aware mobile applications. IEEE Pervasive Computing 4 (2).

Rahman, S. A., & Bhalla, S. (2005). Supporting spatial data queries for mobile services. *The 2005 IEEE/WIC/ACM International Conference on Web Intelligence (WI'05P),* (pp. 696-699).

Raibulet, C., Arcelli, F., & Mussino, S. (2006). Mapping the QoS of Services on the QoS of the Systems Resources in an Adaptive Resource Management System. In *Proceedings of the 2006 IEEE International Conference on Services Computing,* (pp. 529-530).

Raibulet, C., Arcelli, F., Mussino, S., Riva, M., Tisato, F., & Ubezio, L. (2006) Components in an Adaptive and QoS-based Architecture. In *Proceedings of the ICSE 2006 Workshop on Software Engineering for Adaptive and Self-Managing Systems,* (pp. 65-71).

Raibulet, C., Mussino, S., & Ubezio, L. (2007). An Adaptive Resource Management Approach for a Healthcare System. In *Proceedings of the 19ᵗʰ International Conference on Software Engineering & Knowledge Engineering,* (pp. 286-291).

Randell, B. (1998). Dependability - A Unifying Concept. *Computer Security, Dependability, and Assurance: From Needs to Solutions,* (pp. 16-25). IEEE Computer Society.

Ranganathan, A., Al-Muhtadi, J., & Campbell, R. (2004). Reasoning about uncertain contexts in pervasive computing environments. *Pervasive Computing, IEEE, 3*(2), 62-70.

Rao, B., & Minakakis, L. (2003). Evolution of mobile location-based services. *Communications of the ACM, 46*(12), 61-65.

Raubal, M. (2004). Formalizing Conceptual Spaces. In A. Varzi & L. Vieu (Eds.), *Formal Ontology in Information Systems, Proceedings of the Third International Conference (FOIS 2004).Frontiers in Artificial Intelligence and Applications, 114,* 153-164., Amsterdam, The Netherlands: IOS Press.

Rehrl, K., Bruntsch, S., & Mentz, H. J. (2007). Assisting Multimodal Travelers: Design and Prototypical Implementation of a Personal Travel Companion. *IEEE Transactions on Intelligent Transportation Systems, 8*(1).

Reichle, R., Wagner, M., Ullah Khan M., Geihs, K., Lorenzo, J., Valla, M., Fra, Paspallis, N. & Papadopoulos, G.A. (2008). A Comprehensive Context Modeling Framework for Pervasive Computing Systems. In *8th IFIP International Conference on Distributed Applications and Interoperable Systems* (pp. 281-295)

Reiter, M., & Stubblebine, S. (1999). Authentication metric analysis and design. *ACM Transactions on Information and System Security, 2*(2).

Reither, M. K., & Stubblebine, S. G. (n.d). Authentication metric analysis and design. *ACM Transactions on Information and System Security.* ACM Press.

Reithinger, N., & Sonntag, D. (2005). An integration framework for a mobile multimodal dialogue system accessing the semantic web, *Ninth European Conference on Speech Communication and Technology.*

Resource Description Framework (RDF) / W3C Semantic Web Activity. [Online]. Available: http://www.w3.org/RDF/. [Accessed: March 17, 2008].

Riding, R. (2001). Cognitive Style Analysis – Research Administration. *Learning and Training Technology.*

Riecken, D. (2000). Introduction: personalized views of personalization. *Communications of the ACM 43*(8), 26-28. New York, USA: ACM.

Rigole, P. & Berbers, Y. (2006). Resource-driven collaborative component deployment in mobile environments, In *Proceedings of the International Conference on Autonomic and Autonomous Systems* (pp. 1-5).

Rigole, P., Clerckx, T., Berbers, Y. & Coninx, K. (2007). Task-driven automated component deployment for ambient intelligence environments. In *Pervasive and Mobile Computing, 3* (3), 276-299. Elsevier Science Publishers B.V.

Riva, M. (2006). *Exploiting Architectural Reflection to Achieve Adaptivity in Context-Aware Environments.* MSc Thesis, University of Milano-Bicocca, DISCo, Milan, Italy.

Riva, O., and di Flora, C. (2006). Contory: A Smart Phone Middleware Supporting Multiple Context Provisioning

Strategies. In Proceedings of the 26th IEEE International Conference on Distributed Computing Systems Workshops (ICDCSW06).

Riva, O., Toivonen, S. (2007). The DYNAMOS approach to support context-aware service provisioning in mobile environments. Journal of Systems and Software 80(12): 1956-1972.

Robinson, R., Henricksen, K. & Indulska, J. (2007). XCML: A runtime representation for the Context Modeling Language. In *4th International Workshop on Context Modeling and Reasoning (CoMoRea), PerCom'07 Workshop Proceedings*, (pp 20-26). IEEE Computer Society Press

Rodriguez, J., Dakar, B., Marras, F.L. et al. (2001). Transcoding in WebSphere. In: *New Capabilities in IBM WebSphere Transcoding Publisher Version 3.5 Extending Web Applications to the Pervasive World. Everyplace Suite. Chapter 11.* New York: IBM Redbooks, 446 p.

Roman, M., et al. (2003). Dynamic application composition: Customizing the behavior of an active space. In Proceedings of IEEE PERCOM, IEEE Computer Society, p. 169, Washington, DC, USA.

Roman, M., Hess, C., Cerqueira, R., Ranganathan, A., Campbell, R., & Nahrstedt, K. (2002). Gaia: A middleware infrastructure to enable active spaces. *IEEE Pervasive Computing, 1*(4), 74-83.

Román, M., Hess, C., Cerqueira, R., Ranganathan, A., Campbell, R. H. & Nahrstedt, K. (2002). Gaia: a middleware platform for active spaces. SIGMOBILE Mob. Comput. Commun. Rev., ACM, 6, pp. 65-67.

Rosa, L., Lopes, A. & Rodrigues, L. (2008). Modeling adaptive services for distributed systems. In *Proceedings of the 2008 ACM Symposium on Applied Computing* (pp 2174-2180). ACM Press

Rossi, G., Gordillo, S., & Fortier, A. (2005). Seamless Engineering of Location Aware Services. *International Workshop on Context-Aware Mobile Systems, Lecture Notes in Computer Science*.

Roussaki, I., Strimpakou, M., & Anagnostou, M. (2007). Designing next generation middleware for context-aware ubiquitous and pervasive computing. *International Journal of Ad Hoc and Ubiquitous Computing, 2*(3), 197-206.

Roussaki, I., Strimpakou, M., Pils, C., Kalatzis, N., & Anagnostou, M. (2006). Hybrid context modeling: A location-based scheme using ontologies. *3rd Workshop on Context Modeling and Reasoning*, Pisa, Italy.

Rutherford, M., Carzaniga, A., & Wolf, A. L. (2006). Simulation-Based Test Adequacy Criteria for Distributed Systems. *Proceedings of the 14th FSE*, Portland, Oregon, November 2006.

Ryan, N., Pascoe, J., & Morse, D. (1999). Enhanced Reality Fieldwork: the Context Aware Archaeological Assistant. *BAR International Series, 1999*(750), 269–274.

Sacchetti, D., Talamona, A., Cerisara, C., Chibout, R., Ben Atallah, S., & Van Raemdonck. W. (2005). Seamless Access to Mobile Services for the Mobile User. Video at the *3rd International Conference on Pervasive Computing* (Pervasive 2005).

Sadi, S. H., & Maes, P. (2005). *xLink: Context Management Solution for Commodity Ubiquitous Computing Environments*. In Tokyo, Japan.

Sadler-Smith, E., & Riding, R. J. (1999). Cognitive style and instructional preferences. *Instructional Science, 27*(5), 355-371.

Safety Forum – Working Group RTD (2006). Strategic Research Agenda ICT for Mobility. European Commission. Retrieved February 20, 2007, from http://ec.europa.eu/information_society/activities/esafety/doc/esafety_2006/sra_ict_for_mobility_v.3_final.pdf

Saha, D., & Mukherjee, A. (2003). Pervasive Computing: A Paradigm for the 21st Century. *IEEE Computer, 36*(3), 25-31. IEEE Computer Society Press.

Sailesh, S., Pavel, D., & Trossen, D. (2006). Context Service Framework for Mobile Internet. *International Worskshop on System Support for Future Mobile Com-*

puting Applications (FUMCA 2006), September 2006, Irvine, California, USA.

Saint-Andre, P. (2005, December 8). Xmpp-simple feature comparison, *XMPP-SIMPLE Feature Comparison*. Retrieved November 13, 2007, from http://www.jabber.org/protocol/xmpp-simple.shtml.

Salovey, P., & Mayer, J. D. (1990). Emotional intelligence. *Imagination, Cognition and Personality, 9*, 185-211.

Samarati, P., & Vimercati, S. (2001). Access Control: Policies, Models and Mechanisms. *Foundations of Security Analysis and Design*, (pp. 137-196).

Sandhu, R. S., Coyne, E. J., Feinstein, H. L., & Youman, C. E. (1996). Role-Based Access Control Models *Computer 29* (2), 38-47.

Sandhu, R., Coyne, E., Feinstein, H., & Youman, C. (1996). Role-based access control models. *IEEE Computer, 2*, 38-47.

Sasakura, M, & Yamasaki, S. (2007). A Framework for Adaptive e-Learning Systems in Higher Education with Information Visualization. In *Proceedings of the 11th International Conference on Information Visualization*, (pp. 819-824).

Satyanarayanan, M. (2001). Pervasive computing: vision and challenges. *IEEE Personal Communications, 8*(4), 10-17.

Scagnetto, I., Selva, A., Vassena, L., and Rizio, P.Z. (2005). Mobe: Context-aware mobile applications on mobile devices for mobile users. 1st International Workshop on Exploiting Context Histories in Smart Environments, pp.49–54.

Scherp, A., & Boll, S. (2004). mobileMM4U - framework support for dynamic personalized multimedia content on mobile systems. In *Proceedings of Techniques and Applications for Mobile Commerce Track of Multi Conference Business Informatics*, Essen, Germany.

Schilit, B., Adams, N., & Want, R. (1994). Context-Aware Computing Applications. *IEEE Workshop on Mobile Computing Systems and Applications*, Santa Cruz, USA.

Schilit, B., Adams, N., and Want, R. (1994) Context-aware computing applications. In Proceedings of IEEE Workshop on Mobile Computing Systems and Applications, pp. 85-90, Santa Cruz, California. IEEE Computer Society Press.

Schilit, B., Trevor, J., Hilbert, D. & Koh, T. (2002). Web interaction using very small Internet devices. *Computer, 35* (10), 37-45. IEEE Computer Society.

Schilit, B.N. & Theimer, M.M. (1994). Disseminating active map information to mobile hosts. *IEEE Network, 8* (5), 22-32.

Schmidt, A. (2004). Management of dynamic and imperfect user context information. *On the Move to Meaningful Internet Systems 2004: OTM 2004 Workshops*, (pp. 779-786).

Schmidt, A. (2006). Ontology-based user context management: The challenges of imperfection and time-dependence. *On the Move to Meaningful Internet Systems*, (pp. 995-1011).

Schmidt, A., & Van Laerhoven, K. (2001). How to build smart appliances? *Personal Communications, IEEE, 8*(4), 66-71.

Schmidt, A., & Winterhalter, C. (2004). User Context Aware Delivery of E-Learning Material: Approach and Architecture. *Journal of Universal Computer Science (JUCS), 10*(1), January 2004.

Schmidt, A., Aidoo, K. A., Takaluoma, A., Tuomela, U., Van Laerhoven, K., & Van de Velde, W. (1999). Advanced Interaction in Context. *In Proceedings of the 1st international symposium on Handheld and Ubiquitous Computing, September 27-29, 1999, Karlsruhe, Germany*, (pp. 89-101).

Schmidt, A., Beigl, M., & Hans-W, H. (1999). There is more to context than location. *Computers and Graphics, 23*(6), 893-901.

Schneier, B. (2005). Two-Factor Authentication: Too Little, Too Late. *Communication of the ACM, 48*(4).

Schulzrinne, H., & Wedlund, E. (2000). Application-layer mobility using SIP. *Mobile Computing and Communications Review, 4*(3), 47–57. ACM SIGMOBILE.

Schunk, D. H. (1989). Self-efficacy and cognitive skill learning. In Ames, C., & Ames, R. (Eds.), *Research on motivation in education, 3: Goals and cognitions* (13-44), San Diego: Academic Press.

Schuster, M., Domene, A., Vaidya, R., Arbanowski, S., Kim, S. M., Lee, J. W., and Lim, H. (2007). Virtual Device Composition. In Proceedings of the Eighth International Symposium on Autonomous Decentralized Systems (ISADS07), Sedona, Arizona.

SDCARD, (n.d.). *Secure Digital simplified Physical Layer Specification*, from http://www.sdcard.org/about/memory_card/pls/

SDMMC, (n.d.). *SD Card Association*, from http://www.sdcard.org

Seceleanu, T. & Garlan. D. (2005). Synchronized Architectures for Adaptive Systems. In *Proceedings of the 29th Annual International Computer Software and Applications Conference.* (pp. 146-151).

Serafini, L., Giunchiglia, F., Mylopoulos, J., & ernstein, P. (2003). Local relational model: a logical formalization of database coordination. In P. Blackburn, C. Ghidini, & R. Turner (Eds.), *Context'03.*

Shankar, C., & Campbell, R. (2005). A policy-based management framework for pervasive systems using axiomatized rule-actions. *Network Computing and Applications, Fourth IEEE International Symposium on*, (pp. 255-258).

Shaw, M. (2002). Self-Healing Softening Precision to Avoid Brittleness. In *Proceedings of the Workshop on Self-Healing Systems*, (pp. 111-113).

Shehab, M., Bertino, E., & Ghafoor, A. (2005). Efficient hierarchical key generation and key diffusion for sensor networks. *Second Annual IEEE Communications Society Conference on Sensor and AdHoc Communications and Networks*

Shi, J., Bochmann, G., & Adams, C. (2004). *A Trust Model with Statistical Foundation.* Paper presented at the Workshop on Formal Aspects in Security and Trust, Toulouse, France.

Siewiorek, D., Smailagic, A., Furukawa, J., Krause, A., Moraveji, N., Reiger, K., Shaffer, J., and Wong, F. L. (2003). SenSay: A Contect-Aware Mobile Phone. In Proceedings of the 7th IEEE International Symposium on Wearable Computers (ISWC03).

Smith, B. (1982). *Reflection and Semantics in a Procedural Language.* PhD Thesis, MIT Laboratory for Computer Science, Cambridge, MA, USA.

Sorniotti, A., Molva, R., & Gomez, L. (2008). Efficient access control for wireless sensor data. *IEEE International Symposium on Personal, Indoor and Mobile Radio Communications.* 15-18 September, 2008, Cannes, France.

Spanoudakis, N., & Moraitis, P. (2006). Agent Based Architecture in an Ambient Intelligence Context. *Proc. 4th European Workshop Multi-Agent Systems (EUMAS06)*, (pp. 163–174).

Specht, G., and Weithoner, T. (2006). Context-Aware Processing of Ontologies in Mobile Environments. In Proceedings of the 7th International Conference on Mobile Data Management (MDM'06).

SPI, (n.d.). *SPI reference*, from http://en.wikipedia.org/wiki/Serial_Peripheral_Interface_Bus

SPICE. (2006). *Spice d4.1: ontology definition of user profiles, knowledge information and services.* Retrieved February 13, 2008, from http://www.ist-spice.org/documents/D4.1-final.pdf.

SPICE. (2007). *Spice unified architecture.* Retrieved from http://www.ist-spice.org/documents/SPICE_WP1_unified_architecture_Phase%202.pdf.

Spielberger, C. D. (1972). Conceptual and methodological issues in anxiety research. In Spielberger C. D. (Ed.), *Anxiety. Current trends in theory and research* (Vol. 2). New York: Academic Press.

Spielberger, C. D., & Vagg, P. R. (1995). Test anxiety: A transactional process model. In C. D. Spielberger & P. R. Vagg (Eds.), *Test anxiety: Theory, assessment, and treatment* (pp. 3-14). Washington, DC: Taylor & Francis.

Stajano, F. (2002). *Security for Ubiquitous Computing.* John Wiley and Sons.

Stefanidis, K., Pitoura, E. & Vassiliadis, P. (2007b). A context-aware preference database system. *International Journal of Pervasive Computing and Communications,* 3(4), 439-460.

Stefanidis, K., Pitoura, E., & Vassiliadis, P. (2005). On supporting context-aware preferences in relational database systems. Paper presented at the First International Workshop on Managing Context Information in Mobile and Pervasive Environments.

Stefanidis, K., Pitoura, E., & Vassiliadis, P. (2006). Modeling and storing context-aware preferences. *10th East European Conference on Advances in Databases and Information Systems (ADBIS 2006). Thessaloniki, Greece,* (pp. 124-140).

Stefanidis, K., Pitoura, E., & Vassiliadis, P. (2007). Adding context to preferences. The 23rd International Conference on Data Engineering(ICDE), (pp. 846-855).

Steiner, J. G., Neuman, B. C., & Schiller, J. I. (1988). *Kerberos: An Authentication Service for Open Network Systems.* Paper presented at the Usenix, Dallas, Texas.

Sterling, L. & Juan, T. (2005). The Software Engineering of Agent-Based Intelligent Adaptive Systems. In *Proceedings of the International Conference on Software Engineering.* (pp. 704-705).

Strang, T. & Linnhoff-Popien, C. (2004). A context modeling survey. In UbiComp 1st International Workshop on Advanced Context Modeling, Reasoning and Management (pp. 34-41)

Strang, T., & Linnhoff-Popien, C. (2004). A context modeling survey. *Workshop on Advanced Context Modelling, Reasoning and Management, UbiComp,* (pp. 34-41).

Strang, T., & Popien, C. L. (2004). A context modeling survey. In *Workshop on Advanced Context Modelling,*

Reasoning and Management, UbiComp 2004 - The Sixth International Conference on Ubiquitous Computing.

Strang, T., and Linnhoff-Popien, C. (2004). A Context Modeling Survey. Workshop on Advanced Context Modelling, Reasoning and Management, UbiComp 2004.

Strang, T., Linnhoff-Popien, C., & Frank, K. (2003). Cool: a context ontology language to enable contextual interoperability, *Distributed Applications and Interoperable Systems: 4th Ifip Wg6. 1 International Conference, Dais 2003, Paris, France, November 17-21, 2003, Proceedings.*

Strassner, J., O'Sullivan, D., & Lewis, D. (2007). Ontologies in the engineering of management and autonomic systems: a reality check. *Journal of Network and Systems Management, 15*(1), 5-11.

Streitz, N., & Nixon, P. (2005). The disappearing computer. *Communications of the ACM, 48*(3), 32-35.

Strimpakou, M., Roussaki, I., Pils, C., & Anagnostou, M. (2006). COMPACT: Middleware for context representation and management in pervasive computing environments. *International Journal of Pervasive Computing and Communications, 2*(3), 229-246.

Strohbach, M., Bauer, M., Kovacs, E., Villalonga, C., & Richter, N. (2007). *Context sessions: a novel approach for scalable context management in ngn networks.* Newport Beach, California, USA.

Strohbach, M., Kovacs, E., & Goix, L. W. (2007). Integrating ims presence information in a service oriented architecture.

Sun Developer Network (2007). Java 2 Platform, Standard Edition (J2SE). retrieved june 1, 2007 from http://java.sun.com/j2se

Sun Microsystems, Inc. (2000). *Personal Java Application Environment Specification, Version 1.2a* (Final) retrieved from http://java.sun.com/products/personaljava/

Suzuki, J. & Yamamoto, Y. (1999). OpenWebServer: An Adaptive Web Server Using Software Patterns. In *IEEE Communications Magazine, 37*(4), (pp.46-52).

Taiani, F., Fabre, J. C., & Killijian, M. O. (2002). Principles of Multi-Level Reflection for Fault Tolerant Architectures. In *Proceedings on the Pacific Rim International Symposium on Dependable Computing*, (pp. 59-66)

Tan, J. G., Zhang, D., Wang, X., & Cheng, H. S. (2005). Enhancing semantic spaces with event-driven context interpretation, *Pervasive Computing: Third International Conference, Pervasive 2005, Munich, Germany, May 8-13, 2005, Proceedings.*

Tanenbaum, A. S. (2002). *Computer Networks.* Prentice Hall PTR

Tanenbaum, A. S., & Steen, M. V. (2001). Distributed Systems: Principles and Paradigms. *Prentice Hall PTR.*

Thomas, R. K., & Sandhu, R. (2004). Proximity based access control in smart-emergency departments. *Pervasive Computing and Communications Workshops, 5.*

TI, (n.d.). *CC2431 product page*, from http://focus.ti.com/docs/ prod/folders/print/cc2431.html

Toivonen, S., Kolari, J., & Laakko, T. (2003). Facilitating mobile users with contextualized content. *In Proc. Workshop Artificial Intelligence in Mobile Systems.*

Tolone, W., Ahn, G.-J., Pai, T., & Hong, S.-P. (2005). Access control in collaborative systems *ACM Comput. Surv. , 37* (1), 29-41.

Tonti, G., Bradshaw, J. M., Jeffers, R., Montanari, R., Suri, N., & Uszok, A. (2003). Semantic web languages for policy representation and reasoning: a comparison of kaos, rei, and ponder. *The Semantic Web—ISWC,* (pp. 419-437).

Truong, B. A., Lee, Y., & Lee, S. Y. (2005). A unified context model: bringing probabilistic models to context ontology. *Lecture notes in computer science,* (pp. 566-575).

Tsianos, N., Germanakos, P., Lekkas, Z., Mourlas, C., & Samaras, G. (2007). Evaluating the Significance of Cognitive and Emotional Parameters in e-Learning Adaptive Environments. *Proceedings of the IADIS International Conference on Cognition and Exploratory Learning in Digital Age (CELDA2007)*, Algarve, Portugal, December 7-9, 2007, (pp. 93-98).

Tsien, J. (2007). The memory code. *Scientific American Magazine, 297*(1), 52-59.

Tzafestas, S. G., (1997). Editorial: Robot Adaptive and Robust Control. In *Journal of Intelligent and Robotic Systems, 20,* 87-91.

Tzeng, W. G. (2002). A time-bound cryptographic key assignment scheme for access control in a hierarchy. *IEEE Transactions on Knowledge and Data Engineering, 14*(1), 182–188.

U. S. Department of Transportation (1998). Developing Traveler Information Systems Using the National ITS Architecture. Retrieved February 23, 2007, from http://itsdocs.fhwa.dot.gov/jpodocs/repts_te/4163.pdf.

Umlauft, M., Pospischil, G., Niklfeld, G., & Michlmayr, E. (2003). LoL@, a Mobile Tourist Guide for UMTS. *Information Technology & Tourism, 5*(3), 151-164.

UPnP Forum. (2003, December 2). *Upnp device architecture 1.0.* Retrieved from http://www.upnp.org/.

USB, (n.d.). *USB Developers page*, from http://www.usb.org/developers

Vallée, M., Ramparany, F., and Vercouter, L. (2005). Flexible Composition of Smart Device Services. In Proc. of the 2005 International Conference on Pervasive Systems and Computing (PSC'05), Las Vegas, USA.

van Bunningen, A. H. (2004). *Context aware querying: Challenges for data management in ambient intelligence.* (Tech. Rep. No. TR-CTIT-04-51). The Netherlands: University of Twente.

van Bunningen, A. H., Feng, L., & Apers, P. M. G. (2006). Modeling uncertain context information via event probabilities. *The Second Twente Data Management Workshop TDM'06,* (pp. 25-32).

van Bunningen, A. H., Feng, L., & Apers, P. M. G. (2006b). A context-aware preference model for database querying in an ambient intelligent environment. *The 17th International Conference on Database and Expert Systems Applications (DEXA)*, (pp. 33-43).

van Bunningen, A. H., Fokkinga, M. M., Apers, P. M. G., & Feng, L. (2007). Ranking query results using context-aware preferences. *First International Workshop on Ranking in Databases*, (pp. 269-276).

Van Setten, M., Pokraev, S., & Koolwaaij, S. (2004). Context-Aware Recommendations in the Mobile Tourist Application COMPASS. In *Proceedings of Adaptive Hypermedia and Adaptive Web-Based Systems Third International Conference* (pp. 235-244). Eindhoven, The Netherlands

Vetere, G., & Lenzerini, M. (2005). Models for semantic interoperability in service-oriented architectures. *IBM Systems Journal, 44*(4).

Victor, K., Pauty, J. & Berbers, Y. (2007). Context distribution using context aware flooding. In: Braun, T., Mascolo, S., Konstantas, D. & Wulff, M. (eds.), *First ERCIM Workshop on Emobility*, Vol. 1 (pp. 95-106).

Vieira, V., Tedesco, P., Salgado, A.C. & Brézillon, P. (2007). Investigating the Specifics of Contextual Elements Management: The CEManTIKA Approach. In Kokinov, B.; Richardson, D.C.; Roth-Berghofer, Th.R.; Vieu, L. (Eds.) *Modeling and Using Context 6th International and Interdisciplinary Conference, CONTEXT 2007* (pp. 493-506) Lecture Notes in Artificial Intelligence, Springer Verlag

Villanova, M., Gensel, J. & Martin, H. (2003). A progressive access approach for web based information systems. *Journal of Web Engineering, 2* (1&2), 27-57.

Volokh, E. (2000). Personalization and Privacy. *From the Communications of the Association for Computing Machinery, 43*(8), 84.

W3C (2004). SWRL: A Semantic Web Rule Language Combining OWL and RuleML, retrieved may 21, 2004 from http://www.w3.org/Submission/2004/SUBM-SWRL

W3C (2004b). Composite Capability/Preference Profiles (CC/PP): Structure and Vocabularies 1.0, retrieved june 1, 2007 from http://www.w3.org/TR/2004/REC-CCPP-struct-vocab-20040115

W3C. (2003). W3c multimodal interaction framework. *W3C Note*. Retrieved from http://www.w3.org/TR/mmi-framework/.

W3C. (2007). Emma: extensible multimodal annotation markup language. *W3C Working Draft 14 December 2004*. Retrieved from http://www.w3.org/TR/emma/.

Waldner, J. B. (2007). *Nano-informatique et intelligence ambiante: inventer l'ordinateur du XXIe siècle*. Lavoisier.

Wang, Q., & Abu-Rgheff, M. A. (2003). Next-generation mobility support. *Communications Engineer, 1*(1), 16- 19. IET.

Wang, S.-J. (2004). Anonymous wireless authentication on a portable cellular mobile system. *Computers, IEEE Transactions on, 53*(10), 1317 - 1329.

Wang, X., Zhang, D., Gu, T., & Pung, H. (2004). Ontology based context modeling and reasoning using owl. In *Pervasive Computing and Communications Workshops, 2004. Proceedings of the Second IEEE Annual Conference on* (pp. 18-22).

Want, R., Hopper, A., Falcao, V., & Gibbons, J. (1992). The active badge location system. *ACM Transactions on Information Systems, 10*(1), 91–102.

WAP Forum. (2001, October 20). Wag uaprof. Retrieved from http://www.openmobilealliance.org/tech/affiliates/wap/wap-248-uaprof-20011020-a.pdf.

Warren, S. D., & Brandeis, L. D. (1890). The Right to Privacy. *Harvard Law Review, IV*(5).

Web Models s.r.l. (2008). WebRatio Site Development Studio. Retrieved January, 2008, from http://www.webratio.com.

Weiser, M. (1991). The computer for the 21st century. *Scientific American, 265*(3), 94-104.

Weißenberg, N., Gartmann, R., & Voisard, A. (2006). An Ontology-Based Approach to Personalized Situation-Aware Mobile Service Supply. *Geoinformatica 10*, 1 (Mar. 2006), 55-90. DOI= http://dx.doi.org/10.1007/s10707-005-4886-9.

Wermelinger, M. (1998). Towards a Chemical Model for Software Architecture Reconfiguration. In *IEE Proc Software*, *145*(5), 130-136.

Williamson, G., Stevenson, G., Neely, S., Coyle, L., and Nixon, P. (2006). Scalable information dissemination for pervasive systems: implementation and evaluation. In Proceedings of the 4th international workshop on Middleware for Pervasive and Ad-Hoc Computing (MPAC 2006), Melbourne, Australia, ISBN:1-59593-421-9.

Winsborough, W. H., & Li., N. (2002). *Towards Practical Automated Trust Negotiation.* Paper presented at the IEEE Workshop on Policies for Distributed Systems and Networks.

Wolf, J.L., Squillante, M.S., Yu, P.S., Sethuraman, J., & Ozsen, L. (2002). Optimal crawling strategies for web search engines. *WWW Conference 2002*, New York, USA.

Woolf, B. (1997). Null object. *Pattern languages of program design 3*, (pp. 5–18).

World Wide Web Consortium, W3C (2004): Resource Description Framework, W3C Recommendation 10 February 2004, http://www.w3.org/RDF/.

World Wide Web Consortium, W3C (2004b): Web Ontology Language Reference, W3C Recommendation 10 February 2004, http://www.w3.org/TR/owl-ref/.

WSMO Working Group (2004), D2v1.0: Web service Modeling Ontology (WSMO). WSMO Working Draft, (2004). (http://www.wsmo.org/2004/d2/v1.0/).

WSMX Working Group (2007), The Web Service Modelling eXecution environment, http://www.wsmx.org/.

Wullems, C., Looi, M., & Clark, A. (2004). Toward context-aware security: An authorization architecture for intranet environments. *Pervasive Communication and Communication Workshops.*

Xiang, Q. J. Ma, Y. F., Lu, J., Xie, J. P., & Sha, H. Y. (2007). Framework design of highway traveller information system of Jiangsu Province of China. *Intelligent Transportation Systems*, *1*(2), 110-116. IET.

Xynogalas, S., Chantzara, M., Sygkouna, I., Vrontis, S., Roussaki, I., & Anagnostou, M. (2004). Context Management for the Provision of Adaptive Services to Roaming Users. *IEEE Wireless Communications*, *11*(2), 40-47.

Yang, S. & Shao, N. (2007). Enhancing pervasive Web accessibility with rule-based adaptation strategy. *Expert Systems with Applications*, *32* (4), 1154-1167.

Yarvis M. (2001). *Conductor: Distributed Adaptation for Heterogeneous Networks.* Unpublished doctoral dissertation, Los Angeles University, UCLA Department of Computer Science

Yesilada, Y., Harper, S., Goble. C. A., & Stevens, R. (2004). Screen readers cannot see: Ontology based semantic annotation for visually impaired web travellers. In ICWE'04 (pp. 445-458). Munich, Germany: Springer.

Yeung, A. K. W., & Hall, G. B. (2007). *Spatial Database Systems: Design, Implementation and Project Management.* Springer Series: GeoJournal Library, *87*.

Yi, X. (2005). Security of chien's efficient time-bound hierarchical key assignment scheme. *IEEE Transactions on Knowledge and Data Engineering*, *17*(9), 1298–1299.

Yin, J., Alvisik, L., Dahlin, M., & Iyengar, A. (2002). Engineering Web Cache Consistency. *ACM Transactions on Internet Technology*, *2*, 224-259.

Younghee, K., & Keumsuk, L. (2006). A Quality Measurement Method of Context Information in Ubiquitous Environments. *Proceedings of the International Conference on Hybrid Information Technology*, *2*, 576-581. IEEE.

Yu, J., Benatallah, B., Saint-Paul, R., Casati, F., Daniel, F., & Matera, M. (2007). A Framework for Rapid Integration of Presentation Components. In *WWW'07* (pp. 923-932). Banff, Canada: ACM.

Zadeh, L. A. (1973). Outline of a new approach to the analysis of complex systems and decision processes. *IEEE Trans. on Systems, Man and Cybernetics, 3*(1), 28-44.

Zadeh, L.A. (1963). On the Definition of Adaptivity. In *Proceedings of the IEEE*, (pp. 469-470).

Zeadally, S., Siddiqui, F., DeepakMavatoor, N., & Randhavva, P. (2004). SIP and mobile IP integration to support seamless mobility. *Proceedings of 15th IEEE International Symposium on Personal, Indoor and Mobile Radio Communications, 3*, 1927- 1931

Zebedee, J. (2008). *An adaptable context management framework for pervasive computing.* MSc thesis, School of Computing, Queen's University.

Zhang, G., Parashar, M. (2004). Context-aware Dynamic Access Control for Pervasive Applications. *Proceedings of the Communication Networks and Distributed Systems.*

Zhang, W., Das, S., & Liu, Y. (2006). A trust based framework for secure data aggregation on wireless sensor networks. *IEEE Communications Society Conference on Sensor, Mesh and Ad Hoc Communications and Networks.*

ZigBee (n.d.). *Zigbee Alliance*, from http://www.zigbee.org

Zimmer, T. (2006). QoC: Quality of Context – Improving the Performance of Context-Aware Applications, *Pervasive 2006 Conference*, Dublin, Ireland.

Zimmermann, P. (1994). *PGP User's Guide.* Cambridge, USA: MIT Press.

About the Contributors

Dragan Stojanovic is an assistant professor at the Computer Science Department, Faculty of Electronic Engineering, University of Nis, Serbia. He received his PhD, MSc, and BSc degrees in computer science from the University of Nis, in 2004, 1998 and 1993, respectively. His research and development interests encompass context-aware and location-based services, mobile/Web/distributed information systems and services, mobile objects and spatio-temporal data management, and geographic information systems. He has published widely in those and related topics. He successfully participates in several international and national R&D projects in cooperation with academic partners and industry.

* * *

Fabien Bataille has led the "Ambient Services" research team at Alcatel-Lucent Bell Labs, on the topic of innovative mobile services with a focus on Context Awareness. He is also responsible for Alcatel-Lucent Bell Labs definition of work and management of contributions to national and EU research projects: RNRT Safari, FP6 Mobilife, ITEA2 Easy Interactions and ITEA Metaverse1.

Yolande Berbers received her MSc and PhD degrees in computer science from the Katholieke Universiteit Leuven in 1982 and 1987, respectively. Since 1990, she has been an associate professor in the Department of Computer Science at the Katholieke Universiteit Leuven and a member of the DistriNet research group. Her research interests include software engineering for embedded software, ubiquitous computing, service architectures, middleware, real-time systems, component-oriented software development, distributed systems, environments for distributed and parallel applications, and mobile agents. She runs several projects in cooperation with other academic partners and/or industry. She teaches various courses on programming real-time and embedded systems, and on computer architecture.

Jan van den Berg is associate professor of ICT at Delft University of Technology, The Netherlands. He earned his MSc in (Applied) mathematics from the same university and his PhD in Artificial Intelligence from Erasmus University Rotterdam, The Netherlands. He has taught courses in Business Intelligence, Information Security, Computational Finance, Information & Communication Technology, Artificial Intelligence and Information Architecture Design. His research areas of interest include the subjects taught in these courses and more specifically (probabilistic) fuzzy systems, genetic algorithms, neural networks, sustainable development, text mining & knowledge discovery, and computational philosophy. He has published in many international journals.

Tarak Chaari is in a post doctoral position in the Laboratory for Analysis and Architecture of Systems: LAAS-CNRS at Toulouse. His research interests focus on adaptation in the scope of pervasive applications and context–aware systems. He holds a PhD on "adapting pervasive applications in multi-contextual environments" from the National Institute of Applied Sciences of Lyon (INSA Lyon). He teaches information systems modeling and development in INSA Lyon. He is a Member of the French adaption action ADAPT (http://adapt.asr.cnrs.fr) on dynamic adaptation to runtime environments. T. Chaari has published more than 15 peer-reviewed papers in conferences and journals. He is also a reviewer for many international conferences and journals on context-awareness, adaptation and service oriented systems.

Florian Daniel is a post-doc researcher at the University of Trento, Italy. He holds a PhD in Information Technology from Politecnico di Milano and a master in computer engineering (cum laude) from Politecnico di Milano. His research interests include conceptual modeling and design of Web applications, adaptivity and context-awareness in Web applications, component-based user interface design, Web mashups, business processes, and business intelligence applications. Daniel is member of the organizing committee of the international workshop on Adaptation and Evolution in Web Systems Engineering (AEWSE) and the WebML research group. He has been PC member for several international conferences and reviewer for international journals, such as *IEEE Computer, IEEE Internet Computing, ACM Transactions on the Web*.

Semir Daskapan is assistant professor at the ICT department at the School for Technology, Policy and Management (TPM) of Delft University of Technology. He has been involved in several research projects on IT security and published several international papers. Currently he teaches courses in information security, privacy, trust management, computer dependability and complex adaptive systems. Prior to working at Technical University Delft he was ICT (project) manager at the Dutch patent office, the Dutch Ministry of Economic Affairs, and CSN of the Royal Dutch Telecom (KPN). He has a MSc in aerospace engineering, MSc in international economics and a PhD in computer science.

Stefan Dietze is a research fellow at the Knowledge Media Institute of the Open University since June, 2006. His main research interests are in Semantic Web, Knowledge Modelling and Semantic Web Services (SWS). His work has been published throughout major conferences, journals and workshops in the area of Semantic Web, Web Services and SOA. He is currently a key researcher within the EU-framework 6 project LUISA, which applies and extends current SWS technologies to enable context-aware delivery of E-Learning resources. Currently, he is involved in the EU FP6 IP SOA4ALL.

John Domingue is the deputy director of the Knowledge Media Institute at The Open University, UK. He has published over 100 refereed articles in the areas of Semantic Web Services, Semantic Web, ontologies and human computer interaction. Up until last year he was the scientific director of DIP an EU Integrated Project (IP) on Semantic Web Services which involved 17 partners and had a budget of 16M Euros. Also last year he chaired the European Semantic Web Conference. Currently he is the scientific director of SUPER, another EU IP which unites Semantic Web Services and Business Process Modeling. Dr Domingue also currently sits on the Steering Committee for the European Semantic Conference Series, is a co-chair of the WSMO working group and a co-chair of the OASIS Semantic Execution Environment Technical committee.

Heinz-Josef Eikerling got his diploma in computer science from Paderborn University in 1992. Subsequently, he joined the computer science departments at Paderborn University and the University of Tübingen. In 1996 he received the Dr. rer. nat. from Paderborn University for his research conducted in the field of electronic design automation. In 1996 after working for the FZI (Research Center for Information Technology) in Karlsruhe he joined the semiconductors division of the Siemens AG, Munich, where he was a member of the CAD tools team. In 1997 he worked for the Mettenmeier GmbH in the field of geographical information systems. Since 1997 he works at C-LAB, a joint research institute operated by Paderborn University and Siemens IT Solutions & Services as a principal consultant where he is leading the distributed interactive systems group. His primary research interests include distributed/mobile computing, mobile and service-oriented middleware and advanced content processing in mobile networks.

Amr Ali-Eldin has been in IT projects from both academia and industry. His focus is on innovation and development of Technology. He was awared his PhD in information systems from Delft University of Technology, The Netherlands. He worked as an IT innovation architect in a number of high technological ICT projects with the focus on privacy, identity and access management, software engineering and service-oriented architectures. Ali-Eldin joined the Accenture Technology Architecture workforce in Accenture as a technology architect since January 2007. Accenture is a global management consulting, technology services, and outsourcing company. It is registered in Hamilton, Bermuda and is said to be one of the largest Consulting Firm in the world with more than 178,000 people in 49 countries. The company generated net revenues exceeded US$22.39 billion for the fiscal year ended Aug. 31, 2007. Accenture's clients include 91 of the Fortune Global 100 and more than two-thirds of the Fortune Global 500.

Ling Feng is the professor of Computer Science and Technology at Tsinghua University in China. Her research interests include context-aware data management towards Ambient Intelligence, knowledge-based information systems, data mining and warehousing, distributed object-oriented database management systems, etc., and has published over 100 papers in international and national journals and conferences. She serves as the Asian editor of the *International Journal of Informatica*, associate editor of the *International Journal of Data Warehousing and Mining*, on the editorial board of the *International Journal of Neuroscience Methods*, and the *International Journal of Data Analysis Techniques and Strategies*. She received the 2004 innovational VIDI Award by The Netherlands Organization for Scientific Research, 2006 Chinese ChangJiang Professorship Award by the Ministry of Education and Li Jiacheng Foundation, and 2006 Tsinghua Hundred-Talents Award.

Andrés Fortier is doing a jointly PhD in computer science between the University of La Plata and the Universidad Politécnica de Valencia. He is also a teaching assistant of Object Oriented courses at the University of La Plata. He has published several papers on architectures for context-aware systems. His research interests include dynamic languages, metaprogramming, software architectures, mobile computing and context-dependent systems.

Panagiotis Germanakos, PhD, is a research scientist, in the Laboratory of New Technologies, Faculty of Communication & Media Studies, National & Kapodistrian University of Athens and of the Department of Computer Science, University of Cyprus. He obtained his PhD from the University of Athens in 2008 and his MSc in International Marketing Management from the Leeds University Business School in 1999. His BSc was in computer science and also holds a HND Diploma of Technician Engineer in the field of computer studies. His research interest is in Web adaptation and personalization environments and systems based on user profiling / filters encompassing amongst others visual, mental and affective processes, implemented on desktop and mobile / wireless platforms. He has several publications, including co-edited books, chapters, articles in journals, and conference contributions. Furthermore, he actively participates in numerous national and EU funded projects that mainly focus on the analysis, design and development of open interoperable integrated wireless/mobile and personalized technological infrastructures and systems in the ICT research areas of e-government, e-health and e-learning and has an extensive experience in the provision of consultancy of large scaled IT solutions and implementations in the business sector.

Laurent Gomez is a senior researcher at SAP Research in the Department of Security and Trust since 2001. He received his engineer degree in computer science from Ecole Superieure en Sciences Informatiques, Sophia Antipolis, France in 1999. Currently involved in the WASP project, his current research interests lie in the area of secure integration of wireless sensor networks into business application from end-to-end confidentiality of sensor data to contextual access control, including trusted sensor data processing. In the scope of the WASP project, he is actively involved in the development of a secure mediation layer between WSNs and business applications, so called Enterprise Integration Component.

Silvia E. Gordillo is full professor at Facultad de Informatica, UNLP, Argentina and one of the directors of LIFIA. She holds a PhD from Universite Lyon II, France. Her research interests are mobile and pervasive information systems, and aspect-oriented specification of geographic information systems.

Alessio Gugliotta has studied computer science at the University of Udine (Italy) and received his master's degree in March 2002, cum laude, followed by a PhD in computer science at the University of Udine, in March 2006. Since January 2006, he has a position of research fellow in the topic of Semantic Web Services at the Knowledge Media Institute of the Open University (Milton Keynes, UK). His current research is focused on service oriented computing, knowledge representation and Semantic Web Services, and their application within multiple domains such as e-government and e-learning.

Dino Giuli is full professor in Telecommunications at the Department of Electronics and Telecommunications of the University of Florence where he was director of the Department until 2004. Since 1996 he is promoter and scientific co-ordinator of the PhD program in "Telematics and Information Society." His research activities have been principally oriented in the domain of telematics and environmental monitoring systems. Giuli is author of more then one hundred and fifty scientific publications, mainly published on scientific journals and international conference proceedings. He is AEI member of and IEEE senior member.

Carsten Jacob studied computer science and graduated from Humboldt-Universität zu Berlin. He then started working as a research associate at the Fraunhofer Institute for Open Communication Systems (FOKUS). His main research activities pertain to context-aware applications and Semantic Web technologies in service oriented and mobile computing environments. He published multiple scientific papers in these fields of work and has been involved in a number of national and international projects addressing decentralized software architectures, semantics, and future Web applications.

Adrien Joly is a PhD candidate researching in the field of context-awareness / ambient services for the Social Communications Department of Alcatel-Lucent Bell Labs Applications, in collaboration with the CNRS-LIRIS laboratory and under supervision of Pr. Pierre Maret. He received a master's degree in information technology from the Institut National des Sciences Appliquées de Lyon (INSA-LYON, France) in 2006. His current interests cover ambient intelligence, pervasive systems, ubiquitous computing, social networking, Semantic Web, mobile applications, and modular software architecture.

Nikos Kalatzis was born in Athens, Greece, in 1976. He received his diploma on physics by the Physics Department of the University of Ioannina in 2000. In 2002, he received his MSc on information security by the University of London (Royal Holloway College - Department of Mathematics). For the next two years, he worked in industry in the field of IT security. Since 2004, he pursues the PhD degree in the area of computer networks, in the Computer Science Division of National Technical University of Athens (NTUA). Currently, he works as a research engineer at the Computer Networks Laboratory in NTUA. He has participated in some international research projects. His major research interests lie in the field of ambient intelligence, context-awareness, context prediction algorithms, security and privacy on context aware systems. He has several publications on these research fields.

Frédérique Laforest is associate professor in the CNRS UMR 5205 LIRIS Laboratory (Lyon Research Center for Images and Intelligent Information Systems) in Lyon, France. She teaches pervasive information systems and applications modeling at the INSA Lyon high school. Her research interests encompass document-based user interfaces, and adaptation of user interfaces and applications to the context of the end-user. Always applying her works to the healthcare domain, she has proposed research tools for the better access and the easier management of patients' records when the care practitioner is not in office, but in a situation of mobility (home hospitalization, emergency care). Laforest has published more than 50 peer-reviewed articles in conferences and journals.

Annett Laube is a senior researcher at SAP Research France located in Sophia-Antipolis and currently leading the SAP team working in the WASP project. She has more than 10 years of work experience in the IT Industry (IBM Development and Consulting, SAP Development) and in industrial research (IBM Research Center Heidelberg, SAP Research). Annett graduated at TU Dresden University in 1995 in theoretical and applied computer science. She got her PhD in computer science from TU Dresden, Germany in 2000. The areas of her professional interests include context-awareness and security in wireless and mobile applications, applications of sensor networks and their secure integration into enterprise systems.

Zacharias Lekkas is a research assistant and doctoral candidate at the New Technologies Laboratory of the Faculty of Communication and Media Studies of the University of Athens. He holds an Msc in occupational psychology from the University of Nottingham. He is interested in the role of emotions in web-based educational systems, and has conducted empirical research on the effect of human factors such as anxiety, emotional moderation, emotional intelligence, self efficacy, etc. Additionally, his research interests include the field of decision making support in adaptive hypermedia and the design of personalized training systems. His work has been published in conferences, journals and edited books, whilst he is one of the awarded authors (best student paper award) at the Adaptive Hypermedia 2008 Conference.

Yuanping Li received bachelor's degree in automation from University of Science and Technology in Beijing in 2004, and received master's degree in software engineering from Tsinghua University in 2007. He is currently a candidate for doctor degree in computer science in Tsinghua University, Beijing China. His research interest is context-aware data management.

Nicolas Liampotis was born in Athens, Greece, in 1980. He received the Electrical and Computer Engineering Diploma from the National Technical University of Athens (NTUA) in 2005. Since 2005, he pursues the PhD degree in the area of computer network security, in the Communication, Electronic and Information Engineering Division of NTUA. Currently, he works as a research engineer and network administrator at the Computer Networks Laboratory in NTUA. He has participated in a number of national and international research and development projects. His main research interests include mobile and personal communications, security and privacy in pervasive computing, context-awareness, service modelling, and QoS-based network resource management. He is a member of the Technical Chamber of Greece.

Nahuel Lofeudo is a grad student at Facultad de Informatica, UNLP, Argentina and staff researcher at LIFIA. His research interests include embedded systems, mobile web and pervasive computing.

Pierre Maret is a professor in Computer Science at the University of Lyon (Université Jean Monnet) and he is a member of the Laboratoire Hubert Curien. He obtained his PhD thesis in 1995, his Habilitation in 2006 and has been member of the INSA Lyon and LIRIS Laboratory. Pierre Maret is leading research in the field of virtual communities, social networks and ambient intelligence. He cooperates with industrial and academic international partners on several research projects.

Patrick Martin is a professor in the School of Computing at Queen's University. He holds a BSc and a PhD from the University of Toronto and a MSc from Queen's University. He is also a Faculty Fellow with IBM's Centre for Advanced Studies. His research interests include database system performance, Web services, pervasive computing and autonomic computing systems.

Pietro Mazzoleni is a researcher at IBM's Thomas J. Watson Research Center in Hawthorne, New York, USA. Pietro got is PhD in computer science from University of Milan (Italy). During his career, he worked as visiting scholar at Rutgers University (Newark, NJ) and Vrije Universiteit (Amsterdam). Prior to joining IBM he worked for 4 years as assistant professor at University of Milan during which he successfully lead several international research projects. He published several articles in scientific conferences as well as international journals. He also holds two patents in the area of services. His main research interests cover many areas in the fields of service engineering and database systems.

Costas Mourlas is assistant professor in the National and Kapodistrian University of Athens (Greece), Department of Communication and Media Studies since 2002. He obtained his PhD from the Department of Informatics, University of Athens in 1995 and graduated from the University of Crete in 1988 with a Diploma in Computer Science. In 1998 was an ERCIM fellow for post-doctoral studies through research in STFC, UK. He was employed as Lecturer at the Univeristy of Cyprus, Department of Computer Science from 1999 till 2002. His previous research work focused on distributed multimedia systems with adaptive behaviour, quality of service issues, streaming media and the Internet. His current main research interest is in the design and the development of intelligent environments that provide adaptive and personalized context to the users according to their preferences, cognitive characteristics and emotional state. He has several publications including edited books, chapters, articles in journals and conference contributions. Mourlas has taught various undergraduate as well as postgraduate courses in the Dept. of Computer Science of the University of Cyprus and the Dept. of Communication and Media Studies of the University of Athens. Furthermore, he has coordinated and actively participated in numerous national and EU funded projects.

Federica Paganelli is research scientist at the National Interuniversity Consortium for Telecommunications (CNIT) at the Electronics and Telecommunications Department, University of Florence. She holds a PhD in Telematics and Information Society from the University of Florence. Her research interests include context-aware and Ambient Intelligent system, distributed systems and solutions for pervasive computing environments, especially for the eTourism, eHealth and infomobility application domains.

Heiko Pfeffer studied computer science at the Rheinische-Friedrich-Wilhelms-Universität Bonn and the Université Claude Bernard Lyon I. After graduation, he started to work as scientific researcher at the group of Open Communication Systems (OKS) at the Technische Universität Berlin and the Fraunhofer Institut FOKUS. His main research areas comprise the modeling of service collaboration and interaction within service oriented computing environments and the mobile Web. He has been involved in multiple national and international projects within the area of service oriented architectures, mobile computing, and technologies for future Web applications.

Carsten Pils was born in Heinsberg, Germany, in 1971. He received a Dipl.-Inform. degree in 1997 and a PhD in 2005 from the Technical University RWTH Aachen, Germany. Since 2005, he has been working for the Telecommunications Software and Systems Group at the Waterford Institute of Technology in Waterford, Ireland. He has been working on wireless communication systems, distributed systems, mobile agents and context-aware computing. His contributions within a number of German national and European funded R&D projects (AMASE, ParcelCall, VIP, Daidalos, FAST-Integration) included software design and development, standardization, work package and activity management. From 2004 till 2005 he was project manager of the German national project FAST-Integration. His current research interests include context-aware computing, information retrieval systems and graph matching problems.

Manuele Kirsch Pinheiro is associate professor in the "Centre de Recherche en Informatique" of the "Université Paris 1 Panthéon-Sorbonne" since September 2008. Previously, she occupied a post-doctoral position on the Katholieke Universiteit Leuven's Department of Computer Science. She received her PhD in computer science form the "Université Joseph Fourier – Grenoble I" (2006), and her master's degree from the "Universidade Federal do Rio Grande do Sul", Porto Alegre, Brazil. Her research interests include ubiquitous computing, context-aware computing, adaptation (personalization), cooperative work (CSCW), group awareness and information systems.

Wendy Powley is a research associate and adjunct lecturer in the School of Computing at Queen's University. She received her Bachelor of Arts in psychology in 1984, a Bachelor of Education in 1985, and a Masters of Science in computer science in 1990, all from Queen's University. She is also a faculty fellow with IBM's Centre for Advanced Studies in Toronto, ON. Wendy has been involved in numerous research projects, mainly in the area of autonomic computing for web services and database management systems.

Davy Preuveneers received his MSc degree in computer science in 2002, and his MSc in artificial intelligence in 2003 from the Katholieke Universiteit Leuven in Belgium. Since 2003, he is a PhD student and research assistant in the DistriNet research group at the Department of Computer Science of the Katholieke Universiteit Leuven. His research is in the field of component-based software engineering, middleware and service oriented architectures for context-aware adaptation. His research interests also include service composition and interaction in particular in the setting of mobile and ubiquitous computing environments.

Claudia Raibulet is assistant professor at the University of Milano-Bicocca, Italy since 2004. She received the Master degree in Computer Science from the "Politehnica" University of Bucharest, Romania in 1997. In 2002, she received the PhD degree in computer and system engineering from the Politecnico di Torino, Italy. Her research interests include various areas of software engineering: software architecture, distributed systems, dynamic systems, mobile computing, context-aware environments, object-oriented methodologies, and reverse engineering. She is the author of more than fifty scientific publications including book chapters, journal, conference, and workshop papers. Currently, she is a member of various program and organizing committees related to conferences and workshops, as well as a reviewer of different international journals. She is involved in national and international research projects. Furthermore, she is an IEEE member.

Peter Rigole obtained his MSc and PhD degree at the DistriNet research group of the Katholieke Universiteit Leuven in 2001 and 2006 respectively. His research interests include distributed computing, embedded systems, resource-awareness, component-based development and automated deployment of component-based applications. He currently works as a post-doctoral researcher on several projects in cooperation with academic partners and the industry.

Gustavo Rossi is full professor at Facultad de Informatica, UNLP, Argentina and Head of LIFIA. He holds a PhD from PUC-Rio, Brazil and a HDR from INSA-Lyon, France. His research interests are advanced separation of concerns in Web applications, design issues for Web 2.0 applications and interface specification of RIAs.

Ioanna Roussaki was born in Athens, Greece, in 1975. She received the electrical and computer engineering diploma from the National Technical University of Athens (NTUA) in 1997. In 1998, she joined the Computer Networks Laboratory (CNL) of the School of Electrical and Computer Engineering (SECE). Since then, she has participated in many national and international research and development projects. In 2003, she received her PhD in the area of telecommunications and computer networks and became a senior CNL research associate. Since 2008, she is a lecturer in SECE, where she teaches several courses. Her major research interests lie in the fields of mobile and personal communications, ubiquitous and pervasive computing, context-awareness, virtual-home-environment, e-negotiations, mobile agent systems, algorithms and complexity theory. She has over 50 publications on these research fields.

She holds a master's degree on techno-economic studies. She is a member of IEEE and the Technical Chamber of Greece.

George Samaras is a professor in the Department of Computer Science of the University of Cyprus. He received a PhD in computer science from Rensselaer Polytechnic Institute, USA, in 1989. He was previously at IBM Research Triangle Park, USA and taught at the University of North Carolina at Chapel Hill (adjunct faculty, 1990-93). He served as the lead architect of IBM's distributed commit architecture (1990-94) and co-authored the final publication of the architecture (IBM Book, SC31-8134-00, Sept. 1994). His work on utilizing mobile agents for Web database access has received the best paper award of the 1999 IEEE Int. Conference on Data Engineering (ICDE'99) and recently the work on eLearning received the best student paper award of the 2008 Int. Conference on Adaptive Hypermedia and Adaptive Web-Based Systems (AH2008). He has a number of patents relating to transaction processing technology and numerous book chapters, technical conference and journal publications. He has served as proposal evaluator at a national and international level and he has been regularly invited by the European Commission to serve as an external project evaluator and auditor, ESPRIT and IST Programs (FP5, FP6, FP7). His research interest includes eLearning and eServices, Web information retrieval, mobile/wireless computing, context based services, personalization Systems, Database Systems. He also served on IBM's internal international standards committees for issues related to distributed transaction processing (OSI/TP, XOPEN, OMG). He participates in a number of EU's IST projects related to eLearning, mobile and wireless computing as the Scientific coordinator of the Cyprus participation.

Alessandro Sorniotti has a double MSc degree from Politecnico di Torino (Turin, Italy) in computer science and from Institut Eurécom (Sophia-Antipolis, France) in Networking. He also obtained a research master diploma (DOA) in networking and distributed systems from Université de Nice-Sophia Antipolis (Nice, France). Alessandro has won a scolarship and he is a PhD candidate at Ecole Nationale Supérieure des Télécommunications (Paris, France), working as a research associate at SAP Labs France. He is engaged in two EU projects, WASP, that addresses the technology of wireless sensor networks, and TAS3 that focuses on trust and privacy. His current research topic is the study of protocols for secret exchange, secret matching and secret handshake.

Stephan Steglich is director of Competence Center Open Communication Systems (OKS) at Fraunhofer FOKUS. He received his MSc in computer science (1998) and PhD (2003) in Computer Science from the TU Berlin in 2003. His fields of interest include, e.g., context-awareness, user-interaction, and adaptive systems. In 1998 and 1999 he has worked intensively in the research area of intelligent mobile agents. Since 1999 he has started research activities in the area of user-centric communication. He has been involved in a number of projects, which were related to human-machine-interaction, UMTS/VHE, personalization and user profiling. Stephan is managing international and national level research activities and has been an organizer and a member of program committees of several international conferences. He has actively participated in standardization activities in these research areas and gives lectures in 'Mobile Telecommunication Systems', 'Advanced Communication Systems' at the TU Berlin.

Maria Strimpakou was born in Athens, Greece, in 1977. She received her Diploma in Electrical and Computer Engineering from the National Technical University of Athens (NTUA) in 2000. In 2001, she joined the Computer Networks Laboratory (CNL) of the School of Electrical and Computer

Engineering (SECE) and started her doctoral studies, while working as a research engineer. Since then, she participated in several research projects on service and software engineering, e-commerce, mobile agent systems, ubiquitous and pervasive computing, context awareness, ontology design and data management in distributed environments. From 2002 until today, she supervised the laboratory classes of "Communication Networks" and "Computer Networks" undergraduate courses of the Communications, Electronics and Information Engineering Division of the SECE. Results of her research work have been disseminated in numerous international conferences and journals. She is expected to complete her PhD studies before the end of 2008.

Nikos Tsianos is a research assistant and doctoral candidate at the New Technologies Laboratory of the Faculty of Communication and Media Studies of the University of Athens. He holds an MSc in political communication from the University of Athens. His main research area is the incorporation of theories from the psychology of individual differences into adaptive educational hypermedia, the development of corresponding systems and the empirical evaluation of such systems in the context of an experimental psychology methodology. He has published several articles in conferences and journals regarding this field of research, while he has been credited with the best student paper award at the Adaptive Hypermedia 2008 Conference. He is currently editing a book about cognitive and emotional human factors in web-learning.

Yves Vanrompay is a PhD student and research assistant in the DistriNet research group of the Katholieke Universiteit Leuven's Department of Computer Science. He received his MSc degree in Informatics in 2003, and his MSc in artificial intelligence in 2004 from the Katholieke Universiteit Leuven. His research interests include context-aware systems, adaptation, context reasoning and learning.

Koen Victor is a PhD student and research assistant in the DistriNet research group of the Katholieke Universiteit Leuven's Department of Computer Science. He received his MSc degree in informatics in 2005 from the Katholieke Universiteit Leuven. His research is focussed on context enabled distribution techniques for ad-hoc mobile networks, information retrieval based on its context and context addressing.

Kirk Wilson is a research staff member in CA Labs, an organization within CA, Inc that supports academic research. Kirk also serves as CA's primary representative on a number of industry standard technical committees. Kirk has been the editor of OASIS WSDM MOWS and co-editor of the DMTF's WS-CIM specifications. He has over 25 years' experience in information processing, both as a software customer with a Fortune 500 industrial gas and chemicals manufacturer and as a thought leader in the software industry. As a software customer, Kirk received an Innovative Application in Artificial Intelligence award from the American Association for Artificial Intelligence for his work on chemical regulatory compliance. Kirk holds a PhD in philosophy from the University of Massachusetts.

Jared Zebedee is a graduate of Queen's University (Kingston, Ontario) holding bachelor's (BSc) and master's (MSc) degrees in computer science. He now works as an enterprise software engineer and project leader for Procter & Gamble Inc. Jared has also worked on projects involving Web Services and Web services distributed management (WSDM) technology with CA Inc.. He was an exhibitor at CA World 2007 where he demonstrated the Autonomic Web Services Environment (AWSE), a project conducted as part of his research while studying at Queen's.

Lizhu Zhou is a full professor of Department of Computer Science and Technology at Tsinghua University, Beijing, China. Professor Zhou received his Master of Science degree in computer science from University of Toronto in 1983. His major research interests include database systems, digital resource management, web data processing, and information systems. Since 1980's, Zhou has led the completion of more than 20 R & D projects funded by the Natural Science Foundation of China, China's high-tech programs, industries and international organizations. He has published over 100 papers in journals and refereed conferences, and served as program committee member, program committee chair, and conference chair for many international conferences.

Mohamed Zouari, is a PhD student at IRISA Research Laboratory in Rennes at the north of France. His research interests include adaptive systems, distributed systems and data replication. More specifically he works on software architectures for dynamic adaptation to context changes. He holds a master degree in information systems from INSA Lyon on adaptation policies for pervasive systems. He is a member of the French adaption action ADAPT (http://adapt.asr.cnrs.fr) on dynamic adaptation to runtime environments.

Index